PRAISE FOR

Disunion Among Ourselves: The Perilous Politics of the American Revolution

"Eli Merritt deftly explores a revolutionary America rife with divisions and driven by a fear of civil wars on multiple fronts. Deeply researched, wide-ranging, and insightful, *Disunion Among Ourselves* persuades that our national Union began from, and still depends on, fending off the many demons of disunion."
—**Alan Taylor**, University of Virginia, author of *American Revolutions: A Continental History, 1750–1804*

"*Disunion Among Ourselves* is an elegantly written and deeply researched book that challenges long-accepted myths about the origins of the American Union. Merritt shows that the seeds of the Civil War lay in the American Revolution and that the founding fathers had good cause to fear disunion and internecine conflict. The chance to build a new republic might have been fumbled away without superior statecraft—and indeed it nearly was. This suspenseful account supplies a timely lesson for our own hyperpartisan times—that the values of moderation, compromise, and the rule of law are prerequisite to the survival of democracy."
—**Ian W. Toll**, author of *Six Frigates: The Epic History of the Founding of the U.S. Navy*

"*Disunion Among Ourselves* tells an important story that has been missed or skipped over in nearly all histories of the Revolution. It has indeed, as promised, recovered 'a whole area of the Revolution' previously underappreciated, and for that is invaluable."
—**Richard Kreitner**, author of *Break It Up: Secession, Division, and the Secret History of America's Imperfect Union*

"Merritt's insightful work demonstrates that the issue of sectional conflict was 'hard wired' into our nation. Our 'original sin' of slavery was inextricably bound up with the 'original fear' of disunion. For those interested in the original and continuing project of 'We the People,' *Disunion Among Ourselves* is a must read."
—**Nicholas S. Zeppos**, Chancellor Emeritus and Distinguished Professor of Law and Political Science, Vanderbilt University

"Eli Merritt takes a new look at a unique political generation—America's leaders during the Revolution, who found ways to overcome divisions as sharp as any we face today. Those leaders often stumbled, and some of the compromises they made—notably those that maintained the viability of slavery—exacted a heavy price in the long run. Yet that generation managed to win a war and give us a country of our own. Merritt helps us understand how they did it."
—**Melvin Patrick Ely**, College of William & Mary author of *Israel on the Appomattox: A Southern Experiment in Black Freedom from the 1790s Through the Civil War*

"*Disunion Among Ourselves* is a most timely book. With detective-like research and deft storytelling, Eli Merritt rescues important conflicts and compromises occurring in the earliest years of the nation's history from both the shadow of later sectional crises and the glare of founding generation worship. Showing just how unlikely a unity of states was during and after the Revolution—particularly because of regional division over diplomatic challenges long neglected by historians—he displays the essential role played by our first national leaders' character, intelligence, and discipline."
—**Daniel H. Usner**, Vanderbilt University, author of *Native American Women and the Burdens of Southern History*

"Merritt unquestionably contributes to our knowledge of the political rhetoric of the American Revolution by his study of the fear of disunion and civil war. His interpretation helps us understand the politics of the period in both its broader contours and its specifics. This is a significant achievement."
—**Max Edling**, King's College London, author of *Perfecting the Union: National and State Authority in the US Constitution*

DISUNION AMONG OURSELVES

DISUNION AMONG OURSELVES

THE
Perilous Politics
OF THE American Revolution

ELI MERRITT

UNIVERSITY OF MISSOURI PRESS
COLUMBIA

Copyright © 2023 by
The Curators of the University of Missouri
University of Missouri Press, Columbia, Missouri 65211
Printed and bound in the United States of America
All rights reserved. First printing, 2023.

Library of Congress Cataloging-in-Publication Data

Names: Merritt, Eli, author.
Title: Disunion among ourselves : the perilous politics of the American Revolution / Eli Merritt.
Description: Columbia : University of Missouri Press, 2023. | Includes bibliographical references and index.
Identifiers: LCCN 2022047689 (print) | LCCN 2022047690 (ebook) | ISBN 9780826222817 (hardcover) | ISBN 9780826274861 (ebook)
Subjects: LCSH: United States--Politics and government--1775-1783. | United States--Politics and government--1783-1789. | Civil war--United States--Prevention--History--18th century. | United States. Continental Congress--Decision making--History. | Political culture--United States--History--18th century. | Polarization (Social sciences)--Political aspects--United States--History--18th century. | United States--Foreign relations--1775-1783. | Concord.
Classification: LCC E210 .M44 2023 (print) | LCC E210 (ebook) | DDC 973.3--dc23/eng/20221110
LC record available at https://lccn.loc.gov/2022047689
LC ebook record available at https://lccn.loc.gov/2022047690
∞™ This paper meets the requirements of the American National Standard for Permanence of Paper for Printed Library Materials, Z39.48, 1984.

Typefaces: Celestia Antiqua and Caslon

For my father, Gilbert S. Merritt, a federal judge who instilled within me a love of history, ethics, constitutional law, and democratic values.

We have nothing to fear but disunion among ourselves.
Robert Livingston, delegate of New York, October 4, 1775[1]

God grant that the union may not be dissolved, and the good people again involved in all the horrors of war.
Samuel Holten, delegate of Massachusetts, October 9, 1783[2]

CONTENTS

Acknowledgments ix

Introduction 3

PART ONE: FIRST CONGRESS TO THE TRIAL OF INDEPENDENCE

Chapter 1: "Civil Wars Among Ourselves" 19

Chapter 2: "Unite or Die" 41

Chapter 3: South Carolina Withdraws 57

Chapter 4: "A Fatal Issue to Our Union" 77

Chapter 5: "Intestine Wars and Convulsions" 99

Chapter 6: "Colonies Might Secede from the Union" 123

Chapter 7: "A Firm League of Friendship" 135

PART TWO: ALLIANCE, CONFEDERATION, AND CRISIS OF UNION

Chapter 8: The Mississippi and Fisheries 151

Chapter 9: "The Very Salvation of These States" 167

Chapter 10: "North Against South" 185

Chapter 11: The Mississippi and Fisheries Again 209

Chapter 12: Crisis of Union 227

PART THREE: FIRST CONSTITUTION AND THE PERILS OF PEACE

Chapter 13: "The Body Politic Is Sick, Sick Indeed!" 243

Chapter 14: "A Confederation of Very Dissonant Parts" 257

Chapter 15: "The Power of Britain in These States Is Now Broken"	275
Chapter 16: "Symptoms of Disunion"	293
Chapter 17: "Le Washington de la Negotiation"	309
Chapter 18: "The Greatest Empire in the World"	321
Chapter 19: "Stained with the Blood of Her Sons"	337
Chapter 20: "United We Stand, Divided We Fall"	353
Notes	371
Bibliography	411
Index	427

ACKNOWLEDGMENTS

I OWE A DEBT OF GRATITUDE to many people for their support and assistance in bringing *Disunion Among Ourselves* across the finish line. In the introduction I highlight the contributions of academic mentors Howard Lamar and Akhil Amar as well as scholars of the early period David C. Hendrickson, Max M. Edling, James Roger Sharp, Jack P. Greene, Alan Taylor, Cathy D. Matson, Peter S. Onuf, Jack N. Rakove, Edmund Cody Burnett, Merrill Jensen, and Bernard Bailyn. I add to this list of scholars whose writings significantly influenced me Joseph L. Davis, John Richard Alden, Maya Jasanoff, Melvin Ely, Andrew O'Shaughnessy, Joel Richard Paul, Joe Crespino, Richard B. Morris, Jonathan R. Dull, Edmund S. Morgan, Colin Bonwick, John Ferling, Thomas Fleming, George William Van Cleve, Robert A. Rutland, and William M. E. Rachal, among others.

I also wish to thank the stellar team of Vanderbilt faculty who gave me an intellectual home as a visiting scholar for two years as I researched and wrote. They are Nick Zeppos, Jeff Balser, Keith Meador, Marshall Eakin, and Stephan Heckers. Not only did these leaders at Vanderbilt provide me with an office, library access, and an environment of fellowship for the completion of the book. They helped me to forge a career change from the practice of medicine to the writing of history and political analysis. I especially want to thank Nick for his friendship and support over the years.

My gratitude also extends to Andrew Stuart, my book agent, and to Andrew Davidson, Drew Griffith, Robin Rennison, Mary Conley, Deanna Davis, and others at the University of Missouri Press for shepherding *Disunion Among Ourselves* through production to market. Chris Robinson crafted the excellent maps that make the complex geopolitical landscape of the thirteen colonies and trans-Appalachian West visually comprehensible for 21st century readers. Amy Maddox and Susan

E. Benton meticulously copyedited and proofread the final manuscript before it went to press. Travis Wilds and Luchi Carmen Martínez translated dozens of French and Spanish letters from the 1770s and 1780s into English. I thank you all.

Numerous colleagues, friends, and family members read parts of the manuscript, providing critical feedback. For this invaluable help I want to thank Rosana Castrillo Díaz, Harrison Hobart, Charlie Lord, Michael Johns, Christopher North, Martha Ingram, Tom Comitta, Natasha Lasky, Deb Daugherty, Marianne Merola, Michelle Fiordaliso, James Roger Sharp, Jack May, Ian Toll, Daniel Usner, Kathyrn Huarte, Will Lippincott, Geri Thoma, David Colin Carr, John Seigenthaler, Kevin Gutzman, and Bob Massie.

My thanks also go out to the Virginia Historical Society's Mellon Research Fellowship, the North Caroliniana Society's Archie K. Davis Fellowship, and the Program for Cultural Cooperation Between Spain and the United States for supporting and underwriting research.

Others who deserve to be recognized for their longtime cheerleading of *Disunion Among Ourselves* include Rufus E. Fort, Stroud Merritt, Louise Merritt, Fields Livingston, Blyth Lord, Peter Fry, Ben Humphreys, Curt Armstrong, Daniel Kovnat, Don Brode, Matt Joseph, Shan Mohammed, Chris Donohoe, Ted Fischer, Chris Castro, Amy Atkinson, Mark Atkinson, Casey Hanley, David Herschorn, Jonathan Tann, Jordana Tann, Jay O'Connor, Heather Corcoran, and Andrew McAllister.

Most of all, I wish to thank my father, Gilbert S. Merritt, for his contagious love of history and the example he set of constitutional scholarship; my wife, Rosana Castrillo Díaz, whose support and encouragement of my writing and this book have been steadfast and enlivening for decades; and my two sons, Alejandro and Cameron, who tolerated my history lessons from the book at the breakfast table for years.

Alejandro and Cameron, never forget what Winston Churchill said in 1953 about how democracies keep afloat: "Study history, study history. In history lies all the secrets of statecraft." I would add to Churchill's wisdom that the study of history is also the secret to effective citizenship, the second vital force democracies must possess in order to survive and thrive.

DISUNION AMONG OURSELVES

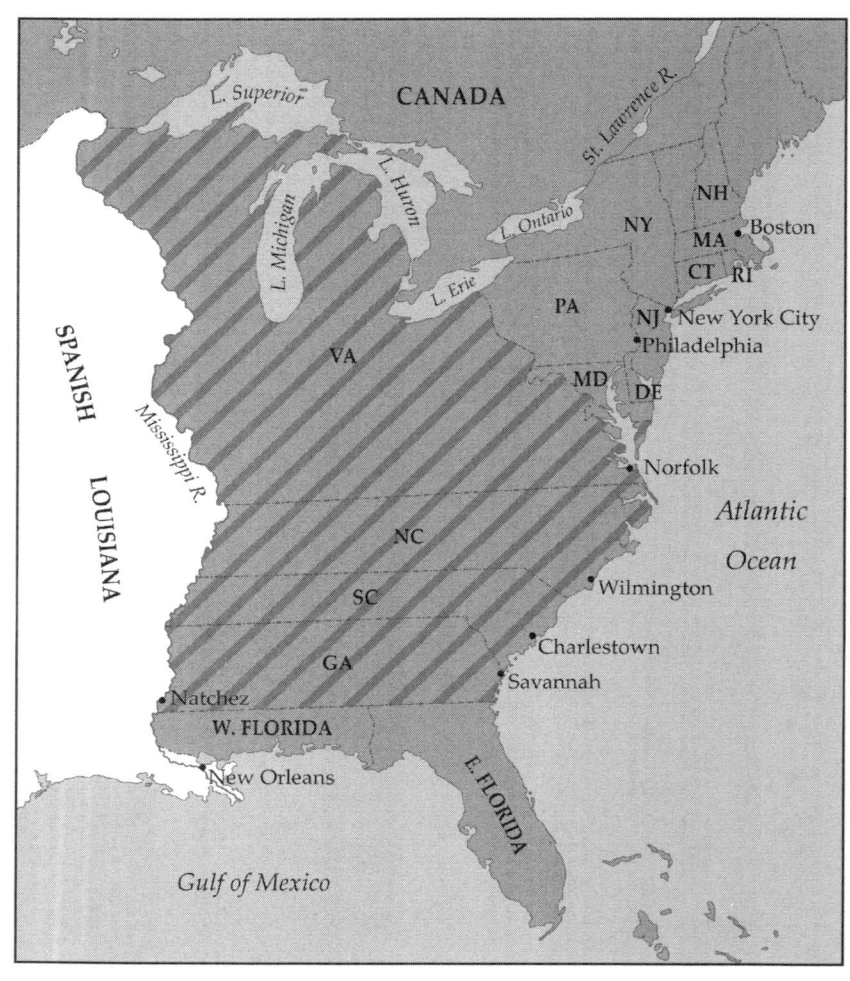

MAP 1. Land Claims of the Southern Colonies, 1774. (Chris Robinson, Cartographer)

INTRODUCTION

This book tells the story of the deep political divisions that beset the Continental Congress during the American Revolution. The politics of those years were filled with distrust, polarization, and, most strikingly, the centrifugal force of disunion. In fact it is almost certain that the founders of the United States would have split the thirteen states into two or three confederacies at the end of the Revolutionary War—Northern and Southern or Northern, Middle, and Southern—if not for one overwhelming fact. Those separate confederacies, the founders were convinced, would rapidly fall into civil wars. And, if this tragic outcome was not enough to put an end to the American experiment in liberty, the armies and navies of Britain and other European nations would soon step in, bleeding the war-torn confederacies to their own advantage and, afterward, restoring colonial status.[1]

The founding of a single United States, therefore, was hardly the easy marriage of thirteen homogeneous, liberty-loving states so often depicted in American history. A single United States was not foreordained or even desired as a matter of first preference by most of the founders. Instead, the American Union was an unwelcome alliance formed by bitterly conflictual colonies and regions for the maintenance of internal and external security. An apt metaphor capturing the spirit of the early republic is that of a shotgun wedding. If the New England, Middle, or Southern states had chosen to walk away from the union of thirteen, civil wars would have broken out. For this reason—the prevention of civil wars—the founders reluctantly bound themselves into one peacekeeping American government under the United States' first constitution, the Articles of Confederation and Perpetual Union.[2]

Throughout the nine years of the Revolution, the founders felt the foreboding guns of disunion and civil wars pointing at their backs. One congressman who crystallized this fact as early as 1776 was John Witherspoon, president of the College of New Jersey, later renamed Princeton. America's foremost scholar of the Scottish Enlightenment, the fifty-three-year-old Witherspoon told his fellow delegates in late July, three weeks after the passage of the Declaration of Independence, that rejecting a single permanent American Union was "madness." In a speech on the floor of Independence Hall, he explained that without a durable political bond of all thirteen states, the present War of Independence was going to be "only a prelude to a contest of a more dreadful nature, and indeed much more properly a civil war than that which now often obtains the name." Witherspoon was comparing the imperial civil war with Britain then taking place—that is, the Revolutionary War—with a far more horrific domestic civil war among the states that would result from disunion. Why should they spend their mutual treasure and blood seeking to obtain independence from the British now, Witherspoon asked, "with a certainty, as soon as peace was settled with them of a more lasting war, a more unnatural, more bloody, and much more hopeless war, among the colonies themselves?"[3]

Without one government to forge nonviolent remedies and compromises, Witherspoon and the other founders knew, Americans would go to war with one another over disputed state boundaries, commerce, massive undivided war debt, state-federal financial accounting, and especially the gold mine of unsettled western territory extending from the crest of the Appalachian Mountains to the Mississippi River. If there was one source of civil bloodshed the founders feared more than any other, it was what they called the "right of soil." Americans would take up arms against one another over land. The hundreds of millions of acres of trans-Appalachian territory, claimed by many of the states in overlapping royal charters and rulings, represented the ripest field for civil wars. But there were numerous other hotly contested territorial trouble spots, such as the Wyoming Valley in modern-day Pennsylvania and the six million acres that later became the state of Vermont. The founders feared a chain reaction. An eruption of violence in one of these volatile domains would pit state against state—and perhaps state against Congress. This circumstance of warfare over land, in the absence of an effective controlling authority to contain it, would force the other states to take sides, spiraling them into separate confederacies that would ultimately break out into the hopeless conflagration Witherspoon described in July of 1776.[4]

Did the founders anticipate that future Americans might fight a civil war to put an end to slavery? The answer to this question depends on what is meant by "civil war." During the Revolution the founders left no records specifically prognosticating that free Northern states would fight slaveholding Southern ones for the explicit purpose of restoring the Union or emancipating enslaved persons. However, fear of large-scale slave rebellion—certainly a type of civil war—was rife, and some observers of the American scene wondered aloud about how slave revolution in the Southern states might combine with outside forces to end the evil practice. One such force was the British army recruiting Black Americans in the South to fight against enslavers by instilling "diabolical notions" into their minds: the promise of freedom and liberty. Keeping down slave insurrections, said one group of Virginians in the spring of 1775, was a matter of the colony's "internal security."[5]

In his *Notes on the State of Virginia*, Thomas Jefferson worries about another outside force that might intervene to abolish slavery and punish enslavers: the "wrath" of God. "Indeed," Jefferson says, "I tremble for my country when I reflect that God is just: that his justice cannot sleep forever." In the *Notes*, Jefferson expresses a hope that the post-Revolution years will effect "a total emancipation" of enslaved persons without bloodshed. Exposing his own palpable fear of a violent uprising of enslaved persons against enslavers, the Southern founder prays "under the auspices of heaven" that emancipation will take place with "the consent of the masters, rather than by their extirpation."[6]

Another American, Joseph Galloway, a Pennsylvania delegate to Congress who later defected from the cause of the Revolution to become a loyalist, predicted that a North-South civil war might combine with the spirit of liberty in Black Americans to deliver a crushing blow to the South. In early 1775 Galloway published a political tract in which he warned the citizens of the thirteen colonies that they must reconcile with England—or else the colonies would be wracked for decades to come by civil wars. In the treatise *A Candid Examination of the Mutual Claims of Great Britain and the Colonies*, Galloway professes that the primary source of civil wars will be disputes over the "right to the soil." However, he also predicts an awful North-South civil war at some point in an independent America. "The northern colonies, inured to military discipline and hardships," Galloway warns, "will, in all probability, be the first to enter the list of military controversy; and, like the northern Saxons and Danes, carry devastation and havoc over the southern, who, weak for want of discipline, and having a dangerous enemy within their own bowels, must, after suffering all the horrors of a civil war, yield to the superior force, and submit to the will of the conquerors." That "dangerous enemy within," of course, was the approximately 430,000 African American people held in bondage in the Southern states. If given the chance, Galloway suggests, Southern enslaved persons would join the Northern troops in the fight against their Southern enslavers.[7]

II

Disunion Among Ourselves fills a gap in our historical understanding of the American Revolution because it is the first book to tell the story of the founders' careful maneuvers to avert disunion and domestic civil wars. It presents compelling evidence that the avoidance of disunion and civil wars was a formidable political and diplomatic force that shaped the founders' decision-making from the First Continental Congress in 1774 to the formal end of the war in 1783, impacting the outcome of historic legislation like the Continental Association of 1774, the Declaration of Independence, the formation of the Continental Army and the election of its commander in chief, the Articles of Confederation, and the Peace of Paris. Evidence is strong, too, that one factor shifting Washington's military strategy southward from New York to Yorktown, Virginia, in August of 1781 was apprehension of disaffection in the Southern states and alarm that if the Continental Army did not soon score a victory there, European powers might coerce the restoration of Georgia, South Carolina, and perhaps North Carolina back into the British empire in a peace treaty.

Once this lens of interpretation is brought to bear on the American Revolution—as well as on the subsequent "critical period" that impelled the disuniting thirteen states to the emergency summit in Philadelphia in 1787—we gain clarity on the underlying life-and-death feelings and motivations that caused the founders to unite, remain united, and compromise in spite of the rampant regional forces propelling them apart. One such example of hard-fought compromise, spurred by disunionist threats within the Continental Congress, is the Declaration of Independence. By the summer of 1776, fourteen long months after the Battles of Lexington and Concord, the time had finally come for the Middle states, literally, to "join or die." So dire was the perceived need for a declaration of independence as a first step toward obtaining a French alliance that especially New Englanders were prepared to abandon the Middle states to their fate if they continued to impede the proclamation. The real story of the summer of '76 is not one of elevated patriotism and American single-mindedness. The reality of that founding moment is that chiefly the Middle states were left with a crucial decision to make, and, under relentless pressure, they chose to go to war *with* New England and the Southern states instead of *against* them. July 2, 1776, the day the states voted in favor of independence, should be viewed not by the light of the founders' well-crafted propaganda of unity. Collective independence, in actuality, was coerced by a clear and present danger of disunion and intercolonial bloodshed. It was indeed a shotgun wedding, one that created a nation.

Two other examples from the book demonstrate how the founders forged great things from perceived risks of disunion and domestic civil wars: the Mississippi-Fisheries Compromise of 1779 and the ratification of the Articles of Confederation in 1781. Regarding the first, in early 1779, the Congress opened up formal debates on the United States' minimal peace terms for ending the war. Quickly the states divided into regional camps, New England standing for fishing and drying rights at the island of Newfoundland as a sine qua non of peace and the Southern states backing Virginia in its twin demands for a western U.S. boundary at the Mississippi River and navigation rights on the waterway along its course to the Gulf of Mexico. For the most part, the Middle states opposed both overreaching claims on grounds that the navigational and territorial greed of New England and the South was going to unnecessarily prolong the war and perhaps sabotage independence altogether. Tortuous debates rife with threats of disunion ensued, resulting in a New England–South compromise to make both the Mississippi and the fisheries ultimatums of European treaties. Together these two regions overcame the opposing votes of the Middle states.

The Mississippi-Fisheries Compromise formally unraveled in Congress two years later, but that did not stop the peace commissioners in Paris from feeling its effects and gearing their diplomatic actions to the known dangers to the Union of unequal treatment of New England and the Southern states in the peace treaty. In the end it was the perils of disunion that drove Peace Ministers John Jay, John Adams, and Benjamin Franklin to fight tooth and nail to obtain both sets of water and territorial rights in the Anglo-American treaty. They succeeded, achieving not only political and economic independence from the British empire but also access to the Newfoundland fisheries for New England and the Mississippi boundary for the Southern states. By bringing the trans-Appalachian

West (as far as the Mississippi) under the domain of the United States, the peace treaty nearly doubled the size of the Atlantic seaboard colonies. Historians broadly agree that the Treaty of Paris was "the greatest triumph in the annals of American diplomacy."[8]

However, try as the peace ministers did, they were unable to secure the free navigation of the Mississippi sought by the Southern states since 1776. An uncooperative Spain possessed both banks of the river at its mouth, enabling it to exert a stranglehold on the free flow of American commerce there. Even so, in a symbolic nod to unity and the compromise of 1779, Jay, Adams, and Franklin refused to sign the peace treaty unless Britain transferred its own erstwhile right to navigate the Mississippi to the new United States. Thus, in Article 8 of the definitive peace treaty signed in September of 1783, Britain illogically awarded the United States a navigation right that it did not technically possess the authority to transfer. "The Navigation of the River Mississippi," Article 8 reads, "from its Source to the Ocean shall forever remain free and open to the Subjects of Great Britain and the Citizens of the United States." Jay, Adams, and Franklin insisted on this article in part to strengthen the hand of the United States in future negotiations with Spain to open the Mississippi. Yet, far more vital to their thinking, Article 8 was conspicuous proof to the leadership of the Southern states that they had done everything in their power to put the navigation of the Mississippi on par with the Newfoundland fisheries in their diplomatic efforts.[9]

Probably the most spectacular success of the founders during the Revolution was the ratification of the first U.S. constitution. Here again the specter of disunion and civil wars proved decisive. Nothing but the prospect of this violent sequela of the Revolution could possibly have bound New England, the Middle states, and the Southern states into one constitutional Union. It was a long, agonizing slog. Franklin proposed the first iteration of the Articles of Confederation in late July of 1775, and not until March 1, 1781, in acute anticipation of the end of the war, did the states finally secure the constitutional bond that most delegates believed was their only hope for survival.

For understandable reasons, historians and constitutional scholars have dismissed the Articles of Confederation as a failed charter, shoddily constructed in the throes of war. It is, of course, undeniable that the Articles of Confederation was structurally inadequate to the cause of a strong and safe Union. Nevertheless, its ratification in 1781 was an accomplishment of epic proportions. Historians and constitutional scholars should look again at the founders' colossal struggle to unite the thirteen states under the Articles of Confederation. Against the odds, they did it. Their success in 1781 was no less a miraculous feat—of desperation—than the ratification of the second constitution in 1788, one that once again rescued the United States from the onrush of disunion and civil wars.

III

Disunion Among Ourselves also casts light on the most tragic aspect of the Revolution. That is, how did the purportedly enlightened founders of the republic possibly perpetuate the crime of slavery during the war years—and thereafter—in spite of the institution's roaring contradictions with the ideals of liberty and freedom that inspired the war? In those first decades of our national history, slavery was the same "irrepressible conflict" it remained for the next seven decades. Yet while liberating themselves from the tyranny of King George and the Parliament, the leaders of the Revolution did not compel the states to liberate those suffering from a form of tyranny unfathomably worse than the Coercive Acts of 1774. Three centuries later we are still confused and angered by the hypocrisy of their decisions. Some historians and commentators attribute the founders' failure to enact some federal plan of emancipation to systemic racism and moral corruption, underpinned by perverse readings of the Bible. Others lay the blame on the entrenched economic systems in both the North and South that enriched white planters and merchants on the profits of the slave trade and slave labor. No matter how heinous these practices were, the economic argument emphasizes, the founders simply could not break their addiction to the lucrative status quo.[10]

These interpretations are correct, but they overlook an additional factor that weighed heavily on the minds of the founders: the belief that any attempt by the federal government to end slavery or the slave trade would tear apart the United States. One significant reason for the founders' inaction on slavery on the federal level is their fear of disunion and civil wars. Antislavery advocates, like John Adams, John Jay, Alexander Hamilton, James Wilson, and Benjamin Franklin, among others, did not dare attempt to mandate even the gradual emancipation of enslaved persons throughout the thirteen states because they were certain that such a move would inflame divisions and disunion between North and South at the very moment they were working so hard to unite the fractious states into one Union—in order, for one thing, to prevent civil wars in the first place.

Because the founders of the United States believed that some, if not all, of the Southern states would secede from the Union if the Northern states demanded a plan of emancipation or an end to the slave trade—and because any such secession would drive the states into bloody mayhem—they faced a stark choice in the 1770s and 1780s. They could either advance a federal program for liberating Black Americans from slavery, or they could secure freedom from civil wars for themselves. They chose the latter, making a grievous devil's bargain. As James Madison explained the decision-making of the Constitutional Convention, referring to the slave trade, "Great as the evil is, a dismemberment of the union would be worse."[11]

In the twenty-first century we are still left to wonder what would have happened to the United States, and to slavery in the South, had some fearless Northern founders refused to unite under one constitution with any Southern state that did not first agree to submit to a plan of abolition. Would disunion actually have taken place? Or would such a demand by Northerners have pressured the weaker Southern states into a compromise that constitutionally freed enslaved persons at some point well before the Emancipation Proclamation? Alternatively, if the Constitutional Convention had broken apart over slavery, as many historians believe it almost did, and the thirteen states had gone on to form separate confederacies, would civil wars in fact have erupted? Or is it possible instead that the founders would have created and sustained separate republics that successfully averted violence between them through diplomacy? In another scenario, might the thirteen states have come back together after a period of disunion into a second constitutional convention, at that point finally implementing a plan to rid the United States of slavery?[12]

We will never know the answers to these questions, but exploration of such historical contingencies helps us to appreciate the realpolitik of slavery, emancipation, and the fears of disunion and civil wars that governed the political and constitutional behavior of the founders in the 1770s and 1780s. *Disunion Among Ourselves*, while not attempting to expiate the founders of their sins, elucidates a tragic dilemma they faced. I hope that scholars and students will explore the nexus of slavery, emancipation, and disunion more fully, testing the propositions put forth here. Moreover, I hope that readers will ponder the contradictions of the founding era at the deepest level, asking themselves, in a speculative exercise, what they would have done to end slavery at the federal level if they had been abolitionist-minded political leaders living in the 1770s and 1780s.

IV

In writing *Disunion Among Ourselves* I owe a debt of gratitude to many historians and constitutional scholars. First among them is Howard Lamar, my mentor at Yale. I first encountered Professor Lamar in an undergraduate seminar on early American westward expansion called "Southern Frontiers." Thereafter he served as an advisor for my senior essay in history about the Mississippi navigation crisis of 1786, encouraging me to submit the paper for publication after graduation. Professor Lamar introduced me to the wide-ranging influence of westward expansion and sectionalism on the psyches of Americans in the prerevolutionary and revolutionary periods of our history. Under his tutelage I revised my essay and published it as "Sectional Conflict and Secret Compromise: The Mississippi River Question and the United States Constitution" in the *American Journal of Legal History*. This book, which began as a narrow investigation of the Mississippi question during the years of the Revolution, is a direct outgrowth of that article. Westward expansion and sectionalism remain at the heart of the story told here, now with the Southern states' pursuit of the navigation of the Mississippi River counterbalanced by New England's even greater fervor for gaining fishing and drying rights at Newfoundland.[13]

I had not one but two academic advisors at Yale. Because my research explored the consequences of westward expansion and North-South sectionalism on the drafting of the U.S. Constitution, Lamar introduced me to Akhil Amar in the law school. Professor Amar embraced my thesis, generously meeting with me once per week for almost a year to discuss the direction of my research. Under his influence I developed a skepticism of secondary sources along with an attendant passion for scouring primary source materials in search of the emotional factors and motives that so often guide the course of history. What I discovered about the 1780s, especially in the person of James Madison, was monumental fear of what was going to happen if the thirteen states did not ratify a new government capable of containing the centrifugal forces of disunion. Founders like Madison foresaw catastrophe. So, with reluctance, they ratified the Constitution of 1787.

Later, to my surprise, when I went on to research the backstory of the Mississippi navigation crisis in the records of the Revolution, I found the same pervasive fears of disunion and civil war and the same efforts to avert them through political compromise and a federal constitution. I owe it in no small part to Professor Amar that both my article on the

Mississippi crisis and this book bring a "constitutional gaze" to the hard work of nation building during the founding years. My father, Gil Merritt, a federal judge who served for forty-four years on the Sixth Circuit Court of Appeals, first introduced me to this unique gaze on history. Professor Amar deepened it, helping me to turn the gaze onto sectional crisis in the 1770s and 1780s and its impact on the making of two U.S. constitutions.

Professors Lamar and Amar directed me down the path of investigating the territorial and disunionist energies that forged the constitutional United States. Along the way, numerous other scholars have enriched the journey. One of them is David C. Hendrickson, author of *Peace Pact: The Lost World of the American Founding*, a tour de force in the interpretative school known as the "unionist paradigm." In a book that spans the years from the Revolution through the ratification of the Constitution, Hendrickson advances the thesis that disunion was "the demon" the founders worked most tirelessly to subvert. In this vein he further claims that the second U.S. constitution was not a happy association of thirteen states destined to become a single nation. Rather it was a partnership, "a peace pact," among dissimilar states rooted in the self-preservation of all. Max M. Edling, in *Perfecting the Union: National and State Authority in the U.S. Constitution*, reaches the same conclusion, presenting the framing and ratification of the federal compact of 1787 as "the outcome of a perceived need to secure the survival of the American union of republics as an independent nation."[14]

Disunion Among Ourselves, joining this unionist/disunionist perspective, explores similar themes in the politics, diplomacy, and constitution making of the Revolution. Perhaps another apt name for this lens of interpretation of American history, which justly applies from 1774 until 1860, when South Carolina became the first state to secede from the Union, is the "survivalist paradigm." In short, American political leaders made the choices they did during that long stretch of history in order to ensure the survival of the nation—as well as themselves and their families. Above all, they had to avert the disaster of disunion because it was the fountainhead of civil wars and international wars. As the pages that follow reveal, the founders believed that international wars would naturally follow civil wars because one or more of the separate confederacies was certain to seek out naval alliances with European powers for self-preservation once disunion happened.

James Roger Sharp, author of *American Politics in the Early Republic: The New Nation in Crisis*, is another historian who turns this interpretative lens to the study of the early years of the Union. In this work Sharp explores the politics of the Federalist years, arguing that the 1790s was a decade of extraordinary sectional danger. In fact he compares its magnitude of "vitriolic sectional suspicions and hostilities" with the 1850s and the Civil War itself, providing convincing evidence that twice during the years 1798 to 1801 the United States stood at the brink of civil war. Similar to my findings on the politics of the Revolution, Sharp defines the origins of the North-South split as taking root in "the Southern and New England dichotomy." Further, he points out a nearly universal flaw in the scholarship of the founding period: historians' faith in the inevitability of the formation and preservation of the United States. "Scholars have dealt with the period," Sharp writes, "as if the fate of the Constitution and the union were never in doubt. They have overemphasized the *continuity* of institutions from the colonial to the national period and have minimized the *dissonance*." The truth of the 1790s, he insists, is something quite different from this picture of inevitability. Rather, the early republic was in constant peril. Fear of civil breakdown was a persistent threat. One consequence of this oversight, Sharp concludes, is that contemporary Americans have not yet understood the enormity of the founders' undertaking and, vitally, how much they struggled and sacrificed to avoid domestic catastrophe.[15]

Historian Alan Taylor extends this narrative of a fragile, bitterly divided America further still in his *American Republics: A Continental History of the United States, 1783–1850*. In this book Taylor casts the United States as an "always-imperiled" country contending with "a dread of internal division." So too do historians Jack P. Greene in his *Understanding the American Revolution: Issues and Actors* and Cathy D. Matson and Peter S. Onuf in their *A Union of Interests: Political and Economic Thought in Revolutionary America*. Greene says that virtually every delegate who set foot in the Congress during the Revolution, radicals and conservatives alike, agreed with the claim of John Witherspoon when he declared on the floor of Congress in 1776, "the greatest danger we have is of disunion among ourselves."[16]

In *A Union of Interests*, a book that is foundational to the emergence of the unionist paradigm, Matson and Onuf establish that, among the founders, fears of a dissolution of the Union into separate confederacies was a critical driver of the Constitutional Convention. Another work by Onuf, *The Origins of the Federal Republic: Jurisdictional Controversies in the United States, 1775–1787*, has a unique resonance with *Disunion*

Among Ourselves because both highlight jurisdictional conflicts between the states—and between Congress and the states—as touchstones for understanding the evolution of American politics and constitutional government during the founding period.[17]

While military histories of the War of Independence abound, political and constitutional histories are in short supply. Seminal works in this narrow field include, among others, *The Continental Congress: A Definitive History of the Continental Congress from Its Inception in 1774 to March 1789* by Edmund Cody Burnett; *The Constitutional Origins of the American Revolution* by Jack P. Greene; *The Articles of Confederation: An Interpretation of the Social-Constitutional History of the American Revolution, 1774–1781* by Merrill Jensen; and *The Beginnings of National Politics: An Interpretive History of the Continental Congress* by Jack N. Rakove. I leaned heavily on all four as I structured the narrative of *Disunion Among Ourselves*.

Finally, one historian more than any other, Bernard Bailyn, influenced the conceptualization of this book. In *The Ordeal of Thomas Hutchinson*, Bailyn describes a process of maturation in the historical understanding of an event like the American Revolution that, over time, advances the dominant narrative from the "heroic" to the "tragic." That is to say, new histories written in the tragic mold point out flaws in the heroes and upset assumptions long associated with brilliant beginnings. Barbara Tuchman calls it revealing "the underside" instead of "setting up marble statues."[18]

So much of what Bailyn concludes about historical interpretation in *The Ordeal of Thomas Hutchinson* broadly applies to *Disunion Among Ourselves*. In his introduction he writes, "For there is in fact a whole area of the Revolution that has been almost completely submerged in the historical literature and that hardly enters at all into our general understanding of what that formative event was all about. And it is not a secondary or incidental part of the story. It is fundamental, and the omission of so basic a part of the story did not come about and was not perpetuated accidentally." Such stories, Bailyn says, are submerged by the "historian's angle of vision," in this case the heroic angle, which shuts out elements that contradict longstanding idealistic views. Further, Bailyn states, "Until we look deliberately at the development from the other side around, we have not understood what the issues really were, what the struggle was all about."[19]

Whereas Bailyn casts his tragic angle of vision at the famous loyalist Thomas Hutchinson, bringing forth fresh insights about the Revolution by telling the story of a well-intentioned but defeated royal governor, I tell the story of the American Union from 1774 until 1783 "from the other side around"—that is, from the angle of disunion and its harrowing consequences. In so doing, I do not pretend to present a comprehensive account of the federal politics of those years. Rather I spotlight "a whole area of the Revolution," to borrow again from Bailyn, that has been lost in the penumbra. My hope is that readers will enjoy a suspenseful story about the uncertainties and dangers of the early American experiment and that historians and constitutional scholars will incorporate my findings into future representations of the founding years in order to render them more complete.

PART ONE

FIRST CONGRESS TO THE TRIAL OF INDEPENDENCE

CHAPTER I

"Civil Wars Among Ourselves"

In september of 1774, when more than four dozen delegates from twelve colonies gathered in Philadelphia to devise a strategy of resistance to the Coercive Acts, they were under no illusion about the extraordinary political challenges confronting them. As thirty-eight-year-old Massachusetts lawyer John Adams wrote to his wife Abigail, "Fifty gentlemen meeting together, all strangers, are not acquainted with each other's language, ideas, views, designs. They are therefore jealous of each other—fearful, timid, skittish."[1]

The four punishing Coercive Acts had been passed in quick succession between March and June. They were, as the delegates agreed, vengeful measures enacted by Parliament to retaliate against Boston for the destructive tea incident in its harbor in December. The Parliament was intent upon demonstrating its supremacy in all matters economic and political, especially to New Englanders, who had been in the vanguard of rebellion against royal authority since the Stamp Act almost a decade earlier. King George III and Lord North acted with such confidence that year in part because reports from America affirmed that a show of force would quickly humble the Sons of Liberty and their mob followers. Thomas Gage, soon to be appointed royal governor of Massachusetts, had said just this to the king only weeks before the acts were passed. The New England rebels would be "lions whilst we were lambs," Gage reported, but would turn "very meek" in the face of overwhelming British bayonets. Gage was encouraged not only by the superiority of the Royal Army but also by the historic fact of American disunity. If it came to war, he and many other observers of the American scene expected New England to stand alone. In a letter written ten days before the First Congress assembled, Gage especially highlighted the probable opposition of Southerners, who "talk[ed] very high" but feared that breaking away from the British empire would leave them defenseless against slave rebellions and Indian attacks on their southwestern frontiers.[2]

The first of the four Coercive Acts was the Boston Port Act. In this measure Parliamentarians in London canceled all trade into and out of one of America's most important water systems: Boston Bay and the hundreds of miles of rivers and coastlines serving the commercial center. The law, to be enforced by the Royal Army and Navy, made illegal the landing, discharging, and shipping of goods and merchandise until the full cost of the British East India Company's lost tea had been compensated. To the seafaring people of Massachusetts, who lived by water, ships, and navigation, this act constituted an unprecedented assault on the rights and freedoms of New Englanders.

FIGURE 1. Boston Harbor, 1774. (Illustration of British warships surrounding Boston. Paul Revere, *A view of the town of Boston with several ships of war in the harbour, vol. I. [detail]*, 1774, engraving, 6.61 x 10.43 in, New York Public Library.)

Next came the Massachusetts Government Act, the Administration of Justice Act, and the Quartering Act. Whereas the Port Act had abolished trade, the Massachusetts Government Act tread upon more treacherous ground still by effectively abolishing colonial government. It abrogated the colony's charter, forbade town meetings, and passed traditional powers of appointment of colonial officials previously enjoyed by the assembly into the hands of King George and his recently appointed military governor,

Gage. The other two bills, the Administration of Justice Act and the Quartering Act, were also unconstitutional in the eyes of self-respecting Americans. One provided for select jury trials to be removed to England or Nova Scotia at the whim of the governor. The other empowered the governor to quarter soldiers where he pleased, when he pleased, and at public expense, again without the consent of the colonial assembly.

These four acts left most of Boston, and much of the rest of colonial North America, in a state of shock. It seemed as if an orderly world of constitutional liberties and republican government was being overturned by forces of tyranny well-known to colonists from recent British history. They remembered the tyranny of Charles I, who ruled by the precept of a king's divine rights before he was beheaded in 1649. They remembered Cromwell, Charles II, James II, and, finally, the installation of Mary and William in the Glorious Revolution that ushered in a new era of legislative supremacy under the English Bill of Rights. Most of all, they remembered the past century and a half of their own liberties and freedoms peaceably guaranteed to them, not by a distant king or Parliament, but by their own elected colonial legislatures. Now the most powerful colony in New England, Massachusetts, was under assault by the king-in-parliament. So to restore their rights and privileges, and avoid war, the Whig faction in the colony organized. Soon an extralegal assembly issued a declaration calling for a congress of all thirteen colonies to meet in Philadelphia in early September. Massachusetts itself nominated five delegates—James Bowdoin, Robert Treat Paine, Thomas Cushing, Sam Adams, and John Adams.

John Adams, for one, readily accepted the honor and the responsibility of service in the Continental Congress, but not without trepidation. As the Massachusetts lawyer shared confidentially with his diary, he was of two alternating mindsets about his role in the coming gathering of colonies. In his virtuous statesman moments of thought, he relished the chance to step upon the world stage as an intrepid lawgiver and sentry of liberty in the mold of Solon, Lycurgus, and other great Greek and Roman statesmen of antiquity. He had long since deemed the highest calling in a citizen's life to be the defense of liberty against despotism. However, just as soon, Adams's mind would shift away from Roman triumphalism and valor to sinking doubt. One day in Massachusetts months before the Congress convened, following a long walk in the countryside, he sat down at his desk and wrote, "I feel unutterable anxiety." Adams worried that even the decisions of "the wisest men upon the continent" might avail nothing in the war of wills with Lord North and his late gauntlet of oppressive measures. "The objects before me are too grand and multifarious for my comprehension," he recorded, going on to express, "A more extensive knowledge of the realm, the colonies, and of commerce, as well as of law and policy, is necessary, than I am master of."[3]

* * * * *

The delegates, of course, did not come to the First Congress with a fixed plan to launch into independence from the empire. On the contrary, their purpose was to enact stiff economic measures that would force Parliament to repeal the four dangerous acts, restoring harmony and goodwill. Nevertheless, everyone present in Philadelphia that early September knew that there were a host of radicals among them, especially from New England, who were privately warm to independence. They further understood that after nearly ten years of protests and boycotts against arbitrary parliamentary measures, circumstances were ripe for a violent rupture. Universally, they believed that if they did not proceed with caution and wisdom at the Congress of 1774, their deliberations might precipitate bloodletting, which would ultimately leave the colonies—or at least some of them—with no choice but to separate from the mother country by way of an awful imperial civil war.

The logic that British violence upon Americans would catalyze independence was especially pervasive in New England, where Boston Harbor was under martial lockdown. But other delegates shared the sentiment. One of them was Colonel George Washington of Virginia, who arrived in Philadelphia on September 4. We know this about Washington because during this period he declared outright in a letter to a fellow Virginian that violent missteps by the British in Boston would bring about the inevitable. The letter was directed to a man Washington considered a traitor, Robert Mackenzie, also a Virginia military man, but one who was now patrolling impounded Boston on behalf of Lord North and royal tyranny. The forty-two-year-old Washington, renowned for his heroism in the late French and Indian War, warned Mackenzie that the moment British troops spilled American blood, everlasting alienation would set in. Restoration of brotherly love would thereafter be futile. And in such a case, Washington asserted, it could not be fairly said that the colonists severed their ties from Britain voluntarily. By killing, the Parliament and King George will have driven America into a righteous independence. "Give me leave to add, as my opinion," Washington concluded the letter, "that more blood will be spilt on this occasion (if the Ministry are determined to push matters to extremity) than history has ever yet furnished instances of in the annals of North America."[4]

Chapter 1: "Civil Wars Among Ourselves"

Americans dreaded this outcome—a decision in favor of independence—for numerous reasons. One was that, as Washington professed, it would bring on a bloody imperial civil war, pitting self-trained provincial militias against one of the most awesome professional fighting forces on earth. Another reason independence was anathema to Americans was their defenselessness against the other warring nations of the world. If the colonies went to war with Britain, they would simultaneously lose the military and naval protection of the empire. When this happened, would other foreign powers like France, Spain, and Russia remain on the sidelines, impartially observing the war of American independence from afar? Or would they exploit it, plundering and conquering on their own behalf as the Anglo-American conflict exhausted both sides month after month?

Another thing the delegates dreaded that September was disunion and civil wars among themselves. So real and ubiquitous was this apprehended sequel of independence that a leading New York politician, Philip Livingston, had warned John Adams about it on his way down the coast to the Congress from Boston. Livingston was a member of the most prominent family in the colony. His namesake father was Second Lord of the Manor, and his brother, William, would later sign the U.S. Constitution. From New York political service, Philip himself would go on to serve three years in Congress and sign the Declaration of Independence. Adams, never one to withhold harsh judgments of others from the pages of his diary, wrote an entry on August 22 describing the fifty-eight-year-old Livingston. More than anything, the New Yorker embodied the propensity common in that city to talk too loud and fast. "Phill. Livingston," Adams said, "is a great, rough, rapid mortal. There is no holding any conversation with him. He blusters away."[5]

Over lunch one day at the table of attorney Zephaniah Platt in his stone townhouse at the tip of Manhattan, Livingston shared with visiting delegates and other guests his certainty that any independence movement would end in domestic civil wars. Honing in on specifics, he contended that New Englanders would be the worst offenders. According to Adams, Livingston foretold that the fierce Puritan coalition of northern America would sack the middle and southern regions of America as the barbarians did poor old Rome. "If England should turn us adrift," Adams quoted Livingston as saying, "we should instantly go to civil wars among ourselves to determine which colony should govern all the rest. Seems to dread N. England—the Levelling Spirit &c. Hints were thrown out of the Goths and Vandals."[6]

FIGURE 2. John Adams, Massachusetts Delegate. (Detail of a portrait of John Adams. John Singleton Copley, *John Adams (1735–1826)*, 1783, oil on canvas, 93.75 x 57.875 in, Harvard University Portrait Collection, Bequest of Ward Nicholas Boylston to Harvard College, 1828.)

Not much later, another distinguished New Yorker, Rev. Samuel Seabury, forty-four-year-old rector of St. Peter's Church in West Chester, went public in the newspapers with a similar prognostication. Echoing what Adams had heard from Livingston, Seabury warned that the protective bond of the colonies with the mother country was each colony's only salvation from its hostile neighbors. "Whenever the fatal period shall arrive, in which the American colonies shall become independent on Great Britain," he envisioned, "a horrid scene of war and bloodshed will immediately commence. The interests, the commerce of the different provinces will interfere: disputes about boundaries and limits will arise. There will be no supreme power to interpose; but the sword and bayonet must decide the dispute."[7]

Also like Livingston, Seabury was most wary of the militant power and might of New England, predicting if the colonies launched themselves into independence, the northernmost colonies would eventually unite themselves into a single "republic" and conquer New York. "It is well known that the province of Massachusetts Bay have carried their opposition to the British government to the most daring height," Seabury wrote in the pages of James Rivington's newspaper, the New York *Gazetteer*. He continued:

> Only now suppose it possible that they should succeed, and become a state independent of Great Britain. The probable consequence would be that the other New England colonies would join them, and together with them, form one Republic. When once they had arrived at this height of power, how long do you suppose they would remain in peace with this government? Certainly only till a fair opportunity offered to attack it with advantage. The New England people have ever cast a wishful eye on the lands of this province. Connecticut, Massachusetts, New Hampshire, have all in their turns encroached upon them; and their encroachments have not only been very troublesome, but also very difficult to remove. A state of continual war with New England, would be the inevitable fate of this province, till submission on our part, or conquest on their part, put a period to the dispute. The consequences of such an event to the landed interest of this colony, need no enumeration.[8]

Another member of the clergy, Thomas Bradbury Chandler, a respected Anglican priest from New Jersey, said something similar in another tract published in 1774. Cautioning faithfulness to England to avoid revolution precipitating rack and ruin, Chandler argued:

> What must be the consequence of a rebellious war with the Mother Country, any person of common sense, if he will take the liberty to exercise it, may easily foresee. Even a final victory would effectually ruin us; as it would necessarily introduce civil wars among ourselves, and leave us open and exposed to the avarice and ambition of every maritime power in Europe or America. And till one part of this country shall have subdued the other, and conquered a considerable part of the world besides, this peaceful region must become, and continue to be, a theatre of inconceivable misery and horror.[9]

Livingston's observation over lunch and the published essays of Seabury and Chandler were hardly isolated, fringe forecasts in the Revolutionary Era. Predictions had long been rampant that an independent America would self-destruct in civil wars. According to conventional wisdom, the only force preventing such mayhem among the colonies was the restraining hand of Parliament and the British king. James Otis, patriot and author of the influential *The Rights of the British Colonies Asserted and Proved*, averred in 1765, "Were these colonies left to themselves tomorrow, America would be a mere shambles of blood and confusion." An English traveler visiting the colonies in 1759 and 1760 observed such great diversity and heated division that he too drew the conclusion: "Were they left to themselves, there would soon be civil war from one end of the continent to the other."[10]

In the year of the Coercive Acts, concrete speculation that maritime New England would rain fury over the other colonies was not limited to New York. It crept into Philadelphia, where the Congress was meeting. As Sam Adams, second cousin to John and thirteen years his senior, reported back to Joseph Warren in Massachusetts, delegates in Philadelphia were whispering that New Englanders had traveled to Philadelphia not simply to fight British tyranny but to spearhead independence. Furthermore, rumors held that a war of independence against the empire would be followed by a civil war of New England conquest southward. Some delegates, Adams wrote to Warren, were actively terrified "that as we are a hardy and brave people we shall in time over run them all." Adams brushed off the claim as "groundless." Still, as he alerted Warren, New Englanders must exert themselves to extinguish the fear, lest it hang as a dark cloud over the prospect of forming a secure, protective American Union to safeguard Massachusetts.[11]

* * * * *

Another celebrated American, Joseph Galloway, forty-three-year-old speaker of the Pennsylvania House, proved to be the most anxious delegate of all to attend the First Congress. The reason for this was that Galloway, like Livingston, Seabury, and others, foresaw American disobedience as a certain pathway not only to the coming of a destructive imperial civil war with England, but also to several species of domestic civil war.

As Galloway soon announced in a widely published manifesto, *A Candid Examination of the Mutual Claims of Great Britain and the Colonies*, independence was a Pandora's box never to be opened. If such folly ever happened, he outlined, first there would be prolonged warfare between England and the colonies, with only slim chances of independence prevailing. The invincible Royal Navy, he promised, would shell every port, burn wharves, fields, barns, and homes, and reduce the colonies to a permanent form of servitude far worse than the Boston Port Act. Moreover, in the chaos that independence would unleash, disorganized, unprofessional rebel American armies would appropriate property belonging to the landed gentry. The colonies would be released into a primitive state of nature. There would be anarchy, rape, murder, and pillage, Galloway said. There would be a takeover of the wealth and property of the landed by the rapacious landless. And not gentlemen, certainly, but the tawdry "unthinking, ignorant" sorts of men among them would rampage the countryside, "ravishing your wives and daughters, and afterwards plunging the dagger in their tender bosoms."[12]

Next in the list of domestic horrors, independence would bring forth two subcategories of geographic civil war: land, border, and boundary wars between individual colonies, and finally, at some point, a bloody conflagration between North and South. This conclusion, he lamented, was not fanciful. It was based on a synthesis of twenty-five years' worth of personal observation and experience of the colonies combined with deep readings of history. The colonies' extraordinary differences of culture, religion, government, economy, and viewpoints of land and maritime rights, already sources of long-standing jealousies and dislikes, Galloway cautioned, made civil wars inevitable.

Livingston and Seabury had specifically highlighted the risk of a New England overthrow of New York. Galloway, a veteran of colonial and ministerial politics since well before the Stamp Act, saw the future differently, underscoring the dangerous fault line between the Northern and Southern colonies. If the North and South did attempt to combine into one union, he said, a day of reckoning was predetermined. Civil war would be written into the bond, and, without doubt, the impotent South would suffer a crushing loss. Galloway viewed the empire as a vital protector of the vulnerable agricultural Southern colonies. Shorn of the external control of the king and Parliament, the maritime Northern colonies would at some point invade.

"The northern colonies, inured to military discipline and hardships," Galloway warned, "will, in all probability, be the first to enter the list of military controversy; and, like the northern Saxons and Danes, carry devastation and havoc over the southern, who, weak for want of discipline, and having a dangerous enemy within their own bowels, must, after suffering all the horrors of a civil war, yield to the superior force, and submit to the will of the conquerors."[13]

FIGURE 3. Joseph Galloway, Pennsylvania Delegate. (Portrait of Joseph Galloway. Thomas Day, *Joseph Galloway*, ca. 1775, watercolor on ivory, 1.5625 x 1.1875 in, National Portrait Gallery, Smithsonian Institution, NPG.92.33.)

In this divination Galloway did not make reference to slavery as a cause of a North-South American civil war. But he did call attention to the "dangerous enemy within"—that is, the half million enslaved persons living in the Southern colonies primed for an uprising against their enslavers. Generally, it was held in the Revolutionary Era that slavery was a decrepit, corrupt institution that rendered the Southern colonies weak and pregnable. Galloway's point was that without outside protection, Virginia, Maryland, North Carolina, South Carolina, and Georgia would be easily vanquished by their Northern counterparts in the event of domestic civil war. It was possible, too, he implied, that the enslaved might rise up for freedom in that war, joining the Northerners in the conquest.

Again, Galloway's forebodings about the perils of North-South disunion and civil war were not singular. These risks were often repeated during the founding years. Another penman, writing for a New York gazette in August of 1773, described a fascinating dynamic between the Northern and Southern colonies whereby their regional differences constituted an "equilibre, so important for the tranquility of the Colonies." The Northern colonies, formidable in resources to build and outfit commercial ships and a navy, were vital to the protection of the "opulent" Southern colonies, which in turn benefited the Northern ones by providing prodigious staple crops of tobacco, indigo, and rice for the carrying trade. What the British empire had to be afraid of, however, was the "natural weakness" of the South. "If the colonies happen to vie," the writer warned, "and try their reciprocal strength with each other, the political force of the Northern Colonies will soon destroy the opulent force of the Southern."[14]

* * * * *

With such anxieties and ill omens in the air, the First Congress convened on Monday, September 5, at the City Tavern on the west side of Second Street. Twelve colonies were represented at the historic gathering in Philadelphia, not thirteen, because the southernmost colony, Georgia, refused to send delegates. In a vote held on August 10 in Savannah, the conservative faction overwhelmed the "violent liberty people" to quash a motion for dispatching a delegation. The assembly in Savannah did adopt resolutions deploring the Coercive Acts and declaring that Americans possessed the same political rights as mainland British subjects. But the necessary majority of Georgia representatives could not be mustered to endorse attendance of the extralegal Continental Congress. Voices rang out across Georgia proclaiming any such present and future gatherings to be "unconstitutional, illegal, and punishable by law." Other outspoken Georgians argued that New Englanders' destruction of British tea was itself a dreadful crime from which they must distance themselves. Because Georgians "had no hand in destroying any teas," one group of concerned citizens from Saint Paul Parish set forth, "they can have no business to make themselves partakers of the ill consequences resulting from such a conduct."[15]

On the first day of the Congress's proceedings, the delegates of the other twelve colonies met at the City Tavern, instead of a formal legislative hall, for a surprising reason. High-ranking host of the Congress, Speaker Galloway, had made plain to each arriving delegate that he had been planning for months for them to unite in the royal chambers of the Pennsylvania State House. That elegant hall, hung with a portrait of King George III, stood for Anglo-American union and empire. For more than fifty years the representatives of the people of Pennsylvania had been deliberating there, pursuing liberty, settling differences, making law, and reconciling divisive disputes with Parliament. The Congress of 1774 should be no different, Galloway contended. Since they were loyal colonists intent upon seeking redress, not independence or war, the State House was the "proper place" to make their petitions.[16]

Rapidly, though, a faction arose to oppose Speaker Galloway and what seemed to many to be cowering in the face of the Coercive Acts. Other delegates, including several attendees from the speaker's own Pennsylvania, recoiled at the suggestion of convening at the State House, promoting instead a neutral space elsewhere, a building or room more consonant with freedom, liberty, civil disobedience, and a people's right to revolution when arbitrary power seizes them, as taught by John Locke.

In this prelude to the First Congress, the delegates split badly on where to deliberate. So as faithful followers of representative government, they postponed its determination to an official vote. That is why, on the first day of Congress, they initially assembled not in a legislative hall but in the large room of City Tavern. There they debated the location of Congress. Soon after, either at City Tavern or in Carpenters' Hall—the historical record is unclear on this point—they reached a majority consensus to forgo the imperial trappings of the State House. More delegates were pleased with the choice of the modest Carpenters' Hall, located on Chestnut at Fourth.

Architecturally, Carpenters' Hall symbolized the ideals of republican simplicity, the everyman, and equality. And, not incidentally, the hall offered the added benefit of quick access to Ben Franklin's Library Company situated only one flight of stairs above on the second floor. The library housed more than two thousand volumes, including Locke's *Two Treatises*, Blackstone's *Commentaries on the Laws of England*, Coke's *Institutes*, Montesquieu's *Spirit of the Laws*, and Trenchard and Gordon's *Cato's Letters*. If the delegates could agree on one thing, it was that they would need the weight and wisdom of these tomes to end the standoff with King George and Parliament without bloodshed.

* * * * *

After selecting Carpenters' Hall as their meeting place, the Congress turned to the first order of business: the election of a president of the legislative body. With no recorded opposition, the delegates named Virginian Peyton Randolph to the post. In light of his long experience as speaker of the House of Burgesses in Williamsburg, the fifty-three-year-old Randolph was a logical choice. However, according to John Adams, there was an additional, and far more important, reason for electing Randolph. The key criterion for determining the leadership of Congress was Randolph's colony of origin: Virginia.

Decades later Adams recorded that the governing philosophy of the American Revolution and the early years of the republic was "the Frankfort advice, to place Virginia at the head of everything." In saying this he was alluding to a conversation that took place on the eve of the First Congress in the small town of Frankfort, just outside Philadelphia. On that day, August 29, 1774, numerous Pennsylvania patriots, forewarned of the impending arrival of the Massachusettsans, had ridden five miles from Philadelphia to Frankfort to intercept them. Dr. Benjamin Rush and Thomas Mifflin, along with several others, constituted a welcoming party of sorts to the First Congress. Yet, in fact, they came bearing preemptive messages about two matters they said that, if not kept contained, would jeopardize the embryonic American Union. What was on their minds was not political subjects like voting power or whether colonial imports or exports should be cut off to force the hand of Parliament in the escalating imperial crisis. Those questions would have to wait several weeks to evoke divisiveness in the Congress.[17]

In Frankfort the first topic at hand was instead a stern warning by the Pennsylvanians to their Massachusetts counterparts not to promote "independence." Gravely, as Adams recalled, Rush and Mifflin exhorted the Massachusetts men to squelch all talk of separation from England. First of all, they pressed, "You must not utter the word independence, nor give the least hint or insinuation of the idea, either in Congress or any private conversation; if you do, you are undone; for the idea of independence is as unpopular in Pennsylvania, and in all the Middle and Southern States, as the Stamp Act itself." The colonies, of course, were not yet states, but this was the language Adams used after the Revolution when describing the episode to fellow politician Timothy Pickering.[18]

Next, Adams records, "We invited them to take tea with us in a private apartment." There, the Pennsylvania contingent shared circulating rumors and prejudices against the Massachusetts men. It was being said that the overwrought New Englanders planned to destroy the empire. Their ambition was not liberty, justice, and peace, but revolution and the dangerous doctrine of independence. The graphic portrait being painted of this approaching radical element was not flattering. "Mr. Samuel Adams was a very artful, designing man, but desperately poor, and wholly dependent on his popularity with the lowest vulgar for his living." John Adams and Thomas Treat Paine were politicians "of no great talents, reputation, or weight, who had no other means of raising themselves into consequence, than by courting popularity." The fourth, Thomas Cushing, "was a harmless kind of man, but poor, and wholly dependent on his popularity for his subsistence." They were, in a word, "four desperate adventurers." To raise themselves up, the rumor was being spread, they and their New England compatriots would throw down the scepter and orb of King George, launching the colonies into the violent storm of independence.

In this recollection Adams was not exaggerating the stereotype so many Americans and Britons carried in their minds of New Englanders. In this period of colonial-imperial troubles over tea taxes, the Puritans and Pilgrims living in the four colonies eastward of the Hudson River were considered by some to be "New-England fanaticks." Other epithets directed at these rabble rousers include "hair-brained fanaticks," "obstinate, hot-headed zealots," and "demagogues." Another accusation leveled at New Englanders in an age when moderate, thinking politicians believed faithfully in the doctrine of balanced government—equal parts monarchy, aristocracy, and democracy—was that they were "rebellious Republicans" whose aim in government was to establish something akin to the dread of pure democracy. By some, they were hated for triggering the wrath of Parliament and the king through their lawless destruction of tea, deploying art and chicanery to induce the other colonies to follow in their "mad schemes." By others, New Englanders were mocked as "the most virtuous people on earth!" whose motto, the "Saints shall inherit the earth," applied to them alone, not to Anglicans, Presbyterians, Baptists, Quakers, and the rest. Worst of all, the people of New England were feared as religious bigots who, if independence happened, might wipe out all the other religions of North America in their Puritan crusade to establish "New-England Republican Government."[19]

Derived in part from these regional stereotypes of New Englanders, the second counsel the Pennsylvanian delegates in Frankfort strongly urged upon Massachusettsans before they entered Philadelphia pertained precisely to the question of what colonies or region of America should take the lead in Congress. What Adams heard was information he remembered indelibly for the rest of his life. He called it the "Frankfort advice": to head off discord and dissension, Pennsylvania advised Massachusetts, New Englanders must perforce place the reins of the Congress in the hands of the vast commonwealth of Virginia.

"You must not pretend to take the lead," they said. "You know Virginia is the most populous state in the Union. They are very proud of their ancient dominion, as they call it; they think they have a right to take the lead, and the Southern States, and Middle States too, are too much disposed to yield it to them."

Adams considered what he heard that day to be catalytic. "It made a deep impression on my mind," he said. The key to the success of the American Union in the early years, he professed, was to defer to Virginia. The Old Dominion was the flagship of the Southern colonies. Therefore, to unite that region to New England, Virginia must be propped up and appeased. "This conversation, and the principles, facts, and motives, suggested in it," Adams said, "have given a color, complexion, and character, to the whole policy of the United States, from that day to this."[20]

Adams went on to underscore that to understand the history of the Revolution and the early period, one must understand the Frankfort advice. Why was a Virginian, George Washington, nominated commander in chief of the Continental army? Why did Virginia, not Massachusetts, first press a motion for independence on the floor of Congress? Why did Virginian Thomas Jefferson author the Declaration of Independence? In his account of the early years of the war, Adams gives a single, unequivocal answer to all three questions: to bind Virginia and therefore the other Southern colonies to the cause of resistance and thus unite the dissimilar colonies into a safe, unified whole.

* * * * *

For the same reason, the First Congress placed a Virginian, Peyton Randolph, in the president's chair. After this election, the delegates named Charles Thomson, forty-five-year-old Pennsylvanian, as secretary. Then they opened up the combustible question of voting power in their deliberations. They were a republican legislative body whose mission in Philadelphia was to enact countermeasures to the Coercive Acts. To do so they would make proposals, hold debates, and, finally, through the sacred tradition of voting, enact the majority, or supermajority, will of Congress. Before casting ballots to determine these measures, of course, they must agree upon a "method of voting."[21]

The central question was: How would they represent the people of their respective colonies on the sensitive, potentially historic resolutions advanced on the floor of Congress? Would it be by colony, one-colony-one-vote, a formula favoring small colonies like New Hampshire and Delaware, or by population or wealth, tilting the power scale by a factor of three or four times to large colonies like Virginia, Massachusetts, and Pennsylvania? And what about enslaved persons? Roughly 40 percent of the South's population was held in bondage. In New England, enslaved and free Black people constituted less than 3 percent of the population. Many in Congress found slavery to be a moral abomination. Even so, to avert polarization and preserve unity, the debates in September 1774 did not hew to moral judgment and criticism of the institution but to the matter of legislative power. If they framed a system of voting based on proportional representation or wealth, were enslaved persons to be deemed property or people, either way perversely bloating the power of the Southern colonies? These were politically and morally fraught questions that would haunt the American experiment until the Civil War.[22]

Virginia delegate Patrick Henry, thirty-eight years old and already famed in the colonies for his fiery resistance to the Stamp Act, was the first delegate to stand up in Carpenters' Hall and take the offensive on voting. By all accounts, at home and in this First Congress, Henry was considered a magisterial speechmaker. Watching him on the floor of Congress, Silas Deane of Connecticut described him as "the completest speaker I ever heard . . . in a letter I can give you no idea of the music of his voice, or the high wrought, yet natural elegance of his stile & manner." James Madison once said that Henry's voice reminded him of a trumpeter on the battlefield calling the troops to a charge. Thomas Jefferson claimed that the master orator "spoke as Homer wrote."[23]

No official transcript of Henry's September 5 speech survives, but several delegates took notes. The thrust of his argument was that a representative Congress must be one *of the people*, counted proportionally, not by colony. He therefore vehemently opposed the rule of one-colony-one-vote. Each individual—by which he meant each white male of standing, owning a defined minimal amount of property—must be given equal voice. This was a self-evident truth of the reigning white male republicanism of the day. If not, the first American Congress, of many to come, Henry projected, would itself be rightly judged as trampling on the sacred principle of the equality of the people. "A precedent ought to be established now," he pressed, "that it would be great injustice if a little colony should have the same weight in the councils of America as a great one."[24]

Henry made this speech toward the end of the day, leaving little time for a well-digested response. As far as is known, only one delegate briefly spoke up against Henry's large colony argument. It was John Sullivan, a thirty-four-year-old attorney from small New Hampshire. Appointed two years earlier as an army major in the New Hampshire militia, Sullivan was the last to speak on the first day. To him equality meant equality of colonies, not equality of the citizens within them. "Major Sullivan," in the

Chapter 1: "Civil Wars Among Ourselves"

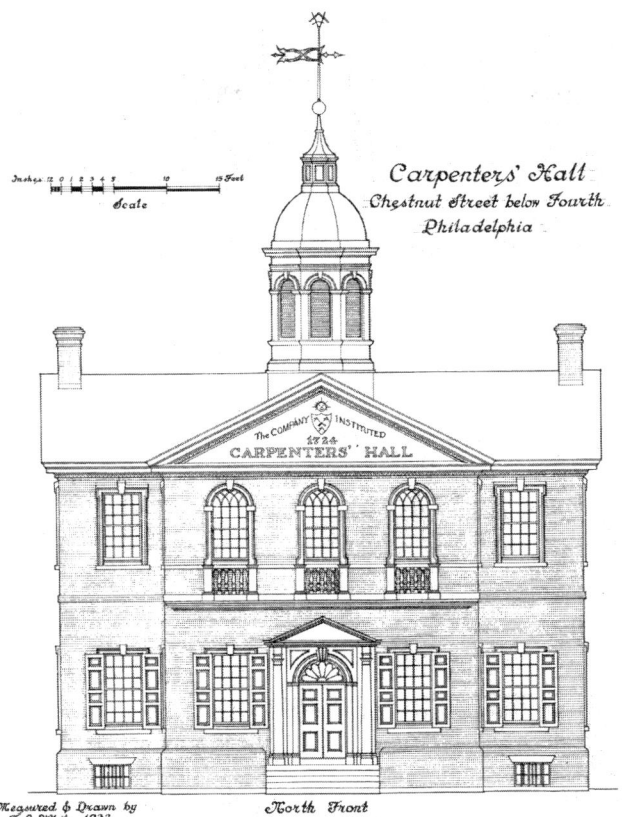

FIGURE 4. Carpenters' Hall, First Continental Congress. (Illustration of Carpenters' Hall. F. L. White, *North front - Carpenters' Company Hall, 320 Chestnut Street & Carpenters' Court, Philadelphia, Philadelphia County, PA*, 1932, print, 19 x 24 in, Library of Congress Prints and Photographs Division, Washington, DC.)

words of John Adams, "observed that a little colony had its all at stake as well as a great one."[25]

After this reply to Henry, the Congress adjourned, postponing further debate until ten o'clock the next morning. Back at his lodgings on Second Street, Adams took some alarm at the proceedings, noting in his diary that the first day of the First Congress had exposed a fault line. "This is a question of great importance," he reflected. "If we vote by colonies, this method will be liable to great inequality and injustice, for 5 small colonies,

FIGURE 5. Patrick Henry, Virginia Delegate. (Portrait of Patrick Henry. J. B. Longacre, *Patrick Henry*, date unknown, print, New York Public Library, EM7772.)

with 100,000 people in each, may outvote 4 large ones, each of which has 500,000 Inhabitants." He continued, "This will lead us into such a field of controversy as will greatly perplex us."[26]

* * * * *

After sleeping on the question overnight, Henry awoke Tuesday morning invigorated to push harder still to settle the matter in favor of the equality of people, not of colonies. This time, Samuel Ward of Rhode Island, forty-nine-year-old statesman who had served for three decades as royal governor, led the charge against Henry's position, arguing in favor of equality of the colonies. Then another Virginian, Benjamin Harrison, stood up and delivered the first speech in U.S. history menacing an action that would later be described as a threat of nullification and secession.

Henry spoke first again, saying that British "fleets and armies" had now invaded New England. This act of war changed everything. America was no longer a sphere of the British empire split into satellite colonies subordinate to the Crown. "We are in a state of nature, sir," he said. Americans were one people fighting tyranny. Thus, they had it in their power to recreate political society according to precepts and rules that honored "the democratical part of the constitution." A genius at turning words, Henry

Chapter 1: "Civil Wars Among Ourselves"

strove to persuade his fellow delegates of the necessity of population-based representation through recourse to a stirring new American patriotism. "The distinctions between Virginians, Pennsylvanians, New Yorkers and New Englanders, are no more," he said. "I am not a Virginian, but an American."[27]

Ward of Rhode Island was unmoved by this rhetoric. Taking the floor, he insisted that the colonies represented in Congress were joined as separate political bodies in the defense of liberty. They were not one mass of citizens. They were a confederation of thirteen equal nation-states. All thirteen might be heading for war, and "the weakest colony by such a sacrifice would suffer as much as the greatest."[28]

At this point, Harrison, forty-eight-year-old future lieutenant of the Charles City County militia and governor of the state, stood up to declare that Congress was treading on dangerous ground. He shared that his mind rebelled at such an inequality of the people as the small colony men were advancing on the floor of the hall. He, Washington, Henry, Randolph, and the other Virginia delegates, Harrison said, had ridden to Philadelphia to succor fellow colonists in distress anticipating representation in the classical tradition of the law. Instead, they were encountering a politically pathological way of thinking sure to shock the sensibilities of all Virginians.

As penned in personal notes by delegate James Duane, forty-one-year-old New York lawyer, Harrison decried the "injustice" of the one-colony-one-vote principle as a poor footing upon which to commence a continental assembly and possible common war. Then the speaker issued a finely honed threat. Were the Virginians in Congress to consent to the iniquitous one-colony-one-vote rule, he promised, they would ride home to a parade of reproach and outrage rather than thanks from their constituents. It was certain, he said, that back in Virginia he would be "censured by his constituents & unable to excuse his want of attention to their interest. And that he was very apprehensive that if such a disrespect should be put upon his countrymen we should never see them at another convention."[29]

Harrison uttered no incivilities. No one was personally vilified. His tone, surely, was modest, not bellicose. Debating the question at hand in Carpenters' Hall, he simply conveyed the subtle message to the other colonies that Virginia, if dishonored and disrespected in such a grave matter of justice and jurisprudence as voting power, might be left with no option but to part ways with the Congress.

Here was an astonishing beginning to the American Union. Samuel Adams later designated the First Congress in Philadelphia to be the formal birth of the American nation. The events of 1774, most notably the Boston Port Act, he remarked, "suddenly wrought a Union of the colonies which could not be [brought] about by the industry of years of reasoning." Now on the second day of that Congress, revealing a deeper truth about the Union, the specter of withdrawal by Virginia raised a vexing silence over the Congress. How would they vote on the measures they must enact in unison in order to banish the Coercive Acts? A prominent Virginian had stated that a determination in favor of one-colony-one-vote might drive the largest, most populous and wealthiest of the thirteen colonies to turn its back on the Union.[30]

Besides this, there was another looming question in the subtext of Harrison's remark. Would Virginia withdraw alone, or would other states follow?

* * * * *

According to Duane, Harrison's speech on the dismal prospects of Virginia attending future American congresses, in the event that voting injustice were served upon them, was a jarring turning point. Abruptly, records indicate, the delegates ceased to argue the merits of each side's political philosophy about voting power and representation. Rather, they sought a conciliating, face-saving rescue from the Virginia position, and by the late afternoon of the same day they landed on one. John Adams, John Jay of New York, and other parliamentary strategists made the argument that time was of the essence in responding to the Coercive Acts. They must move forward, not divide over procedure. Moreover, notwithstanding the validity of everything Harrison and Henry had said, it was impossible to obtain the actuarial data necessary to assign voting by population or wealth. This argument, it turns out, saved the day.[31]

What was the real population of Virginia? Rhode Island? No one knew. They did not have accurate counts on hand. And if they chose to vote based on formulas of wealth instead of population, what was the value of their imports, exports, and land? How much was Virginia tobacco worth? Georgia's rice? Maryland's enslaved persons? Massachusetts's timber and shipyards? How many quintals of cod and haddock did Connecticut ship out each year? No standard had been set for determining answers to any of these questions relating to the population and wealth of each colony. It would all be guesswork, and this, they concluded, would only foster discord and distract them from greater tasks at hand.

Chapter 1: "Civil Wars Among Ourselves" 39

What they could do speedily, however, without research or argument, was to count to twelve. Therefore, with due respect and deference to Virginia, Adams and the other intervening delegates asked the Old Dominion's delegates to make a special exception on voting—for this Congress only.[32]

Reluctantly, the Virginians agreed. In the interest of time, parsimony, and avoidance of conflict, the First Congress adopted a *temporary* rule of one-colony-one-vote. Contrary to everything Henry and Harrison had said, the small colonial population of Rhode Island would enjoy equality with the enormous colonial population of Virginia.

Henry and Harrison had lost the debate, but not entirely. They and other delegates who viscerally opposed the expedient they were approving on paper, considering it "unequal," did so exclusively for the First Congress, adding a codicil of sorts. In the compromise struck late in the day of September 6, the delegates formally agreed that one-colony-one-vote was under no circumstances to be construed as "a precedent" enshrined for future assemblies. In the case that England did not cede ground on the Coercive Acts and the colonies indeed were forced to reconvene for a second congress, the rule should be considered null and void.[33]

So concerned were some about this constitutional misstep into unrepublican voting that one of the delegates, surely a large-colony lawyer, further clarified that a verbal pledge to the agreement would not suffice. He asked that a written entry be made on the journals of Congress to establish beyond any jurisprudential doubt that the decision on voting method had been a one-time dispensation only, not a long-term commitment of Virginia and the other large colonies. They reserved the right, at a later date, to resume debates and rectify the grievous constitutional wrong they were enacting against their better republican judgments.[34]

CHAPTER 2

"Unite or Die"

With the matter of voting powers decided in favor of one-colony-one-vote, the First Congress proceeded to the fundamental business of devising an effective strategy to overturn the Coercive Acts. To this end, the delegates would remain in session at Carpenters' Hall for another seven weeks, typically assembling from 9:00 or 10:00 a.m. until 3:00 or 4:00 p.m., Monday through Saturday. Afterward, on most days, groups of delegates gathered at taverns and the homes of prominent Philadelphians to strategize further and, vitally, to forge personal bonds they hoped would preserve their liberty and safety. During this inaugural period of the American Union, the delegates were, in fact, embarked upon a two-part mission. One was to unite as a political band of brothers. The other was to combine the prudent art of persuasion with the science of economic civil disobedience to impel King George III and Parliament to reverse their autocratic ways and stave off imperial civil war.

Happily for the delegates, a spirit of unity infused the Congress in most things, but least of all on the central question that drew them to Philadelphia. How were they going to force the hand of the Lord North ministry, prompting the Parliament to repeal the Coercive Acts? They would write petitions and declarations, but the only sure way to defeat their opponents in London, they were sure, was an economic shock to the system: a trade embargo enforced at every port from Georgia to New Hampshire. On this they all agreed. The critical point of contention was the nature and form of the embargo. Would it be a pact of nonimportation, nonexportation, or both?

Debates on this topic brought the delegates face to face for the first time with the depth of their economic and commercial differences, particularly those of the diversified, free-labor North and the slaveholding, staple-crop South. One political historian of the Revolution, John Ferling, has called the embargo conflict of 1774 "the first North vs. South clash in American history." Virginia was the first to showcase the divide when it respectfully rebuffed all entreaties to cut off the exportation of tobacco in the short term on grounds of planter economic imperative. Later, toward the end of the Congress, four South Carolina delegates became so enraged at the prospect of a mandate to cease all rice and indigo exports that they walked out of Congress in protest, refusing to return until justice was served upon the white slaveholding peoples of their colony.[1]

This early menace of secession by South Carolina was, of course, a harbinger of things to come, not only in the next century but throughout the Revolution—and not only by South Carolina but by other states and regions in the Union as well. Threats of secession would remain a bedrock of American politics from the First Congress in 1774 until the formal conclusion of the Revolutionary War nine years later—and thereafter in similar fashion until the Civil War finally put the matter to rest.

* * * * *

The first half of September in particular was a time of confidence and good cheer. As John Adams recorded in detail in his diary, the delegates built their affections and alliances with one another over beer, wine, rum, and Madeira as well as dinner tables filled with "everything which could delight the eye, or allure the taste, curds and creams, jellies, sweet meats of various sorts, 20 sorts of tarts, fools, trifles, floating islands, whipp'd sillabubs &c. &c.—parmesan cheese, punch, wine, porter, beer &c. &c." On one occasion, at the home of Dr. Benjamin Rush, after time spent surveying the Delaware River from the top-floor back windows, Adams exulted in "a mighty feast again, nothing less than the very best of Claret, Madeira, and Burgundy. Melons, fine beyond description, and pears and peaches as excellent."[2]

New Englanders like Adams were especially heartened in these first weeks to discover an avid spirit of resistance and unity among the delegates from Virginia, the largest and most populous colony not only of the Southern bloc but of all thirteen. Over the clink of glasses and clank of tankards, the Virginians made unifying pronouncements that reassured them of the great Southern colony's devotion to liberty—and, vitally, to the safety and defense of Boston. At one gathering Benjamin Harrison of Virginia professed that "he would have come on foot," if necessary, to defend the rights of Boston and America. Richard Bland, a cousin of

Thomas Jefferson, and at sixty-three one of the oldest delegates to attend, announced he would have traveled as far as Jericho on the Jordan River. Toasts went up to the "Union of the Colonies," "Unanimity to the Congress," "Liberty," and "Firmness." Richard Henry Lee, early organizer of Virginia committees of correspondence and in a year and a half to stand before the Second Congress to formally introduce a motion for independence, pledged to fight until the Coercive Acts were wiped away and all the king's troops were withdrawn from American soil. In the Southern colonies, reported Silas Deane of Connecticut, Lee was hailed as the "Cicero of America."[3]

The most reassuring announcement of all, according to South Carolinian Thomas Lynch, came from the mouth of George Washington. At a dinner one night at his residence in Philadelphia, Lynch, patriot of old who stood out among the other delegates for his bold sartorial statement of American allegiance—he wore only homemade American cloth, repudiating all British dress until justice was restored—claimed he knew firsthand what Washington had said recently at an assembly held in Williamsburg. "Colonel Washington," he professed, "made the most eloquent speech at the Virginia Convention that ever was made." If England did not back down peaceably, the fearsome hero of the French and Indian War reportedly declared, "I will raise 1000 men, subsist them at my own expense and march myself at their head for the relief of Boston."[4]

* * * * *

Never far from hand in these homes and taverns where the delegates raised their glasses to the new American Union were copies of the *Pennsylvania Journal*, a Philadelphia newspaper whose serpentine masthead bore a stark reminder of the most important work to be done in the aftermath of Parliament's acts. Emblazoned across the top of the front page of the paper were an icon and motto designed to embolden them to stand tall against oppression and, simultaneously, to sacrifice for the cause. The logo was that of a rattlesnake, and the slogan beneath it pronounced in all caps, "UNITE OR DIE." Strikingly, the snake was sliced into nine, not thirteen, contiguous segments: New England, New York, New Jersey, Pennsylvania, Maryland, Virginia, North Carolina, South Carolina, and Georgia.

Distinct from the other colonies, the New England four were depicted on the masthead as a single regional unit comprising the snake's head and possessing its venomous fangs—for good reason. Far more than the

Middle colonies and Southern colonies, this northernmost region was already a tight-knit confederation of like-minded economic actors, possessing a consolidated religious and maritime identity. Massachusetts, Rhode Island, Connecticut, and New Hampshire could be counted upon to move in unison. No one doubted this regional principle in colonial America.

FIGURE 6. "Unite or Die," *Pennsylvania Journal*, 1774. (Political cartoon. Artist unknown, "Unite or Die," November 24, 1774, newspaper, *The New-York Journal; or, The General Advertiser*, 1664.)

Besides this, New England was the feared powerhouse of commercial and shipping strength in the thirteen colonies. New Englanders, hearty and brave indeed, were trained in shipbuilding—hewing, shaping, caulking, joining, trimming, sail making, rigging, and launching—as well as sailing and fishing and the vast "carrying trade" that earned them a livelihood. New England's confidence came from its commerce and from an understanding that professional sailors and ships were the wellsprings of naval power. New England could build a navy, and in the eighteenth century, sea power was the undisputed linchpin to security of life, liberty, and property, not to mention nationhood and independence.

The segmented rattlesnake and the motto "Unite or Die" were not new in America. They derived from the "Join or Die" injunction to the colonies that Benjamin Franklin, then in London lobbying the Parliament to desist in its reckless course that would surely precipitate war, had originated as the rallying cry of Albany Congress twenty years earlier. Every delegate in Philadelphia in 1774 knew the infamous history of that congress. The overarching purpose of the gathering, called by the Board of Trade on the eve of the French and Indian War, was the defense of the American western frontier. In Albany the colonies would empower a central colonial government for this fundamental objective and, on top of this, two significant others: to regulate Indian trade and to settle the nettlesome western land disputes among them. Franklin, who spearheaded the congress on behalf of the Crown, considered it to be a life-or-death mission, since it was unity that would save American lives in a war with France. Yet in spite of this, the Albany Congress failed miserably. All thirteen colonies were invited, but only New England, New York, Pennsylvania, and Maryland attended. The Southern colonies did not show up.[5]

Franklin had come to Albany equipped with a Plan of Union creating an effective central colonial government with a "Grand Council" comprised of forty-eight representatives. The Grand Council would "make laws for regulating and governing" new settlements in the West. To meet these and other federal obligations, the council would further possess "power to make laws, and lay and levy such general duties, posts, and taxes, as to them shall appear most equal and just."[6]

FIGURE 7. Benjamin Franklin, Pennsylvania Delegate. (Portrait of Benjamin Franklin. J. A. Duplessis, *Portrait of Benjamin Franklin*, 1868, engraving, Library of Congress, LC-USZ62-25564.)

What concerned Franklin the most in the 1750s was that the colonial leaders in Albany refused to submit to any centralization of American power whatsoever. Rather, to his dismay, some of the delegates in attendance actually transformed the pressing political occasion into a buying opportunity. Among other land activities taking place during the in-between hours of the Congress, for instance, a Connecticut land-speculating syndicate, the Susquehannah Company, feuded with Pennsylvania's proprietary family for a huge Iroquois cession in the Wyoming Valley. Iroquois representatives caught wind of the gathering and came to town, meeting separately out of doors with company representatives. Before the congress ended, the Susquehannah Company laid out two thousand pounds for the purchase of millions of acres in the Wyoming Valley from the Iroquois, apparently infuriating Pennsylvanians.[7]

The experience left Franklin pessimistic. What he learned in Albany was that Americans cherished their commercial and land freedoms—as well as independence from one another—far too much to surrender to a profit-losing, power-dissipating central authority. In the aftermath of the Albany Congress, he seemed to lose all hope that the colonies would ever voluntarily unite, writing to an English correspondent that only an act of Parliament imposing union stood any chance of drawing the thirteen together.[8]

A few years later the sage of Pennsylvania flatly pronounced that American independence was a geographic, historic, and political impossibility. England had nothing to fear of America, he wrote in a public essay speaking about the separate colonies, because "their jealousy of each other is so great that however necessary an union of the colonies has long been, for their common defense and security against their enemies, and how sensible soever [*sic*] each colony has been of that necessity, yet they have never been able to effect such an union among themselves, nor even to agree in requesting the mother country to establish it for them."[9]

In September 1774, under the specter of a different sort of war, the colonies were trying again. The foe was different—not the French and Indians over the Appalachian Mountains to the west, but a seemingly autocratic Parliament eastward across the Atlantic. Even so, the ruling sentiment was the same: "Unite or Die." Not only the *Pennsylvania Journal* but also the *Massachusetts Spy* and the *New York Journal* carried this potent motto and the snake symbol on their mastheads. Sermons and speeches, too, enjoined Americans to lay aside their differences and unite for the sake of liberty and property.[10]

One preacher in Fairfield, Connecticut, Samuel Sherwood, counseled his parishioners to this effect in late August; then, upon the urging of "public spirited friends," he published his sermon in pamphlet form. Sherwood told Americans that God meant for civil rulers to be just, fair, and charitable. They must therefore resist Lord North's "iron rod of oppression." And to do this they must unite against internal division, which he called "a party separating spirit." He wished that "we may stand or fall together: and not be devoured one of another; nor become an easy prey to foreign enemies who may seek our ruin." Sherwood praised the coming Continental Congress, affirming that he eagerly awaited the issuance of the delegates' wisdom to guide them. His own advice in the meantime, repeated a half dozen times in the sermon, was that Americans fix their "attention upon the common cause, the public good and general interest of the land. Our strength, our glory, and our security depend very much upon our friendly agreement and firm union together."[11]

* * * * *

In the first weeks of the Continental Congress, this oft-repeated counsel of American solidarity was rapidly put to the test. On September 6, the same day the delegates settled the matter of the Congress's mode of voting, an express rider from New Jersey galloped into town bearing news that Boston was under siege after the British killed six townspeople. Reportedly, the melee erupted over contested gunpowder in a town near Boston. "Six of the inhabitants had been kill'd in the skirmish," James Duane of New York recorded the urgent news. "Cannon fired upon the town the whole night."[12]

By the end of the day in Philadelphia, church bells were tolling in collective mourning, and New Englanders were writing home to loved ones begging for news that family and friends were safe. Further, many New England delegates gave glowing reassurances in their letters that the Middle and Southern colonies were rallying to Boston's defense. "This city is in the utmost confusion," Silas Deane, thirty-six-year-old Connecticut lawyer and merchant, wrote to his wife Elizabeth, "all the bells toll muffled, & the most unfeigned marks of sorrow appear in every countenance." And, Deane professed, the provincial leaders in the Congress were uniting one after the other behind Boston and New England. "You may tell our friends that I never met, nor scarcely had an idea of meeting with men of such firmness, sensibility, spirit, and thorough knowledge of the interests of America, as the gentlemen from the Southern provinces appear to be. . . . May New England go hand in hand with them & we need not fear a want of spirit."[13]

John Adams similarly shared with Abigail that America could be counted upon to come to the rescue of New England in case a large-scale war broke out in Boston. A wave of gratitude rushed over him, he said, as he felt the representatives in Philadelphia from South Carolina to Maine unite in the support of Massachusetts. He was touched, he confessed, by "the kindness, the affection" that greeted him. Beyond this, his new friends in Philadelphia were vowing revenge. "WAR! WAR! WAR! was the cry" of Philadelphia, he said. Then, once the delegates learned several days later that Boston was safe and no lives had in fact been lost—it was a false rumor—Adams wept. Tears of relief, he wrote to Abigail, "streamed from my eyes."[14]

During these tense inaugural days, when it appeared that blood had been spilled, Thomas Cushing of Massachusetts dared to propose that the Congress institute a daily prayer to uplift them. As a measure of the religious diversity of the colonies—and the divisiveness of religion—John Jay of New York and John Rutledge of South Carolina immediately opposed the idea as too incendiary. After all, the delegates hailed from at least six different religious backgrounds, including Anglican, Congregationalist, Presbyterian, Quaker, Baptist, and Dutch Reformed churches, and nothing in the broad sweep of history, as they all knew, so divided political bodies as religion. Children of British and European history, the delegates of 1774 possessed intimate knowledge of the millions of lives claimed by Catholic-Protestant religious wars since the mid-sixteenth century. This is one reason why Jay and Rutledge raised a red flag at Cushing's motion, cautioning their colleagues to keep the toxic issue entirely out of the proceedings of Carpenters' Hall.[15]

As John Adams recorded the concern over bowing their heads in prayer in Congress, "We were so divided in religious sentiments, some Episcopalians, some Quakers, some Anabaptists, some Presbyterians and some Congregationalists, so that we could not join in the same act of worship." But Sam Adams stepped forward, protesting that they must search for common ground and transcendence of difference. Persuaded that prayer was a critical spiritual aid to work of unification and valor, he "arose and said he was no bigot, and could hear a prayer from a gentleman of piety and virtue, who was at the same time a friend to his country." This Adams, a devout Congregationalist, then surprised the Congress by advancing the name of an Anglican minister, the Reverend Jacob Duché of Philadelphia's Christ Church. Apparently, this crossing of the aisle by Adams was enough to shift the opinion of the delegates in favor of a devotion. That September 6 the Congress passed a resolution to invite the Anglican reverend to open the next day with prayers. Thereafter Duché became the official chaplain of the united colonies in Philadelphia, serving until October of 1776 when ill health led him to submit his resignation.[16]

Another proof of colonial unity came eleven days later. On Friday, September 16, Paul Revere rode into town with the Suffolk Resolves, seeking the Congress's endorsement of steps taken in Suffolk County, which contained Boston, in response to the Massachusetts Government Act and General Thomas Gage's late buildup of a half dozen regiments of troops. The resolves comprised nineteen acts of resistance, declaring that "it is an indispensable duty which we owe to God, our country, ourselves and posterity, by all lawful ways and means in our power to maintain, defend and preserve those civil and religious rights and liberties, for which many of our fathers fought, bled and died, and to hand them down entire to future generations." Until justice was restored, the people of that county resolved to shut down courts, cease payment of taxes, cut off all imports, and, most provocatively, raise a militia for their self-defense, commencing drilling exercises weekly.[17]

The next day the Massachusetts delegates presented the resolves to the assembled delegates, who received them "with great applause," Sam Adams noted. Then the Congress moved unanimously to endorse all nineteen, passing its own resolution affirming "the united efforts of North America in their behalf." The resolution continued:

> This assembly deeply feels the suffering of their countrymen in the Massachusetts-Bay, under the operation of the late unjust, cruel, and oppressive acts of the British Parliament—that they most thoroughly approve the wisdom and fortitude, with which opposition to these wicked ministerial measures has hitherto been conducted, and they earnestly recommend to their brethren, a perseverance in the same firm and temperate conduct as expressed in the resolutions determined upon.[18]

John Adams, swept with gratitude, recorded in his diary that the Congress's actions that September 16 had erased his fears. "This was one of the happiest days of my life," he wrote. "In Congress we had generous, noble sentiments, and manly eloquence. This day convinced me that America will support the Massachusetts [sic] or perish with her."[19]

* * * * *

In the last week of September, the delegates embarked upon the paramount work of economic civil disobedience, and on this question recent Anglo-American history, more than any other beacon, guided them. As they all knew, the strategy of embargo had worked well before. In March of 1765 the Parliament had passed the Stamp Act, imposing unrepresented taxes on newspaper, pamphlets, and legal documents throughout the colonies. In response, the colonists united in protest, halting all distribution of stamps, refusing to apply them, and ceasing all imports until the act was repealed. Their representatives met in the Stamp Act Congress in New York in October and explained in eloquent manifestos the jurisprudence at the root of their civil disobedience. In February of 1766, enlightening the colonists to the power of unified economic resistance, Parliament repealed the act.

In 1767 the same legislative body in far-off Westminster adopted the Townshend Duties on tea, glass, lead, paper, paint, and other articles, and once again the colonists practiced unified nullification through embargo and economic disobedience. Three years later these taxes, too, were voided by Parliament, all except the one on tea. This special exemption ultimately helped bring on, first, the tea raid in Boston Harbor in 1773 and, now, the present unprecedented martial law oppressing the New England city.

History was instructive, but members of Parliament, it was common knowledge in 1774, were at that moment furious at Massachusetts beyond anything either side of the Atlantic had ever witnessed in a hundred and fifty years of largely amicable relations. That is why New Englanders as a whole, joined by a smattering of Middle and Southern delegates, believed that nothing short of full embargo this time would humble the Parliament sufficiently to compel such massive repeal. The power of America in the current battle of wills with England would be a strict, potent trade embargo: immediate, complete nonimportation and nonexportation of all American commodities, including Southern staple crops.

The thinking of these delegates was logical and systematic. The united colonies must starve the empire of profits, which would, as a direct function of the commercial nature of English government, force the hand of Parliament. Perversely, greed would do the work of liberty. Rich merchants, it was believed, controlled Parliament. Deprived of their accustomed profits from trade with the thirteen colonies, they would lobby

Lord North and George III to restore American rights, rescinding the Coercive Acts. After all, it had happened this way twice before with the Stamp Act and the Townshend Acts.

To New Englanders with war at their doorstep, total embargo was a matter of life and death. Canceling imports alone would represent a mere swipe at England, only angering merchants and parliamentarians, potentially spawning a campaign of violence against them. A complete trade ban, by contrast, would bring England to its knees, force the nation into bankruptcy and capitulation. In this hopeful projection, Boston would be restored to safety and imperial civil war averted.

This was the main point many New Englanders drove home on the floor of Congress in late September soon after Richard Henry Lee of Virginia became the first delegate on record to formally advance a trade strategy. On Monday the 26th, Lee proposed economic resistance by way of nonimportation, making no reference to nonexportation. Fifty-two-year-old Eliphalet Dyer of Connecticut, Yale graduate and lieutenant colonel in the French and Indian War, quickly argued that Lee's proposal was insufficient. He urged that only the combined measures of civil resistance, banning imports *and* exports, would come down "like a thunder clap" on the mother country, overturning her oppression. Another New Englander, Thomas Cushing of Massachusetts, long-serving speaker of the House and a Harvard graduate, three years younger than Dyer, spoke more graphically. Nothing but the full "force" of a total trade ban, he insisted to his fellow delegates, would arrest a slippage into war: "Whoever considers the present state of G. Britain and America must see the necessity of spirited measures. G. B. has drawn the sword against us, and nothing prevents her sheathing it in our bowels but want of sufficient force. I think it absolutely necessary to agree to a Non Importation [and] Non Exportation immediately."[20]

New England was tightly unified in this economic stance, but the region did not stand entirely alone. In the initial debates, Samuel Chase of Maryland and Christopher Gadsden of South Carolina lent support. "Non-exportation [is] of vastly more importance than a Non-importation," Chase insisted. Gadsden concurred, pressing the Congress to go to the extreme of nonexportation to prevent a slippage into Anglo-American civil war. "Boston and New England can't hold out—the country will be deluged in blood, if we don't act with spirit," Gadsden argued. "Don't let America look at this mountain, and let it bring forth a mouse."[21]

* * * * *

The problem with full embargo was that the seven Virginians present in Carpenters' Hall had their hands tied by an official decree of their home colony that expressly prohibited precisely that which New Englanders sought. Virginia, whose Chesapeake Bay was not under assault like Boston's waters, differed starkly on the question of nonexportation and, recognizing the approach of potential conflict ahead in Philadelphia, had already issued a preemptive directive to quash it. It was a tobacco resolve, one standing as a vivid early example of the primacy and potency of colonial rights—later "states' rights"—triumphing over federal deliberations and powers.[22]

That August, prior to the First Congress, after receiving New England's circular letter calling for unity and resistance against the Coercive Acts, the colony of Virginia had called a convention in Williamsburg at the Raleigh Tavern. Roughly one hundred delegates assembled there to deliberate a month before the First Congress. In the proceedings nonimportation evoked little fight, but immediate nonexportation was beaten down. The reason is that it posed far too grave a burden on Virginia's narrow one-crop economy: tobacco. To clarify its position, the convention prepared an explicit order for its delegates to carry to Congress. Virginia would consent to nonexportation only beginning in the last half of 1775, after the current year's harvest had safely shipped. The colony strictly ruled against any and all congressional measures endorsing nonexportation of the crop before that time. The message of the Virginians was that, regrettably, too much was at stake. Tobacco was the nerve center of the colony, and this year's crop simply could not go to rot.

Virginia's decision sprang from a distinctive Southern way of life practiced not only in the largest colony of the thirteen but also in Maryland and North Carolina. It was a slave-based tobacco industry that fed the white elite and sustained their aristocratic identities. As the Virginians gathered in Philadelphia, enslaved persons back home were engaged in a long and lucrative economic tradition of the colony: cutting tobacco and wheeling or floating it to storehouses for drying all along the Potomac, James, Rappahannock, and York Rivers. Under bondage, Black men, women, and children dredged rivers, built piers, and repaired flatboats for later transport of the crop downriver. At shipment time, white overseers would direct enslaved people to bundle the leaf into hogsheads weighing nearly a thousand pounds each and roll them down plantation terraces to piers on rivers for export.

From these docks workers loaded the hogsheads onto wide shallow barges or, where navigation permitted, directly onto oceangoing vessels. From the mouth of each river, these large sloops and schooners sailed into the brackish waters of the Chesapeake and from there into the saltwater of the Atlantic for the two-month journey to British merchant houses in Bristol, Liverpool, or London, where the tobacco was sold on consignment.

In September the crop of 1774 was only half ready, and tobacco was the principal source of income for Virginia, Maryland, and North Carolina. It purchased these colonies the necessities of life, and, pivotal to the Virginia argument, the crop repaid heavy debts owed to British merchants by season's end. In the early 1770s Virginia alone was exporting nearly seventy million pounds of the leaf from the Chesapeake, totaling approximately 40 percent of the exports to Great Britain from all the colonies combined. The plant was "the grand staple of Virginia," touching pocketbooks and nearly every other aspect of society. It served as a medium for commercial transactions and payment of taxes and debts, a symbol adorning paper money, a favorite topic of almanacs and gentlemanly conversation, and a widespread motif of decorative arts. As such, it heavily dominated politics in the Virginia House of Burgesses, which one historian has called "a tobacco planters' club."[23]

Heedful of the displeasure their ruling might evoke in Congress, the Virginia Convention in Williamsburg took pains to elucidate its reasoning for rejecting nonexportation. The convention wished heartily for unanimity and solicited its delegates in Philadelphia to present the colony's position carefully, softening the blow. Chiefly, they explained, the crush of Virginia debt to British merchants, not greed, was at work in their decision and their reciprocal request for the indulgence of Congress:

> The earnest desire we have to make as quick and full payment as possible of our debts to Great Britain and to avoid the heavy injury that would arise to this country from an earlier adoption of the non-exportation plan, after the people have already applied so much of their labor to the perfecting of the present crop, by which means they have been prevented from pursuing other methods of clothing and supporting their families, have rendered it necessary to restrain you in this article of non-exportation; but it is our desire that you cordially cooperate with our sister colonies in General Congress in such other just and proper methods as they, or the

majority, shall deem necessary for the accomplishment of the valuable ends.[24]

On tobacco, thus, Virginia was intransigent. In solidarity with Massachusetts, the largest colony would gladly abstain from all luxury imports immediately. However, notwithstanding the pains of the Boston Bay and risks of partial embargo, the tobacco harvest of 1774 must sail to sea from the Chesapeake Bay. After drying, curing, and bundling, it would not be ripe to load and ship until the summer of 1775.

* * * * *

With little conflict, the Congress settled the matter of nonimportation. On the 27th of September, a Tuesday, the delegates "resolved unanimously" to halt all imports from Great Britain in unified resistance. The date for the commencement of this nonimportation embargo was set for December 1, 1774. Nowhere in the journals of Congress, debate notes, or the letters of delegates is there significant evidence of heated discord or disagreement on this legislative act so deeply and negatively impacting all American trade.[25]

In contrast, on the matter of nonexportation, emotions ran high and feelings struck sore for the remainder of the Congress—and thereafter. No one liked the preemptive, self-regarding Virginia resolution on tobacco, except Virginia and, to a lesser extent, the other Southern colonies whose profits on export crops would benefit by another year's open trade. Imagine if each of the twelve colonies in attendance at the Congress had arrived with a large self-protective exemption from the burden of unified resistance. It would have set them spiraling into confusion. Their commercial protest would emerge as a patchwork shot through with holes rather than as a unified wave pouring over the Coercive Acts. Ultimately, such a patchwork would have confirmed the widespread mockery on American and European shores that true American union was to be a dead letter from day one. Bringing together the self-interested, quarrelsome peoples of the thirteen fractious colonies, the First Congress would only prove, was an impossibility.

Even so, nothing could be done about the Virginia order, except to ask Washington, Henry, Harrison, Lee, Randolph and the other Virginians to dispatch an express rider back to Williamsburg to request an undoing of an unequivocal ruling of their people. Except for in moments of extreme pique, no one seriously entertained this idea. It was impractical, for one, and certain to affront the Old Dominion. Most persuasively, the idea of strenuously requesting a reversal of an established Virginia legislative decision risked a dangerous disharmony between the new collective Congress and the most powerful, self-important colony in the coalescing Union.

So the fifty-five delegates, with so many desperate for nonexportation to be made law of the land immediately, sought effective workarounds. In lieu of delaying *all* colonial nonexportation to Virginia's date of postsummer 1775, what else could be done? One seriously considered proposal was to enact a total embargo on all exports effective December 1, with the single exception of tobacco. The seemingly unavoidable exemption, many argued, need not set a precedent for all American exports. Why should the rest of the colonies erect a weak trade defense, nonimportation only, at a critical moment in history as a function of a single colonial prohibition? No other colony was restrained by legislative mandate. Therefore, twelve of them could act with valor and force. After all, sacrifice for higher constitutional purpose was their purpose in Philadelphia.

But instead of this, an indignant division developed within the South Carolina delegation. Of the five South Carolinians present, Thomas Lynch and Christopher Gadsden were strongly for nonexportation, except tobacco, notwithstanding the presumption of unfairness to the other exporting colonies. Their colleague, young Edward Rutledge, however, was not. This led Rutledge into an open-floor fight one afternoon with the respected Richard Henry Lee of Virginia, seventeen years his senior, and soon Rutledge and three other South Carolinians would stage a dramatic walkout.

No one specifically commented on Rutledge's manner of speech or attitude on September 26 when he confronted the Virginians, but surely it was not one of patience. The South Carolinian, upset by what he regarded as hypocrisy, argued that Virginia must find a way to annul its legislature's mandate on tobacco. To bring home the point, he mocked either Lee or Bland, one of whom had apparently commented earlier that day that all the colonies must practice "generosity" in their collective affairs. "A gentleman from the other end of the room talked of generosity," he said. "True equality is the only public generosity."[26]

More exactly, Rutledge meant equality of sacrifice of Southern exports. After that statement he made the fair and accurate claim that South Carolina depended as much on rice and indigo for its survival as did Virginia on tobacco. He therefore found it unnatural and oppressive to

FIGURE 8. Edward Rutledge, South Carolina Delegate. (Portrait of Edward Rutledge. Henry Bryan Hall, *Edward Rutledge*, 1872, print, New York Public Library, EM1265.)

ask his colony to give up its vital exports while Virginia remained agriculturally comfortable for another nine months. Instead, Rutledge appealed to Virginia to give up tobacco, permitting the entire Congress to endorse a total trade stoppage at the beginning of December.

Richard Henry Lee answered back, arguing that Rutledge's argument of "equality of sacrifice should be laid aside." He drew a horticultural distinction, pointing out that tobacco was a unique, sensitive crop with an extended growing, drying, curing, and shipping season. "Produce of the other colonies," he said in Carpenters' Hall, "is carried to market in the same year when it is raised, even rice."[27]

CHAPTER 3

South Carolina Withdraws

In the midst of the Congress's contentious debates over nonexportation as essential, or not, to rescuing Massachusetts from the approach of bloodshed, Speaker of the Pennsylvania House Joseph Galloway requested floor time to present a comprehensive plan that he promised would restore justice and avert imperial civil war—and resultant domestic civil wars—by a superior means. Accordingly, the delegates set aside Wednesday, September 28, for Galloway's speech. The content he delivered that day became the basis of his highly publicized pamphlet, *A Candid Examination of the Mutual Claims of Great-Britain and the Colonies*, printed five months later in New York. In the published work Galloway prognosticated imperial civil war, colonial border civil wars, and a North-South civil war as the natural consequences of American separation and independence. In the September 28 address delivered in Carpenters' Hall, according to records, he made most of the same arguments in abbreviated form.[1]

On the same day as his speech, Galloway submitted a 550-word Anglo-American constitution of his own writing that he told other delegates was premised on Franklin's Albany Plan of 1754. Galloway called his charter—the first of many constitutions to be proposed in the Revolutionary Era—"A Plan of a Proposed Union between Great Britain and the Colonies." What is most remarkable about Galloway's speech and his Plan of Union, as it became known in shorthand, is the degree to which he rooted the present and future tranquility and safety of the thirteen colonies in the cardinal principle of preserving a single supreme source of constitutional power. For him, to prevent chaos and bloodshed, this source was going to be the British monarch and Parliament. "There must be," he exhorted, "one supreme legislative head in every civil society, whose authority must extend to the regulation and final decision of every matter susceptible of human direction; and that every member of the society, whether political, official, or individual must be subordinate to its supreme will, signified in its laws."[2]

Galloway repeated this golden rule of civil society—that final and supreme power must reside at a central locus, not dispersed into separate regional or colonial governments—at least eight times in his speech, and it was the keystone of the constitution he advanced. As it turns out, after more than a decade of detours and stumbles into decentralized government, this is precisely the organizing principle that the founding fathers returned to and ratified in the U.S. Constitution of 1787—and for the same reasons given by Galloway thirteen years earlier.

Impressed by the prescience of this first constitution advanced to save the American colonies from ruin, historian Maya Jasanoff entertains a fascinating what-if in her book *Liberty's Exiles*: "What would have happened to the thirteen colonies if Galloway's scheme had been adopted?" Possibly, Jasanoff answers, the colonies would have united into a liberal, self-determining government within the British empire, like that formed a century later by their northern neighbors in Canada, New Brunswick, and Nova Scotia. Essentially, Galloway was promoting the principle of "home rule" several generations before its time, one that not only proved a successful accommodation in Canada but also later went on to serve as a template for Ireland, India, and other similar semi-independent British dominions across the globe.[3]

* * * * *

Galloway opened his speech of September 28 by observing that most everything he had heard thus far in the Congress "tended to inflame rather than reconcile—to produce war instead of peace" between Britain and the colonies. Therefore, he felt it was his "incumbent duty to speak plainly, and to give his sentiments without the least reserve." To wit, he averred that the Congress's current scheme to wrest justice from Parliament by way of defiance and a trade embargo, whether of nonimportation alone or nonimportation combined nonexportation, was doomed to failure. He called such economic sanctions "an insult on the supreme authority of the state; it cannot fail to draw on the colonies the united resentment of the mother country." He went on to say:

> If we will not trade with Great Britain, she will not suffer us to trade at all. Our ports will be blocked up by British men of war, and troops

Chapter 3: South Carolina Withdraws

will be sent to reduce us to reason and obedience. A total and sudden stagnation of commerce is what no country can bear: it must bring ruin on the colonies: the produce of labour must perish on their hands and not only the progress of industry be stopped, but industry and labour will cease, and the country itself be thrown into anarchy and tumult.[4]

Galloway proceeded from these introductory remarks to offer two core arguments to persuade the now more than fifty delegates in Congress to lay down their animus and instead pick up an olive branch and a written constitution to forge reconciliation with England. The first was a series of historical and jurisprudential "facts," he called them, that illuminated accommodation as the only pathway to peace and harmony. The second was an acknowledgement of "the real state of the colonies"—that is, their disunity and the perils of setting them loose from Parliament and King George without a replacement central authority to prevent civil wars among them.

Perhaps more than any other delegate in Congress, Galloway saw both sides of the debates that had divided the colonies and the mother country since the Stamp Act of 1765. In this spirit, he presented the "facts" of recent Anglo-American history in a manner that demonstrated sophisticated thinking as well as commitment to compromise with a perceived enemy. He acknowledged that Parliament had grievously erred in enacting its late "obnoxious statutes." But he refused to blame one party in what was clearly a power struggle between righteous men on both sides of the Atlantic. It all began, Galloway said, in the year 1753 when the French and their Indian allies made incursions in the Ohio Valley, threatening Pennsylvania and Virginia land and lives. In this "dangerous situation"—aware of "their incapacity to defend themselves"—the colonies made "supplications to the parent state for its assistance." Soon "Great-Britain sent over her fleets and armies for their protection," expending "millions" of pounds to rescue the colonies and at the same time requesting by urgent bulletins that each colony pay its fair share in arms, munitions, foodstuffs, and money to support a unified war effort.

With this, Galloway established the point of origin of the power struggle with Parliament that had been fostering so much ill will and agony. It was the inability and unwillingness of the colonies to pay an equitable share of the financial burden of the victorious French and Indian War. During the war, England requested material assistance on an emergency basis. "But what was the conduct of the colonies on this occasion,"

Galloway asked the delegates in Congress, "in which their own existence was immediately concerned?" He continued:

> However painful it may be for me to repeat, or you to hear, I must remind you of it. You all know there were colonies which at some times granted liberal aids, and at others nothing; other colonies gave nothing during the war; none gave equitably in proportion to their wealth, and all that did give were actuated by partial and self-interested motives, and gave only in proportion to the approach or remoteness of the danger. These delinquencies were occasioned by the want of the exercise of some supreme power to ascertain, with equity, their proportions of aids, and to over-rule the particular passions, prejudices, and interests, of the several colonies. [. . .] To remedy these mischiefs, Parliament was naturally led to exercise the power which had been, by its predecessors, so often exercised over the colonies, and to pass the Stamp Act.

But after this, Galloway lamented, everything went terribly wrong. Instead of fighting for another decade over the power of taxation, England and American should have embarked upon "a constitutional reformation of the authority of Parliament over the colonies," one honoring the sacred British right of self-taxation while not menacing Parliament's incontrovertible right of legislative supremacy over all the parts of the empire. Instead, the colonies rebelled, stormed homes, and issued declarations of independent rights, alarming the king and Parliament that their true intention was "American Independence." This grave and lasting fear—an independence movement of the colonies—became the ultimate source of the repressive measures that followed, including the Declaratory Act, the Tea Act, and the four Coercive Acts. This was the recent history that had driven England and the colonies to their present crisis.

Next Galloway turned to the colonies' readiness for war, separation, and independence, stating unequivocally that they had no alternative but to reconcile with England due to the certainty of domestic civil wars—and probable French reinvasion—once they lost the binding hand of the Parliament and king together with the protecting shield and sword they wielded. Underscoring his central theme of the categorical need for a single supreme governmental authority to prevent chaos and loss of life, the Pennsylvania delegate characterized the colonies as particularly raw and volatile. "In regard to the political state of the colonies," he said, "you must know that they are so many inferior societies, disunited and unconnected in polity. That while they deny the authority of Parliament, they are, in respect to each other, in a perfect state of nature, destitute of any supreme direction or decision whatever, and incompetent to the grant of national aids, or any other general measure whatever, even to the settlement of differences among themselves." As Galloway sternly warned the other delegates:

> The seeds of discord are plentifully sowed in the constitution of the colonies; that they are already grown to maturity, and have more than once broke out into open hostilities. They are at this moment only suppressed by the authority of the parent state; and should that authority be weakened or annulled, many subjects of unsettled disputes, and which in that case, can only be settled by an appeal to the sword, must involve us in all the horrors of civil war. You will now consider whether you wish to be destitute of the protection of Great Britain, or to see a renewal of the claims of France upon America; or to remain in our present disunited state, the weak exposed to the force of the strong. I am sure no honest man can entertain wishes so ruinous to his country.

It all added up, he contended, to the irrefutable logic of reconciliation with England on the basis of compromise and permanent constitutional reform rather than antagonistic assertions of rights and patchwork coercive economic countermeasures intended to bring the Parliament to heel.

* * * * *

Having thus stated his case, Galloway proceeded to outline his Plan of Union. It had two parts. The bulk of the constitution concerned itself with the formation of a central American government possessing the legislative, executive, and judicial powers and functions typical of an enlightened Anglo-American parliamentary system. It established an American congress elected by the colonies that would meet once per year, more often if necessary, that was, for all intents and purposes, an American branch of Parliament. Galloway explicitly compared the new American congress to England's House of Commons, affirming that it "shall hold and exercise all the like rights, liberties, and privileges as are held and exercised by and in the House of Commons of Great Britain."[5]

The congress's jurisdiction included "regulating and administering all the general police and affairs of the colonies," such as taxation, requisitions in times of war, and Indian affairs. It also gave the congress judicial powers, most critically authority to mediate disputes between any two colonies or groups of colonies in all matters "as well civil and criminal as commercial." The delegates to the new congress would be elected every three years by the separate colonial assemblies, thus gloriously removing the constitutional problem at the root of all Anglo-American troubles since the Stamp Act: taxation without representation. After the adoption of Galloway's charter, Americans would be represented in their own American branch of Parliament, voting up or down all money bills in the constitutional manner they had been demanding for a decade. Furthermore, sensitive to the fact that each colony considered itself a nation-state unto itself, Galloway engrafted a clause in the constitution prohibiting the central government from infringing on the rights and prerogatives of colonies and their sacred assemblies. The congress's powers extended only to continental affairs involving two or more colonies. Otherwise, it guaranteed that "each colony shall retain its present constitution and powers of regulating and governing its own internal police, in all cases whatever."

The Galloway plan additionally provided for an executive branch to implement and enforce continental laws. That branch was to be operated by "a president general" appointed by the king to serve during good behavior. The president further possessed a veto power over legislation as well as the authority to call for special meetings of congress in periods of crisis and emergency. All this—the erection of a separate central government with legislative, judicial, and executive functions on American soil, including full representation by the colonies in their own congress—constituted the concessions that Great Britain would make to the colonies in order to restore peace and harmony in the empire. But, Galloway insisted, the colonies must likewise make concessions to end the standoff with London and bring the two parties back from the brink of civil war in Massachusetts.

In exchange for Britain's grant of these rights and powers to the colonies, Galloway's constitution conceded to the Parliament in London several sources of authority and control over American legislation. Essentially, the Parliament would function as a second chamber of the American congress, much like a senate or house of lords, with the ability to originate bills and disapprove or veto laws passed by the colonies. Legislation could only be made law if both the congress and the Parliament gave their assent. It was, to Galloway, a perfect power-sharing compromise. In point of fact, the constitution he outlined would have granted Americans enormous political autonomy. As Jasanoff observes, "Galloway's plan proposed a greater degree of autonomy for the American colonies than any other British domain enjoyed, including Scotland. His proposed American legislature would have fewer constraints than the Irish parliament, too."[6]

Galloway did make one grave mistake, in American eyes, in his decision to label the American congress "inferior," when in reality it was a coequal legislative chamber. In the second to last clause of his constitution, the Pennsylvanian established that:

> The said president general and the Grand Council [congress] be an inferior and distinct branch of the British legislature, united and incorporated with it for the aforesaid general purposes; and that any of the said general regulations may originate and be formed and digested, either in the Parliament of Great Britain or in the said Grand Council, and being prepared, transmitted to the other for their approbation or dissent; and that the assent of both shall be requisite to the validity of all such general acts and statutes.

The last clause made an exception, granting the congress sole powers during emergencies like the late French and Indian War. "In time of war," the Galloway constitution concluded, "all bills for granting aid to the Crown, prepared by the Grand Council [congress] and approved by the president general, shall be valid and passed into a law, without the assent of the British Parliament."[7]

After Galloway's speech and presentation of plan, the delegates in Congress took two steps before wrapping up their deliberations for the day. They opened the floor for what turned out to be "warm debates." Then they entertained a motion to study the constitution in depth in the days to come—or to table it indefinitely. James Duane, who seconded Galloway's plan, was the first to speak. The New Yorker said he lent his full support to nonimportation, nonexportation, *and* the strategic constitution just presented because he had come to Philadelphia to relieve Boston and Massachusetts of Parliament's unjust measures, but not at all costs. He sought "a lasting accommodation with G. Britain," one that would prevent "a civil war with America, [which] would involve a national bankruptcy." Richard Henry Lee of Virginia stood up next, declaring that he wished not for a new entangling accommodation with England such as Galloway's, but something far more simple: restoration of the old system that existed before the Stamp Act, wherein Parliament entirely kept its hands off American tax money. John Jay of New York backed Duane and Galloway, saying, "I am led to adopt this plan," explaining as his reason that it would safeguard American rights and liberties. Edward Rutledge of South Carolina concurred, calling the constitution "almost a perfect plan."[8]

Patrick Henry, on the other hand, disagreed decidedly, spurning Galloway's plan. After hearing so much praise of it, the Virginian rose from his chair and delivered a tirade that revealed his hidden commitment to American independence as the only route to escape the present quagmire. Henry said he deplored the corruption of the British system of government, and all Galloway's constitution did was promise to despoil the colonies by an ingenious new means: the creation of an inferior American congress still subject to the control of Parliament's hand. "We shall liberate our constituents from a corrupt House of Commons," Henry assailed Galloway's proposal, "but thro[w] them into the arms of an American legislature that may be bribed by that nation which avows in the face of the world, that bribery is a part of her system of government."[9]

Henry declared he would not consent. He instead demanded that the American colonies live by their own constitutions, not by Britain's. John Adams kept notes of Henry's speech, quoting his last words as, "I am inclined to think the present measures lead to war." This sentence is cryptic, but Henry seemed to be saying that, after the passage of the Coercive Acts, Anglo-American civil war was preordained and, moreover, that he embraced it as the only true means of securing American rights and freeing her republican assemblies and peoples of hopeless British corruption.[10]

Since Galloway's plan was only the first iteration of a proposal that the Congress might tender to Parliament to stem the tide of imperial civil war, and because the delegates had not yet completed the critical work of the embargo, they faced a decision at the end of the day. No one contemplated submitting the Plan of Union to an immediate up or down vote that same day. The delegates would either send it to a committee for further debate and revisions, or they would defer the matter altogether to future consideration. They chose the latter course, tabling the Galloway constitution indefinitely by a vote of six to five colonies, with Rhode Island's two congressmen divided.[11]

* * * * *

By the end of September, much remained undone on the Congress's agenda prior to declaring an end to their work. The delegates not only hoped to render final decisions on nonexportation and Galloway's Plan of Union, but they also intended to debate a long list of other items: the possibility of making restitution to the East India Company for the destroyed tea; a continental system to enforce the embargo; preparation for defensive war; a declaration of American rights; a precise delineation of what specific powers Parliament possessed over the colonies, if any—notably the right to regulate colonial trade as opposed to the right to impose taxes for the purpose of raising imperial revenue; and numerous petitions enlisting the support of the king and the peoples of England and America in defeating the Coercive Acts.

First in line, after the tabling of the Galloway constitution, was the still unresolved matter of nonexportation. On September 29 the delegates reopened this debate, and the next day they came to a decision. Historian of the Continental Congress Edmund Cody Burnett describes the debates thus: "When it came, however, to the question of non-exportation, the contest became fierce. Many believed that a scheme of non-exportation would be ruinous, especially to the southern colonies, whose markets were almost wholly in Europe." Even so, on September 30 the delegates, honoring the long deferment of nonexportation required by Virginia's official mandate, set the date for enacting it a year into the future. Logically, ceasing all exports would only come into play if the Parliament did not repeal the Coercive Acts by that time.[12]

In *A Leap in the Dark*, John Ferling describes the embargo agreement of 1774 as a hard-fought North-South compromise. The Southern colonies conceded on nonimportation and the Northern colonies on the one-year delay to nonexportation. "The question was resolved," Ferling states, "by the submission of the northern congressmen, a pattern that was to become habitual during the next couple of decades. In this instance, New England sought—had to have—unity. It settled for non-importation only, although the southern colonies agreed that non-exportation would commence in September 1775 if the imperial crisis had not been resolved."[13]

Not all were satisfied, however. One dissatisfied New England delegate who fought for better terms on nonexportation was John Adams. The absolute postponement of this powerful deterrent to imperial civil war, he confessed in private letters to Abigail and a friend in Boston, left him crestfallen and wracked with anxiety. He wanted to add emergency exceptions to the Virginia position. Though the historical record is not clear as to whether Adams actually presented his contingent provisions on nonexportation on the floor of Carpenters' Hall, we know he drew up formal resolutions highlighting two escape clauses he deemed critical

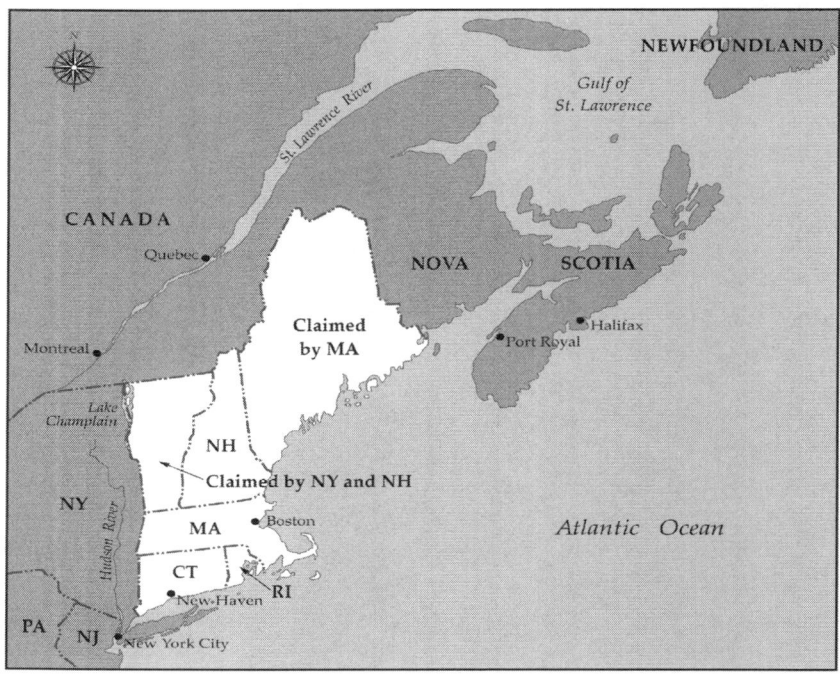

MAP 2. New England, 1774. (Chris Robinson, Cartographer)

to the life and liberty of Massachusettsans. One required that if blood were spilled in the Bay Colony at the hands of the British, all colonies would act forthwith on nonexportation: "Resolved, That in case hostilities should be further pursued against that Province, and submission be attempted to be compelled by force of arms, as soon as intelligence of this shall be communicated to the several colonies, they ought immediately to cease all exportations of goods, wares, and merchandise, to Great Britain, Ireland, and the West Indies."[14]

The other resolution Adams drafted pertained to the prospect of British officials capturing Massachusetts rebels, like himself, on grounds of treason and then dispatching them overseas for trial. In this case, too, Congress must exert the full pressure of nonexportation. Such a violation of American rights, Adams said, "ought to be considered as a declaration of war and a commencement of hostilities against all the colonies, and reprisals ought to be made in all the colonies and held as hostages for the security of the person or persons so arrested; and all exportations of

Chapter 3: South Carolina Withdraws 67

merchandise to Great Britain, Ireland, and the West Indies, ought immediately to cease."[15]

Considering himself a clear-eyed realist, Adams could not reconcile himself to these omissions from the embargo. In his worldview, desperate times called for heroic measures by all. On September 29 he wrote separate letters to Abigail and his friend William Tudor expressing his disappointment. The Congress was counseling Massachusetts to "patience, forbearance, [and] long suffering," he complained to his wife of nine years. "I wish I could convince gentlemen of the danger, or impracticability of this as fully as I believe it myself," he continued. After this, Adams turned more critical, comparing the opposing delegates to ambassadors from hostile foreign nations: "The art and address, of ambassadors from a dozen belligerent powers of Europe, nay of a conclave of cardinals at the election of a pope, or of the princes in Germany at the choice of an emperor, would not exceed the specimens we have seen."[16]

Adams made similar observations to Tudor. "You say you look up to the Congress," he wrote back in reply to a letter he had recently received from his friend. "It is well you should: but I hope you will not expect too much from us." One problem afflicting the Congress was a severe clash of cultures and economic interests, Adams asserted. "Here is a diversity of religions, educations, manners, interests," he said, "such as it would seem almost impossible to unite in any one plan of conduct." Another impediment was that far too many delegates from the Middle and Southern colonies "shudder at the prospect of blood." The outcome was hesitation and partial measures. "We hear, perpetually, the most figurative panegyricks upon our wisdom fortitude and temperance: The most fervent exhortations to perseverance," Adams reported. What Massachusetts needed in Congress instead, of course, was valor—a fighting spirit. "But I tremble for fear, we should fail of obtaining it."[17]

* * * * *

Notwithstanding the imperfections of the two-part staggered commercial resistance plan, the delegates proceeded over the next three weeks to develop a comprehensive strategy for implementing it across the Atlantic seaboard while simultaneously completing numerous declarations and addresses meant to persuade the world of the justice and rightness of American cause. These foundational documents, soon printed widely in newspapers in America and England, included the Declaration and Resolves of Congress, Petition to the King, Address to the People of Great Britain, and Address to the Inhabitants of the Colonies. The universal message of these papers was that Americans were equal, not second-class, citizens within the British empire; the Coercive Acts were unconstitutional and violative of their basic rights as equal citizens; and, therefore, "repeal of them is essentially necessary, in order to restore harmony between Great Britain and the American colonies."[18]

The Declaration and Resolves of Congress has often been described by historians as a precursor to the Declaration of Independence. It decried not only the Coercive Acts but also the maintenance of a British standing army in America in a time of peace, wrongful trials, and other acts of Parliament trampling upon the colonies' "indubitable rights and liberties, which cannot be legally taken from them, altered or abridged by any power whatever, without their own consent, by their representatives in their several provincial legislature." The declaration asserts that "the inhabitants of the English colonies in North-America, by the immutable laws of nature, the principles of the English constitution, and the several charters or compacts, have the following RIGHTS." The Congress followed this claim with a list of ten constitutional demands, including life, liberty, and property not to be infringed "without their consent"; "a free and exclusive power of legislation . . . in all cases of taxation and internal polity"; "a right peaceably to assemble"; and the "inestimable privilege of being tried by their peers of the vicinage, according to the course of that law." In its last lines, the declaration affirms the Continental Congress's intention to pursue "peaceable measures" as it waited patiently for the Parliament to restore the colonies' sacred rights. These were to include an address to the king and the people of Great Britain as well as "a non-importation, non-consumption, and non-exportation agreement."[19]

The delegates held out their greatest hope for rescue from "impending destruction" in Massachusetts in a carefully worded petition to the king. They had no expectation that Lord North and his band of righteous ministers in Parliament would reverse themselves voluntarily. King George III, though, held sway in the councils of government. The Congress wished therefore for his "most gracious sovereign" to intervene on behalf of equal rights for Americans and swift relief of Massachusetts from Parliament's oppressions. Laying out the same constitutional arguments as the Declaration and Resolves, the petition appealed to King George as "the loving father of your whole people" to employ his "royal authority" and "paternal guidance" to broker a peace settlement in London that would restore justice and liberty to America. The delegates communicated, too,

Chapter 3: South Carolina Withdraws 69

that the need for kingly interposition was urgent. The imminent risk was the splintering and destruction of the British empire. By his glory and grace, the king could keep it "united."[20]

FIGURE 9. King George III of England. (Portrait of King George III. William Pether, *Portrait of George III of the United Kingdom*, 1762, mezzotint print, 19.7 x 13.8 in, National Portrait Gallery, Smithsonian Institution, NPG D11286.)

The Congress, in its Address to the People of Great Britain, called for unity of all the peoples of the British empire in the common fight for liberty and freedom taking place in America. It warned that if Americans were suffered to be made the "slaves" of Parliament, other British subjects would be next until finally they would witness together a total degeneration of the greatest form of government in the world. Again listing the crimes of Parliament against the colonies, the delegates professed, "We believe there is yet much virtue, much justice, and much public spirit in the English nation—To that justice we now appeal. You have been told that we are seditious, impatient of government and desirous of independence. Be assured that these are not facts, but calumnies—Permit us to be as free as yourselves, and we shall over esteem a union with you to be our greatest glory and our greatest happiness."[21]

Like the other papers, the Address to the Inhabitants of the Colonies recites one by one the many "outrageous proceedings" of Parliament in relation to America since the termination of the French and Indian War.

The Congress further asked the thirteen colonies to stand firmly behind the "Continental Association," the deliberative body's final package of embargo recommendations to colonial legislatures. Uniquely, however, in this address, the delegates counseled their fellow colonists to beware the approach of a divide-and-conquer strategy by the British in their effort to subvert colonial liberties. The hope of Parliament was that "disunited all may be subdued."[22]

* * * * *

In the same mid-October days that the delegates in Philadelphia were debating and fine-tuning these manifestos, they sought to finalize the centerpiece of their program of resistance: the embargo. Earlier, on September 30, they had rendered the decision to add full-bore nonexportation to their economic strategy if the Parliament did not come to its senses by the summer of 1775. But now, two weeks later, something uncanny happened that tore the fabric of that agreement, throwing the Congress into upset and paralysis. South Carolina reversed its earlier position, contending that a total trade embargo was unfair and unequal to its home colony's staple crops of indigo and rice. Debates resumed on this volatile issue on Saturday, October 15, continuing to dominate the proceedings for another three days. Then crisis struck when four of South Carolina's five delegates walked out of Carpenters' Hall in protest, leaving the rest of Congress to decide whether they should submit to the colony's extortion or proceed instead to enact the embargo without her.[23]

The mechanics of the trade circuits of the British empire that drove South Carolina to this drastic action are complex and nuanced. But what is certain is that four of the five delegates from that colony came to the conclusion that the nonexportation clause, as written, overwhelmingly favored "the Northern Colonies" due to a combination of existing legal patterns of commerce, ship ownership, trade relationships, and those colonies' expertise in smuggling. Crucially, trade in rice and indigo, as "enumerated commodities" burdened with the tightest restrictions of all trade items in the empire, was on course to be decimated while flour, fish, and other Northern exports, they said, would maneuver their way to market and, in so doing, keep the Northern economies healthily afloat. South Carolina, meanwhile, suffering a true total ban on its trade, would descend into penury.[24]

In this state of mind, the South Carolinians demanded a revision of the nonexportation clause, exempting rice and indigo. When other delegates

Chapter 3: South Carolina Withdraws

pushed back, the planters stiffened, declaring not only that they would not sign the embargo without this exemption but also that they would take their leave and return to South Carolina. To evidence their sincerity, they did actually stage a walkout. Effectively, South Carolina nullified the nonexportation ruling and seceded from the Congress for several days. In his *Our Lives, Our Fortunes*, historian Richard R. Beeman has pieced together the chronology, placing South Carolina's walkout on October 16 or 17.[25]

Another historian of the early Congress, Edmund Cody Burnett, explains that the American Union broke apart that mid-October, salvaged only by compromise:

> Now, upon a renewal of the discussion, that delegation (four of them at least, the Rutledges, Lynch, and Middleton; Gadsden seemed quite willing to yield) laid down an ultimatum that, unless South Carolina staples, rice and indigo, should be exempted from the non-exportation provision, they would not sign the Association; and those delegates did in fact withdraw from Congress for the time being. . . . Thereupon, to prevent the break-up of the union, a compromise was effected whereby the South Carolinians yielded their contention with regard to indigo on condition that an exception be made of rice.[26]

The story of South Carolina's first act of disunion is recounted in more detail still in the records of the South Carolina provincial assembly. Not long after the five delegates returned to Charleston, the assembly called upon them to account for the crisis of exports in Congress in October. The moderate, well-liked Christopher Gadsden, who opposed the walkout, spoke first. Calling the rice exemption "obnoxious," he declared it his duty to report with veracity what transpired: "He had not any hand in causing those words to stand in the instrument of association—that, they had well nigh occasioned a division in Congress And, so ill was a proposition of that nature received, that it had occasioned a cessation from business for several days; in order to give our deputies time to recollect themselves." He continued, "When the association was completing, and the members of Congress were signing that instrument, all our deputies, but himself, withdrew." Gadsden asked his colleagues to allow him to sign the continental document on behalf of his entire delegation, but they would not grant this request. The Congress stood in crisis during those days.

Many delegates insisted on signing without South Carolina, arguing that special dispensations offered for disunionist behavior would set an awful precedent. Others deemed compromise, even capitulation, necessary to their avowed higher purpose in Philadelphia to erect and publicize to the world a unified front in the defense of Massachusetts.[27]

In the end, as Gadsden reported, Secretary of Congress Charles Thomson, olive branch in hand, called the four absent South Carolina delegates back into Carpenters' Hall, and a compromise was brokered. The rice exemption would be inserted into the articles of the Association for the purpose of preserving the Union. "Carolina was on the point of being excluded from the association," Gadsden said in his speech, "when our deputies being again summoned by the Secretary, they returned into Congress, yielding up the article of indigo: and that Congress only for the sake of preserving the union of America allowed the article rice to be added to the association."[28]

Next to speak in Charlestown was John Rutledge, future first governor of the state of South Carolina and later member of the Constitutional Convention. In self-defense, Rutledge testified that he and the other delegates had pursued an exemption for one or more of their colony's staple crops out of a spirit of pride and protection of South Carolina's particular interests. The Continental Association, he argued, had been biased in favor of the Northern colonies. And, he professed trenchantly, "he could never consent to our becoming dupes to the people of the North."[29]

Rutledge gave as the reason for his preliminary refusal to sign the embargo—that is to say, without some fair offset to the interests of the "rice Colonies" (South Carolina and Georgia)—"that, as the Northern trade would be but little affected by the association, he saw no reason why ours should be almost ruined; for, nearly all our indigo, and two thirds of our rice, went to the ports of the mother country. That, if we must bear burdens in the cause of America, they ought to be as equally laid as possible."[30]

As a consequence of the South Carolinians' demands and threats, the Congress capitulated on October 18. The delegates agreed to exempt rice, but not indigo. In its final form, adopted on October 20, the nonexportation clause of the Continental Association specified that in the event Parliament did not repeal the Coercive Acts by September 10, 1775, the thirteen colonies would enact full-scale nonexportation to all ports in the British empire, "except rice to Europe."[31]

Chapter 3: South Carolina Withdraws 73

FIGURE 10. John Rutledge, South Carolina Delegate. (Portrait of John Rutledge. Artist unknown, *John Rutledge*, ca. 1891, photographic print, Library of Congress, LC-USZ62-91143.)

In this way, thus, the American Union enacted its first commercial legislation, the Continental Association. The delegates did not know it, but in 1774 they were establishing two fundamental operating principles of American government that would not be fully abandoned until the Civil War. The first was colonial- or state-preemptive legislation—that is, the advance issuance of a formal veto or strict countermeasure by a colonial or state legislature opposing central legislation, like Virginia's resolution on tobacco. The second operating principle was threats of secession, like South Carolina's dramatic walkout. In the early years, like later years, whenever genuine disunion reared its head, Union-saving compromise became the only reliable path forward, even if it left trails of resentment and jealousy in its wake.

* * * * *

In spite of these discords and pitfalls, the First Congress accomplished much. Union gained a footing. Delegates from disparate economies and cultures, breaking bread together week after week, formed lasting friendships. They stated their rights and clarified their demands in public addresses and declarations. For numerous reasons, however, the Congress never did resume formal debates on Galloway's Plan of Union. The first proposed constitution, while admittedly binding the empire and forestalling imperial and civil wars, was anathema to most delegates because it cemented the colonies not only to the mother country but also to one another at a moment when each colony was declaring to the world that in North America, colonial assemblies were the supreme and final arbiters of law and justice. Not only this, the Galloway constitution perpetuated a political system wherein Americans remained "inferior" to those in England. In truth, such a subordinate status was the obnoxious opposite of everything most of the delegates had come to Philadelphia to proclaim and achieve.

Foremost among its achievements, the Congress concluded its impressive trade pact. By the Continental Association, soon published throughout America and Europe, all American harbors would cease imports of all kinds, including slaves, as of December 1, 1774. In a blow aimed at the profiteering company that had triggered the imperial crisis in the first place, the Association also enjoined the thirteen colonies to a total nonconsumption of any tea known at any time, past or present, to have touched the hands of the East India Company. Nonexportation would wait another year. In compliance with Virginia orders, this facet of resistance would not come into execution until September of the next year. In compliance with South Carolina's demands and threats, the commercial agreement would exempt rice permanently. Finally, in a subsequent vote, the delegates established they would reconvene for a Second Congress on May 10, 1775, if Parliament had not begun the process of repealing the Coercive Acts by that time.[32]

On the question of nonexportation, the Congress was acutely aware that many readers of the Continental Association would scratch their heads, wondering why at such a decisive moment, when a highly charged unified commercial resistance seemed to be the only hope for ensuring America's safety and salvation, the delegates had so badly watered down the embargo by delaying this vehicle of resistance for so long. So, wisely, if not candidly, the drafters of the Association provided an explanation.

The reason given by Congress was goodwill toward England. Cognizant of the fact that depriving merchants in the empire of tobacco, indigo, and other Southern staples, as well as vital raw materials from the North,

Chapter 3: South Carolina Withdraws 75

would immeasurably damage British families and fortunes, Congress voted to postpone nonexportation. That is, altruism was the delegates' alibi. "The earnest desire we have not to injure our fellow-subjects in Great-Britain, Ireland, or the West-Indies," the Association read, "induces us to suspend a non-exportation until the tenth day of September, 1775."[33]

Thus, as publicly stated, American sympathy for Britain, not internal cleavage or a tobacco ultimatum, underlay the decision to delay nonexportation. The impression conveyed by the First Congress to the world was that the colonies had unanimously voted to give the Parliament a second chance, enacting nonexportation only if the government carried on its calamitous Port Act, Government Act, and others for another year, despite nonimportation. As portrayed to the king and Parliament, it was a carefully planned, multistage, unanimous decree of American resistance that took into consideration, in the final analysis, clemency toward England. The Association did not offer any rationale whatsoever for the rice exemption. South Carolina's walkout, threatening disunion, was kept a hushed secret.

* * * * *

The proceedings of the First Congress concluded in late October. Among the dozens of toasts and tributes offered at farewell celebrations during the delegates' last two weeks together, one more than others captures the spirit of their endeavors and final parting. After the signing of the Continental Association on Thursday, October 20, Philadelphia held a festive dinner at City Tavern. In the presence of some one hundred delegates, Pennsylvania assemblymen, and other invited guests, someone at the table tendered the sincere hope, "May the sword of the parent never be stain'd with the blood of her children." Nearby sat a table of Quakers, one of whom, overhearing this, stood up and asked to join the political gentlemen in the sentiment. "This is not a toast but a prayer," said the Quaker, and in unison all rose and lifted their glasses.[34]

During his final days in Philadelphia, John Adams entertained a friend visiting from New England with a tour about town. They perused books in the Library Company and afterward sat as spectators at a hearing of the Pennsylvania Supreme Court. On the morning of the 29th, Adams boarded fellow Massachusettsan Thomas Cushing's carriage for the two-week journey back to Boston. His departing fantasy was that no war would come and therefore no further congresses would be required. "It is not very likely," he wrote in his diary, "that I shall ever see this part of the world again, but I shall ever retain a most grateful, pleasing sense of the many civilities I have received in it."[35]

George Washington, in his two months in Philadelphia, had grown in his conviction that petitions and addresses were weak means of redress against inveterate corruption of mind and pocketbook in London. He put his faith in embargo, union, and arms. The colonel hoped Britain would change its unenlightened course, but still he was diligently preparing for war. Before setting out on the road home to Mount Vernon, he bought a new sash and epaulets for his military uniform and inquired with merchants about the prices of muskets. While in Philadelphia, Washington also ordered a book on the science of waging war entitled *A Military Treatise on the Appointments of the Army*, written by Thomas Webb, British brother in arms with him in the late French and Indian War.[36]

As Washington had written to turncoat Robert Mackenzie several weeks before, if the king's army struck first, imperial civil war would become inevitable. To Washington, even this worst species of warfare was a small price to pay for the preservation of liberties and natural rights. His honor and virtue as a Virginia colonel, uniquely skilled in the art of war, would permit nothing less.

CHAPTER 4

"A Fatal Issue to Our Union"

During the same months that fifty-five American delegates were deliberating in Carpenters' Hall in Philadelphia, and then implementing nonimportation of British goods back home, Royal Governor of Massachusetts Thomas Gage was maneuvering in Boston to avert first blood. Gage, a fifty-six-year-old, career military man who by most accounts was moderate and fair-minded in diplomacy and war, found himself in the winter and spring of 1774–75 confronting a predicament. On the one hand, his marching orders from London bid him to enforce the Coercive Acts with an iron hand, brooking no further violent crimes like Boston's pillaging of East India Company tea in December of 1773. On the other hand, Gage was charged with the task of doing nothing to inflame the tinderboxes that were Massachusetts and New England. The governor's unenviable job was to subdue rebellion, restoring law and order in such a way as not to incite imperial civil war. As one of his superiors in London, William Legge, Lord Dartmouth, put it, the British mission in New England was to "quiet the minds of the people, to remove their prejudices, and, by mild and gentle persuasion to induce . . . submission on their part."[1]

Gage's strategy was peaceful disarmament backed by shows of force. To evidence British superiority, the general marched festooned redcoats regularly in Boston and throughout the neighboring countryside. Added to this, he decided that the only real way to head off Anglo-American civil war was to strip the colonists of the firepower that would embolden them to fight back on a massive scale. He would maintain the peace and gain the advantage by keeping as much gunpowder and cannon as possible out of the hands of the rebels who might at any moment take the field.

That is why on April 19, 1775, just before dawn, some two hundred of Gage's light infantrymen under the command of Major John Pitcairn stood face to face with seventy-six New England militiamen on Lexington Green. The objective of the British was to march to Concord, where they were to destroy or appropriate munitions of war. In Lexington, en route to Concord, however, armed Americans lined up, refusing to disperse when commanded to do so by mounted British officers. The standoff lasted several minutes, when a shot of unknown provenance was fired. After this, in a fog of shouted orders on both sides, the British infantry rushed the American line, opening up their guns and bayoneting the fallen. Eight New Englanders died. Ten were wounded. There were no serious British injuries. As historian Rick Atkinson describes this first bloodletting of the Revolution, "Lexington had been not a battle, or even a skirmish, but an execution."[2]

At the North Bridge in Concord four hours later, again there was a tense standoff at close range, and again a shot rang out, spurring battle. This time the New Englanders scored a victory. There were five American casualties, including two dead, compared to eight and three on the British side. The remainder of the day saw the New England spirit soar, as several thousand militiamen from near and far swarmed to the series of roads connecting Concord to Boston, where they harassed, chased, and sniped redcoats all the way back to Mystic River. In total, British casualties reached 273, with 73 dead, out of about 1,800. New England casualties totaled 95, with 49 dead, from an estimated 3,700 who engaged at one time or another in the all-day shooting mayhem of April 19.[3]

* * * * *

Three weeks later the Continental Congress reconvened in Philadelphia. Most of the delegates had attended the First Congress six months earlier. John Adams, Sam Adams, John Dickinson, John Hancock, John Jay, James Duane, Philip Livingston, Philip Schuyler, and Silas Deane were all there. So were George Washington, Patrick Henry, Peyton Randolph, Richard Henry Lee, Edmund Pendleton, Benjamin Harrison, Thomas Lynch, Christopher Gadsden, and John and Edward Rutledge. One notable absence from this second convocation was Joseph Galloway. The most prominent newcomer was the sixty-nine-year-old Benjamin Franklin, who had only five days before the opening of the Second Congress disembarked from the ship *Pennsylvania Packet* after a decade-long stay in England. Galloway and Franklin were old friends and staunch political allies in the fight for Pennsylvania citizens' rights against the proprietary

Penns, the ruling family of the colony. Twenty-five years Galloway's senior, Franklin had mentored the younger man in the early 1750s. Once he left for London in 1764, they corresponded regularly on matters both political and personal.

While still in London, Franklin had circulated Galloway's Plan of Union to high-ranking British officials, including Lord Chatham and Lord Camden. He did this because he viewed the proposed constitution to be an act of good faith by Galloway and his associates in Philadelphia during a period of peril for both sides. Technically speaking, Franklin found little to disapprove of in Galloway's plan. Yet privately he could not stomach it because it would unavoidably draw the colonies into closer contact with a nation he judged to be politically and morally corrupt, perhaps beyond redemption. In late February, Franklin did not mince words in a letter to Galloway:

> When I consider the extreme corruption prevalent among all orders of men in this old rotten state, and the glorious public virtue so predominant in our rising country, I cannot but apprehend more mischief than benefit from a closer union. . . . Here numberless and needless places, enormous salaries, pensions, perquisites, bribes, groundless quarrels, foolish expeditions, false accompts or no accompts, contracts and jobs devour all revenue. . . . I apprehend therefore that to unite us intimately, will only be to corrupt and poison us also.[4]

In Philadelphia, Galloway may not have fundamentally disagreed with Franklin's assessment about the decadence and greed of British government, but he remained unapologetic in his political views. Aghast at the First Congress's rejection of his constitution and adoption instead of a militant trade policy, accompanied by incendiary declarations, he refused to return to service in what he now considered to be a rogue political body. Terrified of the chaos the Congress was certain to unleash, he now dedicated his energies to fighting and delegitimizing the "American demagogues" who were advocating the supremacy of themselves and their assemblies over Parliament. All the while, Galloway continued to promote his Plan of Union, or some similar political reform reconciling America and England, as the only salvation.[5]

Reciprocally, Galloway's disloyalty to the cause of liberty inflamed many American patriots against him. Because he did not retire quietly, someone in Philadelphia harassed him with an invitation to kill himself.

According to Joseph Hewes, North Carolina delegate who recounted the story in a letter back home, Galloway was an "apostate" who on either May 8 or 9, several days before the commencement of the Second Congress, returned to his home in Philadelphia in the presence of several friends to discover a curious box on his doorstep. When the speaker opened it, in Hewes's telling, he was horrified at what he saw inside. It was a rope laced up into a noose. The purveyor of the box accompanied this instrument of suicide with a short note, urging, "All the satisfaction you can now give your injured country is to make a proper use of this and rid the world of a damned scoundrel."[6]

* * * * *

While the newly returned Franklin remained cordial with Galloway, even encouraging him to reconsider his stance on the Congress and instead work from within, the famous scientist-philosopher had by May 1775 drawn drastically different conclusions about what steps the colonies should take to preserve their liberty and dignity. As he told Galloway by letter, Parliament and its merchant masters seemed hopelessly corrupt. He viewed the king and his ministers as small-minded, egotistical, and vindictive. If any single thing could be held under the spotlight now and in the future to explain the present bumbling imperial crisis, Franklin believed, it was the folly of the leading men in London. In contrast, setting him widely apart from his friend Galloway, the doctor found very little to fault in the American performance in the contest so far. The colonists had conducted themselves with honor, patience, and good faith.

For these reasons, Franklin gave up his cherished London life that spring, returning home to Philadelphia to fight, first, for liberty and equality and, second, for the peaceful preservation of the British empire (the reverse of Galloway's ordering of these political values). The doctor was not heartened on the day of his arrival, May 5, when he heard the news of Lexington and Concord. Everywhere in Philadelphia there were harried preparation for war and uneasy talk that reconciliation, after such fatal wrongdoing as the British soldiers' firing on Massachusetts militiamen, was an impossibility. Franklin largely sided with this viewpoint. In a letter to friend David Hartley, Whig member of Parliament, he foretold an interminable war. "You will have heard before this reaches you," Franklin penned, "of the commencement of a civil war; the end of it perhaps neither myself, nor you, who are much younger, may live to see."[7]

Franklin's grief, however, was joined by undaunted political conviction. He accepted appointment to the Continental Congress on May 7, and by the time it was gaveled to order three days later, he came equipped with a forceful, two-part prescription for the preservation of liberty. First, the colonies must arm for self-defense. Second, the colonies must unite into an invincible constitutional Union. In the Second Congress Franklin was going to step into the shoes of Galloway as the foremost advocate of a supreme written charter to safeguard American liberties and ensure domestic tranquility. The difference was that Galloway's constitution incorporated the Parliament and king of England. Franklin's was a pure American constitution, the first proposed in the founding era.

FIGURE 11. Title Page, Articles of Confederation. (U.S. Articles of Confederation. *Articles of Confederation and Perpetual Union Between the States of.* . . . Williamsburg, Virginia: J. Dixon & W. Hunter, 1777, Library of Congress Printed Ephemera Collection, portfolio 178, folder 26.)

Franklin called it the Articles of Confederation and Perpetual Union. In thirteen articles, the constitution provided for all the basic needs of the "United Colonies" in the present and future. It empowered Congress to raise an army, receive and send ambassadors, enter into treaties and alliances, create a treasury, tax the colonies on the basis of voting-age male population, and regulate "general commerce." An Executive Council was established to enforce the law, judicial bodies to be organized ad hoc as domestic disputes arose. Voting was to take place by delegates elected by colonial assemblies, the numbers in Congress to be determined by proportional representation, not equal colony representation. In the event of changing or unforeseen circumstance, Article XII stipulated an amendment process whereby Congress proposed amendments and the colonies approved them by simple majority vote. Essential to colonies famously jealous of centralized power, Article III safeguarded the colonies' existing rights and prerogatives. The federal constitution promised not to obliterate what later came to be defined as "states' rights," meaning the established powers and protections then owned and enjoyed by the colonies in their local assemblies, constitutions, and laws.[8]

Franklin's federal constitution also self-consciously erected bulwarks against American disunion and domestic civil wars. Foremost in this calculus, he mandated that the thirteen colonies bind themselves into a "Perpetual Union." The Articles would unite them perpetually—that is to say, forever. There could be no disunion, secession, or splitting into separate confederacies. Once they acceded to the constitution, the colonies committed to seek legal, not separatist or military, remedies to resolve their differences—*in perpetuity*, not simply so long as one colony, region, or the other found the Union convenient. As a mark of seriousness and emphasis, Franklin used the highly charged word *perpetual* four times in the constitution: in its title and in Articles IV, XI, and XIII. In Article II, for good measure, he added a fifth reminder of permanency, stipulating that the colonies were contractually binding not only themselves but also "their Posterity."

In answer to widespread concerns that Americans were destined to engage in perpetual civil wars over the "right to the soil," Franklin empowered the "general Confederacy" to settle all continental matters of "War and Peace" and "all Disputes and Differences between Colony and Colony." Not only this, Franklin knew that the pristine western lands beyond the Appalachian Mountains, stretching to the Mississippi River, were longstanding battlegrounds of overlapping claims by many colonies. In the 1770s, those lands were ripe for explosive conflict. Therefore, in Article V, he granted the Union, not the colonies, the right to adjudicate the West and erect new colonies there. This would prevent colonies or geographic sections from seceding, declaring separate independence, and then making war on Native Americans or other colonists to conquer those lands for themselves. In Franklin's constitution, the thirteen colonies were uniting into "a firm League of Friendship" in which—and this was the lawmaker's most important aim—there would be a strict policy of perpetual peace with one another. It was a security pact. Implicitly, this meant that there could be no foreign wars, no boundary or commerce wars, and no wars of western territorial expansion undertaken by any colony or region without the express sanction of the supreme Union.[9]

Tactful and patient, Franklin did not rush his Articles of Confederation and Perpetual Union onto the floor of Congress. Rather, he extensively canvassed other delegates first, seeking their advice and endorsement. It was not until more than two months after the Congress commenced, in fact, that the Pennsylvanian finally stood up in person and presented his constitution to his fellow delegates.

Before this, the Congress deliberated on other life-and-death questions. In the aftermath of Lexington and Concord, was there any hope of reconciliation with the king and Parliament? If so, what strategy would obtain it without the self-abasement of Americans as inferior and unequal members of the British empire? Should the Congress raise arms and petition the crown for mercy, or simply raise arms, forcing the king's ministers to step forward with reasonable terms of accommodation? If the Congress did legislate in favor of mustering an army, would it be composed of regional or continental troops? Who would serve as commander in chief and who would pay the army's expenses? And what about essential goods and matériel? With all imports and exports to the British empire cut off, how would Americans survive a war? After a century and a half of living under the yoke of Parliament's restrictive policies, was it finally time to throw open American ports to free trade with France, Spain, Holland, and all the other nations of the world?

* * * * *

In early May, radicals in Philadelphia succeeded in their aim to ostracize Galloway. Soon after an unknown person left the suicide noose on his front porch, the former speaker of the Pennsylvania House took leave of the city, never again serving as a delegate in Congress or the Pennsylvania assembly. In the end, Galloway fled the chaos of imperial dismemberment and civil war, boarding a ship for the safety and security of England. Nevertheless, many other delegates in Congress took up Galloway's cause of reconciling the colonies to king and Parliament, all the while stridently declaiming against the horrors of independence. Among the most prominent representatives of this perspective in the debate chamber was John Dickinson, forty-two-year-old Philadelphia attorney who had earned fame eight years earlier for his erudite "Letters from a Pennsylvania Farmer."

Even after Lexington and Concord, Dickinson was not yet ready to leverage the ultimate Lockean political instrument of revolution against abusive government. Nor was he ready to declare frank American independence from Parliament only while continuing to uphold allegiance to King George in a radically reconstituted constitutional empire, as many delegates were proposing at the time. With the Congress now gathered in the Assembly Room of the State House rather than Carpenters' Hall, Dickinson promoted instead a Plan of Treaty with the Parliament and king. His idea was that the Congress should dispatch commissioners to London to restore peace and finally, for all time, resolve the vexing matter of taxation entirely in the favor of the colonies.

The first critical issue the Congress faced when it reconvened in May was whether it should raise a large offensive army to prove its might and power in the face of tyranny or rather a defensive army only, one whose intent was to wave a white flag and reassure London of the Congress's allegiance to the empire. For several weeks this question was debated only lightly and sporadically in the hall of Congress, until the third week of May when Dickinson stood up and offered a full-scale plea for reconciliation. He spoke for hours on either May 23 or 24, or both, perhaps giving as many as three speeches. As he spoke, Dickinson characterized himself as a patriot seeking both liberty and truth. His intent was not to surrender to tyranny but to follow the path of objectivity and prudence, allowing the facts of empire and colonial unpreparedness for war and independence to speak for themselves.[10]

Now that scores of men had been killed in Massachusetts, Dickinson said, the Congress had before it three avenues for the relief of America and the restoration of liberty. First, "war, without petitioning, or sending agents to England, to treat of an accommodation." Second, "we may prepare as mentioned and also petition, but without sending agents." Third, "we may prepare, petition, and send agents." Dickinson importuned the Congress to enact the third option: peace and liberty together at all costs. The pointed reason he gave for this strategy was that the colonies were too raw and disunited, and therefore too weak, to surmount the multitude of dangers that separation from Britain would unleash. They included "the danger of insurrection by Negroes in Southern Colonies," "incursions of Canadians and Indians upon the Northern Colonies," invasion by "rapacious and ambitious nations of the world," and "civil convulsions among ourselves."

Chapter 4: "A Fatal Issue to Our Union" 85

FIGURE 12. John Dickinson, Pennsylvania Delegate. (Portrait of John Dickinson. Albert Rosenthal, *John Dickinson*, 1888, etching, New York Public Library, EM934.)

Dickinson was racked with guilt as he made these ominous pronouncements about America's future if the Congress unleashed independence. "I'm sorry for it," he said, explaining that he was opposing separation from the empire in full knowledge that "these words are not so pleasing to the ears of some worthy members" gathered in the hall. Nevertheless, he said, "the dictates of my conscience command me boldly to speak on the naked sentiments of my soul in a time of such exigence on a point of such moment to my country."

As Dickinson perceived it, independence was a dark prospect for the colonies. It "presents to me an ocean perpetually tempestuous without bottom & without shore. If there are in it any islands, or spots of terra firma, they are too distant & too small to be discovered by my weak sight. I cannot perceive a speck where a dove might pick up any green [leaf]." He offered the prognostication that even if the colonies won a war for independence against the mother country, happiness would not be their lot. "Success, may to us become a misfortune. Our victories may be worse than defeats—& like the Macedonian monarch, we may conquer—but to weep."

The thirteen colonies were unready in 1775 to form an effective union among themselves, Dickinson argued, and therefore unready to prosecute and win a war against the king's forces. His advice was to pursue an accommodation in the present while waiting for a maturation process to prepare the colonies for a break with England in the distant future. "It would be the height of imprudence to push a quarrel with Great Britain to extremity—until these colonies are grown so strong & united, that in case she should be ruined, we should have nothing to fear from any other power. That time is not yet arrived." He estimated that it would take forty to fifty years of political and economic development before America could safely split from the empire. "Time will settle this matter fully in our favor," Dickinson said. "Let us only keep quiet for 40 or 50 Years."[11]

In support of this plan of reconciliation, the Pennsylvania farmer submitted to Congress resolutions comprising a two-part strategy to achieve peace with London while simultaneously preserving life, liberty, and property at home. First, the colonies must be put in a "state of defense," organized and funded by Congress and supplied with arms and ammunition through the dispatch of covert vessels to France, Holland, and the West Indies to negotiate purchases. Second, King George and the British ministry must understand that the colonies' purpose in organizing an army was self-preservation, not offensive war. America must communicate to London its ardent, heartfelt desire for "a restoration of the harmony formerly subsisting between our mother country & these colonies." In fulfillment of this hope, the Pennsylvanian proposed that the Congress send peace commissioners to London where they would "present an humble & dutiful petition to his majesty."[12]

* * * * *

As Dickinson anticipated, his strategy of caution did not endear him to many delegates in Congress. One of the most ruffled of all was John Adams, a New England hardliner who soon rose to a leadership position within the party opposing reconciliation. Unquestionably, Adams shared Dickinson's preoccupations over the incompatibilities and disunited state of the thirteen colonies. Where he differed was his willingness to throw caution to the wind for the sake of the higher calling of safeguarding constitutional rights. After Lexington and Concord, Adams believed that revolution was necessary, independence inevitable. Therefore, to his worldview, the thirteen colonies had no alternative but to unite and find peaceful constitutional and psychological means now—not in fifty years—to transcend their dissimilarities and tensions, including contests over the right to soil.

Adams knew from personal experience and self-scrutiny just how difficult it was going to be to unite the separate regions of America into a functioning whole. During the First Congress, in fact, he did not highlight others as prime examples of the combustible parochialism and self-superiority that he believed might foil an American Union. Instead he pointed a finger at himself, confessing in his private diary that he himself embodied a destructive New England chauvinism. In an entry penned one October day, he admitted that he was entirely convinced that the people of Massachusetts and the three other New England colonies were superior in most every regard to those from the other nine colonies. "The morals of our people are much better," he said. "Their manners are more polite and agreeable—they are purer English. Our language is better, our persons are handsomer, our spirit is greater, our laws are wiser, our religion is superior, our education is better." During the Second Congress, he shared the same sentiments with Abigail by letter, acknowledging the existence within himself of an "overweening prejudice in favour of New England." But then, looking in the mirror, the founder suddenly asserted that these self-righteous beliefs within himself were an "infirmity, in my own heart" that he must overcome.[13]

Adams attributed these prejudices within himself, as well as those gripping the other delegates in Congress, including the Southern delegates' deplorable attachment to slavery, to the effect on the mind of "Mothers Milk," by which he meant familiar and cultural childhood learnings instilled from birth. In Adams's political psychology, the prejudices lawmakers inherit from their parents and home communities were the worst poisons of politics—and the greatest perils to the incipient American Union. Especially when dissimilar peoples attempt to unite in a cooperative enterprise, he believed, the only way out of conflict and paralysis was transcendence of prejudices, leading to sacrifice of interest in hard-fought compromise.[14]

If only Adams had been able to live up to these ideals in politics, he might not have come to such painful loggerheads with Dickinson so early in the course of the Second Congress. In contrast to the Pennsylvanian, Adams believed that the status quo empire had come to an everlasting end. He would never return to the subjugation of the New England people by a Parliament that had proved itself to be not only obtuse and thieving but also now murderous. Because he and the other New England delegates had traveled to Philadelphia in 1775 to form a war government, not a submissive peace government, Adams simply could not tolerate Dickinson's usurpation of the reins of Congress and his lengthy diatribes about restoring British sovereignty. After all, Boston was burning and his own family members in Braintree feared for their lives. From the first day of Congress, Adams wanted to raise a continental army, appoint officers, and begin a full-bore, painstaking international search for gunpowder, munitions, and arms. Proposals for peace treaties and reconciliation, to Adams, were the stuff of wishful thinking and cowardice. In any event, even if the delegates in Congress intended to negotiate for peace, they must do so from a position of strength.[15]

This clash of priorities drove Adams and Dickinson to a showdown—one that triggered a threat of disunion and later led to a permanent alienation of feeling. In his writings, Adams records an episode in late May, when, having left the State House soon after delivering a speech disputing the wisdom of extending yet another olive branch to England, he was angrily accosted by Dickinson outside the courtyard. In Adams's description, Dickinson shouted at him "in as violent a passion as he was capable of feeling."[16]

"What is the reason, Mr. Adams," Dickinson demanded to know, "that you New England men oppose our measures of reconciliation?" Dickinson then increased his vehemence, laying down a red line. "Look Ye! If you don't concur with us, in our pacific system, I, and a number of us, will break off, from you in New England, and we will carry on the opposition by ourselves in our own way." Adams replied with equal zeal that he had every right in the world to speak his mind to the Congress. He would not be silenced and gagged. After this, they parted ways.

Not long afterward, however, the two men encountered one another again outside the State House, and, according to Adams, Dickinson's disrespect spelled the end of their relationship. They passed one another on Chestnut Street, walking so close that their elbows nearly touched. Adams bowed and pulled off his hat in respect. Dickinson, though, ignored him "haughtily," Adams wrote in his diary later the same day. "He passed without moving his hat, head or hand." Dickinson did not make eye contact. In no way at all did he acknowledge Adams's presence. To the Braintree lawyer, it was an affront that signaled a lasting breach. "We are not to be upon speaking terms, nor bowing terms," he concluded, "for the time to come."[17]

Chapter 4: "A Fatal Issue to Our Union"

And so it was. So bitter and polarizing was the question of American independence, and so deep the two men's prejudices, that Adams and Dickinson never exchanged words in private again. Over the next thirty years, they addressed one another only in public legislative forums. In the end, despite his best efforts, Adams's overweening biases in favor of New England—and independence—seem to have gotten the best of him.[18]

* * * * *

Over the next several weeks the conciliatory and militant wings of Congress struck a bargain. As Dickinson proposed, they agreed to prepare a deferential appeal to King George III, now known as the Olive Branch Petition. Concurrently, they formed the Continental Army and appointed a commander in chief. As both Adams and Dickinson record in separate writings, the Olive Branch Petition was enacted to prevent disunion. In his notes, Dickinson asserts that a refusal by Congress in May and June of 1775 to seek reconciliation might well have proved "a fatal issue to our Union." Elsewhere he underscores that the greatest threat to colonial resistance was the "Doctrine of Disunion." Adams, in a letter to James Warren, president of Massachusetts Provincial Congress, corroborated that the threat of secession of some colonies from the Congress was the overriding reason that the New England delegates and their prowar, proindependence allies from Virginia and other Southern colonies capitulated to the reconciliationists, most of whom hailed from the Middle colonies. Of the Olive Branch Petition, Adams wrote to Warren, "We must have a petition to the king and a delicate proposal of negotiation &c. This negotiation I dread like death. But it must be proposed. We can't avoid it. Discord and total disunion would be the certain effect of a resolute refusal to petition and negotiate."[19]

With its hands thus tied, the Congress formally resolved on May 26 to draft the petition. A week later it appointed a committee, consisting of Dickinson, Franklin, John Jay, Thomas Johnson, and John Rutledge, to draw up the document. Unsurprisingly, Dickinson took the lead, penning most of the language. It began, "We, your Majesty's faithful subjects of the colonies . . . entreat your Majesty's gracious attention to this our humble petition." It continued, "We beg leave further to assure your Majesty, that notwithstanding the sufferings of your loyal colonists, during the course of the present controversy, our breasts retain too tender a regard for the kingdom from which we derive our origin, to request such a reconciliation as might in any manner be inconsistent with her dignity or her welfare." Earnestly, the Olive Branch Petition bespoke "the apprehensions that now oppress our hearts with unspeakable grief." It concluded with a repetition of the plea: "Your Majesty be pleased to direct some mode, by which the united applications of your faithful colonists to the throne, in pursuance of their common councils, may be improved into a happy and permanent reconciliation."[20]

* * * * *

Eleven days after Congress established the committee to petition King George, it passed a resolution to coordinate the military efforts of the thirteen colonies into one unified Continental Army. One day after this, June 15, the delegates named George Washington of Virginia as commander in chief of the army. "George Washington, Esq.," the official *Journals of Congress* attests, "was unanimously elected." True as this might have been on the day of the official vote, this characterization of the election of the American general of the Continental Army—one carefully crafted for release to the newspapers and handed down for centuries in our founding mythology—hardly captures the truth of how and why Washington was chosen. The reality, corroborated by many sources, is that the Southern colonies would not tolerate a Northern general out of fear of New England dominance and the perils of domestic civil war.[21]

As John Adams explained the "out of doors" negotiations that took place to make Washington general, it was the product of "a Southern Party against a Northern and a jealousy against a New England Army under the Command of a New England General." This logic cut deep, and eventually all became persuaded to vote for Washington. For the security of the Union, to quell persisting alarms over domination by New England, and to unite the Southern states into a collective war against England, Adams said, where fighting thus far remained restricted to Massachusetts, they must elect a "Southern General."[22]

Adams was not alone in this interpretation of the geopolitical dynamics that put Washington in charge. Another New England delegate, Eliphalet Dyer, fifty-three years old and a former colonel in the French and Indian War, confirmed it in several letters. One reason Dyer, from Connecticut, was so interested in capturing the rationale of Congress in the selection of Washington is that he had entertained aspirations of serving as commander in chief himself. So in the letters, he was at least in part explaining away his own failure to be appointed.

Whatever the reason, Dyer stated plainly that what clinched the appointment of Washington was a powerful fear in the Southern colonies

Chapter 4: "A Fatal Issue to Our Union"

of too great an accumulation of military power in the Northern colonies and, as a consequence, the subjugation at some point in time of those weaker colonies. A New England general at the helm of a New England army continued to terrify many in Congress. As Dyer described it, the precise sequence of events unnerving the Southern colonists was, first, the formation of a Northern army commanded by a Northern general; second, the victory of that army in the imperial civil war with England; and, third—and this is the flickering vision of the future that frightened them—the Northern army, blood still pumping hard from victory, imposing its will upon the rest, or else.[23]

FIGURE 13. George Washington, Virginia Delegate. (Portrait of George Washington. Charles Willson Peale, *George Washington as Colonel in the Virginia Regiment*, 1772, oil on canvas, 50.5 x 41.5 in, Museums at Washington and Lee University, gift of George Washington Custis Lee, U1897.1.1.)

As Dyer explained Washington's appointment to Joseph Trumbull, Connecticut commissary general who had recently joined the defense of Boston: "It removes all jealousies, more firmly cements the Southern to the Northern, and takes away the fear of the former lest an enterprising eastern New England General proving successful, might with his victorious army give law to the Southern & Western Gentry." In a second letter, this one to his home colony's governor, Jonathan Trumbull Sr., Dyer restated and clarified that the purpose of the appointment was 1) to unify the North and South and 2) to remove deep-seated fears in Southern leaders of the Continental Army being turned against them. Referring to the ascension of Washington, Dyer wrote, "His appointment will tend to keep up the Union & more strongly cement the Southern with the Northern colonies, & serve to the removing all jealousies [an] army composed principally of New Englanders (if happily they prove successful) of being formidable to the Southern Colonies."[24]

So fragile was the American Union in June of 1775, and so uncertain the future, that some patriots took at face value rumors predicting a split up of the colonies into two separate confederacies. Even on the same day of Washington's appointment, one delegate, thirty-five-year-old George Clinton of New York, who would later become governor of the state and vice president of the United States, defended the Congress hardily against such rumors. Five days earlier John McKesson, secretary of the New York Provincial Congress, had written to Clinton on behalf of the dozens of delegates sitting in their home assembly. In his letter McKesson reported that they had recently received credible reports that some of the Southern colonies had recently threatened to secede from the Union if the Congress proposed reconciliation and accommodation with King George under weak, shameful terms. Moreover, McKesson claimed, New Yorkers were hearing that the delegates in Congress were actively debating a scheme to divide the thirteen colonies into separate confederacies. The New York Provincial Congress wanted urgently to know: Were the threats of disunion and the plan to separate into two confederacies real and true?[25]

"False as Hell," Clinton replied in his June 15 letter to McKesson. He said he could affirm with certainty that no order by any Southern colony to withdraw from the Union had ever been discussed in Philadelphia. Neither did he think a secession by any Southern colony had ever been held "in contemplation" by anyone. Respecting the two separate confederacies, he promised he had heard nothing at all in Congress to that effect; it was untrue. "These, sir," Clinton concluded, "are Tory reports calculated to frighten the timid and to create distrust of our proceedings."[26]

Perhaps so. There is no reason to doubt the veracity of Clinton's response to McKesson. But what cannot be doubted is that the Congress elected George Washington as commander in chief for two compelling reasons. One was his virtue, honor, and proven courage on the battlefield. The other was the colony of his birth. Had Washington been a Northerner, he never would have assumed control of the American army. And, as a probable consequence, he likely would not have become the president of the Constitutional Convention and, after that, the first president of the United States. The most crucial reason for Washington's appointment as first general of the Continental Army—and possibly to these other official roles—was the tidal pull of regionalism, notably the necessity of uniting the colonies and averting the emergence of warring separate confederacies.

* * * * *

The next fraught matter on the Congress's docket was the election of subordinate officers and their salaries. Here again, according to John Adams, New Englanders and Southerners sparred. "I have never, in all my lifetime, suffered more anxiety than in the conduct of this business," Adams wrote to Massachusetts merchant and politician Elbridge Gerry on June 18. "The choice of officers, and their pay," he continued, "have given me great distress. [Charles] Lee and [Horatio] Gates are officers of such great experience and confessed abilities, that I thought their advice, in a council of officers, might be of great advantage to us; but the natural prejudices, and virtuous attachment of our countrymen to their own officers, made me apprehensive of difficulties." Both Lee and Gates, British-born veterans of the French and Indian War who had recently settled in Virginia, indeed encountered stiff opposition from New Englanders. Washington intervened in their favor, as well as that of "many of our best friends in the southern colonies," reported Adams. At the conclusion of the tortured voting, Lee and Gates secured high-ranking posts, the former major general and second adjutant general, together with Massachusetts's Artemis Ward as second in command. But, said Adams, the proceedings were "Torment. . . . Dismal bugbears were raised, there were prejudices enough among the weak and fears enough among the timid as well as other obstacles from the cunning."[27]

On the question of officer pay, Adams worried that he was going to incur the wrath of New England when they learned how "amazingly high" it was. He attributed the exorbitant salaries of officers, as compared to that of foot soldiers, to the "Southern Geniuses" in Congress who felt in fact that the compromise pay agreed upon was "vastly too low." In conflict were the egalitarianism of New England and the aristocratic social views of the South. "Those ideas of equality, which are so agreeable to us natives of New England," Adams lamented, "are very disagreeable to many gentlemen in the other colonies." Adams fought against such pay discrepancy "it totis viribus" (with all one's might), he told others, "but in vain."[28]

The Congress rendered these decisions on the Continental Army's military leadership on June 17. Six days later Washington and his entourage set off from Philadelphia for Boston, the scene of war. The delegates of

Congress and citizens of Philadelphia sent them off with music, applause, and a parade of brightly colored troops of light horse. As Joseph Reed, Washington's secretary who traveled with him, commented, they were heading to Massachusetts into "a sea of difficulties."[29]

By this time, Washington had ordered the drafting of his last will and testament, apologized to his wife, Martha, for putting his life and their marriage in harm's way, and predicted to Patrick Henry that the enterprise upon which he was embarked would not likely earn him glory. Instead, as recorded by Dr. Benjamin Rush, Washington told his Virginian colleague, "Remember Mr. Henry, what I now tell you: from the day I enter upon the command of the American armies, I date my fall, and the ruin of my reputation." Washington was devoted to the cause of liberty and freedom. He was willing to die for it. But in June of 1775, the future seemed bleak to the commander in chief. When it all ended darkly, he worried, he would be the central target of censure and scorn.[30]

* * * * *

Throughout these months, John and Abigail Adams kept up a regular correspondence. In one letter Abigail asked her husband to describe the famous Benjamin Franklin. In answer to her, Adams praised his fellow congressman for his unprepossessing manner and dauntless spirit. Adams accentuated that Franklin brought into the Congress a reassuring confidence that the American Union, if pushed to the extremity, could in fact achieve independence and preserve it afterward:

> He does not hesitate at our boldest measures, but rather seems to think us, too irresolute, and backward. He thinks us at present in an odd state, neither in peace nor war, neither dependent nor independent. But he thinks that we shall soon assume a character more decisive. He thinks, that we have the power of preserving ourselves, and that even if we should be driven to the disagreeable necessity of assuming a total Independency, and set up a separate state, we could maintain it.

Adams concluded by saying Franklin was "a great and good man."[31]

Franklin indeed had extraordinary faith in the American spirit and the American Union—but only if that Union was organized and governed by a formidable written constitution. A binding, everlasting code of supreme federal laws was, to him, essential to the war effort and to the domestic peace of the thirteen colonies. The doctor had first proposed a formal American union in 1751 in a letter to a friend and fellow printer from New Jersey. Its purpose was the promotion of trade and peace with Indian nations and the persuasion of those nations to enter alliances, not wars, with the English instead of the French. In the letter, Franklin said he was inspired by the ease with which Native Americans formed confederations among themselves and also surprised by the irony that "a like union should be impracticable for ten or a dozen English colonies, to whom it is more necessary, and must be more advantageous; and who cannot be supposed to want an equal understanding of their interests."[32]

Three years later, the colonies failed at Franklin's grand plan of constitutional union at the Albany Congress of 1754. In 1775, assuming the time was ripe at last in the aftermath of Lexington and Concord, he was ready to try again. So, before the Congress, he put pen to paper at his writing desk at home on Market Street drafting the Articles of Confederation and Perpetual Union. Aware that many delegates in Congress still desperately sought reconciliation, he had to account in his constitution for the possibility of reunion with the mother country. He did this in Article XIII, providing an escape clause. The last paragraph of that article specified that should the two warring parties, Britain and America, achieve "Terms of Reconciliation," the Articles of Confederation would thereby be abrogated, permitting that "the colonies shall return to their former connection and friendship with Britain."[33]

By at least late June, Franklin began to promote his constitution to select delegates of Congress, seeking their approbation and enlisting their support in forming a committee to revise it and bring it to the floor for formal debate. Surely he bent the ear of a dozen or more delegates over the course of the summer, but only one record survives providing a window onto the political forces at work against Franklin's "perpetual" union. Years later, upon the request of François Soulés, a French historian conducting research for a book about the American Revolution, Thomas Jefferson wrote a brief summary of the outcome of the Articles of Confederation in 1775 to aid Soulés with his understanding of what had happened. Delegate Jefferson was a latecomer to the Second Congress, arriving in Philadelphia on June 20. He and Franklin had never met before. Yet with common interests in music, art, architecture, natural philosophy, government, and history, they immediately took a liking to one another. Thirty-two, tall, dignified, and red-haired, Jefferson was an object of celebration that year due to the popularity of his recently published *Summary View of the Rights of British America*. In this short tract Jefferson radically proposed that the British Parliament had no authority whatsoever over the thirteen colonies. The colonists in America owed deference solely to the King of England, as the chief magistrate of the empire.[34]

FIGURE 14. Thomas Jefferson, Virginia Delegate. (Portrait of Thomas Jefferson. A. B. Hall, *Thomas Jefferson*, 1892, etching, in James Grant Wilson and John Fiske, eds., *Appletons' Cyclopædia of American Biography*, vol. 3. New York: D. Appleton, 1888.)

As he penned in the notes to Soulés, Jefferson appreciated Franklin's constitution. He looked favorably upon its foresight, concision, proportional representation, protection of colony rights, and the other republican features certain to deter an overconcentration of central power. Yet, as he told Franklin with regret, he could not lend his support. Jefferson's reasoning was straightforward: any constitution advanced on the floor of Congress at this tender moment in the Revolution would backfire, sowing discord and jealousy instead of unity. To defend liberty and property, the colonies must, of course, combine. That much was certain. But the delegates in Congress had vastly divergent views regarding the need for a constitutional Union and the governing structure and principles underpinning any such formal alliance binding them. They would be unable to agree on trade policy and, critically, on the duration of any such unifying constitution, whether perpetual or merely a compact of convenience scheduled to dissolve upon the termination of hostilities with Parliament.

As Jefferson told Soulés, some of the members of Congress made privy to Franklin's constitution "were revolted at it."³⁵

Paradoxically, Jefferson was arguing, any formal attempt to implement a perpetual constitution risked wrecking the Union. If the Congress attempted to adopt universal rules permanently governing all thirteen colonies, some delegates would shout them down on the basis of the doctrine of colony sovereignty, others the injustice of colonial voting powers (one-colony-one-vote vs. proportional representation), others the exclusion of enslaved populations in representation, others any taxation at all, others the triumph of majority voting over supermajority, others trade restriction unfairness, and still others the constitution's conspicuous overreach in establishing new colonies on western territories rightfully belonging to some colonies by bona fide founding charters. In Franklin's admittedly meritorious project to adopt a perpetual union, consequently, there would be no end to what the delegates would fight about, and now was the time to fight Lord North, King George, and General Gage, not one another.

Jefferson's advice became a quiet though widely accepted operating premise within the early Congress. It counseled a moratorium: to preserve a military Union, a constitutional Union must wait. Most critically, putting the constitution to a vote in 1775 would needlessly disrupt the sensitive war proceedings then advancing within Congress and serving as a forceful continental unifier.

Franklin followed Jefferson's advice, but not entirely. Rather than introduce the charter as formal legislation to submit to a committee and formal vote, he found a middle way. On Friday, July 21, after a week during which members and committees were busy mustering soldiers, tents, corn, and powder, as well as tabulating total numbers dead and wounded at the recent Battle of Bunker Hill, the renowned scientist-politician stood up and tendered the Articles of Confederation to his fellow delegates as food for thought. He presented this first constitution of the united colonies as an object to stir their imaginations, explaining that over time, relations with Parliament might worsen. If so, Franklin counseled, such a perpetual constitution as the one he was submitting into the record might one day become urgently necessary for the Union to enact and survive by.³⁶

CHAPTER 5

"Intestine Wars and Convulsions"

By the time Franklin presented the Articles of Confederation to his fellow delegates in the Continental Congress, the future author of the political manifesto *Common Sense* had made landing on the shore of the Delaware River. Thomas Paine, thirty-seven years old, charismatic, and possessed of one of the most progressive Enlightenment minds of the eighteenth century, had arrived in America for the first time in November of 1774. It was an adventure he undertook upon the advice of Franklin, in fact, who at a meeting in London earlier that year had encouraged the spirited young man, unemployed and recently separated from his second wife, to make a new life in Philadelphia. So he did. Paine had always wanted to be a writer, and by good fortune, while browsing at a Philadelphia bookstore not long after his arrival, he met its owner, Robert Aitken. The bookseller was also a printer with imminent plans to launch a magazine called *The Pennsylvania Magazine; or American Monthly Museum*. In search of work, Paine showed Aitken several unpublished manuscripts, and soon the Philadelphian, impressed by the newcomer's intellect and facile pen, hired Paine as a writer and editor.[1]

Over the ensuing winter, Paine and Aitken worked long hours to launch the magazine. The inaugural issue, running fifty-two pages in length, appeared on January 24, 1775. In the preface, likely written by Paine, the magazine praised freedom of the press, self-improvement as the surest path to happiness, and the high prospects of a bright future for the human species. Turning the pages, readers found a character sketch of Voltaire, an introduction to the natural history of the North American beaver, an essay on suicide, reports on new technological innovations, and the current prices of pork, beef, coffee, butter, Madeira, and other commodities. The issue also contained the full text of the Continental

Congress's October 1774 petition to King George III, begging the sovereign of the British empire to intercede with the North ministry to restore "peace, liberty, and safety" for all. After this first issue, Paine kept writing for the *Pennsylvania Magazine* for another fourteen months, penning at least seventeen and perhaps as many as twenty-six essays and poems.[2]

Aitken declared publicly to the readers of the magazine that its editors were intent upon a stance of neutrality on the twin volatile subjects of politics and religion. But this was not the nature of Thomas Paine. Trim, five feet eight inches in height, dark hair pulled back into a queue, Paine was instead a liberal crusader whose tendency was to steer hard and fast into fields of controversy, advancing always the banner of human progress. By the time of Bunker Hill, Paine wished ardently not only for American independence from vice-ridden Britain for white Americans but also for education and civil rights for women and the emancipation of enslaved people. So moved was he by the plight of American enslaved persons—and the institution's gross incompatibility with the liberty Americans espoused—that he put pen to paper on the subject within months of alighting in Philadelphia. Aitken, it seems, refused to publish Paine's first provocative treatise on an urgent American political and moral theme. So Paine tendered it to *The Pennsylvania Journal and the Weekly Advertiser*, where it appeared on March 8, 1775, under the nom de plume "Justice and Humanity."[3]

FIGURE 15. Thomas Paine, Writer. (Portrait of Thomas Paine. George Romney, *Thomas Paine*, date unknown, etching, National Archives and Records Administration, NAID 530488.)

Chapter 5: "Intestine Wars and Convulsions"

"African Slavery in America," Paine's pioneering piece of progressive political writing, is one of the earliest and most influential essays in the archives of American abolitionist literature. In it Paine begins by deploring slave traders. "That some desperate wretches should be willing to steal and enslave men by violence and murder for gain," he writes, "is rather lamentable than strange. But that many civilized, nay, christianized people should approve and be concerned in the savage practice is surprising; and still persist, though it has been so often proved contrary to the light of nature, to every principle of Justice and Humanity."

Above all, Paine condemns the slave trade in the essay, but he also outlines pathways to emancipation in the here and now. One pressing question of the day, Paine says, is:

> What should be done with those who are enslaved already? To turn the old and infirm free would be injustice and cruelty; they who enjoyed the labours of their better days should keep and treat them humanely. As to the rest, let prudent men, with the assistance of legislatures, determine what is practicable for masters, and best for them. Perhaps some could give them lands upon reasonable rent, some, employing them in their labour still, might give them some reasonable allowances for it; so as all may have some property, and fruits of their labours at their own disposal, and be encouraged to industry; the family may live together, and enjoy the natural satisfaction of exercising relative affections and duties, with civil protection, and other advantages, like fellow men.

This 1,600-word soaring condemnation of slavery, which never draws distinctions on the practice between North and South, met with little fanfare in the colonies. In fact *The Pennsylvania Journal and the Weekly Advertiser* ran it as a postscript at the end of the paper. As far as is known, no other colonial newspaper reproduced it. In contrast, Paine's next groundbreaking political tract would rock the British empire.

* * * * *

Released on January 10, 1776, *Common Sense* was published and republished so many times that by April, more than one hundred thousand copies were in circulation, the equivalent of a runaway bestseller in modern times. No pamphlet in colonial history had ever sold so wildly or struck the hearts of men and women so deeply as Paine's *Common Sense*.[4]

One galvanizing theme of Paine's famous work, addressed pointedly to equivocating leaders in the colonies as well as in the Continental Congress, was "TIS TIME TO PART"—that is, from a tyrannical empire. Another theme Paine confronted head-on in *Common Sense*, one typically overlooked in summaries of the tract, was the abiding apprehension that the thirteen colonies, once detached from the protection of the king of England, would descend into the furies of civil wars. Paine did not dismiss the fear. He admitted it was real. But in answer he promised he had a remedy. First, declare independence "Now," Paine argued, not later, when the chance of forging a successful Union would be greatly diminished. Second, echoing Franklin, Paine stated the free colonies must adopt a "Continental Charter" to restrain them and bind them into a peaceful, perpetual brotherhood.[5]

Common Sense, published anonymously, opens with the author's theory of government. Paine reminds readers that government, "a necessary evil," is an entirely elective instrument of society designed to ensure the health, freedom, and security of the people. Government springs eternal from society, he asserts, and is necessary, among other reasons, as an essential corrective to human vice. Left to their own devices, society's appointed leaders fall into venality, and the people run amok. Government's overriding purpose, beyond providing safety and security, Paine says, is therefore "to supply the defect of moral virtue."[6]

With this foundation laid, Paine declares outright that America has no future hope in the British constitution because it has grown rotten to the core. Breaking British government into its three constituent branches, monarch, House of Lords, and House of Commons, he characterizes the first two hereditary branches as corrupt beyond repair. Paine considers that the House of Commons, representative of the people, is the only bright spot in the British constitution, but this branch, like the others, had also become entrenched in greed and bribery. More than anything, Paine takes aim at the medieval institution of monarchy. Kings and queens, he blasts, are an invention of the "Devil."

These contemporary truths about the British constitution led Paine inexorably to the conclusion that Americans must exercise the right of revolution and separation from nefarious government. Notwithstanding the pain and agony of rupturing ancient bonds, Paine tells Americans they must declare independence and return to virtue, liberty, and freedom. Trumpeting independence as the only means of honorable escape from the colonies' centuries-long "prostitution" to rank kings, queens, and lords, he makes the piercing appeal, "TIS TIME TO PART."

Chapter 5: "Intestine Wars and Convulsions"

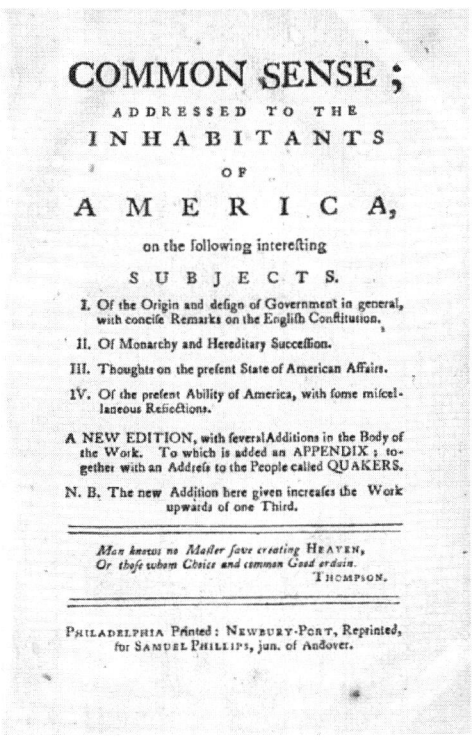

FIGURE 16. *Common Sense*, 1776. (Cover page of Thomas Paine's *Common Sense*. Thomas Paine, *Common Sense*, 1776, 8 x 5 in, pamphlet, National Museum of American History, PL.225292.11.)

In *Common Sense* Paine not only marshals the most cogent arguments for independence ever heard in the British empire and Europe, but he also takes on the counterarguments. Starting with the legions of reconciliationists in the colonies and Congress, those who profess that patience and goodwill on both sides will restore harmony, he regrets to inform them that these hopes are an "agreeable dream." After the bloodshed of Lexington, Concord, and Bunker Hill, Paine says, the breach is irreparable. Quoting Milton in *Paradise Lost*, he explains, "Never can true reconcilement grow where wounds of deadly hate have pierced so deep." Throughout his treatise, Paine keeps up this drumbeat. "I challenge the warmest advocate for reconciliation," he says, "to show a single advantage that this continent can reap by being connected with Great Britain. I repeat the challenge; not a single advantage is derived."

Several paragraphs after these words, Paine turns to the shadow of disunion and civil war so often talked about in print and whispered conversation. To this set of contrarians, he concedes that the risk exists but counters that such a prospect will only be made worse if the colonies wait, dither, and miss the present opportunity now to strike out on their own. Paine calls the window of opportunity presenting itself in 1776 "the seedtime of continental union." In poetic words, he counsels America:

> Youth is the seedtime of good habits, as well in nations as in individuals. It might be difficult, if not impossible, to form the Continent into one government half a century hence. The vast variety of interests, occasioned by an increase of trade and population, would create confusion. Colony would be against colony. Each being able might scorn each other's assistance; and while the proud and foolish gloried in their little distinctions, the wise would lament that the union had not been formed before. Wherefore, the present time is the true time for establishing it. The intimacy which is contracted in infancy, and the friendship which is formed in misfortune, are, of all others, the most lasting and unalterable. Our present union is marked with both these characters: we are young, and we have been distressed; but our concord hath withstood our troubles, and fixes a memorable era for posterity to glory in.

Two clear-cut, inspiring remedies, if adopted by the Congress, Paine promises, will sublimate internal dissension and launch America into a safe independence. One is to replace voracious lords and kings as heads of state with a "Continental Charter, or Charter of the United Colonies"—that is, a written constitution to serve as an everlasting glue to bind and unite them. Outlining its contours, Paine proposes that the constitution should institute a republican government, duly elected from each colony, presided over by a rotating "President" elected for a one-year term, each colony represented in the president's chair every thirteen years. Recognizing the diversity of interests in the colonies and extreme sensitivity on the question of which colony or colonies might rule over the others, Paine counsels against a simple majority for legislation. To head off discord and to ensure the longevity of the constitution and the Union, he recommends a large supermajority for the passage of American federal laws. It should be a voting formula of "not less than three fifths of the Congress," he proposes. Under this calculus, no colony or region could reasonably complain of injustice in the administration of the continental government. This would guarantee the Union's survival and keep the colonies at peace.

The second bulwark against disunion and civil war, Paine proclaims, is the grand project of independence itself. Whereas the naysayers were widely propagandizing that separation from England would free a destructive genie from its bottle, unleashing civil strife in competition for land and commerce, Paine creatively turns this logic on its head. Independence and liberty would become the new Holy Writ to replace empire. "Independence," he maintains, "is the only BOND that can tie and keep us together." Common sacrifice and mutual bloodshed for liberty would unite the diverse colonies into a permanent brotherhood that would shield them from future violence against one another. This was the core of Paine's argument. If victorious, the glory of independence would become the fount of their collective identity and their most potent antidote to internal disruption. It would be the colonies' familial cement, their vow and votary to one another.

Yet, Paine cautions, his strategic plan requires the colonies to act "Now." The secret to achieving union and victory, the author repeats several times in *Common Sense*, is proper timing: immediate, unhesitating separation from Britain not in one year, two years, or a decade, but today. His thesis was novel and unconventional—and the precise opposite of the advice given by John Dickinson. The Pennsylvania statesman had sought to persuade his fellow Americans only six months earlier that a lurch into independence in the eighteenth century was premature. The colonies must wait four to five decades to develop economically, politically, and militarily before separating, Dickinson counseled.

According to Paine, Dickinson had it all wrong. Independence must take place now or never, because civil wars would in fact bloody American soil to the extent the colonists waited. If the colonies did not unite now—in their infancy, in the midst of the great cause of liberty that would make them forever fierce and famous—they would grow tragically apart from one another. With each passing decade their mistrusts would become more deeply rooted, so that by the 1820s or 1830s, Paine specifically forecast, they would be unsheathing their bayonets. By then, the opposing interests of the colonies and their rankling feelings of "superiority" over one another would divide them, and wars would come.

On the other hand, independence, youth, liberty, common cause, and bloodshed—together with a tight-knit constitution to sort out their differences off the battlefield—would tie them peaceably together into the future. All Americans needed to do, Paine urged in his epic summons to liberty and revolution, was to act "Now."

*****

Common Sense hit the thirteen colonies with a tidal force. On reading the rousing declarations of Paine, General Charles Lee, soon to be appointed as commander of the newly formed Southern Department of the Continental Army, wrote to Washington that the author's wisdom was transformative. "Have you seen the pamphlet *Common Sense*? I never saw such a masterly, irresistible performance. It will, if I mistake not, in concurrence with the transcendent folly and wickedness of the Ministry, give the coup de grace to Great Britain. In short I own myself convinced by the arguments of the necessity of separation." Washington himself, at army headquarters in Cambridge, studied the manifesto and dubbed it "unanswerable." Others across the continent agreed. "Who is the author of *Common Sense*?" a correspondent from South Carolina asked in the *Philadelphia Evening Post*. "He deserves a statue of gold."[7]

In spite of its popularity, Paine's essay lacked the power to catalyze an immediate declaration of independence by a slow-moving, ponderous body like the Continental Congress. This would take time. Ever since early September of 1775, when the Congress reconvened in Philadelphia after a monthlong adjournment, in fact, its members had scrupulously avoided the two issues Paine proclaimed to be most indispensable to American freedom and liberty: independence and a constitution. Both topics were too combustible to touch. Consequently, the delegates invested their energies in those matters that seemed urgent but less controversial. One of them was military operations: further organization of the army and recruitment of soldiers, officers, foodstuffs, cannon, gunpowder, and matériel for the war effort. Most pressing in late fall and winter of 1775–1776 was the Continental Army's planned preemptive assault on British Canada. New Englanders in particular fixated on this pursuit, fearing that if they failed to seize the initiative on their northern border, the enemy would invest it with overwhelming firepower and, from there, launch its conquest of America.

The delegates also vigorously debated continental trade policy as it related to yet another "cruel, unjust, unconstitutional" act of Parliament. To punish New England for all its manifold wrongs, Parliament enacted the New England Trade and Fisheries Act in the spring of 1775. Almost as execrable to New Englanders as the Boston Port Act, the Restraining Act, as it was also known, cut off all New England trade with the world. As another blow, the act struck at the backbone of the New England economy, prohibiting New Englanders from fishing in the waters off Newfoundland and most of America's Atlantic coast.[8]

Chapter 5: "Intestine Wars and Convulsions"

This assault on colonial trade spurred the Congress to reassess its commercial policies in the midst of a war demanding every day more arms, ammunition, powder, clothes, tents, meat, and bread. Trade had already become one of the most divisive and disuniting issues in Congress. And so it proved in October when the delegates opened deliberations on whether or not to revise the Continental Association—and perhaps even open American ports to France, Spain, and other foreign powers as a lifeline to survive the oppressions of Britain. The debates, which did not go far, stumbled on the problem of disunion. Not since the trade conflicts over the Continental Association in the First Congress had the delegates warned one another so sternly about the power of regionally biased commercial policy to break the Union.[9]

When Robert Livingston of New York proposed reversing the Continental Association's ban on exports, except for lumber and tobacco, Maryland's Samuel Chase said the people in his colony, Virginia, and North Carolina would never tolerate it. "This will produce a disunion of the colonies," Chase retorted. "The advantage of cultivating tobacco is very great. The planters would complain. Their Negro females would be useless without raising tobacco."[10]

Thomas Willing of Pennsylvania argued that the survival of the war effort depended upon opening select ports on the Atlantic coast, allowing exports to be traded for critical war essentials that would then be shared with the other colonies by internal commerce. Alarmed, Richard Henry Lee of Virginia combated this idea, insisting instead on an absolute equality of trade policy for all colonies. Otherwise, the disadvantaged colonies would cry foul, and resentment would set in. If the Congress favored some colonies in its policies and not others, no matter the rationales offered, Lee explained, "Jealousies and dissensions will arise and disunion and division. We shall become a rope of sand."[11]

Christopher Gadsden concurred with Lee. Trade favors and restrictions laid unequally upon the colonies by Congress "will divide us. One colony will envy another, and be jealous. Mankind act by their feelings."[12]

Livingston professed he was "not convinced." His view was that emergency measures enacted to sustain the war, even if seeming to offer preferential trade advantages to some colonies and ports, would not be the cause of disunion. The thing that would break apart the colonies was the starvation of their essential needs by total embargo. He continued to advocate keeping pressure on the Parliament and its merchants via partial embargo, while otherwise freeing Americans to trade with their British commercial brethren to obtain vital goods. John Adams kept notes on what Livingston said: "[He] thinks the exception of tobacco and lumber would not produce disunion. The colonies affected can see the principles, and their virtue is such that they would not be disunited. Carolina is cultivated by rich planters—not so in the northern colonies. The planters can bear a loss and see the reason of it. The northern colonies can't bear it." Richard Henry Lee corrected him. The truth, he said, is that "the Northern colonies are more fortunate."[13]

FIGURE 17. Robert Livingston, New York Delegate. (Portrait of Robert Livingston. Gilbert Stuart, *Robert R. Livingston*, date unknown, oil on canvas, 35.25 x 28.5 in, Museum of the City of New York.)

Livingston's trade logic also drew a word of caution from John Joachim Zubly, delegate from Georgia. Zubly said that the delegates must be more wise than daring when it came to establishing policy for the Union. They must remember that the commercial self-interest of the colonies could easily overwhelm their virtue. "It is prudent not to put virtue to too serious a test," Zubly pressed. "I would use American virtue, as sparingly as possible lest we wear it out."[14]

In the end, the delegates decided to adhere to the Continental Association of 1774. While waiting out their last hopes of reconciliation with the king and Parliament, they would not stoke "jealousies and divisions" by enacting new trade exceptions. In the meantime, they agreed, the united colonies would satisfy their wartime commercial needs through smuggling and by building bridges with Britain's archrival, France, in the hopes of securing secret assistance.[15]

Chapter 5: "Intestine Wars and Convulsions" 109

* * * * *

Beyond trade, the Congress confronted regional division and distrust on a wide range of other issues that fall and winter. These included slavery, New England domination of the army, pay of officers, views on government, and the twin matters of independence and confederation. Regarding slavery, throughout the fall delegates worried about a concerted British strategy to divide the Northern and Southern colonies at the Hudson River, cutting off all communication between them by way of control of this great artery of North America. Then, according to Sam Adams, the British would direct the bulk of the Royal Army and Navy to an invasion of the North while sending smaller forces into the South with the explicit intent of emancipating enslaved Black people, whom they expected to join the British in the conquest of their rebellious Southern enslavers. By all accounts, South Carolina and Georgia seemed to be the two most vulnerable colonies to such attack. In Philadelphia their own delegates were privately reporting to others in Congress that "1000 regular troops" landing on the coast of those two southernmost colonies, whose officers proclaimed "Freedom to all the Negroes," would quickly have at their disposal an eager army of "20,000 Negroes." As John Adams reported, based on a conversation with a Georgia delegate, "The Negroes have a wonderful art of communicating intelligence among themselves. It will run several hundreds of miles in a week or fortnight."[16]

Not much later, these fears of slave insurrection in the South brought about a clash in the Congress over the enlistment of Black people in the new Continental Army. On September 26, as the delegates were preparing a letter to Washington outlining enlistment procedures, Edward Rutledge of South Carolina made a motion to enjoin Washington to exclude free and enslaved Black people from the army. In this motion Rutledge was "strongly supported by many of the Southern delegates." They lost the point, however, due to powerful opposition. Nevertheless, in Cambridge, at army headquarters, Washington had already handed down an order to do precisely what so many Southern delegates wished. Although small numbers of Blacks had served in the battles of Lexington, Concord, and Bunker Hill, and even though Congress itself had placed no racial restrictions on military service, Washington and his council in Cambridge independently ordered Continental Army officers not to enlist them.[17]

This insistence of so many Southern delegates on keeping free and enslaved Black Americans out of the army begs a question: What were they so afraid of? Clearly, it stands to reason that Southern leaders feared that today's trained, armed Black enlisted men in the North might become tomorrow's ringleaders of slave insurrection in the South. For 150 years, Southerners had believed that the best way to keep enslaved persons down was to keep them uneducated and unarmed. So in 1775, the prospect of Blacks working side by side with whites in the Continental Army flew in the face of ancient teachings. And it was terrifying.

Another prospect that might have flashed in the imaginations of Southern delegates was that of a righteous antislavery New England army of mixed races marching on the Southern colonies in a domestic civil war whose purpose might include emancipation. There is no documentary evidence that connects Rutledge's motion to exclude Blacks from the army with this specific threat, but still, month after month as the war advanced, according to New England delegates, Southerners continued to dread what might happen to their states if the army, or armies, being formed by the Congress became too large, too powerful, and too New England in composition.

As Connecticut's Eliphalet Dyer related to a friend back home, the "Southern gentlemen of the Congress" remained preoccupied by fears that the present civil war between Britain and the colonies would unloose a New England army to invade southward. He contended that Pennsylvanians, nervous that a Connecticut army would trigger the event by first "violently" conquering lands disputed between the two colonies in the river-rich Wyoming Valley, were warning the Southern delegates of this imminent danger. Those Pennsylvanians, Dyer said, "try to possess the minds of Southern gentlemen of the Congress that we are a hardy daring enterprising people & if we prove successful against the ministerial army here we shall after that make our way by force into any of the Southern colonies we please." Dyer specifically named John Dickinson as one of the leading Pennsylvania voices propagating these fears and concerns.[18]

Another New England delegate, fifty-year-old Samuel Ward of Rhode Island, former governor of the colony and a founder and trustee of Brown University, was troubled by the manner in which, to his view, the Southern delegates in Congress were hampering the war effort in New England with their unreasonable, interfering demands for mitigation of New England dominance of the army. "I have several times mentioned to you," Ward wrote to his brother Henry in Rhode Island, "the anxiety I felt on account of the new modelling the army, that cruel jealousy which the southern colonies have of the northern has occasioned all this mischief. The army must be wholly continental, all colonial distinctions must be at an end, the troops must be taught to look up not to their several colonies but to the Continent."[19]

In letters back home, Ward complained frequently about this problem of Southern distrust of New England—and the dangers it posed to life and limb in New England. "Southern gentlemen," he said in another letter to Henry, "wish to remove that attachment which the officers & men have to their respective colonies & make them look up to the continent at large for their support or promotion." This obstructionism was creating "infinite difficulty in reenlisting the army. The idea of making it wholly continental has induced so many alterations disgusting to both officers & men that very little success has attended our recruiting orders. I have often told the Congress that under the idea of new modelling I was afraid we should destroy our army."[20]

FIGURE 18. Samuel Ward, Rhode Island Delegate. (Portrait of Samuel Ward. *Hon. Samuel Ward, May 27, 1725–March 26, 1776, Governor of Rhode Island and Member of the Continental Congress*, date unknown, print, New York Public Library, EM5704.)

"The N. E. colonies are happily united," Ward said in a third letter. "Others see it and knowing them to be brave and enterprising are very jealous especially of the two larger colonies [Massachusetts and Connecticut]." It was jealousy that was wreaking havoc on the organization of the army and therefore severely debilitating it. "If the N. E. colonies had been applied to for their respective quotas of men, had appointed their officers & been permitted to have given a bounty as usual," Ward continued, "we might have had a fine army long since."[21]

So deeply felt were the Southern demands to create a truly diverse, geographically balanced Continental Army that it became one impetus in early October for the dispatch of Benjamin Franklin and two Southern delegates, the youthful Thomas Lynch of South Carolina and middle-aged Benjamin Harrison of Virginia, on a special mission to Washington's headquarters in Cambridge to sort out the sore points and conflicts. As Ward described it, the special commission was organized as an embassy of Southern and Middle colony men sent to dialogue with New Englanders since the overwhelming bias of military officers in Cambridge seemed to be toward New England. Ward and others from his region worked hard to get a fellow New Englander, Eliphalet Dyer, elected to the embassy, but, the Rhode Islander lamented, "we failed." Ward explained that a strict sectional dynamic was at work in the appointment of the commissioners: "Some of the southern gentlemen seem to consider this matter as an affair between New England & the other colonies & upon that plan balloted for gentlemen only of the other colonies. (Colo. Dyer & Colo. Harrison had equal votes at first, upon a second trial another Southern member came in & turned the vote for Colo. Harrison)."[22]

The Franklin-Lynch-Harrison delegation departed Philadelphia for Cambridge on October 4, 1775. Less than five weeks later, on November 7, John Murray, 4th Earl of Dunmore, royal governor of Virginia, issued a proclamation that established martial law in the colony and proclaimed freedom to any enslaved persons willing to escape their plantations and join the British army. Expectations had been that the British ministry would first foment slave insurrection in the poorly guarded colonies of South Carolina and Georgia. But now this specter was striking the largest and richest colony in the Union. Virginians railed at the emancipation proclamation as a "diabolical scheme," labeling Dunmore a "monster." Some called for his assassination, others for stringing him up on the gallows. Hearing the news, North Carolina dispatched four hundred soldiers northward over the border to defend liberty and, ironically, liberty's antithesis, the preservation of slavery in the South.[23]

* * * * *

In the first three months of 1776, the urgency behind the interconnected projects of independence and confederation quickened. Still no formal motions were put on the floor of Congress, but letters and notes on debates reveal that the delegates were despairing more than ever about the split in the body between reconciliationists and radicals now ready to declare independence.

Most menacing was the sense of inevitability that at least some colonies, led by New England, were going to declare independence with or without the others. This feeling of forward movement toward a historic break with the empire was driven by numerous events. One was Paine's acclaimed treatise calling on the colonies to separate "Now." Another was Lord Dunmore's emancipation proclamation in Virginia, proving to Southerners that British royals would stop at nothing to repress and conquer them. Then a week after this, Lord Dunmore led one hundred regulars and twenty loyalists to the first significant defeat of Virginians in the Revolution. At Norfolk, Dunmore's force killed seven and captured eighteen other patriots. According to New Yorker James Duane, this was a wake-up call to Virginians signifying that unity in Congress, not reconciliation with Britain, was the only hope of saving liberty and lives in America.[24]

The most significant accelerator of independence and confederation, however, was the arrival in Philadelphia on January 8 of a copy of King George III's speech delivered to Parliament on October 27, 1775. Already the king had rejected the Olive Branch Petition, with rumors rife in America that he did not deign even to read it. Nonetheless, week after week, many delegates in Congress impatiently waited for word from London that a fair and just accommodation was near at hand. Now, instead of this, Congress received a speech by His Majesty that proclaimed all-out war on the colonies. Accusing them of conspiring to establish "an independent empire," King George announced that the era of "moderation and forbearance" had come to an end. He was preparing the army and navy for conquest, and he had begun negotiations with other powers for "offers of foreign assistance." The king's intention was hardly fair and just constitutional accommodation. His plan was to apply brute force "to put a speedy end to these disorders."[25]

All these developments in the winter of 1775–76 pressed the Congress further toward independence as liberty's only salvation. But still the delegates held back. There were many reasons for the inertia, among them their love of England and their fear of imperial war. Another major force at work, as they voiced in letters, was the certainty of many delegates that the Congress could never form a single constitutional confederation of such discordant colonies. The unresolved fights over commerce, voting power, slave representation, the western lands, and taxation that had taken place during the First Congress remained seared into their memories. Not only this, but the delegates could not agree at all on what the contract of the American Union should look like. Should they unite into a carefully constructed "perpetual" federal government, as Franklin had proposed in the summer of 1775 in his Articles of Confederation? Or should they combine only loosely into a defensive and offensive military treaty and alliance, leaving the colonies free to form thirteen independent republics or perhaps like-minded regional republics, as they saw fit?

In the summer of 1775, Jefferson had warned Franklin that bringing a constitution to the floor for debate was a dangerous idea because it would drive the colonies apart at the very moment they must unite. There was a higher priority: war. This same force was at work in 1776, but with a new priority that had to take precedence over a constitution: independence. Not a single delegate in Congress thought it prudent or preferable that the thirteen colonies should declare independence *first* and only afterward bind themselves into a constitutional Union. But they had no choice. Constitutional confederation was a Pandora's box. They must keep the lid shut on it in order to shield the precarious war effort and now the independence movement from colonial discord and disunion.

It would take until June for the delegates to fully accept that they were going to separate from Britain before uniting themselves by solemn oath and constitutional compact. In the interim, they struggled with the contradictions and contingencies confronting them, puzzling through pathways out of the maze. Carter Braxton of Virginia, for one, was of the opinion that the Congress would never be so foolish as to declare independence in advance of formally confederating because such a step would terminate in domestic bedlam. Independence, he wrote to his uncle Landon Carter, "is an object to be wished for by every American." But, he continued, it must not be risked until Congress possessed "a superintending power" over all the colonies.[26]

"I am convinced the assertion of independence is far off," Braxton said as late as mid-April. "If it was to be now asserted, the continent would be torn in pieces by intestine wars & convulsions." Consistent with past and current predictions by others regarding the underlying causes of American civil wars, the Virginian pointed to the "right to lands" as the certain chief culprit, indicating that bloodletting would probably commence in prized territories like the Wyoming Valley or the forks of the Ohio River, each claimed by more than one colony. Without a salutary constitution enforcing peace among them, Braxton confessed, he was confident in his dire predictions because lust for land was a principle etched into human nature.[27]

Eliphalet Dyer of Connecticut joined Braxton in this focused worry that violent land conflicts between two colonies "may be of almost fatal

Chapter 5: "Intestine Wars and Convulsions" 115

FIGURE 19. Carter Braxton, Virginia Delegate. (Portrait of Carter Braxton. Max Rosenthal, *Carter Braxton*, ca. 1885, print, New York Public Library, EM1063.)

consequence to the whole." Silas Deane assessed the risk of two-colony civil war breaking out in the Wyoming Valley similarly. "Should violences of any kind be committed," he said, "the consequences will be terrible beyond description."[28]

Braxton, like many other delegates, additionally expressed concern over the colonies' divided views on what form of government to institute in an independent America. New Englanders, he said, had no honest interest in reconciling with monarchical Britain for the reigning reason that their ambition was to rid America of monarchy and aristocracy altogether in order to implement democracy. In a letter to his uncle, Braxton distinguished the democratic radicalism of the four New England colonies from the more balanced forms of government in the Southern and Middle colonies:

> Two of the new England Colonies enjoy a government purely democratical, the nature & principle of which both civil & religious are so totally incompatible with monarchy that they have ever lived in a restless state under it. The other two, tho' not so popular in their frame[work], bordered so near upon it that monarchical influence hung very heavy on them. The best opportunity in the world being now offered them to throw off all subjection & embrace their darling democracy, they are determined to accept it.

New Englanders, for their part, gladly admitted they were imbued of a "republican spirit." Reciprocally, they expressed worries that delegates from the Southern and Middle colonies inclined too much toward "the distinctions of an aristocracy" and "monarchy."[29]

This incompatibility of the respective regions' preferred constitutional structures is perhaps one reason so many Americans assumed that the final outcome of a revolution for independence, if it came to pass, would be three republics, not one. Thomas Hutchinson, former royal governor of Massachusetts, went so far in the year of independence to alert others that Congress's grand scheme was separation from the British empire followed precisely by the establishment of "three distinct independent Republics, Northern, Middle, and Southern." This was, he said confidently, the "determined design" of the rebel Congress in Philadelphia.[30]

* * * * *

John Adams, more than any other delegate, was an astute political analyst of these unstable regional dynamics of the American Union. He wrote about them often, enhancing especially our understanding of the New England/South divide in the 1770s. What we find is that publicly Adams denied the incompatibility of the thirteen colonies, whereas privately he admitted to terrible fears that a wrong move by the Congress could end in disaster.

One window into Adams's state of mind is a war of words he conducted with a fellow Bostonian in the *Massachusetts Gazette; and the Boston Post-Boy and Advertiser* after the First Continental Congress. Back home he encountered engrossing doubts about the viability of an independent American confederation. A man he knew well and considered a friend, Daniel Leonard, led this charge in the *Massachusetts Gazette*, dubbing himself "Massachusettensis." Leonard, favorite son of a prominent family from Norton, Harvard graduate, and lawyer, warned that the thirteen colonies were sovereign states of "jarring interests, and opposite propensities." They harbored "deep animosities" toward one another. Leonard contrasted particularly the "tempers and habits of the Carolinians"—that is, the two southernmost planter colonies—with those of Massachusetts, characterizing them to be as discordant as those of "different nations." Not stopping with the planter/seafarer line of division, Massachusettensis said that even the New England colonies, such as Connecticut and Rhode Island, were "rivals to each other in trade." There were risks all around, the writer professed, raising the specter of "violent altercations" and "the sword of civil war."[31]

Considering himself a defender of the American Union, Adams refused to stand by while Leonard misrepresented the hope of the Continental Congress. He took up his pen, responding not once but twelve times in published rebuttals. Adams wrote under the pseudonym "Novanglus," the New Englander, and undermined Leonard's prognostications of civil wars on grounds of recent empirical evidence. Novanglus asked the readers of the *Massachusetts Gazette* to look at the preceding ten years of imperial struggle. Since the Stamp Act Congress of 1765, the colonies had united, shepherded to the defense of liberty as much by the "eminent patriot" Patrick Henry of Virginia as by Massachusetts's own James Otis. When a British standing army in Boston fired on and killed five Americans in the King Street massacre of 1770, the colonies did not divide. They united in "brotherly sympathy." And most recently, as Massachusetts was invaded, Adams testified, the delegates of the Continental Congress in Philadelphia had pledged themselves to the cause of her defense and the sanctity of liberty and property "unanimously."[32]

On this theme of "proofs of union," Adams said more. "Look over the resolves of the several colonies," he said, "and you will see that one understanding governs, one heart animates the whole body." Acknowledging the diversity of interests of the colonies, he bore witness to the fact these had hardly undercut their unity in Philadelphia: "When we consider the variety of climate, soil, religion, civil government, commercial interests, &c. which were represented at the congress, and the various occupations, education, and characters of the gentlemen who composed it, the harmony and unanimity which prevailed in it can scarcely be paralleled in any assembly that ever met." It all signaled, Adams reassured his countrymen, a "cordial, firm, radical, and indissoluble union of the colonies."[33]

Yet there was also a private side to Adams. Once back in Philadelphia sitting in Congress after Lexington and Concord, his letters frequently underscored the same dread and perils of American Union he had refuted so audaciously in newsprint. In the same month, in fact, that that Rhode Islander Samuel Ward was complaining bitterly about Southern obstruction of a successful defense of New England, Adams wrote to a close confidante in Massachusetts, Joseph Hawley, fifty-two-year-old leader of the Provincial Congress, of his preoccupations over the regional and ideological incompatibilities of the colonies. Now Adams was the one to say in a private letter that the delegates from the separate American regions were so different from one another as to constitute "several distinct nations almost." In saying this, he was chiefly referring to the contrasts between democratic New Englanders and his "Southern Brethren," as he sometimes referred to them.[34]

To Hawley, Adams drew sharp attention especially to three troublesome North/South lines of demarcation. They were Southern slavery, Southern class stratification, and the hauteur of the planter. In Philadelphia, listening to and watching incessant clashes of interest in Congress, he came to the forlorn conclusion that if the American tinderbox of North and South were not handled with care, it would all come apart:

> Gentlemen in the other colonies have large plantations of slaves, and the common people among them are very ignorant and very poor. These gentlemen are accustomed, habituated to higher notions of themselves and the distinction between them and the common people than we are.... I dread the consequences of this dissimilitude of character, and without the utmost caution on both sides, and the most considerate forbearance with one another and prudent condescension on both sides, they will certainly be fatal.

Adams had other complaints about the "barons of the South." One problem that seemed never to go away was the New England/South split over army salaries. It occasioned "great debate," according to one delegate. New Englanders wanted something approaching more equity of pay, while other delegates wanted a larger, stratified gap. The Southern delegates primarily, but also the Middle colonies, to some extent, Adams reported, continued to decry the fact that "the pay of the privates is too high and that of the officers too low." The Massachusettsian also shared the common attitude of extreme pique among New Englanders at the demands of Southern delegates to fully integrate Southern officers into the Northern army. "It is altogether absurd to suppose," he wrote his friend John Winthrop, a Harvard professor, "that the council of Massachusetts should appoint gentlemen from the southern colonies, when Connecticut, Rhode Island and N. Hampshire do not." Adams then outlined a litany of disadvantages to this forced integration, including the displacement of officers who are "better qualified," the disgruntlement of Massachusetts privates serving under "strangers," and, generally, the arousal of resentment in the Massachusetts people. He called the mandate a "disgrace" upon his colony.[35]

These political issues governing the military, however, were ultimately surmountable. What preoccupied Adams far more was the gulf between the liberal constitutional mindset of New Englanders and the more feudal one of Southerners. Generally, he believed that America was on the cusp of entering a new progressive era of liberty, equality, and republicanism. The problem was that Southerners were going to hold back the march of progress. Enlightenment concepts of government, Adams wrote to Abigail, were "fully understood by the people at large in New England, but have been attended to in the southern colonies only by gentlemen of free spirits and liberal minds, who are very few." In other words, from the perspective of enlightened government, the South was entrenched in medieval ways. In another letter Adams lamented that "Gentlemen, men of sense, or any kind of education in the other colonies are much fewer in proportion than in N. England," so much so that it was going to require "a miracle" to bring them aboard New England's forward-moving constitutional agenda.[36]

In one impassioned letter, Adams laid bare his belief that "all our misfortunes arise from a single source, the reluctance of the Southern colonies to republican government." They were impeding independence, he emphasized, because independence was a step into a republican future for which they were a poor, incongruous fit. "The difficulty lies in forming constitutions for particular colonies, and a continental constitution for the whole," he wrote to Horatio Gates, expanding his critique to include the Middle colonies. "Each colony should establish its own government, and then a league should be formed, between them all. This can be done only on popular principles and maxims which are so abhorrent to the inclinations of the barons of the South, and the proprietary interests in the Middle colonies, as well as to that avarice of land, which has made upon this continent so many votaries to mammon that I sometimes dread the consequences."[37]

Adams made these observations to Gates during the same month that another delegate, Joseph Hewes, complained to a colleague in his home colony of North Carolina that the tenor of Congress had dramatically shifted from the golden days of 1774 and 1775. "We do not treat each other with that decency and respect that was observed heretofore," Hewes said. "Jealousies, ill natured observations and recriminations take place of reason and argument."[38]

Nevertheless, for Adams, hope sprang eternal. "Patience, fortitude and perseverance, with the help of time," he concluded to Gates, "will get us over these obstructions." In another letter written a few months later to a young lawyer friend in Massachusetts, Adams elaborated on this political science, opening a window onto what he believed was one of signature secrets of leadership. "The first virtue of a politician is patience," Adams said, "the second is patience; and the third is patience."[39]

* * * * *

While John Adams was coping with the slow pace of independence through the exercise of patience, his older cousin Sam was contemplating instead the radical step of forming a Northern confederacy. Sam first broached the topic by letter to John himself, who at the time was on a hiatus from Congress back home in Braintree, five days after the publication of *Common Sense*. In the letter he shared his alarm that delegates in Congress had recently made a motion—yet again—to publicly denounce independence, reaffirming the colonies' commitment to reconciliation. Sam explained that he labored hard to have the motion postponed. Then he told John that he had lately engaged in "some free conversation" with Benjamin Franklin about the necessity of acting quickly to form a constitutional Union. Referring to Franklin, he continued, "We agreed that it must soon be brought on, & that if all the Colonies could not come into it, it had better be done by those of them that inclined to it. I told him that I would endeavor to unite the New England Colonies in confederating, if none of the rest would join in it. He approved of it, and said, if I succeeded, he would cast in his lot among us."[40]

Sam Adams was not the only New Englander in the first half of 1776 to explore liberating New England to confederate and declare independence separately from the other colonies. Elbridge Gerry of Massachusetts, referring to the four New England colonies, wrote to James Warren, "I think it may be demonstrated that the eastern district alone is able of itself to declare independency." Ward of Connecticut, itching to get free of the "unhappy jealousy" held by the Southern colonies toward New England, was also excited to report that Franklin approved the plan. "Dr. Franklin who is full for it," Ward wrote to Henry Ward, "advises the four N. England Governments to enter into one themselves & invite the other colonies to accede to it and let them fall in as they may like. I sometimes think this would be the surest way to induce the other cols. to join us, many important considerations on both sides of the question are to be weighed before we come to a conclusion."[41]

The two Adamses, Franklin, Gerry, and Ward gave consideration to a New England confederation for good reason. British military and naval

FIGURE 20. Samuel Adams, Massachusetts Delegate. (Portrait of Samuel Adams. John Singleton Copley, *Samuel Adams*, ca. 1772, oil on canvas, 49.5 x 39.5 in, Museum of Fine Arts, Boston, deposited by the City of Boston.)

strategy continued to concentrate virtually all its efforts in that geographic section. Therefore, it was a matter of life and death for them. In order to prosecute the war, New Englanders needed not only an efficient, unclogged political machine to obtain money, guns, cannons, gunpowder, ammunition, shirts, shoes, and shovels. It also needed a navy. And the only way to open the floodgates to these necessities was to negotiate formal alliances with Britain's archenemies, France and Spain. And if American political leaders were sure of anything, it was that no foreign power on earth was going to embrace them openly and deploy warships to their shores in support of their cause until the colonies in question confederated as independent states. The way they viewed it, the order of operations was confederation first, independence second, and foreign alliances third, the ultimate bonanza that could only be negotiated after confederation and independence had been proclaimed to the world.

Only because so many risk-averse Southern and Middle colony delegates—and their home governments—balked at confederation and independence month after month did New Englanders seriously contemplate splitting off and going it alone, at least until such time as the other colonies came to their senses and closed ranks. To form a New England confederation and declare its independence from Britain, without the others, was a crucial means to an end. More than anything else, that end was rescue by French and Spanish sea power. As New Englanders saw it, obtaining overwhelming foreign assistance through confederation and independence, one way or the other, was the only course of action that would save the lives of their countrymen and win the war.

CHAPTER 6

"Colonies Might Secede from the Union"

IN EARLY MAY OF 1776 Patrick Henry, James Madison, George Mason, Edmund Randolph, and dozens of other Virginians gathered at the capitol in Williamsburg for the colony's fifth political convention since 1774. The first four conventions had enacted days of fasting and prayer, dispatched proclamations of protest, banned commerce and payment of debts to Britain, appointed committees of safety, called forth militias, requisitioned arms and gunpowder, named delegates to the Continental Congress, and issued at least one order, the Tobacco Act of 1774, that asserted colonial over congressional sovereignty in circumscribed areas of governance and lawmaking.

The fifth convention, which took place from May 6 until July 5, surpassed the others in importance both for the legislation it adopted in favor of independence and for the immense territorial obstacle it erected to the formation of a constitutional Union. The fifth convention is celebrated in American history for its enactment of a resolution calling upon its delegates in Philadelphia to propose a three-part motion on the floor of Congress: to form a constitutional confederation, declare continental independence, and secure foreign alliances. What is less well-known is that Virginia attached a strict state sovereignty clause to its resolution for independence. And, not incidentally, shortly after this the independent commonwealth made legal claim in its state constitution to an incredible landmass almost equal in size to the other twelve colonies combined. On the basis of its colonial charter of 1609, the new "state" announced to the world that its boundaries extended over the Appalachian Mountains to include a western portion totaling more than two hundred thousand square miles, a slice of the earth today divided into the six states of West Virginia, Kentucky, Ohio, Indiana, Illinois, and Wisconsin. As its constitution affirmed, Virginia alone possessed power and authority over this gargantuan swath of land.[1]

The first legislative accomplishment of the convention was the resolution for independence, which was rushed to Philadelphia soon after its adoption on May 15. In fact, it was a four-part act directing its representatives in the Continental Congress to make a formal motion in favor of (1) independence, (2) foreign alliances, (3) confederation, and (4) the preservation to each member state of the confederation of unquestioned sovereignty over its "internal concerns." In the language of the convention, Virginia consented to the first three "provided, that the power of forming government for, and the regulations of the internal concerns of each colony, be left to the respective colonial legislatures."[2]

By the same May 15 resolution, the delegates in Williamsburg ordered the formation of a committee to prepare two charters: a declaration of rights and a constitution. As completed on June 12, the Declaration of Rights affirmed that "all men are by nature equally free and independent, and have certain inherent rights . . . namely, the enjoyment of life and liberty, with the means of acquiring and possessing property, and pursuing and obtaining happiness and safety." After this, the declaration outlined a dozen surpassing rights guaranteed to "the people," including representative government, free and fair elections, trial by jury, freedom of the press, free exercise of religion, and freedom from arbitrary arrest. In section 14 of their bill of rights, the delegates additionally attached a clause prohibiting any political community within the new state from setting up any form of government not subordinate to Virginia: "That the people have a right to uniform government; and, therefore, that no government separate from, or independent of the government of Virginia, ought to be erected or established within the limits thereof." Implicitly, this clause sent a clear message to western settlers and to Congress about which government possessed supreme sovereignty over Virginia's chartered western lands.[3]

Seventeen days later, the convention adopted the first Virginia state constitution, which proclaimed "the government of this country [Virginia], as formerly exercised under the crown of Great Britain, is TOTALLY DISSOLVED." With these words, dated and signed by the delegates on June 29, 1776, the commonwealth of Virginia declared its independence from the British empire. In the constitution, the delegates instituted a republican government with separation of powers into three branches, executive control over the state militia, and legislative control of money bills. In the second to last section of the constitution, running

189 words, Virginia established its sovereignty over its trans-Appalachian western lands. First, it acknowledged that the four states of Maryland, Pennsylvania, North Carolina, and South Carolina were, in fact, within Virginia's original jurisdiction as mapped out in the Royal Charter of 1609. But, in accordance with previous rulings of the Crown and Parliament over the preceding 110 years, the new state formally "ceded, released, and forever confirmed, to the people of these Colonies respectively" separate sovereignty over these four territories.

This logic, however, did not apply to the splendid lands across the Appalachian Mountains also deemed by royal charter to belong to Virginia. Setting the groundwork for fierce disputes for years to come between Virginia and Congress, as well as between Virginia and several states with conflicting claims in the upper Mississippi Valley, the constitution asserted Virginia's sole ownership of the lands in question and its sole authority to dispose of the lands as it wished. The boundaries of western and northern Virginia, it declared, were "fixed" by two unequivocal legal instruments: the Charter of 1609 and the Treaty of Paris of 1763, which ended the French and Indian War. Only the "General Assembly" of the new state of Virginia, the delegates in Williamsburg codified in late June of 1776, had jurisdictional rights and powers over those lands—and no one else.

* * * * *

Three hundred miles away in Philadelphia, delegates in Congress waited impatiently, yet with growing confidence that unity was finally coalescing around confederation and independence. Their optimism sprang from numerous sources. One was a set of two acts Congress passed in the late spring and early summer that seemed irretrievably to commit the colonies to the hazardous pathway of Union and independence. The first act, adopted on April 6, 1776, opened American trade to all the nations of the world except Great Britain. Before this, the Congress was able to argue that Americans were fighting a defensive war only, while earnestly longing for the restoration of peaceful ties with Britain. Now, how could the colonies possibly step back from the privilege—and equal world standing—of free trade with major European powers and the West Indies islands? To many, the prospect of retreat from free trade seemed impossible.

The second act of Congress that seemed to cast the colonies' fate to the winds of independence was its resolution recommending that each colonial legislature formally abolish royal government and institute state government in its place. To one New York delegate, John Jay, this step was indispensable not only for the military defense of the colonies, individually and collectively, but also to stave off domestic disorder. As he shared in a letter to fellow New Yorker Alexander McDougall, Jay believed Americans must "erect good and well-ordered governments in all the colonies, and thereby exclude that anarchy which already too much prevails."[4]

In the same spring and the early summer months, too, a revolution seemed to be taking place in the hearts and minds of Southern delegates. In the winter of 1776, one observer of the politics of independence in Congress had split the colonies into "two parties," one comprised of the "Northern Colonies," by which he meant New England, and the other Southern and Middle colonies (except, the writer said, for some Virginia delegates who "attached themselves to the Northern Colonies"). In other words, the proindependence party was limited to the four New England colonies and Virginia. As spring broke, however, a shift commenced. One by one the Southern colonies threw off hopes for an honorable reconciliation with Britain, warming to independence. The first to move in this direction was the North Carolina Provincial Congress, which on April 12 empowered its delegates in Congress "to concur with the other delegates of the other colonies in declaring Independency, and forming foreign alliances." Virginia's May 15 resolution differed from that of North Carolina in that it ordered the colony's delegates to go beyond mere concurrence to actually spearheading an act on the floor of Congress. By this time, the political leadership of South Carolina and Georgia, without mentioning the word *independence* in their acts, had also removed all restrictions on their delegates in Congress prohibiting such concurrence.[5]

In essence, by May 15, the four southernmost colonies had freed their representatives in Congress to join New England in the issuance of a declaration of independence. As John Adams put it on May 20, "Here are four colonies to the southward, who are perfectly agreed now with the four to the northward. Five in the Middle are not yet quite so ripe." Nevertheless, the future looked bright, Adams reported in another letter: "The Middle colonies have never tasted the bitter cup—they have never smarted—and are therefore a little cooler—but you will see that the colonies are united indissolubly."[6]

* * * * *

Against this backdrop, on Friday, June 7, 1776, Virginia delegate Richard Henry Lee stood up on the floor of Congress and, in compliance with the order of his home convention in Williamsburg, moved "that these

United Colonies are & of right ought to be free & independent states, that they are absolved from all allegiance to the British crown, and that all political connection between them and the state of Great Britain is & ought to be totally dissolved; that measures should be immediately taken for procuring the assistance of foreign powers, and a Confederation be formed to bind the colonies more closely together."[7]

The next day, Saturday, June 8, debates opened, continuing on Monday. According to notes kept by Thomas Jefferson, representatives from the Middle colonies and South Carolina made speeches opposing the polarizing motion for independence on both days. Represented by John Dickinson and James Wilson of Pennsylvania, Robert Livingston of New York, Edward Rutledge of South Carolina, and unspecified "others," these delegates joined their fellow Americans in the sentiment of independence, but, in contrast to the urgency of Lee's resolution on Friday, they insisted upon more time. As Jefferson penned, the delegates opposing the motion argued that "the people of the middle colonies (Maryland, Delaware, Pennsylva., the Jersies & N. York) were not yet ripe for bidding adieu to British connection but that they were fast ripening & in a short time would join in the general voice of America."[8]

But this was not all. The speakers announced that they would not be steamrolled, and they would by no means permit the other colonies to declare independence for them in a majority or supermajority vote. They were themselves "perfectly independent" of the other colonies of North America. Therefore, the Congress had no legal authority to commit them to such a momentous course of action without the express consent of their home assemblies. After making this point, according to Jefferson, the Middle colony and South Carolina delegates drew a bright red line on the floor of Congress: "That if such a declaration should now be agreed to, these delegates must (now) retire & possibly their colonies might secede from the Union: That such a secession would weaken us more than could be compensated by any foreign alliance."

On the "other side," John Adams of Massachusetts and Richard Henry Lee and George Wythe of Virginia, among others, offered rebuttals. Fully embracing the need to act now, they said the situation with King George and the Parliament was irretrievable—"that the question was not whether, by a declaration of independence, we should make ourselves what we are not; but whether we should declare a fact which already exists." Further, they disagreed that unanimity could be achieved in time to save the war-torn colonies from ruin—"that it would be vain to wait either weeks or months for perfect unanimity, since it was impossible that all men should ever become of one sentiment on any question."

Instead, it seems from Jefferson's notes, the New England and Virginia delegates proposed a compromise: a staggered declaration of independence, one permitting the ready colonies to announce immediately and the others to come in over time. To support the viability of this system for securing liberty, the delegates recounted the history of the Dutch revolution of the sixteenth century, where initially only some of the United Provinces signed onto a declaration of independence from the Habsburg empire. It was being said that separation and division among Americans would end in catastrophe. Yet, "the history of the Dutch revolution, of whom three states only confederated at first," one delegate stated, "proved that a secession of some colonies would not be so dangerous as some apprehended."

The two days of debate ended in stalemate. Nursing the hope that New York, New Jersey, Pennsylvania, Delaware, Maryland, and South Carolina might finally reconcile themselves to a declaration of independence, the Congress determined on Monday the 10th "to postpone the final decision to July 1." After this, concluding the day, the delegates appointed a committee to draft a tentative declaration of independence in the meantime, and the next day, June 11, they appointed two other committees in fulfillment of Richard Henry Lee's motion, one "to prepare and digest the form of a confederation to be entered into between these colonies" and the other "to prepare a plan of treaties to be proposed to foreign powers."[9]

* * * * *

One delegate had much more to say privately about the ill-advised New England and Virginia motion for independence. After the first day of debates, on "Saturday Evg 10 o'clock," Edward Rutledge of South Carolina put pen to paper in a letter to his friend and fellow congressman John Jay of New York, then away from Philadelphia. Rutledge reported that "the sensible part of the House opposed the motion," explaining that the proindependence faction had the order of things turned terribly upside down. First the colonies must unite themselves into a confederation and obtain a treaty of alliance with France, and only then, after these critical first two steps, should they proclaim their independence to the world.[10]

Rutledge was amazed that New England and Virginia would consider seeking alliances with foreign nations before the thirteen colonies had formed a confederating alliance among themselves. Arguing that the colonies were on a path to "rendering ourselves ridiculous in the eyes of foreign powers by attempting to bring them into an union with us before we had united with each other," he said a declaration of independence, coming first, was additionally going to abolish American bargaining power with France, forcing the Congress to accept whatever servile terms King Louis XVI demanded for racing to their rescue. Or, by declaring independence in advance of securing an alliance with France, the Congress was giving Britain the opportunity to beat Americans to the negotiating table with France. Possibly, King George and King Louis would sign an Anglo-French alliance, one mutually assuring the destruction of the Continental Army. Evincing a hostility toward New England not uncommon in the Southern and Middle colonies, Rutledge concluded by saying that "a man must have the impudence of a New Englander to propose in our present disjointed state any treaty (honourable to us)" with France or any other power then at peace with England.

Three weeks later, Rutledge shared far more inflammatory sentiments with Jay, this time about the perils of an American Union. He was a member of the committee to draft the Articles of Confederation, and in a 480-word letter written on June 29, he said things to Jay that delegates of Congress rarely committed to paper. For some reason, that Saturday, only two days before the Congress resumed deliberations on independence, Rutledge's animosity toward New England overflowed. It may be that he had recently come from a heated meeting with other committee members, who included New Englanders Samuel Adams, Josiah Bartlett, and Roger Sherman, when he sat down to write Jay. In any event, Rutledge told Jay, who was then in New York, that he must immediately repair to Philadelphia to attend to congressional business because critical matters were coming on fast. They would soon vote on independence, and, not only this, the Articles of Confederation in their current form must also be defeated.

Rutledge dedicated the rest of the letter to warning Jay about the present and future dangers of New England dominating American confederated government. He made explicit reference, too, to the means by which the region would exercise that oppression. One was through military and naval might, the other through power politics exploiting a weak constitution. Bragging that he did not fear losing a civil war against New England, the South Carolinian did insist to Jay that entering into a common confederated government with that region of America risked great perils they must guard against. "The force of their arms I hold exceeding cheap," Rutledge declared, "but I confess I dread their overruling influence in council, I dread their low cunning, and those levelling principles which men without character and without fortune in general possess, which are so captivating to the lower class of mankind, and which will occasion such a fluctuation of property as to introduce the greatest disorder."[11]

Without specifying what he perceived to be the constitution's most egregious defects, Rutledge underscored that the other colonies in the Union needed vast constitutional safeguards against New England before they could or should consent to the Articles. The thrust of Rutledge's argument was that the Articles of Confederation, as then written, was a Trojan horse. Once the apparent gift of a confederated constitution passed the gates of colonial assemblies into Congress, New Englanders would surprise the other states with their illiberal conduct. "If the plan now proposed should be adopted," Rutledge cautioned Jay, "nothing less than ruin to some colonies will be the consequence of it. The idea of destroying all provincial distinctions and making everything of the most minute kind bend to what they call the good of the whole is in other terms to say that these colonies must be subject to the government of the Eastern Provinces."

This dread led Rutledge to a final conclusion about how the colonies must approach the formation of the federal government. At all costs, he said, they must pull together to thwart the transfer of overlarge power from colony—and from Parliament—to Congress in order to protect themselves from New England. So many patriots had been arguing since 1774 that the colonies had nothing to fear but disunion among themselves. To Rutledge, they had nothing to fear but too much union among themselves. As he emphasized to Jay before once again urging him to come to Congress as soon as possible, "I am resolved to vest the Congress with no more power than what is absolutely necessary, and to use a familiar expression to keep the staff in our own hands, for I am confident if surrendered into the hands of others a most pernicious use will be made of it."

* * * * *

On Monday, July 1, 1776, at nine o'clock in the morning, some four dozen delegates gathered in the Assembly Room of the Pennsylvania State House to vote aye or nay on what John Adams called "the greatest question" ever agitated on the North American continent. Adams viewed a successful vote for independence as something more than the liberation of American states from British tyranny; it was the birth of a historic republican confederation. Earlier that morning, before the speeches and debates commenced, he wrote to Archibald Bulloch of Georgia, "May Heaven prosper the new born republic—and make it more glorious than any former republics have been." Still, Adams said he was not naïve. Later in the day he wrote far more chastening words to Samuel Chase of Maryland. "If you imagine that I expect this declaration will ward off calamities from this country, you are much mistaken," he acknowledged. "A bloody conflict we are destined to endure."[12]

Ironically, on this day of expectation, the records of the internal happenings of Congress are scant. The proceedings began with the reading of several letters from George Washington and a report from the army's paymasters in the Southern colonies. Next came an appropriation of funds for the defense of Virginia. After these morning items, Virginian Benjamin Harrison, sitting in the president's seat as presiding officer, called for a resumption of debates on the motion for independence, followed by each colony's vote. Other than this, what survives is one formal speech against independence, given by John Dickinson, and letters and notes by other delegates, one affirming that John Adams offered a proindependence reply and another providing the results of the vote.

We do not know the content of Adams's speech. We only know that he later said that on that day he repeated arguments for an immediate declaration of independence he had presented "twenty times before." Dickinson's speech, on the other hand, has come down to us with elaborate details of his preoccupations and prognostications. Regarding this speech, and perhaps others unrecorded, Adams observed similarly that everything pronounced on the floor of Congress by the opposing side had already been said a "hundred times, for six months past." That is to say, Dickinson's arguments were not the isolated, lone cries of a Cassandra. They were common knowledge—the realpolitik of American independence.[13]

As he stood up to speak that Monday, the forty-three-year-old Dickinson was filled with anguish. He admitted as much in his opening remarks, saying, "The consequences involved in the motion now lying before you are of such magnitude, that I tremble under the oppressive honor of sharing in its determination." After this, he declared July 1 to be a melancholy day for him, one destined to ruin his honor for all time. His opposition to the rashness of independence—that is, if undertaken before securing a constitutional Union and foreign alliances—was going to deliver "the finishing blow," he lamented, to his reputation as an American patriot. Nevertheless, Dickinson said he could not sit down. He must discharge his duty to truth—to the dangers of a declaration of independence unsupported first by a firm confederation and a respectable, not exploitative, treaty of alliance with France. "Silence would be guilt," Dickinson professed. "I must speak, tho I should lose my life, tho I should lose the affections of my c[ountrymen]." Dickinson then offered a prayer: "I do most humbly implore Almighty God, with whom dwells wisdom itself, so to enlighten the members of this house, that their decision may be such as will best promote the liberty, safety and prosperity of these colonies."[14]

In the body of his speech, Dickinson made two overriding arguments against the precipitous motion on the floor of the Assembly Room, both of which coalesced around a singular prescription he implored his fellow Americans to abide: wait. First, the thirteen colonies must negotiate a favorable treaty with France and bind themselves tightly into a lasting confederation. Only then would it be safe to sever ties with the mother country that had historically protected them from foreign invasion and intercolonial strife. To bring home the point, the Pennsylvanian compared a declaration of independence to the launching of a feeble ship onto stormy waters. The ship, he said, must be fortified, strong, united, and well-armed. With no confederation and no alliance in place, what the Congress was on the cusp of doing instead was to brave "the storm in a skiff made of paper."

First Dickinson laid out the myriad dangers of embarking upon independence without the assured cooperation and assistance of a naval power like France. He challenged the chief argument being made on the impetuous proindependence side. It was that only by projecting the "strength & unanimity" of the colonies in a swift, unhesitating declaration would France and perhaps Spain truly believe the colonies were in earnest in their intent to break away from the British empire permanently, rather than merely playing both sides for maximal American advantage. The language being uttered was that "foreign states will not assist us, until we declare independence."

This was a deadly fallacy, Dickinson promised. Instead, France might well view the declaration with "contempt." Why? Because the Congress had only recently dispatched an envoy to Paris, Silas Deane, who would soon take up negotiations with the French foreign ministry of on the subject of Franco-American mutual interests—and a *mutual* decision on the timing of a declaration on independence. The French might deplore the manner in which "we haughtily pursue our own measures" without consulting them. It might wound their "pride." They might scoff, urging that "we will not be hurried by your impetuosity." In the meantime, while France distanced itself from the error of American independence, Great Britain might proceed to sink the American skiff with the force of a cyclone. Nothing would anger George III and Parliament so much as the declaration being proposed. The empire's fury would rise, and the Parliament would vote all the "wealth of London" to the colonies' destruction. "The war will be carried on with more severity," Dickinson recorded in his preparatory notes for the speech. "Burning towns. Letting loose Indians on our frontiers."

Possibly, Dickinson continued, this British revenge on America was not even the worst of it. Another fair prospect was that the Congress would be left entirely bereft of European allies as France, Spain, and England concerted among themselves to suppress the British colonial rebellion across the ocean, divvying up the proceeds. "Suppose on this event G. B. should offer Canada to France & Florida to Spain. . . . Would not France & Spain accept them?" Moreover, if this was not satisfactory reward for a Franco-Spanish-Anglo war on America, Dickinson said, King George and the Parliament would go further. Rather than permit the colonies to secede successfully from the British empire, they would agree to "a partition of these colonies," wherein France and Spain would acquire new territory within them. Dickinson did not specify how the three powers would divide up the colonies, but every delegate in the room knew that France eyed with interest the northern climes of America (Canada, the upper Ohio Valley, and perhaps the unsettled Vermont territory) and Spain the southern ones (the lower Mississippi Valley, the Floridas, and perhaps even Georgia and South Carolina).

The second reason for waiting, Dickinson said, was the fragmented state of the American Union. He found it deeply worrying that the Congress might declare independence and even seek out treaties with foreign powers before they secured a treaty among themselves. "Not only treaties with foreign powers but among ourselves should precede this declaration," Dickinson said. As was not uncommon, the speaker highlighted the large quantity of "unsettled lands" on the continent claimed by one or more colony as particularly explosive. If a declaration of independence happened before the colonies reached accommodations about such matters, he admonished, it might foster "bitterness of soul." Exasperated Americans would ask how the Congress could possibly have been so shortsighted and so derelict of its duty. Dickinson said this even while openly confessing his own pessimism about the ability of the thirteen dissimilar colonies to unite into a single confederation. He had himself sat for weeks on the committee to draft the Articles of Confederation and Perpetual Union, and no project before the Congress seemed so bleak, he admitted. "The Committee on Confederation dispute almost every article," he said. "Some of us totally despair of any reasonable terms of confederation."

According to the outline of his speech, the Pennsylvania jurist did not end on an upbeat note. Quite the opposite. In conclusion, he acknowledged frankly that the past several months of maneuvers on independence had left him feeling deceived by some of his fellow Americans. He now doubted that some delegates in Congress, implicitly pointing the finger at New Englanders, had ever truly aimed at reconciliation. Their scheming, he said, made him wonder what other surprises might be in store for the colonies after a declaration of independence of all thirteen.

"Since they can conceal their views so dexterously," Dickinson said, alluding to New Englanders, he wished to share what he believed the future of independence might hold. Looking into what he called the "Doomsday Book of America," he conjectured that New England would not long remain faithful to the American Union. Rather, "in 20 or 30 Years this commonwealth of colonies may not be thought too unwieldy—& Hudson's River be a proper boundary for a separate commonwealth to the northward. I have a strong impression on my mind that this will take place." That is, New England would disunite from the rest at the Hudson River, and, Dickinson continued, this was something "dreadful" to contemplate. What the congressman meant is that a separation of New England from the American Union at a later date would inevitably bring about a civil war—or wars.

Judging from the votes cast shortly after his address that Monday, Dickinson spoke, at least in part, for many inside the Assembly Room. The colonies of Pennsylvania and South Carolina voted no on independence. Delaware divided, rendering its vote null. New York abstained, because this colony alone remained under an injunction of its legislature prohibiting it from voting. The rest cast their ballots for independence. In the final tally, the grand measure for American independence passed in the affirmative on July 1 with nine votes, supplying the bare minimum supermajority many delegates believed should be the basis for a formal adoption by all.[15]

CHAPTER 7

"A Firm League of Friendship"

AFTER THE LANDMARK VOTE OF July 1 in favor of independence, the delegates confronted a conundrum. By the republican rules of the house, the matter was decided. A supermajority had spoken. But how was the Congress going to handle a public announcement about this historic ruling? If the nine states voting in favor of independence proceeded to adopt and publicize a declaration of independence, what would be the effect of their disunity on the Union, the prospect of future alliances, and the military and diplomatic strategies to be pursued by the British?

We know almost nothing about what was said in Congress during the late afternoon of July 1, after the vote. But we do know that the delegates had three options. First, they could expunge the vote, keep it secret, and resume debates with the intention of forging unanimity at the pace of the most laggard colony among them. That is, as Dickinson had begged them, they could wait—for as long as necessary.

Second, by consensus of all thirteen, the supermajority of colonies that had voted for independence could advance to a formal declaration without the slow movers, allowing Pennsylvania, Delaware, New York, and South Carolina to join the independent United States in a staggered manner at a later date, notwithstanding the chaos this option would engender domestically and internationally.

Third, the supermajority of colonies could abandon the pathway of negotiation and consensus altogether and instead grimly inform the others that they were declaring independence without them—no matter what. Those nine colonies would announce that they had arrived at a final reckoning on July 1. The dissenters must declare themselves either with the proindependence colonies or against them. This third option would particularly ensnare Pennsylvania, Delaware, and New York. If these Middle colonies did not join the independence-now majority, squeezed as they were geographically between the New England and Southern colonies, they might instead become the enemies of those regions. Certainly, if they did not aid New England and the Southern colonies in their war effort, allowing free passage on roads and rivers, as well supplying their armies, chances were that Pennsylvania, Delaware, and New York would become the worst fields of blood on the continent in the expanding British civil war, now potentially pitting American against American.

We do not know what was said—or threatened—that day. Evidence, though, reveals that Edward Rutledge, after his side lost the vote, requested time outside Congress to regroup with the dissenters. We also know the Congress agreed to a revote the following day, July 2, and that many delegates worked tirelessly over the next twenty-four hours to achieve the grail of American revolutionary politics: unanimity, or at least the appearance thereof. It seems, therefore, that what happened on July 1 was something akin to the third option. The supermajority exerted tremendous pressure on the Middle colonies and South Carolina to "Join or Die." Knowing the other colonies, or at least the New England ones, were going to declare independence without them, the dissenters saw clearly that they were caught in an impossible military situation. That is to say, they chose consensus and unanimity only after the supermajority menaced a species of disunion that would be catastrophic for them. Weighing the options, the Middle colonies and South Carolina chose the pathway most likely to preserve their lives, liberty, and honor. They chose independence.[1]

How did the unanimity-seeking Congress do it? How did the body of delegates transform a secret 9-3 vote (New York abstaining) into "the unanimous Declaration of the thirteen united States of America," as publicly expressed three days later in the Declaration of Independence? The answer is subterfuge. For the sake of liberty and self-preservation, they lobbied and maneuvered, probably until late in the night on July 1, until the votes lined up. Then, the next day, back in the Assembly Room, twelve colonies cast aye votes for independence (again, with New York abstaining).[2]

To effect this outcome, South Carolina reversed its stand from Monday. Delaware, by adding a newly arrived member, also switched to aye. So did Pennsylvania, but only after intensive efforts and discreet parliamentary tactics. To help the Congress achieve unanimity, while still not transgressing their principled opposition to declaring

Chapter 7: "A Firm League of Friendship"	137

FIGURE 21. Declaration of Independence, 1776. (Portrait of the Declaration of Independence presented to the Second Continental Congress. John Trumbull, *Declaration of Independence*, 1819, oil on canvas, 12 x 18 ft, U.S. Capitol Rotunda.)

independence before confederation and alliance, John Dickinson and Robert Morris agreed to sit out the July 2 revote. By not showing up to Congress for the ballot, absenting themselves, Dickinson and Morris left the Pennsylvania delegation with five members present: Benjamin Franklin, John Morton, James Wilson, Thomas Willing, and Charles Humphreys. Three voted for independence, two against, barely swinging Pennsylvania to the aye category.[3]

Only abstaining New York did not vote in favor of independence on July 2. Does this mean the Declaration of Independence, issued two days later, misrepresented the truth about unanimity? No, because the Declaration of Independence never mentions voting in its text, and the parchment would not be signed and therefore formally ratified by delegates of all the states until mid-August. Before this, it was published and proclaimed without signatures, and by that time the New York delegates had given every assurance that its assembly was committed to independence and would not disappoint. It only had to overcome a technicality. So the declaration was, effectively, unanimous on July 4, even though the New York legislature did not formally ratify independence until July 9.

In this improvised manner of quiet political maneuvering, as Delaware congressman Thomas McKean later recalled, "Unanimity in the thirteen states, an all-important point on so great an occasion, was thus obtained. The dissention of a single state might have produced very dangerous consequences."[4]

* * * * *

On June 7 Richard Henry Lee of Virginia had presented a three-point master plan for achieving victory in the war against Britain: (1) independence, (2) confederation, and (3) foreign alliance. Four days later, on June 11, while simultaneously advancing the project of independence, the delegates ordered the formation of a committee on confederation to draft a formal compact uniting them. The next day Congress designated further that the committee would be composed of one delegate from each colony. Among those appointed were Sam Adams of Massachusetts, Robert Livingston of New York, John Dickinson of Pennsylvania, Joseph Hewes of North Carolina, and Edward Rutledge of South Carolina.[5]

While delegates differed widely in their views of the nature, purpose, and duration of a continental compact, they all agreed with the singular proposition that they must pledge themselves to one another until at least the end of the war. Most called the entity under consideration a "confederation." Others, like John Adams and Josiah Bartlett of New Hampshire, sometimes referred it as a "continental constitution." Still others saw it as something more akin to a diplomatic agreement signed among thirteen equal sovereign republics, deeming it a "treaty of confederation and union." Whatever the pact was going to be, expectations ran high that they would complete it by the end of the summer. After that, they would rush the continental compact to each state legislature for its approval, where hopefully a spirit of exigency and conciliation would secure collective ratification by the end of the year. Only when all thirteen states had signed on would the supreme continental laws, whether conceived of as a constitution or treaty, go into effect.[6]

According to the surviving records, soon after the appointment of members on June 12, the committee on confederation named John Dickinson, known for his literary talents, as the draftsman of the preliminary agreement. Then, five days later, on June 17, Dickinson presented his twenty-article handiwork to the committee for debate and revision. In it, he borrowed heavily from Franklin's earlier Articles of Confederation and Perpetual Union, read aloud to Congress by the elder statesman in July of 1775. The 1776 compact carried the same formal name as Franklin's but went even further in its efforts to preclude secession, disunion, and civil war. For one, it repeated the word *perpetual* three times. For another, it stated that the member states "hereby severally enter into a firm League of Friendship."[7]

As a vital new element, the states were strictly prohibited from forming subconfederations by Article V. Committee members incorporated this article into the constitution because they viewed subconfederations to be seeds of cooperation among states within a region that might grow into disunion. Nor could any state or states send or receive ambassadors for the purpose of trade or peace treaties or war alliances with foreign nations without Congress's approval. The Articles of Confederation further forbade states from keeping standing armies, and it proscribed them from employing "Force to procure Redress of any Injury or Injustice" against any other member. With regard to boundary disputes and the trans-Appalachian lands, whenever two or more states proved incapable of reconciling their differences peaceably outside Congress, the compact required those states to submit the dispute to the central body for arbitration.[8]

The committee on confederation spent almost a month debating Dickinson's first draft of the Articles. On July 12 it submitted a revised version to Congress. The committee made no pretense to recommend the compact as a finished product. It meant only to deliver raw material to the floor, where the assembled delegates would commence substantive debates, propose amendments, and vote up and down until a compromise compact had been hammered out. The truth is that many committee members felt anguish about the convoluted articles they were delivering to their fellow lawmakers. As John Dickinson expressed in his July 1 admonition against declaring independence before accomplishing the hard work of confederating, "Some of us totally despair of any reasonable terms of confederation." Another committee member, Bartlett of New Hampshire, reiterated the sentiment. The reason was that the Congress had set the bar to the highest notch possible: unanimity. "Without the unanimous consent of all it cannot be established," Bartlett lamented to a colleague in New Hampshire. Therefore, he prayed for intervention by God, whom he called "the Supreme Disposer of all events."[9]

* * * * *

Having received the committee's draft compact on July 12, the Congress ordered it to be printed for the private consideration of each delegate, and over the next ten days they cleared all other matters from the docket. On Monday, July 22, debates on the Articles of Confederation began in earnest, continuing unceasing for a week and a half, then periodically until August 20. In total, the Congress debated the compact twenty full days, investing more than 150 hours into passionate argumentation and strenuous efforts at salutary compromise.[10]

This iteration of the Articles of Confederation comprised some three thousand words, still broken down into twenty articles. The first of them declared that "the name of this Confederacy shall be 'The United States of America.'" The second reinforced the permanent nature of the alliance, one never to be undone: "The said Colonies unite themselves so as never to be divided by any act whatever, and hereby severally enter into a firm League of Friendship with each other, for their common defence, the security of their liberties, and their mutual and general welfare." After this came a large number of uncontroversial articles and clauses, but three in particular landed as bombshells to many of the delegates.[11]

In Article XI the committee addressed the combustible issue of taxation. According to the article, American taxation would be based proportionally on the total count of inhabitants of "every Age, Sex and Quality, except of Indians not paying taxes" in each state, including enslaved persons. In the next contentious article, XVII, paradoxically, the compact upended Franklin's recommended formula for proportional representation, restoring the original equality of colonies agreed to by the First Congress as a stopgap. Article XVII read, "In determining Questions in Congress each Colony shall have one Vote." Finally, in Article XVIII, the Articles of Confederation awarded full discretion and authority over state boundary disputes and the ownership of the western lands to Congress. That meant, for example, that congressional power would override that of the Virginia state constitution, adopted only weeks earlier, which had unequivocally asserted Virginia jurisdiction over the territory of Kentucky and all the lands above the Ohio River it claimed to the "South Sea"—that is, the Pacific Ocean. The federal Articles undid this Virginia power, granting the Congress ultimate authority to limit and define the boundaries of the new states.[12]

The first two matters, representation and taxation, became conflated in the minds of many delegates because both concerned justice and fairness to each colony in terms of tax money and voting power, yet the Articles outlined wildly opposite and contradictory formulas for apportioning each. The one-colony-one-vote revision was upsetting to all Virginians, the Adams cousins, Franklin, and most other delegates from large-state

Massachusetts and Pennsylvania because *the people* of the United States would not be equal in the eyes of Congress and the large states would therefore not be awarded the proportional voting power they deserved.

Reviewing that article, Benjamin Rush, a Pennsylvania medical doctor soon to be named surgeon general of the Middle Department of the Continental Army, was aghast. He billed the one-state-one-vote as a "death warrant" to American government. To such familiar reproofs, delegates from the small states replied that Congress simply had no alternative. Republican political theory aside, under terms of proportional representation, the small states would be trampled on. They would be reduced to utter insignificance, squeezed out of existence by the four large states capturing vastly more than half the voting power on the continent. In light of this hazard, the small states declared they would never budge from the prudent decision rendered by the committee on confederation, now codified in Article XVII.[13]

The large states also complained bitterly at the illogic of the Articles taxing them on the basis of population while refusing to apply the same touchstone for assigning voting power. By this distortion, the large states were to pay greatly more in tax money. However, for all the extra burden, they were supposed to possess equal voting power with the small-population states. In the same debates, the Southern states defended slavery against taxation. Again delegates recoiled against the use of population to determine taxation but not voting power. Further, they complained that enslaved persons were property, not people. Maryland's slaveholding Samuel Chase advised the Congress to set the matter aside immediately, for enslaved persons were not population at all but "a species of property, personal estate." If the Union planned to tax enslaved persons, he insisted, it must also tax New England's rich industry in codfish and haddock, since fish were items of wealth for the New England states in the same way slaves were for the Southern states.[14]

South Carolina's Thomas Lynch concurred, seconding Chase's invitation to table the matter. Then Edward Rutledge joined the chorus. To log enslaved persons as taxable would be highly unjust to the Southern states, because Southern wealth would be taxed but not the wealth of the Northern states. Following Chase, he chose the example of New England, arguing that not only would New England's fish not be taxed but also "the Eastern Colonies will become the carriers for the Southern," earning shipping profits as another source of "wealth for which they will not be taxed." No, Rutledge warned, the Congress's wisest course would be simply to put this question behind them, omitting slavery altogether from consideration in matters of taxation and representation.[15]

* * * * *

The third great issue dividing the Congress that summer was jurisdiction and ownership of the trans-Appalachian western lands. Until now, the matter had rested uneasily on the periphery of Congress. In July of 1776, the Articles of Confederation, by assuming such large territorial powers to itself, forced a nascent North/South divide to center stage. The reason for this regional division was that not only Virginia claimed broad ownership of land in the fertile agricultural sunbelt stretching from the Ohio Valley southward down the Mississippi River. So did North Carolina, South Carolina, and Georgia. Based on charters and land purchases, three Northern states—Massachusetts, Connecticut, and New York—also asserted claims in the trans-Appalachian West. However, the Northern states' visions of expansion and intended use of the lands were starkly different from those of the Southern states.

Unlike the Southern states, the Northern ones had no immediate plans for agricultural expansion into the West. They did not envision enslaved persons tilling the soil to raise a tobacco harvest that would be floated down the Mississippi to Spanish New Orleans, or some other commercial post near the Gulf of Mexico, for exchange. Rather, the lands claimed by Massachusetts, Connecticut, and New York were located in the chilly northern climes of the upper Mississippi and Great Lakes. This latitudinal fact meant that, in the years to come, the peoples of those states would endeavor, as they had for over a century, to bring the rich fur trade of the Great Lakes region back east. From New York and Boston harbors, they would send shiploads of beaver and otter pelts, not corn and tobacco, to ready markets throughout the world.

Article XVIII, permitting Congress to arbitrate disputes over land ownership and state boundaries, was a powder keg especially for Virginia delegates because they eyed it as a constitutional instrument that land companies, other states, and even Congress were going to abuse in order to usurp the colony's chartered territories. In this assumption, they were not wrong. Many other delegates viewed the Virginia claim as grotesquely large, and, with the formation of the new Union, they believed that the western lands should fall into the common treasury. To them, the legal rationales of Virginia and the other landed states crumbled under the immediate fact that the thirteen states were now a brotherhood prosecuting

Chapter 7: "A Firm League of Friendship" 143

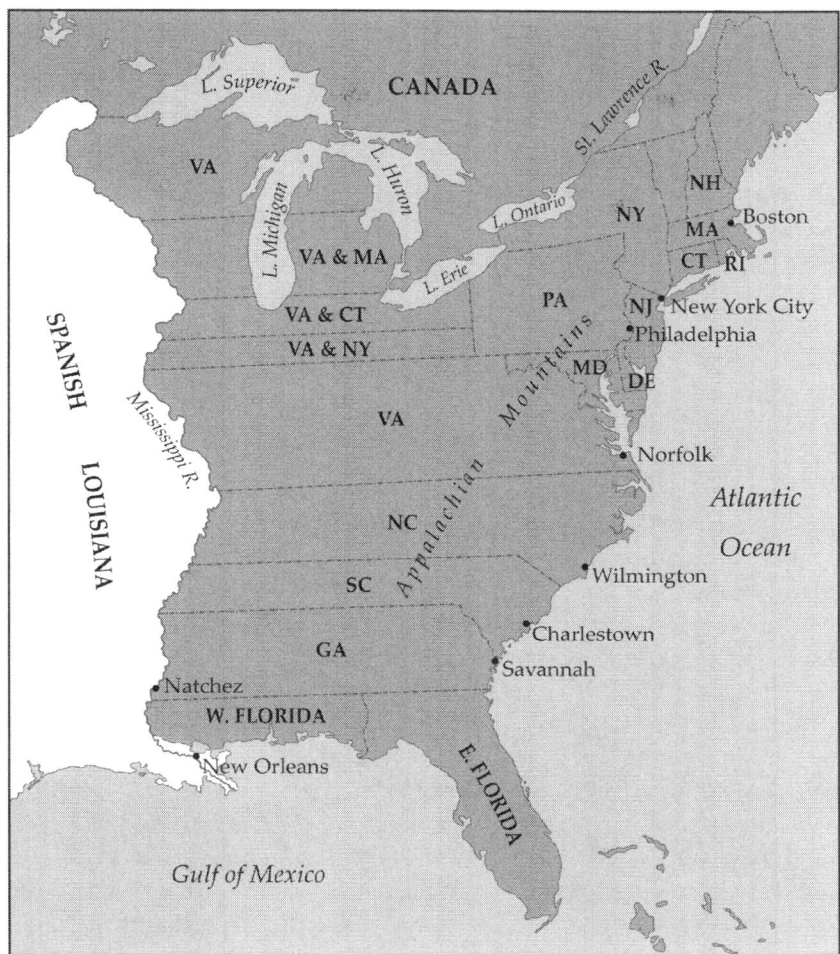

MAP 3. Western Land Claims of the American States, 1776. (Chris Robinson, Cartographer)

the war for independence—and the western lands—together. The states, they argued, were in the midst of a war that scrambled precedents, charters, treaties, boundaries, and colonial identities.

Not only this, some delegates also argued that colonial charters were by no means the superseding law of the war and the Union. Instead, to their view, the unsettled western lands extending to the Mississippi were royal lands—the king's lands, the Parliament's lands, the empire's lands—and if the United States were so fortunate as to win the war and gain some share of that territory in a peace settlement, it should be stamped American, not Virginian or Georgian. Its ownership must be transferred into a U.S. treasury for future sales, for the public good, to the benefit of all.

* * * * *

On the issue of the western lands, like with taxation and representation, the delegates found themselves deeply polarized by the end of July. In fact, optimism about forming a confederation sank to an all-time low after only eight or nine days of debate. Many delegates were so pessimistic that they were ready to throw in the towel, abandoning the notion of a permanent written compact altogether, preferring instead to continue their mutual war for liberty on an ad hoc basis. Joseph Hewes of North Carolina wrote to his governor on July 28. "What we shall make of it God only knows," he lamented, referring to the Articles. "I am inclined to think we shall never model it so as to be agreed to by all the colonies." Hewes apprehended that the colonies would divide forever over the terms of confederation, or, if not this, over their discordant views regarding the conditions required for making alliances with France and Spain. "I think it probable," he continued, "that we may split on these great points. If so our mighty Colossus falls to pieces."[16]

Other letters recorded worries among delegates that the thirteen states were perhaps not well-suited to a single confederation. The best course forward, some said, was to leave the matter of postwar political organizations and structures to future determination. Samuel Chase of Maryland, a leading opponent especially of Virginia's western land claims, disagreed with this assessment, arguing that a failure of confederation would doom any and all hope of securing foreign alliances and therefore the war for liberty itself. Chase was stunned at many delegates' retreat from confederation, writing to Richard Henry Lee, "We do not all see the importance nay the necessity of a Confederacy. We shall remain weak, and distracted and divided in our councils, our strength will decrease, we shall be open to all the arts of the insidious court of Britain, and no foreign court will attend to our applications for assistance, before we are confederated. What contract will a foreign state make with us, when we cannot agree among ourselves?"[17]

John Witherspoon of New Jersey took such alarm at the defection of delegates from the confederation that he pleaded with them to reconsider in an emotional address delivered on July 30. President of the College of New Jersey, later renamed Princeton, and America's foremost scholar of the Scottish Enlightenment, Witherspoon said that repudiating a permanent confederation of all thirteen states was "madness." Enacting some compact binding themselves into mediating rules and laws, he said, was the thirteen states' sole hope of averting "civil war." The professor made this point not once but three times. Without a constitutional Union, a future of civil war was not a matter of speculation, he promised. It was a fact of human nature established in "all history." It was foreordained.[18]

Moreover, Witherspoon alerted those opposed to perpetual unity that the civil war of which he spoke would be of a nature far more horrifying than the present Revolution. Without a lasting brotherhood of all thirteen, he said, today's War of Independence was going to be "only a prelude to a contest of a more dreadful nature, and indeed much more properly a civil war than that which now often obtains the name [the present civil war with Britain]." Why spend their treasure and blood seeking to obtain independence from the British, Witherspoon pleaded, "with a certainty, as soon as peace was settled with them of a more lasting war, a more unnatural, more bloody, and much more hopeless war, among the colonies themselves?"

FIGURE 22. John Witherspoon, New Jersey Delegate. (Portrait of John Witherspoon. Alexander Hay Ritchie, *Rev. John Witherspoon, D.D.*, ca. 1879, print, New York Public Library, EM807.)

What state or states would trigger the American civil war? Witherspoon did not specify, but he affirmed that without a caretaking compact subduing violent tendencies, "one or more of the strongest or largest of the American states" would subjugate the rest. Even before this might happen, he warned, the smaller states would take fright and rush to unite themselves into subconfederations. Then they would take the further logical step of seeking foreign alliances to protect themselves from the larger, wealthier, and more militant American states. If there was to be no confederation of the thirteen, Witherspoon said, referring to the small states, "Will they not be ready to prefer putting themselves under the protection of Great Britain, France or Holland, rather than submit to the tyranny of their neighbours?"

As a concluding point, Witherspoon challenged the dangerous doctrine being circulated by some delegates that the best course of action was for the Congress to postpone the completion of the American confederation "to some future period." Here the professor asked his fellow delegates to understand an essential truth: they must confederate now—or never. Underscoring the same theory of "Now" so central to Thomas Paine's argument for independence and confederation in *Common Sense*, Witherspoon said that delay was a certain formula for failure that would bring about mayhem:

> Alas, nothing can exceed the absurdity of that supposition. Does not all history cry out, that a common danger is the great and only effectual means of settling difficulties, and composing differences. . . . If therefore, at present, when the danger is yet imminent, when it is so far from being over, that it is but coming to its height, we shall find it impossible to agree upon the terms of this confederacy, what madness is it to suppose that there ever will be a time, or that circumstances will so change, as to make it even probable, that it will be done at an after season?

* * * * *

In spite of Witherspoon's plea to enact a permanent confederation now, not later, the Congress gave up the fight for a constitution altogether in August. The last formal day of debates was August 20, when delegates tabled the Articles for consideration to an unspecified future date. Why, it must be asked, when so many Americans believed that a constitutional Union was the key to everything—order, safety, justice, fairness, republicanism, rule of law, foreign alliance, peace among themselves, and, ultimately, victory over England in the war—did they give up so easily? Undoubtedly, many factors contributed to the Congress's reluctant moratorium on confederation, but from the evidence it seems that they backed away primarily in order to prevent a rupture. Their only other option on the explosive issues before them was to call for floor votes and let the majority, or supermajority, decide. And what would be the outcome of this? At best, it would engender lasting antipathy in the Congress, and at worst, it would trigger the secession of some states. In the end, one principle of Revolutionary politics overruled all others. It was that the risk of disunion and civil war in the future, as portrayed by Witherspoon, was infinitely preferable to provoking disunion and civil war today. So they stepped away. They hedged and delayed as the only means they knew for remaining at peace with one another.[19]

Voices from the floor of Independence Hall throughout late July and early August underscore the truth of this strategy of avoidance to forestall disunion. As Thomas Jefferson recorded on the question of voting power, the adoption of either proportional representation or one-state-one-vote by majority vote would have set off a defection of the other side. According to his notes, "The larger colonies had threatened they would not confederate at all if their weight in Congress should not be equal to the numbers of people they added to the confederacy, while the smaller ones declared against a union if they did not retain an equal vote for the protection of their rights." The idea of taxing enslaved Black people as individuals composing population fared no better. "If it is debated whether their slaves are their property," Thomas Lynch of South Carolina regretted to inform his fellow delegates, "there is an end of the confederation."[20]

Jefferson himself entered the fray on the issue of the western lands. "The limits of the Southern colonies are fixed," he declared in an impassioned speech on the states' exclusive rights to their chartered lands. James Wilson from Pennsylvania, a state with no substantial western claims, retorted that he would never agree to such a scheme, singling out Jefferson's Old Dominion for attack. The "extravagant" Virginia charter, he put it bluntly, could never be borne. So long as Virginia held tight to its right to the land, Pennsylvania would cling to a different sort of right. That is, Wilson promised, his state would "not confederate unless those claims are cut off."[21]

So much pessimism had set in by the end of August that Edward Rutledge of South Carolina pronounced the Articles of Confederation to be a "Devil." It was not merely a problem of having made no progress on uniting the thirteen states. The Articles had been so abused and hated, and the current delegates of Congress were now so sour on one another, Rutledge wrote to Robert Livingston on August 19, that the only hope for the Union was to abandon the present compact altogether and appoint a separate special convention of all new members of the states to start over. "If that was done we might then stand some chance of a confederation," the South Carolinian proposed. "At present we stand none at all."[22]

Other congressmen echoed similar views back home to friends and colleagues. Some said the proof was in the pudding that declaring independence before confederating had been a fatal blunder. William Williams of Connecticut said of the American charter, "I fear a permanent one will never be settled." Abraham Clark of New Jersey called the present situation "very alarming." "Nothing but present danger," he wrote to a Presbyterian pastor from his state, "will ever make us all agree, and I sometimes fear that will be insufficient."[23]

PART TWO

ALLIANCE, CONFEDERATION, AND CRISIS OF UNION

CHAPTER 8

The Mississippi and Fisheries

IN 1776 THE CONTINENTAL CONGRESS, though failing to adopt the Articles of Confederation, did successfully launch the ship of independence after months of debate and parliamentary maneuvering. That year the Congress also found its way forward on the all-important matter of foreign treaties with France, Spain, and other European nations. During the same month the delegates organized committees to prepare a declaration of independence and the Articles, it appointed John Adams, Benjamin Franklin, John Dickinson, Benjamin Harrison, and Robert Morris to formulate "a plan of treaties to be proposed to foreign powers." The formation of this committee marks the commencement not of clandestine negotiations with France and Spain to aid the Revolution but of a formal foreign policy of the United States.[1]

At first the committee was highly conservative, merely drafting templates for forming treaties of friendship and commerce, not for entangling military alliances. Soon, however, as American fortunes in the war darkened in the winter of 1776, the delegates revised their treaty templates to include full-bore alliances, binding both nations to fight for agreed upon terms until the bitter end. In this second set of diplomatic instructions, the Congress mapped out for the first time the distinct land and water ambitions of New England and the Southern states—regional war objectives that within several years, once opposed by France, Spain, and many fellow Americans, would trigger explosive debates on the floor of Independence Hall.

* * * * *

The delegates assembled in Congress that summer held out the greatest hopes for friendship and assistance in the war from France, less so from Spain. The reason for this contrast in expectations derived from two sources: political philosophy and geography. On the first of these, France had been in the vanguard of Enlightenment theories of government for the past half century, whereas Spain was far less enamored of liberal political thought. In formally separating from a monarch deemed despotic, Americans were carrying revolutionary torches of "liberty," "equality," and "constitution," not to mention "free trade," a radical economic concept recently reinforced in Adam Smith's *The Wealth of Nations*. Some of Americans' favorite voices of the French Enlightenment were the Baron de Montesquieu, Jean-Jacques Rousseau, and Denis Diderot, all of whom actively promoted natural rights and constitutionalism. Spain, on the other hand, had insulated itself from radical political and economic theories. Considering France's greater participation in the Enlightenment, the delegates of Congress felt sure that King Louis XVI of France was more likely to aid the colonies' rebellion for citizens' rights than was King Charles III of Spain. King Charles might be persuaded to join the war to undercut and embarrass Great Britain, but likely only with considerable prodding by King Louis, a dynastic cousin through the Bourbon bloodline.

FIGURE 23. King Louis XVI of France. (Portrait of Louis XVI of France. Joseph-Siffred Duplessis, *Portrait of Louis XVI, King of France and Navarre (1754–1793)*, ca. 1774–1776, oil on canvas, 31.4 x 24.4 in, Collection of the Palace of Versailles, MV 3966.)

Chapter 8: The Mississippi and Fisheries

The diverging ideologies of France and Spain on matters of government and economy figured prominently in the delegates' assumptions regarding treaty making in the year of independence, but not nearly as much as the map of colonial North America left in wake of the Seven Years' War ending in 1763. The first bloodletting of that protracted contest, the American theater of which is known as the French and Indian War, took place in the trans-Appalachian West near the Ohio River, when young George Washington came to blows with encroaching Frenchmen. At the war's termination nine years later, England emerged the overwhelming victor, acquiring not only the trans-Appalachian West clear to the Mississippi River but also Canada, Florida, Dominica, Grenada, Saint Vincent, the Grenadines, and Tobago.[2]

Significantly, France was ejected from the North American continent altogether, but not Spain. The multiple treaties ending the Seven Years' War transferred to the Spanish king all the land lying west of the Mississippi River—that is, the massive province of Louisiana. The long-shared border along the Mississippi River made Spain and Anglo-Americans uneasy neighbors. Spain, not France, found itself concerned in 1776 that westward-expanding Americans, unfettered by the restraining rule of King George III, would pose a mortal threat to Louisiana. Spanish ministers could not predict the future, but more than a few in Madrid worried that after a successful War of Independence, Americans might turn their lust for land and liberty across the Mississippi to the weakly-held Louisiana.

The linchpin for understanding the objectives of the Southern states during the war, and therefore the diplomacy they advocated in Congress, is preexisting knowledge of the geography and commerce of the lower Mississippi River in the 1770s. The crux of the matter is that Spain had acquired the warm-water port of New Orleans and the Isle d'Orleans on the eastern bank of the river in the Treaty of 1763, thereby empowering the Spanish monarch, owner of both shores of the mouth of the Mississippi for two hundred solid miles upriver, to choke off the trade of the entire Mississippi Valley. That is, even though Anglo-Americans might possess full and fair title to the vast lands between the Appalachian Mountains and the Mississippi, Spain held the key to the agricultural happiness of those lands, because farming demanded commerce to thrive, and commerce, in turn, demanded access to rivers to reach trading posts like New Orleans for exchange of goods from all over the world.

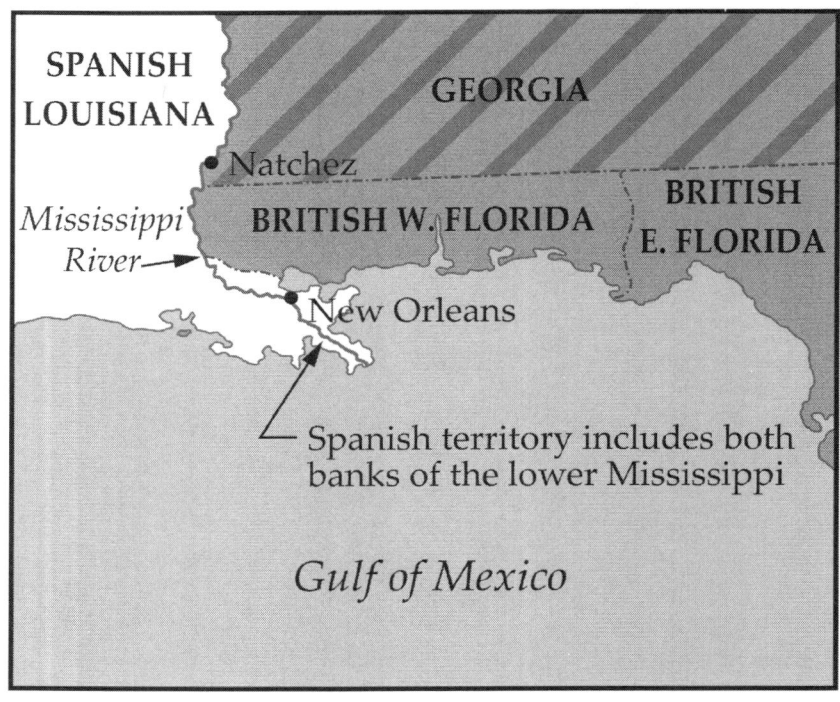

MAP 4. Spanish Control of the Mouth of the Mississippi, based on the Treaty of Paris, 1763. (Chris Robinson, Cartographer)

By Spain's interpretation of international maritime law, this geography of the lower Mississippi gave King Charles III every right to control not only the commerce that passed between his shores extending to the Gulf of Mexico but also all ships and shipping. Within its rights, Spain could prohibit the passage of British ships into its kingdom's Mississippi waters entirely. Or it could permit passage of ships only, with no right of touching the shore, tying to the shore, or making deposits at New Orleans or any other port along the river's mouth (whereby small rivercraft could deposit goods from upriver to be later picked up by seagoing vessels for export to the Caribbean and Europe). As another heavy-handed tactic, Spain could permit passage of ships, with or without a right of deposit, yet charge exorbitant taxes and tolls, effectively decimating the trade of Britain's interior trans-Appalachian lands.

Aware of these dangers, British peacemakers in the early 1760s refused to leave the negotiating tables without a unique proviso embedded

Chapter 8: The Mississippi and Fisheries 155

into the Treaty of Paris guaranteeing their empire the free navigation of the lower Mississippi through Spanish banks. In Article VII of that treaty, Britain consented to incorporate the east-bank territories of New Orleans and the Isle d'Orleans into greater Louisiana *only if* the possessor of the mouth of the river guaranteed Britain unimpeded navigation along those essential last two hundred miles to the sea. By the final documents—Britain's treaty with France, and France's subsequent treaty with Spain—all three European powers entered a new phase of peace with one another in which the Mississippi River navigation was "equally free" to all. Specifically, Article VII stipulated free navigation to England, France, and Spain "in its whole breadth and length, from its source to the sea, and expressly that part which is between the said island of New Orleans and the right bank of that river, as well as the passage both in and out of its mouth."[3]

FIGURE 24. King Charles III of Spain. (Portrait of Charles III of Spain. Anton Raphael Mengs, *Charles III of Spain*, ca. 1765, oil on canvas, 59.4 x 42.9 in, Collection of Museo del Prado, P02200.)

What complicated matters for the Congress in 1776—again notably for the Southern states, which claimed for themselves the lands on the lower Mississippi Britain had acquired in the 1763 treaty—was that Article VII was silent on "Americans" and the "United States." It said nothing about such a people, nor civil disobedience, revolution, or colonial separation from a mother country. Would Article VII apply in international courts of law—in London, Madrid, and Paris—to the United States if the Congress and Continental Army in fact succeeded in achieving political independence from England? A new nation might be formed, but that new nation, plain for all to read, was not recognized in the Treaty of Paris of 1763.

Nothing at all, by any lawyer's or foreign minister's reading of diplomatic precedent in America or Europe, could possibly require Spain to honor treaty obligations to British subjects in America if those subjects no longer formed a part of the British empire. Soon Americans from the Southern states, predominantly Virginia, would begin to ponder the dilemma of the navigation of the Mississippi River in earnest. They would fashion robust Enlightenment arguments in favor of a logical automatic transfer of the Anglo-American right inherent in Article VII to the self-same Americans, notwithstanding the renaming of their country. Yet privately, honestly, most Americans knew this appeal was grasping at straws when it came to hidebound Spain. King Charles and his ministers were not going to look favorably upon a colonial rebellion against a fellow monarch, much less a demand by a new nation for commercial rights within the Spanish empire based upon a treaty signed by the monarchs.

If the United States, first, survived and, second, wished legitimately to navigate the lower Mississippi unmolested by Spanish guns, the delegates in Congress knew there were only two ways forward. They must either obtain such a right directly from King Charles III through diplomacy during the war, or they must wait and somehow wrest the right from the parry and thrust of peace negotiations that would finally end the war.

* * * * *

In the first phase of its diplomacy, focused dominantly on obtaining a treaty of commerce with France, the Congress did not yet mention the navigation of the Mississippi River. Instead the committee of five prepared a template for a common commercial treaty, an agreement that would keep the United States as disentangled as possible from Old World politics. Three objectives underlay the treaty the committee was drafting. First, they hoped the accord would yield open trade between the signatory country on a most-favored-nation basis, including expedited shipments of arms and munitions to sustain the War of Independence. Second, American commercial treaties with European powers of the stature of France and Spain would send a symbolic message of inevitability to Britain. Such treaties would proclaim to King George and Parliament that the United States was a bona fide independent nation formally recognized by powerful commercial allies. In the hopeful view of many Americans, after such treaties materialized, Britain would have little alternative but to grant independence, persuaded that such a milestone rendered even His Majesty's infamous army and navy impotent to reverse the course of history.

The third American objective in signing treaties with France and Spain was to establish the boundaries and domain of the new United States. Anticipating that these world powers might choose to make war on the British empire while it was weakened by colonial rebellion in North America, the Congress wanted to draw up agreed-upon separate spheres of conquest. As finally adopted in mid-September, Congress's treaty template with France (conditions for a treaty with Spain would be adapted from this one) reserved the North American continent and its nearby islands exclusively to Americans. As stipulated in Article IX, France was precluded from invading or claiming not only any part of the thirteen colonies extending to the Mississippi River but also Canada, Florida, and British islands like Newfoundland, Cape Breton, and St. John's. Ambitiously, the Congress asserted its claim to all those North American territories "which now are, or lately were under the Jurisdiction of or Subject to the King or Crown of Great Britain."[4]

This did not mean that there was nothing to be gained by France if it declared war on England. In the event that King Louis of France embarked upon his own separate war against King George, the Congress outlined a sizable sphere of conquest for France. As described in Article XI, France's domain was the entire world of British possessions other than the North American one detailed in Article IX. That included Britain's prized sugar islands in the West Indies as fair game for France.

The plan for treaties, of course, did not neglect to attend to the lifeblood of New England's commerce over the preceding century: the capture, drying, and salting of codfish in the waters and on the shores of the island of Newfoundland. This island was declared off-limits to French or Spanish acquisition. Nor could these foes of Britain privately pursue expanded fishing rights and privileges in these waters in any peace accords with King George. In this determination the Treaty of 1763 came into play, with the Congress guaranteeing to France "the same Rights of Fishery on the Banks of Newfoundland, and all other Rights relating to any of the said Islands, which he is entitled to by virtue of the Treaty of

Paris." These were restrictive rights—which did not include ownership or control of any part of the island itself—and New Englanders meant to keep it that way.

With no apparent discord, the Congress formally approved the plan of treaties on September 17. Nine days later, it appointed three American ambassadors to attend the court of Versailles to commence negotiations with Louis XVI's first foreign minister, Charles Gravier, Comte de Vergennes. As would become routine practice in American diplomacy for the next quarter century, the Congress mandated a mission of three for the express purpose of providing equal representation abroad to the United States' three geographical sections—New England, the Middle states, and the Southern states. The Americans selected for the mission, who would first dialogue with France and only afterward Spain under the advisement of Vergennes, were Silas Deane of Connecticut, Benjamin Franklin of Pennsylvania, and Thomas Jefferson of Virginia. When Jefferson declined the post, owing to illness in the family, Congress replaced him with Arthur Lee of Virginia, a thirty-six-year-old physician-politician and fighter for liberty since the mid-1760s. At the time, Deane and Lee were already stationed in Europe on assignment to procure clandestine munitions and credit for the war back home.

The seventy-one-year-old Franklin had only returned to America from Europe sixteen months before. Now in the service of the new American Union, he agreed to traverse the ocean again. All agreed that Franklin, an acclaimed diplomat-scientist of international standing, was the linchpin to winning the hearts and purses of the two Bourbon powers. So on October 27, 1776, he set sail from Delaware Bay on board the sixteen-gun sloop *Reprisal*. The voyage across the Atlantic was "short but rough," a mere thirty days, Franklin reported back home after his arrival.[5]

* * * * *

The Congress might have been willing to wait patiently to hear how commercial treaties with France and Spain were unfolding in Europe if military catastrophe had not struck George Washington's army in successive waves, culminating in multiple surrenders in October and November. In the face of more than thirty-two thousand British troops on American soil and some 130 ships of the Royal Navy, the overwhelmed Continental Army first abandoned New York City and Long Island in a humiliating retreat across New York. Then, farther north, British forces trounced Benedict

Arnold at Lake Champlain. After this, with the Continental Army continuing its retreat, Lieutenant General Charles Cornwallis captured Fort Washington and Fort Lee on the Hudson and pushed the diminished American army across the Delaware. Five days later, on December 12, apprehensive of imminent invasion, the Congress fled Philadelphia for the safety of the town of Baltimore one hundred miles south.[6]

No analyst of the military history of the American Revolution has concluded anything but that the late winter of 1776 was one of the bleakest periods of the war. Six days before Christmas, Thomas Paine, then serving in the army as an aide to General Nathanael Greene, published the first of thirteen essays—symbolically, one for each state—called *The American Crisis*, in which he acknowledged, "These are the times that try men's souls."[7]

As such, with liberty and independence seeming to rest on a razor's edge, the Congress in Baltimore concluded that "speedy" military alliances with France and Spain were now "indispensably necessary." So on December 24 the delegates appointed a new committee of five—Elbridge Gerry, Samuel Adams, John Witherspoon, Abraham Clark, and Richard Henry Lee—to consider what commercial or territorial offerings might induce maritime France and Spain to declare swift war on England as allied combatants. Four days later, the committee read its report, and two days after that, on Monday, December 30, Congress approved revised instructions to Franklin, Deane, and Arthur Lee, soon dispatching them across the ocean to Paris.[8]

Regarding France, Congress was now ready to a make a hard sacrifice, one to be borne largely by New Englanders. If King Louis XVI entered the war as an ally of the United States, promising not to lay down arms until Britain formally granted American independence, the United States would award France one half of the island of Newfoundland, if won at the peace tables, and full fishing rights in "the cod fishery of America."[9]

In its offer to King Charles III, similarly in exchange for a military alliance, the Congress promised an equally enticing transfer of land: the restoration to Spain of the Florida landmass it had lost to Britain in the Seven Years' War. When the British took control of this Spanish province, they had divided it into East Florida and West Florida for administrative purposes, one centered on the Atlantic and the other extending from the Apalachicola River across the north coast of the Gulf of the Mexico several hundred miles to the Mississippi River. Because many

Southern members of Congress had been hoping to add these two British colonies to the ranks of the Southern states since shortly after Lexington and Concord, in this case they were the ones making a notable sacrifice for the common good.

However, almost certainly under the direction of committee member Richard Henry Lee of Virginia, soon to emerge as the chief spokesperson for the American right to the navigation of the Mississippi, the Congress placed a strict condition on the grant to Spain of the two Floridas. In the language of the new directive dispatched to American ambassadors in Paris in early January of 1777, Spain must reciprocally guarantee to the United States "the free and uninterrupted navigation of the Mississippi and use of the harbor of Pensacola." To the thinking of those delegates in Congress dedicated to obtaining navigation rights on the lower Mississippi River, if the United States fought alongside Spain in the Revolution to reduce the two Floridas, awarding them to Charles III at the conclusion of the war, it seemed only fair to ask Spain to permit Americans free navigation of the Mississippi and, additionally, commercial rights in Pensacola, the capital of West Florida, already a vital port for Anglo-American commerce on the Gulf of Mexico for more than a decade.[10]

FIGURE 25. Richard Henry Lee, Virginia Delegate. (Portrait of Richard Henry Lee. Alonzo Chappel, *Richard Henry Lee*, date unknown, engraving, New York Public Library.)

What was not yet clearly established was the precise definition of "free and uninterrupted navigation of the Mississippi." In this mandate the Congress, following the recommendation of the committee, chose essentially to recapitulate the language of Article VII of the Treaty of 1763, wherein Spain guaranteed free navigation of the river to France and Britain. The broad term "navigation," it was hoped, would include a right to deposit or exchange goods on Spanish land at a location, or locations, accessible to both seagoing vessels and American rivercraft descending from the Ohio River with tobacco and corn. Because flatboats and keelboats from upriver could not possibly battle the high winds and dangerous waves of the ocean, an exchange of commodities and merchandise to seagoing schooners and sloops must take place somewhere on the river.

December 30, 1776, marks a milestone in American history because on that day the Congress established for the first time, in no uncertain terms, that the concrete objectives of the Revolution extended well beyond securing independence for the thirteen seaboard states. On behalf of New England, the war would be waged for independence and water and land rights on the island of Newfoundland. On behalf of the Southern states, the war would be fought for independence, a boundary at the Mississippi, and navigation rights on the same river. Led by the dynamic partnership of committee members Sam Adams of Massachusetts and Richard Henry Lee of Virginia, who had been collaborating closely on all things political for two years, both sets of land and water rights were set forth as nonnegotiable in military alliances. As coming years of congressional debates would highlight recurrently, the Mississippi and Newfoundland fisheries were critical sectional balances for one another. To pursue one as an objective of Congress but not the other was soon to be viewed as an act of betrayal that menaced the Union.

* * * * *

To the disappointment of Congress and the Continental Army, no substantial progress would be made in signing treaties of alliance in Europe for more than a year. During this time the delegates continued their struggle to compromise terms on the Articles of Confederation, and as they worked long days to supply the army with troops, blankets, foodstuffs, arms, and powder, they also fought over who was to blame for the recent military catastrophes in New York and New Jersey. In their private letters, congressmen sought answers for their multiplying failures on the battlefield, often finding them in the defects or cowardice of the peoples of other states and regions.

Caesar Rodney of Delaware described how when the British overtook New York City, New England troops had "behaved in a most dastardly, cowardly scandalous manner." William Hooper of North Carolina registered his agreement. A member of Congress since 1774, Hooper had long since developed a contempt for New Englanders, because in his view they were commoners who had the audacity nonetheless to style themselves as moral and military superiors to the rest. In a letter to Samuel Johnston, a future governor of his state, Hooper opened by saying that what he was about to write was "truly confidential." Underscoring the tendency of delegates to steer clear of committing criticism of their fellow Americans to paper, the North Carolinian went on, "Were it not that my friend Hewes is to be the bearer, I should not trust out of my own hands a letter which may be attended with unhappy consequences should it fall into the power of any one disposed to make an unfriendly use of it."[11]

FIGURE 26. William Hooper, North Carolina Delegate. (Portrait of William Hooper. Henry Bryan Hall, *William Hooper*, date unknown, print, New York Public Library, EM1641.)

With this disclaimer, Hooper stated his truth about what had happened in New York and Long Island. Intrepid Middle and Southern state soldiers stood their ground, while especially the "New England heroes" turned and ran away. New Englanders, he said, had earned themselves "reproach and dishonour—they suffer in the comparison with the troops to the southward of Hudson's River who have to a man behaved well and born the whole brunt on Long Island—and that for which the Eastern troops must be damned to eternal fame." Hooper further specified that "when I commend the Southern troops I except the Philadelphia City Militia who poltroon like deserted their station."[12]

Hooper worried that Washington's defeats in the Middle states signaled the coming of anarchy, and when this happened, officers and troops would forsake the Union and cling to their respective state governments for dear life. Writing to a North Carolina delegate now back home named Joseph Hewes, Hooper begged the recipient to share the letter with no one, except Johnston, again saying that what he had to communicate was "truly confidential." When the Union fell apart, the congressman explained, "venality and corruption will become the road to military honours." And, Hooper asked, what would be the effect of this on New England? "I tremble for the consequences of it," he replied, pointing to the prospect of some species of civil war between New England and the Southern states. "Already such a hatred to the Eastern troops exists in the Southern corps," Hooper continued, "that it requires the utmost exertions of the genl. officers to prevent its breaking out into acts of violence and occasioning a general schism in the army."[13]

That winter Hooper wrote four other surviving letters that exude military and political despair, all of which showcase varying degrees of Southern chauvinism. In one he calls New Englanders "bloodsuckers" who invariably try to bend the organization of the army and Congress's financial support of campaigns to their advantage. Alluding to a funding resolution moved in mid-November by Elbridge Gerry of Massachusetts, he accused New England of "subterfuge." The bill was defeated, Hooper continued, but "my blood still boils with a resentment that language will not find curses to express." In another letter, likewise pertaining to bounties and payments to army recruits, the congressman claimed, "The Eastern gentry are not yet satisfied & wish to screw us up a few pegs higher." And, announcing to Hewes that the British army now threatened Philadelphia, Hooper saw clear to deprecate New England and the Middle states while painting a heroic picture of the Southern ones: "New England skulks within her own bounds. The Middle Colonies shrink into insignificance, & the Southern colonies from their own virtue must decide the contests. I believe sincerely that the virtue of the whole continent has fled to the Southward. Oh clasp her, nourish her until she bless us."[14]

Military defeat also upset Samuel Adams. Though not nearly so hotheaded as Hooper, Adams decried the Middle states for their cowardice in not standing and fighting as General Howe pushed the Continental Army across New Jersey. Writing to James Warren, he celebrated New England for its fortitude in withstanding the "forces of the tyrant" for two full years. Then he asked, "But what will be said of Pennsylvania & the Jerseys? Have they not disgraced themselves by standing the idle spectators while the enemy overran a great part of their country?" The British now occupied Trenton, a short distance from Philadelphia. "If they were as near Boston," Adams put forth, "would not our hardy countrymen cut them all to pieces or take them prisoners."[15]

William Williams of Connecticut joined in the finger-pointing, attributing some of the lassitude in the people of Pennsylvania to their love of "money & that is all the God they worship." He said he looked forward to taking leave of Congress soon because the animosity of so many delegates in Philadelphia toward New Englanders perplexed and wearied him. "There are strange mortals in Con[gres]s be assured," he wrote to Joseph Trumbull, "tis hard to say what some of them aim at, but easy to say a number invariably hate & persecute every N Engld Man, & can embroil matters exceedingly." Again, Pennsylvania stood out as a special case. "This province," Williams lamented, "have a fixed hatred of N. E. & everything that belongs to it."[16]

In contrast, John Adams often dampened the flames of discord and disunion around him, calling upon his fellow Americans to bury their resentments and rise up to their common love of liberty and freedom. Perhaps this is one reason he did not fall into obscurity after the Revolution but instead remained at the helm of American government for decades to come. Somewhat uniquely for a New Englander, in the face of the defeats of the American army in Manhattan and Long Island, Adams turned regional chauvinism upside down, praising the Southerners for valor and voicing his disbelief at "the infamous cowardice of the New England troops."[17]

More than once in his letters, Adams stated, "I am ashamed of my country," alluding to New England, not the new United States. With his eyes wide open, he responded to the military debacles with truth seeking and humor rather than by hurling blame on the Southern and Middle colonies. As he asked of army officer Henry Knox, "Pray tell me, Coll Knox, does every man to the southward of Hudson's River behave like an hero and every man to the northward of it like a poltroon or not?" Adams demanded to know "whether it is true," because if so, he insisted wryly, he was determined to give up his life in New England and "remove to some Southern colony, where I could enjoy the society of heroes, and have a chance of learning sometime or other, to be part of an hero myself."[18]

CHAPTER 9

"The Very Salvation of These States"

In the first half of 1777 Americans battled on, still however without either a binding alliance among themselves or one with France or Spain. What they had accomplished, however, was the Declaration of Independence, and in the view of Benjamin Rush of Pennsylvania, this singular binding act had saved the Union during the Revolution's dark hour. Initially, the declaration had been hard fought in Congress, Rush recorded in private notes, with some delegates professing that it "divided & weakened the colonies" by stoking polarization. Ultimately, though, "the contrary of this was the case," Rush celebrated. "Nothing but the signing, & recognizing of the declaration of independence preserved the Congress from a dissolution in decemr 1776 when Howe marched to the Delaware." Then, auspiciously, Washington's twin victories at Trenton and Princeton served to restore morale to the cause, enabling one New England delegate to herald in early February of 1777, "There is more unanimity in Congress than ever, the little Southern jealousies have almost subsided, & the Dickinsonian politics are banish'd." The first assertion referred to the Southern states' fears of New England political and military dominance and the second to Dickinson's stubborn insistence on reconciliation with Britain.[1]

From the perspective of the politics of the Union, the two most notable events of early 1777 were the commencement of debates about New England's formation of a subcongress and the arrival in Philadelphia of a new North Carolina delegate, Thomas Burke, thirty-year-old physician and lawyer who was destined to become the staunchest defender of states' rights in the early years of the republic. Both of these political forces influenced the next iteration of the Articles of Confederation, finally brought back to the table for discussion in the late spring.

Galvanized at least in part by the failure of the Union to adopt a confederated government, and further fueled by the despair of the last four months of 1776, New England organized a Convention of the New England States, which was held in Providence, Rhode Island, on December 25. The primary objective of the meeting was to adopt measures "for their mutual defence & for regulating trade & commerce." The resolutions they passed were, in fact, quite comprehensive: "They have recommended measures for supporting the credit of the paper currency and for raising an army for defence of the state of Rhode Island. They have also recommended to the [New England] assemblies to fix the prices of a number of necessary articles & have agreed on a farther bounty to encourage the soldiers to enlist in the new army."[2]

In early February New Englanders submitted the various resolutions adopted by the Providence convention to the Continental Congress for its "approbation." Caught by surprise, not only by the suddenness of the move but also by the constitutional propriety of it, most of the delegates from other regions expressed their displeasure. Did the Congress have the right to approve or disapprove the New England convention and its measures? Without a charter of its own to determine constitutionality, what was the place of a vote of the Continental Congress in endorsing or overturning them? Some New England delegates clarified that their purpose in submitting the resolutions was to inform the Congress, not to seek approval. Sam Adams asserted "that a right to assemble upon all occasions to consult measures for promoting liberty & happiness was the privilege of freemen—that it was contested by govr Hutchinson & that it was dreaded only by tyrants." Virginian Richard Henry Lee lent support on constitutional grounds, saying that the delegates in Congress "were not yet confederated—therefore no law of the union infringed."[3]

Other delegates smelled a rat, arguing that by giving the Congress's approbation of the New England convention, they were effectively sanctioning the formation of separate regional confederations. Pennsylvania's Benjamin Rush was the most outspoken in this regard. "I think the meeting is full of great and interesting consequences," he said on the floor of Congress, "and should be regarded with a serious & jealous eye. Their business was chiefly continental, and therefore they usurped the powers of congress . . . it becomes us to remember that arbitrary power has often originated in justice & necessity."[4]

Insisting that the New England convention was a blow to the continental Union, Rush advised against congressional approval. To further justify his position, he leaned on history as well as the obvious necessity of treating the fragile American Union with solemn care, which meant formally disallowing regional subconfederations. In making his case, Rush asked the other delegates to contemplate the nature of the historic Anglo-American union they were currently breaking. For two hundred years the American colonies had honored their bond with the king of England and Parliament, not menacing it. Then—and only when injustice required it—they had seceded from a corrupt British government, as it had become "criminal" not to do so.

In a like manner, Rush said, the thirteen states must now look up to the Continental Congress as the sole central authority governing them. To him, the Providence convention represented an act of New England independence, something alarming and dangerous to the whole. He acknowledged that unknown vicissitudes of events in the future might bring about regional independence, but at the present time, the delegates must deplore any and all steps that might provoke disunion and secession: "The time may come & probably will come when it will be the interest of the united States to be independent of each other, but I can conceive of no temporal punishment to be severe eno' for that man who attempts to dissolve, or weaken the union for a century or two to come."

FIGURE 27. Benjamin Rush, Pennsylvania Delegate. (Portrait of Benjamin Rush. Charles Willson Peale, *Portrait of Benjamin Rush*, 1783, oil on canvas, 49.9 x 39.9 in, Winterthur Museum, Garden and Library, gift of Mrs. Julia B. Henry, 1959.0160 A.)

Unsure what to do, the Congress put the question to a vote. In light of the absence of any supreme law of the Union contradicting it, did the New England convention "stand in need of the approbation of Congress to make it valid"? On February 4 the Congress voted yes—only to appoint a committee and reverse itself a few days later. In the end, the delegates chose to steer clear of any ruling whatsoever on the validity of the convention itself. Rather, they officially approved some of the resolutions of the December 25 meeting, and in registering their disapproval of others, the Congress "recommended" to New England that those points be "referred to the consideration of the other united States." Moreover, in the spirit of equal rights and opportunities, the Congress invited the Middle states and the Southern states to organize similar regional meetings, if they wished, to safeguard their own immediate economic and military interests.[5]

* * * * *

North Carolina delegate Thomas Burke made his debut in Congress in Baltimore in early February. Burke, who possessed a brilliant analytical mind, even if tinged with above-average distrust of government power, deserves to be profiled for several reasons. One is that from the nature and substance of his letters dispatched to North Carolina Governor Richard Caswell, it is evident that he came to Congress not just as an American patriot devoted to the collective cause of freedom, liberty, and independence. Burke was also on a reconnaissance mission, seemingly set in motion by authorities back home, to obtain information about the other twelve states and, conspicuously, the dangers "combinations" of them might pose to the safety of North Carolina. Connected to these calculations, Burke stands out in our early history for the role he played in framing the final version of the Articles of Confederation. Above all, the North Carolinian gave energy to the article on the supremacy of state power in all matters except those specifically ceded to the Congress. Additionally, he was a prime mover of the article divesting the Congress of sovereignty over the trans-Appalachian western lands.[6]

Three days after his arrival in Baltimore, Burke alerted Governor Caswell, "I find a considerable jealousy is entertained of the Northern States." He clarified elsewhere that "Northern" and "New England" were often used synonymously in reference to the four northernmost states. Soon, in another letter, when reporting to Caswell on the "political principles" motivating the various states, Burke said that his fellow delegates kept their long-term ambitions "out of view," but again, generally speaking, "all are under some apprehensions of combination in the Eastern States to derive to themselves every possible advantage from the present war, at the expense of the rest." This seemed true enough, Burke affirmed, yet North Carolina also had much to fear from the Middle states regarding its extensive trans-Appalachian land claims. He suspected those states intended to gain power in Congress and then strip them of that property. Burke explained that if this came to pass, it would be done discreetly, yet intelligently, in a two-step manner. First, the "party" of Middle states would maneuver to enlarge the powers of Congress. After this, they would exercise those powers to "pass resolves injurious to the rights of those states who claim to the South Seas."[7]

FIGURE 28. Thomas Burke, North Carolina Delegate. (Portrait of Thomas Burke. Artist unknown, *Thomas Burke*, date unknown, etching, General Negative Collection, State Archives of North Carolina, Raleigh, NC.)

Continuing in this vein, Burke wrote a remarkable disquisition on government power and its abuses soon after the Congress relocated back to Philadelphia. On March 11, 1777, in a more than 1,800-word letter to Caswell, he professed that the thing wise statesmen must fear most in politics is that "power of all kinds has an irresistible propensity to increase a desire for itself. It gives the passion of ambition a velocity which increases on its progress." He lauded the delegates in Congress for their professions of virtue and disinterest but insisted that even exalted lovers of liberty were not immune from "the delusive intoxication which power naturally imposes on the human mind."[8]

Burke was confident that he understood the first principle of human nature and therefore also of constitution making. It was the inevitability of the "abuse & corruption of power." Therefore, the job of republican statesmen was to exercise "political vigilance & jealousy" over power. And, Burke said, the primary reason North Carolina must withhold power from the new American Congress was that seemingly benign powers awarded today by the states to the central body "will insensibly produce combinations of the states, & such combinations will be fatal to the liberties of many."

What exactly did Burke fear? Was it political combinations of other states that might disadvantage North Carolina through heavy-handed legislation? Or was it military combinations that might violently subdue his home state? It was both of these, and repeatedly he advised the governor not to make the dread mistake of assuming that the "public virtue & spirit" of the present era would last. Rather, he said that the "greatest danger" to North Carolina was for political leaders to permit naïve beliefs in virtue to be the cause of surrendering too much power to Congress.

Burke anchored his argument in the core philosophy that "unlimited power can not be safely trusted to any man, or set of men, on earth." Troubles might begin in the political chamber, but they could end up in disunion, separate confederacies, and civil war. This was his message, and it was of particular importance for the less populated states like North Carolina. The problem for those states, he said, was that "the more powerful states by combining, can doubtless subjugate the more feeble."

In analyzing the arc of the future, Burke concluded that New England by itself posed little direct risk to his home state. It was too remote, and the region lacked "fertile soil," which weakened its military capacity "if uncombined with others." New Englanders did possess maritime strength. "Their principal resources," Burke described, "will always be in commerce & fisheries. This indeed will give them ships & seamen; but they can not support the one, or fit out the others, without the assistance of other states." Therefore, the North Carolinian concluded, referring to four England states acting alone, "their strength may indeed be competent to internal defense, but, I believe, not to foreign conquests." By this, he meant foreign conquests of other American states, like his own.

What worried Burke most was that Massachusetts, Pennsylvania, and Virginia would combine into a confederacy of sorts, leaving the remaining states at their mercy. He presented a domino theory of what would follow if these three conspired to dominate the rest:

> I think the most formidable combination would be Massachusetts, Pennsylvania & Virginia. The first has power sufficient to overawe & consequently to direct the other three New England States. The

second could equally influence Jersey & Delaware. Virginia would be formidable to her Southern neighbours, & Maryland. New York could not resist a combination of Pennsylvania and Massachusetts; Maryland must fall a sacrifice to Pennsylvania & Virginia. Against this powerful confederacy, I fear, we [North Carolina] should not be able to hold out long.

That is, rather than enjoy independence in the aftermath of 1776, Burke worried that North Carolina was going to trade the tyranny of King George and the Parliament in London for the tyranny of the three largest states in the American Union.

* * * * *

Three weeks after Burke dispatched this lengthy letter to Governor Caswell, the Congress at last reopened debates on the Articles of Confederation, setting aside a minimum of two days each week for deliberation until complete. Again they hoped for a speedy resolution of their differences, leading to a binding agreement, and again they met with disappointment. As April passed into May and then into June, July, August, and September, the delegates clashed not only on the troublesome triad of voting powers, taxation, and sovereignty over the western lands but also on the very meaning of *independence* as proclaimed in the late declaration. Were the "United States of America" one independent republic or thirteen separate ones joined together to prosecute the war and afterward only to remain in a confederation for mutual defense and trade advantages? What political entity, or entities, had in fact been declared independent in 1776? The delegates differed in their answers to these questions. No one knew what, exactly, was happening to the power dynamics of the former British colonies. What is clear from their letters is that most members of Congress wanted to have it both ways. They wished to invest their respective states with superior power and at the same time to solidify sufficient concord and justice among themselves to win the Revolution and maintain domestic security.[9]

Not until mid-November did the Congress finally adopt the Articles of Confederation, which would still require the ratification of each state before being formally enacted into law. Between April and the first week of October, instead of deliberating every other day as intended, the Congress addressed the matter of the confederation on average every two weeks. Then, beginning on October 7, debates entered a new forward-moving phase, occurring every day or every other day until hard-fought compromises had been struck. By this time the delegates were no longer in Philadelphia but in the town of York, Pennsylvania, one hundred miles west. In mid-September they had abandoned Philadelphia for a second time, under imminent threat of invasion by the British after Washington's defeats at the Battle of Brandywine and the Battle of the Clouds. On September 28 General Howe captured the American political capital, holding it thereafter for nine months.

Many factors other than the loss of Philadelphia account for the breakthrough on the Articles of Confederation in the months of October and November, but several in particular stand out as decisive. For one thing, the delegates apprehended disunion if they did not soon adopt continental laws to structure the economy and settle conflicts among themselves. As the New England convention had acutely demonstrated, states were demanding unified oversight of monetary policy, trade, credit, and bounties for the recruitment of troops. Besides this, the convention unmistakably revealed to all that when the Congress temporized in the fulfillment of its most essential administrative and military duties, regional confederacies would fill the void.

Another acute worry was interstate violence over territory claimed by New York, New Hampshire, and a self-styled militia known as the Green Mountain Boys. The necessity of a controlling constitution to avert this outcome came to life brightly in January of 1777 when the Green Mountain Boys declared some nine thousand square miles of land between the Connecticut River and Lake Champlain to be the independent state called Vermont. Seven months later they adopted a state constitution. For decades New York and New Hampshire had been contesting the same region, setting up a combustible situation. In the eyes of many it risked erupting into a civil war between New York and New England. Delegates often observed that "New York entertains the most virulent jealousy against her Eastern neighbours," and in either instance—whether New Hampshire appropriated the land for itself or New England and its Vermont allies succeeded in erecting a fifth New England state—it all boiled down, in the view of New Yorkers, to the same thing: unwarranted aggressive acts of New England against their state. As Sam Adams explained it in late June, New York delegates were calling for Congress's intervention "to prevent a civil war between that state and the Green Mountain Men."[10]

Delegates also deemed a formal confederation to be vital to the moment because without it the Congress was impotent to borrow money

Chapter 9: "The Very Salvation of These States" 175

abroad on the credit of a bona fide nation. It seemed obvious that France and Spain were never going to enter into treaties or alliances with the United States so long as a durable American confederation, one capable of honoring its obligations, remained theoretical. All these circumstances reinforced a growing, and urgent, conviction in Congress month after month that the Articles were "necessary to our salvation." Said another delegate, "Many assert that the very salvation of these states depend upon it." Richard Henry Lee summed it up: "This great bond of Union will more effectually than any thing else produce present strength, credit, and success, and secure future peace and safety."[11]

Under the gun after sixteen months of anguished evasion and procrastination, the Congress hammered out the final form of the Articles of Confederation and Perpetual Union in October and November. It was modeled on the Dickinson plan of 1776 yet weakened in many places by delegates, like Burke, who were persuaded that Congress, if not expressly restrained, was going to encroach on the autonomy of the states. On this question of state powers and rights, Dickinson's constitution had merely reserved to the states "regulation and government of its internal police." The final Articles of 1777 departed from this open-ended language, leaving no room for doubt about where primary sovereignty resided in the American state/federal nexus: the states. Article II, adopted without significant opposition, read, "Each state retains its sovereignty, freedom and independence, and every power, jurisdiction and right which is not by this confederation expressly delegated to the United States in Congress assembled."[12]

The delegates also took care to clarify, especially to New England, that regional subconfederations and pacts were expressly prohibited by the constitution, except when explicitly sanctioned by the Congress. This clause appeared in Article VI: "No two or more states shall enter into any treaty, confederation, or alliance, whatever, between them, without the consent of the United States, in Congress assembled, specifying accurately the purposes for which the same is to be entered into, and how long it shall continue."[13]

Dickinson's constitution had empowered the Congress to define state boundaries, including setting limits on their western extents. On this question delegates—notably those from Virginia and North Carolina, the two states most readily poised to expand over the mountains into their western districts of Kentucky and Tennessee—pushed back hard, demanding that the Congress not tread on their states' chartered territorial rights. Other states ultimately conceded the point but only if the Articles spelled out a process for adjudicating land conflicts. This was done in Article IX. By that article, whenever the legislature or executive authority of a state formally petitioned the Congress for a hearing on a territorial dispute involving more than one state, the federal body would appoint a court of appeals to settle the matter. In effect, the delegates devised a jury system wherein they themselves would serve as judges and jurors. Their rulings would be "final and decisive."[14]

It is possible that the Congress's decision to forfeit all federal power to appropriate the western lands into a national treasury was a compromise with the large state of Virginia, which in return consented to the perpetuation of the one-state-one-vote rule. However it came about, the large states gave ground on this issue in Article V, forgoing population or wealth-based representation for equality of states in voting on general legislative matters. On votes pertaining to war and peace, treaties and alliances, and borrowing and appropriating money, a nine-state majority was constitutionally mandated. This supermajority mandate, outlined in Article IX, would prevent impulsive rulings on these most crucial issues of the Union by seven or eight states that might, in fact, represent only one-third or less of the actual population of the United States.

On the last issue that had been obstructing the formation of a constitutional Union for so many months, the basis of continental taxation, the New England and Southern states crossed swords again, as in 1776. The outcome of this dispute was the establishment of a tax on the value of all land and improvements in each state (Article VIII). New Englanders were much aggrieved by this ruling because their land values were considerably higher—by some estimates five times that of Southern states—and as a double hit, this formula left slaves entirely untaxed, even though it was thought that at least one-third of Southern "property" value lay in slave ownership.[15]

As Richard Henry Lee of Virginia explained in a letter to Roger Sherman, delegate from Connecticut then in New Haven, the passage of the taxation provision was yet another example of the sacrifice and compromise required by the states and regions to cement the Union. "We have finished the Confederation," Lee wrote in November, "and it will go forward to the states in a few days, with strong exhortation to consider and return it quickly. In this great business dear Sir we must yield a little to each other, and not rigidly insist on having every thing correspondent to the partial views of every state. On such terms we can never confederate."[16]

On Saturday, November 15, 1777, the Congress formally approved the long-awaited Articles of Confederation, ordering that three hundred copies be struck off at the printer for distribution to the states. Two days later the delegates gave their consent to a circular letter, to be dispatched with the compact, that entreated the executives of each state to convene legislative assemblies without delay to ratify the Articles. Requesting that each state return its ratification to the Congress no later than March 10, 1778, the letter called on "wise and patriotic legislators" to rise above "local attachments." All the states must set their sights on the "happiness and glory of the general Confederacy," which must be "indissoluble" and "permanent." There was no other way forward. The Articles of Confederation, the congressional letter said, was "essential to our very existence as a free people, and without it we may soon be constrained to bid adieu to independence, to liberty and safety."[17]

* * * * *

Across the Atlantic in Paris, American ambassadors Franklin, Deane, and Lee happily greeted the news of a completed, though not yet ratified, Articles of Confederation. A month before the intelligence reached them, though, a messenger brought to their hands a far more transformative bulletin—one from the American battlefield. As they learned during the first week of December, General Horatio Gates of the Continental Army had scored a stunning victory in the Hudson River Valley in mid-October. At the Battle of Saratoga, Continental troops routed the British army under the command of General John Burgoyne, who surrendered his entire corps of soldiers and officers, comprising more than 5,700 men together with 7,000 muskets and 42 brass cannons. It was, by far, the greatest win yet for the Continental Army in the Revolutionary War.[18]

This decisive defeat of the British at Saratoga was a turning point for American affairs at the court of Versailles because it provided living proof that the Continental Army possessed the will and might to prevail. As a result, negotiations with French foreign minister Vergennes quickened, and on February 6, 1778, France and the United States signed two treaties, one of friendship and commerce and the other a military alliance. So vital to the American cause was a French alliance that historian Edmund Morgan has called it "the greatest diplomatic victory the United States has ever achieved." Finally, Americans obtained the international recognition and military and naval support, or at least the imminent promise thereof, they had desperately sought since 1776. Most gratifying of all, King Louis XVI and Vergennes bound the French nation to fight until the independence of the United States was assured. Two articles in the treaty of alliance affirmed this pledge. Article II read, "The essential and direct end of the present defensive alliance is to maintain effectually the liberty, sovereignty, and independence absolute and unlimited of the said United States, as well in matters of government as of commerce." And to underscore the point yet again, Article VIII stated regarding the two signatory nations, "They mutually engage not to lay down their arms, until the independence of the United States shall have been formally or tacitly assured by the treaty or treaties that shall terminate the war."[19]

FIGURE 29. Charles Gravier, Comte de Vergennes, Chief Minister of France. (Portrait of The Count of Vergennes. Antoine François Callet, *Charles Gravier, Comte de Vergennes, Ambassadeur et Ministre, du roy Louis XVI*, 1781, oil on canvas, 62.6 x 50.8 in, Collection of Musée de l'Armée.)

Morgan further asserts that the Franco-American treaties of 1778 "gave the Americans all they could have hoped for and exacted almost nothing in return." Yet in this assessment, he errs in one important regard. As per the December 1776 instructions of Congress, Franklin had directly communicated to Vergennes and his ministerial secretary, Conrad Alexandre Gérard, about the United States' intention not to exit the war without American ownership of at least one half of the island of Newfoundland and unabridged fishing rights in the North Atlantic Ocean. The French, however, had private objectives relating to the final disposition of this jewel of North America and therefore required the treaty of alliance to run silent on Newfoundland and the fisheries.[20]

Chapter 9: "The Very Salvation of These States" 179

In the treaty of commerce, Vergennes called for language on the fisheries that proved highly suspicious and troubling to New Englanders for the remainder of the war. Article IX spelled out clearly that Newfoundland was fair game for either the United States or France. Further, it left no question about the obligations of each party to the other when it came to said island and fishing rights: there were none. More concerning still for Americans interested in these land and water rights, the article outlined in advance that in the event France did possess the island at war's end, or some part or parts of it, American ships were expressly prohibited from fishing, landing, curing, drying, and trading therein:

> The subjects, inhabitants, merchants, commanders of ships, masters and mariners of the states, provinces, and dominions of each party respectively shall abstain and forbear to fish in all places possessed or which shall be possessed by the other party: The most Christian King's subjects shall not fish in the havens, bays, breeks, roads, coasts, or places, which the said United States hold or shall hereafter hold; and in like manner the subjects, people and inhabitants of the said United States shall not fish in the havens, bays, creeks, roads, coasts, or places, which the most Christian King possesses or shall hereafter possess.[21]

In this treaty of friendship, uncertainty about the future of Newfoundland went so far as to evoke the prospect of future Franco-American hostility. This would come about if American ships were found to be in violation of terms of the article. If so, the treaty expressly permitted those ships and their cargos to be apprehended by the French navy. "If any ship or vessel shall be found fishing contrary to the tenor of this treaty," it stipulated, "the said ship or vessel with its lading, proof being made thereof, shall be confiscated."[22]

Such a provision was antithetical to what the Congress had originally proposed in December of 1776. The article Franklin, Lee, and Deane advanced in talks with Vergennes set forth instead that France and the United States should amicably join forces to wrest Newfoundland from Great Britain, and when they met with allied success, "the fishery shall be enjoyed equally and in common by the subjects of his most Christian Majesty and these states" and "half the island of Newfoundland shall be owned by and subject to the jurisdiction of his most Christian Majesty; provided . . . the remaining part of Newfoundland be annexed to the territory and government of the United States."[23]

To be sure, the Franco-American treaties of 1778 constituted an exceptional diplomatic achievement for the United States in all regards—except this one. France joined an alliance, opened her ports, and promised not to lay down arms until American independence had been secured. Yet both the text and subtext of the commercial treaty made it worryingly clear that American fishing, landing, and drying rights on the banks and shores of Newfoundland, of preeminent importance to New England, were in jeopardy.

* * * * *

The American ambassadors, of course, made diplomatic overtures not only to the French at the court of Versailles. Soon after Franklin received the Congress's directive for a Spanish-American military and naval alliance, he dispatched its conditions to the Spanish ambassador at court, Don Pedro Pablo Abarca de Bolea y Jiménez de Urrea, 10th Count of Aranda. In a letter to Aranda dated April 7, 1777, Franklin quoted the Congress's commission word-for-word: "That if his Catholic Majesty will join with the United States in a war against Great Britain, they will assist in reducing to the possession of Spain the town and harbor of Pensacola; provided the inhabitants of the United States shall have the free navigation of the Mississippi, and the use of the harbor of Pensacola."[24]

Thus began American diplomacy with the Spanish over the Mississippi navigation, an odyssey that would not fully accomplish the objectives of those states with economic interests in the river until the Jefferson administration negotiated the Louisiana Purchase a quarter century later. At this juncture, unfortunately for the Southern delegates in Congress so hopeful for cooperative Spanish-American trade on the lower river, Franklin's April letter to Aranda had an effect entirely opposite to that intended. Aranda in Paris forwarded the missive to the desk of his immediate superior in Madrid, José Moñino y Redondo, 1st Count of Floridablanca, chief minister of King Charles III, who read it less as an expected invitation to a desirable friendship and alliance than as a troubling broadcast of American expansionist intentions.[25]

The view in Madrid was that if the rebels on the North American seaboard somehow won the war and became an independent nation or nations, Spain's grand task was going to be to exclude them not only from the banks of the Mississippi River but also from the contested British lands lying between the Mississippi River and the Appalachian Mountains. If Spain joined the war against England, that is to say, why should King George's eastern Mississippi Valley not be a fair field of opportunity for Spanish troops and diplomats? After all, the king and the Spanish ministry held great interest in possessing those hundreds of millions of acres both as a buffer to block American westward expansion and as a lucrative agricultural and trade zone.

Soon the French ambassador at the court of Madrid, Comte de Montmorin de Saint Herem, overheard high-level Spaniards discussing the Continental Congress's insistence on the free navigation of the Mississippi. In a private letter to Vergennes, Montmorin crystallized the worldview of King Charles and Floridablanca. "It is only too apparent," the French ambassador reported to Vergennes, "that Spain looks upon the United States as prospective enemies before too long. In consequence, far from suffering them to approach her possessions, she will omit nothing to keep them away, and specifically from the banks of the Mississippi."[26]

Floridablanca, forty-nine years old, was not a minister of state who acted rashly, compromised lightly, or believed at all in colonial rebellions in a monarch's dominions. A hardline Castilian criminal prosecutor, narrowly devoted to his king, he had only recently replaced a liberal predecessor, El Marqués y Duque de Grimaldi, known to be acquiescent to the progressive policies of Enlightenment France. The austere Floridablanca wished to have nothing to do with such French politics, nor with American colonists who were so enlightened, apparently, that they were burning their king in effigy and breaking apart his empire. It was Floridablanca's understanding that Americans were a cantankerous, untamable people. In his court they carried a reputation for acquisitiveness, disregard for authority, and unruly Protestantism. Americans therefore seemed to pose a material risk to the safety of Spanish Louisiana. Floridablanca worried further that their spirit of revolt against monarchical power might spread to residents of Spain's American colonies. If infected by the same wild notions of liberty, equality, and self-rule, might not King Charles's subjects in Louisiana, Mexico, and Peru emulate the armed anarchy of King George's subjects in Massachusetts and Virginia?[27]

The attitudes of Americans, joined together with their uncomfortable proximity to Spanish Louisiana, set Floridablanca's mind to a cogent diplomatic strategy of exploiting both sides of the Anglo-American conflict. To achieve this, for the moment he spearheaded a foreign policy of consistent, carefully orchestrated yet rare aid and encouragement to the Congress as the surest method to weaken both the mother country and the revolting colonies simultaneously. Hardly raising a glass to the

FIGURE 30. José Moñino y Redondo, 1st Count of Floridablanca, Chief Minister of Spain. (Portrait of José Moñino y Redondo, 1st Count of Floridablanca. Francisco de Goya, *José Moñino y Redondo, conde de Floridablanca*, ca. 1783, oil on canvas, 77.1 x 45.8 in, Collection of Museo del Prado, P003255.)

prospect of a stable and independent new American nation, the count wished to see the original thirteen colonies in perpetual conflict with archfoe England—and with one another. As his state papers reveal, Floridablanca's intent was that the American "republic might remain in such division, with independence between the provinces, and their interests so opposed to each other, that prudently there would not, in time, be the danger of a formidable power in the vicinity" of Spanish Louisiana and the Mississippi River.[28]

All this led Floridablanca to take a watch-and-wait diplomatic approach in the early years of the Revolution. After receiving Aranda's letter informing him of the United States's formal request for an alliance, he chose not to answer. Instead he dispatched a covert agent to the seat of Congress to discover the strengths and vulnerabilities of the American states and their combined government. The order from Madrid, sent to Cuba for implementation, commanded the Spanish informant to collect strategic intelligence "about the state of the war, and its progress, of the gains of each party, of their respective forces, of the dispositions of both sides, and whether or not they might follow them, and learning of any prejudicial designs against Spain and its American colonies." Further, the observer of Congress was to accomplish these goals without betraying any formal connection with the Spanish government whatsoever.[29]

The Spanish ministry directed the order for a covert operation at the American capital to the commander of Cuba, Captain General Diego Joseph Navarro y Valladares, in the fall of 1777. For the job, Navarro selected a wealthy, charismatic, sixty-two-year-old Cuban merchant named Juan de Miralles y Trajan, who had long been one of Havana's most active commercial agents with the thirteen colonies. Miralles departed Havana in December aboard the merchant vessel *Nuestra Señora del Carmen*, landing at Charlestown, South Carolina. From there, the undercover Spanish emissary proceeded overland toward York, where, he told anyone who asked, he planned to open a flour export business.[30]

CHAPTER 10

"North Against South"

WHILE FRANKLIN, LEE, AND DEANE were jockeying at the court of Versailles for alliances and loans of money to sustain the war, patriot leaders in the Continental Congress and the thirteen state legislatures struggled to consummate the bond of Union. In the last week of November 1777, the Congress dispatched its circular letter and copies of the Articles of Confederation to the many states, soliciting prompt ratifications. What did not help matters is that some congressmen were already registering countervailing complaints about the Articles in letters back home to their countrymen, some of whom would soon stand in judgment of the "Constitution of the Congress" in ratifying assemblies. One of the earliest expressions of dissatisfaction with the completed Articles, by a delegate who helped to frame them, came in a November 21 letter from New Hampshire's Nathaniel Folsom to a fellow leader of his state, Meshech Weare. Congressman Folsom said that he was displeased with the formulas adopted for determining both the apportionment of continental taxes and the requisitioning of soldiers for the Continental Army. Both methods had roots in grand bargains struck to get the Articles approved, but, Folsom said, he was left with "great uneasiness" about them.[1]

To Folsom's reading of the final form of the Articles of Confederation, there were blatant injustices served upon the Northern states in these two fixed systems of calculating burdens of war. The pitfalls related to the institution of slavery, not on expressed moral grounds but on that of equity and fairness to the white inhabitants of each state. On the first point, Folsom argued that taxation must be based not solely on land value, as Article VIII outlined, but also on other forms of wealth in a state, namely slavery. "It appears to me that one third part of the wealth of the Southern states," Folsom explained, "which consists in negroes, is entirely left out and no notice taken of them, in determining their ability to pay taxes, notwithstanding it is by them that they procure their wealth." Another wrong to the Northern states could be found in Article IX, which set forth that troop quotas were to be calculated on the basis of each state's "number of white inhabitants." This method of assessing war burdens was unjust, Folsom said, because Northern men would be drained off the land and stripped from their businesses, impoverishing towns and families, whereas the enslaved persons of the Southern states would keep the Southern economies humming. "By their negroes being left at home," Folsom protested, "they can till their lands and git bread & riches."[2]

Similarly, some Southern political leaders judged the Articles of Confederation to be an instrument of unfairness and jeopardy to their region. The basis for this claim was the North-South mathematical makeup of the Union. The structure of the constitution, wherein each state possessed equal voting power, pitted the four agricultural, slaveholding Southern states—or five, if Maryland is included—against the eight merchant, seafaring Northern states. The perils of this balance of power did not escape the notice of South Carolinian William Henry Drayton in his state's ratification debates. Surely he took some solace in the nine-state supermajority required for votes on declaring war, making peace, and adopting foreign treaties. But to Drayton, this was hardly adequate protection for the minority coalition of the Southern states—whether in these vital areas of lawmaking or in manifold others the Congress would take up in coming years. Therefore, the South Carolinian called for a revision of the Articles, changing the nine-state supermajority to an eleven-state protective shield.

On the floor of the South Carolina State House in Charlestown, Drayton laid out explicitly his opinion that the great political divide in the newly forming American Union lay between North and South. And, he warned other South Carolinians, the Southern states must take heed and counteract their overwhelming numerical disadvantage in voting:

> When I reflect, that from the nature of the climate, soil and produce of the several states, a northern and southern interest in many particulars naturally and unavoidably rise; I cannot but be displeased with the prospect that the most important transactions in Congress may be done contrary to the united opposition of Virginia, the two Carolinas and Georgia, states possessing more than one half of the whole territory of the confederacy and forming, as I may say, the

body of southern interests . . . the honor, interest, and sovereignty of the south are in effect delivered up to the care of the north. Do we intend to make such a sacrifice?[3]

Thomas Burke, after a six-month hiatus, returned to Congress from North Carolina in early March of 1778 with similar concerns. Eliphalet Dyer of Connecticut, for one, greeted the congressman's reappearance with extraordinary regret, due to Burke's hardline position on state sovereignty and his brusque political style. Dyer dubbed the North Carolinian "The Disturber," saying his renewed presence in Congress during the season of constitution making had occasioned "universal sorrow" among members. At least one of Burke's fellow North Carolina delegates, Cornelius Harnett, actually echoed the sentiment to North Carolina's governor, Richard Caswell. He singled out Burke as the only delegate in Congress who seemed radically opposed to a constitution. "Every member of Congress seems to wish for a confederacy except my good friend Burke," Harnett wrote, "who laughs at it as a chimerical project."[4]

More aptly characterized, Burke's chief argument was that the acute phase of a war was no time for making a constitution or alliance among the thirteen states because it would force the states into recklessly surrendering more power than they would during a time of peace and tranquility. Harnett disagreed passionately, arguing that a constitutional Union must be secured now—as the sine qua non of the Revolution—because without it, peace with Great Britain was going to bring about bloodletting among the states. As he put it to Governor Caswell, "I think that unless the states confederate a door will be left open for continual contention & bloodshed, and that, very soon after we are at peace with Europe. I heartily wish I may be mistaken."[5]

As expected by many, Burke soon raised a storm of protest against the Articles. He had not been present when Congress approved them, and already in North Carolina he had submitted two formal reports to the state assembly urging numerous amendments and other alterations be adopted prior to North Carolina's ratification. In these briefs he went further than Drayton of South Carolina. He called for a single state nullification power, one affirming a state's authority to override any act of Congress that contravened its interests. This was not a power to veto the act for the other states—only an exemption for the state that provided formal "instructions" from its assembly to the Congress asserting the state's superior right to dissent and therefore not abide. "Without something of this kind," Burke explained, "according to the present constitution of Congress, it may be impossible for the delegates to preserve the independence of the state."[6]

Burke, like Drayton, also drew attention to the distinct economic interests of the Northern and Southern states, declaring his opposition to Article VI prohibiting a state from making its own commercial treaties with foreign nations. He disagreed with this restraint on the basis that "each [state] should be at liberty to increase its wealth and strength as much as possible." Additionally, this freedom of commercial powers was of particular "importance to the Staple States," by which he meant the Southern states, those depending upon staple crops for their economic livelihood. The treaty a state signs with a foreign nation, Burke acknowledged, must not be "inconsistent with treaties entered into by the United States," but short of this, the Articles of Confederation must not strip powers and rights of this kind from the "free commercial people" of any state.[7]

In Congress Burke made these same arguments. Additionally, he deplored overt talk by Maryland delegates of their intentions to block the Articles until the states with chartered claims to the trans-Appalachian lands, like North Carolina, surrendered them into the Union's treasury. Maryland's grievance was hardly an idle one. Delegates primarily from those Middle states with no claims to western lands held in contempt the Articles' omission of a concrete provision empowering the Congress to declare the unsettled lands, which they believed belonged to the British crown, to be the "common stock" of the Union. Many were demanding a reinstatement of this constitutional power—present in the Dickinson version but expunged in this one—and Maryland was the bellwether of the opposition. As plainly expressed in a directive of its assembly to its delegates in Congress, the state of Maryland was "justly entitled to a right in common with the other members of the union, to that extensive tract of country which lies to the westward of the frontiers of the United States."[8]

* * * * *

In its circular letter of November, the Congress had set March 10, 1778, as the target date for the states to submit their ratifications of the Articles, permitting the central body to proclaim the consolidation of the confederated Union to the world shortly thereafter. On that March day, however, only Virginia had complied with the request unconditionally. Other states clogged their ratifications with amendments and other qualifications, most giving their delegates discretion to ratify after debate on whatever terms they deemed exigent to the Union. South Carolina offered twenty-one such nonbinding amendments to the Articles, most designed to augment the power of the states and limit that of Congress. Other state assemblies made ratification contingent on adoption of their amendments. This was the case with Maryland, whose delegates regretted to inform Congress that they were disabled from ratifying unless language was added to the constitution restoring the Union's power to "ascertain and restrict the boundaries of such of the confederated states which claim to extend to the river Mississippi or South Sea."[9]

Not until June 22 did the Congress formally hear amendments to the Articles of Confederation. That same day the delegates voted to reject them all, tabling them for consideration as formal amendments to be proposed after ratification, according to the amendment process outlined in Article XIII. The reasons given for this determination ranged from the logistical to the apocalyptic. If a single change were made to the Articles, the Congress must submit it to all thirteen assemblies for their approval, and by that date in June a half dozen states had already ratified without mandatory conditions. Some argued that not ratifying the Articles as is would forever vanquish the hope for a permanent Union. As Henry Laurens of South Carolina, president of Congress, put it, "Were the various amendments to be fully discussed and alterations made I should not live to see ratification." Other congressmen predicted that a new round of debates aimed at redrafting the Articles—to be submitted yet again to exasperated state assemblies—would precipitate the abandonment of a single American confederacy altogether in favor of "partial confederacies," a grim prospect fraught with "many dangers and evils."[10]

Many delegates privately established a new deadline of July 4, 1778, the second anniversary of the Declaration of Independence, for unanimous ratification. But still on that day, with Congress now back in Philadelphia, five states lacked unconditional powers of ratification. Nevertheless, the congressmen gathered at City Tavern for an anniversary dinner replete with orchestral music, a display of the Declaration of Independence, a crimson flag, and thirteen formal toasts, each coordinated with an outdoor discharge of pistols. After the thirteenth toast, "May the Union of the American states be perpetual," the evening concluded with "a brilliant exhibition of fireworks."[11]

Up against a wall of state delegations proscribed by their assemblies from ratifying the Articles without adoption of amendments first, Congress advanced a plan of partial ratification accompanied by the dispatch of another circular letter imploring the recalcitrant states to submit their stamps of approval. On Thursday, July 9, an engrossed copy of the Articles of Confederation was laid before the Congress and, taking turns, the delegates from eight states—New Hampshire, Massachusetts, Rhode Island, Connecticut, New York, Pennsylvania, Virginia, and South Carolina—signed the compact, formally ratifying on behalf of their constituents. Ratifications from North Carolina and Georgia were expected soon, but without formal papers in hand, their delegates could not yet sign. Congressmen from three Middle states, Maryland, Delaware, and New Jersey, were under injunctions not to ratify without formal incorporation of amendments—most vitally, the thorny one investing the Congress with sovereignty over the western lands. The next day, July 10, delegates approved a letter to the refractory assemblies requesting that "their delegates may be instructed to ratify the confederation with all convenient dispatch; trusting to future deliberation to make such alterations and amendments as experience may shew to be expedient and just." The assemblies were asked to "conclude the glorious compact, which, by uniting the wealth, strength, and councils, of the whole, may bid defiance to external violence and internal dissentions, whilst it secures the public credit both at home and abroad."[12]

Most delegates expected a sanguine outcome from the strategic steps Congress took that July to achieve the goal of unanimous ratification. It had ruled against any and all amendments without discrimination, and it put the wayward states under pressure through its official, ceremonial ratification by eight states on July 9 and its letter. James Lovell and Sam Adams of Massachusetts rightly singled out Maryland as the ringleader of the opposition, assuring themselves that her assembly must inevitably fall in line as soon as New Jersey and Delaware did. "I believe there will [be] no difficulty except with Maryland," Sam Adams wrote, "& she will finally accede."[13]

Other delegates worried that the partial ratification that took place on July 9 portended trouble. It was a strange thing that eight states had ratified a constitution that did not set out a procedure or timetable for its execution and operation. Were the eight states now bound by the Articles of Confederation perpetually—and the other five not? Or were none bound until all thirteen ratified? By agreed-upon policy, the latter was the case. But still New Jersey delegate Nathaniel Scudder had a bad feeling, writing on July 13 to John Hart of his state, a signatory of the Declaration of Independence, to inform him about "an affair to me of the most serious

Chapter 10: "North Against South"

and alarming importance." His concern was that the disarray of a partial confederation of the states would distress the Unites States's new treaty with France and serve as a target of exploitation by the British. Only days earlier, the first French ambassador to the United States, Conrad Alexandre Gérard, had made landing on the American shore. Scudder felt like the glorious compact promised to France was in fact a fraud the ambassador would soon see through:

> These states have actually entered into a treaty with the Court of Versailles as a confederated people, and Monsieur Girard [sic], their ambassador plenipotentiary to Congress, is now on our coast with a powerful fleet of ships. . . . He probably may be landed by this time, and will at all events be in Philadelphia in a few days. How must he be astonished & confounded and what may be the fatal consequences to America, when he discovers (which he will immediately do) that we are ipso facto unconfederated, and consequently, what our enemies have called us, "a Rope of Sand"? Will he not have just cause to resent the deception and may not insidious Britain, knowing the same, take advantage of our disunion?[14]

* * * * *

When Ambassador Gérard arrived in Philadelphia, undercover Spanish agent Juan de Miralles y Trajan had already taken up residence in the city only a few blocks from the Pennsylvania State House. The two envoys had never met. But soon they held a private conference, and thereafter Miralles lobbied Gérard regularly to do Spain's bidding with Congress on the basis that France and Spain were Bourbon blood brothers and King Charles III would never accede to a triple Franco-American-Spanish alliance until Congress first made certain concessions. Some historians have argued that in 1778 and 1779 Ambassador Gérard was the second most powerful personage on American soil, only surpassed by George Washington. Given the ambassador's rank and the lifesaving nature of the French-American alliance, there is truth in this contention. But Gérard was also one of the most unfortunate public servants in America because France had saddled him with impossible, self-contradicting tasks, including the burden of advocating for Spain in the Mississippi Valley.

According to his instructions from Chief Minister Vergennes, the ambassador's highest charge was to shield the Franco-American alliance from any breach that might throw the thirteen colonies, or any divided parts of them, back into connection with George III. Almost as vital, Gérard must maneuver the Continental Congress into postures and policies acceptable to Spain so that Floridablanca and Charles III would declare war against Great Britain as well, joining a triple alliance. As much as members of Congress, Vergennes yearned for a Spanish entry into the war to seal the fate of Britain. More than did the Americans, he feared that the French fleet alone against the guns of the Royal Navy might suffer defeat.

"There is a point of great moment to the king [Louis XVI]," Vergennes delineated in his written instructions, "which will require all the skill of the Sieur Gérard: it concerns the measures to be arranged on behalf of Spain." To effect the triple alliance, Gérard's job was to delicately steer the Congress away from the Floridas, Jamaica, and the Newfoundland fisheries as objects of war or peace, as these were targets of interest to Charles III. Vergennes did not yet mention the western lands and the navigation of the Mississippi River in Gérard's directive, but, adding to the French ambassador's tragic bind, Miralles was soon going to highlight these objects as sine qua non of a Spanish treaty.[15]

FIGURE 31. Conrad Alexandre Gérard de Rayneval, French Ambassador. (Portrait of Conrad Alexandre Gérard. Charles Willson Peale, *Conrad Alexandre Gérard*, 1779, oil on canvas, Collection of Independence National Historical Park, Philadelphia.)

Chapter 10: "North Against South" 193

If these circumstances were not enough to vex the ambassador's mission, Vergennes also formally assigned his diplomat the responsibility of preventing a breakup of the American Union. In his fortieth year of service to the French crown, the first minister of Louis XVI foresaw that disunion between the states would be the undoing of the Franco-American alliance. Gérard therefore must do nothing whatsoever to disrupt "the union and the perfect accord which have so far prevailed among the thirteen confederated states." He said that England's dream was "to sow division among the states." The same disunion was France's nightmare, and Gérard, as ambassador on the ground, was accountable for managing this hazard adroitly.[16]

Over the coming year, the outcome of Gérard's mission, inextricably entwined as it was with the fragility of the American Union and the conflicting war ambitions of New England, the Southern states, and the Middle states, would drive the Congress to political crisis—and Gérard to a nervous breakdown. By opposing New England's claim to the Newfoundland fisheries and the Southern states' claims to the western lands and the Mississippi navigation, Ambassador Gérard would precipitate an aggravated sectional fight that lasted seven long months. As one historian of the Continental Congress, Edmund Cody Burnett, explains it, "On these two questions Congress divided for the most part along geographical lines, the New Englanders standing stoutly for the fisheries, the Southerners for the navigation of the Mississippi, while the intervening states cast their votes partly with one side, partly with the other." Burnett continues, testifying that the struggle over the Newfoundland fisheries "was one of the most protracted, as it was probably the most hotly contested parliamentary battle ever waited in Congress. Without question no other contest stirred so violently the great deeps of Congressional bile."[17]

The Mississippi-fisheries fight was to be the most painful upheaval experienced by the American Union in its five-year history. So debilitating was the crisis for Gérard that he eventually fell ill in what, by all appearances, was nervous exhaustion. Complaining of fevers, sweats, bilious colic, jaundice, kidney pains, extreme weakness, and heat flashes, the seemingly vigorous, tenacious first French minister to the United States, who before Philadelphia had never traveled farther from home than Vienna, would repeatedly solicit a replacement to fill his post and permission to return to France. His regular correspondence increasingly took on a tone of resignation and despair. In the end Vergennes would take pity on him and grant the request.

* * * * *

Gérard's troubles began in the last week of July 1778 when he and Miralles sat down for their first official diplomatic conference. As the French ambassador promptly reported back to Vergennes, he was distressed by what he heard from the Spanish "agent sécret." Not even to Gérard did Miralles overtly divulge his identity as an informer for the Madrid court. Nevertheless, the Frenchman assumed as much early on, a fact later confirmed by Versailles, and during his tenure in Philadelphia he treated the Spaniard as the official-yet-undeclared mouthpiece of Floridablanca and King Charles III.[18]

Whereas France had entered the war to wound Britain and capture the rich commerce of her now self-emancipating states, Miralles represented Spain to Gérard as intent upon core objectives of protecting and enlarging Spanish holdings and, pointedly, depriving the United States of the trans-Appalachian western lands and any and all use of the Mississippi River. During a tense, uncomfortable dialogue, he insisted that by war's end France should be in possession of Canada to the north of the new nation and "Spain everything which the English had acquired by the treaty of 1763 in Florida and on the Mississippi," meaning the eastern half of the Mississippi Valley. This included "the exclusive navigation of the Mississippi." When Gérard expressed his chagrin and puzzlement at the lack of liberality of the Spanish position on the Mississippi Valley and its great river, Miralles explained that the French must understand one essential point: "The Americans will soon be the enemies of Spain."[19]

As he informed Vergennes, Gérard refuted Miralles's assertions with an intensity equal to the Spaniard's. He explained that the described fears of the United States becoming a potent enemy of Spain were unfounded. A dominant opinion in France was that by nature republics were ineffective and inward-looking. Vergennes, in his efforts to usher Spain into war, counteracted Spanish fears of American aggression with promises that the United States was more likely to fall prey to internal discord than external quarrels with neighbors. The nation, he predicted, would "remain quiet with the inertia that is characteristic of all constitutional democracies."[20]

Gérard, in his meeting with Miralles, deployed the same arguments, expressing his gravest concerns about the position Spain was espousing on the Mississippi River. By this time Gérard was already particularly aware of the attitudes of Virginians and North Carolinians regarding their Kentucky and Tennessee districts and the rivers that served them.

To Miralles, he stated flatly and unequivocally that he could not advocate such an extreme stance on the Mississippi. Rather, he enjoined the Spanish agent to inform the court of Madrid that an official policy of excluding the Americans from the navigation would precipitate just what Spain apprehended: hostility. "The Congress would never," Gérard pressed, "willingly consent to give up the navigation of the Mississippi, so necessary as it is as an outlet for the huge settlements the Americans are planning on the Ohio and its tributaries." In momentary deference to Miralles's surmise that Spain and America might become rivals one day, Gérard submitted nonetheless that shutting the Mississippi was fraught with perils in the present. Even if the future might hypothetically see the United States and Spain turn against one another, Gérard admonished, "It would be wise at least to prevent them from becoming so immediately."[21]

* * * * *

In his first several months of service to the French crown in Philadelphia, Gérard's intention was to convert Miralles to a middle position on the trans-Appalachian western lands and the navigation of the Mississippi. He might well have held to this position if not for the unexpected discoveries he made in private conversations with American delegates who seemed, shockingly to the minister, to agree with Miralles. As it happened, by the end of the year it was Gérard who was converted to Miralles's view, not the other way around. Gérard's reorientation on these western concerns of the United States began most forcibly in October when delegate Gouverneur Morris of New York paid him a visit at the new French legation on Chestnut Street. Morris came on official business. The Congress had appointed him chairman of a committee charged with drafting instructions for its newly appointed sole minister to France, Benjamin Franklin. Morris's specific purpose in Gérard's parlor was to inform the Frenchman about the general contents of Franklin's mission. But it is what Morris had to say unofficially—about the West, Mississippi navigation, Canada, Nova Scotia, and the Newfoundland fisheries—that sparked a geopolitical awakening in Gérard. Most striking to him, a preeminent statesmen of the new American republic wished to see the Mississippi closed to the commerce of his fellow statesmen from the South.

Morris began the conference with Gérard with a sincere expression of gratitude for the recent arrival upon her shores of the Count d'Estaing's fleet and the distinguished ambassador himself. From there he entered into a point-by-point description of the new diplomatic instructions

Congress had drafted for dispatch to Franklin, which centered upon an energetically urged plan of attack on Canada to be undertaken by combined American land troops and the French navy. Franklin's instructions were to move with haste to obtain an agreement from Vergennes and Louis XVI to turn their naval might upon Canada, with gaining control and sovereignty over the prized northern fisheries on the coast of Newfoundland included. As specified in the directive to Franklin, the United States' unmistakable intention was to divide Canada into two new American states. And as everyone knew, they would become, for all intents and purposes, Northern in character, economy, and culture.[22]

Morris, sensible that the United States could not with honor ask France to dedicate its navy to this territorial and commercial expansion of the United States with no advantage to itself, came prepared to Gérard's home with justifying arguments and an offer of rewards for King Louis XVI. With Canada, especially Nova Scotia, in British hands, Morris argued, "France would have no hope of acquiring a large part of the Newfoundland fishery," which the New Yorker portrayed as one of the singular treasures of all North America. On the other hand, if Canada and Newfoundland became American, he pressed, the United States and France would freely share the fisheries. In addition to this gain, the French would also obtain access to the lucrative Canadian fur trade, and, after the conquest of Canada, with numerous ships of the line and frigates floating at the ready, the French would be fully equipped and poised for an attack upon the British West Indies. France, of course, not the United States, would become sole master of any such islands conquered in that hemisphere.[23]

After this, the conversation turned to Spain and the Mississippi Valley. And as Gérard put it in a dispatch to Vergennes, what he heard fall from the mouth of Morris was so important that it must "be transmitted in its entirety." Echoing Miralles, the French ambassador expressed his concern that the Mississippi Valley was a tinderbox that might bring Spain and the United States into conflict. Worse, as they both knew, no objective was more critical for France and the United States at the present juncture of the war than bringing Spain into a triple alliance—and in particular, discord over the lower Mississippi Valley might well foil that grand ambition. "Forgoing St. Augustine and Pensacola, Mobile, and even the navigation of the Mississippi," Gérard tempted Morris, "would perhaps alone accomplish such a mutually important objective and firmly establish the trust and friendship of Spain."

Chapter 10: "North Against South"   197

FIGURE 32. Gouverneur Morris, New York Delegate. (Portrait of Gouverneur Morris. J. Rodgers, *Gouverneur Morris, Member of the Federal Convention of 1787*, date unknown, print.)

What stunned Gérard was that Morris swiftly agreed, stating that the American republic would gain great advantage by acquiring Canada and only debilitate itself by expanding toward the Southwest. As he detailed in his correspondence to Vergennes:

> Mr. Morris confessed that in several respects Spain's anxieties might be well-founded . . . that he would nonetheless confide to me that he was of the same view as several of his most enlightened colleagues, who were struck by the need to establish a law of *coercendo imperio* [constraining the size of the empire] [and] that the current provinces of the South were already weakening the confederation; that to expand further in this direction would be to increase the disadvantage beyond measure; that it [the South] was the seat of wealth and weakness; that the austerity and vigor of the North would always be the Republic's safeguard; and that it was in this direction that they ought to expand and consolidate.

Morris was well-read, and in this case it seems he had digested Roman historian Tacitus's *Annals*, in which Emperor Tiberius at the turn of the first millennium calls for a public reading of a decree "advising the restriction of the empire within its present frontiers." In applying this principle of *coercendo imperio* to the United States, Morris also told Gérard that the Mississippi navigation should be closed to Americans in order to solidify the nation's population east and northeast and accordingly strengthen the republic. "He confided to me, moreover," Gérard penned, "that the same persons believed it was in the confederation's interest that navigation rights to the Mississippi from the mouth of the Ohio down belong exclusively to Spain, because it was the only way to keep the large population that would take shape between the Ohio, the lakes and the current settlements in Virginia in subordination to the American Republic."[24]

These were surprising, revelatory words for Gérard. Once Morris's meaning was fully clarified, the ambassador expressed his surprise at the notion of a closed Mississippi, asserting that he knew many men in Congress who "stubbornly believed" an open commerce on the Mississippi to be a nonnegotiable item of American foreign policy. Morris acknowledged this fact yet reiterated that the wisest delegates comprehended "the disadvantages of expanding to the South" and that "the majority of those who insisted on navigation rights to the Mississippi were guided by considerable interests in the new settlements," meaning land speculation and other monetary motivations. The conversation concluded with an expression of optimism by Morris that "there was every reason to hope for satisfactory results should these matters be presented to Congress in their true light."

* * * * *

Meanwhile, during these same fall and winter months, the Congress waited on New Jersey, Delaware, and Maryland to ratify the Articles of Confederation. In mid-July the delegates had sent a letter to those states that had not yet approved the charter, calling forth their patriotism with the promise that "future deliberation" would rectify defects and injustices through an amendment process. However, many of the leaders of these three states were not necessarily in a trusting mood. As Governor William Livingston of New Jersey expressed in a letter to Henry Laurens, president of Congress, he would submit the letter to the state legislature, as requested, but he himself was opposed to ratification. The reason was the western lands—plus common sense about politics and human nature. Not hiding his motivations, Livingston told Laurens, "I sincerely hope that this state will never ratify it, till Congress is explicit in doing us that justice respecting the common lands, which I think no man of common sense, or the least acquainted with human nature would trust to the future deliberations of any body of men (I speak it with the highest respect for that assembly which I verily believe to be the most illustrious upon earth)."[25]

In spite of this initial reluctance of the governor, the New Jersey legislature voted in favor of ratification in the third week of November, allowing its delegates in Congress to affix their signatures to the Articles on the 26th. After this, for some delegates, hope soared. "It's daily expected," Elbridge Gerry wrote when the good news about New Jersey came in, "Maryland & Delaware will follow the example." Other delegates were less sanguine, anticipating lasting obstructionism from these small states. "I wish I could say they were confederated," Congressman William Whipple of New Hampshire wrote with more than a touch of bitterness, "but our froward sister M[aryland] & her little crooked neighbour [Delaware] still stand out." Of the two, Maryland was always denounced as the chief instigator of resistance. Said Francis Lightfoot Lee of Virginia, prospects for a confederation of the thirteen were not bright in mid-December. "Maryland still refuses to confederate," he wrote, "& is going to publish a declaration of their rights & grievances, in a very high & violent tone, it is said."[26]

Lee was not wrong. On December 15 the House of Delegates and Senate of Maryland issued two stinging resolutions, one a set of "Instructions" to its six delegates in Congress, and the other "A Declaration" of its land rights. In these resolves, Maryland's state representatives declaimed against the "avarice and ambition" of the states claiming sole ownership of the West, squarely placing the blame for the United States' "appearance of disunion" not upon Maryland and Delaware but upon the shoulders of states like Virginia, which were grossly violating "Principles of Justice and Equity." The Articles of Confederation, they continued, as currently written, were "incompatible" with these principles as well as the honor, interests, and self-preservation of Maryland. It was not only a question of fairness—that is, what peoples would benefit monetarily from the sales and rents derived from those fertile lands. Confederating under the terms then being required by the landed states, far from an invitation to harmony, was a recipe for ruin, including the probable depopulation of the small states and the growth of the large ones to such "a superiority of wealth and strength" that they would oppress by "open force," if necessary, their "less powerful neighbours" in order to establish hegemony over continental affairs.[27]

Another possible outcome of a state like Virginia retaining such a vast domain was its rapid growth into a nation unto itself. With the Virginia claim large enough to constitute a sizable separate confederacy, its leaders might well break apart its territory into many satellite states, which would be "bound by some alliance, or confederacy" to Virginia as the master state. "Why is the claim to that territory now made and so pertinaciously insisted on?" the Maryland representatives asked, referring to Virginia. Answering, they said, "We can suggest to ourselves but two motives"—both rooted in "the designs of a secret ambition." Either Virginia was altogether deceiving the other states with her promises to relinquish "at some future period a portion of the country," or she planned on quick sales of the land "to reap an immediate profit," leaving little left over to relinquish. Either way, said Marylanders, "We have cooly and dispassionately considered the subject," determining that their state would not ratify the American charter until an article or articles first were added establishing equal jurisdiction and benefit to all the states in the Union from the treasure of the vast western lands.

Three weeks later Delaware delegate Thomas McKean wrote a private letter shedding further light on the dynamics of the Union-for-land demands of the two small states in Philadelphia. By this time the Virginia Assembly had issued a formal proposal to Congress to complete ratification with eleven states only, rather than continue to wait as Maryland and Delaware held the constitutional Union hostage. Virginia had also passed a law allotting bounties of land in its trans-Appalachian West to veterans of the Continental Army. Still, Maryland and Delaware were holding out for an amendment transferring the bulk of the western lands into the Congress's treasury, and McKean felt compelled in the letter to alert Thomas Collins, member of the Delaware Assembly, that pressures and dangers were mounting in Philadelphia that should persuade his home assembly to reverse its position and ratify.

"Many evils are foreboded from the Confederation not being ratified," McKean warned. He then outlined five specific perils of further delay. First, "it holds up a prospect to Great Britain of creating disunion and drawing off some of the states." By this, he meant that Britain would soon identify the disaffected states and, through stealth negotiations, offer them favorable terms to return to the empire, then enlist them against the rebel states. Second, if not this, American disunion would give the British command hope, invigorating them to fight on rather than come to the peace tables. Third, the failure of the American confederation, once widely known abroad, would deter nations from signing alliances with the United States and offering them subsides and credit. Fourth, it created a bona fide justification for France to break its alliance with the United States and conclude a separate peace with Great Britain. Why? Because France could claim, not incorrectly, that "she had been deceived in the treaty; that we had called these states the United States of America, when in reality they had not confederated, nor would confederate."[28]

FIGURE 33. Thomas McKean, Pennsylvania Delegate. (Portrait of Thomas McKean. Charles Willson Peale, *Thomas McKean*, after 1787, oil on canvas, 27.5 x 22 in, National Portrait Gallery, Smithsonian Institution; transfer from the Smithsonian American Art Museum; gift of the collection of George Buchanan Coale, 1926, NPG.66.63.)

Fifth, and most worrisome of all for Delaware, McKean confessed, was a reluctant decision made by the eleven confederated states to conquer Maryland and Delaware instead of sitting by and watching those two small states sabotage the Union and the War of Independence. As McKean's words make clear, this was not an idle rumor he heard mentioned offhandedly once or twice. It was the thing he feared most in January of 1779. It was the chief reason he urged Collins to get to work immediately in Delaware to push through ratification. Further delay, he told his friend, was "a temptation to the confederated states to commence a war against the others, upon some pretence or other (and such pretences are never wanting) and when conquered to annex them to some other, or sell them for the purpose of discharging public debts &c." He continued:

> Upon the whole I am clearly of opinion that it is for the interest of the United States in general, and of Delaware in particular, from its situation, that the confederation should be ratified by us, and should therefore give my voice most cheerfully for the measure. I hope we shall not be the last in coming into it, lest that should be interpreted disaffection . . . and lest it should be assigned as a reason hereafter for not admitting us into the Union, but for subduing us by force.

* * * * *

It did not help matters during that fall and winter, shortly before Ambassador Gérard made a catalyzing announcement to Congress, that trade and economic issues had lately reanimated Southern distrust of centralized power to the point that at least one Southern delegate was menacing walkout and defection from the Union. The trouble began during the summer when, in the view of many Southerners, the Congress grossly overstepped in adopting a continental embargo prohibiting the states from exporting foodstuffs it deemed vitally necessary to feed the army. The list of banned exports included wheat, flour, rye, Indian corn, rice, bread, beef, pork, bacon, and livestock.[29]

John Mathews, thirty-four-year-old South Carolinian lawyer from Charlestown, wrote a letter to Thomas Bee, soon to be appointed lieutenant governor of South Carolina, alerting him that no act of Congress in its short history was so treacherous as this one. The embargo had been rushed through Congress "by artful men," he said, in advance of the ratification of the Articles of Confederation precisely because it was patently unconstitutional by the letter and law of that charter. He deplored the embargo both because it represented a slippery slope in Congress toward a precedent of "unlimited powers" and because it was unjust to the Southern states. In this instance, the burden of sacrifice required by the embargo would fall heavily on those states and, he said, Pennsylvania. New England, New York, and New Jersey would be untouched because they did not run surpluses of the commodities in question.[30]

Mathews also expressed his displeasure at Congress's possession of other powers over finance, such as the making of money and obtaining loans. "For God's sake," he wrote to Bee, "let's stop where we are, & take a breath a little. Let anyone attentively examine, what the powers of Congress are, when they have done this, I cannot persuade myself they will be for giving more, in my poor opinion they are already enormous. That single one of borrowing & making what money they please, & I may truly say without controul, is sufficient for, & I am afraid in the end will, be our destruction."

Congressman Titus Hosmer of Connecticut also reacted to the divisions and distrusts in Independence Hall with fear and "the most melancholy presages" about the future. He lamented to inform the governor of his state that "the opposition between the states and the old prejudices of North against South; and South against North seem to be reviving; and are industriously heightened by some who I fear would be but too well pleased to see our union blasted and our independence broken and destroyed." In this assertion Hosmer was underscoring the economic issues splitting North and South. However, he also found pique in the stubbornness of the Southern delegates on administrative matters, like when to convene Congress. There was much to be accomplished in a deliberative body beset by so many committees and long speeches, and Northern delegates had long since proposed two sessions per day, adding an afternoon gathering to the morning meeting, which typically lasted from nine until two. "The Southern States," though, Hosmer reported, "are fixed against holding Congress more than once a day."[31]

Some congressmen, Hosmer said, seemed willing to "see our union blasted." Who were they? The Connecticut delegate did not indicate, but one Southerner in Congress at the time seems especially to qualify. It was Cyrus Griffin of Virginia. In October Griffin sent Thomas Jefferson an anxiety-ridden letter in which he professed, "It appears to me that Congress will shortly be dissolved." Griffin worried about the bankruptcy of Congress, the worthlessness of American currency, and the sagging fortunes of the Continental Army. Most of all, he shared confidentially, he feared the undoing of the Union by North/South political division. So intolerable were the current injustices to the Southern states, he went on, that he felt that honor might require him, in good faith, to forsake the Congress, taking his leave:

> Great questions are carried every day in favor of the Eastward and to the prejudice of the Southern States. Great questions are now upon the carpet [extending the embargo] and if determined in the affirmative will do excessive damage to Virginia and Maryland

particularly. At present we are under secrecy—perhaps in a little time I shall think myself obligated to quit Congress; I will not sit in a house whose proceedings I cannot assent to with honor, nor is it in my abilities to oppose them with success.[32]

* * * * *

Against this backdrop of an unfederated Union, seeming at times to tilt into North/South disunion, Ambassador Gérard of France wrote a short note on February 8, 1779, to the new president of Congress, John Jay of New York. In it he asked permission to address the assembled delegates in person on "subjects of the highest importance." The next day the Frenchman penned a more detailed memorial to the Congress, announcing exciting happenings across the Atlantic. King Charles III of Spain was throwing down the gauntlet. In order to put an end to the assaults of the British empire on France and America, the Spanish king had decided upon "a decisive and peremptory proceeding." It was a final and absolute offer of mediation to end the war based on independence for the former thirteen colonies. Furthermore, representing more good news still to Americans, if Britain refused the mediation, Charles III would forthwith honor his Family Compact with France and declare war on the British crown. "The place of negotiation is fixed at Madrid," Gérard advised, so the Congress should "furnish immediately" their minimum peace terms and appoint an American minister to represent their interests.[33]

However, the urgent memorial of February 9 had more to say than this. Following his brief description of auspicious tidings, the French minister pressed the Congress neither to delay nor overreach in their demands for peace and independence. Temporizing, he said, would in all probability subvert the mediation and suffer ill effects to the Franco-American alliance. After this, Gérard established two fundamental principles for the Americans to incorporate into their determination of minimum peace terms. First, French King Louis XVI had a limited view of "the object of the revolution"—that is, it was independence for the original thirteen colonies only. And to meet with success, the Congress must consider each term of its instructions "in relation to Spain." Vis-à-vis His Catholic Majesty Charles III, the Congress must take care not to provoke "discontents" in the mediator. This last consideration, to avoid offense to Spain at all costs, was so important that it "ought to be one of the subjects of the positive and definite instructions which the States will give for the conclusion of the peace."[34]

Gérard himself understood only half of what was going on in European negotiations. Days earlier he had opened a letter from Vergennes announcing the Spanish mediation, but what the French foreign minister at Versailles did not reveal was the maneuver's secondary motives. Spain was by no means acting magnanimously on behalf of the United States. On the contrary, the proposed third-party intervention was a calculated move to benefit Spain in numerous ways. In reality, neither Vergennes nor Floridablanca anticipated significant gain from a mediation, even if accepted by England, because, as everyone knew, George III remained angrily opposed to parting with his American colonies. Also, Spain planned to set as the price of its peaceful intercession the restoration to Charles III of Gibraltar and perhaps Minorca and/or the Floridas.[35]

All this doomed the mediation. Nevertheless, advancing it urgently with both Britain and the United States was a prudent move to make on the complex chessboard of diplomacy, one Vergennes and Floridablanca hoped would drive the territorial and water ambitions of both nations to the surface and, with any luck, abridge and reconcile them. The two Bourbons agreed to propose an earnest mediation and then watch carefully what the Americans and British clamored for. Privately, Floridablanca was maneuvering to transform the failed peace talks into a pretext to enter the war—as an ally of France, not the United States. In the months gained by the mediation, Spain would prepare its navy to sail squadrons to the Mediterranean to seize Gibraltar and to the Gulf of Mexico to seize the Floridas, not to the American coastline where George Washington's army desperately needed naval assistance to recover New York and Rhode Island.

At work, too, in the launch of the mediation were critically strained relations between France and Spain. The plan to intercede was a concession from Louis XVI to Charles III as a measure to appease the upset of the latter at France's precipitous alliance with the thirteen colonies after Saratoga, undertaken against Spanish protest and arguably in violation of the Bourbon Family Compact. The Spanish king and Floridablanca were particularly aggrieved by France's agreement in the Franco-American alliance not to lay down arms until the full political and economic independence of the United States had been achieved. Spain did not wish for a successful independence of the former colonies. Its goals in the war were instead to run a spear through the British empire, debilitate it, and recover lost territory and commerce. Months earlier Vergennes had barely managed to convince Floridablanca to make independence a condition of the anticipated mediation effort. The Spanish minister preferred a partial independence, exclusively for those American states not then occupied and controlled by British troops. He had urged that New York and Rhode Island be left in British hands and, according to French ambassador Montmorin in Madrid, went so far as to admit that his court desired to draw a map of North America that left the new American states in a manner of disarray similar to that then existing in Germany.[36]

Vergennes and Floridablanca also did not see eye to eye on the navigation of the Mississippi River. Since a Philadelphia letter was at a minimum distance of at least six to eight weeks by ship and coach to Versailles, often much more, Vergennes had not yet received the intelligence from Gérard on the conviction of Morris and other "enlightened colleagues" that the river should be closed to the United States. He did, however, have on his desk Gérard's midsummer report on Miralles's insistence on the exclusive Mississippi navigation for Spain, a claim that struck him as "amazing." Like Gérard, the French chief of foreign affairs felt that "the liberty of the navigation of the Mississippi" could not in fairness be denied to the Americans if they owned land on the river. Even so, Vergennes knew that the French court had already offended Charles III with its unapproved alliance with the United States and that the French treasury and navy could only hold out for so long alone against Britain. He wanted Spain in the war and frankly did not know what to do about the Mississippi. Spain did, after all, possess both banks at the mouth of the river. Therefore, there was some legal precedence to the Spanish logic that no power on earth required King Charles to grant foreign subjects a riverine commercial easement through His Majesty's undisputed property.[37]

* * * * *

Vergennes said nothing about Spain's hidden motives behind the mediation in his letter to Gérard, but he did provide explicit instructions on the Newfoundland fisheries, Canada, and the Mississippi navigation. His message on the first two was unambiguous. The United States should be content with the large territory and commercial riches it already possessed. There was the real risk that inscribing these northern claims as obligatory American terms of peace—possession of Canada and fishing and drying rights at Newfoundland—would provoke umbrage in both England and Spain, scuttling the mediation before it ever began. Regarding the Mississippi, Vergennes offered no official position of the French ministry whatsoever. His only guidance to Gérard was that he must explore the

Chapter 10: "North Against South" 207

matter thoroughly and, once convinced of the proper course, advance it deftly, irrespective of the grief it might elicit in either Miralles or the American Congress.

Vergennes was clear-cut on this mandate to Gérard. He instructed his representative in Philadelphia to gauge "local considerations" about the Mississippi and to let them make up his mind. If those circumstances strongly supported the Spanish claim, "You must prepare the Americans with skill and dexterity" to agree to the relinquishment. If Gérard concluded Spain must relent, on the other hand, he should instead attend delicately to Miralles, persuading him not to inflame the situation either in Philadelphia, Cuba, or Madrid by protesting the outcome. In this case, Vergennes wrote, "You must encourage the Spanish agent not only to avoid giving alarms to his Court about this object but to present the state of affairs in such a manner that the Court will not find difficulty in consenting to a shared navigation."[38]

By the time Vergennes's directive on the Spanish mediation arrived in Philadelphia in early February, six months of the ambassador's residency in the United States had passed. He had already long been hard at work in the exploration of the "local considerations" touching on the Mississippi navigation. What he had discovered in numerous gatherings and dinners at the French legation and Miralles's house nearby was that Morris's promise that other enlightened members of Congress shared his views on the West was correct. Congress's new president, John Jay of New York, was one of them.

As was customary for the president of Congress, Jay called on Gérard frequently at the legation. In one private conversation, recorded by Gérard as a "very long interview," Jay revealed the presence in Congress of three lines of division on the Mississippi navigation. The largest number of delegates would renounce it entirely. The middle group wanted to find a reasonable compromise with Spain, and the last group, in the minority, "believes that the navigation of the Mississippi is absolutely indispensable." The two last groups in Congress were said to take land-speculating interests in settlements on the eastern bank of the Mississippi from the Ohio and Illinois rivers southward to Natchez in West Florida. As Jay explained further, Gérard recounted, many delegates intended to carve out new states from those swaths of land. Gérard was heartened to say, however, that the president himself agreed with the principle that "there should never be more than 13 states united, unless Canada formed the fourteenth."[39]

CHAPTER 11

The Mississippi and Fisheries Again

On Monday, February 8, 1779, Ambassador Gérard requested an in-person audience with the delegates of Congress. President John Jay responded promptly, and one week later, on February 15, the ambassador delivered a speech to the delegates in Independence Hall in which he announced the news of Spain's intended mediation to end the war and secure American independence and peace for all. He spoke for an hour and fifteen minutes and afterward remained in the hall an extra forty-five minutes for questions and conversation. What Gérard had to say that day not only set into motion a grueling seven-month contest over the role of the Newfoundland fisheries and the navigation of the Mississippi River in a free, just, and equal American independence. The French call for a formal written declaration of the United States' terms for peace also forced delegates to take sides, further solidifying their regional political identities.[1]

Were a state's delegates for or against continuing the war until Britain and France consented to a formal grant of fishing and drying rights at Newfoundland to the United States in a peace treaty? How about the right to navigate the Mississippi? Who would own the Floridas at the end of the war, and would this outcome impact which nation, Britain or Spain, possessed the authority to transfer Americans navigation rights? Would delegates back the fisheries or the Mississippi navigation—one, both, or neither? In the seven months of debates, the only perfect coalition of geopolitical interests was that of the four New England states, whose delegates stood like a Rock of Gibraltar behind the right to catch and dry fish in the northern waters. The Middle states and Southern states, at least initially, were more desultory in their affinities and alignments.

One of the starkest effects of the prolonged and searing Mississippi-fisheries debates of 1779, however, was to coalesce the Southern states into a stronger geopolitical bloc. Many delegates felt that the navigation of the Mississippi was, in fact, only of vital importance to Virginia and North Carolina, since small-population South Carolina and Georgia were decades away from large-scale westward expansion toward the great river. As the Mississippi-fisheries fights intensified, though, it became increasingly clear to the Southern delegates that they must band together to protect common regional interests. Besides this, the debates opened their eyes to their minority voting power in Congress—four or five Southern states versus eight or nine Northern ones. Looking to the future, they realized that they must do everything possible to open the Mississippi River because the states that were going to form on its banks, and those on its major tributaries like the Ohio, would be Southern in identity and economy, thereby growing Southern wealth and influence in the confederation and, critically, boosting the region's voting power in Congress.

* * * * *

No copy of Gérard's address is preserved in the American or French archives, but notes on the event were kept by Secretary of Congress Charles Thomson, South Carolina delegate William Henry Drayton, and Gérard himself. In the speech the ambassador went to great lengths to persuade the delegates that the fate of the United States hung on a thread that might easily snap if they proved to be overambitious and uncooperative with France and Spain. Gérard painted a picture of George III, the British ministry, and Parliament as emboldened to redouble their efforts to conquer America by creditable reports "that divisions prevailed among the members in Congress, and between Congress and some of the States." The British hope, too, was that "discord would arise between the United States and France." Due to these ripe conditions of disunion in the nation and the alliance, George III was determined not to grant an inch to the rebelling Americans. In fact, Gérard reported, recently the English king had gone so far as to initiate talks with the Empress of Russia to provide troops against the Americans and, in return, "a large district [of land] in America would be assigned to the Empress."[2]

Against this long shadow of British intransigence and perseverance, the ambassador depicted the Bourbon monarchs Louis XVI and Charles III as riding into the breach with their monies, ministers, armies, navies, and mediations in one hand and the flag of American independence in the other. To see this revolution materialize, Gérard pressed the delegates hard to draft peace terms restricted to independence alone. "The Court of France had no object in view but the independence of the United States," and "the pride of Great Britain was too high, and her abilities too great, to submit to extraordinary demands at present." The Congress must act swiftly, humbly, and with "concord," Gérard insisted.[3]

In his formal remarks, Gérard did not mention the Mississippi navigation. This topic would come up only after the speech in informal conversation. He did, however, make an oblique reference to the Newfoundland fisheries. To him, it was more than obvious that access to the fisheries should under no circumstances, at this stage in the war and diplomacy, be made an ultimatum of peace by Congress, because neither the United States nor France had subdued the island and therefore there was no valid argument for the claim. Offhandedly, the ambassador admitted that France took enormous interest in the fisheries and, if she conquered them, would offer some form of fishing and curing rights to "her Allies." He did not specify whether the allies in question were the United States, in plural, or the United States and Spain.[4]

As impactful in the day's proceedings as the formal address itself is what Gérard said to the delegates afterward. He stayed on in Independence Hall in further dialogue with a large gathering of delegates, answering questions and elucidating some of his more oblique remarks. Of note, chroniclers Gérard and Drayton both highlighted the importance of Gérard's response to direct questioning by North Carolina delegate Thomas Burke on the subject of the Mississippi navigation. After the speech, Burke sat down in a chair directly beside Gérard for a decorous cross-examination. First the North Carolinian asked politely what rewards the king of France hoped to extract from the mediation. Nothing more than the absolute, unquestioned independence of the United States, Gérard professed. Then Burke commented that the ambassador had "insinuated with great brevity the necessity of conforming to the preferences of Spain," yet without providing details. Burke urged the minister to offer a candid assessment, to speak openly.

At this, Gérard for the first time stated his official position on the Mississippi as it related to France and Spain. What was essential was a peaceful border between Spain and the United States, he offered, explaining that "the possession of Pensacola and the exclusive navigation of the Mississippi could alone fulfill this goal." Americans should grant these securities to Spain to prevent present and future discontents in the hinterland and to bring Spain speedily into the alliance with France and the United States. Gérard went further, however. Far worse than merely derailing the mediation, a congressional sanction of unruly expansion into the Mississippi Valley risked a dramatic shift in Spain's position on the War of Independence from neutrality with surreptitious aid to the United States, joined to the hope of a Spanish declaration of war if mediation failed, to a possible outright rejection of American independence followed by a Spanish alliance with Britain. If the Congress failed to attach Spain to its cause, said Gérard, Charles III might make "common cause against an independent America" with George III. Gérard implied that the Spanish king would go to whatever extreme necessary to obtain his much-sought peaceful boundary in America.

These intimidating words of caution to Burke about the necessity of a peaceable, easy border with Spain in the Mississippi Valley did not settle the matter. Gérard had been warned in advance by delegates friendly to him that if the subject of the Mississippi navigation came up on this day, he could expect opposition. Indeed, when he uttered words regarding the "exclusive navigation" for Spain in response to Burke, numerous delegates in the gathering protested crossly. In Gérard's words, "Several members perorated heatedly for the conservation of the navigation of the Mississippi." William Henry Drayton of South Carolina recorded that "Spain wished to have the territorial claims of the United States terminated. She wished to have the navigation of the Mississippi shut." Despite this flare-up, the conference ended with assurances by most delegates present that the stumbling block of the Mississippi could be surmounted by thoughtful consideration, care, and a spirit of generosity from the Continental Congress equal to that of the king of Spain.[5]

Over the next several days, Gérard felt guardedly optimistic that the problem of the Mississippi would find an amicable settlement in Congress, although one circumstance distressed him. Virginian Richard Henry Lee, known for his inflexible views on Virginia's territorial rights in the West and the necessity of the navigation of the Mississippi to a burgeoning trade there, had not been present in Independence Hall on the day of his presentation and remarks. Lee was then at home at Chantilly-on-the-Potomac on a short leave of absence. Three or four days later, though, he was back in Philadelphia. On the day of his return, Gérard communicated to Vergennes with satisfaction that he, the ambassador, had thus far expertly managed complicated affairs in Congress. He closed the dispatch with a shift in tone, warning, "Mr. Richard Henry Lee just arrived; we must see if he will not succeed in changing things." Shortly, Gérard expressed his further hope that "a great landowner of the South" would not be put in charge of congressional affairs relating to the Spanish-American boundary and other issues in the Mississippi Valley.[6]

* * * * *

On Wednesday, February 17, two days following Gérard's speech announcing the mediation, the Congress established a "committee of five" to deliberate on American peace terms. As was the custom on essential matters of state, the committee members were selected to represent the three regions of New England, the South, and the Middle states. The men appointed were Sam Adams of Massachusetts, Thomas Burke of North Carolina, Meriwether Smith of Virginia, Gouverneur Morris of New York, and John Witherspoon of New Jersey, with Morris named as chair of the committee. When the Congress appointed the committee members, Richard Henry Lee had not yet returned to Philadelphia. Had he been present, he almost certainly would have taken the place of Meriwether Smith, since Lee was both a dominant figure in Congress from the flagship state of Virginia and an acknowledged expert on the trans-Appalachian West and its rivers.[7]

After only five days of deliberation, the committee presented its report, read aloud to the Congress assembled. It included a preamble, a single precondition to be met prior to negotiations, five preliminary articles of a peace treaty, and one desideratum eagerly sought "in case the allies of these United States will agree to support them." Evidencing the success of Spain's obfuscation of its true intents—to enter the war, perhaps, but not by way of an alliance with the United States—the committee members articulated in the preamble that the enumeration of American terms for peace was made immediately necessary by recent intelligence that "his Catholick Majesty is disposed to enter into an alliance with the United States of America." Further, "in consequence of such declaration, the independence of these United States must be finally acknowledged by Great Britain; and immediately thereon a negotiation for peace will be set on foot."[8]

To protect the United States from the machinations of British ministers who, once seated at the negotiating table, might attempt to restore colonial status to the states, the report declared that the Congress would not consent to negotiations until King George's representatives had "first, as a ground and preliminary" acknowledged "the liberty, sovereignty, and independence, absolute and unlimited, of these United States." Once this requisite for opening discussions had been agreed upon, negotiations could begin, wherein the United States would assent to a permanent peace only if Britain satisfied five American ultimatums.

First, the enemy must agree to a northern boundary of the United States along the colonies' historic line of demarcation with Canada, a western boundary at the Mississippi River, and a southern boundary between Georgia and the Floridas from the Atlantic Ocean to the Mississippi. Second, King George must evacuate all British land and sea forces from within these boundaries. Third, the treaty must stipulate "that a right of fishing and curing fish on the banks and coasts of the island of Newfoundland, equally with the subjects of France and Great Britain, be reserved, acknowledged, and ratified to the subjects of the United States." Fourth, it must guarantee "that the navigation of the river Mississippi, as low down as the southern boundary of the United States, be acknowledged and ratified absolutely free to the subjects of the United States," and fifth, "that free commerce be allowed to the subjects of the United States with some port or ports below the southern boundary of the said states, on the river Mississippi, except for such articles as may be particularly enumerated."

These five, plus the unlimited political and economic independence of the thirteen states, constituted the nonnegotiable terms of peace. The hoped-for bonus item, France and Spain willing, related to Britain's Nova Scotia together with Cape Breton Island and the province's many other dependent fishing and drying islands. As stated in this first draft of peace demands, Americans wished to see Nova Scotia either "ceded to the United States, or declared independent." Undoubtedly, Sam Adams was the primary mover on the acquisition of this prized territory, because it was his oft-stated belief that Nova Scotia would serve as a protective shield around the Newfoundland fisheries as well as a base for the development of an American navy.

Nova Scotia, in addition to fishing rights on Newfoundland, Adams felt, was not too much to ask to secure a dignified American peace, for without it the British were bound not only to harass American shipping in the northern waters but also to threaten American independence and sow division in the new nation. His letters from this period reveal that the right of fishing and curing at Newfoundland was a nonnegotiable matter for him and further that "Nova Scotia & Canada would be a great & permanent protection to the fishery.... The cession of those territories would prevent any views of Britain to disturb our peace in [the] future & cut off a source of corrupt British influence which, issuing from them, might diffuse mischiefe and poison thro the states." In this statement, what Adams meant was that if at the end of the war Britain held control over territories dear to some Americans—like Nova Scotia and Canada were dear to New England—but not to other Americans, it would provide the former mother country with a power to set up internal antagonisms in the young nation, dividing public opinion, and perhaps the states, to England's ultimate advantage.[9]

* * * * *

The toughest problem the Congress faced in issuing its ultimatums of peace that February was the navigation of the Mississippi River. Here was a great and confounding diplomatic puzzle, not only because Gérard and Miralles were caviling and menacing on the subject but also because no one could predict how the geography of the Mississippi Delta might be reconfigured by the war's end—and, therefore, what corollary navigation rights might adhere to what landmasses of the redrawn map. The answers to many questions were yet unknown. Would Spain in fact enter into an alliance with the United States, and, if so, would she grant Americans navigation rights on the Mississippi as part of the pact? Or might the Catholic monarch instead declare war on Britain independently, stripping Americans of the chance to use the Floridas as leverage to obtain the navigation through an alliance? If Spain balked on the alliance, would the king and Floridablanca sign a treaty of commerce with the United States opening the Mississippi? Notwithstanding Spanish-American relations, what would become of the Floridas in peace negotiations, notably West Florida, which bordered the Mississippi? Would that river province remain British or be transferred to Spain—or perhaps the United States? All of these unsettled questions left the Americans swirling in a sea of contingencies. Still, though, Gérard had demanded that concrete American peace ultimatums be swiftly delivered.

From the American perspective, there were only two true securities to the United States' future trade down the Mississippi to the Gulf of Mexico. Either Spain must grant the new nation a right of free navigation along its two-hundred-mile stretch of ownership of both banks of the lower river, or the United States must obtain the British colony of West Florida in the peace treaty. That is to say, if Spain proved itself hostile to U.S. trade on the Mississippi, blocking American ships from the ingress

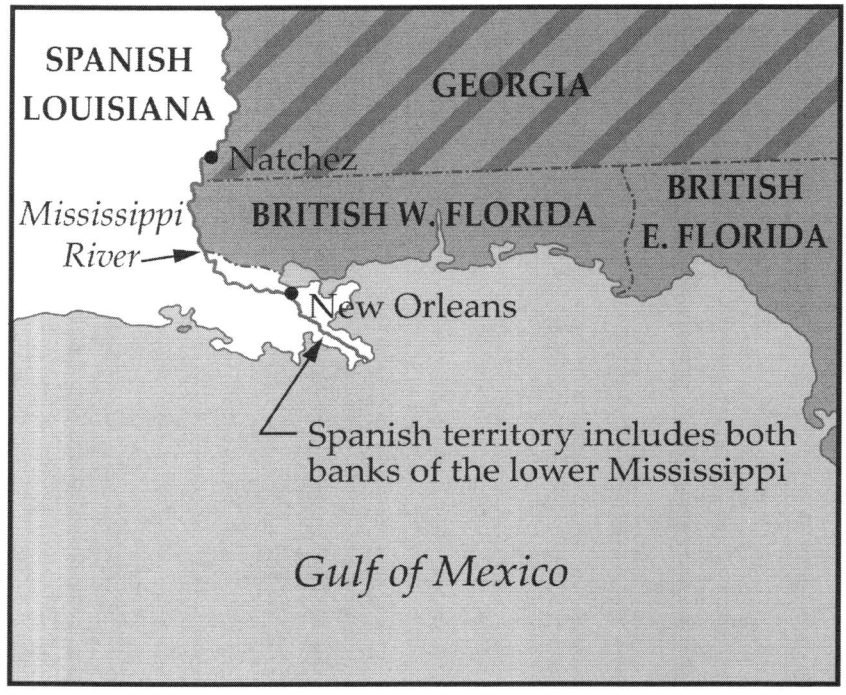

MAP 5. Spanish Control of the Mouth of the Mississippi, based on the Treaty of Paris, 1763. (Chris Robinson, Cartographer)

and egress through the lower river, the Congress must take possession of West Florida. The reason for this is that West Florida contained two routes to the Gulf of Mexico. One was down the great river. The second was by way of the navigable back rivers, bayous, and lakes accessible to shallow-draft craft on the Mississippi at the town of Manchac, or Fort Bute, at the farmost southern border of West Florida. There, at Manchac, the Iberville River split off from the Mississippi, flowing southeast to the Amite River and from there into Lake Maurepas, Lake Pontchartrain, and finally into the Gulf of Mexico on the opposite side of New Orleans.[10]

This labyrinthine water system, together with the uncertainty of the future map of the lower Mississippi, explains why on February 23 the committee on a Spanish mediation proposed not only preliminary articles for a peace treaty with Britain but also intersecting instructions for a Spanish alliance. In the peace demands, the committee required from Britain "that free commerce be allowed to the subjects of the United States with some port or ports below the southern boundary of the said states, on the river Mississippi"—that is, in British West Florida. Whether Kentucky and Tennessee farmers sold their staple crops at Baton Rouge, Manchac, or elsewhere on British soil did not matter. The essential thing was a guarantee in the peace treaty of "free commerce" with a British riverport that itself was accessible to the sea.

Yet, believing that chances were great that Spain would sign an alliance with the United States in Madrid, the committee laid out for the second time its terms for a Spanish-American alliance. This time the Congress offered to reduce the Floridas with an American army of up to six thousand infantrymen in exchange for two things from Spain. One was a subsidy of money, with the amount not yet specified, and the second was "the free navigation of the river Mississippi to the subjects of the United States . . . in the fullest extent of egress and ingress." To the extent that this broad extent of free navigation proved unworkable, American ministers in Europe signing an alliance with Spain must insist that "a port be reserved for the delivery and sale, purchase and lading of all commodities, excepting such articles as shall be particularly enumerated."[11]

* * * * *

Over the next several months, the delegates in Congress divided into several camps on matters of war, peace, the fisheries, the Mississippi, and the general trustworthiness of the French and Spanish in hurrying the United States to deliver minimal, restrictive terms of peace into the hands of Ambassador Gérard. One camp, dubbed the "pro-Gallican" or "pro-French" party by some historians, was represented early on by Gouverneur Morris of New York, who argued that the overriding obligation of the Congress in 1779 was to adhere religiously to the Franco-American alliance. In that lifesaving compact, Morris asserted, France had bound itself to fight for American independence, but nowhere in that document did Louis XVI agree to fight on for a New England right to fish at British Newfoundland and Nova Scotia, or an American right to navigate the Mississippi River. Certainly, because Morris alone in a committee of five could not overcome the dominating influence of Sam Adams on the fisheries and Burke and Smith on the Mississippi navigation, he had consented to present them as preliminary articles of peace for consideration and debate. But this does not mean he agreed with them. He did not. The

New Yorker viewed them instead as territorial and navigational overreach certain to wreck the mediation, disaffect Spain and France, prolong combat, and needlessly spill more American blood.[12]

Morris did not entirely turn his back on these objects of American trade and commercial expansion. He simply disagreed that the Congress should demand them now—in the specific instrument of a peace treaty. A merchant skilled in the art of commerce, Morris proposed other sound ideas for how the United States could succeed in the mediated peace and obtain the fisheries and Mississippi navigation at a later date. To end the war, the peace treaty should be signed without mention of either object, but in separate commercial treaties with Britain and Spain after the peace, the United States would require free use of the fisheries and Mississippi—or else refuse to sign those treaties. By convention, this two-part mechanism of peace treaty followed by commercial treaty is how wars frequently ended in the eighteenth century and how trade resumed between former belligerents. This smart formula for peace, Morris insisted, would sideline flammable issues while additionally allowing the United States to maintain its honor and integrity in not exceeding the war aims contractually agreed upon in the Franco-American alliance. Additionally, Morris maintained, the ruinous war had gone on long enough and American independence was on a tenuous footing. The army was exhausted; if peace were not grasped now, it might never be achieved.[13]

Tough-minded New Englanders like Sam Adams, James Lovell, Elbridge Gerry, Samuel Huntington, William Whipple, and William Ellery, in contrast, had much to say about congressmen like Morris and the weak-kneed policies they advocated at the behest of interfering foreigners like Gérard and Miralles. In the week after February 23, it was specifically Lovell, forty-one-year-old Massachusetts delegate and close collaborator with Adams, who declared that the chief obstacles to a forceful American territorial and navigational foreign policy were not only France and Spain but also the "lickspittles" in Congress.[14]

By this term, Lovell meant fawning subordinates to an admired, superior other, and, in this case, he was almost certainly referring to Gouverneur Morris and President John Jay, also of New York, both of whom seemed to many New Englanders to be serving the interests of France first and America second. Later, in a letter to John Adams, Lovell crystallized his view that the fundamental problem of settling American terms for a peace treaty with England had less to do with divergent viewpoints about the essential territorial and commercial rights of the United States than a lack of political courage in some delegates who refused to unequivocally lay down the law. "In short," Lovell explained to Adams, "the great difference sprung from our varying quantum of obsequiousness to the dictations of a foreigner [Gérard] as they were retailed to us through the mouths of either fear or roguery, and not from our being wide of each other in opinion of our rights."[15]

Sam Adams agreed entirely with Lovell in this assessment. Adams's view of the American Union was that its fundamental purpose was to safeguard the liberties and natural rights of its member states, and no natural right was more essential to the future happiness of New England than that of catching and drying cod and haddock in the North Atlantic Ocean. The fundamental obstacle to obtaining a respectable peace treaty ending the war, in his view, too, was not the obvious Machiavellianism of the kings and ministers of Europe, nor the fearful conjurings of their spokesmen in Philadelphia, but a lack of backbone in Americans. As Adams's letters reflect, the greatest problem he stumbled over in the Congress, year after year, was the "timidity" of other delegates. In part for his own amusement and that of his friend James Warren, he once drew up a sketch of the various classes of temperaments he had encountered in his years in politics, comparing them to a menagerie of animals. Men were "variously class'd," he wrote, as those possessing "the magnanimity of the lion, the generosity of the horse, the fearfulness of the deer, and the cunning of the fox . . . fidelity of the dog . . . the vanity of the ape, the tameness of the ox, or the stupid servility of the ass." What most seemed to Adams to hinder the progress of independence and confederation were those men in Congress who acted like scared deer and servile asses.[16]

* * * * *

The congressional debates over the United States' essential demands for making peace with Britain extended from late February until the middle of October. Similar to the stalemate over the Articles of Confederation, the primary cause of Congress's prolonged paralysis over such a vital matter of state was the emergence of polarization in Independence Hall so extreme that it provoked clear and present threats of disunion. In the middle of March, the delegates easily adopted the committee's recommendations on the boundaries of the new nation and the withdrawal of the British army and navy. Already by the end of the month, however, they were clashing painfully over the Newfoundland fisheries and the Mississippi navigation. At that point, after two days of vitriol, on March

22 and 24, they decided to tackle these sensitive foreign policy issues one at a time—first, the fisheries and, after this, the navigational labyrinth of the lower Mississippi. It was during the first several months of fights over the fisheries that the Congress descended into a severe crisis of disunion, by far the most divisive and paralyzing in its five-year history.

During those first months, non–New England delegates like Gouverneur Morris of New York, Meriwether Smith of Virginia, Thomas Burke of North Carolina, and William Drayton of South Carolina outright refused to make themselves—and the states they represented—parties to an American foreign policy that transformed the War of Independence into a war for fishing rights on the Grand Banks of Newfoundland. All indicators were that peace was near. Spain was going to mediate in favor of American independence. Britain, possibly, was going to lay down arms and formally acknowledge American independence. And now, at this critical juncture, New Englanders were demanding territorial and water rights—entirely outside the bounds of the Franco-American alliance—that were going to shock and affront France, Spain, and Britain, almost certainly leading to a collapse of the mediation. To Morris, Smith, Burke, and Drayton, it was one thing to dispatch an American diplomat to Madrid with instructions to do everything within his creative powers to obtain fishing rights. It was quite another to draw a red line across the mediating tables that proclaimed categorically that full political independence for the thirteen states was insufficient for peace and Britain must also grant Americans fishing rights on its privately held Newfoundland, or else the bloodletting by all nations must continue. Based on the committee's first draft of peace terms, this seemed to be the New England position, and most all the delegates from the Middle and Southern states, with only a few exceptions, deplored it.[17]

That is why on March 22 Morris, Smith, Burke, and Drayton joined forces to advance an amended Article III on the fisheries that emasculated the New England ultimatum. As revised that day while New Englanders looked on and protested, the new fisheries article gave France and Spain the power to veto the desideratum. On this question, as the amended article stipulated, American negotiators in Madrid should request that "an acknowledgment be made by Great Britain of a common right in these States to fish on the coasts, bays, and banks of Nova Scotia, the banks of Newfoundland and gulf of St. Lawrence, the coasts of Labrador and straits of Belleisle; provided always that the allies of these States shall be in circumstances to support them in carrying on the war for such acknowledgment." However, as a compromise measure, the Congress required that "in no case by any treaty of peace the common right of fishing as above described be given up." In other words, France and Spain, not the United States, would decide the fate of American fishing and drying rights in the northern waters and shores of Newfoundland and Nova Scotia.[18]

On March 24 New Englanders responded to this assault, recruiting Sam Adams's close political ally, Richard Henry Lee from Virginia, to make a motion on the floor restoring potency to the fisheries article. Essentially it was the same February 23 ultimatum, weakened only slightly by the removal of Britain's requirement to "ratify" fishing rights. The article introduced by Lee, seconded by Connecticut's Eliphalet Dyer, required "that the right of fishing on the coasts and banks of North America be reserved to the United States as fully as they enjoyed the same when subject to the King of Great Britain, excepting always what shall have been excepted by the treaty of Paris between France and the United States, the whole to be explained by the treaties of Utrecht and Paris with Great Britain and of Paris with the United States of North America."[19]

This advocacy of a New England commercial right by Richard Henry Lee, Virginia's ranking delegate and a nimble power broker in Congress since 1774, would prove decisive in the coming months, facilitating a quid pro quo wherein Lee stood fast for the fisheries in return for New Englanders' support on the navigation of the Mississippi. Soon, another prominent Southern delegate and advocate of unfettered American commerce on the lower Mississippi, Henry Laurens of South Carolina, who had just stepped down as president of Congress, crossed the aisle to become a fierce advocate for freedom of fishing for New England. This early alliance of Lee, Laurens, and New Englanders on the Mississippi and fisheries represented the beginnings of a sectional bargain, one that first took shape in April of 1779 and endured for years thereafter.

The addition of Lee and Laurens to the lobby for the fisheries as an ultimatum of peace hardly diminished the righteousness and determination of Middle and Southern state delegates who opposed it. The latter dug in their heels, claiming that the new nation must launch itself into international affairs on an ethical, legalistic, and faithful footing, not to mention that the New Englanders' demand on the fisheries was a blatant violation of the Franco-American alliance. That rescuing alliance said not a single word about the fisheries—and therefore, obvious to all, the United States had no power on earth, except for that of bad faith, now to assert to its ally that Americans would not desist in the war until Britain granted them the additional bounty of Newfoundland fishing rights. In their view, raising up these commercial rights to the echelon of ultimatums risked terribly disaffecting France and Spain, and these two European powers were the lifeline of the Revolution: the supply centers for arms and munitions, the bank generating subsidies and loans, the only legitimate navy the United States possessed, the wellspring of the United States' credibility and respectability in the world, and the chill running through the veins of England as it faced a potential triple alliance. To alienate France and Spain in any way was, therefore, an act of folly and suicide.

What is more, these Middle and Southern state delegates argued, now was scarcely the moment to impugn the French alliance. The American treasury was empty and its paper currency so worthless that George Washington had recently complained that "a wagon load of money will scarcely purchase a wagon load of provisions." And, clinching the argument that the fisheries must not be made an ultimatum, the United States and France were not presently winning the war. At the beginning of the year the British had redirected their central war strategy to the South and lately had all but captured the entire state of Georgia. That spring British forces held much of New York, Rhode Island, and Georgia. Would the bankrupt Congress hold out for fish in the Northeast while the new nation lay in such a precarious state of conquest? To most congressmen, it was an indefensible, selfish stance for New England to take. They determined that New England must be overruled.[20]

* * * * *

The best way to understand what the Middle and Southern state delegates were up against in the battle over haddock and cod is to peer inside the personal history, character, and lifelong commitments of Samuel Adams, the undisputed leader of the New England bloc in Congress since 1774. The only other New England delegate who had held as much sway over the early Congress was his cousin, John Adams, who in February of the preceding year had left the American coast for Europe to serve as American ambassador, replacing Silas Deane of Connecticut on the three-man commission to negotiate with the French. Still, in those years, Sam, not John, was widely considered to be "the famous Adams" for the reason of his undying advocacy of American political liberty—and commercial liberty—since the Sugar Act in 1764. For his leadership and trenchant writings, Sam Adams qualifies more than any other

Chapter 11: The Mississippi and Fisheries Again

patriot as the father of the American resistance movement and, ultimately, independence. Jefferson once called him "the patriarch of liberty." John Adams, who knew him well, underscored his cousin's political skill set as outstanding for its combination of the art of gentle persuasion, force of will, and talents for parliamentary maneuvering. Sam, he said, "is always for softness, and delicacy, and prudence where they will do, but is stanch and stiff and strict and rigid and inflexible in the cause."[21]

A consummate legislator, Sam Adams was a tireless backroom negotiator who knew the good effects of a public iron will. To his opponents, he was often viewed as a zealot, propagandist, and dogmatist. One newspaper labeled him the "Cromwell of New England." Another charged that Adams had the ability not only to shepherd others to his political causes but also to invest them with a "resolve to conquer or die in the cause they have espoused." In the view of Congressman Joseph Galloway, Adams would stop at nothing to accomplish his aims. As Galloway reported, "He eats little, drinks little, sleeps little, thinks much, and is most decisive and indefatigable in the pursuit of his objects."[22]

All his life Adams had watched New England fishing ships sail from Boston, Marblehead, Gloucester, and Plymouth, returning in the early summer from the Grand Banks of Newfoundland with massive catches of cod, haddock, and capelin. He witnessed these events not only from the shores and wharves of these towns but also from an observatory atop his house on Purchase Street in Boston. His land there stretched almost three hundred feet to Boston Harbor, and on clear days he would climb an outdoor stairway to a rooftop landing specifically designed for viewing the expanse of the harbor, where tall-masted vessels came to shore, fisherman unloaded their catch, and dockworkers began the process of salting and curing. These fish, gathered in greatest abundance on the banks of Newfoundland, were the economic breath of life of New England. In 1768 Adams had already gone on record as asserting that "the fishing grounds" were a "species of property." What made the Grand Banks so special were the swarms of plankton swimming in its shallows, attracting the densest concentration of fish anywhere in the world to feed there.[23]

Indeed, the rocky soils and cold climate of these northern colonies did not permit widespread commercial agriculture, so shortly after the founding of Plymouth, the men and women of New England looked to the sea for their livelihood. Yankee vessels first ventured to the banks off Sable Island and Newfoundland in the middle of the seventeenth century, and by the turn of the eighteenth, more than six hundred vessels manned by some four thousand men were swarming over these rich fishing grounds each year. They caught haddock, halibut, flounder, rosefish, herring, salmon, lobster, and cod in such volume that by the decade before the American Revolution, New England merchants marketed a catch worth about $1 million per year. Especially the mighty cod—adopted some years later as the state symbol of Massachusetts—thrived and drew profits.[24]

Plates of cod and haddock were enjoyed in New England homes and taverns, yet most of it, dried and cured, sailed back out again to serve as the primary currency of New England's trade. In one important loop of commerce, salt fish was exchanged for molasses and sugar in the West Indies. Back in New England distilleries, the molasses or sugar, in turn, became rum, a second prized commodity of the region. Merchants from Marblehead, Gloucester, Plymouth, and Salem also sent cargoes of fish to Pennsylvania for wheat and to the Southern colonies for rice, tobacco, and indigo—or fish was exchanged in the West Indies for slaves, who were then bartered on the Atlantic coast of America for these crops. Since much of the cod and haddock of the Grand Banks was dried and cured locally on the shores of Newfoundland, another wave of trade carried New England rum directly to Newfoundland in exchange for salt fish. The best dried fish of all went to Spain and Portugal, where it commanded a high price in Spanish dollars or the finest of Madeira wines on exchange.

No matter where the cod and haddock were dried, this quadrangular trade of salt fish, molasses, rum, and slaves between New England, Newfoundland, the South, and the West Indies served as an essential source of profits to New England merchants and employment to captains, sailors, and fisherman as well as driers, curers, picklers, and distillers. The fisheries were also inextricably bound to the other major industries of New England: shipbuilding and shipping. Without fish to catch, shipbuilding would decline precipitously, throwing lumberers and carpenters out of work. And the principal purpose of a ship was to conduct commerce. Loss of fish would devastate the New England carrying trade. All in all, at least as Sam Adams viewed it, fish was equally if not more important to New England as tobacco to Virginia and North Carolina and indigo and rice to South Carolina and Georgia.

Grandson of a ship captain, Adams did not view the fisheries as an adjunct to New England independence from Britain. It was instead the marrow and lifeblood of it. After all, one cause of the American leap into independence was Parliament's deplorable New England Restraining Act of 1775, officially known as the New England Trade and Fisheries Act, abolishing, for one thing, all rights of American colonists to take cod, haddock, or any other species in the North Atlantic fisheries. Parliament followed this in the same year with Palliser's Act, deepening the wound by awarding New England's fishing and drying rights at Newfoundland to Ireland and the British islands of Guernsey, Jersey, and Man. To Adams, these acts were final, fatal strikes in the long and oppressive history of parliamentary navigation acts eviscerating New England trade. In Adams's manner of thinking, the Parliament had no more right to take away New England's property in fish, without its consent, than it did its property in tax revenues or in commercial livelihood when it shut down Boston Harbor.

This is the legacy of thought and political activity Adams brought to the Continental Congress in 1779 when Morris, Jay, and other Middle and Southern state delegates refused to consent to Newfoundland fishing and drying rights as an ultimatum for a peace treaty. In the following months, Adams further clarified his point of view in a half dozen letters, underscoring the hollowness of the independence the United States stood to gain if the terms thereof failed to obtain access to the fisheries.

In answer to the counsel he heard in the Congress to moderate the American position, omitting the fisheries in order to obtain a swift peace, Adams said the notion was absurd. His attitudes were righteous and proud: "However desirable this may be, we must not wish for it [peace] on any terms but such as shall be honorable & safe to our country. Let us not disgrace ourselves by giving just occasion for it to be said hereafter, that we finished this great contest with an inglorious accommodation." To him, independence without the fishery would be a bankrupt, destitute independence, at least for New England. It would be to take the name of independence without the strength of economy and navy to safeguard it. In defending his position, he wrote to a colleague that "the name only of independence is not worth the blood of a single citizen."[25]

Adams's allusions to an American navy were not incidental. One powerful reason he insisted upon the fisheries as an ultimatum was the future security of the nation. Large-scale fishing was the wellspring of sailors, ships, shipbuilding, and sailing know-how, and all these in turn were the keystones for erecting a respectable navy for young America. To be a sea power in the future, the United States must enjoy uninterrupted fishing rights on the Grand Banks. Adams, waxing poetic, went to great lengths to inextricably link fish, trade, honor, independence, liberty, happiness, national security, and the future American navy that would preserve them all: "Our happiness depends upon independence. To be prosperous we must have an extensive trade. This will require a respectable navy. Our ships must be mann'd, and the source of seamen is the fishery." Adams now and thereafter for years tied the fisheries to this distinctive taxonomy of independence. The peace would either be honorable or dishonorable, manly or cowardly, and as long as he had breath to give, he would not stand by and watch the child independence he had birthed be debased in the final act of the struggle.[26]

A final argument Adams brought to the fisheries contest, at least in his letters, was that of the necessity of sectional justice. The other states in the Union simply must understand, he asserted, that fish was New England's staple crop, and without this elemental commodity of trade, the commercial happiness of Massachusetts, Connecticut, Rhode Island, and New Hampshire would be decimated. "The fishing banks," he once instructed a fellow Massachusetts delegate to call out loudly to other congressmen, "are at least as important as tobacco yards, or rice swamps, or the flourishing wheat fields of Pennsylvania." Therefore, it would not be "just" to sign a peace treaty that secured the trade of some but not all of the states in the Union.[27]

CHAPTER 12

Crisis of Union

THE SHARP DIVISION OVER AMERICAN access to the fisheries as an ultimatum of peace brought the Congress to its nadir that spring and summer. Numerous sources corroborate that New Englanders formally declared that they would sooner break the American Union than compromise on this aspect of peace with Britain. One source documenting the New England threat of disunion is the papers of John Adams, who returned to the United States in late July. In the months that followed, he was briefed on the congressional crisis over the fisheries by Massachusetts delegates Sam Adams, Elbridge Gerry, and James Lovell. "Debates had run so high," John Adams later recorded, "that the Eastern states had been obliged to give in their ultimatum in writing, and to say they would withdraw if any more was done; and that this [the fishery] was so tender and important, that if not secured, it would be the cause of a breach of the union of the states."[1]

Another chronicler of the disunionist politics taking place within the Congress was Ambassador Gérard, who wrote weekly dispatches to Vergennes in Paris. Delegates like Gouverneur Morris, John Jay, and Daniel of St. Thomas Jenifer of Maryland, among others, kept the French ambassador intimately informed of the debates inside Independence Hall. Soon after Middle and Southern state delegates argued to New Englanders that the Congress must defer to the French in their adoption of ultimatums of peace, Gérard documented, Sam Adams grew angry and remonstrated animatedly against a weak, deferential America. "M. Samuel Adams became so annoyed about this that he put aside his ordinary reserve," the ambassador explained to Vergennes, continuing that the Massachusetts delegate next demanded to know, "What is thus the reason for which we must so strongly tie our interests with those of France?"

Then, pounding his foot on the floor of Independence Hall to indicate the location of the seat and power of American government, Adams proclaimed, "Here . . . [is] where our independence must be consolidated." Several weeks later, after the first severe clash over the fisheries, Gérard recorded specifically that Adams pronounced on the floor of Congress that, owing to their obvious lack of common interests and mutual understanding, a split of the Union into separate confederacies seemed inevitable: "It escaped from the mouth of M. Samuel Adams that everyone could see more and more that it would be necessary that the two empires separate, speaking of those of the East and the South."[2]

This record of what happened in Congress in the midst of the fisheries crisis is not inconsistent with the political theory of Sam Adams as we know it from his later writings. After the war, when a movement was set afoot to create a "national government" sovereign over the states, he rejected it outright on the basis of the incompatibility of the New England and Southern states. As he wrote to his longtime confidant, Richard Henry Lee, he apprehended that if these two distinct regions were too firmly squeezed together under a single national government, one with all-embracing powers over commerce, imposts, and other means of raising revenue, it would be explosive and likely cause civil wars. Adams insisted to Lee that sovereignty must remain in the states:

> Can this national legislature be competent to make laws for the free internal government of one people living in climates so remote and whose "habits and particular interests" are and probably always will be so different? Is it to be expected that general laws can be adapted to the feelings of the more Eastern and the more Southern parts of so extensive a nation? It appears to me difficult if practicable. Hence then may we not look for discontent, mistrust, disaffection to government and frequent insurrections, which will require standing armies to suppress them in one place & another where they may happen to arise. Or if laws could be made, adapted to the local habits, feelings, views & interests of those distant parts, would they not cause jealousies of partiality in government which would excite envy and other malignant passions productive of wars and fighting.[3]

* * * * *

The effect of New England's hardline stance on the fisheries was to profoundly destabilize the Congress and trigger counterthreats by other states that they would join in disbanding the Union if New England continued its self-interested and domineering control over American policy for peace.

In mid-June, Elbridge Gerry of Massachusetts announced on the floor that New England would soften its demand for an absolute right to the fisheries in a peace treaty but only on the condition that the Congress satisfied New Englanders on both a new fisheries ultimatum in that treaty and stern terms for a commercial treaty with England. In this supposed spirit of compromise, Gerry advanced an array of five resolutions on the fisheries that, taken together, constituted a worse affront to the sensibilities of most Southern and Middle state delegates than the original ultimatum. The New Englander still required a positive ultimatum on the fisheries in the peace treaty—for Britain "not to disturb the inhabitants of these States in the free exercise of their common right to the fisheries"—to be followed by the drafting of a separate commercial treaty with Britain that could be adopted only with the "unanimous consent" of all states, not a bare majority or supermajority.[4]

Now New England would control the peace treaty and hamper the signing of a commercial treaty with England, shutting Britain's worldwide ports after the war to the wheat of Pennsylvania, tobacco of Virginia and North Carolina, and rice of South Carolina until New England's demands on fish had been fully satisfied. If not, the nation as a whole would suffer indefinitely the lack of a commercial treaty. If this were not enough, Gerry also moved that the Franco-American alliance be amended by an article of understanding acknowledging the United States' full, unimpeded fishing rights, thus making it a legal peace claim and neutralizing the argument of Morris and others that demanding fish transgressed the alliance. If French foreign minister Vergennes begged to be excused of this article, the American peace minister was thereby prohibited from signing any peace treaty until he had received further instructions from Congress.

According to Gérard, some of the Middle and Southern state delegates answered this affront with their own menace to leave the Union. As Gérard described it to Vergennes, four non–New England states categorically declared that they would "leave the confederation" if a majority of the states adopted negotiating instructions requiring the blood of all to continue to pour for the sole object of New England fishing rights. Then, not much later, Gerry made a new motion. New England would consent to omit all mention of fish in the peace treaty. It would instead make the fisheries an ultimatum of the commercial treaty and, furthermore, no matter the outcome of either treaty with Britain, the Congress would agree by a formal resolution to ignite a second war against England for

FIGURE 34. Elbridge Gerry, Massachusetts Delegate. (Portrait of Elbridge Gerry. Nathaniel Jocelyn, *Elbridge Gerry (1744–1814)*, ca. 1845–1847, oil on canvas, 26 x 19.75 in, Harvard Art Museums / Fogg Museum, Louise E. Bettens Fund, 1943.1816.)

the fisheries if fishing and curing privileges at Newfoundland were in fact disturbed by the Royal Navy or the king's privateers.[5]

Once again, New England incensed the Middle and Southern delegates with what the latter perceived as a false gesture of compromise. In his correspondence with Vergennes, Gérard said this proposal by Gerry stimulated the Southern delegates to their highest degree of animus yet. "The debates on this question were violent," he wrote. "The deputies of the provinces of the South, of Maryland, Virginia, and the Carolinas, accused the authors of this motion of seeking to make war inevitable or at least to make the resumption of commerce with England and the duration of peace depend upon their own whims." The non–New England congressmen declared that any such policy would illegitimately bind the states to territorial and martial goals exceeding the contract for independence in 1776 as well as the terms of the Franco-American alliance in 1778. As such, they refused to participate in this dangerous foreign policy and demanded instead that the New England proposal be put directly to the state legislatures, not to the Congress.[6]

* * * * *

It is not only the feud over the fisheries that explains the intensity of the crisis that struck the Congress during the summer of 1779. The peace treaty debates also took place against the backdrop of numerous other sources of conflict and instability. The most acute were the languishing Articles of Confederation, the disorganized and insolvent state of American finances, a tempest over the appointment of American envoys abroad, the Pennsylvania-Virginia boundary dispute, the statehood movement of the contested Vermont territory, and Britain's further expansion of the war into the South. These problems, too, confronted the delegates with "jealousy & party spirit," "dangerous consequences," "divisions and animosities," and "violent parties." Just at the moment the fisheries debates reached a boiling point, calls rang out from New York that "the Vermont business is now arrived at a crisis." Besides rights of navigation, fishing, and drying of catch, the "right of soil" was always the most troubling category of political conflict confronting the nascent American government. In this case, New York was calling upon the Continental Congress to intervene to prevent the three parties of New England, New York, and Vermont settlers from igniting "the flames of civil war" over rightful boundaries and ownership of the land.[7]

Stirring further despair related to soil, Virginia made a daring proposal to the Congress in response to Maryland's ongoing refusal to ratify the Articles of Confederation. On May 20, 1779, the Virginia delegates introduced resolutions passed earlier by its General Assembly that proposed that a constitutional confederation be formed immediately by whatever states were willing to adopt the Articles of Confederation, whether that number be large or small. This was the first overt endorsement by Virginia of a partial confederation. As such, for some delegates, it engendered panic about the impending formation of subconfederations.[8]

Virginia promised to confederate "with any one or more states" who would join her, leading the three North Carolina delegates, Thomas Burke, William Sharpe, and John Penn, to write an urgent appeal to their governor and state legislature to render a decision. Explaining that a current crisis in congressional affairs relating to the terms of a peace treaty had led some states to declare categorically that if their conditions for peace were trespassed they would "neither submit or confederate," the delegates asked their home state to take up the "solemn requisition" of Virginia without delay. In light of these circumstances, should North Carolina sign on to a permanent confederation with Virginia? Referring to that state glowingly as "our favored, and favoring sister Virginia, whose interests, habits, manners and inclinations are so similar and consenting with ours," the North Carolinians requested to know the state's position.[9]

A month later, as the crisis over the fisheries deepened, Virginian William Fleming wrote to Governor Thomas Jefferson that New Englanders continued to block the peace treaty, and this obstruction was contravening the Franco-American alliance, wearing out the patience of Ambassador Gérard, and generally debilitating the Union and prospects for independence. To Fleming, it seemed that the U.S. Congress had been constituted for the explicit purpose of doing the most important work of the war and the Union, and, at present, it was failing miserably at two of its most fundamental objectives: confederation and a clear delineation of United States' terms of peace. By the third week of June, circumstances in Philadelphia seemed so dire to Fleming that he told Jefferson, "I think it high time for Virginia to look to her own importance and to provide for her own security, in case of disunion."[10]

* * * * *

The American Union was held together that anguished spring and summer of 1779 by three dynamic forces. One was the delegates' undiminished determination to secure liberty and freedom from British tyranny in the collective War of Independence. Second, they were confident that, as much as the thirteen states might seem to be a poor fit for a single harmonious republic, disunion into separate confederacies was only going to amplify the agony and bloodshed of the American continent by adding domestic civil wars to the imperial civil war already afflicting them. And third, the Union was maintained that year by a powerful cross-regional coalition known in the annals of the early republic as the Lee-Adams coalition.

One of the most important political alliances in American history, this collaboration, engineered by Richard Henry Lee and Sam Adams, had been in operation since the First Congress. It married the two most populous, influential states of the thirteen—Virginia and Massachusetts, leaders of the South and of New England, respectively—into a potent unity. Of great moment to the events of the Revolution, Sam Adams and Richard Henry Lee were dear friends and close political associates extending back to the burning of the Gaspée in 1772. After this, they had acted in concert as the regional ringleaders of the First Continental Congress, Suffolk Resolves, nonimportation, nonexportation, foreign treaties, state constitutions, the opening of American ports to world trade, and, their most hard-fought battle, independence. They were, in their own eyes and those of many others, the general managers of Congress. It was said that the two ruled the Congress "as absolutely as the Grand Turk does in his own Dominions."[11]

Historians generally agree that the Lee-Adams coalition did not hold the same sway over congressional affairs in 1779 as it had in 1776. Nevertheless, by recruiting Henry Laurens of South Carolina into its leadership, the coalition managed to thwart the general will of the Middle and Southern states on the fisheries. And through its tenacity, it ultimately forged a striking sectional bargain, one of the most fascinating in U.S. history, most appropriately given the name the Mississippi-Fisheries Compromise—or the Compromise of 1779. This coalition of New Englanders, Lee, and Laurens, whom Lee called "the Southern Chief," raised up the banner of both the Newfoundland fisheries and the navigation of the Mississippi River as inalienable rights of the United States that must therefore, one way or the other, be fought for tooth and nail at the negotiating tables in Europe with France, England, and Spain. The coalition would brook no compromise on a three-part formula for American peace: independence, the fisheries, and the navigation of the Mississippi.[12]

In support of all three, consummate politician Richard Henry Lee spearheaded a public relations campaign in which he promoted the idea that the fisheries and Mississippi navigation were as essential to American independence as a human being's two legs to a strong and able body. The peace ending the war would be the defining moment of the future of America. "In this," he contended, referring to the peace treaty, "I shall ever include the fisheries and the navigation of the Mississippi—These Sir are the strong legs on which N. America alone can walk surely in independence." The Mississippi and fisheries were not secondary to independence and therefore something to be sacrificed at the negotiating table, as Gérard and so many delegates declaimed. As Lee repeated in at least nine letters in 1779 and early 1780, they were nonnegotiable, immanent "strong legs" of a comprehensive independence.[13]

Several of these letters went to South Carolinian Henry Laurens when Lee was on hiatus from Congress. A fifty-four-year-old merchant and rice planter who would later be tapped for high diplomatic office in Europe, Laurens turned out, more so even than Lee, to be a profile in courage in the battle for the fisheries. The reason for this designation of political courage is because Laurens was harassed and pilloried for his profisheries stance not only by other Southern delegates but also by his very own fellow South Carolina delegate, William Henry Drayton. Early on, the North Carolina delegates tried to force Laurens's hand on the fisheries through a menacing ploy. They wrote a letter to the governor of their state declaring that Henry Laurens of South Carolina was at once voting in Congress against ending the war swiftly—that is, he was voting in favor of making the fisheries an ultimatum of peace—and simultaneously entreating North Carolina to increase its dispatch of troops and munitions to South Carolina, then under threat of British takeover. In the letter the North Carolina delegates flatly recommended to Governor Caswell of their state that, in the face of Laurens's illogical, self-contradictory advocacy of the fisheries, he immediately withdraw all North Carolina troops from service in South Carolina and "no more battalions should be raised in our state for the purpose of being sent thither."[14]

The North Carolina delegates did not send the letter. Instead, on the same day, they dispatched a copy to Laurens and Drayton together with an intimidating cover letter affirming their intention to mail it immediately if Laurens did not reverse his stance on the fisheries. Laurens was outraged by this action of Burke, Sharpe, and Penn, an attempt to use bloodshed on the field of the mutual war as blackmail to control his vote, and so decided himself to write to the governor of North Carolina. "I am not answerable to any man or set of men but to my self & my constituents," he told the governor. "Let justice be done, though heaven should fall."[15]

Letters like this one, with Drayton initially siding with the North Carolinians, went back and forth until Laurens finally put his foot down to all parties. Giving ample reasons for his support of the fishery as an ultimatum, notably that it was "the capital source from whence we are to supply our future navy," Laurens did not budge an inch. Reprimanding the other delegates for their political and ethical overreach, he declared he was a man who voted his "conscience." In the end, as Laurens himself recorded for posterity, his unrelenting self-defense on the basis of republican independent-mindedness finally "put an end to the farce & produced much politeness & many assurances of good will & esteem from the delegates of North Carolina."[16]

* * * * *

From March until early August, the Lee-Adams coalition's major accomplishment was to halt the forward-moving wheels of a peace treaty that dishonored and disunited the thirteen states by forfeiting either of its strong legs. Then, serendipity intervened to rescue the Continental Congress from its monthslong paralysis on the Mississippi and fisheries. In the second week of August, a ship ascended the Delaware River with news that quickly relieved tension and rewrote the equation of American foreign policy. Newspapers and letters rang out with the announcement: Great Britain had rejected the Spanish mediation and, consequently, Spain would at long last join the war. As New Hampshire delegate Nathaniel Peabody expressed this fortuitous development to the governor of his state, "This moment I am inform'd from good authority, Great Britain has actually refused the mediation of Spain, that His Catholic Majesty has declar'd he will no longer be an idle spectator in the present contest—that he has actually join'd in alliance with France and these United States."[17]

Even though American delegates wrongly interpreted events in Europe to mean that Spain was heading rapidly toward an alliance with the United States, this was thrilling news. Not only did it proclaim to the world that Britain now faced three formidable foes, the United States, France, and Spain—because King Charles III had in fact declared war on Britain in June as an ally of France—but it also freed the American Congress from the vice grip of the Spanish mediation. The United States no longer had to devise terms of peace in full deference to Spain, for fear that both France and Spain might abandon the cause of independence if the Congress caused grave offense. Spain was formally in the war, allowing the Congress to assume its full authority and dignity as an independent belligerent.

Even though the Spanish mediation had unraveled, the prospects for peace had not. With Spain in the war, a peace treaty was, in fact, more probable now than ever. So the Congress immediately went to work completing its long-sought terms for that treaty as well as those for a treaty of alliance with Spain. After this, it appointed American ministers to sail to France and Spain in their defense. Regarding the fisheries, the Lee-Adams coalition was at long last persuaded by the other delegates in Congress that an ultimatum in the peace treaty itself overtly breached the Franco-American alliance. Therefore, the instructions, as approved in August, required that under no circumstances could a peace treaty be signed forfeiting that right. The document must either stipulate a positive American right granting access to the fisheries or say nothing at all, allowing Americans to fish and dry as freely as before the war by the purposeful omission of a prohibition.[18]

This was the first security to the New England interest. There were three more—and a final one hoped for. Second, the United States would engage in no trade at all with England until a positive right to the fisheries was formally granted in a commercial treaty. Third, if in the interim between a peace treaty and a commercial treaty Great Britain did molest American boats and fishermen, the United States as a nation would respond with the much-discussed second declaration of war, a war for cod and haddock. The fourth aspect of the new diplomacy of the fisheries was a requirement of Franklin to advance an amendment to the Franco-American alliance of 1778 at Versailles incorporating the fisheries as a shared privilege of France and the United States as a casus foederis. That is, if Britain interfered with either French or American fishing at any time after peace, the military and naval alliance would be reactivated. Each nation would defend the right of the other, and, if necessary, new wars would be carried on until fishing was restored. The fifth security to American access to the Newfoundland fishery the Lee-Adams coalition intended to wrest from the Congress was appointment of a New Englander as ambassador in chief of peace negotiations.

*****

In those negotiations, as always, the foreign policy of the navigation of the Mississippi River remained the most vexing. In March Richard Henry Lee had risen to his feet in Independence Hall with a proposed resolution that he affirmed was the only sure pathway forward in European negotiations to achieve unobstructed American navigation of the river. Lee had not formally trained as a lawyer, but more than anyone in Congress, at least until James Madison joined the body the next year, he was the United States' most brilliant legal and geographical mind when it came to the lower Mississippi River and the Treaty of 1763, which had opened the river's commerce to Spain, France, and Britain fifteen years earlier.

Lee's resolution inserted an ultimatum into U.S. terms for peace with Britain, stating categorically "that the navigation of the river Mississippi be acknowledged and ratified absolutely free to the subjects of the United States." Lee understood that he was asking King George to award to the United States a commercial right His Majesty in fact had no right to give—navigation through twin Spanish banks at the mouth. Nevertheless, Lee was more farseeing and crafty than were most of the other delegates. In order to end the War of Independence with the new nation's right to freely navigate the Mississippi secured, he wanted to strengthen the American hand as much as possible. When the time came to engage in diplomatic battles with the cagey Spanish minister Floridablanca over the

Mississippi, he wanted the United States to have a fighting chance. And that defense was going to be a competing international treaty already signed by England and the United States affirming that King George had formally passed along his right to navigate the lower river to his American descendants at the moment of their emancipation, like an inheritance. American ministers would wave this treaty at the Spanish and refuse to back down.[19]

The strategy was a clever one, and it might have worked. The problem was that the Congress rebuffed it. Only a handful of delegates, including Lee's brother, Francis Lightfoot, rallied to support the motion, leaving it to die a quick death. By August and September, though, when the time had come to reach a final determination about the Mississippi navigation, the Lee-Adams coalition put it on a similar footing with the fisheries, consenting to exclude the matter entirely from the peace treaty with Britain only if the right were elevated to the status of an ultimatum in a treaty with Spain. Like fish in the commercial treaty with England, the coalition wanted American ministers to sign no treaty or alliance with Spain until Charles III granted full freedom of navigation of the Mississippi to the United States from the river's source to the sea. This was the vital sectional quid pro quo that lay at the heart of the Mississippi-Fisheries Compromise.

The Lee-Adams coalition had to fight hard for this ultimatum on the Mississippi navigation because Gouverneur Morris of New York and John Witherspoon of New Jersey led a contingency of delegates who stridently opposed it. In their belief, the ponderous American demand to sail between Spanish shores was ill-founded and potentially ruinous. As an ultimatum, it might derail negotiations with Charles III and possibly destroy all hopes for the Spanish-American military alliance now so propitiously awaiting them in Europe. The coalition responded to this Middle state intransigence by calling on New Englanders to stand resolutely behind the Southern navigation, and with the backbone of both New England and the South behind it, the ultimatum passed on September 17.[20]

The two delegates who moved the Mississippi ultimatum most aggressively on the floor of Congress were Elbridge Gerry of Massachusetts and Samuel Huntington of Connecticut. Within days of the September 17 decision, Gérard and Miralles independently observed, with astonishment, that the New England states had voted robustly in favor of this hardline stance on the river. As the Spanish agent wrote back to the court of Madrid:

The Congress has agreed upon the points which will be presented to the Court of the King [Charles III], our Sire, by the Minister Plenipotentiary whom they will name to represent them there. I have learned that they are the same points that I have had the honor of reporting to Your Excellency, except that now they claim free entrance and egress on the Mississippi River. This claim has been advanced by the members from the northern provinces, which actually are the provinces to which that privilege is least profitable. I have tried as well as I am able, lacking authority to do so otherwise, to inform and to convince them that our King will never accede to that demand, and Monsieur Gérard has helped me by doing the same.[21]

* * * * *

To close out the tortuous foreign policy work of 1779, all that remained to be done was to appoint two ministers, an American peacemaker and an ambassador to Spain. To the delegates, these elections were nearly as important as the formal instructions because diplomats in that era bore extremely broad powers on their missions conducted an ocean away. The critical issue was the slowness of trans-Atlantic communication. Negotiations typically moved more quickly than the bare minimum of the three to four months necessary to complete back-and-forth letters, leaving an ambassador much to his own devices. Hence, the character and commitments of the U.S. representative abroad seemed almost as crucial as the ultimatums and other directives the Congress had formally prescribed.

The Lee-Adams coalition wanted both posts—the peace position for John Adams, cousin of Sam, and the Madrid ambassadorship for Arthur Lee, brother of Richard Henry. The party of Morris, Jay, and other opponents of the Mississippi and fishery ultimatums, after having given so much ground already, fought these appointments fiercely. They promoted instead then-president of Congress, John Jay, for peace minister. There were "great debates," according to New Jersey delegate John Fell, and again a compromise was forged. The Lee-Adams advocates would relinquish the post of American ambassador to Spain to the Morris-Jay party if the Congress agreed to Adams as peace minister. This "accommodation scheme," reached in the last week of September, left the coalition elated over the accession of John Adams but fretting over the precariousness of putting the Spanish negotiation into the hands of a Middle state delegate who had decisively opposed the Mississippi navigation as an ultimatum from the beginning. James Lovell of Massachusetts, chagrined by the irony and folly of the appointment, penned an exasperated letter to John Adams on the day of Jay's appointment. In the letter he cuttingly derided "the parliamentary propriety of appointing a man to carry into effect by all the powers of skillful negotiation a measure to which he has been opposed tooth & nail in the whole preparatory progress of it."[22]

Miralles and Gérard, on the other hand, were highly satisfied at the selection of Jay for Madrid. "The choice of Jay leaves nothing to be desired," Gérard wrote to Vergennes. "To much intelligence and the best intentions, he joins an amiable and conciliatory temper." Miralles similarly expressed pleasure to his court that Jay, a pro-France and pro-Spain man, had been appointed, notwithstanding the troublesome instructions Congress had saddled upon him. To Miralles, Jay had consistently shown a sympathetic attitude toward His Catholic Majesty and was therefore the ideal choice for the representation of America.[23]

Jay set sail from America for the coast of Spain aboard the thirty-six-gun frigate *Confederacy* with his wife, Sarah, in late October. Less than a month later, peace ambassador John Adams shipped out with aides and his two sons, John Quincy and Charles, on the similarly outfitted French frigate *Sensible*. Adams had only returned to the United States from Paris four months earlier, after Congress replaced the three-person commission to Versailles with Franklin as sole French ambassador. Now Adams embraced a second mission abroad, and to prepare him for success, the Lee-Adams coalition barraged him with information about the seven-month Mississippi-fisheries debates, together with exhortations about what they expected him to accomplish. In September, October, and November, his friends and allies within the coalition condemned the Congress's weak-willed, bowdlerized ultimatums and revealed full details of the political fights that had taken place, including New England's written threat to withdraw from the Union if the fisheries were not honored. Effectively, Sam Adams, Lovell, Gerry, and Lee signaled to John, one of their number, that regardless of the official ultimatums, his real mission at the peace tables in Europe was to obtain independence, the Mississippi boundary and navigation, and the fisheries by whatever means necessary.

In support of these highly important objectives, James Lovell went to the most trouble of all. In November he duplicated the records of Congress pertaining to the Mississippi and fisheries, placing them directly into Adams's hands before his departure. In the diplomatic correspondence, there are twenty-two such entries all under the same rubric, "Proceedings of Congress as to Conditions of Pacification, and Particularly as to the Mississippi and Fisheries." Adams received these papers while onboard the *Sensible* and awaiting ripe winds to sail into the Atlantic, scribbling a note on them, "Recd on Board *Le Sensible* Novr. 17. 1779. Debates and Votes about the Fisheries and the Mississippi." Lovell included with the copies an explanatory cover letter requesting his friend to study the records well and to assert American rights daringly in peace negotiations. He encouraged Adams not to heed the counsel of those who would make the United States cower and pay court to the every wish and demand of France. He closed with a succinct statement of one of the driving philosophies of the coalition: "The way to insure the lasting regard of France is by showing independent virility instead of colonial effeminacy."[24]

Before the ship weighed anchor, Adams also heard from Richard Henry Lee. The Virginian was "well pleased," he wrote, with his Massachusetts friend's appointment as peace commissioner, adding that it was "the crowning work" of a year's labor. In the letter to Adams, Lee also took special care to advance his case that the best strategy for obtaining the Mississippi navigation was likely going to be to etch this right into the peace treaty, not relying on the success of an uncertain Spanish treaty. "I heartily wish you success in your negotiation," Lee urged, "and that whilst you secure one valuable point for us (the fisheries), you will not the less exert your endeavors for another very essential object, the free navigation of the Mississippi, provided that guilty Britain should remain in possession of the Floridas. I totally despair of this navigation from any other advocation."[25]

PART THREE

FIRST CONSTITUTION AND THE PERILS OF PEACE

CHAPTER 13

"The Body Politic Is Sick, Sick Indeed!"

By the early months of 1780, Peace Minister John Adams and ambassador to Spain John Jay had made no significant progress in their negotiations in Europe to obtain treaties that secured American independence together with the prized triad of the trans-Appalachian western lands, navigation of the Mississippi, and fishing and drying rights at the island of Newfoundland. At home, meanwhile, these same matters, plus the ever-elusive Articles of Confederation, continued to divide the United States politically.

Nothing, except for supplying the Continental Army, was more crucial to the security of the thirteen states than finally ratifying the federal compact, and here, as always, the bitter contest over the western lands stymied the Congress. Completing that bond of Union was imperative, Congressman William Churchill Houston of New Jersey explained by letter to Robert Morris of Pennsylvania, because "postponing it to the arrival of peace will leave the states in danger of a dreadful separation." Philip Schuyler of New York was more explicit about the consequences of a failure to ratify an American constitution. He said, as had so often been expressed before, that a state of postwar disunion would precipitate civil wars. "I contemplate with anxious concern," Schuyler wrote to Jeremiah Wadsworth of Connecticut, "that if ever the enemy should be reduced, a few years will bring on civil contests which will deluge this country in blood." Schuyler was clear to assert that the only solution that could arrest the advance of this catastrophe was "a Constitution for Congress." In spite of these incessant forebodings, however, Maryland continued to rebuff the Articles until Virginia first ceded most of its western territory to the national treasury. Maryland had long since drawn an unyielding line: no land, no Union. And by all appearances in 1780, her state legislature and delegates in Congress had no intention of backing down.[1]

In the view of many Americans, the proud state of Virginia, not Maryland, was the true source of the constitutional crisis paralyzing the Congress and imperiling the Union. The Old Dominion matched Maryland in its intransigence on the western lands; in the summer of 1779, with the state/federal land conflicts far from resolved, the Virginia assembly had passed an act opening a land office in Williamsburg whose purpose was to commence selling portions of the state's unappropriated western acreage. In Philadelphia, news of this provocation "produced much uneasiness, dispute and controversy." Houston of New Jersey reported that "the Virginians and our Southern friends" were being "roasted and basted" in Congress on account of their western pretensions, most notably the Virginia delegates after their state's late preemptive move to open the land office. Some solution to the land issue, Houston encouraged, was vital for the "peace of the Union." Another delegate, Gouverneur Morris, went public with his outrage over the land office and Virginia's monstrous claims, declaring in the *Pennsylvania Packet* that the new United States could never brook such inequality and land greed as Virginia's in the founding of a just republic.[2]

An incisive writer, Morris issued a diatribe against Virginia and her late "pre-emption," arguing that the western lands were an inalienable right of all thirteen states, not only one of them:

> What, my countrymen and fellow-citizens have twelve of the United States done that they should be excluded an equal participation of the lands in that immense Western country? And what extraordinary effort has the thirteenth (or Virginia) State made that she should at once grasp and rapaciously seize on one hundred and twelve millions of acres . . . whilst all the other States of America, who have bled at every pore, and their very uttermost penny taxed for the exigencies of the general good, are deprived of their unquestionable and unalienable right?[3]

Calculating the state's dubious western claim to be near 112 million acres, worth the "enormous sum" of $149.3 million, or £44 million, he called the Virginia claim "contrary to the spirit of the confederation." It would work "evils" and operate "to the prejudice of the others, who have equally fought and bled for them." While the rest of the states would expand little or remain geographically as they were, Virginia would grow to a "great superiority" in the Union. If congressional lawmakers did not defeat the Virginia claim, Morris declared, the despotism of King George was going to be replaced by the despotism of Virginia.

In response to the land office and the furor it sparked in Philadelphia, Congress passed a resolution, over the objections of Virginia and North Carolina delegates, asking the Old Dominion to shut down the divisive office and desist in all sales of plots. Dispatched by circular letter to all thirteen states, the resolution read:

> Whereas the appropriation of vacant lands by the several states during the continuance of the war, will, in the opinion of Congress, be attended with great mischiefs; therefore, Resolved, That it be earnestly recommended to the State of Virginia, to re-consider their late act of assembly for opening their land office; and that it be recommended to the said State, and all other states similarly circumstanced, to forbear settling or issuing warrants for unappropriated lands, or granting the same during the continuance of the present war.[4]

For Virginia and North Carolina, the two states with the largest western claims and most imminent plans to expand over the Appalachians to live and profit by them, this act by Congress was wrongful on two counts. First, the Congress had no jurisdiction over the internal matters of a state, which included the management and disposition of its chartered lands. Second, as delegates knew, something more than attention to the public good was at work in the Congress's gesture to close the land office. Behind the scenes, land speculating companies like the Vandalia and Indiana Companies were lobbying Congress to oppose especially the Virginia claim because it conflicted with the companies' past territorial purchases from Native Americans and other acquisitions made over the years through convoluted corporate combinations. The land companies, whose promoters hailed primarily from Pennsylvania and Maryland, intended to cash in on their holdings after the termination of the war. Therefore, they were doing everything in their power to corner Congress into validating them. James Madison, a Virginian soon to arrive in Philadelphia for his first term as a congressman, deplored the operators of these companies and the congressmen associated with them as "land mongers." In the constitutional analysis of Virginians, all questions of law and justice on the matter were clear. Neither land companies nor Congress had any right whatever to breach a state's sovereign territorial rights.[5]

Many of the same delegates in Congress who were fighting Virginia's land claims and its precipitous opening of the land office were firmly of the opinion, too, that the Congress had erred when it dispatched Ambassador Jay to Spain with his hands tied on what John Hanson of Maryland once called "the cursed claim set up to the free navigation of the Mississippi." The Spanish treaty was too important to be sabotaged by the folly of an ultimatum favoring only a handful of states and of no immediate benefit to the military prosecution of the Revolution. Therefore, only a month after the Congress adopted Jay's orders on the navigation, a keystone of the Mississippi-Fisheries Compromise, two leading antagonists to the ultimatum, Morris of New York and John Witherspoon of New Jersey, made a motion on the floor of Congress granting Jay the authority "to recede from the claim of a free navigation of the river Mississippi . . . if the obtaining such navigation shall be found an insuperable bar to the proposed treaties of amity and commerce between these states and his Catholick Majesty."[6]

The motion failed, but it was polarizing and damaging to the Union. To Virginians and other Southerners interested in the Mississippi navigation, the Morris-Witherspoon attempt to surrender the Mississippi was a red flag indicating that their states' essential maritime and territorial rights were not safe in the hands of Congress. South Carolinian Henry Laurens was still in Philadelphia at the time, keeping watch over the Mississippi-Fisheries Compromise. Chief framer of the compromise, Richard Henry Lee, back in Virginia, frequently inquired with Laurens about its status, reminding his colleague that the United States must obtain treaties ending the war "without the loss of either of our legs." After the attempted reversal of the Mississippi ultimatum by Morris and Witherspoon, Laurens replied, "The two Legs are made Ult[timatums], but yesterday there was a proposition for reconsidering & expunging the Southernmost, I opposed it, after an hours debate."[7]

Laurens revealed further to Lee that he had personally confronted Morris on his impure motives for desiring to deprive the Southern states of the Mississippi navigation. "I told the advocate for expunction, I had long since heard every word he had offered in support of his motion-out of doors." Presumably Laurens was referring to the open secret in Philadelphia, often promoted by Morris, that the Congress should close the Mississippi River to American commerce for the sake of preventing

Southern expansion and population growth at the expense of the Northern seaboard states. One fear of some Northern delegates was that an open Mississippi River, added to the western lands' cheap sales prices, would trigger an unprecedented boom of migration southward to the territories later to become the states of Kentucky and Tennessee, depopulating their states, depreciating land values, and sinking their economies into depression. As Morris had also privately confided to Ambassador Gérard a year earlier, almost certainly with the corrupting influence of slavery in mind, "The current provinces of the South were already weakening the confederation . . . the austerity and vigor of the North would always be the Republic's safeguard; and that it was in this direction that they ought to expand and consolidate." The New York congressman was referring to his hope that the United States would expand, not in a southwestern direction, but northeasterly into the territories of Canada, Maine, Acadia, Nova Scotia, and the Gulf of Saint Lawrence.[8]

* * * * *

Political leaders in Virginia universally disdained the Congress's meddling in their state's territorial affairs, and they worried that any acts of usurpation by the Congress would threaten the Union. Therefore, once again, as it had done in its formal resolution in 1776 calling upon the Congress to declare independence, the Virginia Assembly passed an act drawing a stark line between matters of state and federal sovereignty. In 1776 the commonwealth consented to break away from the British empire and join a confederation of independent states "provided, that the power of forming government for, and the regulations of the internal concerns of each colony, be left to the respective colonial legislatures." In December of 1779, with cries growing louder in Congress to strip Virginia of its western patrimony, and with Maryland blocking the ratification of the Articles of Confederation on this basis, the state reasserted the inviolable principle of state prerogative on all internal matters, most obviously relating to its chartered territory. The assembly did this by way of a formal act entitled Remonstrance of the General Assembly of Virginia to the Delegates of the United American States in Congress Assembled, soon dispatched north to its delegates in Philadelphia.[9]

Virginia had been the first state to ratify the Articles of Confederation two years earlier, and in the language of the December 1779 act, the assembly now highlighted that Article IX of that document was unambiguous on the question of jurisdiction over land ("no State shall be deprived of territory for the benefit of the United States"). That is, the taking of a state's property, or land, was patently unconstitutional by that federal charter. "When Virginia acceded to the Articles of Confederation," the remonstrance of 1779 asserts, "her Rights of Sovereignty and jurisdiction within her own territory were reserved & secured to her, & cannot now be infringed or altered without her Consent."[10]

The Virginia act made no specific suggestion of actions the state might take if Congress violated this covenant, but it did avow generally that disastrous internal consequences would follow any such federal self-arrogation of power, including civil violence. "In the process of time," the remonstrance pressed, such acts "must degenerate into an intolerable despotism." The precedent of stripping a state of its land would shake the foundations and sanctity of property rights, and, if tolerated, "a general confusion must ensue; each State would be subjected, in its turn, to the encroachments of the others, and a field opened for future wars and bloodshed."

By late 1779, members of the Virginia Assembly were also keenly aware of the insecure state of the navigation of the Mississippi in Congress. So in order to block future attempts by Morris, Witherspoon, and other Middle state delegates to unravel the ultimatum, they adopted a companion act on the river. Recognizing that no constitutional argument could be set forth on the question of the Mississippi, since Virginia had no real jurisdictional claim to it between Spanish shores, the assembly refrained from issuing a high-toned mandate to Congress forbidding it to surrender a right to navigate. Instead, they issued a binding order on Virginia delegates in Philadelphia—and, only by implication, on the federal body itself. The act carried the title Resolution Instructing Delegates in Congress, in Treaty with Spain to Stipulate for Free Commerce of Mississippi.

In any treaty with Spain, the act charges, the Virginia delegates in Philadelphia were bound to demand "an express stipulation in favour of the United American States, for the free navigation of the river Mississippi to the sea, for the purpose of trade and commerce, with the right of mooring vessels to the shores of said river." The Assembly also required a free port or ports accessible to seagoing vessels, and, underscoring the immediacy of their commercial aspirations on the river, it requested a consulate in whatever town was chosen as the American free port. In the language of the act, any treaty with Spain should stipulate "the free navigation of the gulph of Florida between the said river and the Atlantic ocean, with a free port, or ports, in the Island of New Orleans, or some other convenient place or places for exportation and importation, and the privilege of a consul to reside there."[11]

In order to safeguard its western interests—and the Union—Virginia also continued to advocate in favor of ratifying and implementing the Articles of Confederation without Maryland, which more than one delegate in Congress found to be an intolerable proposition. The Virginia assembly had approved this course of action in late 1778, and in May of the next year the state's delegates had formally advanced it on the floor of Congress. North Carolina, for one, gave the prospect of a "partial Confederacy" serious consideration in the same months Virginia was adopting its resolutions on the western lands and the Mississippi navigation. Initially the North Carolina assembly approved the measure. But days later it reversed itself after Thomas Burke made an impassioned plea to his countrymen that a partial confederation risked a prolongation of the war and possibly disunion.[12]

Burke's worries centered on future regional conflict over the ratification of a peace treaty, stemming from a troublesome constitutional technicality. According to the Articles of Confederation, a supermajority of nine states in Congress was required to formally ratify any peace treaty signed by American diplomats in Europe. This nine-state balance reflected an underlying formula of a two-thirds majority, meaning that if the Union were composed of thirteen states, five were empowered to reject such a treaty, keeping all the rest in the war at their whim. Burke considered this minority control over a peace treaty to be a "dangerous power." What he had in mind was the power of the New England states to keep the other states on the battlefield without end until Britain finally awarded the United States their coveted Newfoundland fishing rights. In the event of a partial confederation of twelve, as proposed by Virginia, Burke expected the Congress to recalculate the votes needed to approve a peace treaty, still using the two-thirds principle. This was the critical point. If twelve states composed the constitutional Union, this math would shift the number needed to defeat a peace treaty from five to four—handing the four states of New England an absolute regional veto.[13]

Burke deplored this prospect. Generally, as he told his fellow North Carolinians, "a partial Confederacy must be followed by confusion." It would be the source of "divided councils" and "may lay the foundation of disunion." Burke's appeal on these grounds was successful. The North

Carolina assembly rescinded its resolution permitting its delegates in Congress to enter into a partial confederation. Adopting a wait-and-watch approach to the constitutional Union, it decided instead to defer the matter to future consideration.

* * * * *

In the winter and spring of 1780, with England now at war with naval behemoths France and Spain as well as the thirteen independent states, many American patriots felt optimistic that King George and members of Parliament would come to their senses and seek peace. If not, the great empire stood to lose not only its American colonies and several West Indies islands in a protracted war, but possibly also the Floridas, Gibraltar, Minorca, and numerous other of its global possessions. "If Britain unsupported by friends or allies, and rent asunder by domestic jars and discontents," New York Congressman James Duane wrote to Washington, "can continue an unjust and unpopular war against the joint efforts of America, France and Spain, she will exhibit an example of obstinacy and of vigour unparallelled in history." Yet that is precisely what happened. Britain fought on, and, unexpectedly, 1780 turned into the darkest year of the war yet for Americans. A perfect storm of economic, military, and constitutional crises struck the fragile United States with the worst existential dread it had experienced since the end of 1776. As British forces adopted an aggressive new Southern war strategy, many delegates were predicting the end of the Union of thirteen. Driven by necessity, some Northern delegates advocated the radical remedy of preserving the independence of as many Northern states as possible, even if it meant sacrificing Southern ones to the cause, restoring them to the empire.[14]

By March the American economy had descended into mayhem. For the Congress and the Continental Army, what paper money they possessed had become worthless due to ruinous hyperinflation. By one calculation, it cost $20,000 to buy a horse and $400 to acquire a hat. With no real gold or silver coin in Congress's coffers, the American people, the states, and even most delegates were losing faith altogether in the Continental dollar, originated as paper currency in 1775 as part of a larger financial scheme to tax the states to back the new federal money. Worsening the crisis, expectations ran low that the institution of the Congress would survive long enough to meet its obligations to redeem the bills for specie. The expression "not worth a Continental" entered the lexicon at this time.

The states did not comply with Congress's requisitions of tax money, and as prices rose and a bona fide financial panic set in, farmers hoarded life-saving foodstuffs for themselves and their communities, refusing to sell even to the Continental Army. "The want of money for public use and the distress arising from that source," Rhode Island delegate Ezekiel Cornell wrote, "is beyond the power of my pen to describe."[15]

Perhaps most demoralizing to the patriotic delegates serving the Union under personal duress far from home, currency speculators throughout the states, preying on vulnerable bill holders fearful that the dollar's value would continue to plummet, were stepping in to harvest the bills for pennies, further eroding the people's trust in the Union and the Congress. In the early days of the Revolution, the Continental dollar had been championed as "a new bond of union to the Associated Colonies." Four years later William Whipple, a New Hampshire delegate, accused "speculating miscreants" of "sucking the blood out of their country." David Ramsay, a Charlestown physician and later one of the first historians of the Revolution, commented on the depressing state of affairs: "A spirit of money-making has eaten up our patriotism. Our morals are more depreciated than our currency."[16]

The financial crisis, of course, did not exist apart from the Congress's failure to ratify a constitution legitimizing itself. As John Sullivan of New Hampshire reminded a correspondent, the languishing of the Articles of Confederation, a weak instrument of government in any event, deepened the pessimism. His worry emanated from a confluence of factors: "Our Confederation is not in force & even if acceded to would be found weak & perhaps far from answering the designs, our treasury is empty, our credit low, our finances deranged & the people at large suspicious of every species of our paper emissions." General Washington, who was no alarmist and rarely complained to politicians, wrote regarding the army, "We have not at this day one ounce of meat, fresh or salt, in the magazine." And, the commander in chief advised, "Certain I am that unless Congress speaks in a more decisive tone, unless they are vested with power by the several states competent to the great purposes of war . . . our cause is lost."[17]

Alexander Hamilton, aide-de-camp to Washington, concurred with his superior's assessment, telling James Duane, delegate from New York, "The fundamental defect is a want of power in Congress." In the same letter, Hamilton reported that the Continental officers and soldiers were justifiably aggravated by the inability of the Congress to pay wages.

"Without a speedy change," Hamilton said, referring to the dysfunctions of Congress, "the army must dissolve; it is now a mob, rather than an army, without clothing, without pay, without provision, without morals, without discipline. We begin to hate the country for its neglect of us."[18]

* * * * *

Another threat facing the United States was a seismic shift in British war strategy. Until 1780 the commanders of the king's army and navy had largely concentrated their forces and engagements with the enemy in the Northern states. No part of the South was under British control, with the exception of the port of Savannah and swaths of Georgia, placed under royal arms in the winter of 1778–79. By the end of 1779, however, the Northern war was deadlocked, leading the British ministry to call for an invasion of the South, a region long considered a hotbed of underground loyalist support and fertile ground for slave rebellions and enlistments. Accordingly, in late December of 1779, Lieutenant General Henry Clinton, commander in chief of British forces in America, launched an expedition of ninety transports carrying 8,500 troops to the coast of South Carolina. By February most of this convoy had landed at a location some twenty-five miles south of Charlestown, with the intent of laying siege to the seaport.[19]

In Congress news of this expedition and its landing on the South Carolina coast set off a wave of alarm that the British high command meant to wrest Charlestown from American hands as a first blow in a grand strategy aimed at the "Conquest of the Southern States," as Congressman James Madison put it by letter to Governor Thomas Jefferson. Madison was hardly alone in assuming that Clinton's purpose in grasping Charlestown was to establish a base from which to sweep northwest across South Carolina and from there into North Carolina and Virginia. South Carolina delegate John Mathews likewise perceived the triggering of a domino effect in the event of the fall of Charlestown. The countryside of South Carolina would not last long, he told Robert Livingston, and the next target would certainly be North Carolina. "I see nothing to prevent it," Mathews said in an anxious letter, "& I believe our enemy have at last seen their true interests, & the conquest of the Southern States is now become their object, & a settled plan formed to effect it." John Sullivan, a New Hampshire delegate and major general in the Continental Army, wrote to Washington about the ultimate outcome of a successful British strategy, one eventually reaching into Virginia.

"I fear the loss of the four Southern States will be the consequence," he projected.[20]

If the Congress had been a formidable, united political body, it could have weathered the quadruple traumas of financial crisis, constitutional crisis, a dissipated army, and now an invasion of South Carolina expected to portend the downfall of the Southern states. But instead, the Congress was a polarized, disunited body beset by a lack of faith in its future. Ezekiel Cornell of Rhode Island attributed much of the dysfunction of the government to the destructive habit of delegates blaming one another for every problem and setback. "I suppose there is not a set of men on earth more fond of charging their blunders to other people's fault than we are," he wrote to Nathanael Greene of his state. To Cornell and many other delegates, it appeared in the spring and summer of 1780 that the Continental Congress was in its death throes. Henry Laurens wrote to Richard Henry Lee that "the body politic is sick, sick indeed!" Pointing to a failure of virtue in the delegates as the primary cause of disorder, Laurens continued, referring to his fellow congressmen, "The servants of the house are more & more riotous & unless relief be immediately administered by wise exertions of the better branches of the family a dissolution or violent convulsion will infallibly be the consequence." Philip Schuyler of New York also felt hopeless about the American government. The loss of South Carolina, he wrote to Robert Livingston, also a delegate from New York, "will superadd to the difficulties we already abundantly experience." Schuyler echoed the sentiment that Congress lacked "wisdom and virtue," which exposed "the political ship to the danger of becoming a wreck thro the incompetency of the pilots. I need not tell you that our affairs are running rapidly to some violent crisis, that the present disorders do not seem to admit of remedy."[21]

In turn Livingston, at home in New York at the time attending to the birth of a child, wrote to a third New York delegate, James Duane, confidentially sharing his view that the Continental Congress was beyond recovery. His letter was cryptic, but Livingston seems to be indicating to Duane that a Northern confederation might be the only lifeline:

> I may condole with you on the new scenes of trouble and anxiety which have opened upon you . . . God send you that spirit of firmness & decision, which becomes every hour more necessary. I am greatly mistaken if daily experience will not teach you that the bond which ties us together is too weak for the exertion that our

circumstances require, and that the confederation even if agreed to, would only prove a nominal union. Greater powers must lodge somewhere, or our efforts will continue to be what they have hitherto been, weak & disjointed, & as the respect for a powerless body will every day diminish, the evil will every day increase till the voice of the people shall vest elsewhere what Congress are unwilling to trust themselves with.[22]

Perhaps more than any other delegate, Cornell of Rhode Island had grown exhausted by the internal struggles of the United States of America. His faith remained unshakeable in New England, he reported in numerous letters in the first half of 1780. But he had lost faith in both the Southern states and the Congress. "The fate of these United states are pregnant with the most alarming events that ever attended them since the commencement of this unnatural war," he wrote to the governor of his state. Singling out the Southern states as weak elements wholly dependent on the Northern ones for their survival, and specifically Virginia for deplorably investing its energies in the defense of its western lands rather than in the common war against the British, Cornell said that the Middle states were roused "upon the principles of honour, virtue, or danger, to make a common defence," together with New England, but not the Southern ones. "In a word," he summarized, "we have but little to expect south of Maryland, the once patriotic state of Virginia weighs but little at present in the scale of defence, or furnishing of men or supplies, her whole attention is ingrossed in making sale of her out lands." He added that lately the Congress had called for revisions of several articles in the Franco-American treaty of amity and commerce, wrongheadedly awarding enhanced powers to France to impose duties on American commerce, "for which we may thank our Brethren in the Southern states." The Union was dissolving, Cornell said, because too many states were "turning all their views to their own advantage without consulting the common good."[23]

In this zeitgeist the delegates generated three potential solutions to avert the impending dissolution of the United States' weak wartime republican government. One was to turn over the management of the war and the federal government to a "Dictator." Cornell said this emergency measure was widely discussed in Philadelphia in mid-1780. In one letter, he explained, "The different policy of the several states and too many of them turning all their views to their own advantage without consulting the common good, cause some able politicians to think that our political salvation in a great measure depends on a controuling power, over the whole, being lodged in some person or persons." In a second letter he clarified exactly what and who he meant. "The necessity of appointing General Washington, sole Dictator of America, is again talked of as the only means under God by which we can be saved, from destruction."[24]

A second remedy contemplated by some Northern delegates in a hushed manner was a Northern confederacy. As the subject of a regional confederation was taboo, even treasonous, most congressmen dared not put words to paper in communication about it. Historians instead find frequent promises in letters to reveal private thoughts and happenings only in person, due to the politically sensitive nature of the content. "I have a thousand things to say to you, which prudence forbids being committed to paper," declared one delegate. "To answer your letter fully wou'd be to commit to paper that which I dare not by any means do," reasoned another. "I fear the most fatal consequences will follow. I cannot give you particulars at this time," said a third. Nevertheless, rare letters survive that shed light on the plans of some delegates to resolve the desperate challenges and polarizations of an ungainly Union of thirteen by paring it down to a smaller, more homogeneous republic.[25]

In this instance, with the Southern states under threat of imminent conquest by the British, one New Englander, John Collins of Rhode Island, wrote to the governor of his state to assert that the moment was clearly fast approaching, in May of 1780, when they must cut the American republic down to size. Collins, like others, wished not to print treasonous intentions in overtly plain English, so he employed a metaphor of a ship with thirteen masts, by which, he told the governor, "you will understand me." In tempestuous weather, Collins said, the American ship of state was rapidly approaching rocks and shoals, and she would soon run aground for want of proper rigging to hold all thirteen masts upright and avert disaster. The shipwreck "will carry away her thirteen masts," he continued the metaphor, but when this occurred, Rhode Islanders should not despair because the hull will be made sound and "we will rig her anew, with fewer masts and move, shrowds and stays, I have no fear but she will weather the storm."[26]

A final solution to the tempestuous storm menacing the breakup of the United States was the ratification of the Articles of Confederation. Once adopted by all thirteen states, the Articles would constitutionally outlaw disunion and the formation of separate confederacies, thereby averting secession and domestic civil wars. Two days after Collins announced that the critical moment might have arrived to rebuild a smaller American republic out of the wreckage of the Continental Congress, New York delegate James Duane wrote to Washington that he was laboring to secure "a federal alliance." In early May, Duane reported, he was "much engaged in another attempt to get the Confederation accomplished." He continued, "It gives me great pleasure to assure your Excellency that the delegates from Virginia are warmly disposed to give it all the aid in their power: & I indeed have the fullest expectation that our joint exertions will succeed: and the future safety and tranquillity of the states be fixed on a permanent basis."[27]

Duane was working intimately on this project of ratification of the Articles with senior Virginia congressman Joseph Jones, who soon announced to Governor Jefferson that the salvation of America depended upon the swift adoption of a permanent constitutional Union. Finally, after years of resistance, Jones and other Virginians were realizing the only way to achieve this safe harbor was for their home state to cede her western lands northwest of the Ohio River to the federal treasury. This act of cession from Virginia would satisfy Maryland and thereby cement the Union. "The present is the season for accomplishing the great work of Confederation," Jones told Jefferson. "If we suffer it to pass away I fear it will never return."[28]

CHAPTER 14

"A Confederation of Very Dissonant Parts"

IN THE MIDST OF THE many difficulties besetting Congress in 1780, intelligence came onto George Washington's desk in early May, and shortly thereafter into the hands of delegates, that a French fleet densely packed with fighting men was expected to arrive on American shores sometime during the summer. This was the famous Expédition Particulière of seven ships of the line, three frigates, and a cutter under the naval command of Chevalier de Ternay carrying on board some 3,000 French marines as well as General Comte de Rochambeau and 5,500 land troops. This was brilliant news, but, remarkably, it further aggravated the bond uniting the thirteen states because a question quickly emerged in Congress relating to American war strategy that pitted perceived Northern interests against Southern ones.[1]

In light of the fact that British commander Clinton had recently deployed roughly one-third of British military and naval strength to Charlestown, it might seem obvious that General Washington and his top advisers would speedily meet force with force, redirecting Continental troops and French allied ships down the Atlantic coast to offer relief to the largest and most prosperous seaport in the Southern states. But Clinton had left a reduced naval presence in New York Harbor, under British arms since 1776, at the very same moment that Ternay and Rochambeau were crossing the water. Therefore, a critical question presented itself: Should American and French forces be coalesced and concentrated in the South to raise the siege on Charlestown and thereby thwart Britain's intended conquest of the Southern states, or should they rush into New York Bay where the moment was ripe at last for the recovery of New York and the lower Hudson, one of the most important cities and commercial river systems in the North?

Unsurprisingly, three New York delegates, James Duane, Philip Schuyler, and Robert Livingston, advocated strongly in Congress that recovering New York and the Hudson River constituted the brightest hope of undercutting the British and winning the war. Duane heralded a combined operation of Continental and French troops and ships on New York, perfectly timed to take advantage of fresh augmentation by Ternay and Rochambeau, as a "golden opportunity to draw the war to a successful period." Together, these three New Yorkers launched a quiet campaign to persuade first Washington and then the Congress to adopt this policy, notwithstanding the almost certain consequence of the fall of Charlestown. They went daringly further, too, than a proposal for all new American enlistments and French forces to join in the campaign for New York. To ensure success, they wished to recall Maryland soldiers and those under the command of General Charles Lee, all recently deployed southward. Washington was not opposed to the New York operation, as he himself believed that the decisive blow should take place at the mouth of the Hudson. Still, aware of the sensitivity of the matter, he asked Schuyler, who met with him for several days in mid-May at Morristown, to take the measure of Congress and seek consensus. Schuyler wrote to Duane, and in Congress Duane and Livingston agreed to conduct political reconnaissance in hopes of winning congressional approval.[2]

This effort of Duane and Livingston in Congress proved short-lived because they found no Southern delegates willing to go along with such a politically and geographically combustible project. Duane reported back to Schuyler in the third week of May, "We have privately stated the subject to some of the Southern Gent. who tho' I believe convinced of the propriety of the measure did not choose, after great deliberation to have it adopted, much less to propose it." He went on to explain that some delegates from the Southern states had come to believe that the Congress, if given the chance, would sign a peace treaty with Britain granting independence to eleven states only, in exchange for Congress's restoration of South Carolina and Georgia to the British empire. Given this circumstance, Duane said, no Southerner would touch the project. "That the reinforcements ordered to the southward should be halted is obvious for the reasons you assign," Duane wrote to Schuyler, "but do you expect such a proposition from a Northern member deeply interested in strengthening the main army? It is a question of the utmost delicacy and even danger: for, however groundlessly, an opinion has been propagated that Congress meant to sacrifice the two southernmost states & it has been productive of great animosity and discontent."

Chapter 14: "A Confederation of Very Dissonant Parts" 259

FIGURE 35. James Duane, New York Delegate. (Portrait of James Duane. John Trumbull, *James Duane*, 1805, oil on canvas, New York City Hall Portrait Collection.)

Similarly, Livingston informed Schuyler at army camp that obtaining congressional consent to sacrifice Charlestown for New York was a dead letter. "I have laboured hard to bring about a recall of the Maryland Line but without success," he warranted. He went on to say:

> To move it myself would have lost us the confidence of the Southern States & excited an opposition which would have effectively deprived us of the power of being useful upon other occasions. I endeavored to prevail on Mr. Jones or Mr. Matthews to make the proposal, in which case we could have supported it with so much force as to have overborne all opposition. They were brought to wish it, but did not dare to move it when it came to the point.[3]

Days later Livingston was so bold as to present a motion himself to recall General Lee's corps of troops, but he immediately withdrew it when Southerners and New Englanders opposed it in unison. Livingston explained that New England stood with the Southern states in this case in order to maintain their "confidence." What he meant is that the New England delegates were siding with Southern interests to ensure the favor would be returned whenever New England interests came onto the floor—that is, the Newfoundland fisheries as an ultimatum of European treaties.[4]

Some Southern members of Congress were indeed raw about Congress's seeming inattention to the Southern states at a moment of life-and-death exigency. John Mathews of South Carolina, for one, was livid over his fellow delegates' early refusal to deploy reinforcements to Charlestown to prevent a disaster. Attributing this resistance to a combination of outright prejudice in favor of the Northern states and congressional inertia, he wrote to General Horatio Gates that "were an angel from heaven to perch on the back of the president's chair & proclaim the immediate annihilation of the southern states, unless something vigorous, & effectual was done, & even point out the mode, I sincerely believe, as soon as he had taken his flight, & the surprise had subsided, they would just sink again into the same torpid state in which he found them."[5]

Aggrieved, Mathews further told Gates that he could write a volume on the subject of Congress's injustices to the Southern states—and he did. The South Carolinian pushed hard for a "Southern campaign" to safeguard Charlestown, expecting the assembled delegates in Congress to take up their rightful mantle of "guardians of the United States." His fellow congressmen did give consideration to such a campaign, he reported, but it was short-lived because regional selfishness overwhelmed public interest:

> As soon as selfishness, and the apprehension of danger to these [Northern] states, from the adoption of such a plan, had repossessed their minds, every art & contrivance was made use of, to silence the just demands of the Southern states for support, & the business was at last got rid of by the old, stale trick of proposing a committee to go to camp to consult with the General. . . . Thus you'll see, my dr. sir, how little is to be hoped from the best plan that human genius can invent, whilst men's minds are warped by self-interest, & the danger is at a distance.

Mathews asserted that justice required the Northern states to offer the Southern ones the same succors in 1780 that Southerners had provided to the common cause in first years of the Revolution. He recounted:

> In the beginning of this war, whilst the efforts of the enemy were pointed to the reduction of the Northern States, men were drawn from every state in the Union (except So. Carolina & Georgia,

whose local circumstances you well know would not admit of it) for the defence of those states in danger, & some of the people of the Southern States, undertook a march of 1000 miles, & underwent the fatigues of it with cheerfulness to effect so laudable & so desirable a purpose, & those that did not send men contributed their aid of money & with great good will, & an affectionate zeal, & would have with alacrity done anything in their power towards the support of the common cause. How the scene is changed. The war is most evidently transferred from the Northern to the Southern States, & in my opinion their conquest there are meant to be solid & permanent. Then have not those states, now the theater of war the same right to expect, the support of the united efforts of the other states? Should not the grand army be now employed there, as it has heretofore been here?

The dispute over the deployment of the French fleet, however, was soon made moot. The reason is that in the beginning of June the Congress learned that all was lost at the Southern seaport of Charlestown. On May 12, after six weeks of bombardment from land and sea, American major general Benjamin Lincoln surrendered 5,700 American soldiers and 1,000 sailors. It was the largest capitulation of troops in the war thus far—and of American history until the Civil War—leaving the Congress in despair. William Churchill Houston of New Jersey called the news "a bitter cup of ill tidings." Henry Laurens reported to Richard Henry Lee that "every man is praying to Jupiter."[6]

James Lovell of Massachusetts expressed his pessimism in a letter to Abigail Adams, attributing the loss of the gem of Charlestown to the corrosive influence of slavery on the Southern fighting spirit. "Only last night could we determine that Charlestown was taken," he said. "It is a fatal blow indeed to that country in particular as well as injurious to the common interest of the Union. Look for the cause in the aristocratic temper of mind which must of course be generated in the rich masters of many slaves." Describing the Union as "a Confederation of very dissonant parts," Lovell professed that the remaining hope of the Revolution resided in "extraordinary exertions in the Middle and Eastern States." It was left to them to counteract the failure of the Southern states to rouse to their own defense.[7]

The fall of Charlestown put an end to the hope for a surprise Franco-American attack on New York for two reasons. First, Continental troops must now unquestionably be deployed to the Southern states to check

British incursions into the South Carolina countryside and North Carolina. Second, British commander Clinton discovered in late May that the Ternay-Rochambeau expedition was on its way to America. Therefore, as soon as his army and navy secured Charlestown and locked down American captives, he ordered the preponderance of his ships and men back to New York to reinforce the mouth of the Hudson. These twin developments dashed the United States' "golden opportunity," as James Duane had described it, to recover New York in the summer of 1780.

* * * * *

One source of dispiriting news for the Southern states that year was the fall of Charlestown and the rumor that the British intended to proceed swiftly to invade North Carolina and Virginia, with unknown consequences for the independence of the Southern states in peace negotiations in Europe. Specifically, as Nathanael Greene, American commander of the Southern Department, soon wrote to Jefferson, a British sweep across the South put "the Independence of the Southern States" at risk. There was yet another concurrent blow to Southern interests, though. It was bad news on the Mississippi navigation. In the second week of August, Congress broke the seal on a forty-page dispatch from Ambassador Jay, dated May 26, that reported on his first conference with Foreign Minister Floridablanca.[8]

Floridablanca's message to Americans was unambiguous. They would never attain treaties of alliance and commerce with King Charles III unless they first reversed their stance on the navigation of the Mississippi River through Spanish shores. As Jay recorded in a careful précis, the minister observed at their meeting that "there was but one obstacle from which he apprehended any great difficulty in forming a treaty with America, and plainly intimated that this arose from the pretensions of America to the navigation of the Mississippi." Jay defended the American right as best he could, but Floridablanca would not back down. "He spoke amply of the king's anxiety, resolution, and firmness on this point," Jay continued, "and insinuated a wish that some method might be fallen upon to remove this obstacle. . . . [It was] a point from which his majesty would never recede."[9]

Jay had been president of Congress during the long and tortuous months of the Mississippi-fisheries debates of 1779. As well as anyone, he understood the delicacy of the Mississippi navigation in American sectional politics. So in his report, perhaps hedging, he left room for hope. And underscoring that his role was to act as an agent of Congress,

Chapter 14: "A Confederation of Very Dissonant Parts" 263

he expressed his wish to exercise no independent judgment or authority whatsoever:

> What passed in the course of this conference needs no comment, though it calls for information and instructions. If Congress remains firm, as I have no reason to doubt, respecting the Mississippi, I think Spain will finally be content with equitable regulations, and I wish to know whether Congress would consider any regulations necessary to prevent contraband as inconsistent with their ideas of free navigation. I wish that as little as possible may be left to my discretion, and that as I am determined to adhere strictly to their sentiments and directions, I may be favored with them fully and in season.

Many delegates assumed such a bulletin alerting Congress to the fact that the Mississippi navigation alone was blocking an alliance with Spain would precipitate a political crisis. "There is a capital question respecting our western extent & free navigation on the Mississippi suddenly to come on," John Armstrong of Pennsylvania soon wrote to a colleague. However, for several reasons, the Congress responded to the news with equanimity and unanimity, electing to remain stiff on the navigation. One reason the Congress did not fall into crisis over the Mississippi is that Virginia responded to the diplomatic setback with a timely introduction of its Resolution Instructing Delegates in Congress, in Treaty with Spain to Stipulate for Free Commerce of Mississippi. Adopted by the Virginia assembly ten months earlier, the state's delegates had strategically held the resolution in reserve for deployment at a moment of threat like this one. On August 22, 1780, the Virginia delegates formally presented the resolution prohibiting them from consenting to a surrender of the navigation. It was read aloud in Independence Hall, then referred to a committee charged with formulating a reply to Jay's letter.[10]

There is a more compelling reason, though, for the Congress's unanimous decision to stand by the Mississippi-Fisheries Compromise of 1779. It stems from a project of that body even more vital to the survival of the Revolution than Spanish money, troops, and ships. By chance, Jay's report arrived in Philadelphia during the same period a committee of Congress was intensely negotiating with the Virginia delegates to yield their state's claims to the Northwest Territory as the means of finally cementing a perpetual constitutional Union of all thirteen states. Senior statesmen James Duane of New York and Joseph Jones of Virginia took the lead in the committee, and both men were entirely persuaded that the Articles of Confederation must be ratified soon—or else the United States as a Union of thirteen would be lost forever.

To put pressure on Virginia, the New York Assembly had adopted a resolution in February ceding its claim to western lands in the Great Lakes region to Congress. The assembly titled the resolution, An Act to Facilitate the Completion of the Articles of Confederation and Perpetual Union among the United States of America, and in its text New York affirmed that only "a federal Alliance" could preserve "the Tranquility and Safety of the United States of America." On June 26, Duane in Congress moved for the formation of a committee to study the New York cession together with the twin opposing acts of Virginia and Maryland on the western lands for the purpose of forging a compromise—one that would, to his mind, rescue the United States from dissolution. Congress approved the committee, appointing five members, Duane, Jones, John Henry of Maryland, Roger Sherman of Connecticut, and Willie Jones of North Carolina. The committee was still in the heat of deliberations when Jay's news on the Mississippi navigation came to hand. Duane, Jones, and the other committee members would not submit their final recommendations on how to rescue the Confederation until September 6.[11]

For the Congress to have provoked a confrontation with Virginia over the navigation of the Mississippi at this critical juncture of the Union itself would have been political suicide. It was simply too much to ask Virginia to cede 60 million acres of its chartered land for the sake of the Union and to request that it also give up the navigation of the Mississippi in a treaty with Spain. This would have been folly of the highest order, as the delegates in Philadelphia understood with clarity.

So by tacit agreement among committee members—Jones served on both the committee on confederation and the committee on Spain and the Mississippi established on August 21—the Congress would present a unified front on the Mississippi in order not to blow up the precarious land-for-Union deal on the Confederation. This logic explains why in the early fall the Congress robustly reaffirmed Jay's mandate on the Mississippi and why, shortly after, it tapped James Madison Jr. to write a comprehensive diplomatic treatise laying out the legal, economic, and political justifications for Congress's claims of both the navigation and a U.S. boundary placed at the eastern bank of the river. The reinvigorated instructions to Jay bid him to "adhere to his former instructions respecting the right of the United States of America to the free navigation of the river Mississippi into and from the sea," including a port.[12]

Chapter 14: "A Confederation of Very Dissonant Parts" 265

The Congress dispatched the instructions accompanied by Madison's explanatory treatise, a 3,600-word tour de force on the United States' western interests written for the eyes of not only John Jay in Spain but also any Spaniard, Englishman, Frenchman or fellow delegate in Congress who doubted the American states' rightful claims to the Mississippi boundary and navigation. In the first half of the paper, Madison marshals six proofs of point to defend American ownership of the trans-Appalachian territory, combating the popular argument that these lands in fact belonged to King George III, not the individual states that claimed them based on royal charters. First, Madison says, the king never actually owned the lands. He was always merely a representative of the people who held them in trust for Americans. In 1776 the thirteen United States had canceled the king's representation of them in government, Madison insists, not their just rights or property claims on the Atlantic seaboard or on the Mississippi River. Second, scores of Americans already lived beyond the mountains (in the future states of Kentucky and Tennessee), and these citizens "could not by voluntary transfer be subjected to a foreign jurisdiction without manifest violation of the common rights of mankind and of the genius and principles of the American Governments."[13]

FIGURE 36. James Madison, Virginia Delegate. (Portrait of James Madison. John Vanderlyn, *Retrat de James Madison*, 1816, oil on canvas, 26 x 22.1875 in, White House Collection / White House Historical Association.)

Third, Americans had expended blood and treasure in the French and Indian War for the sake of the western lands, and, more recently, the military triumphs of Virginian George Rogers Clark and the successful erection of Fort Jefferson at the confluence of the Mississippi and Ohio Rivers had earned Americans fair title. Fourth, the Franco-American alliance of 1778 guaranteed to America its western possessions. Fifth, the Mississippi was the most "natural" boundary between Spanish America and the United States, and if another line of demarcation were to be adopted by treaty, it would be the source of future "disputes." The Congress could not prevent "intrusions" by its citizens, interrupting harmony between the two nations. Lastly, Madison made the strange but constitutionally valid argument that Congress, and therefore Ambassador Jay in Spain, did not have the authority to delimit any of the states—and, if it did so, it would be treading on hazardous ground. In Madison's words: "As this territory lies within the charter limits of particular States and is considered by them as no less their property than any other territory within their limits, Congress could not relinquish it without exciting discussions between themselves & those States concerning their respective rights and powers which might greatly embarrass the public councils of the United States and give advantage to the common enemy."

As for the navigation of the Mississippi, Madison laid out a separate litany of reasons why Spain should permit trade. First, the Peace of 1763 ensured freedom of passage as an inviolable right to Anglo-Americans. Second, if Spain wished for the friendship of the United States, as purported, the navigation must be shared. Otherwise the country would be blatantly placing the United States in "a worse condition" on the river than her enemy, Britain, a nation that had enjoyed navigation rights for more than a decade. Third, natural law and international law both favored the American position because closing a major river to an inland nation would "contravene the clear indications of nature and providence, and the general good of mankind." And, by precedent, a nation holding the mouth of a river could offer no greater impedance to an inland nation's trade than "the right of imposing a moderate toll." Fourth, a free port was required due to the geography and contours of the river and the shape and engineering of boats and ships; trade could simply not exist without it.

Fifth and last, American commerce floating into that free port would one day be colossal, Madison said. The "commercial sagacity" of Charles III should therefore lead him to avail his nation of the opportunity rather than force American trade northward into the Great Lakes and

Canada, benefiting England. Madison asked Spain instead to unite with the United States as an ally at a free port like New Orleans in order to deliver "a decisive blow" to the British empire's maritime preeminence and tyranny over the seas.

* * * * *

The Congress sent off these communications to Jay at the end of October. Almost as soon, circumstances of diplomacy and war put the navigation of the Mississippi back into jeopardy. Even on the same day of the formal adoption of Madison's treatise on the river and lands, an unpromising update from Spain was read to the assembled Congress. It said, "This court manifests a strong desire of excluding every other nation from the navigation of the Mississippi, and, indeed, of the Gulf of Mexico." Thus began a steady flow of correspondence from Jay that fall and winter announcing repeatedly that the navigation was the "sole obstacle" to a Spanish treaty and to obtaining subsidies and loans of money to the United States to sustain the war.[14]

Acting in synergy with this intelligence from Spain, European diplomats on the ground in Philadelphia were lobbying the Congress to overturn the ultimatum on the river, and in the last months of 1780, disturbing news came to the city of an unexpected proposal by Catherine the Great to bring the war to a speedy conclusion in a Russian mediation. By this time French Ambassador Gérard had returned to France, and Spanish observer Miralles had died of pulmonic fever. Miralles's secretary, Francisco de Rendon, took over the informal Spanish consulate in Philadelphia, keeping Floridablanca and King Charles III apprised of American affairs. Gérard was replaced by Anne-César de La Luzerne, a former major general of the French army distinguished in battle in the Seven Years' War. Ambassador Luzerne brought with him a chargé d'affaires and secretary of legation named François Barbé-Marbois. These three European envoys concerted their efforts to persuade the Congress to give up the ill-founded claim to the navigation of the Mississippi through Spanish shores. Moreover, they aggressively challenged the "Charters of the Southern States," claiming that the lands lying east of the Appalachians were British, not American.[15]

French ambassador Luzerne warned openly that if the United States did not release its obstinate clutch on the western lands and Mississippi, it might never see Spain send a single ship to American shores. More subtly, he hinted that France might in equal proportion to such American

FIGURE 37. Anne-César de La Luzerne, French Ambassador. (Portrait of Anne-César de La Luzerne. Henry Bryant Hall, *The Chevalier de la Luzerne*, 1857, etching, New York Public Library, EM14022.)

stubbornness tighten its grasp on its money, guns, and ships, drying up its support of the Revolution. Therefore, he told congressmen, the United States must desist in these overblown claims, and "it would be advisable to restrain the southern states from making any settlements or conquests in those territories." Barbé-Marbois circulated a position paper in Philadelphia entitled "Observations Sur Les Points Contestes de la Négociation Entre L'Espagne et Les Etats-Unis," in which he argued that only conquest or settlement, not insubstantial ancient charters, could convey true title to land. The chargé d'affaires further clarified that "settlement" meant actual occupancy, not temporary incursions. Such occupancy must be demonstrated "by building of houses, clearing & inhabiting the land." Barbé-Marbois called on the Congress to acknowledge the realpolitik of the Revolution. Spain had no need whatsoever of treaties with the United States. She was strong and powerful, while the United States was, by contrast, "a patient extremely ill." In return for American acquiescence in matters vitally important to her, the Spanish king would acknowledge independence, open his commerce, turn his resources to the aid of the states, and support American claims at the peace tables.[16]

Meanwhile, reports from Europe revealed the formation of plans by Empress Catherine of Russia to mediate a truce to end the fighting on the basis of uti possidetis, a principle of international law permitting each combatant to retain all lands held under its arms on the day hostilities ended. This formula would almost certainly force South Carolina and Georgia back into the British empire once a peace treaty was signed. Within months, these accounts in Philadelphia, promoted by the French and Spanish envoys, would be authenticated: Catherine the Great and Emperor Joseph II of Austria were indeed offering to Britain, France, and Spain a co-mediation grounded precisely on this resolution to the crisis between England and her colonies.[17]

In Europe at this time, French minister Vergennes was facing extraordinary pressure from other enlightened monarchs to adopt a face-saving policy toward America that would bring George III to the bargaining table, even if that meant abrogating the Franco-American alliance's promise of independence for all thirteen states. One proposal on the table was an agreement wherein some of the Southern colonies would be united with the two British Floridas to form a logical, staple-rich regional bloc of English colonies to replace the original thirteen. Vergennes was grappling with this tough compromise, recognizing, however, that the Congress would never surrender New York City and the mouth of the Hudson River in a treaty based on uti possidetis. He was less sure, though, about the Congress's willingness to part with South Carolina and Georgia, where intelligence in Europe held that the spirit of independence was feeble. Some reports from America additionally warned of growing animosities between the Northern and Southern states. According to one alert that came onto Vergennes's desk, the Southern states were at one point forming an army to fight against the North, then felt by some Southerners to be neglecting the weaker planter states in their hour of greatest need.[18]

These conditions led to a surprising turn of events in Philadelphia. In November several congressmen took to the floor of Independence Hall to denounce the ultimatum on the Mississippi, calling for its immediate revocation. This time the supplicants were not Middle states delegates but two from Georgia, George Walton and Richard Howly. They had decided the time had finally arrived to raise the white flag on the long-contested river. Accordingly, on November 18 Walton and Howly moved to rescind the ultimatum, and so desperate were they for Spanish rescue from the prospect of a settlement of the war on the basis of a severance of the lower Southern states from the Union that they also proposed that the United States transfer to Spain a strip of land on the eastern bank of the Mississippi extending almost two thousand miles from the Georgia border with the river to its headwaters near the Great Lakes. This would be given in a lifesaving quid pro quo. In return, the Georgians asked Spain not only to sign an alliance but also to provide the United States an annual subsidy of half a million pounds sterling for twenty-five years or a loan of double that sum annually during the war.[19]

Two "whereas" clauses that precede the resolution explain the Georgians' fears and reasoning. The first declaims against a partition of the states in any peace treaty: "Whereas a powerful armed neutrality hath been formed in Europe . . . and a congress of the neutral powers is said intended to be held in the ensuing winter, by which it is not improbable overtures of peace may be made and that the principle, uti possidetis, may be the foundation, a principle utterly inadmissible by these States." The second demonstrates that they viewed the surrender of the Mississippi as the salvation of the occupied Southern states because it would cause Spain finally to consent to an alliance:

> Whereas it has been represented that the only bar to an alliance with Spain, which it is our great interest to effect, is, the navigation of the river Mississippi. . . . Resolved, therefore, that Mr. Jay be instructed, in case he shall find it indispensably necessary, to yield in his instructions heretofore given, upon this subject, and that he be empowered to cede to the Crown of Spain the entire Navigation of the river Mississippi, together with a tract of territory.

The motion was read in Congress that Saturday. Delegates postponed further consideration of it until the coming Wednesday, November 22.[20]

* * * * *

No one in the Continental Congress was more shell-shocked by the Georgians' precipitous abandonment of the navigation of the Mississippi, along with the radical idea of selling its eastern bank, than James Madison. Unfortunately, when the event happened, Joseph Jones, his close collaborator on all matters pertaining to the trans-Appalachian West, had returned to Virginia on a mission to persuade the assembly to cede the Northwest Territory to Congress to cement the constitutional Union. Worse than Jones's absence, the only other Virginia delegate in Philadelphia at the time, Theodorick Bland, joined Georgia in the defection. So, too, did the South Carolina delegates. Bland argued to Madison that the time had come for Virginia to make the sacrifice. Independence and the other states had waited long enough, he said. The Mississippi must be surrendered for the good of sister states Georgia and South Carolina—for the Revolution and for the Union. The danger of the partition of the states outweighed the value of the Mississippi.[21]

Madison, who grew up on the western frontier of Virginia, refused to go along, and a quarrel of many weeks' duration between the two Virginians ensued. A skeptic, Madison told Bland and others that he doubted the authenticity of the recent diplomatic maneuvers in Europe. He doubted a partition stood any chance of success in European chancelleries. What was happening instead was that Spain and France were playing on the United States' fears in a prostrate moment of war to exact from them the Union's most precious rights and resources. That is, there was a strong element of trumped-up, manufactured crisis in all that Floridablanca, Vergennes, Luzerne, and Barbé-Marbois were pushing, and, in response, the Congress must keep a cool head. In a letter to Jones, Madison said that he had done everything possible to persuade Bland to change his position. He explained that Spain's inflexibility and the threats of a partition of the states were "artifices for securing her objects on the Mississippi." He said that John Adams's correspondence confirmed that the Spanish were masters of "ministerial finesse."[22]

From Richmond, Jones soon wrote back to Bland, urging him that he must step back into line on the Mississippi. "The navigation of the Mississippi is of the first consequence to all the southern states," he stressed, emphasizing that the water right would be even more essential to the formation of new states on the Mississippi in the years to come. By now Jones had come to identify the navigation of the Mississippi not only with a specific "part" of the United States—that is, the South—but also with Southern expansion over the Appalachians, which would lead to the creation of more Southern states to augment the region's economic and political power. The navigation, he admonished Bland, should "not to be relinquished upon any consideration but absolute necessity, which alone can justify the sacrificing the clear and evident convenience and interest of a part of the states, for the advantage of the whole." Jones added that westward expansion into the Ohio Valley could not be stopped, and if the Congress gave up the navigation now, it would mean war with Spain, and perhaps, later, France. Jones predicted, with certainty, that western Americans in Kentucky and Tennessee would never respect a treaty giving up their natural rights. "Those people who will settle on and near the waters of the Mississippi, in the United States," he told Bland, "will use the river, and a rupture must inevitably follow; better it would be for them and America to settle the terms of this use now, so as to prevent future contest about it."[23]

The Congress was scheduled to commence debates on the Georgia motion on Wednesday, November 22, 1780. But that day passed and almost two weeks more with no mention of the Mississippi or Spanish negotiations in the congressional record. During this tense period Madison remained confident that the Mississippi would remain safe. As he explained by letter to Jones, there were two reasons for this optimism. One was that it would be dangerous to the Union for the Congress to disregard Virginia's Resolution Instructing Delegates in Congress, in Treaty with Spain to Stipulate for Free Commerce of Mississippi. As significant, he placed great confidence in the tacit but powerful and enduring Mississippi-Fisheries Compromise of 1779. He predicted to Jones that the New England delegates, who were watching the diplomacy of the Mississippi carefully, would surely stand up against the Georgia motion if for no other reason than to assure themselves of Virginia's support whenever the fisheries as an ultimatum of peace next came to the floor. If the Mississippi were traded away for a Spanish treaty, Madison said, "The Eastern States must on the first suggestion take the alarm for their fisheries. If they will not support other states in their rights they cannot expect to be supported themselves when theirs come into question."[24]

* * * * *

Madison stood his ground for the next several weeks, when on December 4 he sat at the Virginia table in Independence Hall and listened to the content of three more dispatches from Jay and William Carmichael, the ambassador's secretary in Madrid. What he heard was disheartening. Still the Mississippi was the sole impediment, the source of an unbridgeable rift between Spain and the United States. This intelligence reanimated the Georgia motion, which the Congress debated in full the next day, December 5. Madison entered the hall steeling himself to combat the proposed revocation of the ultimatum. As he wrote to Jones that morning, "Both my principles & my instructions will determine me to oppose it."[25]

Madison offered his best arguments that day, but the majority in Congress refused to back him. In response, three days later, Madison countered the Georgia motion with one of his own. At a loss on how to proceed, but determined to avoid a crisis between his state and the Congress, Madison pushed onto the floor a resolution to desist all further consideration and action on the matter of the Mississippi until the Virginia Assembly could be informed and allowed to respond. "Resolved," read Madison's December 8 motion, "that the further consideration of the said propositions be suspended until such of the proceedings of Congress and of the communications from their ministers in Spain as relate to this matter together with the said propositions shall have been transmitted by the Delegates from Virginia to the Legislature of that State, and their ultimate sense thereon be made known to Congress."[26]

Congress granted this wish, and four days later Madison posted a letter with enclosures to Governor Jefferson in Richmond, requesting that he deliberate on the predicament of the Mississippi and Spanish treaty with the General Assembly. Madison asked the executive and legislature of his state to answer three questions. First, in exchange for a Spanish treaty, if nothing else would avail it, would Virginia permit its delegates to abandon the American claim to the full navigation of the Mississippi River? Second, was the state willing to give up any of its chartered land on the river to Spain, as Georgia had proposed, for the same purpose? The final question, of far more serious concern to Madison, related to the problem of state versus federal sovereignty. What if the people of Virginia said no, and Congress nevertheless carried on "without their concurrence" and, in the name of the United States, surrendered the river and/or land to Spain? Madison did not wish to be present in Philadelphia on such a day, and if he were to be there, he wanted to possess carefully constructed instructions from his constituents on exactly what to do.[27]

This final question to Jefferson and the assembly was pregnant with peril. Implicitly, Madison was asking if the Virginia delegates should simply submit or, more likely, respond to any override of the state's Mississippi order with political force, such as an ultimatum asserting that it would not cede western territory to the federal treasury until the Congress reciprocally supported the vital water rights of Virginia. Or the state might issue a stern warning, as it had done before on the western lands, that a congressional trespass of its sovereignty risked civil strife and bloodshed. At this time there was no court system to arbitrate federal/state conflicts, no supreme court for final appeals. There was not even a constitution, since the Articles of Confederation remained unratified and therefore inert in its exercise of influence over the Congress and states.

In such a circumstance, the most immediate powers of resistance a state possessed were the powers of protest and refusal to consent. If this failed to arrest an unwanted action of Congress, the only remaining instruments of leverage were threats of disunion. This strategy, after all, had worked many times before. At that very moment, Maryland was refusing to join a constitutional Union until justice was done on the matter of the western lands. In 1779 New England had menaced withdrawal and disunion if the Union did not back up its demands for fishing rights in Newfoundland in a peace treaty. And before that, South Carolina had walked out of Congress in order to pressure the other colonies into safeguarding its right to continue the rice trade in the Continental Association of 1774. Clearly, threats of disunion worked—together with implied civil war—when nothing else would.

CHAPTER 15

"The Power of Britain in These States Is Now Broken"

In early January of 1781 Virginia relented on both the Mississippi navigation and a sizable cession of western lands to the United States. The Old Dominion's motives for these capitulations derived from multiple sources. One was legitimate fear of an impending truce wherein British negotiators would fight with grit for the recovery of some or all of the Southern states. To surrender the Mississippi to Spain, according to credible reports from Congress, meant that King Charles III was going to swiftly embrace an alliance with the United States, rushing to their defense and thereby mitigating the risk of a partition of the thirteen in a peace settlement. This was a powerful inducement to Virginia at a juncture in the war when the manifest object of the British command was the subjugation of the Southern states.

On the matter of the western lands, Virginians, like other Americans, were by now persuaded that Maryland was going to hold out forever—even to the point of witnessing the thirteen states descend into chaos with no constitutional superstructure to rescue them. It was not hard to imagine what might happen if Vergennes and the other European ministers of the warring nations declared a truce on the principle of uti possidetis at the same time that the Southern states were largely in British hands and, as the coup de grâce, those same states were politically disunited from the Northern ones. Under diplomatic duress, the Northern states might be forced to separate from the Southern states. Foreign powers would argue that the Northern and Southern states were incompatible anyway, and further they were bound by no formal alliance or constitution requiring them to negotiate and act in unison.[1]

With the Articles of Confederation unratified, these arguments would be unassailable, at least as seen through the lens of international law and diplomatic tradition. No legal recourse could be made to the Declaration of Independence, either, because it created thirteen "Free and Independent States," not one nation-state. The Declaration twice makes reference to "the united States of America," and the lowercase "united" is hardly accidental. In 1776 the two-step plan of Congress was to declare the independence of thirteen separate republics and, in short order, to bind them up into a single offensive and defensive alliance, or confederation, to fight the war and resolve their differences. Still, in early 1781, almost five years later, the loose-knit states remained disunited. They were not bound to one another by any legally binding contract, and so, as the apprehensive thinking of that year went, the North-South bond of good faith might easily break apart at the negotiating table if British diplomats offered the Northern states attractive terms.

Fears of a partition of the thirteen states at the peace tables weighed heavily on the minds of Virginians in the winter of 1780–81. Yet a more acute military-naval event accounts for the timing of the assembly's twin reversals on the Mississippi and western lands on the same day, January 2, 1781. In the third week of December Jefferson received Madison's letter informing him of the extraordinary pressure Congress was exerting on Virginia to revoke its ultimatum on the navigation of the Mississippi. On December 25 Jefferson laid this letter before the Virginia Assembly for consideration, and five days later, on a Sunday, an express rider delivered news to Jefferson that the turncoat Benedict Arnold, now a brigadier general in the British army, had the day before steered a large fleet into the Chesapeake Bay. Arnold's forty-four-gun *Charon*, the *Fowey*, four frigates, three sloops, two brigs, and sixteen other vessels carried eight hundred men.[2]

Rumors circulated that the fleet intended to sack either Petersburg or Richmond, stirring unrest and dread in the capital but not yet an order by Jefferson to abandon the city or deploy the militia to its defense. Confirmation that Arnold's target was indeed Richmond reached Jefferson on Tuesday, January 2, near 10:00 a.m. On that same day, literally in the midst of panic and impending invasion, the Virginia Assembly forfeited the Mississippi and western lands. As they wrapped up this legislative business, Jefferson and assistants were hurriedly carting away confidential public documents, transporting them across the river to Manchester. Jefferson was one of the last to leave Richmond. He departed in the early morning of January 5, only hours before Arnold seized the town, raiding, burning, destroying, stealing, and freeing slaves at nearby plantations.

Chapter 15: "The Power of Britain in These States Is Now Broken" 277

Until this point Virginia had not been invaded by the British. Now, for the first time, enemy forces laid waste to a major city, ransacking the capital of the state. Afraid and humbled that January 2, Virginia passed resolutions on the Mississippi and western lands that it hoped would save the United States—and itself.

FIGURE 38. Benedict Arnold, Brigadier General in the British Army. (Portrait of Benedict Arnold. Henry Bryant Hall, *Benedict Arnold*, 1865, engraving, New York Public Library, EM3893.)

The first act adopted by the assembly ceded all its land holdings in the trans-Appalachian West to the federal treasury with the exception of the territories that later became the states of Kentucky and West Virginia. This meant that the commonwealth yielded to the United States some 260,000 square miles of land north and west of the Ohio River—a region roughly the size of the original thirteen seaboard colonies. The act explained that Virginia chose to make this massive grant because "the happiness, strength and safety of the United States depend, under Providence, upon the ratification of the articles for a Federal Union." However, the state affixed strict conditions upon the cession, the most controversial of which was a prohibition against Congress ever awarding in any manner whatsoever Virginia's ceded lands to private individuals or land companies that might claim ownership of them on grounds of previous royal grants or purchases from Native Americans. All such outside claims, the Virginia act required, must "be deemed and declared absolutely void and of no effect" by the Congress. This was a powder keg that would soon provoke new crisis in Philadelphia.[3]

After passing the resolution on land, the assembly freed its delegates in Congress to break the United States' ultimatum on the lower Mississippi. The succinct act on the river abandoned all demands for navigation rights between Spanish shores. It only required that Spain acknowledge the right of each American state that abutted the river to navigate that portion of the water "co-extensive" with it. In the language of the act:

> Resolved that the navigation of the river Mississippi ought to be claimed by Virginia only, as co-extensive with our territory, and that our delegates in Congress be instructed to procure for the other States in the Union, the free navigation of that river as extensively as the territorial possession of the said States reaches respectively. And that every further or other demand of the said navigation be ceded, if insisting on the same is deemed an impediment to a treaty with Spain.

With these words, the assembly released its delegates in Philadelphia from any and all obligation to protest a Spanish-American alliance that closed the mouth of the Mississippi to American trade. Nonetheless, Virginia did not give up all hope. In a concluding provision, the assembly ordered its congressmen to fight for a free port, even though not as an ultimatum. In spite of the relaxed nature of the new instructions, Virginia delegates in Congress should "use their endeavor to obtain, on behalf of this State, or other States, having territory on the said river, a free port or ports below the territory of such States respectively."

* * * * *

These two landmark Virginia acts, one sacrificing territory and the other western trade rights, reached Philadelphia during the last days of January. The Virginia delegates formally presented them to the Congress on the 29th. Since Annapolis was on the road between Richmond and Philadelphia, the leading citizens of Maryland learned of the land cession days earlier, and on February 2 its assembly formally approved the Articles of Confederation. Delegates in Congress heard the news and rejoiced. "It is with great pleasure I can inform you that the state of Virginia has ceded to Congress for the use of the United States, all their claims to that tract of country to the westward of the River Ohio," William Floyd of New York wrote to a correspondent, "and that the Legislature of Maryland has agreed to ratify the Confederation—this we consider as a most capital event in favour of this country, and have every reason to expect that many good consequences will result from it."[4]

James Varnum of Rhode Island marveled at the enormity of the grant: "The state of Maryland have acceded to the Confederation, reserving to herself a common right in the wild lands. Virginia have ceded to the United States all their claims west of the Ohio, including nearly sixty millions of acres." James Duane celebrated the news of the Virginia cession and Maryland's approval of the Articles to George Washington, while a separate letter from Joseph Jones of Virginia informed the general of the assembly's simultaneous anguished relinquishment of navigation rights on the lower Mississippi. "I presume you must have been informed," Jones wrote to Washington, "that Virga. has receded from her former instructions to her delegates in Congress respecting the claim on her part to the free navigation of the Mississippi which if approved by Congress will probably bring about an alliance with Spain and an acknowledgment of our Independence. No doubt this event if it takes place will give us more credit in Europe but we pay dear for it."[5]

In early February the Maryland assembly voiced its approval of the Articles of Confederation, but the Maryland delegates had not yet affixed their signatures to the constitution, giving it life. Nor had the Congress dispatched new orders to Ambassador Jay in Spain allowing him to remove the stricture on the navigation of the lower Mississippi. These final steps sealing the fate of Virginia's western interests and the American Union followed swiftly in the remaining weeks of February and early March.

The work of the Mississippi was completed first, in mid-February, when Madison penned a set of revised instructions to Jay permitting him to recede from the ultimatum. In accordance with Virginia's instructions, the Congress did exhort the ambassador to exert every possible effort to obtain "a free port or ports" on the lower river, but such a center of deposit and exchange was discretionary, not mandatory. Delegates approved this now third set of diplomatic instructions on the Mississippi on February 15. Three states were opposed, registering strong nay votes: North

Carolina, Massachusetts, and Connecticut. North Carolinians Thomas Burke and Samuel Johnston simply could not be convinced to trade away the navigation of the river for a Spanish treaty, and the New Englanders, whose people had no vested interest in western commerce, intended for their states to go on record as officially opposed to Congress's bartering away valuable water and navigation rights for any reason whatsoever, fearful the precedent might spur an unraveling of the ultimatum on the fisheries too.[6]

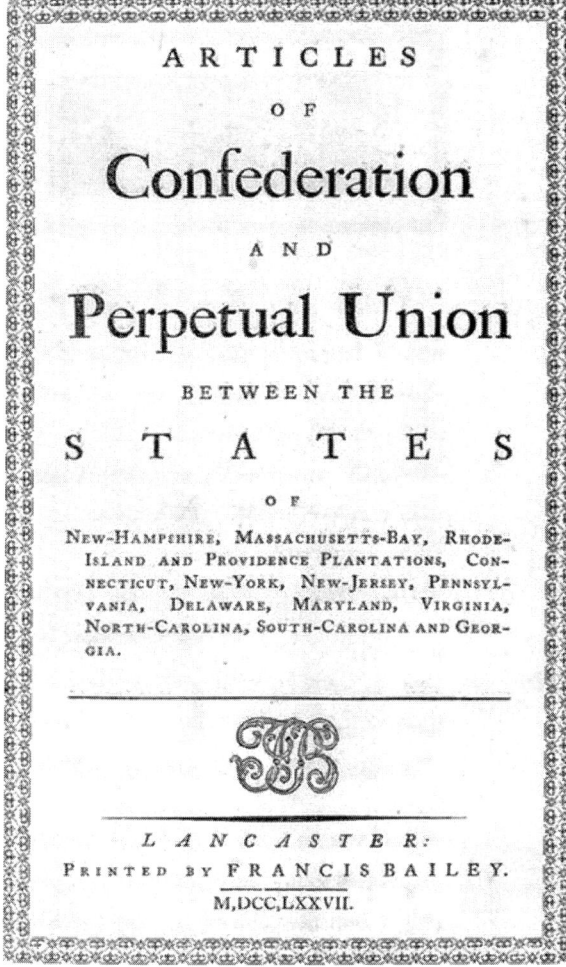

FIGURE 39. Articles of Confederation and Perpetual Union, 1781. (United States Continental Congress. *Articles of Confederation and Perpetual Union Between the States of* . . . . Lancaster, Pennsylvania: Francis Bailey, 1777, Chapin Library of Rare Books, Williams College, Williamstown, MA.)

Two weeks later, on March 1, John Hanson and Daniel Carroll of Maryland signed the Articles of Confederation on behalf of their state, formally inaugurating the United States' first constitutional government. After the signing, there followed the ringing of bells, a banquet, toasts to "The United States of America," the firing of a cannon on land (one boom for each of the thirteen states), a "feu de joye" on water from the frigate *Ariel*, and fireworks in the evening. The *Pennsylvania Packet* exclaimed, "Thursday, the first of March, will be a day memorable in the annals of America to the latest posterity, for the final ratification in Congress of the articles of confederation and perpetual union between these states." The *Pennsylvania Gazette* heralded "a Union, begun by necessity, cemented by oppression and common danger, and now finally consolidated into a perpetual confederacy of these new and rising States."[7]

Thomas Rodney of Delaware described that "great joy appeared in every countenance" on March 1. Theodorick Bland of Virginia said the signing was "accompanied with every demonstration of joy by all ranks of people in this place." The following day, March 2, the president of Congress, Samuel Huntington, informed the governors of the thirteen states by circular letter of the formal ratification, adding, "We are happy to congratulate our constituents on this important event, desired by our friends but dreaded by our enemies." John Mathews of South Carolina wrote to William Livingston of New York that the ratification of the Articles would avert "evil consequences." The new constitution, he said, gave him hope. "My expectations are highly flattered by this important event, & anticipate in my own mind the most happy consequences resulting from it."[8]

*****

The ratification of the United States' first constitution represented a milestone. It put in place a perpetual bond among the states that strictly prohibited secession, subconfederation, and resort to arms as means of resolving differences. It created a constitutional infrastructure for representation, voting, and dispute resolution as well as for building out formal departments of finance, war, and foreign affairs. Over the next six months, the most sweeping administrative reform took place in the treasury. The Congress appointed merchant-financier Robert Morris of Philadelphia to the prestigious new post of superintendent of finance. Morris, not afraid of bold initiatives, set about at once to transform the disorganized American treasury into a sophisticated financial machine, similar in his hopes to that of Great Britain. To create order while simultaneously uniting the states monetarily, he launched a program to lay the entire public debt upon the Congress, and he called upon the states to grant Congress the power to levy and collect taxes, a power egregiously absent in the Articles of Confederation. Additionally, Morris spearheaded the Bank of North America, which would provide loans and issue federal notes to serve as a medium of exchange for all thirteen states.[9]

Even with a perpetual charter and a reforming treasury, political and military leaders of course remained riven by jealousies and clashing views on how much power the states should grant the new confederation. On the military front, the Southern states were bearing the full brunt of the war, with some Southern leaders continuing to harbor no little resentment toward their Northern counterparts for failing adequately to relieve them. As British forces continued to make new inroads into Virginia throughout the spring and summer, torching homes and fields, Madison was inundated with letters expressing shock and bitterness at the perceived neglect. Madison's correspondents argued that the sudden invasion of Virginia caught the state virtually defenseless because for the past two years it had exhausted its resources by deploying troops, munitions, and foodstuffs southward to succor North Carolina and South Carolina. Now, in Virginia's hour of need, many of the state's leaders felt betrayed by Congress and the Northern states.

David Jameson, lieutenant governor of Virginia, wrote to Madison about these matters several times in 1781. "We have the burthen of four states on us," Jameson complained, "at least so far as respects money and necessaries to subsist the principal army, without aid from our Northern brethren. This was not the case when the enemy bent their force against Massachusetts or N York. Every state in the Union contributed at that time, and this, very largely."[10]

In another letter, Jameson recounted recent pillages of the British and Virginia's desperate need for arms, ammunition, wagons, salt, beef, port, corn, and flour. In these dire circumstances, the state's militiamen had been resorting to the deplorable tactic of impressment in order to feed themselves. Jameson said these raids on citizens were disaffecting many Virginians from the cause of the Revolution. And it was a grave injustice:

And when they reflect that their brethren to the North & East of them have a free & open trade, free from invasion and living in ease, & affluence—and will afford them no assistance, their sufferings become more grievous. Virginia freely contributed when her sister states were in distress—why is she left not only to struggle for herself under many difficulties, but required to bear the burthen of the whole Southern War?[11]

High-ranking Virginia officials George Mason, Richard Henry Lee, David Ross, Thomas Nelson, and Edmund Pendleton also complained to Madison about the neglect of Virginia by the Northern states and Congress. Of them, senior statesmen Pendleton, a lawyer and former delegate to Congress, wrote to him with the greatest vehemence. Mirroring Jameson, he asked, "Do Congress mean to leave the weight of this Southern War entirely upon Virginia?" Since the federal body in Philadelphia seemed so deaf to the state's needs, he told Madison, the Virginia Assembly had lately prepared a formal protest "against the Northern States." The manifesto declared that the burden of the Southern war was being unjustly borne by Virginia. Listing the many Northern battles joined by Virginia, and the many Southern battles in which the Northern states had contributed little, the assembly called for an urgent restructuring of the army and a new, invigorated war strategy to furnish Virginia with immediate "aids of men, money, and every warlike munition. If they are denied, the consequences be on the heads of those who refuse them." Ultimately, the assembly chose not to dispatch this inflammatory manifesto to the halls of Congress as a formal document. Pendleton instead sent it to Madison with the request that he privately convey its sentiments to Congress, but he should not publish it.[12]

The letters from Pendleton, however, kept pouring in. In one he alerted Madison to the fact that rumors were circulating in the state that Pennsylvania was holding back soldiers and supplies from Virginia because its leaders wished to undercut the Old Dominion's outsized claims to territory and preeminence within the confederation. "Our people are made very angry," Pendleton said to Madison, "by a report that the Pennsylvania [line], instead of forwarding their troops with that celerity, which their duty & the situation of things demanded, were throwing out insulting speeches that Virginia was too grand—let her be humbled by the enemy, & such like."[13]

Pendleton also shared with Madison his dismay that the Virginia Assembly had reversed its resolution on the Mississippi navigation, an object "of such inestimable importance to us." Why had this happened? Pendleton asked. What he was hearing from fellow Virginians was

FIGURE 40. Edmund Pendleton, Virginia Judge and Statesman. (Portrait of Edmund Pendleton. Henry Bryant Hall, *Edmund Pendleton*, 1872, engraving, New York Public Library, EM6254.)

that the project for ceding the Mississippi had been hatched not by the Spanish, but by delegates in Congress with interests inimical to those of Virginia. In this allegation, the writer was likely alluding to the known desire of some Americans to close the river in order to thwart the western expansion of Virginia and the other Southern states and therefore limit their growth in size and power. Pendleton further explained his understanding that there was a "cabal against Virginia" in Congress that knowingly dispatched New Yorker John Jay, America's ambassador in Spain, to do its bidding in negotiations with King Charles III. The cabal's objective seemed to be to obtain an advantageous treaty and alliance with Spain by giving up the river—with the double benefit of stripping Virginia of power and wealth. Pendleton reported that he had always had a good opinion of Jay and hoped this rumor of his treason to sister states proved false. If true, however, he told Madison that Jay should be "recalled & Sus. Per Coll."—that is, recalled from Spain and then hanged by the neck.[14]

* * * * *

In Philadelphia, Madison and the other Virginia delegates did not ignore these pleas and moods of despair in their countrymen. Several correspondents warned that if the Northern army did not soon come to the rescue of Virginia, disaffection would set in with unknown consequences. George Mason declared his "attachment to the cause of liberty" to be unfazed, but fatigue and pessimism were spreading in Virginia such that political leaders would be unable "to keep our people firm much longer." Jameson professed that since the siege of Charleston began in early 1780, the Middle states had done little to aid the Southern states—New England nothing at all. Without specifying his precise meaning, the lieutenant governor predicted "fatal consequences" would result if this policy did not change. Richard Henry Lee wrote to the Virginia delegates that "the unhappy crisis of our country's fate demands the closest attention of all her sons, and calls for the united wisdom and the strongest exertions of all others who may be affected by our ruin." Lee then called upon the Congress immediately to send George Washington and the Continental Army to Virginia, arming the general with "dictatorial power" to save the state from ruin.[15]

Such letters and reports prompted the Virginia delegates to action. On April 18 Madison proposed a motion on the floor of Congress calling upon Washington to reinforce the Southern states. In support of this, Meriwether Smith, also of Virginia, offered a solemn emotional logic in a speech to fellow delegates. He said that for "two or three years past" Virginians had worried that in the event their state were invaded by the British, the Northern states would give it up. If this came to pass, Smith warned, Virginia would thereafter consider those abandoning states to be the commonwealth's lifelong enemies. And infused with the wrath of betrayal, Virginia would join the British army and take up arms against the Northern states. As Thomas Rodney of Delaware, who kept notes on Smith's speech that day, precisely penned this assertion, "If they were neglected & were forced to give up to the enemy this consideration would make them very inveterate against those states and willingly help to conquer them."[16]

After hearing Smith's speech, the Congress referred the Virginia motion for Southern reinforcements to a committee of three. The fate of the motion is unknown, since no vote on it appears in the extant congressional records. Still, a powerful message was communicated, and not much later, Virginia congressman Joseph Jones directly wrote to Washington, a close friend, conveying similar sentiments. Jones alerted the commander in chief, then in New York, to the deteriorating situation of the Southern states, highlighting in particular that "Virga. receiving so little aid from the North occasions many of her citizens in their letters to the delegates to insinuate that as they are at ease and in safety they care not for the southern states." Jones declared that the ongoing burdens of war weighing so heavily on Virginians "may shake their fidelity and attachment to the cause." In this letter and one other to Washington written in May, he requested large-scale reinforcements be deployed to their home state, including French naval support.[17]

* * * * *

A second source of strain on the delegates during the six months after the formal inauguration of the Articles of Confederation was the inability of Congress to compel the states to comply with federal requisitions for money, military supplies, and troops. By all accounts, the Congress had perpetually united the thirteen states under a constitution that was "inadequate to the purposes of carrying on a vigorous war," as Jones summed up the problem. The powers awarded to the Congress by the Articles, his fellow Virginian Theodorick Bland concurred, were "totally inefficient to work the general weal." Specifically, the Congress lacked the authority to collect taxes, which was pushing the confederation to "the abyss of ruin" because the states were withholding payments. "To this cause alone," Bland continued, "is owing the embarrassed state of our finances—to this is owing the low conditions of our navy, to this the weakness of our army, and the scantiness of its supplies." One historian, Jack Rakove, aptly describes the government of the United States under the Articles of Confederation as a "Union Without Power."[18]

Of all the delegates who put their minds to the weakness of the confederation after ratification, none thought more clearly than James Varnum of Rhode Island. "There are two obstacles to that energy and vigor which are absolutely necessary in the United States," Varnum wrote to his governor. "In the first place, the United States have not vested Congress, or any other body, with the power of calling out effectually the resources of each state. The Articles of Confederation give only the power of apportioning. Compliance in the respective states is generally slow, and in many instances does not take place." The second obstacle, tied to the first, was what the Rhode Islander called "an extreme, tho' perhaps well meant jealousy, in many members of Congress." Congressmen were constantly engaged in combatting the "abuse of power" by Congress, Varnum observed, disabling the body from finding the crucial middle ground necessary to win the war.[19]

Varnum was terribly worried that spring and summer. As he wrote to the governor of Rhode Island, the consequences of the defective structure

Chapter 15: "The Power of Britain in These States Is Now Broken"

of the Articles of Confederation "may be fatal." Apologizing for his pessimism, yet affirming that it was his duty to speak the truth about impeding dangers, Varnum predicted that "the time is not far distant when the present American Congress will be dissolved, or laid aside as useless, unless a change of measures shall render their authority more respectable." The only path to avoiding this outcome, he urged, was to strengthen the Articles of Confederation, and the only way to accomplish this feat against the odds was "to form a convention." Members of Congress should be largely excluded from the convention, Varnum advised, because their prejudices would injure its hopes of success. "It should be the business of this convention," Varnum said, "to revise & reframe the Articles of Confederation, to define the aggregate powers of the United States in Congress assembled, fix the executive departments, and ascertain their authorities." The Rhode Island delegate knew such a proposal would offend, if not madden, many Americans, so he thought up a way to gain their acquiescence in the plan. The promoters of the convention should declare in advance that the new government would be temporary, not permanent. The powers granted would "expire at a given or limited time."[20]

Varnum, at least privately, put forward this avenue of escape from the power deficiencies of the Articles of Confederation. Other delegates, also grappling with the problem, proposed different solutions. One was John Mathews of South Carolina, who pronounced in late May that, upon careful consideration, it was his view that the only cure to the Union's ills was the immediate transfer of "dictatorial powers" to Congress. He preferred to award this temporary power not to any single individual, but to the duly elected federal body. "Something like this must soon be done, or as I am clearly convinced," Mathews alerted Nathanael Greene, commander of the Southern theater of the war, "our affairs will grow from bad to worse, which must end in our utter ruin."[21]

One of the scenarios of disaster Mathews foresaw was a forfeiture of some of the Southern states back to Britain as a means of ending the war. But this, he said, was a fool's errand for any Northern delegates considering it. "However they may amuse themselves with the idea of sacrificing some for the good of the whole," he told Greene, "the hypothesis will prove fallacious." The reason the strategy would fail was that if the Southern states collapsed, the Northern ones would fast follow, Mathews said. Referring to the Northern states, which might cut off some of the Southern states to gain independence for themselves, the South Carolinian said, "They will too late find, when the house falls, they will inevitably be crushed in its ruins. We must either stand or fall together."

Mathews, unlike Smith in his speech to Congress a month earlier, did not specify that conquered Southerners, reunited with the British empire, might put on red coats and march against the North. But, by inference, this seems clearly to have been his meaning. "Divide et impera is an axiom that will prove as certain, as it is old," Mathews concluded the letter.

Three Virginians—Madison, Jones, and Bland—were also hard at work trying to crack the code of the constitution's power inadequacies. With Varnum, Madison served on one committee studying the matter intensely in March. Bland joined another in May. Jones and Madison, always working in lockstep, believed that the only realistic remedy was an amendment to the Articles that empowered the Congress to coerce recalcitrant states, by force if necessary, to execute the lawful determinations of the Union. The amendment they supported did not mince words:

> It is understood & hereby declared that in case any one or more of the Confederated States shall refuse or neglect to abide by the determinations of the United States in Congress assembled or to observe all the Articles of the Confederation . . . the said United States in Congress assembled are fully authorised to employ the force of the United States as well by sea as by land to compel such State or States to fulfill their federal engagements.[22]

Jones promoted this amendment so urgently because he was of the opinion that the current Articles of Confederation, if left unamended for too long, would terminate in disunion. "Danger may spring from delay," he wrote in a letter he intended to share with Jefferson, Pendleton, and George Wythe, a high-ranking Virginian who signed the Declaration of Independence and would go on to serve in the Constitutional Convention. And, "We may fall a prey to our own follies and disputes." On the other hand, a good constitution, if adopted while the "common danger" of war still actively united the states, would prove more durable and lasting. The window of opportunity to obtain such a well-functioning constitution was short, though, Jones contended, and "if suffered to pass away it may never return."[23]

Similarly, Madison laid out his thoughts in a letter to Governor Jefferson. In it he argues that the "coercive powers" of the amendment would have a double benefit for the Union. First, it would cause the states to comply with federal orders. Second, it would empower the federal government to protect the Southern states from acts of Northern militancy. As Madison saw it, the Northern maritime states possessed the capacity to outfit and fully operate their own navy. The Southern states had neither the materials nor the know-how to do this. Therefore, assuming the United States would soon organize a formidable navy, Madison wanted to see it manned by citizens from all thirteen states and available at all times to defend the Southern states. As he put it to Jefferson, "A navy so formed and under the orders of the general Council of the States would not only be a guard against aggressions & insults from abroad; but without it what is to protect the Southern States for many years to come against the insults & aggressions of their N. Brethren."[24]

Bland was not so sure of Madison's logic. To him the Congress was caught in the throes of a Catch-22, because coercion of the states by a central authority itself risked disunion and civil war. In private notes, perhaps prepared for a speech, Bland asked the fundamental question, "Is Congress capable of legislating for 13 states, whose laws, whose constitutions, whose administrations, whose genius differs in so many respects?" He continued, "Would not the first attempt to legislate—if opposed—produce a civil war—must not coercion be used—what powers of coercion have Congress in their hands?" In consideration of this, Bland concluded that even if the amendment were adopted, as soon the American navy menaced a disobedient member of the confederation, that state might "strengthen itself with alliances of other states," launching a civil war of more than one state against the federal government. "Wd. not this effectually break the Union," Bland asked.[25]

* * * * *

In mid-August, at least in part heeding the calls of the Southern states for urgent rescue, General Washington ordered a major military and naval operation against the British in Virginia. Abandoning his famous obsession with recovering New York before all other objects, the commander in chief led some 2,500 Continental troops, half of his army holding the Hudson Highlands, and 5,000 French troops under the Comte de Rochambeau southward to rendezvous with 1,200 men under Lafayette and a French fleet of twenty-eight ships of the line, four frigates, and 3,500 men commanded by the Comte de Grasse expected to arrive on the coast of Virginia in early September.[26]

The allied Franco-American armies decamped from New York on August 21, and nine days later momentous news came to Washington's hand. Cornwallis, aware neither of the movements of Continental and French troops southward to Virginia nor of de Grasse's fleet sailing northward from the Caribbean, had ordered his army to fortify a base at Yorktown, a defensive position situated on a high bluff overlooking the York River and Chesapeake Bay. Washington read the bulletin with rising confidence and delight. Possessing intimate knowledge of the geography of the Yorktown Peninsula and the bay, he envisioned a decisive victory. Cornwallis's army of some 8,500 would be pinioned on the peninsula, with de Grasse blockading and bombarding by water and the combined ground forces of French and Americans laying siege to the fort by land.[27]

By combined serendipity and skill, events unfolded in precisely this manner in September and October. De Grasse's convoy reached the mouth of the Chesapeake Bay in late August and on September 5 soundly defeated naval forces under British Admiral Sir Thomas Graves in the Battle of the Virginia Capes. This gave the French mastery of the Chesapeake, enabling de Grasse to block any escape by sea of Cornwallis. Meanwhile, the French admiral disembarked heavy siege guns and met with Washington and Rochambeau in mid-September to plot strategy. By the end of the month, allied forces had Cornwallis surrounded. On October 9 Washington lit the fuse of the first cannon, and Cornwallis's unconditional surrender of more than 8,000 British troops followed ten days later. Only once before during the war had Continental troops forced a total capitulation of a British army—at Saratoga four years earlier when John Burgoyne surrendered 5,500 men to Horatio Gates. Yorktown was the greatest victory of the Revolution. And it came at a historic juncture of weariness and sinking morale for British high command, King George, and the Parliament. The catastrophic loss in the Chesapeake Bay effectively put an end to the war, largely because it robbed the British of their last best hope of winning by defeating the Southern states.[28]

That evening Washington wrote a sober, unemotional letter to Congress informing delegates "that a reduction of the British army under the command of Lord Cornwallis is most happily effected." He called the surrender an "important event." The soldiery, however, was not so reserved. The next day, according to one American officer, the fighting men celebrated with "laughing . . . jumping and dancing and singing as they went about." Not far off, when a group of Virginia militiamen heard news of the decisive capitulation, they threw their hats into the air and shouted, "America

Chapter 15: "The Power of Britain in These States Is Now Broken" 291

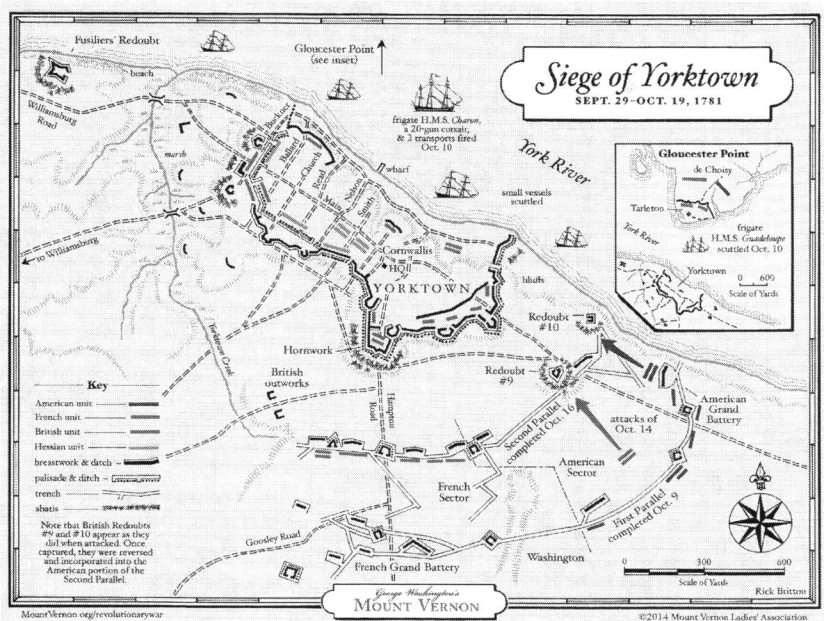

MAP 6. Siege of Yorktown, 1781. (Map of the Siege of Yorktown. Rick Britton, *The Siege of Yorktown*, 2014, digital image, 8.5 x 11 in, courtesy of Mount Vernon Ladies' Association.)

is ours." On October 22 word of the triumph reached Philadelphia, where letters of delegates rejoiced at "this great event" and "the glorious success of the allied arms." One congressman underscored the finality of the battle, saying that "the power of Britain in these states is now broken, I trust it will soon be annihilated." Another declared, "Would to God that a deep sense of gratitude may follow this remarkable smile of heaven at this critical era." And yet another letter designated October 19 as "a day which will ever hereafter be famous in the annals of American history."[29]

When Congress received Washington's official dispatch on Wednesday, October 24, the delegates decreed the day to be one of thanksgiving. As the Connecticut delegation recounted to their governor, members of Congress walked as one body from the State House to the Lutheran Church at 2:00 p.m., where they were joined by French dignitaries, representatives of the Pennsylvania Assembly, and other Philadelphia citizens. Congressional chaplain George Duffield delivered a sermon, and "in the evening the city was illuminated." That night, almost every Philadelphian put a candle in a window to honor the victory. The hope of patriots everywhere was that the vanquishment of the British army at Yorktown would "prepare the way for the establishment of an honorable peace."[30]

CHAPTER 16

"Symptoms of Disunion"

In one manner of thinking, the weeks and months following the Yorktown victory should have been a time of relief and renewed confidence in the United States. The Articles of Confederation had been ratified in perpetuity, and Cornwallis's capitulation in Virginia secured the Southern states, removing the apprehensions of some Americans that a cease-fire based on uti possidetis might result in the coerced relinquishment of some of those states back into the British empire. And more generally, the consensus was that the war was over—the United States had won. In spite of all this, ease of mind hardly predominated in the halls of Congress. Most menacing, delegates doubted the durability of the Union due to the Articles' inadequacies and the states' manifold differences and tenuous commitments to a single centralizing power. Immediately exacerbating this feeling, the Yorktown victory coincided with two tender contests over the right to soil, one of which threatened civil war and the other disunion. The first was a worsening of the prolonged jurisdictional fights over the territory of Vermont. The second was a forceful legal challenge in Congress, spearheaded by the combined forces of land companies and some delegates, to the terms of the Virginia cession of its territory northwest of the Ohio River.

As New Jersey delegate Elias Boudinot expressed the dangers of the jurisdictional chaos in Vermont, a misstep by Congress might "involve the states in a bloody civil war at a very critical & important period." Boudinot was alluding to the prospect that Congress might soon exert powers inherent in the Articles of Confederation to settle the boundary dispute, but this, he repeated again, was "likely to involve the states in a civil war." The concern over impending bloodshed in the Green Mountains first resurfaced in Congress in late July, when New York delegates requested the federal body's intervention, and remained a consistent worry in New York delegates' letters for the next two years.[1]

Madison referred to it as "the thorny subject of Vermont" and "the labyrinths of Vermont" because the situation seemed inextricable. Two states, New York and New Hampshire, claimed the territory in question, and in 1777 the people residing in Vermont, who had long wished to transform the disputed region into a fourteenth colony, declared it an independent state. That same year Vermonters held a convention to adopt a constitution, the first in American history to abolish slavery within its sovereign bounds. The territory comprised at least twenty-eight towns with thousands of residents backed by a fierce militia known as the Green Mountain Boys. The geopolitics were considered explosive largely because all parties understood that the hardy people of the Green Mountains would rather die on the battlefield than surrender their newfound state to New York, New Hampshire, or the Congress. In the era of the American Revolution, Vermonters wanted their territory recognized as a sovereign state, equal to any other, followed by admission into the Union as a fourteenth member. Even more than this desire for unification with the original thirteen states, however, Vermont leaders were committed to political independence from New York and New Hampshire, and to obtain such independence, they were privately corresponding with British military commanders in Canada—something of which the Congress was well aware—about the possibility of Vermont joining the British empire instead.[2]

For the U.S. Congress, the situation in Vermont was a lose-lose. On the one hand, were the congressional delegates to rule in favor of the territory's statehood, it would spark a furor not only in New York but also in other states, notably the Southern ones, which were sharply opposed to investing Congress with a power to dismember any state in the Union. New Hampshire, for its part, strongly disputed the right of Vermonters to establish a new state in lands it had contested with New York since the 1740s. Dramatically weakening the New Hampshire position, however, King George III had settled the dispute in New York's favor in 1764. All of Vermont, by the king's ruling of that year, was deemed the sovereign terrain of New York, subject to the jurisdiction of its government. Therefore, in reality, there were only three committed contenders for authority over the Vermont territory: Vermonters, New Yorkers, and the Congress.[3]

By this time most New Hampshirites, in fact, sided with Vermont statehood for the reasons that most of the territory's inhabitants were

New Englanders, and its admission into the Union would add a fifth New England state to the region's voting power in Congress. Massachusetts had itself led the way in proclaiming New England's support of Vermont statehood on March 8, when it surrendered its own loose claims over part of the territory, simultaneously asserting that Vermont "should be a sovereign independent State." However, here again the Southern states were roundly opposed. In their view, New England as one bloc, and the Northern states as another, had power enough in the Union. Adding Vermont would mean the current "balance of power" of five Southern states against eight Northern states would deteriorate to five versus nine, threatening Southern interests all the more. Soon Arthur Lee of Virginia made the prediction that "with the admission of this little State the confederation will end; its present inequality being as much as it can bear."[4]

Still, this was not the worst outcome in the contest over Vermont. By consensus among delegates, including those from New York, civil war would break out imminently in the region if Congress ruled in favor of New York, proclaiming the territory officially subject to New York laws and land grants, just as George III had in 1764. Such an act abolishing the independent republic of Vermont would in all probability align Congress, New York, and the states from Pennsylvania southward to Georgia against Vermont—and possibly against all New England, perhaps on the battlefield. No one knew precisely how the states might split if a civil war ignited by Congress over Vermont expanded. After all, the Union was fragile, and Massachusetts had already come out in support of Vermont statehood. In *The Origins of the Federal Republic: Jurisdictional Controversies in the United States, 1775–1787*, Peter Onuf analyzes these territorial dynamics. "In case of conflict," he posits, "there was good reason to believe that New Englanders would offer at least covert assistance to the rebels [Vermonters]."[5]

Complicating matters further, a division of opinion existed in New York. In light of the certainty of a civil clash in the event of a congressional attempt to overrule Vermont's declaration of independent statehood, some New Yorkers were coming to the conclusion that their state's interests would be best served by surrendering all claims to the contested area in order to erect the territory as a new Northern state. As New York jockeyed for position in rapidly shifting state alliances, these political leaders argued that New York should cut its losses in order to secure the friendship of New England, which war against Vermont would preclude. In consideration of New York's long-term political and economic interests, they preferred to see the state take sides with New England rather than the Southern states.[6]

For these reasons, the Congress heard the arguments of all parties involved in the Vermont controversy and, wisely, chose to pursue the path of inaction. Month after month, delegates procrastinated in making a federal ruling on it, for fear that doing so might invite a dreadful rupture of the United States.

* * * * *

More than any other delegate who left written records during these months, James Madison revealed in notes and letters the precarious state of the Union as it relates to the Virginia cession of territory and land companies' attempts to infringe it. Madison, thirty years old, possessed not only a perceptive intelligence but also an anxious temperament that absorbed and processed dangers of disunion more than that of the average delegate. Unlike some, he did not practice the power of positive thinking. Madison was instead chronically apprehensive that missteps by delegates in Philadelphia would trigger backlash in a state like Virginia that would cascade into disunion and civil war. One notebook he kept at a young age, perhaps while studying at the College of New Jersey, hints at the way he thought about leadership in times of disunionist crisis. In the notebook Madison pens over 2,500 words summarizing his key insights from reading a popular work of French political philosophy and statecraft about internal political crisis and civil wars. The book, *Memoirs of the Cardinal de Retz: Containing the Particulars of His Own Life, with the Most Secret Transactions at the French Court During the Administration of Cardinal Mazarin, and the Civil Wars Occasioned by It*, analyzes the five-year civil war in France known as La Fronde.

Retz, archbishop of Paris and later a cardinal, wrote the memoir as a denunciation of the manifest errors committed by King Louis XIV, Richelieu, and their ministers that led to bloodshed. Madison pored over this lesson in history, noting that the best way to save nations from such internal combustion is through skillful leadership. A principal theme of the Virginian's notetaking was the means by which nations slip insidiously into civil war. This happens, Madison records, when political leaders are blinded by impetuosity and overconfidence, at one extreme, or timidity and complacency, at the other. Both sets of traits, he writes, deceive political actors into the fatal belief about incipient disunion and civil war that "the danger is not real." As a consequence, rulers either proceed into tumultuous, delicate affairs with a "blind rashness," which precipitates civil war, or a timorous, self-denying inaction, which fails to prevent it.[7]

There is no evidence that Madison had this book of notes with him in Philadelphia during his years of service in Congress. Nevertheless, he practiced every leadership skill at his disposal when in early October a special committee of Congress assigned to consider the land cessions of Virginia, New York, and Connecticut formally requested the Virginia delegates to exhibit proof of the validity of their claims to the Northwest Territory. The committee found little objectionable in the cessions of New York and Connecticut, but it disagreed entirely with Virginia's assertion of authority and privilege to restrict the Congress's disposition of its conceded federal lands—that is, Virginia's mandate prohibiting the federal body from awarding any portion of those lands to land companies or any other entities or individuals. Behind the scenes, Madison and most other delegates knew what was going on. The committee was advancing the interests of land speculators associated with the United Illinois and Wabash, the Indiana, and the Vandalia Companies, in which not a few of the committee members owned shares. Should Virginia submit to what amounted to a subpoena by the committee to submit evidence, Madison reasoned, the state would be tacitly sanctioning the power of Congress to reject the conditions of cession in the first place.[8]

This demand of a special committee spelled the approach of a constitutional crisis of grave magnitude, because under the Articles of Confederation, the Virginia cession was the linchpin holding the American government together. Virginia had ceded the rich territory northwest of the Ohio River for no other reason than to cement the Union. Maryland had refused to confederate without the cession—and only ratified the Articles after Virginia completed it. If now the Congress rejected the state's ultimatum that no private individual or company may profit in any manner whatever from the cession, what was Virginia going to do? The correct response, Madison and the other Virginia delegates confirmed in letters back home, was to revoke the cession, reclaiming the land. Yet how would Maryland—and possibly other states—react to this aggressive countermand by a state already widely denounced as too grandiose and expansive? Would those states withdraw from the Union? In the fall of 1781, Madison foresaw a fearsome chain reaction that could only end in disunion.[9]

The first step Madison and the other Virginia delegates took to counteract this progression of events was to stand before the committee and verbally protest its requisition of evidence. According to Madison, they presented themselves to the committee for three days arguing this point, to no avail. Therefore, on October 10, they submitted a formal written remonstrance, declaring that in this case the congressional committee lacked constitutional authority to examine Virginia's "territorial rights" and to require Virginia delegates to exhibit evidence in defense of them. This, too, failed to deter the committee, so six days later, the day before Cornwallis raised a white flag of surrender over the British fort at Yorktown, the Virginians moved a resolution in which they declared categorically—and correctly—that the committee lacked constitutional jurisdiction to settle a territorial dispute between land companies and a state. The companies must petition the state of Virginia, they insisted, not Congress, if they wished to resolve conflicting claims. Only in Virginia—not Philadelphia—could these disputes be adjudicated in a court of law. In the remonstrance the Virginia delegates drew a red line: "Congress are interdicted by the Confederation from the cognizance of such claims." The usurpation under contemplation by the committee "derogates from the sovereignty of a State."[10]

Never before had Madison been so alarmed at the proceedings of Congress. From mid-October until mid-November, he and his fellow Virginia delegate, Edmund Randolph, felt themselves and their state to be under assault. Their letters warned fellow Virginians about an escalation of "hostile machinations" and "calumnies" and "aggression on Virginia" and "injury to her rights." Madison, in a letter to Edmund Pendleton that quickly dispensed "fervent congratulations on the glorious success of the combined arms at York & Glocester," went on to explicate fully the risks to their home state's territorial integrity posed by "the enemies of Virginia." One circulating tract, by Thomas Paine, specifically refuted the legitimacy of Virginia's claims above the Ohio River. Another, by Thomas Wharton, delegate of Delaware and principal in the Indiana Company, went further. This manifesto, entitled *Plain Facts*, denied that Virginia at any time possessed a valid claim to any land beyond the crest of the Appalachians, including Kentucky.[11]

Randolph, twenty-eight years old and a graduate of William and Mary before reading law, informed the governor of Virginia, Thomas Nelson, that the western land conflict in Congress risked a rupture. The proceedings in Congress were wracked by "disgust and jealousy." A "fraud" was being committed against Virginia, one that "derogates from the dignity of a sovereign state," one that would undercut "her rank in the political world." The "enmity" Randolph observed was unprecedented, he said, and "tho' produced originally by her extent of soil," it now pervaded almost every transaction in which Virginia raised a hand to participate.[12]

Into this emotional environment the special committee on cessions delivered its report on November 3. A nightmare for the Virginians, the committee decreed the state's offer of cession "altogether inadmissible." Virginia's land claims in the West, including Kentucky, were untenable, and the conditions of the cession represented an unacceptable encumbrance, one "incompatible with the Honor, Interests & Peace of the United States." The report called upon Virginia to make a new offer, renouncing "all Claims & pretensions of Claim to the Lands & Country beyond a reasonable western Boundary . . . free from any Conditions & restrictions whatever." And equally disturbing, the committee recommended that Congress acknowledge the validity of the land grants to the Indiana and Vandalia Companies and reimburse with federal funds the American citizen shareholders among the patentees.[13]

Madison and Randolph responded with despair accompanied by a determined strategy of caution in their communications with political leaders back home. They took care with their words due to their knowledge that, referring to Virginia, "Our country is highly inflamed against the congress." They feared that news of a pending rejection of the cession would provoke state leaders in Richmond to adopt a "wrathful measure," one that might give rise to "symptoms of disunion." They did not further describe the nature of the wrathful measure they feared, but a threat of secession by Virginia must surely have been on their minds. Madison, taking the pulse of Congress and determining that every day more and more delegates seemed to be lining up behind a vote to reject the encumbrances Virginia placed on its cession, wanted only to know if the federal body would be so reckless as to pursue this policy. The honor and interests of Virginians were at stake, and at this critical juncture, Madison wondered "what course their honor and security required them to take." Both men urged state leaders to contain, rather than inflame, the controversy, at least until a peace treaty securing independence had been obtained. "The late capture of the British army opens the avenue to peace," Randolph wrote to Governor Nelson. "It will be instantaneously shut up, if Great Britain should have a single glance of a fracture in the American chain." Therefore, Randolph advised, Virginia should not pass or threaten any legislative act "beyond a protest against the authority, now exercised by congress, and a repeal of our cession."[14]

Madison, daily strategizing with Randolph, joined him in these sentiments, writing his most foreboding letter to Jefferson. All efforts by Virginia in Philadelphia to prevent the Congress from overstepping its rights and prerogatives, he wrote to his friend on November 18, were "in vain." It now seemed sure that the Virginia cession would be rejected, leaving the state with no choice but to revoke or suspend it, reissuing a manifesto to Congress against federal interference in cases of state "jurisdiction." Madison advised Jefferson that ultimately Virginia must not yield its rights—and that the probable outcome state leaders in Richmond must prepare for was a rupture of the Union.[15]

The confederation was a critical instrument of war and peace and must therefore endure until a definitive treaty came to American shores, Madison advocated. Virginia should suppress "intemperate measures" and hold the Union together during this critical period, while simultaneously and prudently planning for "its probable dissolution after it." State leaders, he repeated for a second time to Jefferson, "ought in all their provisions for their future security, importance & interest to presume that the present Union will but little survive the present war."

* * * * *

Amid these uncertainties, the Congress nevertheless still bore responsibility for securing the best terms possible in a peace treaty with Great Britain. In 1779, after acrimonious debates, delegates had struck a compromise naming John Adams as American peace minister and John Jay as ambassador to Spain. In his assignment Adams was charged with obtaining a peace treaty that roughly affirmed the same wide boundaries for the United States as those won by Anglo-Americans in the French and Indian War. Congress also bound Adams to an ultimatum prohibiting him from forfeiting the right of fishing on the banks of Newfoundland—and, after securing this first treaty, from signing a commercial one with Britain that did not include an overt positive statement of American fishing rights. Moreover, if in the interim between a peace treaty and a commercial treaty Great Britain interfered with American fishing rights, the United States agreed by resolution to respond with war—a war for cod and haddock.[16]

Jay carried instructions to Madrid strictly forbidding him from agreeing to any treaty with King Charles III that interfered with the same boundaries, except for ceding the Floridas to Spain. By way of ultimatum, the Congress also required the Spanish king to grant Americans free navigation through the mouth of the Mississippi for purposes of trade. In early 1781, under threat of the impending ruin of the Southern states, however, Southern delegates in Congress reluctantly yielded on this point, facilitating the overturn of the navigation as ultimatum. To prevent the loss of Southern states to the British empire in a peace settlement, Congress issued new instructions fully empowering the ambassador to trade away the Southern commercial right in return for the lifesaving alliance with Spain so long delayed, reportedly, by the stumbling block of the Mississippi.

The year 1781 was a decisive one not only for the ratification of a constitutional Union under the Articles of Confederation, the American victory at Yorktown, and the reversal on the navigation of the Mississippi River. During the summer, four months before the decisive victory at Yorktown, the British subjugation of the Southern states—combined with French distaste for John Adams—had also driven the Congress to a radical rewriting of the 1779 ultimatums for peace. At Versailles chief minister Vergennes found Adams to be impossible to work with. In letters to his ambassador in Philadelphia, Anne-César de La Luzerne, Vergennes regretted the necessity of asking his plenipotentiary to speak the bald truth to the American Congress. Adams was entirely ill-suited to the art of peacemaking, "because he has a rigidity, an arrogance, and an obstinacy that will cause him to form a thousand unfortunate incidents and to drive his co-negotiators to despair." Vergennes deplored Adams's "too ardent imagination, his stubbornness, and his pride."[17]

Luzerne received the first of Vergennes's letters in mid-May and soon reported back that he was aggressively lobbying Congress to make a change. One argument the ambassador was advancing in conversations with congressmen, Luzerne told Vergennes, was that Adams was blinded by an implacable regional attachment to the Newfoundland fisheries. As the 1779 peace instructions stood, Adams alone was empowered with "prolonging the present war at his pleasure." And this state of affairs was perilous for not only French interests in negotiations but also the interests of the other states in the Union. Adams, Luzerne further told delegates of Congress, "is infatuated with the interests of the Eastern states, to the point of wishing at any price to assure them a right to the fisheries, and who, for this single object, could destroy a negotiation on which depends the happiness and the tranquility of this whole continent."[18]

At Vergennes's behest, Luzerne also announced to the Congress that Britain had at last agreed to a co-mediation by Catherine the Great of

Russia and Emperor Joseph II of Austria; the moment was therefore ripe for defeating King George's scheme to carve up the states to retain a subset in his empire. But success in the mediation meant stripping the toxic Adams of his unilateral powers and placing the Congress's trust in France to fulfill its promise made in the alliance of 1777 to make no peace with Britain that did not acknowledge the independence of the United States. Of his own accord, Luzerne further hinted that a failure by Congress to comply with his sovereign's request might terminate, tragically, in a decision by France to abandon the American cause and "leave you at the mercy of your enemies."[19]

At the time Luzerne made these overtures to Congress, the Southern states were largely under British arms, with fears running rampant that the European powers indeed might reach a peace settlement based on the surrender of some of them back to Britain. So catastrophic a scenario was this for a majority of the delegates in Philadelphia that they swiftly adopted the policy espoused by Luzerne. On June 6 John Witherspoon and William Churchill Houston of New Jersey introduced a motion to this effect, rescinding the multiple 1779 ultimatums for peace and replacing them with only two. The treaty must provide for the complete political and economic independence of the thirteen states, and, in negotiating it, Adams must act in lockstep with the French, obtaining their "concurrence" on every article and clause. As for the western boundary at the Mississippi River, the Witherspoon-Houston motion canceled this ultimatum. It directed Adams to work closely with the French on this controversial matter, using his "own judgment and prudence in securing the interest of the United States."[20]

A majority of delegates gave support to the new peace instructions to Adams, but others were indignant. To them, the Witherspoon-Houston motion symbolized the infirmity and inferiority of the United States, not the independence and strength of a rising confederation. The making of peace ending the historic Revolution was an august act requiring courage and honor, they argued. The New Jersey motion was pusillanimous. It made the United States an obsequious puppet to a new European master, France. It would wound the dignity of the states and the Congress. Added to this, as a second source of discontent, the dissenting delegates protested the size and structure of the commission. The Witherspoon-Houston motion proposed emasculating the peace demands *and* leaving the fate of the western and southern boundaries, and the navigation of the Mississippi, in the hands of a single New England man. Were the

Congress to adopt the motion in question, they argued that their fellow delegates must counterbalance its impotence by expanding the peace commission to three Americans in Europe.[21]

On June 11 the Congress consented to this request, nominating six candidates to negotiate alongside Adams, among them Benjamin Franklin, John Jay, and Thomas Jefferson. Two days later Jay was elected, and either at that point or the following day, vehement debates ensued. It seems that in a first ballot Franklin won election over Jefferson, and complaints went up promptly that the Southern states had no representation in a delegation composed of Adams, Franklin, and Jay. In the horse trading of "claims espoused by different quarters of the U.S.," sure to collide at the peace tables, it was said that Adams had a New England "impartiality." Jay was disagreed to as a New Yorker who, unbound from congressional ultimatums, would actually be "interested in such [peace] arrangements as would deprive the U.S. of the navigation of the Mississippi," as this would divert water trade from the Ohio Valley and Great Lakes through his state into the Hudson River rather than down the Mississippi. The validity of these accusations was hotly challenged on the floor of Congress. But it could not be gainsaid that neither Franklin nor Jay were "connected with the So. States." Therefore, to appease those states, on June 14 the Congress agreed to broaden the commission to five, accepting Franklin and voting in Jefferson and Henry Laurens of South Carolina to represent the South. The next day, only after sorting out this geographical representation of the commission, did the Congress adopt a modified version of the Witherspoon-Houston motion.[22]

* * * * *

All this political maneuvering left one delegate more than any other rattled and therefore energized to rectify the grievous error of Congress's override of the Mississippi-Fisheries Compromise of 1779. That delegate was James Madison, who argued that the carefully constructed compromise of that year took into account not only ultimatums for peace but also those for a commercial treaty with Britain and a Spanish-American alliance. And now, seen from the perspective of those terms of treaties, New England had all the advantages, and the Southern states none. The fisheries remained protected by other ultimatums: American negotiators could not sign a commercial treaty that did not guarantee American fishing rights, and, no small matter, the United States was going to declare a second war on the British if they interdicted American boats from those waters. Madison never agreed with the relinquishment of the Mississippi navigation to Spain in a treaty, and the Congress's surrender of the ultimatum on the western boundary at the Mississippi in June upset him even more. He deplored the fact that the boundary and navigation had been cast to the fates while the Newfoundland fisheries remained cast in stone as a foreign policy ultimatum.

In advancing this point of view on the trans-Appalachian West and the fisheries, Madison was not only standing up for the interests of Virginia and the Southern states. More fundamentally, he was also asking the other delegates in Congress to join him in placing the preservation and safety of the Union before all other considerations. Madison feared an unequal peace that would excite centrifugal forces. He was managing the politics of disunion. What was going to happen, after all, if a peace settlement should be reached obtaining the fisheries but truncating the United States at the crest of the Appalachian Mountains or some other line of demarcation far from the Mississippi? New England towns would blare in jubilation at their triumph, while Virginia, North Carolina, South Carolina, and Georgia would smart at the one-sidedness of the postwar gains. To Madison's mind, this was a dangerous path. Such a peace treaty would tend toward the disintegration of the new Union rather than its invigoration. For Madison, union building undergirded by pervasive feelings of sectional fairness and justice constituted the most urgent policy of the confederation.[23]

Since June 6, when Witherspoon introduced his motion to reverse the peace ultimatums of 1779, Madison had been fighting against his proposals vigorously. On three successive days the Virginian took to the floor of Independence Hall to reason with the other delegates who were so recklessly hurrying to conform to the wishes of Luzerne. They must, one way or the other, reinstate the Mississippi boundary as an ultimatum. One alternative Madison pressed was for the boundary to be made a separate, secret instruction to be kept from the eyes of the French and Spanish, so as not to alienate them. This proposal having been defeated, he drafted a motion for the signing of a treaty for independence devoid of a defined boundary, deferring its settlement to a separate postpeace negotiation, similar to that planned for New England's fishing rights. At a firm minimum, it seemed reasonable to Madison that the boundary of Virginia's sparsely settled Kentucky and the territory captured by Virginian George Rogers Clark should be made an ultimatum somehow. Again Madison's motions, which often gained support only from fellow Virginians and North Carolinians, met with defeat.[24]

Even after the Congress adopted and dispatched the new peace instructions to Europe, Madison kept up his campaign to reform American foreign policy to ensure sectional fairness of effort, it not outcome. His choice lay between rallying the Congress to reinstate the Mississippi boundary as an ultimatum or a campaign to expunge the special instruction on the fisheries that was the source of the injustice. The first appealed more, so on June 29 he moved to use the strength of the fisheries ultimatum to raise back up the western boundary to high status—as an ultimatum in the commercial treaty with Britain, on par with the fisheries. His motion called for an "Additional instruction" on the boundary equalizing it to the fisheries in this treaty. It failed. Undeterred, Madison, joined by North Carolina lawyer William Sharpe, introduced a resolution to revoke altogether the instructions for fishing rights in a commercial treaty. Accompanying this, new orders would require the peace ministers to "use their most strenuous endeavors" to obtain the fisheries and the boundary in the peace treaty. Finally, a Madison motion passed. Equality had been achieved. Sectional balance had been restored. After adoption, the Congress forwarded this final rendering of peace instructions to the peace commissioners on July 21.[25]

In this small legislative victory, Madison had restored at least a semblance of sectional balance to the United States' peace demands. The motion afforded the occasion to send another explicit message to American diplomats overseas that the Mississippi boundary and fisheries should be treated as equals in the rough and tumble of redrawing maps and commercial accords to end the war. Madison had by now become one of the most alert and farseeing protectors of the American Union in Congress. He understood that despite the panicked exigencies of war and diplomacy, there was a fragile aftermath soon to come: peace itself, when the bands of the confederation would be tested as never before. New cements of the Union were critically necessary, and at the least, one of them must be a feeling across the thirteen states of the sectional fairness and justice of the peace treaty engineered by the Congress. By all appearances, Madison believed that the survival of the Union depended upon it.

* * * * *

By the end of the summer, Congress had revised the peace instructions in a manner that Madison felt to be conducive to the internal security of the Union. By the time of the Yorktown victory in October, though, a new threat to American interests in the Mississippi Valley had emerged. It was the critical problem that one of the two Southern peace ministers,

Jefferson, was not going to serve. The reason Madison's friend declined is that the summons to Europe came to him at a despondent moment. The year 1781 was the annus horribilis not only of the Revolution but also of Jefferson's life thus far. From June until the end of December, the ex-governor was under the shadow of an investigation by the assembly for executive mismanagement and deficit of valor as the commander in chief of the commonwealth of Virginia. Under Jefferson's governorship Virginia had been hard hit by the British. The governor and assembly had been chased once from Richmond, then again the next year from the same capital to Charlottesville, and finally, in flight from Cornwallis and Tarleton's dragoons, from Charlottesville over the Blue Ridge Mountains to the safety of Staunton in the Shenandoah Valley. For these supposed transgressions, the assembly launched an inquiry, leaving Jefferson depressed and fighting for his political reputation. Years later he related that the humiliation of the inquiry was so grievous that it "could only be cured by the all healing grave."[26]

In Philadelphia Madison exhibited patience with Jefferson, frequently writing him letters of comfort and support. The same cannot be said for Madison's Virginia colleague in Congress, Edmund Randolph, who happened to be Jefferson's second cousin. At the time of the appointment of the peace commission, the delegates were aware that the other Southerner minister, Henry Laurens, was imprisoned in London. The British had captured him at sea in September of 1780, and on grounds of orchestrating a rebellion against the mother country, King George incarcerated him in the Tower of London. Delegates in Philadelphia had expected Laurens to be released or exchanged in short order, but a year later he remained behind bars.

To Randolph's thinking, this placed a double burden on Jefferson to throw off his melancholia and self-pity for the sake of the Southern states. In one letter written in October, Randolph stated this concern precisely, underscoring that if Jefferson continued to refuse to serve, two choices lay open to Virginians. They could either hazard Southern interests to the care of Adams, Jay, and Franklin or embark on a renewed campaign in Congress to reinstate them as ultimatums. "If you can justify this resolution to yourself," Randolph leveled at Jefferson, referring to his decision to stay home, "I am confident that you cannot to the world. There remains now no alternative, but either to consign southern interests wholly to the management of our present ministers, or to interdict them from the exercise of all discretionary power."[27]

Eventually Jefferson did yield to the entreaties of Randolph, Madison, and others to cross the ocean to join the negotiations. But his decision to travel to Paris came too late. The Virginia peacemaker made his way to Baltimore, where he confirmed by letter to Madison that he understood his purpose. It was to secure "our right to the fishery, to the Western country, & the navigation of the Mississippi." As he waited for his sailing vessel, the *Romulus*, to come to port, bona fide news came into the harbor that American and British negotiators at Versailles had already signed the preliminary draft of the Treaty of Paris. Learning of this development at nearly the same time as Jefferson, the Congress canceled his mission.[28]

In the end, neither Jefferson nor Laurens made any meaningful contribution to the peace treaty concluding the War of Independence. Jefferson remained in America, and Laurens arrived in Paris only after the other three commissioners had come to terms with the British. Jay, Franklin, and Adams would negotiate the all-important peace treaty with no input at all from Southern representatives of the United States.

CHAPTER 17

"Le Washington de la Negotiation"

On the same day representatives of the United States and Britain would sign the preliminary articles of the Treaty of Paris ending the War of Independence, John Adams penned an entry in his diary. The New Englander was typically not shy to censure or lampoon others in those private pages, and not infrequently he gloated over his own accomplishments. This was not the case on the day of the signing. Instead of congratulating himself, he awarded credit to his fellow peace minister John Jay, comparing the New Yorker's skills at the negotiating table to those of Washington on the battlefield. As Adams recounts, Frenchmen at Versailles, impressed by the Massachusetts man's diplomatic prowess, were calling him, Adams, "le Washington de la Negotiation." In his journal, the founder corrects this misattribution, cautioning future readers not to confuse French flattery with reality. Lauding his fellow commissioner Jay, Adams affirms that anyone privy to the New York lawyer's dexterities during the peace talks would undoubtedly award him, not Adams, the title "Le Washington de la Negotiation." The accolade, he says, is "a very flattering compliment indeed, to which I have not a right, but sincerely think it belongs to Mr. Jay."[1]

The historical record bears out Adams's assessment. By consensus, diplomatic historians of the Revolution agree that Jay was the master strategist of the treaty, by degrees more important to its final outcome than Franklin or Adams. This impact had something to do with Jay's commitment to freeing the United States not only from the monarchical clutch of King George III but also from that of Louis XVI and Charles III. Jay was famously stubborn in the pursuit of his aims. He admitted as much himself at age thirty, once committing to paper a self-analysis. Looking in the mirror, Jay saw a man who was "hard" and "pertinacious," quick to stiffen at "indignities" and "prone to sudden resentment." He wondered if a core "bashfulness and pride" were not at the root of things, if somehow these were not the source of his implacability and "warm passions." Whatever the origins of these traits, Jay emerged in Paris as a brilliant, militant patriot in the quest for independence. The endgame he sought in Paris was a durable, safe, praiseworthy peace that would ensure, as he expressed to Washington, that "these states will be great and flourishing."[2]

This image of John Jay as a warrior of American foreign policy in Europe stands in marked contrast to the low impression many observers in Philadelphia recorded about him at the end of 1779 when he was first elected ambassador to Spain, especially as far as the navigation of the Mississippi is concerned. Jay appeared to be an illogical, perplexing choice for the assignment at the court of Madrid largely because he was a known antagonist to making the navigation an ultimatum of a treaty with Spain in the first place. For this slack attitude toward an essential American right, delegates like James Lovell, Sam Adams, Henry Laurens, and Richard Henry Lee pilloried Jay as one of a party of "lickspittles" who took his marching orders from French and Spanish envoys rather than from fellow Southern delegates, whose futures would depend upon the great waterway for access to the sea.[3]

In 1779 Jay had indeed voted against the ultimatum on the Mississippi navigation. With many other delegates in Congress at the time, he thought it too absolute, too hand tying. And, critically, it risked the loss of a vital alliance with Spain, one of the world's greatest naval powers, for the sake of obtaining distant navigation rights that would fuel an expansive spirit of westbound population shift that he and others legitimately feared would destabilize the fragile republic.

What happened is that Jay, by his own admission, underwent a transformation after departing American shores for Spain. As he later recollected about his years as Spanish ambassador, he had been sanguine and overly idealistic about human nature before his first diplomatic assignment in Europe. Encounters with French and Spanish court officials, however, gradually eroded his naïveté. As he wrote to his sister-in-law, a "variety of trials"—"tricks and machinations" and "trouble and indignation"—had opened his eyes. "Happiness" had given way to "prudence." Jay's awakening began as early as the trans-Atlantic crossing aboard the thirty-six-gun frigate *Confederacy*. On board he learned to his perplexity that King Charles III and Floridablanca, unlike Louis XVI and Vergennes, had declared a separate war on Great Britain without first forming an alliance with the United States. Not only this, a fellow passenger on the ship, the retiring French ambassador Gérard, hounded him regularly on the life-and-death nature of a Spanish-American treaty and alliance. The Frenchman reiterated ad nauseam that Congress's ultimatum on the Mississippi River would "ruin the business."[4]

The *Confederacy* made landing at the port of Cádiz on January 20, 1780, and already by early March Jay's letters were starting to take on the peremptory, muscular tone of a Samuel Adams or Richard Henry Lee. On the third of the month, he pointedly made it known to Congress that he no longer held the views he had espoused in Philadelphia. Gérard was lobbying for an American renunciation of the river, but now the Mississippi seemed to Jay too valuable and too important to the Union to be "quitted," even for a treaty with one of the most powerful nations in the world. "Indeed, as affairs are now circumstanced," he recommended to Congress, "it would, in my opinion, be better for America to have no treaty with Spain than to purchase one on such servile terms. There was a time when it might have been proper to have given that country something for their making common cause with us, but that day is now past. Spain is at war with Britain."[5]

* * * * *

Gérard sharply influenced Jay's new outlook on European diplomacy and the United States' essential rights, but nowhere near as much as King Charles III's first minister of state, José Moñino y Redondo, 1st Count of Floridablanca. Jay spent two and a half demeaning, supplicating years on Spanish soil, and this experience, more than any other, served as the laboratory of learning that later inspired fierceness within him at the court that mattered most, the peace court at Versailles.

Floridablanca was an old-school negotiator who employed Machiavellian techniques of gamesmanship, menace, and false promises. While Jay initially viewed the minister and his king as hopeful allies and trading partners, Floridablanca looked upon Jay and the United States as pawns on a chessboard on which the Spanish were playing for far more valuable pieces than a treaty with rebelling colonies. Over time, Jay came to discern the stratagems of the Spanish minister, and in Paris he would deploy many of them himself to gain the upper hand, seeking his revenge.

The first phase of Jay's negotiations with Floridablanca took place between early March of 1780 and mid-September of 1781. During this period Jay was bound by Congress's ultimatum to sign no treaty that did not grant the United States free navigation of the Mississippi through Spanish shores. The first augury of things to come was Jay's degraded status at the five Spanish courts where he would be petitioning Count Floridablanca for loans of money and an alliance with the confederated states. The diplomatic corps in attendance at the court of Charles III did not remain in one place. Instead, dozens of ministers, ambassadors, and envoys followed King Charles on his annual pilgrimage to five palaces. The king had been in power for two decades, and his yearly calendar seldom changed: January to El Pardo, Easter at Aranjuez, summers at San Ildefonso, autumn to El Escorial, and by December back to the Royal Palace in Madrid. These constant translocations represented an extraordinary hardship for Jay and his wife, Sarah, because they barely possessed sufficient funds to maintain a single residence in Madrid. It would have been less of a "painful situation," as Jay put it, had Floridablanca been willing to advance the United States loans and credit. But the minister hedged and parried these entreaties, just as he did Jay's other diplomatic requests.[6]

Floridablanca diminished Jay's status at court by denying him adequate loans of money to live in customary diplomatic style and, more directly, by denying him the privilege of being recognized in Madrid or at any of Charles III's other outlying royal palaces as a titled minister. From Cádiz, Jay announced his arrival by letter to Floridablanca, describing himself as a plenipotentiary of the United States fully empowered to treat with the king on all matters of diplomacy and commerce. Writing back, the Spanish first minister told Jay he was welcomed to approach the court with assurances of "the sincerity and good dispositions of his majesty towards the United States." But until a treaty had formalized relations, Congress's envoy would be deemed a distinguished private visitor only, not an ambassador. Jay's secretary, William Carmichael, described this as an arrangement wherein the two Americans in Spain would be "treated as strangers of distinction."[7]

Jay traveled to Spain with four overarching aspirations. First, he hoped that King Charles III, like his Bourbon cousin Louis XVI, would recognize the United States as a free, independent, and sovereign nation of the world. This required an appropriate title for Jay and the adoption of a treaty of commerce or alliance, both symbolizing Spain's acknowledgement of the fact of American independence. Second, Jay sought the swift dispatch of Spanish ships to American shores to succor the United

Chapter 17: "Le Washington de la Negotiation"

States against the common enemy, Great Britain. Third, he needed urgent financial assistance, because in Cádiz Jay learned to his chagrin that the Congress was drawing bills of credit upon him, all to be paid within the year in Madrid. Congress took this extraordinary step on the presumption of forthcoming liberality from Charles III. Fourth, Jay felt certain Spain and the United States could come to an amicable agreement on the navigation of the lower Mississippi, even if that meant American consent to reasonable regulations imposed by the king in exchange for the right to conduct trade on the river's Spanish shores.[8]

Floridablanca rebuffed Jay on all four items. Regarding naval assistance, the Spaniard told Jay that the king would take the solicitation under consideration, but first His Majesty wished for the American visitor to prepare and transmit encyclopedic information to the court about each state in the Union and reliable details as to how the United States intended to "indemnify Spain" for its support. By this time Jay had already been in Spain for five months, and now Floridablanca confronted him not with a pathway forward but with extensive homework and, shockingly, a counterrequest for "ships of war" built in America to be dispatched to Spain "without loss of time." Floridablanca repeated the counterproposal three months later, specifying the king's desire for "four good frigates and some other lighter vessels." They should be constructed, equipped, and manned in the United States and sailed to Bilbao, Ferrol, or Cádiz, where "under Spanish colors" the American vessels and sailors would be employed to intercept the convoys of the English East India Company, thereby weakening the British war effort in Europe. The principle behind this request, according to Floridablanca, was that the United States should "reimburse in some shape the expenses already incurred by his Catholic majesty" on behalf of America before asking for new issuances—that is, repayment for clandestine dispatches of cannons, guns, mortar, tents, and utensils Spain had been sending to the thirteen states since 1776.[9]

In response, Jay reminded Floridablanca that "the war against the United States has raged without intermission for six years already." The country is "invaded," and "the Congress are in great want of money for the immediate purposes of self-defense, for the maintenance of their armies and vessels of war, and for all the other expenses incident to military operations." The United States did have the capacities and desire to build frigates for Spain, but "neither the timber, the iron, the masts, nor the other articles can be procured without money." Jay wondered at Floridablanca's state of mind and questioned his good faith. "Sir," he wrote to the minister, "their necessities will not permit them to supply money to those purposes [frigates], and I should deceive your excellency with delusive expectations were I to lead you to think otherwise."[10]

On the matter of financial relief, it is hard to overstate the magnitude of Jay's anguish over this issue during his two and a half years in Spain. He suffered for his wife as well as for the credibility of the United States as a new borrower in the world of international finance. In May Jay asked Floridablanca to extend loans to the United States to cover bills of credit drawn on him from Congress, coming due at once. The Spanish minister demurred, saying the royal coffers were presently near empty on account of the great expenses the king was incurring in the war. He explained further that the royal treasury was itself negotiating loans to shore up its own precarious finances. The most he could do, therefore, was to aid Jay to find private financiers for the bills. Possibly, too, he would have it in his power to offer a loan of 25,000 to 40,000 pounds sterling—in six or seven months. Jay characterized the state of affairs as "humiliating." He barely had enough money to pay his various rents on the itinerary of royal palaces and broadly felt that he had become a beggar at court, while he had intended to evince strength and self-respect.[11]

The situation did not improve over the course of the next six months. Under the assumption that the Spanish chief minister and king would provide loans to the United States, if not sign an alliance, Congress continued issuing one bill of credit after another in Jay's name to be redeemed by the American ambassador in Madrid within months. As he was unable to pay his current debts and new ones continued to roll onto his desk every fortnight, Jay fell into deeper financial straits. By August $50,000 worth of bills had been presented for him to pay, Floridablanca having accepted only $14,000. This left Jay to worry that the financial catastrophe in Spain might inflict an irreparable wound to American credit and therefore its ability to prosecute the war. So, left with no alternative, the American ambassador in Spain turned to Chief Minister Vergennes in Paris for relief.

In a long letter the American expressed his mortification at the imposition. "Sir: I have never taken up my pen," Jay wrote to Vergennes, "with so much reluctance as I now do. . . . But, sir, there are few sensations more painful than those which they experience who, already covered with benefits, are impelled by cruel necessity to ask for more. Such is my present situation and hence proceeds my regret." He reviewed his discontents in Spain, expressing gratitude to France for being "our first, and is still

Chapter 17: "Le Washington de la Negotiation"

our best, and almost only friend." Louis XVI had treated with America on "terms of equality, neither taking nor attempting to take ungenerous advantages of our situation." Jay went on to solicit $50,000, spelling out that "the honor of Congress, suspended on the fate of these bills, now hangs as it were by a hair."[12]

* * * * *

Floridablanca, a seasoned minister with years of experience in the art of subterfuge and double-dealing in the courts of Europe, was skilled at exploiting the vulnerabilities of low-ranking ambassadors like Jay. One might take issue with his methods, or morality, but in the case of the Anglo-American civil war then taking place between the British colonies and mother country, the artful minister was simply advancing the interests of his sovereign as he understood them. The British, including John Jay and the other renegade colonists in America who sought independence, were the inveterate enemies of Spain. They represented a threat to Spanish interests not only in Europe and the coast of Africa but also in the Western Hemisphere extending from the Caribbean, Gulf of Mexico, and the Mississippi Valley to Central and South America. Unlike that of France, Spain's empire spread across the Americas, and silver from Mexico and Peru constituted the chief source of King Charles's wealth. At the time of the American Revolution, the value of silver production and transport across the Gulf of Mexico was a stunning 21.5 million pesos per year and rising.[13]

It was Floridablanca's job to safeguard those shipping lanes, and success in this endeavor meant, first, keeping Americans distant from Louisiana and the Mississippi River and, second, pursuing a foreign policy designed to weaken the British people, if possible, through internal division. On the first objective, Spanish Louisiana had only a small population, less than thirty thousand inhabitants, but it was the giant standing guard over Mexico and the vital transport lanes connecting their silver mines via the Gulf of Mexico to the Gulf Stream and Cádiz. Most of the world's silver traveled from inland Mexico by wagon to the Gulf Coast and thence in galleons northeast along the Texas shoreline, past the mouth of the Mississippi, toward the Atlantic. Floridablanca and the king worried that American emigration over the Appalachian Mountains into what they considered Spain's eastern Louisiana was a threat not only to western Louisiana and control of the Mississippi but also to the security of their silver commerce and the colonies that exported the precious metal.[14]

In some ways, Floridablanca understood Americans better than they understood themselves. Jay was approaching the Spanish king as an ambassador of goodwill and friendship, while throughout the world Americans were famous for being rebellious, disorderly, brazen, land-obsessed, and particularly contemptuous of kings and other forms of central authority. Floridablanca saw the future, perceptively, as one at high risk of American menace, a suspicion corroborated by the Congress's demand of navigation rights on the Mississippi since the beginning of the war. To Floridablanca, this nonnegotiable stance of the United States was glaring evidence of what he feared most for Louisiana: the imminent swarming of Americans over the mountains toward Spanish possessions.

This is one reason Floridablanca would not budge on the navigation. Another reason, entwined with the first, was that he knew that this point of American diplomacy was an explosive political and sectional issue in Congress. Miralles's official intelligence over more than a year and a half and in a five-hour meeting with Gérard in early 1780 shined a bright light for Floridablanca on the sectional divide in America, over not only the navigation of the Mississippi but also the Newfoundland fisheries. The minister hoped that Spain's hard line on the Mississippi would help to contain Americans east of the Appalachian Mountains while simultaneously fostering discord and disunion among them, thwarting the rise of a powerful united confederacy whose outward-directed aggressions might otherwise soon advance over the mountains southwest toward the Spanish empire in America.[15]

* * * * *

As he peregrinated from one royal palace to another, Jay never perceived the full extent of Floridablanca's intentions in his foreign policy with the United States. But he did grow wiser month after month, eventually arriving at two hypotheses to explain the minister's delays and deceptions. First, Jay conjectured that Spain was in fact procrastinating all forward motion with Americans while it engaged in earnest talks with British negotiators to make a separate peace with England conditioned upon the surrender of Gibraltar to King Charles III. If this happened, Spain would divorce itself from the war and thus commensurately reduce the probability of a Franco-American victory. In this conjecture, Jay was correct. Since the American ambassador's arrival, Floridablanca had been in regular talks with covert British agents. One of "the spies of Britain," as Jay called them, had orders to divide Spain from the Americans decisively, with the offer of West Florida to Floridablanca. In exchange Spain would agree to unconditional neutrality in the war: no treaty with the United States, no money, no arms, no trade, and no ambassador at court. Another plan submitted to Floridablanca proposed that in return for the restored neutrality of the Spanish empire, England would award Gibraltar to Charles III, and if the king would take the bolder step of aiding England in suppressing the revolution with Spanish arms, George III was ready to cede Florida and the right to fish on the Grand Bank.[16]

Seeking to maximize Spanish territorial gain while also diminishing the threat of western expansion of Americans into the Mississippi Valley, Floridablanca prepared his own outline of a treaty for King George to sign. It boiled down to Gibraltar, the Floridas, Campeche, and Honduras for Spain, and for England a near guarantee of terminating the revolution and restoring the colonies to dependent status. Floridablanca drew a radiant picture of the primary advantage to the British empire from an immediate peace with King Charles: Spain would never ally with the colonies and would immediately recall its navy from all engagements, freeing the British Royal Navy to concentrate its forces on America.[17]

Jay's second hypothesis was that Floridablanca was coldly scheming to wear down the United States and its ambassador in Spain in order to squeeze from it the prized navigation of the Mississippi. As he reported to Congress, the chief minister hoped to undercut the creditworthiness of the American confederation and Jay's own self-confidence in the "expectation that our distresses would render us more pliant and less attached to the Mississippi."[18]

In another letter, Jay counseled the Congress to trust and rely on Spain no longer and to pursue instead a course independent of foreign nations generally, especially of monarchies. To illustrate the deviousness of Floridablanca's diplomacy on the Mississippi navigation, the ambassador called to the minds of congressmen the biblical story of Jacob and Esau, with Spain playing the role of the former and the United States the latter. In the parable, the powerful, domineering Jacob exploits his brother, Esau, who is in danger of starvation, extorting from him his entire inheritance and wealth for one meal of pottage. Jay said the United States must find its strength, keeping up its "violent exertions" against the British enemy and meanwhile forbearing to trade away its inheritance on the Mississippi River for the meager returns of a treaty with Spain. "In my opinion," Jay wrote, "we should endeavor to be as independent on the charity of our friends as on the mercy of our enemies. Jacob took advantage even of his brother's hunger, and extorted from him a higher price than the value of the Mississippi even for a single dinner. The way not to be in Esau's condition is to be prepared to meet with Jacob's."[19]

To John Adams, then in Paris, Jay added that if Floridablanca and King Charles III were unintelligent enough to disaffect the United States at this critical moment in its rise to power, the breach might become permanent. The United States might ally with old Britain, instead of Spain, he seemed to relish, and "the power of the united States added to that of Britain, and under her direction, would enable her to give law to the western world, and that Spanish America and the islands would then be at her mercy."[20]

* * * * *

By the fall of 1781, one final test of Floridablanca's sincerity remained. From the start, aware of the Congress's ultimatum on the Mississippi navigation, the minister had lamented that a Spanish-America treaty was flatly impossible without a reversal of that stringency. It was the "sole obstacle" to a treaty. It was "the principal object to be obtained by the war." But then the delegates in Congress, under the pressure of Britain's war on the South, made the much-demanded sacrifice. In September at the palace of San Ildefonso sixty miles northwest of Madrid, Jay formally presented Congress's new instruction to Floridablanca, in spite of the fact that he now severely disagreed with giving up the navigation. On September 19 Jay wrote the minister once. Then again on September 22. In response Floridablanca did not invite the American to a parley to hammer out the terms of the treaty stalled now for a year and a half. He instead announced a reorganization of negotiations, designating his secretary, Bernardo del Campo, as formal court representative in further dialogues with the United States on the treaty. Then all of October and November passed without forward motion. After this, the winter came on and broke into the spring and the spring into the summer of 1782. Still, nothing from del Campo or Floridablanca—not one inch of progress made in spite of the American relinquishment of the Mississippi. If ever there was any doubt, Jay now had definitive proof of Spanish duplicity. The myth of a forthcoming treaty *only if* the United States ceded to His Majesty control of the river was exploded. Negotiations with Floridablanca, Jay concluded, were a sham.[21]

In his final six months on Spanish soil, Jay kept his counsel, combating bills of credit and eventually defaulting on many of them. But there were consolations. In those same six months, he celebrated America's victory at Yorktown and the birth of a healthy new daughter. Also, the Congress, acutely aware of Jay's trials against formidable odds in Spain, had months earlier voted for a formal measure of approbation of his conduct as ambassador, informing him of the accolade by official correspondence. Moved, Jay replied to this vote of confidence by his compatriots, penning a heartfelt letter to the president of Congress. "I do not recollect to have ever received a letter that gave me more real pleasure," Jay wrote to the American body. His experience in Spain had been one of "painful perplexities and embarrassments." He found himself

> often at a loss to determine where the line of prudence was to be found, and constantly exposed by my particular situation to the danger of either injuring the dignity and interest of my country on the one hand or trespassing on the overrated respectability and importance of this court on the other—I say, sir, that on considering these things, the approbation of Congress gave me most singular and cordial satisfaction.[22]

Not much later Jay opened another letter from Congress. This one turned him upside down. The delegates in Philadelphia announced to Jay his election as one of five ministers plenipotentiary to negotiate a peace treaty with Britain to end the War of Independence. This was flattering news, of course. But the explicit instructions Congress issued requiring the five-man commission to bend passively to the French in all aspects of the peace treaty excited so much upset in Jay that he wrote back to Philadelphia asking to be delisted and replaced by someone else. The instructions mandated that the American peacemakers "undertake nothing in the negotiations for peace or truce without their knowledge and concurrence." Jay was incredulous at this straightjacket. There was no ambiguity: the Americans must inform and consult Vergennes at every step along the way in the manner of children to a parent. Once intrepid orders of Congress had safeguarded the Mississippi boundary, the Mississippi navigation, and the Newfoundland fisheries, but now they were replaced by the single ultimatum of independence. Everything else was left to the approval and veto power of Vergennes and King Louis XVI.[23]

To Jay it was a contemptible role that he wished to cast off. Chafing, he wrote an emotional, patriotic letter to the president of Congress, Thomas McKean of Delaware, requesting to be removed from the commission on grounds of personal and national honor. He wished his nation to be *independent*, not *dependent* upon the king of France or any other head of state except the Congress itself. He had enlisted in the "Service of my Country" in 1776, he said, determined to faithfully execute any orders in any station to which Congress appointed him. "This resolution, for the first time, embarrasses me." To lie down servile to France, he remonstrated, "occasions sensations I never before experienced." He continued: "Sir, as an American, I feel an interest in the dignity of my country, which renders it difficult for me to reconcile myself to the idea of the sovereign independent States of America submitting in the persons of their ministers to be absolutely governed by the advice and opinions of the servants of another sovereign, especially in a case of such national importance."[24]

In his letter to McKean, Jay asked to be rid of the yoke. He requested that the Congress demote him to any other post in Europe or America, one of obvious lesser prestige and import but one he could fulfill honorably and in good conscience. Due to geographical distance, duty, and "love for our country and zeal for her service," he refused to resign outright, but he would expectantly await his reappointment elsewhere by return mail from Philadelphia at McKean's earliest convenience.

To the good fortune of the United States, the Congress never satisfied Jay in his appeal for dismissal from the peace commission. The ambassador remained in Spain until the early summer, when a letter from Benjamin Franklin landed on his desk urging him to hasten to Paris for the commencement of peace talks. By this time the Austro-Russian co-mediation by Frederick II and Catherine the Great had long since unraveled, foundering on the twin rocks of independence and Gibraltar. John Adams had refused to consider opening peace negotiations in Vienna without independence as a precondition, and Floridablanca issued a similar mandate on Gibraltar. Seeing this from London, George III and Lord North sent notice that they would not attend, putting the co-mediation to a quiet death. Then came the American victory at Yorktown. All this meant that the four belligerents—the United States, France, Spain, and Britain—would settle their various treaties at the palace of Versailles without interfering mediators.

At liberty to start anew in France, Jay, who by now had accepted his role as peace minister in spite of Congress's constraints on American autonomy, set off with his family from Madrid towards the Pyrenees on May 21.

CHAPTER 18

"The Greatest Empire in the World"

W HEN JAY ARRIVED IN PARIS in late June of 1782, Benjamin Franklin had been present in the capital for five and a half years. The third American peacemaker who would materially affect the outcome of negotiations, John Adams, was in Amsterdam negotiating a treaty of commerce with the Dutch. Adams would not appear in Paris until late October, at which time he would ally himself with Jay against the pro-French soft diplomacy of the seventy-six-year-old Franklin.

The three diplomats had different styles and histories. Notably, one thing Jay and Adams had in common was intimate knowledge of the searing fights over the Mississippi River and the Newfoundland fisheries in the summer and fall of 1779. Both men understood that at the end of Union-threatening debates, Congress had forged a compromise that elevated the navigation and fisheries to equal status as ultimatums of various European treaties. Jay had sat as president of Congress during the seven months of acrimonious debates, and Adams had been fully briefed on them in October and November of 1779, before disembarking for Europe. Franklin, on the other hand, had not touched American soil since October of 1776. By this time a celebrity in Paris with intimate friendships in high French circles, he wished ardently not to offend the great ally without whom the United States never could have won the Battle of Yorktown or found itself on the brink of independence in the first place.

* * * * *

The same day of his entrance into Paris, Jay traveled by coach several miles out of town to the village of Passy to pay a visit to Franklin. The famous scientist and man of letters lived at the elegant Hôtel de Valentinois, set upon on a hill and conveniently located on the diplomatic road to Versailles.

In greeting Jay, the elder diplomat already had clear-cut knowledge of his colleague's sentiments on France and Congress's late instructions to do nothing in peace negotiations without the consent of Vergennes, because Jay had written to him numerous times from Madrid. In those letters, the New Yorker had given Franklin every assurance that as much as he disdained the Congress's handcuffs, he would honor them—but only so long as Vergennes reciprocated and acted always in good faith. Jay had an exalted view of "duty" and "principles of action" when it came to both personal relationships and alliances between nations. What he abhorred were "secrecy" and "cunning," he told Franklin. As long as France remained "fair, firm, and friendly" and "faithful," he would abide.[1]

The next day, June 24, the two Americans rode together to Versailles. There, in an agreeable conference with Vergennes, topics ranged from the current state of negotiations with the British to Spain's ongoing pursuit of the Rock of Gibraltar and the whereabouts of fellow American commissioners Adams, Jefferson, and Laurens. On the first of these, in spite of the loss at Yorktown and extraordinary backlash within the Parliament, the administration of Charles Watson-Wentworth, 2nd Marquis of Rockingham, the new prime minister in the wake of North's resignation, remained implacable. Independence was out of the question. Instead, Rockingham sought to terminate the war by means of "a constitutional reconciliation," one comprising home rule for the Americans under a loose British-American federal union. One idea being floated in Parliament was the establishment of two American congresses, one for the North and one for the South, independent of one another but not of the English monarch. The two congresses would be granted separate constitutional powers, yet both would continue to be administered by the British scepter and throne as final arbiter.[2]

Meanwhile, the Straits of Gibraltar teemed with Spanish and French warships and waterborne batteries now in their third year of an attempted siege of the prized fortress for the Spanish. Twice before, the Royal Navy had plowed through the blockade with massive squadrons of frigates and ships to resupply the British garrison, breaking the siege. Still, Floridablanca would not give up. The Spanish monarch had lost this vital Mediterranean naval base to England in 1713, and its recovery was the minister's paramount objective in the war. He put pressure on Vergennes to reinforce the siege and overawe a third British assault in the expectation that if the garrison at Gibraltar remained under Spanish and French cordon at the moment of peace, Britain would have no alternative but to

Chapter 18: "The Greatest Empire of the World"   323

FIGURE 41. Palace of Versailles. (View of Versailles. Israel Silvestre, *Château de Versailles seen from the forecourt*, from *Chalcographie du Louvre*, vol. 22, 1682, reprinted ca. 1360, etching, 14.9375 x 19.8125 in, The Metropolitan Museum of Art, Harris Brisbane Dick Fund, 1930.)

surrender the prize. This was the overriding hope and concerted strategy of Floridablanca and Charles III in the spring and summer of 1782.

As for the missing peace ministers, Adams was then at the Hague awaiting the finalization of a treaty that granted the United States much-needed international recognition and a loan of guilders equal to $2 million. Laurens would arrive only at the eleventh hour, and the other Southern negotiator, Jefferson, never sailed from American shores. Laurens would not alight in Paris until days before the signing. This left him time only to endorse the treaty's contents and add a clause pertaining to slavery that the South Carolinian considered vital to Southern interests.[3]

* * * * *

Jay arrived in France that June reinvigorated to stand up for three non-negotiable conditions of a peace treaty with Britain: independence, the Mississippi boundary, and the Newfoundland fisheries. He also had the navigation of the Mississippi much on his mind, but the conundrum of Spain's ownership of both banks of the lower river remained. Likely by now he was persuaded that if the Spanish continued to be obstinate on the Mississippi, he and the other commissioners must negotiate with the British to somehow undermine them. Prepared to fight for all four objects, Jay unexpectedly fell ill with a serious case of influenza soon after his first meeting with Vergennes and Franklin at Versailles. Placed in virtual quarantine at his quarters in Paris by a doctor, forbidden outside business or social visits, Jay missed much of the first formal month of peace talks with the British. During this interval, Franklin advanced negotiations alone.[4]

Even before Jay fell ill, Franklin had held dozens of hours of dialogue with two British representatives in Paris, Richard Oswald, a Scottish-born merchant, and Thomas Grenville, son of former Prime Minister George Grenville, discovering what he considered to be nefarious intentions. The British negotiators' purpose, as revealed in talks in April, May, and June, was to detach the United States from its alliance with France, settling a separate, gainful Anglo-American peace and driving a wedge between the allies. The ambition of Oswald and Grenville was to promote the prospect of a reconciliation with the colonies, be it denominating them a dominion in the British empire or reluctantly an independent nation. What they most wanted was a restoration of American commerce and a return to the Anglo-American status quo *ante bellum*—that is, a map of the globe that deprived France and Spain of the Floridas, West Indies islands, the fisheries, Gibraltar, Minorca, Dunkirk, and at-risk trading posts in Africa and India. Better than any other tactic, a separate peace with the Americans would redraw the old map, upholding British honor and self-respect while, as a boon to the British empire, reestablishing lucrative trade with America and pushing France out of the equation. Believing in the future prosperity of the thirteen colonies, most Britons wanted to obtain the golden ring of American trade even if those colonies were lost from the empire. What England gained, France would lose.[5]

Franklin let Jay know that he abhorred this notion. "The thing is impossible," he told Jay. "We can never agree to desert our first and our faithful friend on any consideration whatever. We should become infamous by such abominable baseness." To Franklin's conception of justice, a separate peace with the enemy would be an unforgivable contravention of the Franco-American treaties, as well as of Congress's instructions, not to mention a breach in the wellspring of gratitude the United States owed to France for five years of aid and assistance in the war. He could not imagine such a flagrant reneging on the United States' promises and obligations to France, no matter the gains in territory or navigational or fishing rights that might ensue from it.[6]

Franklin continued to maintain this posture in July when news of the sudden death of Rockingham on the first of the month quickened the pace of negotiations. The prime minister's exit from power provoked a split in the antiwar party in Parliament and the ascension to the post of William Petty, 2nd Earl of Shelburne. In Shelburne, a Whig friendly to America had at last risen to the helm. A liberal political thinker, Shelburne had opposed the Stamp Act, the Declaratory Act, and the Proclamation Line of 1763. To America's favor, Shelburne's policy was to end the war as speedily as possible.[7]

On July 10 Franklin and Oswald met for two hours. Perceiving a golden opportunity in the recent regime change in London to advance American interests, Franklin read to the British envoy "a few hints" for a peace treaty from a prepared memorandum. Uncomfortable with opening formal negotiations without French involvement or the consent of the other American peace commissioners, Franklin offered his framework for a treaty not officially but as a conversation starter with the new prime minister. Franklin divided the terms of peace into the two categories of *necessary* and *advisable* articles. The three necessary ones were independence, settling of boundaries, and access to the Newfoundland fisheries. The advisable articles were monetary reparations made for British vandalism of American property, a formal apology for British wrongs committed against their kin, a free-trade compact, and the cession of Canada to the United States.[8]

What stands out in this set of proposals is the fact that, except for independence, there is only one other unambiguous prerequisite of peace: American free use of the Newfoundland fisheries, the flower of New England. The Mississippi boundary is glaringly absent. Franklin soft-pedaled this issue as a necessary article, only stating what was obvious to all—that Britain and the United States must settle boundaries in the treaty. The peace minister did not include the Mississippi boundary—or the navigation—as necessary articles of peace. Only American catching of cod and haddock achieved this premier status alongside independence.

Franklin never left records to account for the omissions and inclusions of his necessary articles of peace, but his archives suggest that correspondence from Philadelphia and New England might have played a role. On the question of the boundary, he had lately received contradictory letters from Congress and its new secretary for foreign affairs, Robert Livingston of New York. One asserted that the peace commissioners in Paris should strive for the boundary at the Mississippi and fishing rights, with the expectation that France would back both claims. Yet Livingston dispatched another missive that diplomatic historian Richard B. Morris calls "a curious letter, in which he manages to advance and retreat at the same time." In it, the foreign secretary asserts that American title to the territory east of the Mississippi appears justifiable. However, he simultaneously demonstrates a willingness to cede the lands in the event that other nations' diplomats at the table refuse that boundary. In such a circumstance, he tells Franklin that he, Jay, and Adams might press instead for an awarding of the area lying between the Appalachians and the Mississippi to the Native Americans who currently inhabit it, a land grant mutually guaranteed by France, Spain, Britain, and the United States. In communicating this, Livingston was not espousing a novel concept in international relations. Geographical buffer zones to prevent direct contact and conflict between rival powers were commonplace. As a bonus, Livingston also proposed in the letter to Franklin that the belligerent parties should agree that the neutral Indian territory "be open to the trade of those whose lands border upon them."[9]

Setting the Newfoundland fisheries apart from the Mississippi boundary and navigation, Franklin never received any extant letters from America with contradictory guidance on New England's historic land and water rights. In fact, on the contrary, numerous letters arrived in Passy alerting Franklin of the perils of sending home a peace treaty with England that failed to grant the United States unfettered fishing and drying rights in the northern waters. One of them came from the same Secretary Livingston, who warned Franklin of looming dangers of disunion on January 7. "All the New England States are much interested in this point," he cautioned Franklin. "They will see with pain their sister states in the full enjoyment of the benefits which will result from their Independence, while their own commerce is checked, and their state impoverished." Livingston continued, alluding to New Englanders, "They will consider their interests as sacrificed to the happiness of others, and can hardly forbear to foster discontents which may excite the most dangerous divisions."[10]

Influential representatives from Massachusetts sounded the same alarm. One who wrote to Franklin was a longtime friend and political correspondent, Thomas Cushing, a founder of the resistance movement in the early days and speaker of the Massachusetts House in the year of the Boston Massacre. At the time of the writing, he was lieutenant governor of the state. The fifty-six-year-old Cushing had reveled in the news of Yorktown for only a few hours when he sat down in Boston to dedicate a short, forceful communiqué to Franklin about this matter so vital to "the Northern States." Congratulating Franklin on the "glorious news" of Yorktown, Cushing informed the peace minister that Americans were now expecting "a beneficial permanent and honorable peace. However, I am confident it will not be thought *so* by the Northern States unless their share of the fishery upon the banks of Newfoundland are secured to them." The peace commissioners must, Cushing explained further, "secure this important branch of business, as important to the Northern States as tobacco, wheat and rice are to the Southern."[11]

These letters, and several others Franklin received on the imperative nature of the fisheries, impacted him. As he saw it, those commercial rights were not only an economic necessity to New England but also a political necessity to the United States. The Union was at stake. For this reason, at least in part, he sent Oswald back to London with terms marking out fishing rights in the waters of Newfoundland as a necessary and nonnegotiable article in no case to be ceded. If England did not agree, the war would continue. The argument must be made and won, the distinguished scientist believed, or else the United States' independence might turn out to be but the beginning of separatism and disunion.

* * * * *

The superseding interest of all the American peace representatives in Paris was the preservation of the Union of the states. The expansive claims they made and fought for reflected less territorial and commercial greed than the pursuit of a balanced peace treaty that would ensure sectional justice and stability in the mold of the Mississippi-Fisheries Compromise of 1779. This is why Jay, once he emerged from his sickbed in late July, fought for the Mississippi boundary and the Mississippi navigation with the same tenacity Franklin put forth for the fisheries. Throughout the year he had given Franklin his word that he would honor the Congress's egregiously misguided instructions to prostrate themselves to the French by seeking Vergennes's approval of an Anglo-American treaty before signing it—but only on the condition that France supported the United States in its essential claims. In August and September, the New York peace minister discovered evidence of what he perceived to be a betrayal by Vergennes that posed immediate risk to the triad of the fisheries, the boundary, and the navigation. So it was with great reluctance that Jay unilaterally made the decision to violate the instructions of Congress for the sake of the greater interests of the confederation.

The first prod to Jay's break with the French came from negotiations with Don Pedro Pablo Abarca de Bolea Conde de Aranda, sixty-two-year-old Spanish ambassador at the court of Versailles. At Vergennes's request, Jay undertook one-on-one conversations with Aranda in early August in a renewed attempt to forge a Spanish-American treaty. With Franklin's support, Jay complied, soon learning that the Spaniard contested not only an American right to navigate the Mississippi but also the Mississippi boundary. In their first formal meeting, Aranda laid out on the table a copy of Dr. John Mitchell's famous map of America, asking Jay where he would draw his dividing line between the United States and New Spain. The American lawyer answered that no map was necessary. The frontier was already marked out by nature and the treaty of 1763 ending the Seven Years' War: the Mississippi River.[12]

Later Aranda countered with a copy of the same map with a bold red line etched roughly down the crest of the Appalachians, some five hundred miles and millions of acres away from the Mississippi, ending in St. Mary's River in eastern Georgia. Floridablanca, during his years in Spain, had never once overtly contested the Mississippi River as the United States' western boundary, but, for that matter, nor had he ever agreed to the boundary, either, leaving Jay and the Congress to assume that the only obstacle to settling a treaty between them was the Mississippi navigation. Now Aranda defined a massive new acquisition for Spain, justifying it on the basis of another perversion of Spanish-American goodwill. When Spain had declared war on Britain in 1779, instead of offering direct aid to the United States, Floridablanca swiftly dispatched a flotilla under Bernardo de Gálvez up the Mississippi River to take possession of Natchez, Baton Rouge, and Fort Manchac in the name of King Charles III. This objective accomplished, Gálvez next laid siege to British West Florida in the first months of 1780. Aranda explained to Jay that these conquests laid the foundation for a fair and valid Spanish claim of eastern Louisiana running fifteen hundred miles up the river eastward to the Appalachians. Reminiscent of the loathed British Proclamation Line of 1763, Aranda's boundary excluded the United States from possession of the entire trans-Appalachian West, except for a small patch in the vicinity of modern-day Akron and Cleveland, Ohio.[13]

Aranda's map of the future North America privately enraged Jay, but it was the behavior of the French that persuaded him that a grand anti-American betrayal was taking shape. This shift came on August 10. On that day Jay met with Franklin, Vergennes, and Joseph Matthias Gérard de Rayneval, Vergennes's undersecretary, at Versailles to confer about the twin issues of the Spanish-American boundary and how to approach the tender issue of independence with London, since so many in the British ministry still wished for a dominion status of some kind for the thirteen colonies, along the lines of Ireland. In a long conversation, Vergennes offered no support whatsoever on the Mississippi boundary. He listened to the American claim but remained "very cautious and reserved." His undersecretary said little too, but more than Vergennes. As Jay reported to Congress, Rayneval simply expressed his disappointment that "we claimed more than we had a right to."[14]

On the question of American independence, Jay demanded that this singular concession of London be a prerequisite of peace—not a mere condition on par with other interests like boundaries, commerce, and land exchanges. Without this, he foresaw overwhelming odds stacking against the United States as the English, French, and Spanish battled out the new map of the world. In the haggling, independence might even be bartered away. From the start, the New York lawyer was absolute on this point. Independence for all thirteen states was a hard, fast *precondition* of peace, not a bargaining chip to be left on the table for abuse and exploitation by enemies or allies. At the conference at Versailles, Vergennes counseled the Americans to moderate an unreasonable demand. He did not agree with the perceived dangers. The allies must negotiate together, not organize a separate, special conclave on independence to precede the rest. So long as independence was made an article of the final treaty, the United States should be satisfied.[15]

From this interview, Jay rushed to the judgment that the French were double-dealing to undermine independence, the boundary, or both. France, he decided, was not a trusted ally. Her allegiance was to herself and Spain, not the United States. Jay told Franklin as much in an impassioned debriefing the same day at his fellow commissioner's home in Passy. They had ridden together by carriage back from Versailles, discussing the state of negotiations. Then Jay stopped off for some time at Franklin's hotel, where he announced that thanks to the mysterious, dubious behavior of the Frenchmen, he was setting his sights on a new course of action. Churning, he argued that the contemptible instruction to make France master of the United States in peace negotiations was going to sabotage American interests and defeat them in their own Revolution, handing the advantage to the Europeans. To assure the peace and independence of the

United States, he said, he would abandon the instruction, abandon the allies, and negotiate independently with the British.[16]

Franklin pushed back, asserting that the Congress's directive to negotiate in tandem with France was uninfringeable and that Jay would not only be violating an act of Congress in pursuing a separate treaty—he would also be risking the alliance. Would he do these things? Franklin asked. As history hands down the events of that day, Jay gave his answer in an abrupt show of anger. Removing the pipe from his mouth, or pocket, he cocked back his arm and proclaimed that if the instruction of Congress were an instrument of dishonor, injury, and indignity to the American Union, he would gladly smash it to pieces. With this, Jay hurled the clay pipe with all his might into Franklin's fireplace, where it exploded into fragments.[17]

* * * * *

Had Vergennes come around to the American position on the boundary, navigation, and fisheries over the next month, Jay might not have fulfilled his promise to break from the French and from Congress's explicit order on Franco-American cooperation on the peace treaty. But indications of a misalignment of interests and outright cunning became even more glaring in September. By the middle of the month, the American peace minister obtained what to him was decisive proof that the French and Spanish planned to deprive the United States of all three. And, critically, Jay was negotiating alone during this time period because now Franklin had fallen ill. In the third week of August, the senior member of the negotiating team was confined to his bed for what Franklin himself believed was fatal abdominal pain. Certain he would die, he called in French doctors and requested Jay draft his last will and testament. In the end, the diagnosis was kidney stones. Franklin was to live another eight years, but for six full weeks he was incapacitated. With Adams not arriving until October 26, this cleared the way for Jay to exercise his influence with little input or interference from any other commissioner.

It was the events of September 6–10 that set Jay on an irrevocable path to a separate peace with the British. First, Rayneval delivered to Jay a long memo entitled "Suggestion Concerning the Manner of Determining and Discussing Boundaries between Spain and the United States from the Banks of the Ohio Toward the Mississippi." The intention of the paper, the French spokesman said, was to help Louis XVI's two allies work out a suitable compromise. Instead, Jay read the manifesto, one proclaiming that the states had "no right" to either the western lands or the Mississippi navigation, as official, subversive French policy. To him, its pronouncements were evidence of what was to come if Vergennes were left in charge of the United States' future. It confirmed that the French intended to mark out the United States as a small coastal republic—one with no access to the Mississippi or the fisheries. Jay also worried that Vergennes might place independence in jeopardy by way of a negotiated truce.[18]

One day after this, Rayneval left for London. Vergennes hid this sudden departure of his undersecretary from American eyes, and when Jay found out about it through private channels two days later, on September 9, he joined the memo and the secret mission together into a compelling theory. A cynical diplomat, Jay was certain that Rayneval had crossed the channel to bring Shelburne into a French-made "underhand bargain" on the trans-Appalachian West wherein the United States would be shorn of all or most of its western acreage and the Mississippi navigation. The next day, September 10, Jay made another eye-opening discovery. By chance or calculation, a British citizen passed into his hands an intercepted letter written five months earlier to Vergennes by François Barbé-Marbois, the secretary of the French legation in Philadelphia. Entirely devoted to the Newfoundland fisheries, the missive was, to Jay, highly seditious and powerfully confirmatory of all he was imagining.[19]

In the letter Barbé-Marbois attacked Sam Adams and other New Englanders for stirring up wrath to obtain the fisheries, declaring their claims to be meritless, insisting that Vergennes should keep with agreed-upon policy to oppose an American right to the Newfoundland waters. Most vicious to Jay and later to Congress, Barbé-Marbois even recommended a method for humbling the New Englanders out of their grasping mania for the fisheries. France should act deliberately yet quietly to delay the evacuation of British troops from America until the Congress and its peace ministers abroad relented.[20]

These were crucial days for Jay. As he himself wrote to a friend on the 26th of the month, employing a sailor's metaphor, "There is a tide in human affairs which waits for nobody, and political mariners ought to watch and profit it and avail themselves of its advantages."[21]

* * * * *

Freed of the albatross of the French and Spanish, Jay intensified his meetings with two British envoys, Oswald and a newly-arrived negotiator, political economist Benjamin Vaughan, making them aware that if King

George satisfied the United States on the quartet of independence, the fisheries, the boundary, and the navigation of the Mississippi, he would turn his back on France and Spain. Jay also promised to fight to restore Anglo-American commercial relations in such a manner as to benefit King George III in preference to Louis XVI and Charles III. These arguments were persuasive. Over the next seven weeks, Jay, Oswald, and Vaughan worked out the broad outlines of the Treaty of Paris, one that included the quartet he considered so vital to the future domestic harmony and flourishing of the United States.

Article I of the treaty, as signed in preliminary form in late November, made the colonies "free Sovereign and independent States." Article II secured the western lands, setting the western boundary of the United States in the middle of the Mississippi River. Article III obtained fishing rights in the North Atlantic, affirming that "the People of the United States shall continue to enjoy unmolested the Right to take Fish of every kind on the Grand Bank, and on all the other Banks of Newfoundland . . . and that the American Fishermen shall have Liberty to dry and cure Fish in any of the unsettled Bays Harbors and Creeks of Nova Scotia, Magdalen Islands, and Labrador."[22]

Most remarkable in Jay's handiwork, he persuaded the British to award the United States the free navigation of the Mississippi not only on the stretches of the river where Great Britain had a legitimate claim, but also through Spanish shores on the lower river, where it entirely lacked jurisdiction. Jay did this as a calculated diplomatic maneuver to strengthen the hand of the United States in its future dealings with Spain; it would permit the United States to claim that Britain had handed down to its birth child the same navigational rights Spain had granted to King George in the Treaty of 1763 ending the Seven Years' War. Article VIII of Jay's treaty laid out the American right in no uncertain terms: "The Navigation of the River Mississippi from its Source to the Ocean shall for ever remain free and open to the Subjects of Great Britain and the Citizens of the United States."

Article VIII was not the only step Jay took in the fall of 1782 to secure the Southern states the navigation of the Mississippi. To supplement this, he penned a secret article of the treaty, one that promised to provide the United States a guarantee of free navigation while also exacting revenge on Spain for its deceptions and treacheries over the past three years. In this article, so secret that it should never be exposed to the French and Spanish under any circumstance, Jay offered the British an inducement to redirect its naval forces to the mouth of the Mississippi in order to reconquer West Florida before signing a treaty with Spain. This would more legitimately empower Britain to share navigation rights, because by the spirit of the Treaty of 1763, those rights inhered in West Florida. The inducement was land. If King George did not retain West Florida by the time of ending its war with King Charles, the Americans would demand from the British a southern boundary of the United States at the thirty-first parallel, whereas if Britain repossessed it, they would be far more liberal, agreeing to a boundary upstream of that by ninety miles at the mouth of the Yazoo River running due east to the Apalachicola River. This afforded England tens of thousands of extra acres of land as a bonus for success in vanquishing the Spanish in West Florida.[23]

In one conference with Oswald on the subject of the trade of the lower Mississippi, Jay sold the British expedition against West Florida to the envoy as a grand commercial prospect for both nations. With peace between an independent United States and England now assured, Jay said that George III no longer had any purpose for maintaining some twenty thousand British soldiers and seamen in the occupied American cities of New York and Charlestown. Cut them loose, he encouraged, and sail them down the coast, around the tip of East Florida, to make a violent, surprise attack on Spanish-held West Florida.

So awed was Oswald at Jay's aggressive attitude toward purported ally Spain that he took verbatim notes, dispatching them to London. As the British envoy recorded, Jay enthusiastically repeated that he wished for the Spanish to be dislodged from West Florida. He even scolded England for not acting immediately. "What are you doing with 20,000 men (he called them so many) lying idle, spending of money in New York and Charles Town," Oswald quoted Jay, "and keeping up a jealousy and animosity between you and us at a time when we are here endeavoring to bring about a restoration of friendship and good will? Why not employ some of those troops to recover that colony?" The feat could easily be accomplished, Jay pressed, and when completed it would remove the last obstacle to a flourishing Anglo-American partnership in the lower Mississippi Valley.[24]

* * * * *

If the extent to which North/South politics and fears of an imbalanced peace treaty motivated the three American diplomats in Paris in 1782 has not been sufficiently understood in U.S. history, John Adams left behind an illuminating record of a conversation he held with Franklin ten days before the signing of the preliminary articles. Adams made it to Paris in late October, and on November 20, as he wrote in his diary, "Dr. Franklin came in, and we fell into conversation." Among other topics, they discussed the Newfoundland fisheries and the navigation of the Mississippi. Well aware that Franklin scrupulously disagreed with the preference of Jay and Adams to override the most recent instructions of Congress, the New Englander made certain Franklin understood the gravity of the "great debates in Congress" of 1779. Recounting details of the fights between the sections of the Union and the zealous attitudes and oratory of Sam Adams, Gouverneur Morris, William Henry Drayton, and Henry Laurens, Adams told Franklin everything he knew. Regarding the struggle over the fishery, New Englanders had submitted an ultimatum in writing declaring that they would withdraw from the Union if the Congress did not stand behind American fishing and drying rights. "This point was so tender and important," Adams said, "that if not secured it would be the cause of a breach of the Union of the States."[25]

A failure to secure the fisheries in the peace treaty risked disunion, Adams was clear to communicate to Franklin. So would the loss of the Mississippi navigation. He conjectured that France's intent in both acts of deprivation of water rights was to foment disunion in the United States, perpetuating its subordinate status and keeping the former colonies under the thumb of Louis XVI. In Adams's words, France's ambition in excluding the expanding United States from Newfoundland and the Mississippi was "to lay the foundation for a rupture between the States, when in a few years they should think them grown too big. I could see no possible motive they had, to wish to negotiate the Mississippi into the hands of Spain, but this."

In this tête-à-tête with Adams, Franklin succinctly confirmed his understanding of the Mississippi-fisheries bargain of 1779—and the necessity of reinforcing it in the peace treaty. "The Fisheries and the Mississippi could not be given up," the scientist-diplomat asserted. "That nothing was clearer to him that the Fisheries were essential to the Northern States, and the Mississippi to the Southern and indeed both to all."[26]

* * * * *

Franklin never fully agreed with the strategy of overriding the orders of Congress on the peace treaty, but the logic of a secure Union, combined with the insistence of Jay and Adams, persuaded him to go along and keep quiet. In November the peace ministers finalized the articles of the preliminary treaty. Adams's major contributions to the peace process were twofold. Most important, he backed up Jay, aligning with him on all points of the treaty as well as on the New Yorker's inspired tactic to negotiate separately from the French. This enabled Jay and Adams to overrule Franklin on Congress's order to seek the approval of Vergennes before signing. Second, while Adams was impressed by Jay's rough draft of the fisheries article, a New York lawyer could not be expected to craft international law on the waters of Newfoundland with the same nuance as a barrister from New England ten years his senior. After carefully considering Jay's proposed Article III, Adams realized that the Middle state commissioner did not adequately understand the geography, seasonal weather patterns, and migrations of fish in that part of the world. Jay had not specified by name fishing rights in the Gulf of the St. Lawrence or drying rights in the harbors and creeks of Nova Scotia, the Magdalen Islands, and Labrador, where after the breakup of winter, Americans would be able to fish alone for several months to great profit. Adams added these.[27]

Before the signing, the British and American negotiators concluded several unsurprising articles, too. One related to prewar American debts owed to British creditors and another to the debts supposedly owed in the same direction for the Loyalist estates confiscated by Americans at the outset of the war. For weeks Franklin, Adams, Jay, Oswald, and Vaughan debated these money matters until finally the American trio yielded. Both would be repaid. In light of the millions of acres of land Britain was awarding to them in the trans-Appalachian West and the bountiful masses of cod and haddock American fishermen would soon be capturing, they seemed to Jay, Franklin, and Adams to be fair concessions. Finally, Henry Laurens appeared on November 28, two days before the signing. His major contribution was to insert a clause into the peace treaty disallowing British armies and fleets from carrying away captured or liberated enslaved people upon their withdrawal from America.[28]

On Saturday, November 30, Franklin, Adams, Jay, and the newly arrived Laurens gathered at Oswald's lodgings on Rue des Petits Augustins to affix their signatures to the preliminary treaty, including the secret article. The agreement was deemed preliminary because at this stage it might still be rejected by Congress or Parliament, or altered in one clause or another before being ratified as the definitive peace. No one, however, suspected this would be the case, since it might cause one party to renege on crucial terms, possibly reigniting the war. Following the signing at

Oswald's house, seals were attached to duplicate copies of the treaty, and one original was turned over to each party for transmission to their principals. With the ceremony concluded, the participants rode out to Passy together to celebrate and dine at Franklin's table. They were joined by several French guests, one of whom predicted grandly that "the Thirteen United States of America would form the greatest empire in the world."[29]

Not much later, the carefully constructed articles of peace set sail from the coast of France destined for the United States in an American vessel appropriately named the *Washington*. John Jay had indeed played the role of the "le Washington de la Negotiation" at the Court of Versailles. But back home in Philadelphia his brazen self-determination on behalf of the United States—and particularly his blatantly Anglophilic secret article—would not be fully appreciated.

CHAPTER 19

"Stained with the Blood of Her Sons"

THE TREATY TO END THE War of Independence navigated up the Delaware River aboard the U.S. packet ship *Washington* on the morning of Wednesday, March 12, 1783. On the same day, it was read aloud in Independence Hall, where over the next two weeks delegates gave its nine formal articles and one secret article a full hearing. With few exceptions, the congressmen publicly heralded the four articles on independence, the Newfoundland fishery, the western boundary at the Mississippi, and the Mississippi navigation. "Congratulations on this happy event," Theodorick Bland penned to a Virginia political colleague later in the day. Stephen Higginson of Massachusetts claimed that the American peacemakers in Paris had "performed wonders in obtaining such a treaty." President of Congress Elias Boudinot of New Jersey extolled the treaty to George Washington as having "opened a new scene in this Western World." Alexander Hamilton, military hero of Yorktown who had taken his seat in Congress for the first time in November, proclaimed that the bounty acquired by the United States "exceeded the hopes of the most sanguine." Soon, when writing personally to Jay to congratulate him, Hamilton exulted that Americans were giving his fellow New Yorker much credit for the treaty. Notably, the lieutenant colonel said, the Newfoundland article was winning Jay high honors in the New England states. So appreciative were they, Hamilton said, that "the New England people talk of making you an annual fish-offering as an acknowledgement of your exertions for the participation of the fisheries."[1]

Many delegates, however, felt differently about the three peacemakers' overt violation of Congress's order to negotiate in good faith with France, seeking Vergennes's approval prior to signing. Madison recorded that the "separate & secret manner" in which the Americans had negotiated the treaty generated angst in Congress because it risked subverting the Franco-American alliance. Delegates like Madison took pains that March to reconcile with French ambassador Luzerne and his secretary of legation, Barbé-Marbois, in Philadelphia, inquiring of them whether King Louis XVI intended to remonstrate against the Congress for the breach of trust. Barbé-Marbois answered that "great powers never *complained* but they *felt & remembered*." Even so, Luzerne did protest. Expressing the French king's "great indignation" at the slight, he presented formal letters of disapproval and objection to Robert Livingston, the new U.S. secretary of foreign affairs. In Paris Vergennes and the king deemed the Anglo-American treaty a failure of allied obligation. Above all, the French foreign minister was stunned by the enormous concessions made by George III to the United States, suspecting quite rightly that the true intent of the king and his cabinet in Whitehall was to win back the heart and purse of America to England, marginalizing or excluding France from trade benefits.[2]

The secret article on West Florida and the lower Mississippi elicited far greater upset in Philadelphia. It was a bizarre, underhanded concoction that no one in Congress ever expected to see in a treaty. Jay's purpose in the article was to save American western commerce from a Spanish chokehold. He had risked his reputation on it for the sake of the Southern states' interest in trade on the Mississippi. He had done it for the good of the Union, to buttress and solidify the Mississippi-Fisheries Compromise of 1779. Yet "the most judicious members" of Congress, as Madison called them, singled out the deceptive article for special denunciation—and annulment. It was "offensive." It gave extra land to Great Britain, the United States' enemy, if that enemy reconquered or otherwise reacquired land from Spain, a fellow belligerent and France's closest ally. While perhaps appreciative of Jay's creative effort to wrest navigation rights from the labyrinth of the lower Mississippi Valley, these delegates feared the secret article, once discovered by Vergennes and King Louis XVI, would infuriate them, possibly driving them to break the alliance. The result might be a premature withdrawal of French military and naval support from America, leaving the thirteen states to complete the project of independence on their own. There might be "a renewal of the war," some feared, with the United States standing alone. At least one delegate fantasized that a furious King Louis XVI might unite with George III to punish France's erstwhile American ally, dividing the thirteen colonies between them.[3]

As soon as the misbegotten article was read on the floor of Independence Hall, it became the Congress's most tightly held secret in years. Not a

Chapter 19: "Stained with the Blood of Her Sons" 339

word of it was committed to the official journal. Madison felt duty-bound to inform the governor of his state and other high-ranking Virginians about the article, but he decided the risk was too great, even if communicated in cipher. Like other delegates, Madison did everything he could to suppress knowledge and awareness of the article. To Edmund Randolph, his closest confidante after Jefferson, he would only say that a most unfortunate blunder had scarred an otherwise splendid peace, one that might propel the United States into new dangers. "In this business," he apprised Randolph correctly, "Jay has taken the lead & proceeded to a length of which you can form little idea. Adams followed with cordiality. Franklin has been dragged into it."[4]

For Madison and other members of Congress, anxiety over the secret article would not be relieved until notice of the Anglo-Spanish treaty reached America at the end of the year. Britain never did launch a naval assault on West Florida. The territory remained under Spanish arms, and in that treaty, George III awarded to Charles III not only West Florida but also all of East Florida extending along the Gulf of Mexico around the panhandle to the Atlantic Ocean. In the end, Spain did not regain Gibraltar. The two Floridas, the lower Mississippi, and the trade of the Gulf of Mexico constituted Spain's grand winnings from the war.

Once the new map of America was redrawn, King Charles retained all of Spain's original Louisiana, giving him exclusive title to the west bank of the Mississippi running 2,500 miles upriver. With the acquisition of West Florida, the Spanish now also claimed two hundred miles of the east bank, making American navigation impossible without Spanish permission. This outcome of the treaty rendered Jay's secret article moot. It also meant that after seven years of diplomatic effort, the Congress had failed in its quest to stand America up on its two "strong legs," as Virginian Richard Henry Lee promoted the navigation of the Mississippi and the Newfoundland fisheries in 1779. Unless King Charles and Floridablanca acquiesced on the Mississippi in future diplomacy, the Southern states' trans-Appalachian western territories would remain effectively landlocked, deprived of access to the Gulf of Mexico to engage in world trade.

* * * * *

In Paris in the fall of 1782, Great Britain and the United States had brought the war to a tentative close. All that remained to mark the formal establishment of the newly independent American nation was the ratification of the preliminary treaty on both sides of the ocean, followed by the formal signing of a definitive treaty back in Paris. For Americans, these two cross-ocean exchanges and signings translated into a nine-month wait, until December of 1783, before George Washington could lay down his sword and submit his resignation to Congress.

During those nine months the United States confronted the greatest domestic trials of its existence. As American political leaders had anticipated for years, the end of the war released pent-up energies of state sovereignty, regionalism, westward expansion, and disunion. In Congress delegates fought over land, including the western territorial cessions and statehood for Kentucky and Vermont, as well as money—how much each state owed the federal treasury and how otherwise to pay off the massive war debt, whether through land sales, taxes, or duties. Delegates also fought over the Articles of Confederation. The loose-knit United States desperately needed a federal charter that empowered a government to fund itself, contract and discharge debt, administer foreign affairs, and settle conflicts among member states. But the instrument it had adopted in perpetuity in early 1781 was a weak legislative body with diffuse, ineffective executive and judicial functions. And making matters more desperate, every effort thus far to strengthen the constitution with amendments had met with states' rights fire and fury and the impossible barrier of Article XIII's requirement for unanimity. By the Articles, no amendment could come into force until ratified by the legislature of every state in the Union. The effect of this was paralysis to the point that many delegates felt suffocated by the constitution with no escape other than either disunion into separate confederacies or the calling of a convention to write a new constitution. Both pathways were fraught with risk. The former would lead to civil wars. The latter, a constitutional convention, would in all probability disband in discord, terminating in the same wretched outcome.

None of these political issues was new in 1783. The decisive difference was the loss of a unifying common purpose: the War of Independence. In this new phase of the American experiment, every political difference and conflict in the Congress seemed to amplify not only the incompatibility of the thirteen states but also the self-defeating nature of their pursuit of a muscular controlling federal authority that, as a first point of priority, must scrupulously avoid infringing upon the independence and freedom of each separate state. The founders were caught in this trap, one made all the more inextricable by states' rights firebrands who declared openly in

Chapter 19: "Stained with the Blood of Her Sons" 341

home legislatures and Congress that they would rather die than surrender the dual powers of purse and sword to a federal behemoth that, once in possession of these, would almost certainly devolve into tyranny.

* * * * *

If these problems were not vexing enough, a latent force present since the First Continental Congress surfaced spiritedly after the war appeared to be won. It was geopolitical rivalry between the Northern and Southern states—or, depending on who was forecasting the future, between New England and the other states or between Virginia and the rest of the Union. Fears of the rising superiority of one state (Virginia) or one geographic section (New England), leading to its despotism over the others, ran rampant. The founders of the United States were well-schooled in balance-of-power political theories as outlined in works like Thucydides's *History of the Peloponnesian War*, Hobbes's *Leviathan*, and Vattel's *Law of Nations*. And beginning in 1781, they had begun to apply these theories to themselves and the competing interests of different geographic regions. The two most obvious fonts of geographic rivalry were New England, perhaps united with New York, against the rest of the states and, alternately, the eight Northern commercial states versus the five Southern agricultural, slavery-based states, including Maryland.

Particularly with the coming of peace, many delegates in Congress felt it was their most urgent task to keep the peace between these rival regions, which meant maintaining "the federal balance of power" between them. The Massachusetts delegation alerted their assembly to this doctrine so vital to the survival of the Union after striking a compromise on the location of the federal capital. In a letter written by Elbridge Gerry on behalf of his congressional delegation, addressed to Sam Adams, president of the Senate, and Tristram Dalton, speaker of the House of Representatives, the Massachusettsians argued that compromises between North and South were compulsory to preserve that balance of "federal power," which in turn was the only hope for preserving the Union. On the other hand, Gerry continued, "The loss of the balance, should it ever happen, must be naturally followed by a change of government, which might involve us in greater calamities than the establishment of our Independence."[5]

In particular, the contest over Vermont exemplified the geopolitical rivalries present within the Congress. The Southern states and some Middle states were opposed to Vermont statehood on grounds of the preponderance of power it would award to New England, expanding the region's voting bloc in Congress from four states to five. In the months following Yorktown, Southern delegates increasingly rallied to the defense of the "Southern interest" against that of the "commercial states," in this case signifying all the Northern states, including Pennsylvania due to the merchant class that controlled Philadelphia. Sometimes Southern delegates worried about overlarge power accruing in New England and at other times in the eight Northern states. The South Carolina members, for one, placed the Vermont question in the larger context of a North/South divide when they explained why they were fighting so hard to prevent its statehood. "This we mean to oppose," they wrote to Governor John Rutledge, referring to Vermont entering the Union, "as greatly detrimental to our state by weakening the Southern interest and throwing too great a weight into the opposite scale."[6]

As these geopolitical rivalries surged into the consciousness of delegates, it also became clear that the balance-of-power maps they held in their heads might transpose neatly into separate confederacies whose boundary lines were easy to draw. This was another dangerous pitfall for nation builders like Gerry, Madison, Hamilton, Duane, Witherspoon, and others. They must manage the balance-of-power tinderbox in Congress without drawing too much attention to the fact that—as seen on the geopolitical map, comprising differences in soil, weather, river access, economics, political systems, and views of slavery—the regions in question might, by some measures, be better off split into two or three nation-states rather than forcibly united into one.

Some of the most faithful founders of the United States believed with anguish in the spring and summer of 1783 that disunion and catastrophe might be fast approaching. Secretary of Congress Charles Thomson, present as an observer of the closed-door politics of America since 1774, warned his wife, Hannah, that they must prepare for a violent future. "I confess," he told her by letter, "I have great apprehensions for the union of the states, & begin to fear that America will experience internal convulsions, and that the fabric of her liberty will be stained with the blood of her sons. Those jarring principles which were kept down by common danger begin to operate, and pride & passion seem to occupy the seat of reason."[7]

Hamilton and Madison shared these forebodings. After actively observing the Congress and participating in its politics for four months, Hamilton wrote to Washington that "the centrifugal is much stronger

Chapter 19: "Stained with the Blood of Her Sons" 343

than the centripetal force in these states—the seeds of disunion much more numerous than those of union." Madison conveyed to Randolph that the United States had reached a crossroads. The first half of 1783, he predicted, would determine "whether prosperity & tranquility, or confusion and disunion are to be the fruits of the revolution. The seeds of the latter are so thickly sown that nothing but the most enlightened and liberal policy will be able to stifle them."[8]

* * * * *

During the nine months preceding Washington's resignation as commander in chief, three intersecting issues inflamed the states and regions. Two were familiar—federal finances and territorial rights. The third was new to the debate chamber—the location of a permanent federal capital. Discord over all three was chiefly a manifestation of Americans' distrust and fear of centralized power—and of one another. Delegates did not believe that their compatriots from different states and regions could be relied upon to exercise power fairly and justly in the service of the diverse economic and political interests within the Union. Many also apprehended that in a republican form of government, once granted large powers from the states, members from New England and the South would jockey for superiority and hegemony over the rest by whatever means possible. Therefore, in the eyes of many, the best strategy seemed to be to withhold power altogether. This would safeguard each state from oppression by a central government dominated by states indifferent or hostile to its interests.

On the other hand, without vigorous authority to steer the ship of the United States, most delegates knew, the Union was destined for ruin. This was the paradox, or trap, of the developing American system. Delegates perceived tragic outcomes on both sides of congressional decision-making, whether over money matter, land disputes, or the location of a permanent capital. Remarkably, their maneuvering to find common ground between perceived extremes of too much and too little power lodged in the federal government resulted in compromises that seemingly saved the Union from dissolution in the same year the War of Independence formally ended.

The first and most divisive field of conflict in 1783 was the Union's finances. Most immediately, a promising plan of finance was collapsing, leaving the treasury bankrupt and with no system in place either to fund the government or to repay the states' staggering debt, estimated to be

$35,327,769. That plan, first adopted by Congress in February 1781, was an amendment to the Articles of Confederation empowering it to levy a 5 percent tariff on imports throughout the thirteen states. Sixteen months later, eleven states had acceded to the amendment. Only Rhode Island and Georgia remained uncommitted, with the latter exempt because its assembly was then unable to convene due to conditions of war. That is when delegates from Rhode Island, led by David Howell and backed by Jonathan Arnold, made it clear to other lawmakers in Congress that Rhode Island would never consent to such a federal encroachment on state sovereignty as the 5 percent impost. Howell called the amendment an act of "tyranny" and "oppression & violence," unfair in the burden it placed on the Northern states, especially small commercial Rhode Island.[9]

In debating the amendment, Howell openly acknowledged that his condemnation of the federal power stemmed, at least in part, from motives of state self-interest. The impost was to be a direct tax on trade goods—that is, it taxed not only imports for domestic use and consumption but also all of the merchants' buying and selling of all manner of items. So, he concluded, the Northern states would be hit the hardest and, among them, Rhode Island the worst of all. His poorly diversified small "maritime" state lived uniquely out of the profits of its "merchants, manufacturers & tradesmen," he argued.[10]

In speeches, letters, and conversations with others, Howell swore that the eleven states in the Union that had ratified the impost had mortally erred by endorsing a "fatal measure" attended by "evils." He went so far as to say that the matter of the impost was a "cause in which I have felt myself disposed to suffer as well as die." It invaded "the sovereignty and independence of the State." It trampled upon "the principles on which the Revolution was founded, the free constitutions of the respective States & the sacred obligation of the Confederation" to reserve to the states the all-important powers of trade and purse. He also warned that the amendment would be a catalyst for disunion and civil war. If at war's end the Congress invaded the rights of the states, the people would defect from the Confederation. "Every measure," Howell professed, "which tends to grieve one member of the Union, tends to a dissolution; for nature teaches to seek redress: And self-preservation, among laws, is Lord paramount."[11]

How would the amendment spark civil war? Once in possession of this power, Howell explained, the federal government would grasp for more power, moving next to the imposition of land taxes, poll taxes, and excises. Naturally, the states would rebel, but by then it would be too late, because the Confederation would have grown too powerful and rich. "Would it not be in the power of Congress, having the *perpetual revenue* at their disposal," he continued, "and having the command of your armies & navies to block up your harbors, and bring war into your state?" This was a danger they must contemplate. If such a tax were to go into effect, "it would require a military force to execute it, and bring in standing armies."[12]

To many delegates, Howell was engaging in overheated demagoguery. Elias Boudinot of New Jersey, who became president of Congress in November—and who himself feared "civil war among ourselves" more than most—considered the Rhode Island congressman personally to be a far greater danger to the Union than any legislation the Congress might pass. After listening to his tirades for half a year, Boudinot said of the Rhode Island hothead, "He has been the means of giving these United States a shock she will feel for years to come, and which indeed I think threatens our Union more than all the arms of G[reat] B[ritain]."[13]

Delegates in Congress like Boudinot, desperate for a unifying revenue plan, understood that the task at hand was not to persuade Howell and Arnold to reverse their positions; they must instead obtain a change in the hearts and minds of the Rhode Island governor and assemblymen who controlled their votes in Congress. Therefore, in late December of 1782, the Congress dispatched a delegation of three to lobby Rhode Island to ratify the impost if for no other reason than to preserve the Union. The delegation set out from Philadelphia on December 22, but en route the traveling members learned that Virginia had rescinded its ratification of the amendment and Maryland, it was rumored, was going to do the same. Hearing this news, the delegation turned back. As 1783 dawned, the impost amendment seemed irretrievably lost.[14]

* * * * *

Madison, Hamilton, and other delegates regarded the first six months of 1783 as decisive to the future of the United States because if the Congress grossly mishandled either finances or the western lands, it might well dissolve the Union. In February Hamilton, for his part, was making a contingency plan for disunion. In the event the United States broke apart, he feared for the fate of his home state, New York. Possessing the coveted Hudson River, with the broils in Vermont still simmering, Hamilton was confident that New York would be ripe territory for civil war. As he wrote to the governor of the state, George Clinton, on February 14, "It is the first wish of my heart that the Union may last; but feeble as the links are, what prudent man would rely upon it? Should a disunion take place, any person who will cast his eye upon the map will see how essential it is to our state to provide for its own security." Almost certainly, what Hamilton foresaw "upon the map" was an invasion by a New England army determined to gain access to the Hudson, if not take control of the entire state.[15]

To deter such aggressions, Hamilton proposed to Governor Clinton that New York warmly welcome military men of all stripes to move into the state and establish themselves as bulwarks of safety. In the letter he urged that New York should offer a gift of land to every officer and soldier in the Continental Army to win their favor. A bounty of land should be exchanged for an oath of allegiance to New York by each military person. "In this position of things," Hamilton wrote, referring to dangers of disunion, "it will be wise in the state of New York to consider what conduct will be most consistent with its safety and interest. I wish the legislature would set apart a tract of territory, and make a liberal allowance to every officer and soldier of the army at large who will become a citizen of the state. A step of this kind would not only be politic in the present posture of affairs, but would embrace important future consequences."[16]

Hamilton was not alone in these projections. Eleven days later, Madison wrote a long letter to Edmund Randolph reporting on the failed state of finances in the Union, alerting him to the perils of a New England/South civil war. A headstrong new Massachusetts delegate, Nathaniel Gorham, had taken his seat in Congress the preceding Friday. Debates ensued wherein delegates Arthur Lee and John Francis Mercer of Virginia, as wary of centralized power as Howell and Arnold of Rhode Island, shrilly declaimed against investing Congress with the twin powers of taxation and coercion to pay by sword. Lee also disputed the account books of Secretary of Finance Robert Morris, which, for example, purported that Virginia owed the Congress $1,307,594 for the year 1782 alone and had only paid $35,710 of this total. Lee said Morris's balance sheet was biased against Virginia, inflating the debt it owed to the treasury. The accounting, by contrast, favored the secretary's own state of Pennsylvania, which would be "enriched" by the plum of Virginia labor and wealth.[17]

After this, Mercer rose and spoke in support of Lee. The "Prince of the South," as one New Hampshire delegate later labeled Mercer, said he would fight to the death any financial system that empowered the Congress not only to lay taxes on Virginians but also to lift the sword and

Chapter 19: "Stained with the Blood of Her Sons" 347

FIGURE 42. Alexander Hamilton, New York Delegate. (Portrait of Alexander Hamilton. John Trumbull, *Alexander Hamilton*, 1806, oil on canvas, 30.625 x 24.625 in, Museum of Fine Arts Boston, Bequest of R. C. Winthrop.)

bayonet on them to enforce collection. These prerogatives belonged to the states. No federal tax collectors, Mercer assured his fellow delegates, would be marching into Virginia now or in the future to enforce obedience to the dictates of the Union. If it were so, "if he conceived the federal compact to be such as it had been represented he would immediately withdraw from Congress & do every thing in his power to destroy its existence."[18]

This encounter took place in Independence Hall on February 21. As Madison reported on it, Gorham responded to Lee and Mercer with his own counterthreat of disunion. If the Southern states were unwilling to form a government on the basis of equity and fairness pertaining to the war debt, granting it a collective power over the purse to balance the books, Gorham warned, some states would withdraw from the present government and form a new one. New Englanders were of the determined opinion that in almost a decade of war, they had paid into the federal treasury a much larger share of wealth than had the Southern states. Unless rectified, this violated "justice," Gorham proclaimed. "The Eastern states," Madison further documented, "particularly Massachusetts, conceive that compared with the Southern they are greatly in advance in the general account." This led Gorham openly to threaten that "if justice was not to be obtained thro the general confederacy, the sooner it was known the better [so] that some states might be forming other confederacies adequate to the purpose."¹⁹

Gorham thus announced one solution to the Confederation's polarizing financial woes: disassociation into separate confederacies. Did his words also constitute a veiled threat that his confederacy might proceed then to obtain justice from the Southern states by other means, such as warfare? Madison certainly seems to have thought so. After hearing Gorham's diatribe, he worried that if the states separated at that juncture an angry New England would use wartime accounting and payment injustice as "a ready pretext for reprisals." A "powerful and rapacious" New England, inflamed over matters of money, would attack. The "opulent and weak" South, without any other recourse, would cry out for aid from England or France, Madison projected. The European enemy of that ally would take the side of New England, and a terrible war, or wars, would follow.[20]

This is why, for Madison, a legislative solution to the financial crisis was a life-and-death mandate. In the letter to Randolph, he said that if the Congress failed yet again to obtain a remedy, disunion was more than a possibility. It was a certainty. "Unless some amicable & adequate arrangements be speedily taken for adjusting all the subsisting accounts and discharging the public engagements," Madison wrote, "a dissolution of the union will be inevitable." Then, given the sore feelings involved, given the money at stake, war would ensue.[21]

* * * * *

Several months later, on April 1, during advanced negotiations over a tax bill under consideration to replace the impost amendment, Gorham revealed to the Congress that at the instigation of the governor of Massachusetts, New England and New York were in fact intending to hold a separate convention in Hartford, Connecticut, "for regulating matters of common concern." He further said that if the federal Congress passed a revenue plan before the Northern convention met, it would consider that plan and "probably cooperate with Congress in giving effect to it."[22]

Was this disunion brinksmanship—a warning to delegates that if they did not break the impasse over a federal revenue system and a means of collection in the states, then the convention in Hartford might in fact transform itself into the beginnings of a separate independent Northern confederacy? Gorham did not say this in so many words, but every congressman in the hall knew such an outcome to the Union was a tangible risk. Virginian Mercer, who soon stood up to reply to Gorham, clearly seems to have understood it this way. Mercer asked to simply know the truth. Had some Northern delegates in fact already decided to break the Union? First the Virginian condemned the separate convention as "a dangerous precedent." Then, referring to Gorham, he gave notice that "it behooved the gentleman to explain fully the objects of the convention, as it would be necessary for the Southern states to be otherwise very circumspect in agreeing to any plans on a supposition that the general confederacy was to continue."[23]

Soon, perhaps reflecting the intentions of men like Gorham, delegate Samuel Holten, himself from Massachusetts, confessed privately in a letter that what frightened him most in the politics of Congress was his own countrymen. Some Massachusetts delegates, he wrote, "are so dissatisfied with the proceedings of Congress" that he worried they would break the Union. Holton continued, "God grant that the union may not be dissolved, and the good people again involved in all the horrors of war."[24]

Samuel Osgood of Massachusetts spoke next. He was a delegate who acknowledged the dangers of centralized federal powers but, like Holten, advocated that American leaders must "choose the least evil": a single Union. In his remarks Osgood, confirming the plan for the Hartford convention, nevertheless assured Mercer and the others in the hall that careful attention was going to be paid to the Articles of Confederation and that nothing would be pursued in Hartford that contravened them. Not persuaded, Richard Bland of Virginia denounced the convocation as pregnant with danger. It had the smell of a separate northern government, he said. And it certainly violated the spirit, if not the letter, of the constitution binding them. In these comments, Bland was alluding to Article VI of the Articles, prohibiting subconfederations: "No two or more States shall enter into any treaty, confederation or alliance whatever between them, without the consent of the United States in Congress assembled, specifying accurately the purposes for which the same is to be entered into, and how long it shall continue." Nothing in this language prohibited New England delegates from organizing a friendly meeting in a Northern city like Hartford, but were they to take the opportunity during such an assembly to adopt an agreement among themselves "for regulating matters of common concern," as Gorham had said, without the consent of Congress, it would be unconstitutional in the extreme.[25]

The exchange that early April day ended with a call for temperance by Madison and Hamilton. Together they stepped forward to deplore all such "partial conventions" as "exciting pernicious jealousies." Hamilton promoted instead a convention of all thirteen states to "strengthen the federal constitution." Higginson of Massachusetts concurred. Phillips White of New Hampshire declared that his state would not participate in any separate political assemblies like the Hartford convention.[26]

Seventeen days later the delegates in Philadelphia, having abandoned the impost as futile, passed a compromise constitutional reform and taxation bill that finally broke the stalemate. Giving up altogether on a strict impost amendment, they hewed more closely to powers already granted in the Articles of Confederation. By Article VIII Congress possessed the right to fund the treasury for "the common defense or general welfare" through a land tax—to be levied by the sole authority and direction of the state legislatures, not federal collectors. Madison, who served on the drafting committee with Gorham, Hamilton, Thomas Fitzsimmons, and John Rutledge, wrote what was an omnibus compromise bill, arguing to his Southern colleagues that a balanced revenue plan was going to protect their states from New England domination rather than unleash it. He made the same argument to them that he conveyed privately to Jefferson in the spring of 1781. The army and navy of the federal government was going to protect the Southern states from the New England states. "Virginia, in common with the Southern States, as likely to enjoy an opulent and defenseless trade," Madison now told others openly, "is interested in a general revenue as tending to secure her the protection of the Confederacy against the maritime superiority of the Eastern States."[27]

This multifaceted amendment called for a revocation of Article VIII, the land tax, and, in its place, the institution of various duties on rum, spirituous liquors, wine, tea, pepper, sugar, molasses, coffee, and human population, with enslaved people counted as "three-fifths" of whites. It also incorporated a guarantee by North Carolina, South Carolina, and Georgia that they would imitate Virginia and make liberal cessions of western lands, and it permitted states to appoint tax collectors. Finally, vital to the bill's success, it stipulated an expiration date for itself at twenty-five years after ratification, alleviating delegates' apprehensions about the imposition of permanent federal monetary control. To come into effect, the bill required the "unanimous accession" of all thirteen states, at which point it would become "irrevocable." Amazed at what they had wrought, Stephen Higginson of Massachusetts called the compromise bill "a strange, though artful, plan of finance, in which are combined a heterogeneous mixture of imperceptible and visible, constitutional and unconstitutional taxes."[28]

What mattered is that the United States passed a promising finance bill, restoring hope in the Union. Soon after its adoption, the convention in Hartford was called off, and even the hot-tempered Mercer converted to the cause. By April 24 the Virginian was confessing to others that the compromise amendment was necessary for preserving harmony and peace in the United States. Without it, the states would witness "scenes of confusion." Such mental pictures, combined with the safety ensured by the twenty-five-year limit on the new federal taxes, had convinced Mercer. That April he lent his support to the finance bill in Independence Hall, and, once back in Virginia, he continued his advocacy, likely offering similar lines of reasoning to state leaders in Richmond.[29]

CHAPTER 20

"United We Stand, Divided We Fall"

Another chronic worry of delegates that winter and spring was that restive officers and soldiers in the Continental Army, upset at the dysfunctional Congress's failure to pay them long overdue wages, would take matters into their own hands. This was hardly an unfounded apprehension, because in the same month Congress received the preliminary articles of peace in Philadelphia, a military cabal at army headquarters on the Hudson River advanced a plan of mutiny against Washington, one portending a march on Philadelphia to demand justice by bayonet. Washington suppressed the plot, known as the Newburgh conspiracy, in mid-March. Delivering an emotional speech urging the officers in attendance to honor the supremacy of civilian constitutional government before all else, the commander in chief urged them not to heed the call of any person "who wickedly attempts to open the flood gates of civil discord, & deluge our rising empire in blood."[1]

By virtue of Washington's intervention in Newburgh, the United States escaped a moment that many historians believe could have ended, at least temporarily, in a military takeover of the Congress. But this disarming of one insurgency on the Hudson did not save the delegates in Philadelphia from similar unrest in the Pennsylvania line of the Continental Army, whose troops were divided into two encampments, one in Philadelphia and the other in Lancaster sixty miles away. On June 17, sick to death of the army's deprivation of funds, five or six sergeants and some eighty soldiers in Lancaster mutinied, setting off down the road to Philadelphia "to obtain justice." To this end, rumors swirled, they intended to combine with more than three hundred fellow soldiers stationed in Philadelphia in a raid on the national bank or the U.S. treasury.[2]

Three days later, on the morning of Friday, June 20, the men marched into Philadelphia and soon took possession of the powder house and public magazines, installing sentinels to guard them. On Monday, however, instead of attacking the bank, approximately four hundred militant soldiers wielding fixed bayonets surrounded the Pennsylvania State House. Inside, there were congressmen from six states, including Madison and Hamilton, as well as many members of the Pennsylvania Assembly meeting in the same building. They were kept "prisoners," in President Boudinot's words. Outside, drums were beating and fifes playing. The message of the mutineers was that they would "no longer be fed by promises." Some jeered and shouted obscenities. Madison, sitting in Independence Hall, witnessed soldiers "wantonly pointing their muskets to the windows of the hall of Congress." Soon, they sent in a paper drafted by the sergeants declaring that if action were not taken to redress their grievances, "an enraged soldiery" would be released upon them.[3]

The standoff ended peaceably that Monday only after a local well-respected Pennsylvania officer, Major General Arthur St. Clair, arrived on the grounds of the State House, negotiating with the leadership of the rebellion for two hours, providing every assurance that Congress would eventually fulfill its obligations. The soldiers withdrew, allowing the delegates to leave the State House unharmed. But still the mutineers remained in town, their drums and fifes continuing to be heard for several more days. Boudinot reported to William Livingston that Philadelphia remained "in great danger." To Washington, he urged "no one can tell when it will end." He feared "the worst is yet to come." Madison observed fluctuations of sentiment on the streets, sometimes alcohol induced, with the soldiers at times penitent and the next moment "meditating more violent measures." Rumors spread that a new plot had been hatched. Soldiers were planning to seize members of Congress and hold them hostage until justice had been served.[4]

On June 24 these conditions led Boudinot to order Congress to abandon Philadelphia and relocate to Princeton, New Jersey, fifty miles away. Members complied, packing up and taking leave of the Revolution's historic capital. In the end, some delegates downplayed the risk of the mutiny and raid, describing the four days as a prolonged affair of bluster and grandstanding. Others believed concretely that missteps by the Congress or General St. Clair would have triggered bloodshed. North Carolina delegates Hugh Williamson and Benjamin Hawkins wrote to their governor, Alexander Martin, that shadows such as those that passed

Chapter 20: "United We Stand, Divided We Fall" 355

FIGURE 43. Arthur St. Clair, Major General in the Continental Army. (Portrait of General Arthur St. Clair. Charles Willson Peale, *Portrait of Arthur St. Clair*, ca. 1782, oil on canvas, 221 x 191 in, Independence National Historic Park.)

over the Congress for four menacing days must rouse the United States to guard for its future. "From your general acquaintance with civil history," they wrote in the aftermath of the uprising, "you must have observed that the cases are numerous in which armies have overturned the liberties of a nation whom they had been hired to defend. More than half of the empires now on the face of the earth have been formed, not like ours by the choice of the people, but by the swords of a mutinous or victorious army."[5]

* * * * *

Toward the end of June, the Congress settled into Nassau Hall at the College of New Jersey in Princeton. In July, during a period of nervous anticipation over the fate of Virginia's cession of land northwest of the Ohio River and therefore the preservation of the Articles of Confederation, Secretary of Congress Charles Thomson penned two letters to his wife, Hannah, that are remarkable for the portrait he paints of the United States' future. In spite of Congress's recent breakthrough on a revenue plan, Thomson was not optimistic. "When I look forward," he wrote, "I see a dark cloud and gloomy prospects for America." The secretary, who was once given the honorary title, "The Man of Truth," wrote to Hannah frequently, and confidentially, about the happenings of Congress. One day, looking down at the lengthy paragraphs he had written to her on the tangles of American politics, the secretary stopped the narrative to apologize. "You see, my dear, what it is to have a politician for a husband," he said. "Instead of love letters you are only to be entertained with business or politics."[6]

The second of the two letters, written before breakfast on Friday, July 25, is the most telling. In it Thomson lays out in detail his vision of an America wracked by three, four, perhaps five confederacies, some of them well-defined and tightly united and others loose and volatile. The cause of disunion was going to be the same "local prejudices, passions and views" that divided Americans in his day, he told Hannah. Nine years earlier, at the outset of the war, Joseph Galloway had made a similar prediction, foretelling a devastating internecine war between the North and South, among other civil broils. Thomas Paine in *Common Sense* promised that American pride in liberty, independence, and the Revolution itself would cement them forever; civil wars would come upon them, likely in the 1830s, *only if* they waited and did not unite in the crucible of war against England "Now." John Dickinson in the year of the Declaration of Independence acknowledged publicly that in his "Doomsday Book of America" he foresaw New England separating from the rest and embarking upon war to gain the Vermont territory and other swaths of New York that stood in the way of their control of the Hudson River.[7]

Thomson had similar ideas, but no one until this time had so comprehensively outlined on paper the probable future boundaries of American confederacies and the nature of the wars they would fight. For almost a decade he had witnessed New Englanders at close range, and, like Dickinson, Thomson envisioned a divided America would undoubtedly bring forth a New England union. Also like Dickinson, the Pennsylvanian predicted that the nation of New England would not rest until it had obtained on its western frontier "the keys of the country"—that is, the Hudson River and Lake Champlain. New Englanders would unite into one confederacy on the basis of the similarities of "their manners, customs and governments" and because "they are an unmixed people, being all sprung from a common stock without any great accession of strangers or foreigners." But "the Eastern Confederacy" would, in fact, be a union of six states, including Vermont and New York, in spite of the latter's cultural differences. For the purpose of securing the Hudson waterway, "New York," Thomson said, "will be compelled to join this confederacy either voluntarily or by force." Vermont will be kept by New Englanders "as a rod over the head of N.Y. &, if necessary, used to chastise & compel it into the Eastern Confederacy."[8]

Chapter 20: "United We Stand, Divided We Fall" 357

In the future of America, there would also be a "middle confederacy" comprised of New Jersey, Pennsylvania, Delaware and Maryland, small states that would band together for the material purpose of expansion and growth into the Ohio Valley. However, Virginia would stand in their way, and this is where a civil war would break out—on the waters of the Ohio River. Thomson did not envisage an immediate Southern confederacy. Instead, gigantic Virginia would make a union of itself. "The haughtiness of Virginia, its great extent," he projected, "and its boundless claims will induce it to set up for itself. And if ever royal government is set up in N. America, here it will first erect its throne." Yet in this vision, Thomson pondered the possibility that western territories like Kentucky and Tennessee might not submit to Virginia. Instead, they might unite to declare independence as a separate republic, soliciting alliance and military aid from the Middle union to defend itself against Virginia. At this point Virginia would be outnumbered and outmanned militarily, so it would be left with no alternative but "to form an alliance with the Eastern Confederacy or the three Southern states."

FIGURE 44. Charles Thomson, Pennsylvania Delegate. (Portrait of Charles Thomson. Joseph Wright, *Charles Thomson*, ca. 1783, oil on canvas, Tudor Place Historic House and Garden, Georgetown, Washington, DC.)

In these fluid and highly contingent prognostications, Thomson singled out South Carolina as the wild card. The four Southern states would encounter unending difficulty in forming a Southern confederacy because this untamable state would never submit to higher rule until she was ultimately required to do so through chastening. "For such is the fiery pride of South Carolina," he wrote to Hannah, "such the dissipation of her morals & her insolence occasioned by the multitude of slaves, that she will not cordially join in any Union till she is taught wisdom by sore suffering."

At the end of the letter, Thomson, who was pressed to head out for breakfast, hastily signed off. "But where am I wandering?" he asked. "I sat down only to tell you I am well and am hurried on I know not how into scenes of fairyland from which I am recalled by Miss Nancy's invitation to breakfast. So I bid you Adieu. Take care of your health. I am, with sincere affection, your loving husband, Charles Thomson."

* * * * *

By midfall Thomson would revise the boundary lines of these separate confederacies, but this reassessment came only after the Congress broke its standoff over the Virginia land cession and waded deeply into the conundrum of the location of a permanent federal capital. On the first issue, after five years of resisting demands by other states for a liberal surrender of its extensive western domain, Virginia had finally ceded all its claims northwest of the Ohio River to the federal treasury in early January of 1781. The Grand Dominion had made this sacrifice for the sake of the Union, because Maryland refused to ratify the Articles of Confederation until the vast state cut itself down to size while simultaneously funding the government with the salable land. Maryland quickly ratified the Articles, bringing the formal constitutional government into existence in March.

The Virginia cession, though, came with a stiff precondition requiring the Congress never to award individuals or land companies even one square inch of the territory granted. One hundred percent of the land must go into the treasury; at no point could the Congress later entertain lawsuits from land companies, adjudicating in their favor. This proscription, written into the cession, commenced a new standoff, one lasting two and a half years. At the behest of land company shareholders from Maryland, Pennsylvania, and New Jersey, some of whom were delegates, the Congress declined to accept the Virginia cession as is. Instead it set up one committee after another to investigate and advise members on how to respond without touching off a firestorm. Virginia accused the interfering land speculators of greed and manipulation in their lobbying to secure Virginia land for the national domain when their true purpose was to hustle the state and the Union out of the territory, enriching themselves. Company members and their supporters in Congress, in turn, called out Virginia and other Southern states for hypocrisy. Land speculators in those states were going to cash in on their holdings in the trans-Appalachian Southwest. Why should Middle state companies and citizens not reap similar benefits in the great domain northwest of the Ohio?

What decided the matter in the fall of 1783 was not the logic of jurisdiction, jurisprudence, or fairness in Congress's distribution of benefits to land companies. It was the emergency of averting catastrophe from a Virginia nullification of its cession, perhaps collapsing the constitutional Union when Maryland responded in kind by nullifying its ratification of the Articles of Confederation. Chiefly, it was threats of this nature emanating from Richmond that persuaded the latest committee on the cession, composed of five members, including Madison, to recommend acceptance without controversial alterations.[9]

Indeed, according to notices sent to Madison from Jefferson, Randolph, Pendleton, and Jones, anti-Congress sentiments were running high in the Virginia state capital, with prospects of a repeal of the cession heating up steadily since the summer of 1782. In Philadelphia Madison feared the hot tempers and rash decisions of his own fellow elected representatives in Richmond more than those of other political leaders in the Union. In the House there were 152 Virginia state officials and another 25 in the Senate. In the vanguard of anti-Congress dissent were "two great commanders," Richard Henry Lee and Patrick Henry, who, fed up with the Congress's longstanding intransigence on the Virginia gift of nearly a half million square miles of land, were calling upon the state to rescind the offer. Outside the chambers of the Virginia Assembly on the streets of Richmond, officers of the state militia and state Continental Line were propounding repeal as well—as the only sure avenue to the state's fulfillment of its obligation to them of grants of land beyond the Ohio for their long service in the war.[10]

Some overwrought members of the Virginia Assembly were formulating fanciful scenarios of what was going to happen if the states continued to capitulate to the Congress's "lusting after power." Many viewed the massive federal allotments of money from states mandated by the late congressional revenue plan as "alarming, and of dangerous tendency." If not Lee and Henry, other patriot leaders in the assembly tied together the Congress's desire to obtain Virginia's land and this new taxation bill, also before them to approve or not, into a knot of near paranoia. They did not want to send Congress Virginia money because that money might be turned against them as funding source for future "offensive measures" against the state's western lands. With state money in hand, the federal government would build itself up. It would establish the merchant class as the head of the confederation, ultimately diverting Virginia's tax dollars from its intended target of debt relief to one invention after another to consolidate its dominance over the states. This was the basis of Virginia's "aversion" to a federal revenue, Pendleton told Madison. When set against "the ardor of congress to grasp that territory," Randolph added, it seemed ludicrous to many Virginians that they should willingly fund and empower the very federal government and Continental Army that might, as soon as adequate preparations could be made, turn its arms against Virginia to take away her western lands.[11]

Jefferson, who as a recent two-term governor of Virginia possessed intimate knowledge of the state's politics, feared that agitators in Richmond would gain the upper hand, passing legislation and adopting policies that would spur "internal contests." That is why he passionately lobbied Virginia statesmen committed to strengthening the Union to serve in the assembly. Virginia must honor its land cession, he argued. It must ratify the financial bill and other Union-fortifying measures. Jefferson's concern was that he saw "the pride of independence taking deep and dangerous hold of the hearts of individual states." State leaders were too intent upon retaining sovereignty, a habit they must "unlearn." No nation-building statesman was more impatient than Jefferson to enlarge the powers of Congress. And, as he wrote to Randolph in early 1783, it must be done "instantly before we forget the advantages of union, or acquire a degree of ill-temper against each other which will daily increase the obstacles to that good work."[12]

Similar to Madison, Jefferson strove to persuade Virginians that a strong Union, one endowed with powers "to enforce their decisions," was essential to their safety. The only way to prevent disunion and civil wars, he said, was to grant the Congress proper authority to intervene to keep peace among the states. If deprived of a central power of coercing the states to abide by federal laws and rulings, "What will be the case? They will not be enforced. The states will go to war with one another in defiance of Congress." Instead of permitting this future to unfold, Jefferson beseeched Randolph, "Lay your shoulder to the strengthening the band of our confederacy and averting those cruel evils to which its present weakness will expose us."[13]

Edmund Pendleton was of the same mindset. The "moment of peace" was upon them, he wrote to Madison. Therefore the states must perceive the "necessity of mutual concessions & good offices to preserve the federal strength & give it dignity among nations." Recalling the first days of the war, he said Americans must continue to adhere to "an adage so often mentioned at the commencement of the dispute." It was the motto of the Revolution, "United we stand, divided we fall." Randolph professed that this doctrine was "no less true in war than in peace."[14]

Determined not to tip the combustible Virginia Assembly into dangerous provocations, Madison and the other members of the committee in Philadelphia acted dexterously to bring their recommendation on the land cession to the floor of Congress at a time when the lineup of states was favorable to approval. In Nassau Hall on September 13, after motions by Maryland and New Jersey delegates to derail the recommendation failed, Congress formally approved the Virginia cession, with minor alterations, by a vote of eight states to two (Maryland and New Jersey dissenting). The cession's all-important Article VI stood, prohibiting the Congress from later consigning any portion of the land grant to companies. The Northwest Territory was to be earmarked as "a common fund for the use and benefit of such of the United American States" and "for no other use or purpose whatsoever."[15]

Congressmen consented to Virginia's hard terms, according to New Yorkers James Duane and Ezra L'Hommedieu, because the extraordinary gain of land was deemed a godsend to a bankrupt, debt-ridden federal treasury and because, persisting unresolved, the cession "might have been a source of internal contentions and convulsions." The same day as the vote, John Francis Mercer of Virginia wrote to Henry Tazewell, a member of the state's assembly, of the relief experienced by many delegates. Referring to the adoption of the cession after so many years of jeopardy, he said, "The moment it was effected I perceiv'd an instant operation on the very being of Congress—a total change of politics in all the states will be a necessary consequence. I begin to hope for the best."[16]

* * * * *

The last divisive issue facing the Congress before Washington's resignation was the location of a permanent "federal town." On April 1 delegates received an offer from the township of Kingston, New York, on the Hudson River, endorsed by the New York Assembly, to grant the central government a tract of land on the river for a federal site. Three days later Congress established a committee, and less than a week after that, Virginia delegates proposed to their home government that their state combine with Maryland to make a more generous counteroffer on the Potomac River. Maryland submitted a plan to Congress offering Annapolis in late May, and on June 10 the president of Congress, Elias Boudinot, dispatched a circular letter to the states informing them of the details of these the two offers, Kingston and Annapolis, advising them that Monday, October 6, had been selected as the official date for Congress to commence formal deliberations.[17]

The location of the federal capital was a tender issue in the United States. Many delegates viewed the decision as determinative of the future direction of the nation, whether toward consolidation of power and values in republican New England, the commercial Middle states, or the westward-expanding, aristocratic, slaveholding South. The capital would become a flourishing, rich city, influencing all aspects of the growth and development of the United States. So concerned was one New Englander, William Gordon, with the inevitability of the expanding South and the consequent placement of the capital there, that he advised John Adams in the fall of 1782 that New England should for this reason shun a tight Union altogether in favor of a loose "collection of republics, and not become an empire." A South-dominated confederation, he warned, would monopolize and debase the Northern states, and "freedom will languish and die." New England must therefore retain its "sovereignty." As Gordon explained the risks to Adams, "If America becomes an empire, the seat of government will be to the southward, and the Northern States be insignificant provinces. Empire will suit the southern gentry! They are habituated to despotism by being the sovereigns of slaves: and it is only accident and interest that has made the body of them the temporary sons of liberty."[18]

For the most part, Gordon was reading the vision of empire of Southern political leaders correctly. In Congress they made numerous arguments publicly in favor of a capital on the waters of the Chesapeake, while reserving others for private communication. Overt reasons given for this temperate zone location included its geographic centrality between New Hampshire and Georgia, its favorable climate, easy accessibility by water, and the necessity of demonstrating to the Southern states that in spite of their minority standing in Congress, the Northern states would not exert power politics in all instances where sheer numbers enabled them to do so. Northern delegates must instead comprehend the coming population growth of territories like Kentucky and Tennessee, whose leaders would resent such a far distant capital as Kingston on the Hudson. Looking at the map, envisioning the peopling of the western halves of South Carolina and Georgia, too, these regions of America would perceive great injustice in the location of a capital so far north as New York State.[19]

The Chesapeake Bay was the logical choice geographically for the territory obtained in the preliminary Treaty of Paris, Southern delegates argued, and its selection would foster trust. *Justice* was a watchword Southerners leaned on frequently in these debates. As expressed by Benjamin Harrison, governor of Virginia, the choice of a Northern capital "will fix this state in an opinion that there is a decided majority against the southern states, and that they are not to expect that justice they are entitled to." Southern delegates also contended that a vote for a "Southern position" of the capital would encourage reciprocity when it came time to vote on matters like finance and cessions of land from North Carolina, Georgia, and South Carolina. Aside from this, there were old wounds to heal. "The southern states have suffered more than any others by the ravages of the enemy," wrote one merchant from Baltimore, "and are entitled to more consideration from those to the eastward than to be put to greater inconveniences than they, merely because they are unfortunately the minority." Perceived neglect in last years of the war still rankled. Therefore, delegates said openly on the floor of Congress, the Northern states should vote for a capital on Chesapeake waters because of "the soothing tendency of so Southern a position on the temper of the So. states."[20]

Privately, however, some Southern delegates underscored that a capital in the Chesapeake Bay would also bring power and wealth to the Southern states. Already, as the newspapers announced, "emigration from abroad prevails much more in the Southern States than those of the eastward, especially in the back settlements; no one therefore can falsely venture to predict which part of the Continent will be consequential [in] a century." Reinforcing this general expectation, a Southern capital would be a boon to the region's rise to preeminence. As two North Carolina delegates, Benjamin Hawkins and Hugh Williamson, admitted to their governor, Alexander Martin, they felt "zeal for fixing Congress on the waters of Chesapeake Bay." A Southern capital would redound to "the honor and prosperity of the Southern States." The capital would thrive and with it the political and economic power of that part of the United States. "The trade of Europe must ever be drawn in a particular manner to that part of the empire where Congress resides," Hawkins and Williamson urged. "Hence by removing Congress to the Southward the progress of population must be increased in those States and their consequent wealth."[21]

* * * * *

By early October the various states had offered at least eight locations for the capital, including Kingston, New York; Annapolis, Maryland; Williamsburg, Virginia; Trenton, New Jersey; Georgetown, Maryland; Germantown, Pennsylvania; and, alternatively, two cessions of raw land, one at the falls of the Delaware River and the other at the falls of the Potomac River, where Congress could build government buildings. On Monday, October 6, debate commenced, with the day spent canvasing delegates on their preferred states for the site. By the end of the day there were two overwhelming top contenders: the New Jersey shore near the falls of the Delaware River, favored strongly by the Northern states, and the Maryland shore near the falls of the Potomac, a vote with equal strength of preference by the Southern states.[22]

The next day, Tuesday, with the field narrowed to two, delegates from New Jersey and Pennsylvania rushed the Delaware location to the floor. Numerous motions were made to block this, including one to reinstate the Hudson, another to select Maryland, and another to postpone debate altogether. All these failed. So in accordance with procedural rules, Congress voted on the falls of the Delaware as the future site of the U.S. capital. It won. By a strict sectional vote on October 7, eight Northern states overruled four Southern states (with Georgia absent) to establish the permanent capital on the Delaware River. On this question, only a simple majority, not supermajority, was required. The vote was fully legal, scrupulously adhering to the spirit, letter, and parliamentary guidelines set forth in the Articles of Confederation. Even so, as Boudinot related to Robert Livingston, "This mortified the Southern members." Debates and voting closed with the appointment of a committee of five "to repair to the falls of Delaware, to view the situation of the country in its neighbourhood, and report a proper district for carrying into effect the preceding resolution."[23]

No extant records document the content of conversations or strategy sessions held outside Congress over the next sixteen hours before the doors of the debate chamber at Nassau Hall opened again on Wednesday morning. What is known is that Southern delegates chose Hugh Williamson of North Carolina and Jacob Read of South Carolina to spearhead a motion for reconsideration. As the first order of business that October 8, Williamson and Read advanced a resolution to set aside the vote of the preceding day on the basis of "justice" to the Southern states. In the wording of the motion, Congress should "fix on some other place that shall be more central, more favourable to the Union, and shall approach nearer to that justice which is due to the southern states." Williamson called for a vote, and once numbers were tallied, the sectional divide persisted. His motion went down to defeat, seven to five. The majority had rendered its opinion. The determination stood: the United States capital was to be situated on the Delaware somewhere near the city of Trenton, New Jersey.[24]

What happened next in Princeton is a marvel of political maneuvering. Arthur Lee of Virginia began closed-door dialogues with Elbridge Gerry of Massachusetts, and together they fashioned a New England–South coalition to overrule the Middle states on a grand bargain that afforded justice to the Southern states. Most critically, Gerry became persuaded that the survival of the Union was at stake. Therefore, he lobbied his fellow New Englanders to come to the South's rescue. It took ten days to obtain critical mass, but the New England and Southern states together forged what seemed to Gerry to be Union-saving compromise.

Gerry acted on a belief, similar to Madison's, that the Union was on a precipice, and only enlightened statesmanship could save it from tipping over. Gerry saw what was happening around him. Delegates were discussing disunion as well as contingency plans for self-preservation when a separation took place. One such delegate, in addition to Hamilton, was his fellow Massachusetts delegate Stephen Higginson. Shortly before the debates over the capital, Higginson told Gorham that if the present "confusion" of Congress persisted, "a dissolution of the Union shall take place, and separate alliances be formed by the several states with different powers in Europe; in which case some of the Southern States, if not all of them, will certainly be connected with France." Needless to say, not only a desire for restoring robust commercial ties would press New Englanders into an alliance with Britain. "Habits, language, and every circumstance will lead to it," said Higginson.[25]

Gerry, thus energized to avert disunion, chose to break with the Middle states on the earlier vote assigning the federal capital exclusively to the falls of the Delaware River. On Monday, October 20, he made a motion to establish a second U.S. capital "at or near the lower falls of Potomac or Georgetown," Maryland. Pronouncing that the Southern states would never agree to a single Northern capital, Gerry argued that the Congress must adopt a compromise resolution such as this to safeguard the Union and maintain "the federal balance of power." The Massachusettsian explicitly stated these motivations in the whereas clauses of the motion:

> Whereas the resolutions of Congress of the 7 instant, to erect buildings for their use at or near the falls of the Delaware, are not satisfactory to a respectable part of the United States, five of which, on the 8th instant, voted for a re-consideration of the said resolutions: And whereas Congress have no prospect of a general assent to any one place for their residence, and there is every reason to expect that the providing buildings for the alternate residence of Congress in two places, will be productive of the most salutary effects, by securing the mutual confidence and affections of the states, and preserving the federal balance of power: It is therefore resolved [to adopt a second federal capital on the Potomac].[26]

The next day, with overwhelming support from New England, Gerry's measure passed. By majority rule, it was decreed on October 21 that the U.S. Congress would thereafter divide its time equally between a Southern capital on the Potomac and a Northern one on the Delaware. Congressional agents should set out immediately to reconnoiter each river and survey the lands to commence construction at the earliest date possible. In the interim, Congress would split its legislative seasons between Annapolis and Trenton. It was a surprising outcome, as the Massachusetts delegates confessed to the members of their General Assembly, but an unavoidable one. The second capital was necessary, they said, to "preserve the Union" and avert "greater calamities than the establishment of our Independence."[27]

Not everyone agreed with this viewpoint. The president of Congress, Boudinot of New York, who voted against the Gerry resolution, looked at the map and thought that Congress had hardly united North and South with its two-capital solution. Rather the dual residencies had unwittingly set the stage for a neat breakup of the Union. "It gives me real distress," Boudinot shared with Robert Morris, "as I fear it is laying a solid foundation for future divisions." In a letter to Robert Livingston, the New Yorker elaborated, comparing the twin American sites of government to "Rome & Constantinople," capitals formed by the partition of the Roman Empire in the fourth century. "I augur great evil from this measure," he told Livingston, by which he evidently meant the evil of a bloody division of the United States into North/South confederacies, each of which would already possess an established federal capital.[28]

As for Secretary of Congress Charles Thomson, nothing he had ever seen before in American politics so markedly convinced him of the inevitability of a dissolution of the United States as the October debates over a federal capital. He felt persuaded as he sat and watched hours of "reproaches & altercation" that it was "the order of providence that this world should be divided into a number of separate & distinct governments." It seemed to be destiny, Thomson told Hannah. In July he had expressed to her his opinion that upon disunion there would be a New England–New York union, a Middle state union, a Virginia union unto itself, and only a loose connection between the other Southern states. By mid-October his thinking had evolved.[29]

As the sectional votes on the capital question testified, the Southern states, including Maryland, were a unified bloc. Without qualification, therefore, Thomson presently declared that there would be three American confederacies: "Eastern, Middle, and Southern." Thomson still feared "calamities" between them but felt a new tug to abide by the dictates of providence, culture, and economy in allowing for a controlled separation along these natural contours. "All things considered," he mused, "I do not know but this may be for the general good & the best that can [be] done for the interest and happiness of the whole." The one condition the secretary set upon the breakup of the United States into three republics was that they "confederate together for the purpose of general defense."[30]

* * * * *

George Washington, of course, was fully aware of these dangers of disunion. As he led the army, he made it a point to receive confidential news about debates in Congress and, more generally, the tempers of political leaders throughout the states. Not only this, the commander in chief spent all of September and October at the estate of Rocky Hill only a few miles outside Princeton. He was at the seat of Congress that fall on official business, where he conferred frequently with delegates about military and civil matters, including the October debates that ended in the two-capital solution to the North/South divide. Then, on November 1, while still in Princeton, Washington was handed an official letter announcing the signing of the definitive Treaty of Paris seven weeks earlier. The long war was over at last. The states had won their independence.

Washington could now disband the Continental Army and return home to Mount Vernon. To others, he expressed "my warmest congratulations" on "this happy event."[31]

Over the next month Washington oversaw the British evacuation of New York. Then, in early December, he bid an emotional farewell to his fellow officers at Fraunces Tavern at the tip of Manhattan before proceeding southward to Annapolis, the temporary capital to which Congress had recently relocated. At Fraunces Tavern, on December 4, he raised a toast to the thirty to forty officers gathered in the room, saying, "With a heart full of love and gratitude I now take leave of you. I most devoutly wish that your latter days may be as prosperous and happy as your former ones have been glorious and honorable." What followed in the tavern was a "mournful silence," punctuated by weeping, during which time Washington embraced the officers one by one, saying goodbye.[32]

The Maryland State House in Annapolis was the location set for Washington's formal resignation. There, on December 23, Secretary of Congress Thomson received the commander in chief, escorting him to the legislative chamber. Members of Congress occupied the floor; the galleries were filled with Maryland politicians and other citizens who had come to witness the historic transaction. A military hero was surrendering power to a civilian government in spite of an uncertain future for thirteen discordant, dissimilar states. Thomson ordered silence, whereupon Washington rose from his seat on the dais, bowed to Congress, and made a short speech. "Having now finished the work assigned me," the general said, "I retire from the great theatre of action, and bidding an affectionate farewell to this august body under whose orders I have so long acted I here offer my commission and take my leave of all the employments of public life." With this, Washington drew his commission from his coat pocket and delivered it to the president of Congress. The same day he departed for Mount Vernon. In his own words, he planned to spend the remainder of his life as "a private citizen on the banks of the Potomac."[33]

During Washington's travels that November and December, he had stopped over at dozens of towns, where he often gave remarks similar to those at Fraunces Tavern and the State House in Annapolis. Already, though, while still at Newburgh, he had put down on paper a formal farewell address to the people of the United States. A "Circular Letter to the States," the address had been widely disseminated through reprinting and publication in newspapers by the time of his retirement. Washington said it contained "the legacy" he wished to leave behind. In it the retiring

Chapter 20: "United We Stand, Divided We Fall" 369

general provided advice to present and future generations of Americans on the means for ensuring the "political happiness" and "social happiness" of the United States.[34]

FIGURE 45. Washington's Resignation of Military Commission, 1783. (Portrait of Washington Resigning His Commission. John Trumbull, *General George Washington Resigning His Commission*, 1826, oil on canvas, 12 x 18 ft, U.S. Capitol Rotunda.)

First and foremost, Washington said, the people of the thirteen states must unite under one federal government, never succumbing to those who promote "a dissolution of the Union." Beware "a spirit of disunion," he counseled, for such an unraveling of the states would unleash "anarchy and confusion," destroying the liberty and independence that had been gained by mutual sacrifice during the war. Further, as the United States was then concluding a long imperial crisis with Great Britain, it was entering into a new domestic one: a political crisis over the distribution of government power between the states and Congress. The outcome of "the present crisis," as Washington called it, would determine whether the United States would "be respectable and prosperous, or contemptible and miserable as a nation." The states must grant the federal government a "proportion of power," he affirmed, adequate to its survival—and therefore that of the states. There must "be lodged, somewhere, a supreme power, to regulate and govern the general concerns of the confederated republic, without which the Union cannot be of long duration." This central question, Washington urged, would decide "whether the revolution must ultimately be considered as a blessing or a curse." It would determine whether the United States "will stand or fall."

Finally, the fifty-one-year-old statesman said that one other commitment of Americans was "essential to the well-being, I may even venture to say, to the existence of the United States as an independent power." In order to overcome their differences, Americans from the thirteen states must "entertain a brotherly affection and love for one another." They must possess "charity, humility and pacific temper of mind."

As he entered retirement that year, Washington called for "the prevalence of that pacific and friendly disposition among the people of the United States which will induce them to forget their local prejudices and policies, to make those mutual concessions which are requisite to the general prosperity, and, in some instances, to sacrifice their individual advantages to the interest of the community." Sustaining a single government under one constitution, for the purpose of safeguarding liberties and rights and keeping the peace, Washington laid down as his last words, required comity and goodwill among the people and the states. This disposition of heart, he said, was one of the vital "pillars" of American independence.

NOTES

For many reasons, notably due to today's rapid online access to primary source materials, I have made minor corrections and adjustments to the wide variability of the founders' spellings and misspellings of words, capitalizations, cryptic abbreviations, and punctuations of sentences. Without ever adding or subtracting words or altering meaning, I have done this for the sake of the readability of quotations, aware that any scholar with a special interest in linguistics can easily access all the letters and speeches quoted in the book at online sites like the Library of Congress and Founders Online. I made these minor edits in quotations from letters and notes on debates only, not in those from newspaper articles or government documents. Those appear as in the original.

ABBREVIATIONS USED IN THE NOTES
Primary and Secondary Sources

AAM	Ferling, *Almost a Miracle*
APYLS	Avalon Project, Yale Law School
ARWPD	Wood, *The American Revolution: Writings from the Pamphlet Debate*
CC	Burnett, *Continental Congress*
DAJA	Butterfield, Faber, and Garrett, *Diary and Autobiography of John Adams*
DAR	Bemis, *Diplomacy of the American Revolution*
EEAI	Evans Early American Imprint Collection

EN	Giunta, *Emerging Nation*
FO	Founders Online
JCC	*Journals of the Continental Congress*
JJUP	*John Jay: Unpublished Papers*
LDTC	*Letters of Delegates to Congress*
LRHL	*The Letters of Richard Henry Lee*
OLL	Online Library of Liberty
PBF	*The Papers of Benjamin Franklin*
PJJ	*The Correspondence and Public Papers of John Jay*
PJM	*The Papers of James Madison*
PTJ	*Papers of Thomas Jefferson*
RDC	*Revolutionary Diplomatic Correspondence*
WJA	*Works of John Adams*
WOTR	Ward, *The War of the Revolution*
WSA	*Writings of Samuel Adams*

Founders

AA	Abigail Adams
AH	Alexander Hamilton
BF	Benjamin Franklin
GW	George Washington
JA	John Adams
JJ	John Jay
JM	James Madison
RHL	Richard Henry Lee
SA	Samuel Adams
TJ	Thomas Jefferson

EPIGRAPH

1. "We have nothing": "Robert Livingston as cited in John Adams, notes of debates, October 4, 1775, *Letters of Delegates to Congress* 2, https://memory.loc.gov/ammem/amlaw/lwdglink.html. John Witherspoon similarly said, "The greatest danger we have is of disunion among ourselves." Witherspoon as cited in JA, notes of debate, July 30, 1776, *LDTC* 4.

2. "God grant": Samuel Holten to John Kettell, October 9, 1783, *LDTC* 21.

INTRODUCTION

1. "Continental Congress": Here I use "Continental Congress" to signify the American congresses that met from 1774 until 1789, including the new phase of government that began on March 1, 1781, under the Articles of Confederation that historians often distinguish as the "Confederation Congress."

2. "Articles": Articles of Confederation, March 1, 1781, Avalon Project: Documents in Law, History, and Diplomacy, Yale Law School, https://avalon.law.yale.edu/18th_century/artconf.asp.

3. "Madness": John Witherspoon, speech in Congress, July 30, 1776, *LDTC* 4.

4. "Right of soil": November 13, 1777, August 7, 1781, and November 22, 1782, *Journals of the Continental Congress* 9, 21, 23, https://memory.loc.gov/ammem/amlaw/lwjclink.html. See also Joseph Galloway, *A Candid Examination of the Mutual Claims of Great-Britain, and the Colonies: With a Plan of Accommodation, on Constitutional Principles*, 1775, Evans Early American Imprint Collection, https://quod.lib.umich.edu/e/evans/N11095.0001.001?rgn=main;view=fulltext; as well as James Duane to George Clinton, June 12, 1779, *LDTC* 13; James Lovell to Samuel Adams, September 29, 1779, *LDTC* 13; and New York delegates to the New York Legislature, March 31, 1779, *LDTC* 12.

5. "Diabolical" and "internal": Municipal Common Hall to Lord Dunmore, April 21, 1775, cited in Ray Raphael, *The People's History of the American Revolution* (New York: New Press, 2002), 310. Raphael provides an overview of insurrections during the Revolution in chapter 6, "African Americans," 309–79. See too Alan Taylor, *Internal Enemy: Slavery and War in Virginia, 1772–1832* (New York and London: W. W. Norton, 2013).

6. "Wrath": Thomas Jefferson, *Notes on the State of Virginia*, APYLS, https://avalon.law.yale.edu/18th_century/jeffvir.asp.

7. "Right to soil": Galloway, *Candid Examination*, EEAI; statistic on slavery population: Raphael, *People's History*, 311.

8. "The greatest": Mark C. Dillion, *The First Chief Justice: John Jay and the Struggle of a New Nation* (Albany, NY: SUNY Press, 2022), 43.

9. "The Navigation": "British-American Diplomacy Preliminary Articles of Peace," November 30, 1782, APYLS, https://avalon.law.yale.edu/18th_century/prel1782.asp.

10. "Irrepressible": William H. Seward, "On the Irrepressible Conflict," Rochester, New York, October 25, 1858, New York History Net, www.nyhistory.com/central/conflict.htm.

11. "Great": James Madison, "Slave Trade and Slaveholders' Rights," June 17, 1788, Founders Online, https://founders.archives.gov/documents/Madison/01-11-02-0091.

12. See Sean Wilentz, *No Property in Man: Slavery and Antislavery at the Nation's Founding* (Cambridge, MA, and London: Harvard University Press, 2018), especially 14–16, for his speculations about the division of the thirteen states into separate confederacies over the question of slavery. Wilentz underscores that a chief cause of the perpetuation of slavery by the Constitutional Convention was the general lack of abolitionist spirit even within the Northern states. "The hard fact is," he writes, "that antislavery disunionist sentiment was far from common among free northerners," 15.

13. Eli F. Merritt, "Secret Conflict and Sectional Compromise: The Mississippi River Question and the United States Constitution," *American Journal of Legal History* 35, no. 2 (April 1991).

14. "The demon": David C. Hendrickson, *Peace Pact: The Lost World of the American Founding* (Lawrence: University Press of Kansas, 2003); "the outcome": Max M. Edling, *Perfecting the Union: National and State Authority in the U.S. Constitution* (New York: Oxford University Press, 2021), 8–9. Here I will not recapitulate the astute and exhaustive historiographical analyses of the unionist model that can be found in these two books as well as in Edling, "Peace Pact and Nation: An International Interpretation of the Constitution of the United States," *Past & Present* 240, no. 1 (August 2018): 267–303. Both books and Edling's article are required reading for scholars and students interested in this paradigm. Of note, Hendrickson credits Peter S. Onuf with the fullest explication of the complex thought behind the unionist paradigm; see *Peace Pact*, chapter 3, "The Unionist Paradigm," 310n2.

15. "Vitriolic": James Roger Sharp, *American Politics in the Early Republic: The New Nation in Crisis* (New Haven and London: Yale University Press, 1993), 2; "the Southern": Sharp, *American Politics*, 21; "Scholars": Sharp, *American Politics*, 5. For Sharp on the years 1789 to 1801 as comparable to the Civil War, see 12–13. Another notable work about early North-South political sectionalism is Joseph L. Davis's *Sectionalism in American Politics: 1774–1787* (Madison: University of Wisconsin Press, 1977). Davis, while not primarily concerned with disunity or the risk of civil war, highlights the relentless pace and growth of North-South consciousness and conflict during and after the Revolution. His book provides a blow-by-blow account of such critical North-South confrontations in the 1780s as the fight over the location of the U.S. capital, the Mississippi River Crisis, and the question of simple majority vs. supermajority vote requirements in Congress to approve commercial legislation. See also John Richard Alden, *The South in the Revolution: 1763–1789* (Baton Rouge: Louisiana State University Press, 1957); Forrest McDonald, *E Pluribus Unum: The Formation of the American Republic, 1776–1790* (Indianapolis, IN: Liberty Fund, 1979); and Michael J. Klarman, *The Framers' Coup: The Making of the United States Constitution* (New York and Oxford: Oxford University Press, 2016).

16. "Always-imperiled": Alan Taylor, *American Republics: A Continental History of the United States, 1783–1850* (New York and London: W. W. Norton, 2021), 7; "a

dread": Taylor, *American Republics*, 36; "the greatest": Speech of Witherspoon, John Adams, notes of debate, July 30, 1776, *LDTC* 4. Greene discusses this speech in Jack P. Greene, *Understanding the American Revolution: Issues and Actors* (Charlottesville: University of Virginia Press, 1995), 152–53.

17. Cathy D. Matson and Peter S. Onuf, *A Union of Interests: Political and Economic Thought in Revolutionary America* (Lawrence: University Press of Kansas, 1990). See especially chapter 5, "Union or Disunion," 82–100. Peter S. Onuf, *The Origins of the Federal Republic: Jurisdictional Controversies in the United States, 1775–1787* (Philadelphia: University of Pennsylvania Press, 1983), viii. See Edling, "Peace Pact and Nation," 279.

18. "Heroic": Bernard Bailyn, *The Ordeal of Thomas Hutchinson* (Cambridge, MA, and London: Belknap Press of Harvard University Press, 1974), viii; "The underside": Barbara Tuchman, *Practicing History: Collected Essays* (New York: Alfred A. Knopf, 1981), 90.

19. "For there": Bailyn, *Ordeal*, viii; "historian's angle": Bailyn, *Ordeal*, viii; "Until we": Bailyn, *Ordeal*, x.

CHAPTER 1

1. "Fifty Gentlemen": JA to Abigail Adams, September 25, 1774, *LDTC* 1. John wrote but seemingly never sent this letter to Abigail. We do not know why, but one hypothesis is that he was controlling the message. He of course wanted to promote an image of the Congress as a harmonious unified body. Friends and family commonly solicited political news from letter recipients like Abigail, and sometimes letters, or at least those paragraphs that contained public news, were read aloud to small groups. John knew this.

2. "Lions": King George III to Lord North, cited in John R. Alden, *General Gage in America: Being Principally a History of His Role in the American Revolution* (New York: Greenwood, 1969), 200; Gage held an interview with the king on February 4, 1774, which the king described to North by letter; "talk[ed] very high": Thomas Gage to William Barrington, August 27, 1774, in Alden, *General Gage*, 212. John Ferling makes the same argument regarding American disunity, the Coercive Acts, and British confidence. See Ferling, *Almost A Miracle: The American Victory in the War of Independence* (New York: Oxford University Press, 2007), 26.

3. "I feel": JA, diary entry, June 25, 1774, L. H. Butterfield, Leonard C. Faber, and Wendell D. Garrett, eds., *Diary and Autobiography of John Adams*, 4 vols. (Cambridge, MA, and London: Belknap Press of Harvard University Press, 1962), 2; "the wisest" and "A more": June 20, 1774, *DAJA* 2; "The objects": June 25, 1774, *DAJA* 2.

4. "Give me leave": George Washington to Robert Mackenzie, October 9, 1774, *LDTC* 1.

5. "Phill. Livingston": JA, diary entry, August 22, 1774, *DAJA* 2.

6. "If England": JA, diary entry, August 22, 1774, *DAJA* 2.

7. "Whenever": A. W. Farmer, *Rivington's New-York Gazetteer*, November 28, 1774, EEAI, https://quod.lib.umich.edu/cgi/t/text/text-idx?c=evans;idno=N10730.0001.001;rgn=div1;view=text;cc=evans;node=N10730.0001.001:2.

8. "Republic": Farmer, *Rivington's Gazetteer*, November 28, 1774, EEAI, https://quod.lib.umich.edu/cgi/t/text/text-idx?c=evans;idno=N10730.0001.001;rgn=div1;view=text;cc=evans;node=N10730.0001.001:2.

9. "What must": Thomas Bradbury Chandler, "What Think Ye of the CONGRESS Now?," 1774, EEAI, https://quod.lib.umich.edu/e/evans/N10953.0001.001?rgn=main;view=fulltext.

10. "Were these" and "Were they": Edmund S. Morgan, *The Birth of the Republic 1763–89* (Chicago and London: University of Chicago Press, 1977), 5.

11. "That as we are": SA to Joseph Warren, September 25, 1774, *LDTC* 1. SA's letter counseling Warren that New Englanders must project themselves to the other colonies as moderate and cooperative equals, as opposed to warriors in the vanguard of independence, is one of the first letters of the Revolution, of many, that reflect the presence of a concerted public effort by New Englanders to maintain a low profile in order not to foment resentment and jealousy by conveying a sense of their regional dominance or superiority. See, for other examples, JA to Samuel Osgood, November 15, 1775, *LDTC* 2, and SA to Elbridge Gerry, September 26, 1775, *LDTC* 2.

12. "Unthinking": Joseph Galloway, *Candid Examination*, EEAI, https://quod.lib.umich.edu/e/evans/N11095.0001.001?rgn=main;view=fulltext. For Galloway's essay, also given as a speech in Congress, see too Ferling, *A Leap in the Dark: The Struggle to Create the American Republic* (New York: Oxford University Press, 2003), 116–19, and Richard R. Beeman, *Our Lives, Our Fortunes, and Our Sacred Honor: The Forging of American Independence, 1774–1776* (New York: Basic Books, 2013), 123–34.

13. "The northern": Galloway, *Candid Examination*, EEAI. Quotations below from Galloway, unless otherwise cited, are derived from the same source.

14. "Equilibre": Anonymous letter, *Rivington's Gazetteer*, August 13, 1773, *Early American Newspapers: Series 2, 1758–1900: The New Republic*, https://www.readex.com/products/early-american-newspapers-series-02-1758-1900-new-republic.

15. "Violent Liberty" and other quotations: Mary Beth Norton, *1774: The Long Year of Revolution* (New York: Alfred A. Knopf, 2020), 156–57.

16. "Proper place": Galloway to William Franklin, September 5, 1774, *LDTC* 1.

17. "The Frankfort advice": JA to Timothy Pickering, August 6, 1822, in *Works of John Adams, Second President of the United States*, ed. Charles Francis Adams, 10 vols. (Boston: Little, Brown, 1850–56) vol. 2.

18. "Independence": JA to Pickering, August 6, 1822, *WJA* 2. See also J. Adams, diary entry, August 29, 1774, *LDTC* 1. Quotations below by Adams, unless otherwise cited, are derived from the same source

19. "New-England fanaticks": Chandler, "A Friendly Address," in Gordon S. Wood, ed., *The American Revolution: Writings from the Pamphlet Debate, 1764–1776* (New York: Library of America, 2015), 2:295; "hair-brained": Chandler, "Friendly Address," *ARWPD* 2:293; "obstinate": Chandler, "Friendly Address," *ARWPD* 2:305; "demagogues": Chandler, "Friendly Address," *ARWPD* 2:310; "rebellious": Chandler, "Friendly Address," *ARWPD* 2:293; "mad schemes": Rev. Samuel Seabury, "The Congress Canvassed," in *ARWPD*, 2:266; "the most virtuous":

Seabury, "Congress Canvassed," *ARWPD* 2:262; "Saints": Seabury, "Congress Canvassed," *ARWPD* 2:257; "New-England Republican": Chandler, "Friendly Address," *ARWPD* 2:311.

20. "It made": JA to Pickering, August 6, 1822, *WJA* 2.

21. "Method of voting": JA, diary entry, September 5, 1774, *LDTC* 1.

22. Slavery population statistics: Table 2, "Regional Differences in Population, 1700–90," Jack P. Greene and J. R. Pole, eds., *The Blackwell Encyclopedia of the American Revolution* (Cambridge, MA: Basil Blackwell, 1991), 42.

23. "The completest": Silas Deane to Elizabeth Deane, September 10, 1774, *LDTC* 1; JM's description of Patrick Henry as trumpeter: William Wirt, *The Life of Patrick Henry* (Philadelphia: Thomas Desilver, 1836), 246; "spoke as Homer": Henry Mayer, *A Son of Thunder: Patrick Henry and the American Republic* (Charlottesville and London: University Press of Virginia, 1991), 85.

24. "A precedent": JA, diary entry, September 5, 1774, *LDTC* 1.

25. "Major Sullivan": JA, diary entry, September 5, 1774, *LDTC* 1.

26. "This is": JA, diary entry, September 5, 1774, *LDTC* 1.

27. "Fleets" and "We are": JA, notes of debates, September 6, 1774, *LDTC* 1; "the democratical": James Duane, notes of debates, September 6, 1774, *LDTC* 1; "The distinctions": JA, notes of debates, September 6, 1774, *LDTC* 1.

28. "The weakest": Duane, notes of debates, September 6, 1774, *LDTC* 1.

29. "Injustice": Duane, notes of debates, September 6, 1774, *LDTC* 1.

30. Adams, Samuel, *Writings of Samuel Adams*, edited by Harry Alonzo Cushing, 4 vols (New York: G. P. Putnam's Sons, 1904–08).

31. Impact and shift after Harrison's speech: Duane, notes of debates, September 6, 1774, *LDTC* 1.

32. Absence of actuarial data for establishing method of voting and the Congress's decision-making: September 6, 1774, *JCC* 1; Duane, notes of debates, September 6, 1774, *LDTC* 1; and JA, diary entry (August 30–September 5), September 5, 1774, *LDTC* 1.

33. "Unequal" and "a precedent": Connecticut delegates to Gov. Jonathan Trumbull, October 10, 1774, *LDTC* 1.

34. Entry in journal: Connecticut delegates to Trumbull, October 10, 1774, *LDTC* 1. For the agreement on voting, see too September 6, 1774, *JCC* 1; Duane, notes of debates, September 6, 1774, *LDTC* 1; and JA, notes of debates, September 6, 1774, *LDTC* 1.

CHAPTER 2

1. "The first": Ferling, *Leap*, 116.

2. "Everything which": JA, diary entry, September 8, 1774, *LDTC* 1; "a mighty feast": JA, diary entry, September 14, 1774, *LDTC* 1.

3. "He would have": Benjamin Harrison, *Oxford Dictionary of National Biography*, https://www.oxforddnb.com/view/10.1093/ref:odnb/9780198614128.001.0001/odnb-9780198614128-e-68567; "Union," other toasts, and Virginians' fervor for resistance: JA, diary entry, August 30–September 5, 1774, *LDTC* 1; "Cicero": Silas Deane to Elizabeth Deane, September 10, 1774, *LDTC* 1.

4. "Colonel Washington": JA, diary entry, August 30–September 5, 1774, *LDTC* 1.

5. "Unite or Die": Franklin coined the motto first as "Join or Die" in the period before the French and Indian War. It took root and was recurring thereafter in colonial protests. See H. W. Brands, *The First American: The Life and Times of Benjamin Franklin* (New York: Anchor Books, 2000), 234; Lester C. Olson, *Benjamin Franklin's Vision of American Community: A Study in Rhetorical Iconology* (Columbia: University of South Carolina Press, 2004), 27–70; and Daniel P. Stone, "Join, or Die: Political and Religious Controversy over Franklin's Snake Cartoon," *Journal of the American Revolution*, January 10, 2018, https://allthingsliberty.com/2018/01/join-die-political-religious-controversy-franklins-snake-cartoon/.

6. "Grand Council": Albany Plan of Union 1754, APYLS, https://avalon.law.yale.edu/18th_century/albany.asp. See also Fred Anderson, *Crucible of War: The Seven Years' War and the Fate of Empire in British North America, 1754–1766* (New York: Alfred A. Knopf, 2000), 77–85.

7. Two-thousand-pound purchase: Anderson, *Crucible*, 78.

8. Franklin's letter to English correspondent: Anderson, *Crucible*, 85.

9. "Their jealousy": Brands, *First American*, 297.

10. "Unite or Die": Stone, "Join, or Die."

11. "Public spirited": Samuel Sherwood, *Scriptural Instructions to Civil Rulers*, August 31, 1774, ConSource, https://www.consource.org/document/scriptural-instructions-to-civil-rulers-by-samuel-sherwood-1774-8-31/.

12. "Six of the inhabitants": James Duane, notes of debates, September 6, 1774, *LDTC* 1.

13. "This city": S. Deane to E. Deane, September 6, 1774, *LDTC* 1.

14. "The kindness": JA to AA, September 18, 1774, *LDTC* 1.

15. Religious backgrounds of delegates: Beeman, *Our Lives*, 59.

16. "We were so divided": JA to AA, September 16, 1774, *LDTC* 1.

17. "It is an indispensable": Suffolk Resolves, September 17, 1774, *JCC* 1; Gage's regiments: Derek W. Beck, *Igniting the American Revolution: 1773–1775* (Naperville, IL: Sourcebooks, 2016), 39, 42, 49.

18. "With great applause": September 17, 1774, *JCC* 1:39 n. 1; "united efforts": September 17, 1774, *JCC* 1.

19. "This was": JA, diary entry, September 17, 1774, *LDTC* 1.

20. "Like a thunder" and "force": JA, notes of debates, September 26–27, 1774, *LDTC* 1.

21. "Non-exportation" and "Boston": JA, notes of debates, September 26–27, 1774, *LDTC* 1.

22. Virginia tobacco resolve: "The Association of the Virginia Convention," Articles V and IX, August 1–6, 1774, APYLS, https://avalon.law.yale.edu/18th_century/assoc_of_va_conv_1774.asp. See also "Instructions by the Virginia Convention to Their Delegates in Congress," August 6, 1774, FO, https://founders.archives.gov/documents/Jefferson/01-01-02-0092.

23. "The grand staple of Virginia": T. H. Breen, *Tobacco Culture: The Mentality of the Great Tidewater Planters on the Eve of Revolution* (Princeton, NJ: Princeton University Press, 1985), 57; Virginia tobacco statistics: John E. Selby, *The Revolution in Virginia, 1775–1783* (Charlottesville: University of Virginia Press, 1988) 26, 31; "a tobacco planters' club": Merrill D. Peterson, *Thomas Jefferson and the New Nation: A Biography* (New York and Oxford: Oxford University Press, 1970), 37.

24. "The earnest": "Instructions by the Virginia Convention," August 6, 1774, FO. The Virginia prohibition against agreeing to nonexportation prior to August 10, 1775, is laid out in "Association of the Virginia Convention," APYLS. The accompanying "Instructions," a letter from the Virginia Convention to the delegates attending Congress, explain the rationale behind its decision.

25. "Resolved unanimously": September 27, 1774, *JCC* 1.

26. "A gentleman": JA, notes of debates, September 26–27, 1774, *LDTC* 1.

27. "Equality": JA, notes of debates, September 26–27, 1774, *LDTC* 1.

CHAPTER 3

1. Galloway's speech and plan: Galloway, *Candid Examination*, EEAI, https://quod.lib.umich.edu/e/evans/N11095.0001.001?rgn=main;view=fulltext. Informative secondary sources include Norton, *1774*, 195–99; Beeman, *Our Lives*, 123–34; Edmund Cody Burnett, *The Continental Congress: A Definitive History of the Continental Congress from Its Inception in 1774 to March 1789* (New York: Norton Library, 1964), 47–50; and especially Ferling, *Leap*, 116–26; Ferling is also the author of *The Loyalist Mind: Joseph Galloway and the American Revolution* (University Park and London: Pennsylvania State University Press, 1997).

2. "A Plan": September 28, 1774, *JCC* 1; Galloway on plan premised on Albany Plan: "Joseph Galloway's Proposed Resolution," September 28, 1774, *LDTC* 1; "There must be": September 28, 1774, *JCC* 1.

3. "What if": Maya Jasanoff, *Liberty's Exiles: American Loyalists in the Revolutionary World* (New York: Vintage Books, 2011), 27.

4. "Tended to inflame": September 28, 1774, *JCC* 1. Quotations below from Galloway, unless otherwise cited, are derived from the same source.

5. "Shall hold": "Joseph Galloway's Plan of Union," September 28, 1774, *LDTC* 1. Quotations below from Galloway, unless otherwise cited, are derived from the same source.

6. "Galloway's plan": Jasanoff, *Liberty's Exiles*, 26.

7. "Inferior": "Joseph Galloway's Plan of Union," September 28, 1774, *LDTC* 1.

8. "Warm debates": "Joseph Galloway's Statement on His Plan of Union," September 28, 1774, *LDTC* 1; "a lasting accommodation": JA, notes of debates, September 28, 1774, *LDTC* 1.

9. "We shall liberate": JA, notes of debates, September 28, 1774, *LDTC* 1.

10. "I am": JA, notes of debates, September 28, 1774, *LDTC* 1.

11. Vote of Congress: Ferling, *Leap*, 119.

12. "When it came": Burnett, *CC*, 46. The language of the resolution was "Resolved, That from and after the 10th day of Septr., 1775, the exportation of all merchandize and every commodity whatsoever to Great Britain, Ireland and the West Indies, ought to cease, unless the grievances of America are redressed before that time." September 30, 1774, *JCC* 1.

13. "The question was": Ferling, *Leap*, 116.

14. "Resolved, That in case hostilities": Resolutions of John Adams, September 30, 1774, *JCC* 1:52 n. 1.

15. "Ought": Resolutions of John Adams, September 30, 1774, *JCC* 1:52 n. 1.

16. "Patience": JA to AA, September 29, 1774, *LDTC* 1.

17. "You say": JA to William Tudor, September 29, 1774, *LDTC* 1.

18. "Repeal": Declaration and Resolves of Congress, October 14, 1774, *JCC* 1.

19. "Indubitable": Declaration and Resolves of Congress, October 14, 1774, *JCC* 1.

20. "Impending": Petition to the King, October 26, 1774, *JCC* 1.

21. "Slaves": Address to the People of Great Britain, October 21, 1774, *JCC* 1.

22. "Outrageous": Address to the Inhabitants of the Colonies, October 21, 1774, *JCC* 1.

23. Records on second round of debates on nonexportation: October 15, 17, 18, 19, 20, 1774, *JCC* 1; "South Carolina Delegates' Report to the Carolina Provincial Congress," January 11, 1775, *LDTC* 1; and Burnett, *CC*, 55.

24. "The Northern": "South Carolina Delegates' Report," January 11, 1775, *LDTC* 1.

25. Beeman chronology: Beeman, *Our Lives*, 155.

26. "Now": Burnett, *CC*, 55. Burnett states that the date of the South Carolina walkout is October 20, the date the Continental Association was signed. This appears to be in error. It is inconsistent with the statement of Christopher Gadsden that the demand to exclude rice and indigo "occasioned a cessation of business for several days." This leads to the conclusion that the walkout happened on October 17 or 18. See "South Carolina Delegates' Report," January 11, 1775, *LDTC* 1. See Beeman, *Our Lives*, 155, for more accurate dating.

27. "Obnoxious": "South Carolina Delegates' Report," January 11, 1775, *LDTC* 1. For another letter expressing passionate feelings about the exemption, see Henry Laurens to John Rutledge, December 1, 1777, *LDTC* 8.

28. "Carolina": "South Carolina Delegates' Report," January 11, 1775, *LDTC* 1.

29. "He could never": "South Carolina Delegates' Report," January 11, 1775, *LDTC* 1. See too on feelings of injustice Edward Rutledge to Ralph Izard, October 29, 1774, *LDTC* 1. The South Carolina delegates were fearful of undue Northern influence in the First Congress even before it commenced; see Norton, *1774*, 150–51.

30. "Rice": "South Carolina Delegates' Report," January 11, 1775, *LDTC* 1.

31. "Except": October 20, 1774, *JCC* 1.

32. The Continental Association: October 20, 1774, *JCC* 1.

33. "The earnest": October 20, 1774, *JCC* 1.

34. "May the Sword": JA, diary entry, October 20, 1774, *LDTC* 1.
35. "It is not very likely": JA, diary entry, October 26, 1774, *LDTC* 1:247 n. 1.
36. Washington's orders in Philadelphia: Ron Chernow, *Washington: A Life* (New York: Penguin, 2010), 174; and Joseph J. Ellis, *His Excellency: George Washington* (New York: Alfred A. Knopf, 2004), 65.

CHAPTER 4

1. "Quiet the minds": Lord Dartmouth to Thomas Gage, April 9, 1774, Rick Atkinson, *The British Are Coming: The War for America, Lexington to Princeton, 1775–1777* (New York: Henry Holt, 2019), 40.
2. Battle of Lexington: Thomas Fleming, *Liberty! The American Revolution* (New York: Viking Penguin, 1997), 106–14; Ferling, *AAM*, 31-32; Christopher Ward, *The War of the Revolution*, 2 vols. (New York: Macmillan, 1952), 1:26–38; David H. Fischer, *Paul Revere's Ride* (New York and Oxford: Oxford University Press, 1994), 191–95; "Lexington": Atkinson, *British*, 63.
3. April 19 total casualties and numbers: Ward, *WOTR* 1:50.
4. "When I consider": Benjamin Franklin to Joseph Galloway, February 25, 1775, FO.
5. "American demagogues": Galloway, *Candid Examination*, EEAI, https://quod.lib.umich.edu/e/evans/N11095.0001.001?rgn=main;view=fulltext.
6. "Apostate": Joseph Hewes to Samuel Johnston, May 11, 1775, *LDTC* 1.
7. "You will have heard": BF to David Hartley, May 8, 1775, *LDTC* 1.
8. "Articles of Confederation": BF, Articles of Confederation, July 21, 1775, *JCC* 2. Quotations below from BF, unless otherwise cited, are derived from the same source.
9. "Right": Galloway, *Candid Examination*, EEAI.
10. Three speeches: John Dickinson, notes for a speech in Congress, May 23–25(?), 1775, *LDTC* 1. This source reveals three separate sets of papers outlining notes for formal addresses and one containing resolutions. Unless otherwise noted, all citations in reference to Dickinson's speech or speeches are derived from two separate entries in *LDTC*, both titled "John Dickinson's Notes for a Speech in Congress [May 23–25? 1775]," *LDTC* 1.
11. Fear that independence would catalyze disunion and civil wars among the colonies was deep-seated in Dickinson. As early as 1765 he wrote to William Pitt that all history dictated this dismal outcome. In the end, he said, the bloody chaos of independence would be pacified by the imposition of the tyranny by a conqueror. Alluding to the achievement of independence by the colonies, Dickinson wrote, "But what, sir, must be the Consequences of that Success? A Multitude of Commonwealths, Crimes, and Calamities, of mutual Jealousies, Hatreds, Wars and Devastations; till at last the exhausted Provinces shall sink into Slavery under the yoke of some fortunate Conqueror." Dickinson to Pitt, December 21, 1765, cited in Greene, *Understanding*, 59.
12. "State of defense": Dickinson, proposed resolutions, May 23–25(?), 1775, *LDTC* 1.

13. "The morals": JA, diary entry, October 9, 1774, *LDTC* 1; "overweening" and "infirmity": JA to AA, October 29, 1775, *LDTC* 2.

14. "Mothers milk": JA to Joseph Hawley, November 25, 1775, *LDTC* 2.

15. JA's attitudes towards reconciliation: Burnett, *CC*, 84–87; Ferling, *John Adams: A Life* (New York: Henry Holt, 1996), 122–23; David G. McCullough, *John Adams* (New York: Simon & Schuster, 2001), 87, 94–95.

16. "In as violent": May–June 1775, *DAJA* 3:318. Quotations below from Dickinson, unless otherwise cited, are derived from the same source.

17. "Haughtily": September 16, 1775, *DAJA* 2:173.

18. Lasting estrangement of JA and Dickinson: May–June 1775, *DAJA* 3:318.

19. "A fatal issue": Dickinson, notes of debate, May 23–25(?), 1775, *LDTC* 1; "Doctrine of Disunion": Dickinson to Samuel Ward, January 29, 1775, *LDTC* 1; "We must have": JA to James Warren, July 6, 1775, *LDTC* 1.

20. Chronology of the Olive Branch Petition: John Jay, draft petition to the king, June 3–19(?), 1775, *LDTC* 1 n. 1; "We, your": Petition to the King, July 8, 1775, APYLS.

21. "George": June 15, 1775, *JCC*.

22. "Out of doors": July–August 1775, *DAJA* 3:322; "A Southern Party": July–August 1775, *DAJA* 3:321.

23. Dyer on North-South dynamics and fear of civil war: Eliphalet Dyer to Jonathan Trumbull Sr., June 16, 1775; and Dyer to Joseph Trumbull, June 17, 1775, *LDTC* 1.

24. "It removes all": Dyer to J. Trumbull, June 17, 1775, *LDTC* 1; "His appointment": Dyer to J. Trumbull Sr., June 16, 1775, *LDTC* 1. According to Dyer, one acute source of concern for the Southern delegates was that a Connecticut-Pennsylvania civil war over the disputed Wyoming Valley would lead to a greater New England invasion of the Southern colonies. See Dyer to William Judd, July 23, 1775, *LDTC* 1.

25. McKesson letter: June 10, 1775, cited in George Clinton to John McKesson, June 15, 1775, Note 1, *LDTC* 1 n. 1.

26. "False as Hell": Clinton to McKesson, June 15, 1775, *LDTC* 1.

27. "I have never": JA to Elbridge Gerry, June 18, 1775, *LDTC* 1; "Torment": JA to Warren, June 20, 1775, *LDTC* 1.

28. "Amazingly high": JA to Cotton Tufts, June 21, 1775, *LDTC* 1; "Those ideas": JA to Gerry, June 18, 1775, *LDTC* 1; "It totis": JA to Tufts, June 21, 1775, *LDTC* 1. See also JA to Warren, June 20, 1775, *LDTC* 1. "Southern Genius's" changed to "Southern Geniuses" for clarity.

29. Philadelphia send-off: JA to AA, June 23, 1775, *LDTC* 1; Chernow, *Washington*, 188–90; "a sea": Chernow, *Washington*, 190.

30. "Remember": Chernow, *Washington*, 188.

31. "He does": JA to AA, July 23, 1775, *LDTC* 1.

32. "A like union": BF to James Parker, March 20, 1751, FO.

33. "Terms": BF, Articles of Confederation, July 21, 1775, *JCC* 2.

34. TJ's summary penned to François Soulés: "Answers to the Queries of M. Soules," August 3, 1786, OLL, https://oll.libertyfund.org/titles/802#Jefferson_0054-05_533.

35. "Were revolted": TJ, "Answers to the Queries," August 3, 1786, OLL. For BF's Articles of Confederation, see too Carl Van Doren, *Benjamin Franklin* (New York: Penguin Books, 1991), 534–35; Brands, *First American*, 501–2; Burnett, *CC*, 90–91; and editors' note, "Proposed Articles of Confederation, [on or before 21 July 1775]," FO, https://founders.archives.gov/documents/Franklin/01-22-02-0069.

36. Franklin's presentation of the "Articles of Confederation": BF, Articles of Confederation, July 21, 1775, *JCC* 2.

CHAPTER 5

1. Paine background: John Keane, *Tom Paine: A Political Life* (Boston: Little, Brown, 1995), 92–96.

2. "Peace": October 26, 1774, *JCC* 1.

3. "African Slavery in America": Thomas Paine, March 8, 1775, OLL, https://oll.libertyfund.org/titles/paine-the-writings-of-thomas-paine-vol-i-1774-1779; quotations below from Paine, unless otherwise cited, are derived from the same source. Paine's writings: Keane, *Tom Paine*, 92–96.

4. Statistics on Common Sense: Chernow, *Washington*, 214–15; Burnett, *CC*, 131; and Fleming, *Liberty*, 159–60. Fleming estimates that the three-month release of *Common Sense* was equivalent to fifteen million if sold in the modern age.

5. "TIS TIME": *Paine, Common Sense Unabridged* (Mineola, NY: Dover, 1997).

6. "A necessary": all citations from this work are from Paine, *Common Sense*.

7. "Have you seen": Major General Charles Lee to GW, January 24, 1776, FO, https://founders.archives.gov/documents/Washington/03-03-02-0128; "Unanswerable": Burnett, *CC*, 132; "Who is": McCullough, *John Adams*, 96.

8. "Cruel": JA, notes of debates, October 20, 1775, *LDTC* 2.

9. October debates on commerce: See especially JA, notes of debates, October 4, 5, and 20, 1775, *LDTC* 2.

10. "This will produce": JA, notes of debates, October 3, 1774, *LDTC* 2.

11. "Jealousies and dissensions": JA, notes of debates, October 3, 1774, *LDTC* 2.

12. "Will divide us": JA, notes of debates, October 5, 1774, *LDTC* 2.

13. "Not convinced": JA, notes of debates, October 3, 1774, *LDTC* 2.

14. "It is prudent": JA, notes of debates, October 5, 1774, *LDTC* 2.

15. "Jealousies": JA, notes of debates, October 12, 1774, *LDTC* 2.

16. Sam Adams on British strategy: SA to Samuel Cooper, April 3, 1776, *LDTC* 3; "1000": JA, diary entry, September 24, 1775, *LDTC* 2.

17. "Strongly": Richard Smith, diary entry, September 26, 1775, *LDTC* 2. For background on these proceedings, see Note 2, chapter 5. Washington's order was issued July 10, 1775.

18. "Southern": Eliphalet Dyer to William Judd, July 23, 1775, *LDTC* 1.

19. "I have several times": Samuel Ward to Henry Ward, December 27, 1775, *LDTC* 2. For Ward and Southern fears of regional imbalance in the army, see six letters from S. Ward to H. Ward: September 30, November 2, November 21, December 27, December 31, 1775, *LDTC* 2, and February 9, 1776, *LDTC* 3.

20. "Southern": S. Ward to H. Ward, November 21, 1775, *LDTC* 2.

21. "The N. E. Colonies": S. Ward to H. Ward, December 31, 1775, *LDTC* 2.

22. "We failed": S. Ward to H. Ward, September 30, 1775, *LDTC* 2.

23. "Diabolical" and statistics: Ferling, *Leap*, 150.

24. Norfolk statistics: Selby, *Revolution*, 64; Duane on Virginians: James Duane to Robert R. Livingston Jr., December 20, 1775, *LDTC* 2.

25. "An independent": "His Majesty's Most Gracious Speech to Both Houses of Parliament," Friday, October 27, 1775, Library of Congresss, https://www.loc.gov/resource/rbpe.10803800/.

26. "Is an object": Carter Braxton to Landon Carter, April 14, 1776, *LDTC* 3.

27. "I am": Braxton to Carter, April 14, 1776, *LDTC* 3.

28. "May be": Dyer to Judd, July 23, 1775, *LDTC* 1; "Should violences": Silas Deane to Zebulon Butler, July 24, 1775, *LDTC* 1.

29. "Two of the": Braxton to Carter, April 14, 1776, *LDTC* 3; "Republican": Oliver Wolcott to Samuel Lyman, March 26, 1776, *LDTC* 3.

30. "Three distinct": Thomas Hutchinson, "Strictures upon the Declaration of the Congress at Philadelphia in a Letter to a Noble Lord, &c.," October 15, 1776, Online Library of Liberty, https://oll.libertyfund.org/pages/1776-hutchinson-strictures-upon-the-declaration-of-independence.

31. "Jarring": Massachusettensis [Daniel Leonard], OLL. The letters, first published in 1774–75, were later bound into a pamphlet in 1776. The quotations are from "Letter VIII: To the Inhabitants of the Province of Massachusetts-bay," January 30, 1775.

32. "Eminent": Novanglus [JA], No. IV, OLL; "brotherly" and "unanimously": Novanglus, No. III, OLL.

33. "Proofs": Novanglus, No. III, OLL.

34. "Several distinct": JA to Joseph Hawley, November 25, 1775, *LDTC* 2; quotations below from JA, unless otherwise cited, are derived from the same source. "Southern Brethren": JA to Samuel Osgood, November 15, 1775, *LDTC* 2.

35. "Barons": JA to Horatio Gates, March 23, 1776, *LDTC* 3; "great": Richard Smith, diary entry, March 15, 1776, *LDTC* 3; "the pay": JA to Hawley, November 25, 1775, *LDTC* 2; "It is": JA to John Winthrop, October 2, 1775, *LDTC* 2. Pay of soldiers and officers was a constant source of disagreement between Northern and Southern delegates. See also Duane, notes of debates, February 22, 1776, *LDTC* 3, and Wolcott to Roger Newberry, June 4, 1776, *LDTC* 4.

36. "Fully understood": JA to AA, February 18, 1776, *LDTC* 3; "Gentlemen": JA to Hawley, November 25, 1775, *LDTC* 2.

37. "All our": JA to Gates, March 23, 1776, *LDTC* 3. Another observer present in Philadelphia in early 1776, Lord Thomas Drummond, an incognito envoy of Britain sent to seek reconciliation, explicitly commented on "two Partys" in Congress

in January, one composed of the "Northern colonies," by which he meant the New England colonies, and the other "the Middle and Southern ones." Drummond, notes, January 3–9(?) 1776, *LDTC* 3. See also Drummond, minutes, January 5 and January 14, 1776, *LDTC* 3.

38. "We do not": Joseph Hewes to Samuel Johnston, March 20, 1776, *LDTC* 3.

39. "Patience, fortitude": JA to Gates, March 23, 1776, *LDTC 3*. "The first": JA to Oakes Angier, June 12, 1776, *LDTC* 3.

40. "Some free": SA to JA, January 15, 1776, *LDTC* 3.

41. "I think": Elbridge Gerry to James Warren, May 1, 1776, *LDTC* 3; "unhappy": S. Ward to H. Ward, February 19, 1776, *LDTC* 3.

CHAPTER 6

1. "State": Constitution of Virginia, June 29, 1776, APYLS, https://press-pubs.uchicago.edu/founders/documents/v1ch1s4.html. This square mileage is based on Virginia's justifiable claim in 1776 in light of both its colonial charter and the Treaty of Paris ending the Seven Years' War, which awarded Britain the land east of the Mississippi River and Spain the land west of the river.

2. "Provided": Preamble and Resolution of the Virginia Convention, May 15, 1776, APYLS, https://avalon.law.yale.edu/18th_century/const02.asp.

3. "All men": Constitution of Virginia, June 29, 1776, APYLS; quotations below, unless otherwise cited, are derived from the same source.

4. Resolution: May 10, 1776, *JCC* 4; "erect": John Jay to Alexander McDougall, April 11, 1776, in Walter Stahr, *John Jay: Founding Father* (New York and London: Hambledon and London, 2005), 58.

5. "Two parties": Lord Drummond, notes, January 3–9(?), 1776, *LDTC* 3; "to concur": Burnett, *CC*, 154. See Burnett, *CC*, 154–56, for a chronology of the colonies' adoption of positions towards independence.

6. "Here are four": JA to James Warren, May 20, 1776, *LDTC* 4; "The Middle": JA to Benjamin Hichborn, May 29, 1776, *LDTC* 4.

7. "That these": TJ, proceedings in Congress, June 7, 1776, *LDTC* 4.

8. "The people": TJ, proceedings in Congress, June 8 and 10, 1776, *LDTC* 4; quotations below, unless otherwise cited, are derived from the same source.

9. "To prepare": June 11, 1776, *JCC* 5.

10. "Saturday": Edward Rutledge to JJ, June 8, 1776, *LDTC* 4; quotations below from Rutledge, unless otherwise cited, are derived from the same source.

11. "The force": Rutledge to JJ, June 29, 1776, *LDTC* 4; quotations below from Rutledge, unless otherwise cited, are derived from the same source.

12. "The greatest": JA to AA, July 3, 1776, *LDTC* 4; "May Heaven": JA to Archibald Bulloch, July 1, 1776, *LDTC* 4; "If you": JA to Samuel Chase, July 1, 1776, *LDTC* 4.

13. "Twenty times": JA, *Autobiography*, cited in Beeman, *Our Lives*, 374; "hundred": JA to Chase, July 1, 1776, *LDTC* 4.

14. "The consequences": John Dickinson, notes for a speech in Congress, July 1, 1776, *LDTC* 4; quotations below from Dickinson, unless otherwise cited, are

derived from the same source. Two records in *LDTC* contain Dickinson's prepared speech and notes: this one and "Colonies in their Limits, In the Hand of John Dickinson, Endorsed 'Arguments agt. the Independence of these Colonies-in Congress,'" July 1, 1776, *LDTC* 4.

15. For the votes, delegates, and rules of Congress relating to independence, see Burnett, *CC*, 175–82; and Beeman, *Our Lives*, 369–75. Beeman poses a question: Was the July 1 vote merely a "straw vote" (374)? It was not. It was a formal vote of Congress. We know this at least in part from a letter written by JA at the end of the day in which he states that regarding the vote, "the question was carried in the affirmative." JA to Chase, July 1, *LDTC* 4. I find nowhere an official record of the Congress stating that the question of independence would be decided by a supermajority vote, but letters of delegates and most historians who address the question reinforce the fact that a supermajority was the assumed standard and threshold. That same day, July 1, Maryland delivered revised instructions to its delegates in Philadelphia empowering them to vote in favor in independence.

CHAPTER 7

1. Rutledge and decision to revote: TJ, proceedings in Congress, July 14, 1776, *LDTC* 4. In this document TJ recounts the events of Congress from July 1 to July 4.

2. Votes of July 2: July 2, 1776, *JCC* 5.

3. Voting and maneuvering of July 1 and 2: see Beeman, *Our Lives*, 369–81; Burnett, *CC*, 180–85; and Charles Rappleye, *Robert Morris: Financier of the American Revolution* (New York: Simon & Schuster, 2010), 71–2.

4. "Unanimity": Thomas McKean to Caesar Rodney, September(?) 22, 1813, in Burnett, *CC*, 1. For New York, see Beeman, *Our Lives*, 415–16.

5. The best secondary sources on the history of the Articles of Confederation are Jack N. Rakove, *The Beginnings of National Politics: An Interpretive History of the Continental Congress* (Baltimore and London: Johns Hopkins University Press, 2019); Burnett, *CC*; Merrill Jensen, *The Articles of Confederation: An Interpretation of the Social-Constitutional History of the American Revolution, 1774–1781* (Madison: University of Wisconsin Press, 1940); and the editorial notes and footnotes contained in *LDTC* and FO.

6. "Continental constitution": Josiah Bartlett to John Langdon, June 17, 1776, and JA to John Winthrop, June 23, 1776, *LDTC* 4; "treaty of": Nicholas Cooke to GW, July 16, 1776, FO, https://founders.archives.gov/?q=confederation%20Dates-From:1776-06-01&s=1111311111&sa=&r=20&sr=.

7. "Perpetual": draft Articles of Confederation, June 17–July 1(?), 1776, *LDTC* 4, https://memory.loc.gov/cgi-bin/query/r?ammem/hlaw:@field(DOCID+@lit(dg004186)):.

8. Article V: "No two or more Colonies shall enter into any Treaty, Confederation, or Alliance whatever between them without the previous and free Consent & Allowance of the Union," draft Articles of Confederation, June 17–July 1(?), 1776, *LDTC* 4. This was not the last time the matter of subconfederations reared its head during the war. See discussion of the "Convention of the New England States" in Providence, Rhode Island, in chapter 9 as one example.

9. "Some of us": John Dickinson, notes for a speech in Congress, July 1, 1776, *LDTC* 4; "Without the": Bartlett to Nathaniel Folsom, July 1, 1776, *LDTC* 4.

10. Printing and dates: July 22, 1776, *JCC* 5; and Burnett, *CC*, 213–29.

11. "The name": July 12, 1776, *JCC* 5.

12. "Every Age": July 22, 1776, *JCC* 5; "South Sea": JA, notes of debates, August 2, 1776, *LDTC* 4.

13. "Death warrant": Benjamin Rush, notes for a speech in Congress, August 1 1776, *LDTC* 4.

14. "A species": JA, notes of debate, July 30, 1776, *LDTC* 4. The delegates considered taxing states based on population as units of wealth, and during these debates Benjamin Harrison proposed the formula of counting two slaves as equal to one freeman, on the basis of labor productivity. See Burnett, *CC*, 226.

15. "The Eastern": JA, notes of debate, July 30, 1776, *LDTC* 4.

16. "What we": Joseph Hewes to Samuel Johnston, July 28, 1776, *LDTC* 4.

17. "We do not all": Samuel Chase to Richard Henry Lee, July 30, 1776, *LDTC* 4.

18. "Madness": John Witherspoon, speech in Congress, July 30, 1776, *LDTC* 4; quotations below from Witherspoon, unless otherwise cited, are derived from the same source.

19. By August 20 the delegates had accomplished a third revision of the Articles, with a significant change made: the clause that gave Congress control over boundaries, charter claims, and unallocated lands was omitted; the delegates did not agree on the document, vote, or submit it to the states, but again they ordered copies be made for the private consideration of delegates. See August 20, 1776, *JCC* 5, for the revised Articles presented that day and ordered to be copied. See Jensen, *Articles*, 139, for a summary of the changes made. After August 20 no debates on the Articles took place for another six months.

20. "The larger": TJ, proceedings in Congress, July 30, 31, and August 1, 1776, *LDTC* 4; "If it is debated": JA, notes of debate, July 30, 1776, *LDTC* 4.

21. "The limits": JA, notes of debates, July 25, 1776, *LDTC* 4.

22. "Devil": Edward Rutledge to Robert R. Livingston, August 19, 1776, *LDTC* 4.

23. "I fear": William Williams to Oliver Wolcott, August 11, 1776, *LDTC* 4; "very alarming": Abraham Clark to James Caldwell, August 1, 1776, *LDTC* 4.

CHAPTER 8

1. "A plan": June 12, 1776, *JCC* 5.

2. Treaty of 1763: Samuel F. Bemis, *The Diplomacy of the American Revolution* (Bloomington and London: Indiana University Press, 1957), 5–10.

3. "Equally free": Treaty of Paris, 1763, APYLS. Britain signed a treaty first with France. Afterward France transferred Louisiana to Spain in a separate treaty, along with the guarantee of free navigation.

4. Treaty template: September 17, 1776, *JCC* 5.

5. "Short": Brands, *First American*, 527.

6. British troops and ships: Ferling, *AAM*, 124–25.

7. "These": Thomas Paine, *The American Crisis,* December 1776. Library of Congress (https://www.loc.gov/resource/cph.3b06889/).

8. "Speedy": Committee of Secret Correspondence to American Commissioners, December 30, 1776, FO, https://founders.archives.gov/documents/Franklin/01-23-02-0056.

9. "The cod fishery": December 30, 1776, *JCC* 6.

10. "The free": December 30, 1776, *JCC* 6.

11. "Behaved": Caesar Rodney to Thomas Rodney, September 25, 1776, *LDTC* 5; "truly": William Hooper to Samuel Johnston, September 26, 1776, *LDTC* 5.

12. "New England Heroes": Hooper to Johnston, September 26, 1776, *LDTC* 5.

13. "Truly": Hooper to Joseph Hewes, November 5, 1776, *LDTC* 5.

14. "Bloodsuckers": Hooper to Hewes, November 16, 1776, *LDTC* 5; "The Eastern": Hooper to Hewes, November 19, 1776, *LDTC* 5; "New England": Hooper to Hewes, November 29, 1776, *LDTC* 5.

15. "Forces": SA to James Warren, December 4, 1776, *LDTC* 5.

16. "Money": William Williams to Joseph Trumbull, October 7, 1776, *LDTC* 5.

17. "The infamous": JA to William Tudor, September 20, 1776, *LDTC* 5.

18. "I am ashamed": JA to Tudor, September 20, 1776, *LDTC* 5; "Pray": JA to Henry Knox, September 29, 1776, *LDTC* 5. See also JA to Tudor, September 26, 1776, *LDTC* 5.

CHAPTER 9

1. "Divided": Benjamin Rush, notes, April 8, 1777, *LDTC* 6; "There is": William Whipple to Josiah Bartlett, February 7, 1777, *LDTC* 6.

2. Convention: Gerry and SA to the Council of Massachusetts, January 31, 1777, *LDTC* 6; "for their mutual": Abraham Clark to John Hart, February 8, 1777, *LDTC* 6; "They have recommended": Roger Sherman to Jonathan Trumbull Jr., January 30, 1777, *LDTC* 6. For further discussion of this convention, see Jensen, *Articles*, 170–71.

3. "Approbation": Benjamin Rush, notes of debates, February 4, 1777, *LDTC* 6.

4. "I think": Rush, notes of debates, February 4, 1777, *LDTC* 6; Quotations below from Rush, unless otherwise cited, are derived from the same source. See also Rush's notes for February 14, 1777, *LDTC* 6.

5. "Stand in need": Rush, notes of debates, February 4, 1777, *LDTC* 6. Also see February 4, 5, and 6, 1777, *JCC* 7; "recommended": February 15, 1777, *JCC* 7. See also February 12, 13, and 14, 1777, *JCC* 7.

6. Burke's role in shaping these two articles: Thomas Burke to Richard Caswell, April 29, 1777, *LDTC* 6; and Jensen, *Articles*, 150–76. Jensen provides an excellent discussion of Burke's impact particularly on reshaping the sovereignty article. For Burke's important contributions to congressional debates on the Articles of Confederation, see Rakove, *Beginnings*, 164–82.

7. "I find": Burke to Caswell, February 4, 1777, *LDTC* 6; "Northern": Burke to Caswell, April 29, 1777, *LDTC* 6; "political": Burke to Caswell, February 16, 1777, *LDTC* 6; "pass": Burke to Caswell, February 16, 1777, *LDTC* 6.

8. "Power": Burke to Caswell, March 11, 1777, *LDTC* 6; quotations below from Burke, unless otherwise cited, are derived from the same source.

9. Minimum of every two days: April 8, 1777, *JCC* 7.

10. "New York": Burke to Caswell, April 29, 1777, *LDTC* 6; "to prevent": SA to RHL, June 29, 1777, *LDTC* 7.

11. "Necessary": Daniel Roberdeau to Thomas Wharton, October 14, 1777, *LDTC* 8; "Many assert": Cornelius Harnett to Caswell, October 10, 1777, *LDTC* 8; "This great": RHL to SA, July 12, 1777, cited in SA to RHL, July 22, 1777, *LDTC* 7 n. 1.

12. "Regulation": Jensen, *Articles*, 254; "Each state": Jensen, *Articles*, 263. See the appendix in Jensen, *Articles*, for both the Dickinson Articles and the final form of the Articles (taken from November 15, 1777, *JCC* 9). Jensen's *Articles* offers a detailed account of the evolution and politics of the first constitution from 1774 to 1781.

13. "No two": November 15, 1777, *JCC* 9.

14. "Final": November 15, 1777, *JCC* 9.

15. Statistics: Jensen, *Articles*, 149.

16. "We have finished": RHL to Sherman, November 24, 1777, *LDTC* 8.

17. "Wise": November 17, 1777, *JCC* 9.

18. Military statistics: Benson Bobrick, *Angel in the Whirlwind: The Triumph of the American Revolution* (New York: Simon & Schuster, 1997), 280.

19. "The greatest": Morgan, *Birth*, 83; "The essential": Treaty of Alliance Between the United States and France, February 6, 1778, APYLS.

20. "Gave": Morgan, *Birth*, 83.

21. "The subjects": Treaty of Alliance Between the United States and France, February 6, 1778, APYLS.

22. "If any ship": Treaty of Amity and Commerce Between the United States and France, February 6, 1778, APYLS, https://avalon.law.yale.edu/18th_century/fr1788-1.asp.

23. "The fishery": December 30, 1776, *JCC* 6.

24. "That if": Benjamin Franklin to Count of Aranda, April 7, 1777, *Revolutionary Diplomatic Correspondence* 2, https://memory.loc.gov/ammem/amlaw/lwdc.html.

25. Diplomacy of Spain: See Bemis, *DAR*, 41–57.

26. "It is only": Count of Montmorin to Comte de Vergennes, November 12, 1778, in Richard B. Morris, *The Peacemakers: The Great Powers and American Independence* (New York: Harper & Row, 1965), 220.

27. The Count of Floridablanca: Bemis, *DAR*, 55–56 and 75–77; and Morris, *Peacemakers*, 49.

28. "Republic might remain": Light T. Cummins, *Spanish Observers and the American Revolution, 1775–1783* (Baton Rouge: Louisiana State University Press, 1991), 56.

29. "About the state": Cummins, *Spanish*, 106.

30. Juan de Miralles y Trajan's mission and voyage: Cummins, *Spanish*, 115–31.

CHAPTER 10

1. "Constitution": Thomas Burke, remarks on the Articles of Confederation, December 16, 1777, *LDTC* 8; "great": Nathaniel Folsom to Meshech Weare, November 21, 1777, *LDTC* 8.

2. "It appears": Folsom to Weare, November 21, 1777, *LDTC* 8; "number of white": Articles of Confederation, APYLS.

3. "When I reflect": William Henry Drayton, January 14, 1778, in John R. Alden, *The First South* (Baton Rouge: Louisiana State University Press, 1961), 51.

4. "The Disturber": Eliphalet Dyer to William Williams, March 10, 1778, *LDTC* 9; "Every member": Cornelius Harnett to Richard Caswell, March 20, 1778, *LDTC* 9.

5. Burke's argument: Jensen, *Articles*, 185; "I think": Harnett to Caswell, March 20, 1778, *LDTC* 9.

6. "Instructions": Burke, report on the Articles of Confederation, ante December 16, 1777, *LDTC* 8.

7. "Each": Burke, report on the Articles of Confederation, December 18, 1777, *LDTC* 8.

8. "Common stock": Burke to Caswell, March 12, 1778, *LDTC* 9; "justly": Votes and Proceedings of the House of Delegates of the State of Maryland, October 1777, cited in John Henry to Nicholas Thomas, March 2, 1778, *LDTC* 9 n. 2.

9. South Carolina amendments: Jensen, *Articles*, 187; "ascertain": Jensen, *Articles*, 192.

10. "Were": Henry Laurens to Rawlins Lowndes, June 23, 1778, *LDTC* 10; "partial": Maryland delegates to the Maryland Assembly, June 22, 1778, *LDTC* 10.

11. July 4 target date: John R. Alden, *The American Revolution, 1775–1783* (New York: Harper & Brothers, 1954), 174; "May": Samuel Holten, diary entry, July 4, 1776, *LDTC* 10 n. 1.

12. Deliberations of July 9, 1778: Burnett, *CC*; and Jensen, *Articles*, 195; "their delegates": July 10, 1778, *JCC* 11.

13. "I believe": SA to James Warren, July 15, 1778, *LDTC* 10. See also James Lovell to William Whipple, July 14, 1778, *LDTC* 10.

14. "An affair": Nathaniel Scudder to John Hart, July 13, 1778, *LDTC* 10.

15. "There is a point": memorandum of instructions for the Sieur Gérard, March 29, 1778, in Ruth S. Hudson, *The Minister from France: Conrad-Alexandre Gerard, 1729–1790* (Euclid, OH: Lutz, 1994), appendix D, 217–22.

16. "The union": memorandum of instructions for Gérard, March 29, 1778, in Hudson, *Minister*, 217–22.

17. "On these two": Burnett, *CC*, 433.

18. "Agent sécret": Conrad Alexandre Gérard to Comte de Vergennes,, July 16, 1779, in John J. Meng, *Despatches and Instructions of Conrad Alexandre Gérard, 1778–1780: Correspondence of the First French Minister to the United States with the Comte de Vergennes* (Baltimore: Johns Hopkins Press, 1939). See also Gérard to Vergennes, July 25, 1778, in Meng, *Gérard*.

19. "Spain": Gérard to Vergennes, July 25, 1778, in Meng, *Gérard*. The correspondences of Meng were translated with the assistance of Travis Wilds, MA French Literature, PhD candidate, University of California, Berkeley.

20. "Remain quiet": Paul C. Phillips, *The West in the Diplomacy of the American Revolution* (Victoria, Aus.: Leopold Classic Library, 2020), 82; Views of Vergennes and Gérard: Phillips, *West*, 82 and 93; and Bemis, *DAR*, 174–75.

21. "The Congress": Gérard to Vergennes, July 25, 1778, in Meng, *Gérard*. For records on the missions of Gérard and Juan de Miralles y Trajan, see also Phillips, "American Opinions Regarding the West, 1778–1783," *Mississippi Valley Historical Association* 7 (1914): 286–305; and James A. James, "Oliver Pollock and the Free Navigation of the Mississippi River," *Mississippi Valley Historical Review* 19, no. 3 (1932): 331–47.

22. Franklin's instructions: Gérard's dispatch to Vergennes describes the instructions article by article. Gérard to Vergennes, October 20, 1778, in Meng, *Gérard*. The formal instructions, with actual dates and numbers of troops, is contained in *JCC* 12, October 22, 1778.

23. "France would": Gérard to Vergennes, October 20, 1778, in Meng, *Gérard*; quotations below from Gérard, unless otherwise cited, are derived from the same source. For an English language account of Morris's meeting with Gérard, see Phillips, *West*, 220–21.

24. "Advising": Tacitus, *Annals* I.

25. "I sincerely": William Livingston to Henry Laurens, July 17, 1778, cited in Laurens to William Livingston, July 18, 1778, *LDTC* 10, n. 2. Georgia formally ratified on July 24, 1778; see Jensen, *Articles*, 195.

26. "It's": Whipple to Weare, November 24, 1778, *LDTC* 10; "I wish": Whipple to Josiah Bartlett, January 3, 1779, *LDTC* 11; "Maryland": Francis Lightfoot Lee to RHL, December 15, 1778, *LDTC* 11.

27. "Instructions" and "A Declaration": December 15, 1778, cited in Samuel Huntington, "Enclosing Papers Relating to Western Claims by the States," September 10, 1780, editors' note, FO, https://founders.archives.gov/documents/Jefferson/01-03-02-0722. Quotations below, unless otherwise cited, are derived from the same source.

28. "Many evils": Thomas McKean to Thomas Collins, January 8(?), 1779, *LDTC* 11; quotations below from McKean, unless otherwise cited, are derived from the same source.

29. Embargo of 1778: June 8, 1778, *JCC* 11.

30. "By artful": John Mathews to Thomas Bee, August 30, 1778, *LDTC* 10; quotations below from Mathews, unless otherwise cited, are derived from the same source.

31. "The most": Titus Hosmer to Jonathan Trumbull Sr., August 31, 1778, *LDTC* 10. Quotation below from Hosmer is derived from the same source.

32. "It appears": Cyrus Griffin to TJ, October 6, 1778, *LDTC* 11. For the debates on extending the embargo then taking place, see Laurens to Lowndes, October 6, 1778, *LDTC* 11 n. 1. See too Lovell to Francis Dana, October 9, 1778, *LDTC* 11. "Great disgust" was taken by the non-New England states at a seeming preference of Congress in awarding New England shipping permits.

33. "Subjects": Gérard to President of Congress, February 8, 1779, *RDC* 3; "a decisive": Gérard to President of Congress, February 9, 1779, *RDC* 3.

34. "The object": Gérard to President of Congress, February 9, 1779, *RDC* 3.
35. Spanish mediation: Phillips, *West*, 96–98; and Bemis, *DAR*, 77–80, 172–76.
36. The Count of Floridablanca's desire for disarray: Phillips, *West*, 92–94.
37. "Amazing": Vergennes to Gérard, October 26, 1778, in Meng, *Gérard*.
38. "Local considerations": Vergennes to Gérard, October 26, 1778, in Meng, *Gérard*.
39. "Very long": Gérard to Vergennes, January 18, 1779, in Meng, *Gérard*. See also Gérard to Vergennes, January 19, 1779, in Meng, *Gérard*.

CHAPTER 11

1. Excellent accounts of the diplomacies of Conrad Alexandre Gérard and Juan de Miralles y Trajan in America in 1778–79 are Phillips, "American Opinions"; and James, "Oliver Pollock."
2. "That divisions": William Henry Drayton's notes of proceedings, February 15, 1779, *LDTC* 12.
3. "The Court": Drayton's notes of proceedings, February 15, 1779, *LDTC* 12.
4. "Her Allies": Gérard to Vergennes, February 17, 1779, in Meng, *Gérard*; quotations below from Gérard, unless otherwise cited, are derived from the same source.
5. "Spain wished": William Henry Drayton, notes of proceedings, February 15, 1779, *LDTC* 12.
6. "Mr. Richard": Gérard to Vergennes, February 18, 1779, in Meng, *Gérard*. See also Hudson, *Minister*, 133; and Gérard to Vergennes, March 3, 1779, in Meng, *Gérard*.
7. "Committee of five": February 17, 1779, *JCC* 13.
8. "In case": February 23, 1779, *JCC* 13; quotations below, unless otherwise cited, are derived from the same source.
9. "Nova Scotia": SA to Samuel Cooper, April 29, 1779, in *Writings of Samuel Adams*, ed. Harry Alonzo Cushing, 4 vols. (New York: G. P. Putnam's Sons, 1904–08), vol. 4.
10. The Iberville River is now called Bayou Manchac. For the navigation of the lower Mississippi and West Florida, see Daniel H. Usner, *Indians, Settlers, and Slaves in a Frontier Exchange Economy: The Lower Mississippi Valley Before 1783* (Chapel Hill: University of North Carolina Press, 1992), 122.
11. "The free": February 23, 1779, *JCC* 13.
12. "Pro-Gallican party": Morris, *Peacemakers*, 8. See also Gouverneur Morris to Robert Morris, July 22, 1779, *LDTC* 13.
13. Morris on the fisheries: "Proceedings of Congress as to Conditions of Pacification, and Particularly as to the Mississippi and Fisheries," March 22 and March 24, 1779, *RDC* 3.
14. "Lickspittles": James Lovell to Horatio Gates, March 1, 1779, *LDTC* 12.
15. "In short": Lovell to JA, November 1, 1779, *LDTC* 14. Regarding JJ as a "lickspittle," JJ's own biographer, Walter Stahr, concludes that Lovell was likely referring to JJ in this portion of the letter to Gates. See Stahr, *John Jay*, 96.
16. "Timidity": SA to JA, January 15, 1776, *WSA* 3; "variously": SA to James Warren, January 7, 1776, *WSA* 3.

17. The first two articles were settled by March 19. See "Proceedings as to Conditions of Pacification," March 19, 1779, *RDC* 3.
18. "An acknowledgement": "Proceedings as to Conditions of Pacification," March 22, 1779, *RDC* 3.
19. "That the right": "Proceedings as to Conditions of Pacification," March 24, 1779, *RDC* 3.
20. "A wagon load of money": GW to JJ, April 22, 1779, in Stahr, *John Jay*.
21. "The famous": Ira Stoll, *Samuel Adams: A Life* (New York: Free Press, 2008), 9; "the patriarch": Stoll, *Samuel Adams*, 257; "is always": Stoll, *Samuel Adams*, 51.
22. "Cromwell": Mark Puls, *Samuel Adams: Father of the American Revolution* (New York: Palgrave Macmillan, 2006), 195; "resolve": Puls, *Samuel Adams*, 191; "He eats": Stoll, *Samuel Adams*, 133.
23. "The fishing": House of Representatives of Massachusetts to Dennys D. Berdt, January 12, 1768, *WSA* 1.
24. Statistics: Robert Greenhalgh Albion, William A. Baker, and Benjamin W. Labaree, *New England and the Sea* (Mystic, CT: Mystic Seaport Museum, 1994), 27, 29.
25. "However": SA to Thomas McKean, August 29, 1781, *WSA* 4.
26. "Our Happiness": SA to Cooper, April 29, 1779, *WSA* 4.
27. "The fishing banks": SA to McKean, August 29, 1781, *WSA* 4.

CHAPTER 12

1. "Debates": November 20, 1782, *DAJA* 3:65.
2. "M. Samuel": Conrad Alexandre Gérard to Comte de Vergennes, March 10, 1779, in Meng, *Gérard*; "It escaped": Gérard to Vergennes, April 4, 1779, in Meng, *Gérard*.
3. "Can this national": SA to RHL, December 3, 1787, *WSA* 4.
4. "Not to disturb": "Proceedings of Congress as to Conditions of Pacification, and Particularly as to the Mississippi and Fisheries," June 19, 1779, *RDC* 3.
5. "Leave the confederation": Gérard to Vergennes, July 14, 1779, in Meng, *Gérard*.
6. "The debates": Gérard to Vergennes, July 31, 1779, in Meng, *Gérard*.
7. "Jealousy": Nathaniel Peabody to Josiah Bartlett, July 3, 1779, *LDTC* 13; "dangerous": Virginia House of Delegates, December 12, 1778, cited in Virginia delegates to Joseph Reed, February 6, 1779, *LDTC* 12, Note 1; "divisions": JJ to George Clinton, June 1, 1779, *LDCT* 13; "violent": William Floyd to Clinton, January 5, 1779, *LDTC* 11; "the Vermont": Clinton to New York delegates, May 29, 1779, cited in New York delegates to Clinton, June 1, 1779, *LDTC* 13, n. 1; "right": James Lovell to SA, September 29, 1779, *LDTC* 13; "the flames": JJ to Clinton, September 21, 1779, *LDTC* 13.
8. Virginia motion: May 20, 1779, *JCC* 14.
9. "With any": May 20, 1779, *JCC* 14; the Virginia motion proposed in Congress on May 20 had been adopted by the Virginia Assembly on December 18, 1778; "neither": North Carolina delegates to Richard Caswell, May 20, 1779, *LDTC* 12.
10. "I think": William Fleming to TJ, June 22, 1779, *LDTC* 13.

11. "As absolutely": John C. Miller, *Sam Adams: Pioneer in Propaganda* (Stanford: Stanford University Press, 1960), 352.

12. "The Southern": RHL to William Shippen Jr., April 18, 1779, *LDTC* 12.

13. "In this": RHL to Henry Laurens, August 1, 1779, in *The Letters of Richard Henry Lee*, 2 vols., ed. James C. Ballagh (New York: Macmillan, 1912–14), vol. 2. For the nine letters on the Mississippi and fisheries he wrote between June 1779 and March 1780, see the index of vol. 2, "Mississippi, navigation of."

14. "No more": North Carolina delegates to Caswell, April 2, 1779, *LDTC* 12.

15. "I am not": Laurens to Caswell, April 4, 1779, *LDTC* 12.

16. "The capital": Laurens to the North Carolina delegates, April 4, 1779, *LDTC* 12; "conscience": Laurens to the North Carolina delegates, April 8, 1779, *LDTC* 12; "put an end": Laurens to the North Carolina delegates, April 8, 1779, *LDTC* 12, note appended to the letter.

17. "This moment": Nathaniel Peabody to Meshech Weare, August 10, 1779, *LDTC* 13.

18. Fisheries and final instructions: August 14, 1779, *JCC* 14.

19. "That the navigation": "Proceedings of Congress as to Conditions of Pacification," March 22 and 24, 1779, *RDC* 3.

20. For records of peace negotiations related to the Mississippi navigation, see Thomas Burke, draft report, August 5(?), 1779, *LDTC* 13; North Carolina delegates to Caswell, August 5, 1779, *LDTC* 13; Laurens, note on negotiating instructions, August (?), 1779, *LDTC* 13; Laurens, notes on a treaty with Spain, September 9–17, 1779, *LDTC* 13; John Fell, diary entry, September 10–11, 1779, *LDTC* 13; Lovell to JA, September 14, 1779, *LDTC* 13; Lovell to Arthur Lee, September 17, 1779, *LDTC* 13; and Gérard to Vergennes, September 10, 1779, in Meng, *Gérard*.

21. Gerry and Huntington: September 10 and 17, 1779, *JCC* 15. "The Congress has": Juan de Miralles y Trajan to Jose de Galvez, Minister of the Indies, September 24, 1779, cited in Laurens, notes on a treaty with Spain, September 9–17, 1779, *LDTC* 13, n. 2. See also Gérard to Vergennes, September 10, 1779, and Gérard's entry for September 17, in Meng, *Gérard*.

22. "Great debates": Fell, diary entry, September 26, 1779, *LDTC* 13; "accommodation scheme": Lovell to JA, September 27, 1779, *LDTC* 13; "the parliamentary": Lovell to JA, September 27, 1779, *LDTC* 13. For the appointments of Adams and Jay, see also September 25–27, 1779, *JCC* 15; Laurens, notes of debates, September 25–27, 1779, *LDTC* 13; and Fell, diary entry, September 27, 1779, *LDTC* 13.

23. "The choice": Gérard to Vergennes, September 27, 1779, in Morris, *Peacemakers*, 13.

24. "The way": Lovell to JA, November 1, 1779, *LDTC* 14.

25. "Well pleased": RHL to JA, October 7, 1779, *LRHL* 2.

CHAPTER 13

1. "Postponing": William Churchill Houston to Robert Morris, March 6, 1780, *LDTC* 14; "I contemplate": Philip Schuyler to Jeremiah Wadsworth, July 16, 1780, *LDTC* 15.

Notes to Chapter 13   395

2. "Produced much uneasiness": October 30, 1779, *JCC* 15; "The Virginians and our Southern friends": Houston to R. Morris, October 2, 1779, *LDTC* 14.

3. "Pre-emption": Gouverneur Morris to the Public, September 4(?) 1779, *LDTC* 13; quotations below by Morris, unless otherwise cited, are derived from the same source.

4. "Whereas": October 30, 1779, *JCC* 15; Circular letter: Samuel Huntington to the States, October 30, 1779, *LDTC* 14.

5. "Land mongers": JM to Joseph Jones, October 17, 1780, in *The Papers of James Madison*, ed. William T. Hutchinson, William M. E. Rachal, and Robert Allen Rutland, 17 vols. (Chicago and London: University of Chicago Press, 1962–1991), vol. 2. See Onuf, *Origins*, 79–83; and Jensen, *Articles*, 211–18, for detailed treatments of the western land and land companies in Congress.

6. "The cursed claim": John Hanson to Charles Carroll of Carrollton, October 30, 1780, *LDTC* 16; "to recede": October 13, 1779, *JCC* 15. See also Henry Laurens to RHL, October 12, 1779, *LDTC* 14.

7. "Without": RHL to Laurens, September 19, 1779, *LRHL* 2; "The two Legs": Laurens to RHL, October 12, 1779, *LDTC* 14. The motion was made on October 12; see October 12, 1779, *JCC* 15.

8. "I told": Laurens to RHL, October 12, 1779, *LDTC* 14; "The current": Conrad Alexandre Gérard to Comte de Vergennes, October 20, 1778, in Meng, *Gérard*. See also Theodore Roosevelt, *American Statesmen: Gouverneur Morris* (Boston and New York: Houghton Mifflin—Riverside Press Cambridge, 1916), 363. See Melanie Miller, *An Incautious Man: The Life of Gouverneur Morris*, Lives of the Founders (Wilmington, DE: Intercollegiate Studies Institute, 2008), 119 and 159–61, for further documentation of Morris's well-known biases towards Northern interests and Northern expansion.

9. "Provided": Preamble and Resolution of the Virginia Convention, May 15, 1776, APYLS, https://avalon.law.yale.edu/18th_century/const02.asp; "Remonstrance": Remonstrance of the General Assembly of Virginia to the Delegates of the United American States in Congress Assembled, December 10, 1779, ConSource, https://www.consource.org/document/the-remonstrance-of-the-general-assembly-of-virginia-to-the-delegates-of-the-united-american-states-in-congress-assembled-1779-12-10/.

10. "No State": Articles of Confederation, APYLS; "When": Remonstrance, December 10, 1779, ConSource. Quotations below from the Remonstrance, unless otherwise cited, are derived from the same source

11. "An express stipulation": Resolution Instructing Delegates in Congress, in Treaty with Spain to stipulate for Free Commerce of Mississippi, October 22, 1779, in William Waller Hening, *Statutes at Large: Being a Collection of All the Laws of Virginia from the First Session of the Legislature, in the Year 1619*, transcr. Freddie L. Spradlin (Torrance, Calif.: Freddie L. Spradlin, 2009), 10:537, http://vagenweb.org/hening/vol10-25.htm.

12. "Partial": Thomas Burke to the North Carolina Assembly, October 25(?) 1779, *LDTC* 14.

13. "Dangerous": Burke to the North Carolina Assembly, October 25, 1779, *LDTC* 14, n. 19. In this letter Burke discusses New England and the fisheries. Note 19 contains the resolution of the North Carolina assembly of October 28, 1779, and Burke's written appeal to the assembly of October 31, along with the state's reversal on a partial confederation. Quotations below by Burke, unless otherwise cited, are derived from the same source.

14. "If Britain": James Duane to GW, May 4, 1780, *LDTC* 15.

15. Statistics on inflation: Ferling, *AAM*, 399; "The want": Ezekiel Cornell to William Greene, December 10, 1780, *LDTC* 16.

16. "A new bond of union": Burnett, *CC*, 81; "speculating miscreants": William Whipple, in Burnett, *CC*, 408; "A spirit of money-making": Ferling, *AAM*, 415.

17. "Our Confederation": John Sullivan to Meshech Weare, October 2, 1780, *LDTC* 16; "We have not": Chernow, *Washington*, 368; "Certain": Chernow, *Washington*, 369.

18. "The fundamental": AH to Duane, September 3, 1780, FO, https://founders.archives.gov/documents/Hamilton/01-02-02-0838.

19. Expedition to South Carolina: Ward, *WOTR*, 696.

20. "Conquest": JM to TJ, June 6, 1780, *PJM* 2; "I see": John Mathews to Robert R. Livingston, April 24, 1780, *LDTC* 15; "I fear": Sullivan to GW, November 12, 1780, *LDTC* 16.

21. "I suppose": Cornell to Nathanael Greene, July 29, 1278, *LDTC* 15; "the body": Laurens to RHL, August 1, 1780, *LDTC* 15; "will superadd": Schuyler to Livingston, April 23, 1780, *LDTC* 15.

22. "I may condole": Livingston to Duane, May 2, 1780, cited in Livingston to Marquis de Barbé-Marbois, May 3, 1780, *LDTC* 15, n. 3.

23. "The fate": Cornell to W. Greene, May 30, 1780, *LDTC* 15; "upon the principles": Cornell to W. Greene, June 18, 1780, *LDTC* 15.

24. "The different": Cornell to W. Greene, June 18, 1780, *LDTC* 15; "The necessity": Cornell to W. Greene, August 1, 1780, *LDTC* 15.

25. "I have": Mathews to Livingston, April 24, 1780, *LDTC* 15; "To answer": Samuel Holten to Joseph Palmer, May 5, 1780, *LDTC* 15; "I fear": Cornell to N. Greene, September 19, 1780, *LDTC* 16.

26. "You will": John Collins to N. Greene, May 2, 1780, *LDTC* 15.

27. "A federal": Duane to GW, May 4, 1780, *LDTC* 15.

28. "The present": Jones to TJ, June 30, 1780, *LDTC* 15.

CHAPTER 14

1. Expédition Particulière: Ferling, *AAM*, 394 and 397.

2. "Golden opportunity": James Duane to Philip Schuyler, May 21, 1780, *LDTC* 15. Quotations below by Duane, unless otherwise cited, are derived from the same source.

3. "I have": Robert Livingston to Schuyler, May 21, 1780, *LDTC* 15.

4. "Confidence": R. Livingston to Schuyler, May 26, 1780, *LDTC* 15.

Notes to Chapter 14

5. "Were an angel": John Mathews to Horatio Gates, March 14, 1780, *LDTC* 14. Quotations below by Mathews, unless otherwise cited, are derived from the same source.
6. Statistics on Charlestown: Ferling, *AAM*, 427; "a bitter": William Churchill Houston to William Livingston, June 5, 1780, *LDTC* 15; "every man": Henry Laurens to RHL, August 1, 1780, *LDTC* 15.
7. "Only last night": James Lovell to AA, June 13, 1780, *LDTC* 15.
8. "The Independence": Nathanael Greene to TJ, November 20, 1780, *PJM* 2.
9. "There was": Report on conference with the Count of Floridablanca, May 11, 1780, contained in JJ to president of Congress, May 26, 1780, *RDC* 3. Jay's dispatch was read on August 14, 1780. Quotations below by Jay, unless otherwise cited, are derived from the same source. See, too, August 14, 1780, *JCC* 17.
10. "There is": John Armstrong Sr. to Joseph Reed, August 30, 1780, *LDTC* 15; Virginia resolution introduced in Congress: August 22, 1780, *JCC* 17. See also Ezekiel Cornell to William Greene, August 22, 1780, *LDTC* 15, n. 4. This note states that the resolution read was dated Nov. 5. 1779. This is explained by the fact that the Virginia archives show two entries for the resolution, one October 22, 1780, and also November 5, 1780.
11. "An Act to Facilitate": February 19, 1780, Documents of the Senate of the State of New York 3, https://www.google.com/books/edition/Documents_of_the _Senate_of_the_State_of/TKclAQAAIAAJ?hl=en&gbpv=0; committee of June 26: June 26, 1780, *JCC* 17. See also a detailed "Editorial Note" on the western lands and the Confederation preceding Motion Regarding the Western Lands, September 6, 1780, *PJM* 2.
12. "Adhere": October 4, 1780, *JCC* 18.
13. "Could not": October 17, 1780, *JCC* 18. Quotations below, unless otherwise cited, are derived from the same source.
14. "This court": William Carmichael to the Committee of Foreign Affairs, May 28, 1780, *RDC* 3; "sole": Carmichael to Committee of Foreign Affairs, August 22, 1780, *RDC* 4. Carmichael was Jay's secretary.
15. "Charters": "Notes on Observations of Barbé-Marbois on Western Boundary of the United States," October 6–16, 1780, *PJM* 2.
16. "It would be": January 31, 1780, *JCC* 16; "settlement": "Notes on Observations of Barbé-Marbois," October 6–16, 1780, *PJM* 2. See also Phillips, *West*, 182–84.
17. Mediation of Catherine the Great: Morris, *Peacemakers*, 158–63; Bemis, *DAR*, 179–81; and Jonathan R. Dull, *A Diplomatic History of the American Revolution* (New Haven and London: Yale University Press, 1985), 130–31. See, too, Comte de Vergennes to Ambassador Luzerne, March 9, 1781, in Mary A. Giunta, J. Dane Hartgrove, and Mary-Jane M. Dowd, eds., *The Emerging Nation: A Documentary History of the Foreign Relations of the United States Under the Articles of Confederation, 1780–1789*, 3 vols. (Washington, D.C.: National Historical Publications and Records Commission, 1996), 1.

18. Uti possedetis and partition: Morris, *Peacemakers*, 94, 106, 149, 169, 179; Vergennes: Morris, *Peacemakers*, 171, 179–80; Vergennes and Southern states: Morris, *Peacemakers*, 171, 180–81.
19. Georgia motion: November 18, 1780, *JCC* 18.
20. "Whereas a powerful": November 18, 1780, *JCC* 18.
21. Madison and Bland on Georgia motion: JM to Joseph Jones, November 25, 1780, *PJM* 2; and JM to Jones, December 5, 1780, *PJM* 2.
22. "Artifices": JM to Jones, November 25, 1780, *PJM* 2.
23. "The navigation": Jones to Theodorick Bland, January 2, 1781, in *The Bland Papers*, https://archive.org/stream/blandpapersbein00campgoog/blandpapersbein00 campgoog_djvu.txt.
24. "The Eastern": JM to Jones, November 25, 1780, *PJM* 2.
25. "Both my": JM to Jones, December 5, 1780, *PJM* 2.
26. "Resolved": motion on instructions to JJ, December 8, 1780, *JCC* 18.
27. "Without": Virginia delegates in Congress to TJ, December 12, 1780, *PJM* 2.

CHAPTER 15

1. Uti possedetis: Morris, *Peacemakers*, 94, 106, 149, 169, 179; and, especially for the risk of American loss of Georgia, South Carolina, and perhaps North Carolina at the peace tables, John E. Ferling, *Winning Independence: The Decisive Years of the Revolutionary War, 1778–1781* (New York: Bloomsbury, 2021), xxii and 385. Historians have argued that, had George III not been almost pathologically opposed to hearing discussion of any independence whosoever for any of the American colonies, some dismemberment of the thirteen may well have been the outcome of a successful Austro-Russian joint mediation. See Bemis, *DAR*, 184; and Morris, *Peacemakers*, 168.
2. Madison's letter to Jefferson: Virginia delegates in Congress to TJ, December 13, 1781, and n. 3, *PJM* 2; Arnold's raid: Selby, *Revolution*, 221–23; Dumas Malone, *Jefferson and His Time*, 6 vols. (Boston: Little, Brown, 1948–1970), 1:336–38; and Jon Meacham, *Thomas Jefferson: The Art of Power* (New York: Random House, 2012), 133–35.
3. "The happiness": "Journal of the House of Delegates of the Commonwealth of Virginia," January 2, 1781, Internet Archive, https://archive.org/details/journalof houseof17771780virg/page/n773/mode/2up. Quotations from the act below, unless otherwise cited, are derived from the same source.
4. "It is with": William Floyd to Unknown, January 30, 1781, *LDTC* 16. For the acts presented to Congress, see Virginia delegates in Congress to Thomas Jefferson, January 30, 1781, *PJM* 2.
5. "The state": James Varnum to William Greene, January 29, 1781, *LDTC* 16; "I presume": Joseph Jones to GW, February 21, 1781, *LDTC* 16. The referenced letter from Duane is James Duane to GW, January 29, 1781, *LDTC* 16.
6. "A free": February 15, 1781, *JCC* 19. The votes are tallied in this entry.
7. "Feu de joye" and other quotations and details of the celebrations: Burnett, *CC*, 500–501.
8. "Great": Thomas Rodney, diary entry, March 1, 1781, *LDTC* 17; "accompanied": Theodorick Bland to RHL, March 5, 1781, *LDTC* 17; "We are": Samuel

Huntington to the States, March 2, 1781, *LDTC* 17; "evil": John Mathews to William Livingston, March 6, 1781, *LDTC* 17.

9. Morris and financial reform: Richard B. Morris, *The Forging of the Union, 1781–1789* (New York: Harper & Row, 1987), 40.

10. "We have": David Jameson to JM, April 7, 1781, FO, https://founders.archives.gov/documents/Madison/01-03-02-0027.

11. "And when": Jameson to JM, August 15, 1781, FO, https://founders.archives.gov/documents/Madison/01-03-02-0113.

12. "Do Congress": Edmund Pendleton to JM, April 7, 1781, FO, https://founders.archives.gov/?q=%22southern%20war%22%20pendleton%20madison&s=1111311111&sa=&r=2&sr=; "against the": Pendleton to JM, March 26, 1781, FO, https://founders.archives.gov/?q=Project%3A%22Madison%20Papers%22&s=1511311111&sa=pendleton&r=18. See other letters cited below in these endnotes as well as David Ross to Virginia delegates, May 18, 1781, *PJM* 2; Thomas Nelson to Virginia delegates, July 26, 1781, *PJM* 2; and Jameson to JM, August 10, 1781, *PJM* 2. Madison's cousin, Rev. James Madison, also wrote him warning that many Virginians were on the brink of defection. See Rev. James Madison to JM, March 9, 1781, *PJM* 3. Additionally, Virginia dispatched a leading statesman, Benjamin Harrison, from Richmond to Philadelphia to argue the case that Congress act immediately to relieve "the Southern states." See Virginia delegates to TJ, February 20, 1781, *LDTC* 16.

13. "Our people": Pendleton to JM, May 28, 1781, FO, https://founders.archives.gov/documents/Madison/01-03-02-0067.

14. "Of such": Pendleton to JM, October 8, 1781, FO, https://founders.archives.gov/documents/Madison/01-03-02-0136.

15. "Attachment": George Mason to Virginia delegates, April 3, 1781, *PJM* 3; "fatal": Jameson to JM, August 15, 1781, FO, https://founders.archives.gov/documents/Madison/01-03-02-0113; "the unhappy": RHL to Virginia delegates, June 12, 1781, https://founders.archives.gov/documents/Jefferson/01-06-02-0090.

16. "Two": Rodney, diary entry, April 18, 1781, *LDTC* 17.

17. "Virga.": Jones to GW, May 31, 1781, *LDTC* 17; "may shake": Jones to GW, May 16, 1781, *LDTC* 17.

18. "Inadequate": Jones, undated letter, cited in JM to TJ, April 12, 1781, *LDTC* 17, n. 1; "totally": Bland to St. George Tucker, May 11, 1781, *LDTC* 17; "Union Without Power": Rakove, *Beginnings*, 333.

19. "There are": Varnum to W. Greene, April 2, 1781, *LDTC* 17.

20. "May be": Varnum to W. Greene, April 2, 1781, *LDTC* 17.

21. "Dictatorial": Mathews to Nathanael Greene, May 20, 1781, *LDTC* 17. Quotations below by Mathews, unless otherwise cited, are derived from the same source.

22. "It is": Proposed Amendment of Articles of Confederation, March 12, 1781, FO, https://founders.archives.gov/documents/Madison/01-03-02-0007.

23. "Danger": Jones, undated letter, cited in JM to TJ, April 12, 1781, *LDTC* 17, n. 1. On this letter Jones wrote "Copy letter to Pendleton, Wythe, Jefferson."

24. "Coercive": JM to TJ, April 12, 1781, *LDTC* 17.

25. "Is Congress": Bland's queries, cited in Bland to Tucker, May 11, 1781, *LDTC* 17, n. 3.

26. Statistics and movements of troops and navies: Ferling, *AAM*, 524–27; Clifford J. Rogers, Ty Seidule, and Samuel J. Watson, eds., *The West Point History of the American Revolution* (New York: Simon & Schuster, 2017), 180–86; Chernow, *Washington*, 406–8; and Ward, *WOTR* 2:881–83.

27. For the timing of Washington's discovery of Cornwallis's fortification of Yorktown, see Ferling, *AAM*, 526.

28. Battle of the Virginia Capes and Battle of Yorktown: Ferling, *AAM*, 528–40; and Chernow, *Washington*, 408–10.

29. "That a reduction": GW to Thomas McKean, October 19, 1781, FO, https://founders.archives.gov/?q=%20Author:%22Washington,%20George%22%201781%20Dates-From:1781-10-18&s=1111311111&r=10&sr=; "laughing": Ferling, *AAM*, 539; "America": Ferling, *AAM*, 539; "this great event": Connecticut delegates to Jonathan Trumbull Sr., October 25, 1781, *LDTC* 18; "the glorious" and "Would to God": Elias Boudinot to Elisha Boudinot, October 23, 1781, *LDTC* 18; "the power": McKean to William Heath, November 3, 1781, *LDTC* 18; "a day": Elias Boudinot to Lewis Pintard, October 23, 1781, *LDTC* 18.

30. "In the evening" and "prepare": Connecticut delegates to Trumbull, October 25, 1781, *LDTC* 18. See Ferling, *AAM*, 540–41, for details of October 24.

CHAPTER 16

1. "Involve": Elias Boudinot to William Livingston, August 25, 1781, *LDTC* 17. For concerns over civil war in Vermont, see also Samuel Livermore to Meshech Weare, August 14, 1781, *LDTC* 17; James Duane to Robert R. Livingston, August 11, 1781, *LDTC* 17; and Onuf, *Origins*, 113–15. A committee on Vermont was established on July 9. The Congress passed a resolution on August 7. The most concise single primary document tracing the chronology of the Vermont controversy from 1779 until early August of 1781 is "New York Delegates' Memorial," August 3, 1781, *LDTC* 17.

2. "The thorny": JM to Edmund Pendleton, February 7, 1782, *LDTC* 18; "Labyrinths": JM to Joseph Jones, September 19, 1780, *LDTC* 16.

3. The unconstitutionality of admitting Vermont: Ezra L'Hommedieu to George Clinton, September 8, 1781, *LDTC* 18.

4. "Should be": "Resolution of the General Court of Massachusetts," March 8, 1781, Making of America, https://quod.lib.umich.edu/m/moa/AJA2015.0001.001/211?rgn=main;view=image; "Balance of power": South Carolina delegates to John Rutledge, January 27, 1782, cited in "Vermont Report," January 28, 1782, *LDTC* 18, n. 1; "With the admission": Arthur Lee to SA, April 21, 1782, cited in Onuf, *Origins*, 121. For the North-South dynamics of the Vermont controversy, see also L'Hommedieu to Clinton, September 8, 1781, *LDTC* 18.

5. "In case of conflict": Onuf, *Origins*, 115.

6. Strategic considerations of New Yorkers in the Vermont controversy: Onuf, *Origins*, 117–18.

7. "The Danger": "Abstracts from the Memoirs of the Cardinal de Retz," December 24, 1759, in *Commonplace Book*, *PJM* 1.

8. On October 2, 1781, a committee on the western land cessions, organized on January 31, reported. The Congress then formed a new committee, composed of Elias Boudinot of New Jersey, James Mitchell Varnum of Rhode Island, Daniel of St. Thomas Jenifer of Maryland, Thomas Smith of Pennsylvania, and Samuel Livermore of New Hampshire, to replace it. The best single source for tracking these committees and the controversies over the western lands in 1781 is *PJM*. Because Madison was so central in these affairs, the editors in editorial notes and footnotes provide extraordinary detail. For the events of October 2, see Virginia delegates to Thomas Nelson, October 9, 1781, *PJM* 3, and notes. See also Jensen, *Articles*, 206–10; Onuf, *Origins*, 75–102; and Irving Brant, *James Madison:*, vol. 2, *The Nationalist, 1780–1787* (Indianapolis and New York: Bobbs-Merrill, 1948), 89–103.

9. For Madison's fears of disunion in October and November of 1781, see especially JM to Pendleton, October 30, 1781, *PJM* 3, and JM to TJ, November 18, 1781, *PJM* 3.

10. "Territorial": "Protest of Virginia Delegates," October 10, 1781, *PJM* 3; "Congress": "Motion of Virginia Delegates on the Western Lands," October 16, 1781, *PJM* 3.

11. "Hostile machinations," "calumnies," "aggression," and "injury": The citations are, respectively, from JM to TJ, November 18, 1781, *PJM* 3; Virginia delegates to Nelson, October 16, 1781, *PJM* 3, and JM to Pendleton, October 30, 1781, *PJM* 3; "fervent": JM to Pendleton, October 30, 1781, *PJM* 3; Paine: Thomas Paine, *Public Good*, 1780, *PJM* 3:14n17; Wharton: Thomas Wharton, *Plain Facts*, 1781, *PJM* 3:47n2.

12. "Disgust": Edmund Randolph to Nelson, November 7, 1781, *LDTC* 18.

13. "Altogether": Papers of the Continental Congress, November 3, 1781. The editors of the *PJM* cite this document, *PJM* 3:304–6n1. Debate was delayed on the committee's report until April 18, 1782, and the matter not finally put to rest until March 1, 1784.

14. "Our country" and "Wrathful": Virginia delegates to Nelson, October 23, 1781, *PJM* 3; "Symptoms": JM to Pendleton, October 30, 1781, *PJM* 3; "What course": JM to Pendleton, November 13, 1781, *PJM* 3; "The late capture": Randolph to Nelson, November 7, 1781, *LDTC* 18.

15. "In vain": JM to TJ, November 18, 1781, *PJM* 3. Quotations below by JM, unless otherwise cited, are derived from the same source.

16. Mississippi-Fisheries Compromise: See chapters 8 and 11 of this book for full details of the compromise and its unraveling.

17. "Because": Comte de Vergennes to Ambassador Luzerne, March 9, 1781, *EN* 1; "Too ardent": Vergennes to Luzerne, April 19, 1781, *EN* 1.

18. "Prolonging": Luzerne to Vergennes, June 11, 1781, *EN* 1. See also *Bemis*, *DAR*, 184–86; Thomas Fleming, *Perils of Peace: America's Struggle for Survival after*

Yorktown (New York: Smithsonian Books, 2007), 74–77; Dull, *Diplomatic History*, 118–20; and Ferling, *AAM*, 472–74.

19. "Leave you": Luzerne to Vergennes, June 11, 1781, *EN* 1.

20. "Concurrence": June 6, 1781, *JCC* 20.

21. These attitudes are described in Luzerne to Vergennes, June 23, 1781, *EN* 1.

22. "Claims": Notes on debates, December 30, 1782, *PJM* 5. On this day the Congress reviewed in detail the debates and decisions from June of 1781. Madison took notes of what was recounted. The best sources for tracing the history of the peace instructions and commission are June 6–15, 1781, *JCC* 20; and June 6–15, 1781, *PJM* 3.

23. Madison and sectional justice on fisheries and boundary: Motion on instruction on Treaty of Commerce, June 29, 1781, *PJM* 3, editorial note and n. 3. JM and boundary: June 6, 7, and 8, 1781, *JCC* 20.

24. Madison's fight to reinstate the Mississippi boundary as ultimatum: see five separate sets of notes on the peace instructions, May 28, 1781, and June 6, 7, 8, and 9–15, 1781, *PJM* 3.

25. "Additional instruction": June 29, 1781, *JCC* 20; "Use their": July 12, 1781, *JCC* 20. The second motion passed on July 12, 1781. See this date in *JCC* 20 and *PJM* 3 and notes.

26. "Could only": Peterson, *Thomas Jefferson*, 242.

27. "If you can": Randolph to TJ, October 9, 1781, *LDTC* 18.

28. "Our right": TJ to JM, February 14, 1783, *PJM* 6.

CHAPTER 17

1. "Le Washington": November 30, 1782, *DAJA* 2. See also November 10, 1782, and November 12, 1782, *DAJA* 2.

2. "Hard": JJ to Robert Livingston, January 1, 1775, *The Correspondence and Public Papers of John Jay*, ed. Henry Phelps Johnston, 4 vols. (New York: G. P. Putnam's Sons, 1890), vol. 1; "these states": JJ to GW, April 21, 1779, *PJJ* 1.

3. "Lickspittles": James Lovell to Horatio Gates, March 1, 1779, *LDTC* 13.

4. "Variety": JJ to Catherine W. Livingston, July 20, 1783, *PJJ* 2; "ruin": JJ to president of Congress, March 3, 1780, *RDC* 3.

5. "Quitted": JJ to president of Congress, March 3, 1780, *RDC* 3.

6. "Painful": JJ to president of Congress, November 6, 1780, *RDC* 4; King Charles and palaces: Jon Kukla, *A Wilderness So Immense: The Louisiana Purchase and the Destiny of America* (New York: Alfred A. Knopf, 2003), 24–25 and 65–67. Kukla's work recounts the history of the Louisiana Purchase, linking this history to the pursuit of the free navigation of the Mississippi beginning in the 1780s.

7. "The sincerity": Count of Floridablanca to JJ, February 24, 1780, *RDC* 3; "treated": William Carmichael to JJ, February 26, 1780, in *John Jay: Unpublished Papers*, ed. Richard B. Morris, 2 vols. (New York: Harper & Row, 1975–80), vol. 1.

8. Financial statistics: "The First Phase of the Spanish Mission," *PJJ* 1:715–18, editorial note. Also see Morris, *Peacemakers*, chap. 11, "Jacob's Bargain." *Peacemakers*

provides a detailed history of the diplomacy of the American Revolution. See also Fleming, *Perils*; and Phillips, *West*.

9. "Indemnify": Questions from Floridablanca, March 9, 1780, contained in JJ to president of Congress, May 26, 1780, *RDC* 3; "four good": Floridablanca to JJ, June 7, 1780, in JJ to president of Congress, November 6, 1780, *RDC* 4.

10. "The war": JJ to Floridablanca, June 9, 1780, contained in JJ to president of Congress, November 6, 1780, *RDC* 4.

11. Floridablanca and finance: Aranjuez, May 11, 1780, in JJ to president of Congress, May 26, 1780, *RDC* 3; "humiliating": JJ to Robert Livingston, May 23, 1780, *JJUP* 1.

12. "Sir:": JJ to Comte de Vergennes, September 22, 1780, *RDC* 4.

13. Statistics on silver: Kukla, *Wilderness*, 33.

14. Population of Louisiana: Usner, *Indians*, 115, table 3. This table reveals that the total population of the Lower Mississippi Valley in 1785 was 30,471.

15. Conrad Alexandre Gérard's meeting with Floridablanca: JJ to the president of Congress, November 6, 1780, *RDC* 4. JJ communicates that dissension among Americans about the Mississippi navigation, well-known in Spain, was weakening his negotiating hand. See also Hudson, *Minister*; and Meng, *Gérard*.

16. "The spies": JJ to Francis Dana, August 19, 1780, *JJUP* 2. For covert British agents, see Morris, *Peacemakers*, 56–64.

17. Floridablanca's plan: Morris, *Peacemakers*, 56–64.

18. "Expectation": JJ to president of Congress, November 6, 1780, recounting events of early September 1780, *RDC* 4.

19. "Violent": JJ to president of Congress, November 6, 1780, *RDC* 4.

20. "The power": JJ to JA, June 4, 1780, *PJJ* 1.

21. "Sole obstacle": Carmichael to Committee of Foreign Affairs, August 22, 1780, *RDC* 4; "the principal": JJ to Samuel Huntington, November 6, 1780, *PJJ* 1; last phase of JJ's mission in Spain: *JJUP* 2; and *RDC* 4 and 5, especially JJ to Robert Livingston, April 28, 1782, *RDC* 5.

22. "I do not recollect": JJ to president of Congress, October 3, 1781, *RDC* 4.

23. "Undertake": Morris, *Peacemakers*, 215. JJ received the Congress's June 1781 orders on a peace treaty in September. For JJ in Spain during these months, see Morris, *Peacemakers*, 245–48.

24. "Service of my": JJ to Thomas McKean, September 20, 1781, *PJJ* 2. Quotations below by JJ, unless otherwise cited, are derived from the same source.

CHAPTER 18

1. "Duty": JJ to BF, July 17, 1780, in *The Papers of Benjamin Franklin*, ed. Leonard W. Labaree et al., 42 vols. (New Haven and London: Yale University Press, 1959–2017), vol. 33; "faithful": JJ to BF, March 29, 1781, *PJJ* 2. Both letters reveal JJ's attitudes on the alliance.

2. "A constitutional": Morris, *Peacemakers*, 271; North and South congresses: Morris, *Peacemakers*, 271. For conference of BF, JJ, and Vergennes at Versailles, see JJ to president of Congress, June 25, 1782, *RDC* 5.

3. Adams at the Hague: McCullough, *John Adams*, 271.

4. JJ's illness and the first month of negotiations: JJ to Robert Livingston, August 13, 1782, *PJJ* 2; and JJ to Comte de Montmorin, June 26–July 19, 1782, *PJJ* 2.

5. Advantages of a separate peace: Morris, *Peacemakers*, 261, 273, 292, 349.

6. "The thing": BF to JJ, January 19, 1782, *PJJ* 2:138.

7. Earl of Shelburne: Morris, *Peacemakers*, 258–60.

8. "A few": Morris, *Peacemakers*, 287; see also Brands, *First American*, 617.

9. "A curious": Morris, *Peacemakers*, 290; "be open": Morris, *Peacemakers*, 290. Livingston wrote to Franklin on January 7, 1782. The other instruction is dated January 22.

10. "All the New": Livingston to BF, January 7, 1782, *PBF* 36.

11. "The Northern": Thomas Cushing to BF, October 26, 1782, *PBF* 35. More letters came to Franklin's hand with the same emphasis on cod and haddock as crucial not only to the health of the New England economy but also to the health of the American Union. See Samuel Cooper to BF, October 27, 1782, *PBF* 35. For more background on the fisheries and New England sentiments, see also Ambassador Luzerne to Comte de Vergennes, January 5, 1782, *EN* 1; Luzerne to Vergennes, January 29, 1782, *EM* 1; and Marquis de Barbé-Marbois to Vergennes, March 13, 1782, *EM* 1. Some New Englanders were declaring, "No peace without the fisheries." See Barbé-Marbois to Vergennes, March 13, 1782, *EM* 1.

12. Maps and boundary lines: *PJJ* 2:271, 382–84, editorial notes.

13. The Count of Aranda kept a journal of negotiations: Boundary Discussions Between Jay and Aranda, August 3–30, 1782, First Session, August 3, 1782, *PJJ* 2.

14. "Very cautious": Morris, *Peacemakers*, 307; Semi-independence similar to Ireland: Fleming, *Perils*, 216.

15. JJ and Vergennes on independence: Morris, *Peacemakers*, 307.

16. JJ's suspicions: One historian more than any other, Richard B. Morris, conducted deep research to discover the extent to which JJ's suspicions about France's intentions in negotiations were accurate. In *The Peacemakers: The Great Powers and American Independence*, Morris marshals evidence that strongly supports most of JJ's foreboding conclusions. See Morris, *Peacemakers*, 309, 326–28. See also *PJJ* 2:333–36, editorial note.

17. Passy discussion and pipe shattering: Morris, *Peacemakers*, 309–10; and Stahr, *John Jay*, 153.

18. "No right": "Suggestion Concerning the Manner of Determining and Discussing Boundaries between Spain and the United States from the Banks of the Ohio Toward the Mississippi," September 6, 1782, *PJJ* 2.

19. "Underhand bargain": Benjamin Vaughan to Shelburne, September 11, 1782, *PJJ* 2.

20. Barbé-Marbois letter: Barbé-Marbois to Vergennes, March 13, 1782, *EN* 1. For Jay's theory of Joseph Matthias Gérard de Rayneval's mission to Shelburne, see also Richard Oswald to Shelburne, September 11, 1782, *PJJ* 2; Morris, *Peacemakers*, 333–34; and JJ to Livingston, November 17, 1782, *RDC* 4. For Barbé-Marbois's letter, see also notes on debates, December 24, 1782, *PJM* 5, n. 2.

21. "There is a tide": JJ to Chevalier de Bourgoing, September 26, 1782, *PJJ* 2.

Notes to Chapter 19   405

22. "Free": British-American Diplomacy Preliminary Articles of Peace, November 30, 1782, APYLS, https://avalon.law.yale.edu/18th_century/prel1782.asp. The secret article is missing from this record. Quotations below, unless otherwise cited, are derived from the same source.

23. Secret article: Preliminary Articles: Second Draft, November 4–7, 1782, *PJJ* 2.

24. "What are": Oswald to Thomas Townshend, October 2, 1782, *PJJ* 2. Oswald states that he is recounting JJ's words verbatim.

25. "Dr. Franklin": November 20, 1782, *DAJA* 3. Quotations below by Adams, unless otherwise cited, are derived from the same source.

26. "The Fisheries": October 20, 1782, *DAJA* 3. Adams is citing Franklin in his diary.

27. Adams on fishery: Morris, *Peacemakers*, 373–74.

28. Henry Laurens and clause on enslaved persons: Fleming, *Perils*, 236–37.

29. "The Thirteen": Morris, *Peacemakers*, 382.

CHAPTER 19

1. "Congratulations": Theodorick Bland to St. George Tucker, March 12, 1783, *LDTC* 20; "performed": Stephen Higginson to SA, June 10, 1783, *LDTC* 20; "opened a new": Elias Boudinot to GW, March 17, 1783, *LDTC* 29; "exceeded": AH to George Clinton, June 1, 1783, *LDTC* 20; "the New England": AH to JJ, July 25, 1783, *LDTC* 20. For Congress's receipt of the preliminary articles, see JM, notes on debates, March 12–15, *PJM* 6. They were not fully laid out in the *JCC* until April 15, 1783, the day they were ratified.

2. "Separate": JM, notes on debates, March 12–15, *PJM* 6; "great powers": JM, notes on debates, March 12–15, *PJM* 6. Italics are original. For French reactions to Anglo-American preliminary treaty, see also Morris, *Peacemakers*, 383–84.

3. "The most": JM, notes on debates, March 12–15, *PJM* 6.

4. "In this business": JM to Edmund Randolph, March 18, 1783, *PJM* 6. Madison's letter is written in cypher with some uncertainty as to whether he is referring generally to the ministers' separate negotiations with the British or specifically to the secret article. I conclude that he is pointing directly to the secret article because it was inarguably the most shocking aspect of the treaty, and Madison uses the language "to a length of which you can form little idea."

5. "The federal": October 20, 1783, *JCC* 25; "federal": Massachusetts delegates to the Massachusetts Assembly, October 23, 1783, *LDTC* 21.

6. "Southern": Hugh Williamson to Alexander Martin, March 25, 1782, *LDTC* 18; "commercial": JM to Randolph, December 17, 1782, *PJM* 5; "This we mean": South Carolina delegates to John Rutledge, February 18, 1782, *LDTC* 18.

7. "I confess": Charles Thomson to Hannah Thomson, July 6, 1783, *LDTC* 20.

8. "The centrifugal": AH to GW, March 24, 1783, *LDTC* 20; "whether prosperity": JM to Randolph, February 25, 1783, *PJM* 6.

9. Debt statistics: notes on debates, January 27, 1783, *PJM* 6, n. 13; "tyranny": Rhode Island delegates to William Greene, October 15, 1782, *LDTC* 19.

10. "Maritime" and "merchants": David Howell to W. Greene, July 30, 1782, *LDTC* 18; perceived negative impact of impost as greater on Northern than

Southern states: JM to Randolph, December 17, 1782, *PJM* 5. See also notes on debates, January 29, 1783, *PJM* 6. For attitudes and philosophies of government of Howell contained in this chapter, see, in addition to the letters cited, Howell to Robert Morris, July 31–August 2 (?), 1782, *LDTC* 18; Howell to Welcome Arnold, August 3, 1782 and October 3, 1782, *LDTC* 19; and Howell to Theodore Foster, October 9, 1782, *LDTC* 19. For the impost and Rhode Island, also see Burnett, *CC*, 480, 530, 533, and 570; and Morris, *Forging*, 41–45.

11. "Fatal" and "cause": Howell to Foster, October 12, 1782, *LDTC* 19; "evils": Howell to W. Greene, July 30, 1782, *LDTC* 18; "the sovereignty": Howell to W. Greene, July 30, 1782, *LDTC* 18; "the principles": Howell to Nicholas Brown, October 2, 1782, *LDTC* 19; "Every": Howell to Brown, October 30, 1782, *LDTC* 19.

12. "Would it": Rhode Island delegates to W. Green, October 15, 1782, *LDTC* 19.

13. "Civil war": Boudinot to William Livingston, October 23, 1782, *LDTC* 19; "He has": Boudinot to John Lowell, March 19, 1783, *LDTC* 20.

14. Delegation to Rhode Island: Burnett, *CC*, 533.

15. "It is the first": AH to Clinton, February 14, 1783, *LDTC* 19.

16. "In this position": AH to Clinton, February 14, 1783, *LDTC* 19.

17. "Enriched": notes on debates, February 21, 1783, *PJM* 6; statistics on Virginia debts for 1782: Virginia delegates to Benjamin Harrison, July 7, 1783, *PJM* 6, n. 2.

18. "Prince": Abiel Foster to Jonathan Blanchard, March 30, 1785, in Kukla, *Wilderness*, 51; "if he conceived": notes on debates, February 21, 1783, *PJM* 6.

19. "Justice": JM to Randolph, February 25, 1783, *PJM* 6. See also notes on debates, February 21, 1783, *PJM* 6.

20. "A ready pretext": JM to Randolph, February 25, 1783, *PJM* 6.

21. "Unless": JM to Randolph, February 25, 1783, *PJM* 6.

22. "For regulating": notes on debates, April 1, 1783, *PJM* 6.

23. "A dangerous": notes on debates, April 1, 1783, *PJM* 6.

24. "Are so dissatisfied": Samuel Holten to John Kettell, October 9, 1783, *LDTC* 21.

25. "Choose the least": Samuel Osgood to Lowell, January 6, 1783, *LDTC* 19; "No two or more": Articles of Confederation, March 1, 1781, APYLS.

26. "Partial": notes on debates, April 1, 1783, *PJM* 6.

27. "The common defense": Articles of Confederation, March 1, 1781, APYLS, https://avalon.law.yale.edu/18th_century/artconf.asp; "Virginia": notes on debates, February 26, 1783, *PJM* 6. In a long footnote written by Madison indicated by "*," he explains this as a dominant rationale for empowering a federal government. He repeats the logic under entries for each of the Southern states, presenting the arguments that were being used to persuade them of the necessity of accepting a federal revenue.

28. "Three-fifths": April 18, 1783, *JCC* 24; "a strange": Higginson to Theophilus Parsons, April 7–10, 1783, *LDTC* 20.

29. "Scenes": John Francis Mercer to Daniel Morgan, April 24, 1783, *LDTC* 20.

CHAPTER 20

1. "Who wickedly": Washington to officers of the Army, March 15, 1783, FO, https://founders.archives.gov/documents/Washington/99-01-02-10840.

2. "To obtain": Colonel Richard Butler and William Henry to the Pennsylvania Council, June 17, 1783, *LDTC* 20, n. 3. History of the June insurrection of the Pennsylvania Line is derived from the many letters cited here plus Elias Boudinot, draft statement on the mutiny, June 23, 1783, *LDTC* 20; notes on debates, June 21, 1783, *PJM* 7, nn. 1–8; and Ron Chernow, *Alexander Hamilton* (New York: Penguin Books, 2004), 180–83.

3. "Prisoners": Elias Boudinot to Elisha Boudinot, June 23, 1783, *LDTC* 20; "no longer": North Carolina delegates to Alexander Martin, August 1, 1783, *LDTC* 20; "wantonly": notes of debates, June 21, 1783, *PJM* 6; "an enraged": Elias Boudinot to GW, June 21, 1783, *LDTC* 20.

4. "In great": Elias Boudinot to William Livingston, June 23, 1783, *LDTC* 20; "no one": Elias Boudinot to GW, June 21, 1783, *LDTC* 20; "meditating": JM to Edmund Randolph, June 30, *PJM* 7.

5. "From your general": North Carolina delegates to Martin, August 1, 1783, *LDTC* 20.

6. "When I": Charles Thomson to Hannah Thomson, October 19, 1783, *LDTC* 21; "The Man": Samuel Hazard, "The Man of Truth," *Hazard's Register of Pennsylvania* (Philadelphia: W. F. Geddes, 1831–35), 8:169.

7. "Local": C. Thomson to H. Thomson, July 25, 1783, *LDTC* 20. "Now": Paine, *Common Sense*; "Doomsday Book": "Colonies in their Limits, In the Hand of John Dickinson, Endorsed 'Arguments agt. the Independence of these Colonies-in Congress,'" July 1, 1776, *LDTC* 4.

8. "The keys": C. Thomson to H. Thomson, July 25, 1783, *LDTC* 20. Quotations below by C. Thomson, unless otherwise cited, are derived from the same source.

9. Committees on cession: notes on debates, June 4 and 10, 1783, and notes, and JM to TJ, September 20, 1783, and notes, *PJM* 7.

10. "Two great": Jones to JM, June 14, 1783, *PJM* 7.

11. "Lusting" and "alarming": Jones to JM, June 14, 1783, *PJM* 7; "offensive": Randolph to JM, May 9, 1783, *PJM* 7; "aversion": Edmund Pendleton to JM, May 4, 1783, *PJM* 7; "the ardor": Randolph to JM, May 9, 1783, *PJM* 7.

12. "Internal": TJ to Randolph, February 15, 1783, in *The Papers of Thomas Jefferson*, ed. Julian P. Boyd et al., 45 vols. (Princeton: Princeton University Press, 1950–2021), vol. 6.

13. "To enforce": TJ to Randolph, February 15, 1783, *PTJ* 6.

14. "Moment": Pendleton to JM, April 14, 1783, *PJM* 6.

15. "A common": September 13, 1783, *JCC* 25. For voting maneuvers, see JM to TJ, September 20, 1783, *PJM* 7, n. 3.

16. "Might have been": New York delegates to George Clinton, September 19, 1783, *LDTC* 20; "The moment": John Francis Mercer to Henry Tazewell, September 13, 1783, *LDTC* 20.

17. "Federal town": C. Thomson to H. Thomson, October 20, 1783, *LDTC* 21. For activities of April, May and June, see also Virginia delegates to Benjamin Harrison, April 10, 1783, *LDTC* 20; New York delegates to Clinton, April 9, 1783, *LDTC* 20; Elias Boudinot to the states, June 10, 1783, *LDTC* 20; and "Instructions to Virginia Delegates in re Permanent Site for Congress," June 28, 1783, *PJM* 7.

18. "Collection of republics": William Gordon to JA, September 7, 1782, FO, https://founders.archives.gov/documents/Adams/06-13-02-0186.

19. Southern arguments relating to the location of a capital: Harrison to Virginia delegates, July 4, 1783, *PJM* 7; Pendleton to JM, July 21, 1783, *PJM* 7; and notes on Congress's place of residence, October 14, 1783, *PJM* 7.

20. "Will fix": Harrison to Virginia delegates, October 25, 1783, *PJM* 7; "Southern": JM to Randolph, July 28, 1783, *PJM* 7; "The southern": George Lux to Theodorick Bland, November 17, 1782, cited in Virginia delegates to Harrison, April 10, 1783, *LDTC* 20, n. 3; "the soothing": notes on Congress's place of residence, October 14, 1783, *PJM* 7.

21. "Emigration": July 29, 1783, *Maryland Journal*, cited in Davis, *Sectionalism*, 67; "zeal": North Carolina delegates to Martin, October 24, 1783, *LDTC* 21.

22. Canvasing of October 6: October 6, 1783, *JCC* 25. See also JM to Randolph, October 13, 1783, plus notes, *PJM* 6.

23. "This mortified": Elias Boudinot to Robert Livingston, October 23, 1783, *LDTC* 21; "to repair": October 7, 1783, *JCC* 25.

24. "Justice": October 8, 1783, *JCC* 25.

25. "Confusion": Stephen Higginson to Nathaniel Gorham, August 5, 1783, *LDTC* 20.

26. "At or near": October 20, 1783, *JCC* 25.

27. "Preserve": Massachusetts delegates to the Massachusetts Assembly, October 23, 1783, *LDTC* 21. See also Burnett, *CC*, 586–87.

28. "It gives me": Elias Boudinot to Robert Morris, October 23, 1783, *LDTC* 21; "Rome": Elias Boudinot to R. Livingston, October 23, 1783, *LDTC* 21.

29. "Reproaches": C. Thomson to H. Thomson, October 20, 1783, *LDTC* 21; "the order": C. Thomson to H. Thomson, October 15, 1783, *LDTC* 21.

30. "Eastern," "calamities," and "All things": C. Thomson to H. Thomson, October 14, 1783, *LDTC* 21.

31. "My warmest": GW to Rochambeau, November 1, 1783, FO, https://founders.archives.gov/?q=Author:%22Washington,%20George%22%20Dates-From:1783-08-01%20Dates-To:1783-12-31&s=1111311113&r=183. For GW's awareness of debates on the location of the capital, see GW to Duc de Lauzun, October 15, 1783, FO, https://founders.archives.gov/?q=Author:%22Washington,%20George%22%20Dates-From:1783-08-01%20Dates-To:1783-12-31&s=1111311113&r=146.

32. "With a heart" and "mournful": Chernow, *Washington*, 452.

33. "Having": GW, speech, December 23, 1783, "Editorial Note: George Washington's Resignation as Commander-in-Chief," FO, https://founders.archives.gov

/documents/Jefferson/01-06-02-0319-0001; "a private": GW to Von Steuben, December 23, 1783, FO, https://founders.archives.gov/?q=george%20washington%20%22give%20my%20final%20blessing%20to%20that%20country,%20%22%201783%20june&s=1111311111&sa=&r=1&sr=. The editorial note and Chernow, *Washington*, 454–57, are the two most comprehensive sources recounting Washington's surrender of his commission.

34. "The legacy": GW to the states, June 1783, FO, https://founders.archives.gov/?q=george%20washington%20%22give%20my%20final%20blessing%20to%20that%20country,%20%22%201783%20june&s=1111311111&sa=&r=1&sr=. Quotations below by Washington are derived from the same source.

BIBLIOGRAPHY

ONLINE PRIMARY SOURCES

Avalon Project: Documents in Law, History, and Diplomacy. Yale Law School. https://avalon.law.yale.edu.

ConSource. https://www.consource.org.

Evans Early American Imprint Collection. https://quod.lib.umich.edu/e/evans/.

Founders Online. https://founders.archives.gov.

Journals of the Continental Congress. https://memory.loc.gov/ammem/amlaw/lwjclink.html.

Letters of Delegates to Congress. https://memory.loc.gov/ammem/amlaw/lwdglink.html.

Library of Congress. https://www.loc.gov.

Making of America. https://quod.lib.umich.edu/m/moagrp.

New York History Net, www.nyhistory.com/ central/conflict.htm.

Online Library of Liberty. https://oll.libertyfund.org.

Oxford Dictionary of National Biography. https://www.oxforddnb.com.

Revolutionary Diplomatic Correspondence. https://memory.loc.gov/ammem/amlaw/lwdc.html.

PRINTED PRIMARY SOURCES

Adams, Abigail, and John Adams. *The Letters of John and Abigail Adams.* Edited by Frank Shuffelton. New York: Penguin Books, 2004.

Adams, John. *Diary and Autobiography of John Adams.* Edited by L. H. Butterfield, Leonard C. Faber, and Wendell D. Garrett. 4 vols. Cambridge, MA, and London: Belknap Press of Harvard University Press, 1962.

———. *Works of John Adams, Second President of the United States.* Edited by Charles Francis Adams. 10 vols. Boston: Little, Brown, 1850–56.

Adams, Samuel. *Writings of Samuel Adams.* Edited by Harry Alonzo Cushing. 4 vols. New York: G. P. Putnam's Sons, 1904–08.

Bernard, Francis, Thomas Gage, and Samuel Hood. *Letters to the Ministry from Governor Bernard, General Gage, and Commodore Hood: And Also Memorials to* the Lords of the Treasury, from the Commissioners of the Customs. With Sundry Letters and Papers Annexed to the Said Memorials. Boston: Andesite Press, 2015.

Blount, John Gray. *The John Gray Blount Papers, 1764–1795*. Edited by Alice B. Keith. 2 vols. Raleigh, NC: State Department of Archives and History, 1952–59.

Burr, Aaron. *Memoirs of Aaron Burr: With Miscellaneous Selections from His Correspondence*. Edited by Matthew L. Davis. 2 vols. London: Forgotten Books, 2012.

Curwen, Samuel. *Journal and Letters of the Late Samuel Curwen Judge of Admiralty, Etc., a Loyalist-Refugee in England, During the American Revolution. To Which Are Added, Illustrative Documents and Other Eminent Men*. Edited by George A. Ward. Charleston, SC: Nabu Press, 2010.

Deane, Silas. *The Deane Papers, 1774–1790*. Edited by Charles Isham. New York: New York Historical Society, 1923.

Dickinson, John. *Empire and Nation: Letters from a Farmer in Pennsylvania*. Edited by Forrest McDonald. Indianapolis: Liberty Fund, 1999.

———. *The Writings of John Dickinson: Political Writings, 1764–1774*. Edited by Paul Leicester Ford. Philadelphia: Historical Society of Pennsylvania, 1895.

Ford, Worthington C., Gaillard Hunt, John Clement Fitzpatrick, Roscoe R. Hill, Kenneth E. Harris, and Stephen D. Tilley, eds. *Journals of the Continental Congress, 1774–1789*. 34 vols. Washington, DC: Government Printing Office, 1904–37.

Franklin, Benjamin. *The Papers of Benjamin Franklin*. Edited by Leonard W. Labaree, William B. Willcox, Claude A. Lopez, Barbara B. Oberg, and Ellen R. Cohn. 42 vols. New Haven and London: Yale University Press, 1959–2017.

Giunta, Mary A., J. Dane Hartgrove, and Mary-Jane M. Dowd, eds. *The Emerging Nation: A Documentary History of the Foreign Relations of the United States under the Articles of Confederation, 1780–1789*. 3 vols. Washington, DC: National Historical Publications and Records Commission, 1996.

Hamilton, Alexander. *The Papers of Alexander Hamilton, 1768–1792*. Edited by Harold C. Syrett and Jacob Ernest Cooke. 27 vols. New York and London: Columbia University Press, 1961–87.

———. *The Revolutionary Writings of Alexander Hamilton*. Edited by Richard B. Vernier. Indianapolis: Liberty Fund, 2008.

Harley, Lewis R. *The Life of Charles Thomson: Secretary of the Continental Congress and Translator of the Bible from the Greek*. London: Forgotten Books, 2018.

Hazard, Samuel. *Hazard's Register of Pennsylvania*. 9 vols. Philadelphia: W. F. Geddes, 1831–35.

Henry, William W. *Patrick Henry: Life, Correspondence, and Speeches*. London: Forgotten Books, 2018.

Iredell, James. *The Papers of James Iredell, 1767–1783*. Edited by Don Higginbotham, Donna E. Kelly, and Lang Baradell. 3 vols. Raleigh, NC: Division of Archives and History, Dept. of Cultural Resources, 1976–2003.

Jay, John. *The Correspondence and Public Papers of John Jay*. Edited by Henry Phelps Johnston. 4 vols. New York: G. P. Putnam's Sons, 1890.

———. *John Jay: Unpublished Papers*. Edited by Richard B. Morris. 2 vols. New York: Harper & Row, 1975–80.
Jay, William. *The Life of John Jay*. Vol. 1. New York: J. & J. Harper, 1833.
Jefferson, Thomas. *Letters and Addresses of Thomas Jefferson*. Edited by William B. Parker and Jonas Viles. New York: Grosset & Dunlap, 1903.
———. *Notes on the State of Virginia*. Edited by William Peden. Chapel Hill and London: University of North Carolina Press, 1954.
———. *The Papers of Thomas Jefferson*. Edited by Julian P. Boyd, Mina R. Bryan, L. H. Butterfield, Charles T. Cullen, John Catanzariti, Barbara Oberg, James P. McClure, Martha J. King, and Tom Downey. 45 vols. Princeton, NJ: Princeton University Press, 1950–2021.
Jefferson, Thomas, and James Madison. *The Republic of Letters: The Correspondence between Thomas Jefferson and James Madison, 1776–1836*. Edited by James M. Smith. 2 vols. New York and London: W. W. Norton, 1995.
Jensen, Merrill. *Tracts of the American Revolution, 1763–1776*. Indianapolis and Cambridge: Hackett, 1966.
Jones, Joseph. *Letters of Joseph Jones of Virginia, 1777–1787*. Edited by Worthington C. Ford. Washington, DC: Dept. of State, 1889.
Lee, Richard Henry. *The Letters of Richard Henry Lee*. Edited by James C. Ballagh. 2 vols. New York: Macmillan, 1912–14.
Lengel, Edward G. *This Glorious Struggle: George Washington's Revolutionary War Letters*. New York: Harper Collins, 2007.
Machiavelli, Niccolò. *The Letters of Machiavelli: A Selection of His Letters*. Edited by Alan Gilbert. New York: Capricorn Books, 1961.
Madison, James. *The Papers of James Madison*. Edited by William T. Hutchinson, William M. E. Rachal, and Robert Allen Rutland. 17 vols. Chicago and London: University of Chicago Press, 1962–91.
Marshall, John. *Correspondence and Papers, November 10, 1775–June 23, 1788. Account Book, September 1783–June 1788*. Vol. 1 of *The Papers of John Marshall*. Edited by Herbert A. Johnson, Charles T. Cullen, and Charles F. Hobson. Chapel Hill: University of North Carolina Press, 1974.
McIlwaine, H. R., and John Pendleton Kennedy, eds. *Journals of the House of Burgesses of Virginia: 1752–1755, 1756–1758*. Richmond, VA: Colonial Press, E. Waddey, 1909.
Pendleton, Edmund. *The Letters and Papers of Edmund Pendleton, 1734–1803*. Edited by David John Mays. 2 vols. Charlottesville and London: University Press of Virginia, 1967.
Rosenfeld, Richard N. *American Aurora: A Democratic-Republican Returns*. New York: St. Martin's, 1997.
Rowland, Kate M. *The Life of George Mason, 1725–1792: Including His Speeches, Public Papers and Correspondence*. Whitefish, MT: Kessinger, 2006.
Sandoz, Ellis, ed. *Political Sermons of the American Founding Era, 1730–1805*. Indianapolis: LibertyPress, 1991.
Sherman, Roger. *Collected Works of Roger Sherman*. Edited by Mark D. Hall. Indianapolis: Liberty Fund, 2016.

Smith, Paul Hubert, ed. *Letters of Delegates to the Continental Congress, 1774–1789.* Washington DC: Library of Congress, 1976–2000.

United States Continental Congress. *Papers of the Continental Congress, 1774–1789.* Washington, DC: National Archives & Records Administration, Central Plains Region, 1957–59.

United States Dept. of State, ed. *The Revolutionary Diplomatic Correspondence of the United States.* Vol. 2. Washington DC: Arkose Press, 2015.

Wood, Gordon S., ed. *The American Revolution: Writings from the Pamphlet Debate, 1764–1776.* New York: Library of America, 2015.

SECONDARY SOURCES

Achenbach, Joel. *The Grand Idea: George Washington's Potomac and the Race to the West.* New York: Simon & Schuster, 2004.

Adams, William H. *Gouverneur Morris: An Independent Life.* New Haven and London: Yale University Press, 2003.

———. *The Paris Years of Thomas Jefferson.* New Haven and London: Yale University Press, 1997.

Albion, Robert Greenhalgh, William A. Baker, and Benjamin W. Labaree. *New England and the Sea.* Mystic, CT: Mystic Seaport Museum, 1994.

Alden, John R. *The American Revolution, 1775–1783.* New York: Harper & Brothers, 1954.

———. *The First South.* Baton Rouge: Louisiana State University Press, 1961.

———. *General Gage in America: Being Principally a History of His Role in the American Revolution.* New York: Greenwood, 1969.

———. *The South in the Revolution, 1763–1789.* Baton Rouge: Louisiana State University Press, 1957.

Allen, Michael. "The Mississippi River Debate, 1785–1787." *Tennessee Historical Quarterly* 36, no. 4 (1977): 447–67.

Allen, Thomas B. *Tories: Fighting for the King in America's First Civil War.* New York: HarperCollins, 2010.

Alley, Robert S., ed. *James Madison on Religious Liberty.* New York: Prometheus Books, 1985.

Allgor, Catherine. *A Perfect Union: Dolley Madison and the Creation of the American Nation.* New York: Henry Holt, 2006.

Amar, Akhil R. *The Bill of Rights: Creation and Reconstruction.* New Haven and London: Yale University Press, 1998.

———. *The Words That Made Us: America's Constitutional Conversation, 1760–1840.* New York: Basic Books, 2021.

Ammon, Harry. *James Monroe: The Quest for National Identity.* Charlottesville and London: University Press of Virginia, 1990.

Anderson, Fred. *Crucible of War: The Seven Years' War and the Fate of Empire in British North America, 1754–1766.* New York: Alfred A. Knopf, 2000.

Armitage, David. *The Declaration of Independence: A Global History.* Cambridge, MA, and London: Harvard University Press, 2007.

Atkinson, Rick. *The British Are Coming: The War for America, Lexington to Princeton, 1775–1777.* New York: Henry Holt, 2019.
Avlon, John. *Washington's Farewell: The Founding Father's Warning to Future Generations.* New York: Simon & Schuster, 2017.
Bailyn, Bernard. *The Ideological Origins of the American Revolution.* Cambridge, MA, and London: Belknap Press of Harvard University Press, 1976.
———. *The Ordeal of Thomas Hutchinson.* Cambridge, MA, and London: Belknap Press of Harvard University Press, 1974.
Banning, Lance. *The Sacred Fire of Liberty: James Madison and the Founding of the Federal Republic.* Ithaca and London: Cornell University Press, 1995.
Beck, Derek W. *Igniting the American Revolution, 1773–1775.* Naperville, IL: Sourcebooks, 2016.
Beeman, Richard R. *Our Lives, Our Fortunes, and Our Sacred Honor: The Forging of American Independence, 1774–1776.* New York: Basic Books, 2013.
———. *Plain, Honest Men: The Making of the American Constitution.* New York: Random House, 2010.
Beeman, Richard R., Stephen Botein, and Edward C. Carter, eds. *Beyond Confederation: Origins of the Constitution and American National Identity.* Chapel Hill: North Carolina Press, 1987.
Bemis, Samuel F. *The Diplomacy of the American Revolution.* Bloomington and London: Indiana University Press, 1957.
———. *Pickney's Treaty: America's Advantage from Europe's Distress,* 1783–1800. New Haven and London: Yale University Press, 1960.
Benton, Geoff. *The Fight for Tom Cod: Newfoundland in the American Revolution.* Rhinebeck, NY: Epigraph Books, 2020.
Billington, Ray A. *Westward Expansion: A History of the American Frontier.* 2nd ed. New York: Macmillan, 1960.
Blumrosen, Alfred W., and Ruth G. Blumrosen. *Slave Nation: How Slavery United the Colonies and Sparked the American Revolution.* Naperville, IL: Sourcebooks, 2005.
Bobrick, Benson. *Angel in the Whirlwind: The Triumph of the American Revolution.* New York: Simon & Schuster, 1997.
Bonwick, Colin. *The American Revolution.* Charlottesville and London: University Press of Virginia, 1991.
Boorstin, Daniel J. *The Americans: The Colonial Experience.* New York: Vintage Books, 1958.
———. *The Lost World of Thomas Jefferson.* Chicago and London: University of Chicago Press, 1948.
Bowen, Catherine D. *Miracle at Philadelphia: The Story of the Constitutional Convention, May to September 1787.* New York: Little, Brown Books, 1986.
Bradley, James E. *Popular Politics and the American Revolution in England.* Macon, GA: Mercer University Press, 1986.
Brands, H. W. *The First American: The Life and Times of Benjamin Franklin.* New York: Anchor Books, 2000.

Brant, Irving. *James Madison*. 5 vols. Indianapolis, New York: Bobbs-Merrill, 1941–61.
Breen, T. H. *Tobacco Culture: The Mentality of the Great Tidewater Planters on the Eve of Revolution*. Princeton, NJ: Princeton University Press, 1985.
Broadwater, Jeff. *James Madison: A Song of Virginia and a Founder of the Nation*. Chapel Hill: University of North Carolina Press, 2012.
Brodie, Fawn M. *Thomas Jefferson: An Intimate History*. New York: W. W. Norton, 1974.
Brooke, John. *King George III*. London: Constable, 1972.
Brookhiser, Richard. *Founding Father: Rediscovering George Washington*. New York: Free Press, 1996.
———. *James Madison*. New York: Basic Books, 2011.
Brown, Charles R. *A Dissertation Presented to the Faculty of Princeton University in Candidacy for the Degree of Doctor of Philosophy*. London and Oxford: Princeton University Press, 1915.
Browning, Andrew H. *The Panic of 1819: The First Great Depression*. Columbia: University of Missouri Press, 2019.
Brumwell, Stephen. *Turncoat: Benedict Arnold and the Crisis of American Liberty*. New Haven and London: Yale University Press, 2018.
Burnett, Edmund Cody. *The Continental Congress: A Definitive History of the Continental Congress from Its Inception in 1774 to March 1789*. New York: Norton Library, 1964.
Burstein, Andrew, and Nancy Isenberg. *Madison and Jefferson*. New York: Random House, 2010.
Butterfield, L. H., Leonard C. Faber, and Wendell D. Garrett, eds. Diary and Autobiography of John Adams, 4 vols. Cambridge, MA, and London: Belknap Press of Harvard University Press, 1962.
Cheney, Lynne V. *James Madison: A Life Reconsidered*. New York: Penguin Books, 2015.
Chernow, Ron. *Alexander Hamilton*. New York: Penguin Books, 2004.
———. *Washington: A Life*. New York: Penguin Books, 2010.
Chorlton, Thomas P. *The First American Republic, 1774–1789*. Bloomington, IN: AuthorHouse, 2012.
Collier, Christopher, and James Lincoln Collier. *Decision in Philadelphia: The Constitutional Convention of 1787*. New York: Ballantine Books, 1987.
Commager, Henry S., and Richard B. Morris, eds. *The Spirit of Seventy-Six: The Story of the American Revolution as Told by Participants*. New York: Da Capo Press, 1995.
Conklin, Carli N. *The Pursuit of Happiness in the Founding Era: An Intellectual History*. Columbia: University of Missouri Press, 2019.
Crane, Verner W. *Benjamin Franklin and a Rising People*. Boston: Little, Brown, 1954.
———. *The Southern Frontier, 1670–1732*. New York and London: W. W. Norton, 1981.

Cummins, Light T. *Spanish Observers and the American Revolution, 1775–1783*. Baton Rouge: Louisiana State University Press, 1991.
Cunningham, Noble E., Jr. *In Pursuit of Reason: The Life of Thomas Jefferson*. New York: Ballantine Books, 1988.
David, Huw. *Trade, Politics, and Revolution: South Carolina and Britain's Atlantic Commerce, 1730–1790*. Columbia: University of South Carolina Press, 2018.
Davis, David B. *The Problem of Slavery in the Age of Revolution, 1770–1823*. New York and Oxford: Oxford University Press, 1999.
Davis, Joseph L. *Sectionalism in American Politics, 1774–1787*. Madison: University of Wisconsin Press, 1977.
DeRose, Chris. *Founding Rivals: Madison vs. Monroe, the Bill of Rights, and the Election That Saved a Nation*. Washington, DC: Regnery, 2011.
Dillion, Mark C. *The First Chief Justice: John Jay and the Struggle of a New Nation*. Albany, NY: SUNY Press, 2022.
Din, Gilbert C. "The Death and Succession of Francisco Bouligny." *Louisiana History: The Journal of the Louisiana Historical Association* 22, no. 3 (1981): 307–15.
Draper, Theodore. *A Struggle for Power: The American Revolution*. New York: Times Books, 1996.
Dull, Jonathan R. *A Diplomatic History of the American Revolution*. New Haven and London: Yale University Press, 1985.
Dunn, Susan. "Revolutionary Men of Letters and the Pursuit of Radical Change: The Views of Burke, Tocqueville, Adams, Madison, and Jefferson." *William and Mary Quarterly* 53, no. 4 (1996): 730–54.
Edling, Max M. "Peace Pact and Nation: An International Interpretation of the Constitution of the United States." *Past & Present* 240, no. 1 (August 2018): 267–303.
———. *Perfecting the Union: National and State Authority in the U.S. Constitution*. New York: Oxford University Press, 2021.
Elkins, Stanley, and Eric McKitrick. *The Age of Federalism: The Early American Republic, 1788–1800*. New York and Oxford: Oxford University Press, 1993.
Ellis, Joseph J. *American Creation*. New York: Alfred A. Knopf, 2007.
———. *American Dialogue: The Founders and Us*. New York: Alfred A. Knopf, 2018.
———. *American Sphinx: The Character of Thomas Jefferson*. New York: Alfred A. Knopf, 1998.
———. *The Cause: The American Revolution and Its Discontents, 1773–1783*. New York: Liveright, 2021.
———. *First Family: Abigail and John Adams*. New York: Vintage Books, 2010.
———. *Founding Brothers: The Revolutionary Generation*. New York: Alfred A. Knopf, 2000.
———. *His Excellency: George Washington*. New York: Alfred A. Knopf, 2004.
———. *The Quartet: Orchestrating the Second American Revolution, 1783–1789*. New York: Vintage Books, 2015.
Farrand, Max. *The Framing of the Constitution of the United States*. New Haven and London: Yale University Press, 1913.

———, ed. *The Records of the Federal Convention of 1787*. 2 vols. New Haven and London: Yale University Press, 1911.

Fehrenbacher, Don E. *Sectional Crisis and Southern Constitutionalism: Compromising the South and Three Sectional Crises and Constitutions and Constitutionalism in the Slaveholding South*. Baton Rouge: Louisiana State University Press, 1995.

Feldman, Noah. *The Three Lives of James Madison: Genius, Partisan, President*. New York: Random House, 2017.

Ferguson, Robert A., ed. *The Federalist*. New York: Barnes & Noble Books, 2006.

Ferling, John E. *Almost A Miracle: The American Victory in the War of Independence*. New York: Oxford University Press, 2007.

———. *The Ascent of George Washington: The Hidden Political Genius of an American Icon*. New York: Bloomsbury, 2009.

———. *Jefferson and Hamilton: The Rivalry That Forged a Nation*. New York: Bloomsbury, 2013.

———. *John Adams: A Life*. New York: Henry Holt, 1996.

———. *A Leap in the Dark: The Struggle to Create the American Republic*. New York: Oxford University Press, 2003.

———. *The Loyalist Mind: Joseph Galloway and the American Revolution*. University Park and London: Pennsylvania State University Press, 1997.

———. *Winning Independence: The Decisive Years of the Revolutionary War, 1778–1781*. New York: Bloomsbury, 2021.

Finkelman, Paul. "Slavery at the Philadelphia Convention." *This Constitution*, no. 18 (1988): 25–30.

Fischer, David H. *Bound Away: Virginia and the Westward Movement*. Charlottesville: University of Virginia Press, 2000.

———. *Paul Revere's Ride*. New York and Oxford: Oxford University Press, 1994.

———. *Washington's Crossing*. New York and Oxford: Oxford University Press, 2004.

Fleming, Thomas. *Liberty! The American Revolution*. New York: Viking Penguin, 1997.

———. *The Perils of Peace: America's Struggle for Survival after Yorktown*. New York: Smithsonian Books, 2007.

———. *Washington's Secret War: The Hidden History of Valley Forge*. New York: Smithsonian Books, 2006.

Forman, Samuel A. *Dr. Joseph Warren: The Boston Tea Party, Bunker Hill, and the Birth of American Liberty*. Gretna, LA: Pelican, 2012.

Fowler, William M., Jr. *American Crisis: George Washington and the Dangerous Two Years after Yorktown, 1781–1783*. New York: Walker, 2011.

Fraser, Antonia. *Marie Antoinette: The Journey*. New York: Anchor Books, 2001.

Fraser, Kathryn M. "Fort Jefferson: George Rogers Clark's Fort at the Mouth of the Ohio River, 1780–1781." *Register of the Kentucky Historical Society* 81, no. 1 (1983): 1–25.

Freehling, William W. *The Road to Disunion*. Vol. 1, *Secessionists at Bay, 1776–1854*. New York and Oxford: Oxford University Press, 1990.

Freeman, Douglas S., and Richard Harwell, eds. *Washington: An Abridgement in One Volume by Richard Harwell of the Seven-Volume George Washington by Douglas Southall Freeman*. New York: Charles Scribner's Sons, 1968.

Fried, Stephen. *Rush: Revolution, Madness, and the Visionary Doctor Who Became a Founding Father*. New York: Crown, 2018.

Fritz, Jean. *The Great Little Madison*. New York: Puffin Books, 1998.

Gaines, James R. *For Liberty and Glory: Washington, Lafayette, and Their Revolutions*. New York and London: W. W. Norton, 2007.

Graebner, Norman A. "The Illinois County and the Treaty of Paris of 1783." *Illinois Historical Journal* 78, no. 1 (1985): 2–15.

Greene, Jack P. *The Constitutional Origins of the American Revolution*. Cambridge, New York: Cambridge University Press, 2011.

———. *Understanding the American Revolution: Issues and Actors*. Charlottesville: University of Virginia Press, 1995.

Greene, Jack P., and J. R. Pole, eds. *The Blackwell Encyclopedia of the American Revolution*. Cambridge, MA: Basil Blackwell, 1991.

Gregory, Anthony. "Formed for Empire: The Continental Congress Responds to the Carlisle Peace Commission." *Journal of the Early Republic* 38, no. 4 (2018): 643–72.

Gutzman, Kevin R. C. *James Madison and the Making of America*. New York: St. Martin's Griffin, 2012.

———. *Thomas Jefferson, Revolutionary: A Radical's Struggle to Remake America*. New York: St. Martin's, 2017.

Haw, James. *John and Edward Rutledge of South Carolina*. Athens and London: University of Georgia Press, 1997.

Hemphill, W. E. "The Jeffersonian Background of the Louisiana Purchase." *Mississippi Valley Historical Review* 22, no. 2 (1935): 177–90.

Henderson, Archibald. "The Spanish Conspiracy in Tennessee." *Tennessee Historical Magazine* 3, no. 4 (1917): 229–49.

Hendrickson, David C. *Peace Pact: The Lost World of the American Founding*. Lawrence: University Press of Kansas, 2003.

Hening, William Waller. *Statutes at Large: Being a Collection of All the Laws of Virginia from the First Session of the Legislature, in the Year 1619*. Transcribed by Freddie L. Spradlin. 13 vols. Torrance, CA: Freddie L. Spradlin, 2009. http://vagenweb.org/hening/index.htm.

Hibbert, Christopher. *Charles I: A Life of Religion, War, and Treason*. New York: Palgrave MacMillan, 2007.

———. *Redcoats and Rebels: The American Revolution through British Eyes*. New York: W. W. Norton, 1990.

Hoffman, Ronald, and Peter J. Albert, eds. *Peace and the Peacemakers: The Treaty of 1783*. Charlottesville and London: University Press of Virginia, 1986.

Hogan, Margaret A., and C. James Taylor, eds. *My Dearest Friend: Letters of Abigail and John Adams*. Cambridge, MA, and London: Belknap Press of Harvard University Press, 2007.

Holton, Woody. *Abigail Adams*. New York: Free Press, 2009.
———. "The Ohio Indians and the Coming of the American Revolution in Virginia." *Journal of Southern History* 60, no. 3 (1994): 453–78.
———. *Unruly Americans and the Origins of the Constitution*. New York: Hill and Wang, 2007.
Hudson, Ruth S. *The Minister from France: Conrad-Alexandre Gérard, 1729–1790*. Euclid, OH: Lutz, 1994.
Hughes, Jonathan. *American Economic History*. 3rd ed. Glenview, IL, and London: Scott Foresman, 1990.
Hutson, James H. *John Adams and the Diplomacy of the American Revolution*. Lexington: University Press of Kentucky, 1980.
Hyland, William G., Jr. *George Mason: The Founding Father Who Gave Us the Bill of Rights*. Washington: Regnery History, 2019.
Irvin, Benjamin H. *Clothed in Robes of Sovereignty: The Continental Congress and the People Out of Doors*. New York and Oxford: Oxford University Press, 2011.
Isaacson, Walter. *Benjamin Franklin: An American Life*. New York: Simon & Schuster, 2003.
James, James A. "Oliver Pollock and the Free Navigation of the Mississippi River." *Mississippi Valley Historical Review* 19, no. 3 (1932): 331–47.
Jasanoff, Maya. *Liberty's Exiles: American Loyalists in the Revolutionary World*. New York: Vintage Books, 2011.
Jensen, Merrill. *The Articles of Confederation: An Interpretation of the Social-Constitutional History of the American Revolution, 1774–1781*. Madison: University of Wisconsin Press, 1940.
———, ed. *Regionalism in America*. Madison: University of Wisconsin Press, 1952.
Keane, John. *Tom Paine: A Political Life*. Boston: Little, Brown, 1995.
Kenyon, Cecelia M., ed. *The Antifederalists*. Boston: Northeastern University Press, 1966.
Ketcham, Ralph. *James Madison: A Biography*. Charlottesville and London: University Press of Virginia, 1990.
Ketchum, Richard M. *Divided Loyalties: How the American Revolution Came to New York*. New York: Henry Holt, 2002.
———. *Saratoga*. New York: Holt, 1997.
Klarman, Michael J. *The Framers' Coup: The Making of the United States Constitution*. New York and Oxford: Oxford University Press, 2016.
Kreitner, Richard. *Break It Up: Secession, Division, and the Secret History of America's Imperfect Union*. Boston: Little, Brown, 2020.
Kukla, Jon. *A Wilderness So Immense: The Louisiana Purchase and the Destiny of America*. New York: Alfred A. Knopf, 2003.
Kurlansky, Mark. *Cod: A Biography of the Fish That Changed the World*. New York: Penguin Books, 1997.
Larson, Edward J., and Michael P. Winship. *The Constitutional Convention: A Narrative History from the Notes of James Madison*. New York: Modern Library: 2005.
Litwack, Leon E. *Been in the Storm So Long: The Aftermath of Slavery*. New York: Vintage Books, 1979.

Lyon, E. W. *The Man Who Sold Louisiana*. Norman: University of Oklahoma Press, 1942.
Maier, Pauline. *American Scripture: Making the Declaration of Independence*. New York: Alfred A. Knopf, 1997.
———. *Ratification: The People Debate the Constitution, 1787–1788*. New York: Simon & Schuster, 2010.
Main, Jackson T. *The Anti-Federalists: Critics of the Constitution, 1781–1788*. New York and London: W. W. Norton, 1974.
Mallock, Daniel L. *Agony and Eloquence: John Adams, Thomas Jefferson, and a World of Revolution*. New York: Skyhorse, 2016.
Malone, Dumas. *Jefferson and His Time*. 6 vols. Boston: Little, Brown, 1948–70.
Maltz, Earl M. "The Idea of the Proslavery Constitution." *Journal of the Early Republic* 17, no. 1 (1997): 37–59.
Manning, Susan, ed. *J. Hector St. John De Crèvecoeur: Letters from an American Farmer*. New York and Oxford: Oxford University Press, 2009.
Mason, Matthew. *Slavery and Politics in the Early American Republic*. Chapel Hill: University of North Carolina Press, 2006.
Matson, Cathy D., and Peter S. Onuf. *A Union of Interests: Political and Economic Thought in Revolutionary America*. Lawrence: University Press of Kansas, 1990.
Mayer, Henry. *A Son of Thunder: Patrick Henry and the American Republic*. Charlottesville and London: University Press of Virginia, 1991.
McCoy, Drew R. *The Last of the Fathers: James Madison and the Republican Legacy*. New York and Cambridge: Cambridge University Press, 1989.
McCullough, David G. *1776*. New York: Simon & Schuster, 2006.
———. *John Adams*. New York: Simon & Schuster, 2001.
McDonald, Forrest. *E Pluribus Unum: The Formation of the American Republic, 1776–1790*. Indianapolis, IN: Liberty Fund, 1979.
———. *States' Rights and the Union: Imperium in Imperio, 1776–1876*. Lawrence: University Press of Kansas, 2000.
McGaughy, J. K. *Richard Henry Lee of Virginia: A Portrait of an American Revolutionary*. Lanham, MD: Rowman & Littlefield, 2004.
McLynn, Frank. *The Year Britain Became Master of the World*. New York: Grove Press, 2004.
Meacham, Jon. *Thomas Jefferson: The Art of Power*. New York: Random House, 2012.
Meng, John J. *Despatches and Instructions of Conrad Alexandre Gérard, 1778–1780: Correspondence of the First French Minister to the United States with the Comte de Vergennes*. Baltimore: Johns Hopkins Press, 1939.
Merritt, Eli F. "Secret Conflict and Sectional Compromise: The Mississippi River Question and the United States Constitution." *American Journal of Legal History* 35, no. 2 (April 1991): 117–71.
Middlekauff, Robert. *Washington's Revolution: The Making of America's First Leader*. New York: Alfred A. Knopf, 2015.
Miller, John C. *Alexander Hamilton: Portrait in Paradox*. New York: Harper & Brothers, 1959.

———. *Sam Adams: Pioneer in Propaganda*. Stanford: Stanford University Press, 1960.

Miller, Melanie. *An Incautious Man: The Life of Gouverneur Morris*. Lives of the Founders. Wilmington, DE: Intercollegiate Studies Institute, 2008.

Morgan, David T., and William J. Schmidt. *North Carolinians in the Continental Congress*. Winston-Salem, NC: John F. Blair, 1976.

Morgan, Edmund S. *Benjamin Franklin*. New Haven and London: Yale Nota Bene, 2003.

———. *The Birth of the Republic, 1763–89*. Chicago and London: University of Chicago Press, 1977.

Morgan, Ted. *Wilderness at Dawn: The Settling of the North American Continent*. New York: Simon & Schuster, 1993.

Morris, Richard B. *The Forging of the Union, 1781–1789*. New York: Harper & Row, 1987.

———. *The Peacemakers: The Great Powers and American Independence*. New York: Harper & Row, 1965.

———. *Seven Who Shaped Our Destiny: The Founding Fathers as Revolutionaries*. New York: Harper & Row, 1973.

Mulford, Carla, and Lester C. Olson. "Benjamin Franklin's Vision of American Community: A Study in Rhetorical Iconology." *American Historical Review* 111, no. 1 (2006): 157–58.

Murchison, William. *The Cost of Liberty: The Life of John Dickinson*. Washington: 2013.

Nagel, Paul C. *John Quincy Adams: A Public Life, a Private Life*. Cambridge, MA, and London: Harvard University Press, 1997.

Newcomb, Benjamin H. *Franklin and Galloway: A Political Partnership*. New Haven and London: Yale University Press, 1972.

Norton, Mary Beth. *1774: The Long Year of Revolution*. New York: Alfred A. Knopf, 2020.

Olson, Lester C. *Benjamin Franklin's Vision of American Community: A Study in Rhetorical Iconology*. Columbia: University of South Carolina Press, 2004.

Onuf, Peter S. "Liberty, Development, and Union: Visions of the West in the 1780s." *William and Mary Quarterly* 43, no. 2 (1986): 179–213.

———. *The Origins of the Federal Republic: Jurisdictional Controversies in the United States, 1775–1787*. Philadelphia: University of Pennsylvania Press, 1983.

———. *Statehood and Union: A History of the Northwest Ordinance*. Notre Dame, IN: University of Notre Dame Press, 2019.

O'Shaughnessy, Andrew. *The Men Who Lost America: British Leadership, the American Revolution, and the Fate of the Empire*. New Haven and London: Yale University Press, 2013.

Paine, Thomas. *Common Sense Unabridged*. Mineola, NY: Dover, 1997.

Paul, Joel R. *Unlikely Allies: How a Merchant, a Playwright, and a Spy Saved the American Revolution*. New York: Riverhead Books, 2009.

Peterson, Merrill D. *Thomas Jefferson and the New Nation: A Biography*. New York and Oxford: Oxford University Press, 1970.
Phillips, Paul C. "American Opinions Regarding the West, 1778–1783." *Mississippi Valley Historical Association* 7 (1914): 286–305.
———. *The West in the Diplomacy of the American Revolution*. Victoria, Aus.: Leopold Classic Library, 2020.
Piecuch, Jim. *Three Peoples, One King: Loyalists, Indians, and Slaves in the Revolutionary South, 1775–1782*. Columbia: University of South Carolina Press, 2013.
Puls, Mark. *Samuel Adams: Father of the American Revolution*. New York: Palgrave Macmillan, 2006.
Rakove, Jack N. *The Beginnings of National Politics: An Interpretive History of the Continental Congress*. Baltimore and London: Johns Hopkins University Press, 2019.
———. *James Madison and the Creation of the American Republic*. New York: Longman, 1990.
———. *Original Meanings, Politics and Ideas in the Making of the Constitution*. New York: Alfred A. Knopf, 1996.
———. *Revolutionaries*. Boston: Mariner Books, 2010.
Randall, Willard S. *Alexander Hamilton: A Life*. New York: HarperCollins, 2003.
Raphael, Ray. *The People's History of the American Revolution*. New York: New Press, 2002.
Rappleye, Charles. *Robert Morris: Financier of the American Revolution*. New York: Simon & Schuster, 2010.
Rasmussen, Dennis C. *Fears of a Setting Sun: The Disillusionment of America's Founders*. Princeton, NJ: Princeton University Press, 2021.
Readex Microprint Corporation. *Early American Newspapers: Series II, 1758–1900: The New Republic*. Chester, VT: Readex, 2004.
Richards, Leonard L. *Shays's Rebellion: The American Revolution's Final Battle*. Philadelphia: University of Pennsylvania Press, 2003.
Roberts, Cokie. *Founding Mothers: The Women Who Raised Our Nation*. New York: HarperCollins, 2005.
Rogers, Clifford J., Ty Seidule, and Samuel J. Watson, eds. *The West Point History of the American Revolution*. New York: Simon & Schuster, 2017.
Rohrbough, Malcolm J. *The Trans-Appalachian Frontier: People, Societies, and Institutions, 1775–1850*. New York and Oxford: Oxford University Press, 1978.
Roosevelt, Theodore. *American Statesmen: Gouverneur Morris*. Boston and New York: Houghton Mifflin—Riverside Press Cambridge, 1916.
Rosenfeld, Richard N. *American Aurora: A Democratic-Republican Returns. The Suppressed History of Our Nation's Beginning and the Heroic Newspaper That Tried to Report It*. New York: St. Martin's, 1997.
Rossiter, Clinton, ed. *The Federalist Papers*. New York: Signet Classics, 2003.
Rutland, Robert A., ed. *James Madison and the American Nation: An Encyclopedia, 1751–1836*. New York: Simon & Schuster, 1994.

———. *James Madison: The Founding Father*. New York: MacMillan; London: Collier Macmillan, 1987.
Schachner, Nathan. *Thomas Jefferson: A Biography*. New York and London: Thomas Yoseloff, 1951.
Sedgwick, John. *War of Two: Alexander Hamilton, Aaron Burr, and the Duel That Stunned the Nation*. New York: Berkley Books, 2015.
Seelye, John. *Beautiful Machine: Rivers and the Republican Plan, 1755–1825*. New York and Oxford: Oxford University Press, 1991.
Selby, John E. *The Revolution in Virginia, 1775–1783*. Charlottesville: University of Virginia Press, 1988.
Sharp, James R. *American Politics in the Early Republic: The New Nation in Crisis*. New Haven and London: Yale University Press, 1993.
Signer, Michael. *Becoming Madison: The Extraordinary Origins of the Least Likely Founding Father*. New York: PublicAffairs, 2015.
Smith, James M., ed. *The Republic of Letters: The Correspondence between Thomas Jefferson and James Madison, 1776–1826*. New York and London: W. W. Norton, 1995.
Smith, Jean E. *John Marshall: Definer of a Nation*. New York: Owl Books, 1996.
Spence, Richard D. "John Donelson and the Opening of the Old Southwest." *Tennessee Historical Quarterly* 50, no. 3 (1991): 157–72.
Stahr, Walter. *John Jay: Founding Father*. New York and London: Hambledon and London, 2005.
Stewart, David O. *Madison's Gift: Five Partnerships That Built America*. New York: Simon & Schuster, 2016.
———. *The Summer of 1787: The Men Who Invented the Constitution*. New York: Simon & Schuster, 2007.
Stoll, Ira. *Samuel Adams: A Life*. New York: Free Press, 2008.
Stone, Daniel P. "Join, or Die: Political and Religious Controversy over Franklin's Snake Cartoon." *Journal of the American Revolution*, January 10, 2018. https://allthingsliberty.com/2018/01/join-die-political-religious-controversy-franklins-snake-cartoon/.
Szatmary, David P. *Shays' Rebellion: The Making of an Agrarian Insurrection*. Amherst: University of Massachusetts Press, 1980.
Taylor, Alan. *American Colonies: The Penguin History of the United States*. New York: Viking Penguin, 2001.
———. *American Republics: A Continental History of the United States, 1783–1850*. New York and London: W. W. Norton, 2021.
———. *Internal Enemy: Slavery and War in Virginia, 1772–1832*. New York and London: W. W. Norton, 2013.
Taylor, Elizabeth D. *A Slave in the White House: Paul Jennings and the Madisons*. New York: Palgrave Macmillan, 2012.
Taylor, Robert M., Jr., ed. *The Northwest Ordinance, 1787: A Bicentennial Handbook*. Indianapolis: Indiana Historical Society, 1987.
Thompson, C. Bradley. *John Adams and the Spirit of Liberty*. Lawrence: University Press of Kansas, 1998.

Toll, Ian W. *Six Frigates: The Epic History of the Founding of the U.S. Navy.* New York and London: W. W. Norton, 2006.
Tuchman, Barbara W. *Practicing History: Selected Essays.* New York: Alfred A. Knopf, 1981.
Turner, Frederick J. *The Frontier in American History.* New York: Henry Holt, 1921.
Tyson, Troy. *The Yankee Way: The Blueprint That Created America.* Greenwood, IN: Courant, 2018.
Unger, Harlow G. *America's Second Revolution: How George Washington Defeated Patrick Henry and Saved the Nation.* Hoboken, NJ: John Wiley & Sons, 2007.
———. *Dr. Benjamin Rush: The Founding Father Who Healed a Wounded Nation.* New York: Da Capo Press, 2018.
———. *Lion of Liberty: Patrick Henry and the Call to a New Nation.* Philadelphia: Da Capo Press, 2010.
Usner, Daniel H., Jr. *Indians, Settlers, and Slaves in a Frontier Exchange Economy: The Lower Mississippi Valley Before 1783.* Chapel Hill: University of North Carolina Press, 1992.
Van Cleave, George. *We Have Not a Government: The Articles of Confederation and the Road to the Constitution.* Chicago and London: University of Chicago Press, 2017.
Van Doren, Carl. *Benjamin Franklin.* New York: Penguin Books, 1991.
Varon, Elizabeth R. *Disunion! The Coming of the American Civil War, 1789–1859.* Chapel Hill: University of North Carolina Press, 2008.
Vile, John R. *The Declaration of Independence: America's First Founding Document in U.S. History and Culture.* Santa Barbara: ABC-CLIO, 2019.
Ward, Christopher. *The War of the Revolution.* 2 vols. New York: Macmillan, 1952.
Warren, Wendy. *New England Bound: Slavery and Colonization in Early America.* New York and London: Liveright, 2016.
Weber, David J. *The Spanish Frontier in North America.* New Haven and London: Yale University Press, 1992.
Whitaker, Arthur P. *The Spanish-American Frontier, 1783–1795: The Westward Movement and the Spanish Retreat in the Mississippi Valley.* Lincoln: University of Nebraska Press, 1927.
Wilentz, Sean. *No Property in Man: Slavery and Antislavery at the Nation's Founding.* Cambridge, MA, and London: Harvard University Press, 2018.
Wills, Garry. *James Madison.* The American Presidents Series. New York: Times Books, 2002.
Wilson, David K. *The Southern Strategy.* Charleston: University of South Carolina, 2005.
Wirt, William. *The Life of Patrick Henry.* Philadelphia: Thomas Desilver, 1836.
Wood, Gordon S. *The American Revolution: A History.* New York: Modern Library, 2002.
———. *The Americanization of Benjamin Franklin.* New York: Penguin Books, 2004.
———. *The Creation of the American Republic, 1776–1787.* New York and London: W. W. Norton, 1972.

———. *Friends Divided: John Adams and Thomas Jefferson.* New York: Penguin Press, 2017.
———. *The Radicalism of the American Revolution.* New York: Vintage Books, 1993.
Wood, W. J. *Major Battles and Campaigns: Battles of the Revolutionary War, 1775–1781.* Cambridge, MA: Da Capo Press, 1990.
Wright, Louis B. *The Cultural Life of the American Colonies, 1607–1763.* New York and Evanston: Harper & Row, 1962.

INDEX

Page numbers in *italics* indicate images

Abarca de Bolea, Pedro Pablo. *See* Aranda, Count of (Pedro Pablo Abarca de Bolea)
abolition of slavery, 5, 10, 294
An Act to Facilitate the Completion of the Articles of Confederation (New York), 264
Adams, John, *24*; and confederation term, 138; and Continental Army failures, 164–65; on Convention of the New England States (1776), 168; as delegate, 21–22, 75–76, 78; on delegates, 19, 67; delegates on, 31–32; and embargo proposal, 65–67; and fishery rights, 227; and foreign alliances committees, 151, 156–58, 159; on Franklin, 94; and French alliance negotiations, 222; on Henry, 64; and independence debates, 126, 127, 130–31, 386n15; on Jay, 309; on Livingston, 23, 107–8; and Netherlands credit, 323; and New England chauvinism, 87; on officer election and pay, 93; and peace negotiations, 7–8, 238–40, 300–303, 306–7, 309, 320, 321, 333–36; on prayer, 48; and reconciliation, 86–89; on skill of Spanish diplomats, 271; on slaves, 109; on Treaty of Paris (1783), 333–36, 339; on unity prospects, 48, 49, 67, 75–76, 116–20, 131; and voting representation, 35–36, 140; on Washington, 90
Adams, John Quincy, 239
Adams, Samuel, *121*; and Articles of Confederation committee, 138; on birth of America, 38; on Continental Army failures, 163–64; as delegate, 21, 78; on delegates, 219; delegates on, 31–32; and domestic civil war fears, 26; on emancipation threat, 109; and fishery rights, 214–15, 219–25, 227–28, 232–36; and foreign alliances committee, 159, 161; Lee-Adams coalition, 232–40, 246; on Maryland's delay of ratification, 190; and Northern confederacy proposal, 120–22; patriotism of, 222–23; on prayer, 48–49; and Spanish mediation offer (1779), 213, 214–15, 217, 219–25, 227–28, 232–33; on Suffolk Resolves, 49; two-state theory, 228; on Vermont conflict, 174; and voting representation, 140
Address to the Inhabitants of the Colonies, 68, 69–70
Address to the People of Great Britain, 67–68, 69
Administration of Justice Act, 20–21
"African Slavery in America" (Paine), 101
Aitken, Robert, 99–100
Albany Congress/Plan, 44–46, 57, 95
The American Crisis (Paine), 159
Annapolis, as temporary capital, 368
apologies, 325
Aranda, Count of (Pedro Pablo Abarca de Bolea), 180, 328
armies. *See* Continental Army; militias and armies

Armstrong, John, 263
Arnold, Benedict, 158–59, 276, *277*
Arnold, Jonathan, 344
Articles of Confederation and Perpetual Union: Article II, 175; Article V, 176; Article VI, 175, 188, 349; Article VIII, 176, 185–86, 350–51; Article IX, 175–76, 186, 247; committee on, 138–39, 175; debates on, 139–48, 173–77, 231; Dickinson draft (1776), 134, 138–39, 175; and fears of Northern domination, 129–30; formal approval of, 177; Franklin's proposal for, 8, 81–83, 94–97, 114, 137–38; limits on federal power in, 286–89; in overview, 3–5, 8–10; pessimism over, 134, 141–48; state powers in, 170–73, 187–88; and taxation, 140, 141–42, 147, 173, 176, 185–86, 350–51; tensions on post-independence, 340; and territorial rights, 139, 140, 142–44, 147, 170, 173, 175–76, 198, 199–200; and voting representation, 140–41, 147, 173, 176, 186–87
Articles of Confederation ratification: by bulk of states, 190; by Delaware, 190, 198, 199, 200–202; delays of as dangerous, 200–201, 255–56; early struggles over, 185–89; expectations of, 138, 177; final, 281; and foreign alliances, 191, 201; and Maryland, 190, 198, 199–200, 243–44, 247, 249, 278–79, 281, 358; by New Jersey, 190, 198–99; in overview, 8; partial ratification, 189–91, 200, 249; secession threats over, 202, 203–4; territorial rights of Virginia as blocking, 188, 189, 199–200, 243–44, 247–49, 254, 256, 263–64, 275–78, 297, 358; by Virginia, 188, 190
Austro-Russian mediation proposal, 301–2, 320, 398n1

Baltimore, as Continental Congress site, 159
Bank of North America, 282
Barbé-Marbois, François, 267–68, 331, 338
Bartlett, Josiah, 138, 139

Bill of Rights, English, 21
Black people: and Continental Army service, 109–10; percentage of population, 34. *See also* slavery
Bland, Richard, 42–43, 286, 288, 289, 349
Bland, Theodorick, 270–71, 281, 337
Boston: Boston Tea Party, 19, 20, 50, 65; King Street massacre (1770), 117; skirmish rumors (1774), 47–48
Boston Port Act, 20
Boston Tea Party, 19, 20, 50, 65
Boudinot, Elias: and capital site selection, 362, 364, 366; and Continental Army mutiny, 354; on Howell, 345; and land cessions committee, 401n8; on Treaty of Paris (1783), 337; and Vermont issue, 293
boundaries. *See* Mississippi River as boundary; national boundaries; state boundaries
Bowdoin, James, 21
Brandywine, Battle of, 174
Braxton, Carter, 114, *115*, 115–16
Britain: Address to the People of Great Britain, 67–68, 69; and Anglo-French alliance fears, 129, 133; attempt to cut France out of peace negotiations, 324; collusion with France, 331; fear of war with, 22–26; Franklin on corruption of, 79, 80; and Mississippi navigation rights, 7–8, 154–56, 161, 236, 265; Paine on government of, 102; potential restoration of colonies to, 6, 200–201, 258, 269, 287–88, 301, 302; rejection of Olive Branch petition, 113; rejection of Spanish mediation offer, 235; Russian military aid talks, 210; Spain as enemy of, 315; Spain's covert talks with, 316–17; Spain's declaration of war on, 310–11, 328; and territorial claims in Treaty of Paris (1783), 332–33, 336, 338–39; territorial gains from French and Indian War, 153, 159. *See also* Florida, East/West; Gibraltar; peace negotiations; reconciliation proposals; Revolutionary War; Treaty of Paris of 1763; Treaty of Paris of 1783

Index

British East India Company, 20, 65, 74
Burgoyne, John, 177, 290
Burke, Thomas, *171*; criticism of Articles of Confederation, 187–88; and fishery rights, 220; and Mississippi River navigation rights, 280; and partial confederation proposal, 231, 249–50; and Spanish mediation offer, 211–12, 213, 217, 220; and states' rights, 167, 170–73

Campeche, 317
Canada: cession of, 325; and Franco-American alliance, 195–97; and Revolutionary War assault, 106, 196; and Spanish mediation offer, 206, 214; and Vermont issue, 294. *See also* fishery rights
A Candid Examination of the Mutual Claims of Great Britain and the Colonies (Galloway), 5–6, 26–29, 57
capital, selection of, 341, 343, 361–67, 368
Carmichael, William, 312
Carpenters' Hall (Philadelphia), 30, *35*
Carroll, Daniel, 281
Catherine the Great, 267, 268–69, 301–2, 320
Champlain, Lake, 159
Chandler, Thomas Bradbury, 25
Charles III, *155*; anger at France, 205, 206; courts of, 312; and likeliness of an alliance, 152, 313. *See also* Spain; Spanish alliance negotiations; Spanish mediation offer (1779)
Charlestown, siege of, 252, 257–62
Charter of 1609, 125
charters, colonial: and Mississippi River navigation rights, 265; and territorial claims, 125, 141–43, 147, 267; and Virginia's land cession, 278
Chase, Samuel, 51, 107, 141, 144
Chesapeake, Battle of, 289–92
City Tavern (Philadelphia), 29, 30
civil war. *See* domestic civil war
Clark, Abraham, 148, 159
Clark, George Rogers, 266
Clinton, George, 92
Clinton, Henry, 252, 257, 262

Clouds, Battle of the, 174
Coercive Acts, 19–21, 60, 68, 77
Collins, John, 255, 256
Common Sense (Paine), 101–6
Compromise of 1779. *See* Mississippi-Fisheries Compromise
Concord, Battle of, 78
Confederation Congress. *See* Continental Congress, Second
confederations: committee on, 128, 138–39; Convention of the New England States (1776) as, 167–70; Hartford convention (1780) as, 348–49, 351; need for in debates, 144–46, 174–75; Paine on Continental Charter, 102, 104; partial confederation proposal, 231–32, 249–50; as preceding/following independence, 114, 121, 132, 133–34; terms for, 138; Virginia's resolution on (1776), 123–24. *See also* Articles of Confederation and Perpetual Union; constitution proposals, early; multiple confederations; subconfederations
Connecticut: Hartford convention (1780), 348–49, 351; land cessions by, 297; and Mississippi River navigation rights, 280; and ratification of Articles of Confederation, 190; territorial claims of, 142
constitutional conventions, calls for: by Hamilton, 350; post-independence, 340; by Varnum, 287
constitutional histories, scholarship on, 12–15
constitution proposals, early: and Albany Congress, 44–46, 57, 95; challenges of, 113; Constitution of 1787, 58; Dickinson draft, 138–39, 175; and form of government debates, 115–16; Franklin's Articles of Confederation proposal, 8, 81–83, 94–97, 114, 137–38; Franklin's first union proposal (1751), 95; Galloway's Plan of Union, 57–58, 61–64, 74, 79; and independence as preceding/following confederation, 114, 121, 132, 133–34; Paine on need for Continental

constitution proposals, early (*continued*)
 Charter, 102, 104; and Virginia's resolution on confederation (1776), 123–24
Continental Army: and Black people, 109–10; Canadian assault (1775-1776), 106, 196; finances, 251–52, 353–55; formation of, 89–90; and French military aid, 258–62; and land bounties, 200; mutiny over wages, 353–55; New York and New Jersey battles, 158–59, 161–65, 167, 177; and North/South tensions, 83, 88, 93, 109–12, 118, 161–64; officer election, 93–94; pay, 93, 109, 118, 163, 353–55; shift to South, 6, 250, 252–53, 255, 282; troop quotas, 186; Washington's appointment to, 90
Continental Association, 6, 41–42, 50–56, 63, 65–67, 70–75, 107–8. *See also* embargoes
Continental Congress, First: accomplishments of, 73–75; examples of unity in, 42–44, 46–49; fears of, 22–33; first meeting, 29; and food, 42; formation of, 19, 21–22; meeting locations, 29–30; number of delegates, 29; religious diversity of, 48–49; schedule, 41; sociability in, 41, 42–43, 73–74; Southern leadership in, 30–33. *See also* independence; reconciliation proposals
Continental Congress, Second: delegate list, 78; meeting places, 84; move to New Jersey, 354, 355; move to York, 174; reconvening date, 74. *See also* Articles of Confederation and Perpetual Union; constitution proposals, early; economics and finances; fishery rights; foreign alliances; Franco-American alliance; independence; Mississippi River as boundary; Mississippi River navigation rights; peace negotiations; reconciliation proposals; territorial rights; voting representation
Convention of the New England States (1776), 167–70

Cornell, Ezekiel, 251, 253, 254–55
Cornwallis, Charles, 159, 290
credit and foreign alliances: and need for confederation, 174–75, 201; and Netherlands, 323; and Spanish-American alliance negotiations, 217, 312, 313, 314, 317; and Spanish mediation proposal, 222; and Treaty of Paris (1783), 335
currency, 168, 222, 250–52
Cushing, Thomas, 21, 31–32, 48, 51, 326–27

Daniel of St. Thomas Jenifer, 401n8
d'Arsac, Charles-Henri-Louis. *See* Ternay, Chevalier de (Charles-Henri-Louis d'Arsac)
Lord Dartmouth (William Legge), 77
Deane, Silas: and alliance negotiations, 158, 159–61, 177–80; as delegate, 78; on delegates, 47–48; on domestic civil war, 115; on Henry, 34; and independence debates, 132–33; on Richard Henry Lee, 43
Declaration and Resolves of Congress, 67–68
Declaration of Independence, 6–7, 65, 68, 137–38, 167, 276
Declaratory Act, 60
Delaware: and independence proposal, 134, 136; and ratification of Articles of Confederation, 190, 198, 199, 200–202
Delaware River and capital site selection, 364–67
del Campo, Bernardo, 318
Dickinson, John, 85; and Articles of Confederation committee, 134, 138–39, 175; as delegate, 78; and domestic civil war fears, 84, 356; and foreign alliances committee, 151, 156–58; and independence proposal, 127, 131–34, 137; and reconciliation proposal, 83–90, 105, 113
dictator proposals, 254–55, 287
diplomacy and diplomats: John Adams on skill of Spanish diplomats, 271; restrictions on states, 139; tensions

Index

over appointments, 158, 231, 238–40. *See also* Franco-American alliance; peace negotiations; Spanish alliance negotiations; Spanish mediation offer (1779)

disunion: Franklin on, 46; John Adams on unity prospects, 48, 49, 67, 75–76, 116–20, 131; overview of issues, 3–12; scholarship on unionist/disunionist paradigm, 12–15; Washington on, 369–70. *See also* domestic civil war; economics and finances; fishery rights; foreign alliances; Mississippi River as boundary; Mississippi River navigation rights; multiple confederations; North/South tensions; secession and secession threats; subconfederations; territorial rights

domestic civil war: in Articles of Confederation, 139; and deference to South, 30–33, 90–93; and Dickinson, 84, 356; and fears of New England, 23–26, 27, 110, 163, 346–47, 356; and Franklin's Articles of Confederation proposal, 82–83; and Galloway, 5–6, 26–29, 57, 60–61, 356; and Hamilton, 345–46; and John Adams, 118; and Lee-Adams coalition, 232; and limits of Congressional power, 289; and Madison, 296–97, 346–47; need for confederation to prevent, 4–6, 114–15, 145–46; and Paine, 102, 103–5, 356; and post-independence tensions, 345–46, 348, 356; and potential restoration of colonies to Britain, 269; and ratification delays, 201–2, 243; and reconciliation proposals, 5–6, 26–28, 57, 60–61, 84; and slavery, 5–6, 10, 28, 110, 118; and territorial claims, 4, 27, 110, 114–15, 174, 231, 248, 293–96, 382n24; and Witherspoon, 4, 13, 145–46

Drayton, William Henry, 186–87, 211, 212, 220, 234

Drummond, Thomas, 384n37

Duane, James, *259*; on battles and War, 47, 113, 250; as delegate, 78; and embargo debate, 63; and French military aid, 258, 262; on Galloway's Plan of Union, 63; on ratification, 256, 279; and territorial rights, 263–64, 361

Duché, Jacob, 48–49

Duffield, George, 291

Lord Dunmore (John Murray), 112, 113

Dyer, Eliphalet: on Burke, 187; on domestic civil war fears, 110, 114–15; and embargo proposal, 51; and fishery rights, 221; and regional control of Continental Army, 90–92, 112

economics and finances: and Articles of Confederation, 282, 344; and capital site selection, 363–64; as contentious issue, 4, 231; and hyperinflation, 250; and information on state wealth, 38; Morris as superintendent of finance, 281–82; North/South differences in, 41–42, 44; and Revolutionary War costs, 250–52; and slavery, 9; tensions on post-independence, 340, 343–48, 359–60; and tobacco, 52–53; and wage mutiny by Continental Army, 353–55. *See also* credit and foreign alliances; fishery rights; Mississippi River navigation rights; taxation

Edling, Max M., 12

emancipation: by Britain, 109, 112, 113; and domestic civil war fears, 110; inaction on, 9–10; Jefferson on, 5; Paine on, 100–101

embargoes: Continental Association (1774), 6, 41–42, 50–56, 63, 65–67, 70–73, 74–75, 107–8; foodstuffs embargo (1778), 202–4; Galloway on inefficiency of, 58–59; nonexportation, 41–42, 51–56, 63, 65–67, 70–73, 74–75; nonimportation, 41, 50, 51, 54, 63, 74; and Stamp Act, 50; and Townshend Duties, 50

English Bill of Rights, 21

Enlightenment, 119, 152, 156, 181

executive branch: in Franklin's Articles of Confederation proposal, 81; in Galloway's Plan of Union, 62; in Paine's proposal for Continental Charter, 104; in Virginia state constitution, 124

Expédition Particulière, 257–62

fear of other countries: and independence, 23, 25, 61, 84, 133; and need for foreign alliances, 157; and territorial claims, 271–72
Fell, John, 238
fishery rights: British restrictions on, 106, 224–25; and commercial treaties, 218, 229, 236, 300, 303; and Franco-American alliance, 157–58, 159, 161, 178–80, 221–22, 229, 235–36; importance of, 223–25; and Lee-Adams coalition, 232–36, 246; and naval development, 225–26, 234; New England Trade and Fisheries Act, 106, 224–25; North/South tensions over, 193, 220–22, 227–30, 232–36; and peace negotiations, 7–8, 239–40, 300–305, 325–27, 331, 332, 334, 335, 339; and Samuel Adams, 214–15, 219–25, 227–28, 232–36; and Spanish alliance negotiations, 272; and Spanish-British covert talks, 317; and Spanish mediation offer, 206, 209–10, 211, 214, 217–26, 227–30, 232–34; in Treaty of Paris (1763), 157–58; in Treaty of Paris (1783), 7–8, 332, 334, 335, 337; and triple alliance, 192–93, 195–97, 206–7. *See also* Mississippi-Fisheries Compromise
Fleming, William, 232
Florida, East/West: and French triple alliance policy, 192, 194; and peace negotiations, 269; and Spanish alliance negotiations, 159–60, 180, 217, 300; and Spanish-British covert talks, 317; and Spanish mediation offer, 205–6, 209, 211, 214, 215–17; and Treaty of Paris (1783), 333
Floridablanca (José Moñino y Redondo), *182*; and alliance negotiations, 180–83, 262–63, 311–18; and Austro-Russian mediation proposal, 320; and focus on Spanish territories during War, 328; and French triple war alliance attempts, 192; and intelligence operatives, 182–83; and Jay, 311–18; and mediation offer, 205–6

Floyd, William, 279
Folsom, Nathaniel, 185–86
food: and Continental Congress, 42; foodstuffs embargo (1778), 202–4
foreign alliances: Anglo-French alliance, fears of, 129, 133; committees, 151–53, 156–58, 159–61; importance of, 121–22, 156–57; and independence debates, 128–29, 131–33; and need for confederation and ratification, 146, 174–75, 191, 201; and Northern confederacy proposal, 121–22; restrictions on states seeking, 139, 188; and trade, 107; treaty template, 156; and triple alliance hopes, 191–98, 206–7; Virginia's resolutions on, 123, 124, 248–49, 263–64, 272, 273–74. *See also* credit and foreign alliances; France; Franco-American alliance; Spain; Spanish alliance negotiations
France: and Anglo-French alliance fears, 129, 133; and Austro-Russian mediation proposal, 301–2; coordination with Spain on American policy, 181, 191, 194–95, 268–69; and foreign alliances committee, 151–52; and independence debates, 128–29, 132–33; Jay's break with, 327–31, 337–38; and Louisiana, 387n3; and Mississippi border rights, 328–29; and Mississippi navigation rights, 155, 161; and Northern confederacy proposal, 121–22; territory losses from Seven Years' War, 153; trade with, 108; and triple alliance hopes, 191–98, 206–7. *See also* French and Indian War; peace negotiations
Franco-American alliance: and Austro-Russian mediation proposal, 302; and Declaration of Independence, 6; as diplomatic success, 177, 180; and Franklin, 158, 159–61, 177–80, 195–96; hopes for, 152; instructions to Gérard, 191–98; and military aid, 177–78, 196, 257–62; and Morris, 195–98; negotiations for, 157, 158, 159–61, 177–80, 195–96; and peace negotiations, 235–36, 324, 337–38; and ratification

Index   433

of Articles of Confederation, 191, 201; revision proposals, 236, 254; Spanish dislike of, 205–6; and Spanish mediation offer, 217, 221–22, 229, 235; and territorial rights, 266; and Treaty of Paris (1783), 337–38
François Joseph Paul, Count de Grasse. *See* Grasse, Comte de (François Joseph Paul)
Franklin, Benjamin, *45*; and Albany Congress/Plan, 44–46, 57, 95; Articles of Confederation proposal, 8, 81–83, 94–97, 114, 137–38; on British corruption, 79, 80; and British territorial claims in Treaty of Paris (1783), 339; and Continental Army control, 112; as delegate, 78, 80–83; and foreign alliances committee, 151, 156–58; and Franco-American alliance, 158, 159–61, 177–80, 195–96; and Galloway, 78–79, 80; health of, 330; and independence proposal, 137; and Jefferson, 95; John Adams on, 94; and Library Company, 30; and Northern confederacy proposal, 120; and Olive Branch Petition, 89; and peace negotiations, 7–8, 303, 307, 321–22, 324–27, 330, 334–36; pessimism about unity, 46; and Plan of Union, 79; and Spanish alliance negotiations, 180; and voting representation, 140
Frederick II, 320. *See also* Austro-Russian mediation proposal
French and Indian War, 45, 59–60, 153, 159, 266. *See also* Treaty of Paris of 1763
fur trade, 142, 196

Gadsden, Christopher, 51, 55, 71–72, 78, 107, 380n26
Gage, Thomas, 19–21, 49, 77–78
Galloway, Joseph, *28*; and domestic civil war fears, 5–6, 26–29, 57, 60–61, 356; and Franklin, 78–79, 80; and meeting locations, 29–30; move to England, 83; reconciliation and Plan of Union, 5–6, 26–28, 57–64, 74, 79, 100; on Samuel Adams, 223; threats to, 79–80
Gálvez, Bernardo de, 328

Gates, Horatio, 93, 177, 290
George III, *69*; anger of, 210; and Austro-Russian mediation proposal, 320; Olive Branch petition rejection, 113; opposition to independence, 398n1; Petition to the King, 67–69; and Vermont dispute, 294. *See also* Britain; peace negotiations
Georgia: and first Continental Congress meeting, 29; and impost debate, 344; and Mississippi River navigation rights, 269–73; potential restoration to Britain, 6, 258, 269; and ratification of Articles of Confederation by, 190; and Revolutionary War, 222, 252; support for independence by, 126; territorial claims by, 142
Gérard de Rayneval, Conrad Alexandre, *192*; and Franco-American alliance, 178, 191–98; and Jay, 239, 311; return to France, 267; and Spanish mediation offer, 204–7, 209–12, 227, 229–30
Gérard de Rayneval, Joseph Matthias, 329, 330–31
Gerry, Elbridge, *230*; on balance of power, 341; and capital site selection, 365–66; and fishery rights, 229; and foreign alliances committee, 159; and funding resolution, 163; and Mississippi River navigation rights, 237–38; and Northern confederacy proposal, 120; on ratification, 199
Gibraltar, 205–6, 316, 317, 320, 322–23, 339
Gondi, Jean-François-Paul de. *See* Cardinal Retz
Gordon, William, 362
Gorham, Nathaniel, 346, 347–48, 349
government: call for state governments, 125–26; form of government debates, 115–16; Paine on role of, 102. *See also* Articles of Confederation and Perpetual Union; confederations; constitution proposals, early
Grand Council, 45
Grasse, Comte de (François Joseph Paul), 289, 290

Graves, Thomas, 290
Gravier, Charles. *See* Vergennes, Comte de (Charles Gravier)
Greene, Nathanael, 262
Green Mountain Boys, 174, 293–94
Grenville, Thomas, 324
Griffin, Cyrus, 203–4

Hamilton, Alexander, *347*; call for constitutional convention, 350; and Continental Army funds, 251–52, 354; and fears of dissolution, 342, 345–46; and regional confederation crisis, 349–50; on Treaty of Paris (1783), 337
Hancock, John, 78
Hanson, John, 246, 281
Harnett, Cornelius, 187
Harrison, Benjamin: and capital site selection, 363; and Continental Army control, 112; as delegate, 78; and foreign alliances committee, 151, 156–58; and independence debates, 42, 131; and need for Virginia's support, 399n12; and taxation of slavery, 387n14; and voting procedures, 36–39
Hartford convention (1780), 348–49, 351
Hawkins, Benjamin, 354–55, 363–64
Henry, Patrick, 34, *36,* 36–39, 64, 78, 117, 359
heroic *vs.* tragic narrative, 14–15
Hewes, Joseph, 80, 119, 138, 144
Higginson, Stephen, 337, 350–51, 365
Holten, Samuel, 349
home rule: in Galloway's Plan of Union, 58, 61–64; in peace negotiations, 322, 329
Honduras, 317
Hooper, William, *162,* 162–63
Hosmer, Titus, 203
Houston, William Churchill, 243, 244, 261, 302–3
Howell, David, 344–45
Howly, Richard, 269–70
Hudson River: and domestic civil war concerns, 345–46; French military aid in, 257–62; and Northern confederacy concerns, 357

Humphreys, Charles, 137
Huntington, Samuel, 237–38, 281
Hutchinson, Thomas, 14–15, 116

impost debate, 344–48
impressment, 282
independence: committee on, 128; debates on, 22–26, 42–43, 114, 121, 126–34; and fear of other countries, 23, 25, 61, 84, 133; and fear of war with Britain, 22–26; George III's opposition to, 398n1; and Henry, 64; and Lee-Adams coalition, 233; and North/South tensions, 31, 134; Paine on, 101–6; in peace negotiations, 322, 323, 324, 325, 327, 329, 332; as preceding/following confederation, 114, 121, 132, 133–34; and reconciliation, 84–86; and Spanish mediation offer, 204–7, 209, 212, 233; staggered proposal, 128, 135; as term, 173; threats to proceed without Middle colonies, 6–7, 135–36; in Treaty of Paris (1783), 332; as unifying, 105, 167; Virginia's resolution on (1776), 123–24, 125; votes on, 134–38
Indiana Company, 297, 298, 299
indigo, 42, 55–56, 70–73
inevitability lens, 13

Jamaica, 192
Jameson, David, 282–83, 285
Jay, John: alliance negotiations with Spain, 262–63, 264, 267, 300–301, 310–18; appointment as ambassador to Spain, 238–39; break with Vergennes, 327–31; and call for state governments, 126; as delegate, 78; delegates and others on, 218, 284, 309–10, 336; finances of, 312, 314, 318; on Galloway's Plan of Union, 63–64; health of, 324; and Mississippi navigation rights, 207, 264, 279, 310–11; and Olive Branch Petition, 89; and peace negotiations, 7–8, 303, 307, 309–10, 319–24, 327–34, 337–39; and religion, 48; and Treaty of Paris (1783) draft, 332–33
Jefferson, Thomas, *96*; and alliance negotiations with France, 158; and

Index

capture of Richmond, 276–77; and deference to Virginia, 33; on emancipation, 5; and Franklin, 95; on Franklin's Articles of Confederation proposal, 95–97, 114; on Henry, 34; inquiry into, 306; and Mississippi River rights, 276; and peace negotiations, 303, 305–7, 323; on power of Congress, 360; on Samuel Adams, 223; and Virginia's land cession, 360
Fort Jefferson, 266
Johnson, Thomas, 89
Johnston, Samuel, 280
"Join or Die" slogan, 44
Jones, Joseph: and federal power, 286, 288; and Mississippi River navigation rights, 270, 271–72; and reinforcements in South, 285–86; and Virginia's territorial rights, 256, 263–64, 279
Jones, Willie, 264
Joseph II, 302. *See also* Austro-Russian mediation proposal
judiciary: in Franklin's Articles of Confederation proposal, 81–82; in Galloway's Plan of Union, 61–62
jury trials, 21

Kentucky: growth of, 247, 265, 363; and Mississippi River navigation rights, 217, 271, 304; and multiple confederacies, 357; and statehood, 340; and Virginia's land cession, 277; and Virginia's territorial claims, 140, 175, 194, 298, 299
Kingston, New York, as capital site, 361, 363
King Street massacre (1770), 117

land bounties, 200, 346
land cessions: of Canada, 325; committee on, 297–99; by Connecticut, 297; by New York, 264, 297; by North Carolina, 350; by South Carolina, 350; tensions on post-independence, 340, 350; by Virginia, 275, 277–78, 293, 296–300, 358–61; and Wyoming Valley, 46
land confiscations, 335

land speculating companies, 46, 142, 245, 293, 296–300, 358–61; and Albany Congress, 46; and Virginia's land cession, 293, 296–300, 358–61; and Virginia's territorial claims, 142, 245
land tax powers, 350
Laurens, Henry: on Charlestown, 261; on delegates, 253; and fishery rights, 221, 233–34; imprisonment of, 306; and Mississippi River navigation rights, 246; and peace negotiations, 303, 306, 307, 322, 323, 335; on ratification by South Carolina, 189
Lee, Arthur: and capital site selection, 365; on financial powers of Congress, 346; and Franco-American alliance negotiations, 158, 159–61, 177–80; and Spanish alliance negotiations, 180; and Spanish ambassadorship, 238; on Vermont, 295
Lee, Charles, 93, 106, 258–59
Lee, Francis Lightfoot, 199, 237
Lee, Richard Henry, *160*; on Articles of Confederation passage, 176; on Convention of the New England States (1776), 168; as delegate, 78; and embargo proposal, 51, 55, 56, 107, 108; and fishery rights, 221, 232–34, 339; and foreign alliances committee, 159, 160, 161; on Galloway's Plan of Union, 63; and independence, 43, 126–27, 128, 138; on John Adams, 240; Lee-Adams coalition, 232–40, 246; and Mississippi navigation rights, 236–37, 246, 339; on need for confederation, 175; and Spanish mediation offer, 212–13, 221, 232–34; and Virginia's cession of lands, 359; on Virginia's war burden, 283, 285. *See also* Mississippi-Fisheries Compromise
Fort Lee, Battle of, 159
Lee-Adams coalition, 232–40, 246
Legge, William, 77
legislature: in Franklin's Articles of Confederation proposal, 81–82; in Galloway's Plan of Union, 61–62, 63; in Paine's proposal for Continental Charter, 104; state-preemptive legislation and

legislature (*continued*)
  embargo debate, 73; in Virginia's state constitution, 124
Leonard, Daniel, 116–17
Lexington, Battle of (1775), 77–78, 80
L'Hommedieu, Ezra, 361
Library Company, 30
Lincoln, Benjamin, 261
Livingston, Philip, 23, 78
Livingston, Robert, *108*; and Articles of Confederation committee, 138; and France relations, 338; and French military aid use, 258–60; and independence, 127; and Northern confederacy, 253–54; and peace negotiations, 325–26; on trade embargo, 107–8
Livingston, Samuel, 401n8
Livingston, William, 23, 198–99
Long Island, Battle of, 158, 162
Louisiana: Louisiana Purchase, 180, 402n6; as Spanish territory, 153–56; transfer to France, 387n3. *See also* Mississippi River as boundary; Mississippi River navigation rights
Louis XVI, *152*; coordination with Spain, 192, 205; hopes for alliance with, 152; and independence, 204; reaction to peace negotiations, 338. *See also* France; Franco-American alliance
Lovell, James, 190, 218–19, 239–40, 261
lumber, 107, 108
Luzerne, Anne-César de La, 267–68, *268*, 301–2, 338
Lynch, Thomas, 43, 55, 78, 112, 141–42, 147

Mackenzie, Robert, 22
Madison, James, *265*; on Charlestown attack, 252; and Continental Army mutiny over wages, 354; and disunion fears, 296–300, 303–5, 342–43; and domestic civil war fears, 296–97, 346–47; on Henry, 34; on land speculation, 245; and Mississippi River navigation rights, 264–67, 270–73, 304–5; and multiple confederations fears, 342–43, 349–50; and peace negotiations, 303–5; and power of Congress, 288–89; revenue plan, 350; on slavery, 10; and Spanish alliance negotiations, 264–67, 270–73; and Treaty of Paris (1783), 338, 339; on Vermont, 294; and Virginia's land cession, 296–300, 359; and Virginia's War costs, 282–84
Madison, Rev. James, 399n12
majority/supermajority voting: and Articles of Confederation, 147, 176, 186; and capital site selection, 364, 365, 366; and First Continental Congress, 33; in Franklin's Articles of Confederation proposal, 82; and independence vote, 127, 134, 135–36; Jefferson on, 97; Paine on, 104; and treaties, 229, 249. *See also* voting representation
Maryland: and Albany Congress, 45; and capital site selection, 362, 364–67, 368; exclusion from Virginia's territorial claims, 125; and independence proposal, 386n15; and ratification of Articles of Confederation, 188–90, 198–200, 243–44, 247, 249, 256, 264, 278–79, 281, 297, 358; recall of soldiers proposal, 258, 259
Mason, George, 283, 284–85
Massachusetts: delegates and interest in independence, 21, 31–33; and Hartford convention (1780), 348–49, 351; and Mississippi River navigation rights, 280; and ratification of Articles of Confederation, 190; and Suffolk Resolves, 49; territorial claims of, 142; and Vermont issue, 295
Massachusetts Government Act, 20–21
Mathews, John, 202–3, 252, 260–61, 281, 287
McKean, Thomas, 138, 200–202, *201*
McKesson, John, 92
Mercer, John Francis, 346–47, 349, 351, 361
Middle colonies: as bloc, 209; and capital site selection, 362, 364–67; confederacy of rumors, 357; consolidation of Congressional powers in, 171, 172–73;

Index   437

and Continental Army losses, 162–64; and Continental Army pay, 118; and Continental Army in South, 285; and domestic civil war fears, 201–2; and form of government debates, 115–16; and independence debate, 6–7, 126, 127, 135–36; and reconciliation proposal, 88, 89; and republicanism, 119; secession threats over fishery rights by, 229–30; and Vermont statehood, 341–42

military aid: and break with France in Treaty of Paris (1783), 338; and Franco-American alliance, 177–78, 196, 257–62, 289–90; and Spanish-American alliance negotiations, 217, 312–14, 328

militias and armies: and Convention of the New England States (1776), 168; removal of in Spanish mediation terms, 214, 219; restrictions on states in Articles of Confederation, 139. *See also* Continental Army

Miralles y Trajan, Juan de: coordination with Gérard, 191, 192, 194–95; death of, 267; intelligence gathering by, 183, 316; on Jay, 239; on Mississippi navigation rights, 206, 207

Mississippi-Fisheries Compromise: in overview, 7–8; and peace negotiations, 7–8, 239–40, 246; and Spanish alliance negotiations, 272; and Spanish mediation offer, 206–7, 209–12, 214–26, 227–30, 232–40; and Treaty of Paris (1783), 334. *See also* fishery rights; Mississippi River as boundary; Mississippi River navigation rights

Mississippi River as boundary: in map of Spanish control, *154*; in overview, 7–8; in peace negotiations, 7–8, 304, 325–26, 327–32; and Spanish alliance negotiations, 153–56, 328; and Spanish mediation offer, 210, 212–13, 214; and triple alliance, 192

Mississippi River navigation rights: and Britain, 8, 154–56, 161, 236, 265; economic importance of, 153–54, 156, 180, 266–67; and Lee-Adams coalition,

233, 236–40; map of Spanish control, *154, 216*; and North/South tensions, 195, 196–98, 210, 233–40, 246–47, 284, 403n15; in overview of conflicts, 7–8; and peace negotiations, 236–40, 246–49, 304–5, 325, 327–32, 334, 339; South's need for, 153–54, 156, 180; South's reversal on, 275–80, 283–84, 301; and Spanish alliance negotiations (1776-1779), 153, 160–61, 180, 237; and Spanish alliance negotiations (1780-1782), 262–74, 275–80, 283–84, 300–301, 304, 310–13, 315–18, 382; and Spanish/French triple alliance, 192, 193, 194–98; and Spanish mediation offer (1779), 206–7, 209–12, 214–26, 227–30, 232–40; and Treaty of Paris (1763), 154–56, 161, 266, 332; and Treaty of Paris (1783), 8, 332–33, 334

molasses, 224, 350

Moñino y Redondo, José. *See* Floridablanca (José Moñino y Redondo)

Montmorin de Saint Herem, Armand Marc, 181

Morris, Gouverneur, *197*; and fishery rights, 196, 220; and Mississippi River navigation rights, 195–98, 237, 246–47; and Spanish mediation offer, 213, 217–18, 220; and Virginia's territorial claims, 244–45

Morris, Robert, 151, 156–58, 281–82, 346

Morton, John, 137

multiple confederations: in Articles of Confederation debates, 146, 174; and capital site selection, 366–67; and form of government differences, 116; and Hartford convention (1780), 348–49, 351; and Northern confederation rumors and plans, 120–22, 167–70, 249, 253–54, 255, 348–49, 351, 356; in overview, 10; and post-independence tensions, 342, 348, 356–58; and reconciliation, 92. *See also* subconfederations

Murray, John (Lord Dunmore), 112, 113

national boundaries: and peace negotiations, 325–26, 327–32, 333; and Spanish

national boundaries (*continued*)
  mediation terms, 214, 219; in Treaty of Paris (1783), 332, 333. *See also* Mississippi River as boundary
Native Americans: and Albany Congress, 45, 46; fear of attacks by, 20, 84; and Franklin's first union proposal (1751), 95; and land cessions by Virginia, 278; territory grant in peace negotiations, 326
Navarro y Valladares, Diego Joseph, 183
navy: naval development, 225–26, 234; and North/South tensions, 289
Nelson, Thomas, 283, 298
Newburgh conspiracy, 353
New England: and Albany Congress, 45; Black population of, 34; as bloc, 43–44, 209; and Continental Army control, 110–12; and Continental Army failures, 162–63, 164; and domestic civil war fears, 23–26, 27, 110, 163, 346–47, 356; domination of Congress by, 129–30, 172–73, 350; economic strength of, 44; egalitarianism of, 93; and embargo debate, 50, 51; fears of confederation by, 120–22, 167–70, 249, 253–54, 255, 348–49, 351; and form of government debates, 115–16; and Franco-American alliance negotiations, 179–80; and independence proposal, 6–7, 128, 134, 135–36; map of, 66; and Mississippi River navigation rights, 237–38, 272, 280; as most rebellious region, 19; and partial confederation, 249; perceptions and stereotypes of, 31–32, 87; and reconciliation debates, 88, 89, 92; and Restraining Act, 106, 224–25; and subconfederations, 167–70, 348–49, 351; Vermont territory as addition to, 294–95, 341–42. *See also* fishery rights; Mississippi-Fisheries Compromise
New England Trade and Fisheries Act, 106, 224–25
Newfoundland. *See* fishery rights
New Hampshire and ratification of Articles of Confederation, 190. *See also* Vermont

New Jersey: and capital site selection, 364; and ratification of Articles of Confederation, 190, 198–99; Revolutionary War battles in, 159, 161, 164, 167
New Orleans, right to access, 153, 154, 155, 249, 267
New York: and Albany Congress, 45; and capital site debate, 361, 363, 364; and domestic civil war preparations, 345–46; and Hartford convention (1780), 348–49, 351; and independence proposal, 127, 136, 137; and ratification of Articles of Confederation, 190; Revolutionary War in, 158–59, 161–63, 167, 177, 222, 257–62; and Spanish mediation offer, 206; territorial claims and cessions, 142, 264, 297. *See also* Vermont
Norfolk, Burning of (1775), 113
North: Northern confederation rumors and plans, 120–22, 167–70, 249, 253–54, 255, 348–49, 351, 356; and Revolutionary War focus, 120–21; Rutledge's dislike of, 129–30. *See also* New England; North/South tensions
North Carolina: land cessions by, 350; and Mississippi River navigation rights, 279–80; and partial confederation proposal, 231–32, 249–50; potential restoration to British control, 6; Provincial Congress, 126; and ratification of Articles of Confederation, 190; as Revolutionary War arena, 262; territorial claims of, 142, 175; and Virginia's territorial claims, 125
North/South tensions: and administrative matters, 203; and appointments, 158, 231, 238–40; and capital site selection, 361–67; and Continental Army, 83, 88, 93, 109–12, 118, 161–64; and deference to South, 30–33, 90–93; and economics, 41–42, 44; and embargoes, 41–42, 50–56, 65, 70–73, 107–8, 202–4; and Enlightenment values, 119–20; and fears of domination of Congress, 129–30, 170–73, 186–87, 202–4; and First Continental Congress, 23–33; and fishery rights, 193,

Index

220–22, 227–30, 232–36; and form of government debates, 115–16; and French military aid, 257–62; and independence debate, 31, 134; John Adams on, 118–19; and military power, 90–93, 129; and Mississippi River navigation rights, 195, 196–98, 210, 233–40, 246–47, 284, 403n15; and navy development, 289; and peace negotiations, 303, 305–7, 333–34; post-independence, 253–56, 340, 341–42, 343–51; and potential restoration of colonies to Britain, 6, 258, 269, 287–88; and ratification of Articles of Confederation, 202–4; and Revolutionary War burdens, 185–86, 250, 282–86, 363; Samuel Adams on, 228; and taxation of slavery, 141–42, 176; and territorial rights, 142–44; and Treaty of Paris (1783), 333–34; and Vermont issue, 341–42. *See also* domestic civil war; Mississippi-Fisheries Compromise
Northwest Territory. *See* territorial rights of Virginia
Novanglus, 117
Nova Scotia, 195–97, 214–15, 220–21. *See also* fishery rights

officer election and pay, 93–94, 109, 118
Olive Branch Petition, 89–90, 113. *See also* reconciliation proposals
Osgood, Samuel, 349
Oswald, Richard, 324, 325, 327, 331–32, 333, 335
Otis, James, 26, 117

Paine, Robert Treat, 21
Paine, Thomas, *100*; delegates on, 31–32; and domestic civil war, 102, 103–5, 356; and land cession by Virginia, 298; move to Philadelphia, 99; writings by, 99–106, 159
Palliser's Act, 225
peace negotiations: by Adams (1779-1781), 235–40, 246–49, 300–305; by Adams, Franklin, and Jay (1781-1782), 7–8, 303–7, 309–10, 319–36, 337–39;

Austro-Russian mediation proposal, 301–2, 320, 398n1; and break with France, 327–31, 337–38; challenges of, 303–7; and fishery rights, 7–8, 239–40, 300–305, 325–27, 331, 332, 334, 335, 339; and Franklin, 321–22, 324–27, 330; French control of, 319–20; home rule in, 322, 329; instructions, 305, 319–20, 321, 325–26; Jay as key strategist in, 309–10, 336; Jay's appointment to, 319–20; Jay's approach to, 321–24; and Jefferson, 303, 305–7, 323; and John Adams, 7–8, 321, 331–36; and Lee-Adams coalition, 235–40; and Mississippi River as boundary, 7–8, 325–26, 327–32; and Mississippi River navigation rights, 236–40, 246–49, 304–5, 325, 327–32, 334, 339; restrictions on states and foreign alliances, 139; Russian mediation proposal, 267, 268–69; Witherspoon-Houston motion, 302–3. *See also* Spanish mediation offer (1779); Treaty of Paris of 1783
Pendleton, Edmund, 78, 283–84, *284*, 360, 361
Penn, John, 231
Pennsylvania: and Albany Congress, 45; boundary with Virginia, 231; and Continental Army losses, 164, 174; delegates meeting with MA delegates, 31–33; exclusion from Virginia's territorial claims, 125; and independence proposal, 127, 134, 136, 137; and ratification of Articles of Confederation, 190; support for Virginia in war, 283; territorial claims of, 147. *See also* Wyoming Valley
The Pennsylvania Magazine, 99–100
Pensacola, 160, 180, 196, 211
Petition to the King, 67–69, 100
Petty, William. *See* Shelburne, Earl of (William Petty)
Philadelphia: capture of (1777), 174; and Continental Congress sites, 29–30, 84, 159; and mutiny over wages, 354–55
Pitcairn, John, 78
Plan of Union, 57–58, 61–64, 74, 79

population, uncertainty about, 38
power: Burke on, 167, 170–73, 187–88; and capital site selection, 362, 363–64; centralization of, 57–58, 59, 60–61; in Dickinson's constitution draft, 175; economics and financial powers, 282; federal power as limited, 286–89; federal powers as overreaching, 343–51, 360; regional balance of powers, 170–73, 202–4, 340, 341–42, 346; state powers in Articles of Confederation, 170–73, 187–88; Washington on, 369–70. *See also* states' rights
prayer, 48–49
presidency: in Galloway's Plan of Union, 62; in Paine's proposal for Continental Charter, 104
Princeton, Battle of (1777), 164

Quartering Act, 20–21

Ramsay, David, 251
Randolph, Edmund, 298–300, 306, 360, 361
Randolph, Peyton, 30, 33, 78
Rayneval, Joseph Matthias Gérard de. *See* Gérard de Rayneval, Joseph Matthias
Read, Jacob, 364–65
reconciliation proposals: decline in interest in, 112–13, 126; by Dickinson, 83–90, 105, 113; and Franklin, 95; by Galloway, 5–6, 26–28, 57–64, 74, 79, 100; and John Adams, 87–89; Paine on, 103; and peace negotiations, 324; and Samuel Adams, 120; secession threats over, 88, 89, 92
religious practices in Continental Congress, 48–49
Remonstrance of the General Assembly of Virginia, 247–48
Rendon, Francisco de, 267
reparations, 325
representation. *See* voting representation
republicanism, 119, 124, 152
Resolution Instructing Delegates in Congress (Virginia), 248–49, 263–64, 272, 273–74, 278, 279

Restraining Act, 106, 224–25
Cardinal Retz (Jean-François-Paul de Gondi), 296
Revere, Paul, 49
Revolutionary War: and Canada, 106, 196; finances and economics of, 250–52; and French military aid, 257–62; in Massachusetts, 77–78, 80; in New Jersey, 159, 161, 164, 167; in New York, 158–59, 161–63, 167, 177, 222, 257–62; in North Carolina, 262; Northern focus, 120–21; North/South tensions and blame for losses, 161–64; North/South tensions over burdens of, 185–86, 250, 282–86, 363; North/South tensions over military deployment, 257–62; in Pennsylvania, 164, 174; in South, 6, 222, 250, 252–53, 255, 282; in South Carolina, 252, 257–62; Spain's entering of, 235; as unifying colonies, 232; in Virginia, 113, 276–77, 282–86, 290–92, *291*, 293, 305–6. *See also* Continental Army; Treaty of Paris of 1783
Rhode Island: British control of, 222; and impost debate, 344–45; and ratification of Articles of Confederation, 190; and Spanish mediation offer, 206
rice, 42, 55–56, 70–73, 74–75
Richmond, Virginia, capture of, 276–77
rights: in Declaration and Resolves of Congress, 68; Virginia's declaration of, 124; women's, 100. *See also* states' rights
Rochambeau, Comte de (Jean-Baptiste Donatien de Vimeur), 257, 289, 290
Rockingham, Marquis de (Charles Watson-Wentworth), 322–23, 325
Rodney, Caesar, 162
Rodney, Thomas, 281, 285
Ross, David, 283
rum, 224, 350
Rush, Benjamin, 42, 141, 167, 168–69, *169*
Russia: Anglo-Russian talks on Russian military aid, 210; mediation proposals, 267, 268–69, 301–2, 320, 398n1
Rutledge, Edward, 56; and Articles of Confederation, 138, 141–42, 147–48; as

Index 441

delegate, 78; and embargo proposal, 55–56; and exclusion of Black people from Continental Army, 109; on Galloway's Plan of Union, 64; and independence proposal, 127, 128–30, 136; and taxation of slavery, 141–42
Rutledge, John, 48, 72, 73, 78, 89

St. Clair, Arthur, 354, 355
Saratoga, Battle of, 177, 290
Savannah, Georgia, 252
Schuyler, Philip, 78, 243, 253, 258
Scudder, Nathaniel, 190
Seabury, Samuel, 24–25
secession and secession threats: in Articles of Confederation, 139; over Articles of Confederation, 146–48; over Articles of Confederation ratification, 202, 203–4; over capital site selection, 365–67; over Continental Association trade embargo, 42, 55–56, 70–73, 75; over fishery rights, 227–30; in Franklin's Articles of Confederation proposal, 82; and independence debate, 6–7, 127, 134, 135–36; over Mississippi River navigation rights, 274; over reconciliation, 88, 89, 92; over Southern campaign, 285–86; over taxes and federal finances, 344–48, 359–60; over Virginia's land cession, 299, 359–61; over voting procedures, 36–39
Seven Years' War, 153. *See also* French and Indian War; Treaty of Paris of 1763
Sharpe, William, 231, 305
Shelburne, Earl of (William Petty), 325, 331
Sherman, Robert, 264
Sherwood, Samuel, 47
shipbuilding, 224
shipping, 224
silver, 315
slavery: and Articles of Confederation, 140, 186; and Continental Army, 109–10; and domestic civil war potential, 5–6, 10, 28, 110, 118; duties on, 350; as economic system, 9, 224; emancipation and abolition, 5, 9–10, 100–101, 109, 110, 112, 113, 294; fear of slave rebellions, 5, 6, 20, 84, 109–10; Jefferson on, 97; and nonimportation embargo, 74; and Paine, 100–101; and South's reliance on Britain, 20, 28; and taxation, 140, 141–42, 147, 176, 185–86; and tobacco, 52–53; and Treaty of Paris (1783), 323, 335; and troop quotas, 186; and Vermont, 294; and voting representation, 33–34; as weakening the South, 5–6, 27–29, 261
Smith, Adam, 152
Smith, Meriwether, 213, 220
Smith, Thomas, 401n8
South: and Albany Congress, 45; as bloc, 209–10; chauvinism of, 163; deference to, 30–33; and fishery rights, 229–30; and form of government debates, 115–16; interest in Florida, 160; as least rebellious region, 19–20; as militarily and morally weak, 5–6, 27–29, 254, 261; potential restoration to British control, 6, 258, 269, 287–88, 301, 302; and reconciliation, 88, 89, 92, 126; reliance on Britain, 19–20, 27–28; and republicanism, 119; as Revolutionary War arena, 6, 250, 252–53, 255, 282; Southern confederacy rumors, 357–58; and Vermont issue, 294–96, 341–42; Virginia as dominating, 33. *See also* Mississippi-Fisheries Compromise; Mississippi River navigation rights; North/South tensions
South Carolina: and Articles of Confederation amendments, 188–89; and Articles of Confederation ratification, 190; Charlestown siege, 252, 257–62; exclusion from Virginia's territorial claims, 125; and independence, 126; and independence debates, 127, 134, 136; land cessions by, 350; and Mississippi River navigation rights, 270; potential restoration to British control, 6, 258, 269; as Revolutionary War arena, 262; territorial claims of, 142; trade embargo and secession threats, 42, 55–56, 70–73, 75; and Vermont statehood, 342

sovereignty, state: in Articles of Confederation, 175; Jefferson on, 97; and Mississippi River navigation rights, 273; and tariffs, 344–48; tensions on post-independence, 340, 344–48; and Vermont, 294; and Virginia's land cessions, 298; and Virginia's resolution on independence, 123–24, 125. *See also* states' rights

Spain: coordination with Britain, 212, 316–17; coordination with France, 181, 191–92, 194–98, 268–69; declaration of war on Britain, 310–11, 328; fear of, 133; and intelligence operatives, 182–83, 316; Revolutionary War entry, 235; and Seven Years' War, 153, 159. *See also* Florida, East/West; Gibraltar; Mississippi River as boundary; Mississippi River navigation rights

Spanish alliance negotiations: approach to, 152–53, 157, 159–61; and credit, 217, 312, 313, 314, 317; and Florida territory, 159–60; and foreign alliances treaty committee, 152–53; and independence debates, 132; and intelligence operatives, 182–83, 316; and Jay, 328; and Mississippi as boundary, 153–56, 328; and Mississippi navigation rights, 8, 153, 180, 237, 262–74, 300–301, 310–11, 315–18, 328; and Northern confederacy proposal, 121–22; and potential enmity between Spain and States, 180–83, 194, 266, 271–72, 315–16, 318

Spanish mediation offer (1779): committee for terms, 213–15, 216–17; debates on, 217–22, 225–26, 227–35; and Lee-Adams coalition, 232–35; presentation of by Gérard, 204–7, 209–12; rejection of by Britain, 235

Stamp Act, 50, 59, 60

state boundaries: arbitration of in Articles of Confederation, 142, 387n19; in Dickinson's constitution draft, 175; and domestic civil war potential, 27; in overview, 4; and Virginia's territorial claims, 125

state nullification powers, 187–88

state of defense proposal, 86

states' rights: in Article II, 175; and ban on states making foreign treaties, 188; Burke on, 167, 170–73; in Dickinson's constitution proposal, 175; in Franklin's Articles of Confederation proposal, 82; in Galloway's Plan of Union, 62; and Virginia's land cessions, 298; and Virginia's territorial claims, 245–46, 247–49

subconfederations: ban on, 139, 168, 175, 349; and Convention of the New England States (1776), 167–70; and Hartford convention (1780), 348–49, 351; and partial confederation proposal, 231–32, 249–50. *See also* multiple confederations

Suffolk Resolves, 49

sugar, 224

Sullivan, John, 34–35, 251, 252–53

Summary View of the Rights of British America (Jefferson), 95

supermajority voting. *See* majority/supermajority voting

survivalist paradigm, 12–15

Susquehannah Company, 46

taxation: and Articles of Confederation, 140, 141–42, 147, 173, 176, 185–86, 350–51; in Dickinson's reconciliation proposal, 84; in Galloway's Plan of Union, 62; import tariff post-independence, 344–48; and inflation, 250–51; land tax powers in Articles of Confederation, 350; Morris on, 282; *vs.* regulating trade for revenue, 65; and slavery, 140, 141–42, 147, 176, 185–86

tea: Boston Tea Party, 19, 20, 50, 65; and nonimportation embargo, 74; Tea Act, 60

Tea Act, 60

Tennessee: and Mississippi River navigation rights, 217, 247, 271; and multiple confederacies, 357; and territorial claims, 175, 194

Ternay, Chevalier de (Charles-Henri-Louis d'Arsac), 257

Index

territorial rights: and Albany Congress, 45, 46; and Articles of Confederation, 139, 140, 142–44, 147, 170, 173, 175–76, 198, 199–200; committee on, 264; in Dickinson's constitution draft, 175; and domestic civil war potential, 4, 27, 110, 114–15, 174, 231, 248, 293–96, 382n24; and fears of other countries, 157; and Franklin's Articles of Confederation proposal, 82–83; and French and Indian War, 153, 159, 266; Jefferson on, 97; John Adams on, 119; and Madison, 264–67; map of land claims, *143*; and need for confederation, 133–34; in overview, 4; and Spanish/French triple alliance, 193, 194–98; and Spanish mediation offer, 205–7, 209–10, 211–13; tensions on post-independence, 340, 357; in Treaty of Paris (1783), 7–8, 332–33, 336, 338–39; and uti possidetis, 268–69, 270, 274–76. *See also* Mississippi River as boundary

territorial rights of Virginia: and Articles of Confederation debates, 140, 142–43, 147; as blocking ratification of Articles of Confederation, 188, 189, 199–200, 243–44, 247–49, 254, 256, 263–64, 275–78, 297, 358; and independence resolution, 123–24, 125; and land cessions, 175–76, 256, 275, 277–78, 293, 296–300, 358–61; and land office, 244–45; and Spanish alliance negotiations, 263–64, 272, 273–74; and Spanish mediation offer, 210

Thomson, Charles, 33, 72, 342, 355–58, *357*, 367, 368

tobacco, 42, 52–56, 74, 107, 108

Tobacco Act of 1774, 123

Townshend Duties, 50

trade: and Albany Congress, 45; ban on British trade, 236; ban on states making foreign alliances, 139, 188; and Boston Port Act, 20; as focus for Continental Congress, 4, 65, 83, 106–7, 152; Jefferson on, 97; opening of to other countries, 125; and peace negotiations, 325, 332, 338; quadrangular, 224; and Spanish alliance negotiations, 152, 161; and Treaty of Paris (1783), 338. *See also* embargoes; fishery rights; Mississippi River navigation rights

tragic *vs.* heroic narrative, 14–15

treaties: ban on states making foreign treaties, 139, 188; foreign alliances treaty committee, 151–53, 156–58; and Virginia's territorial claims, 125. *See also* Franco-American alliance

Treaty of Paris of 1763: and fishery rights, 157–58; and Mississippi River navigation rights, 154–56, 161, 266, 332; and Virginia's territorial claims, 125

Treaty of Paris of 1783: articles of, 332–33; and break with France, 337–38; finalization of, 335; and fishery rights, 7–8, 332, 334, 335, 337; hearings and debates over, 337–39; John Adams on, 333–36, 339; and Mississippi navigation rights, 8, 332–33, 334; ratification of, 339–40; signing of, 307, 335–36, 340; and slavery, 323, 335; and territorial rights, 7–8, 332–33, 336, 338–39. *See also* peace negotiations

Trenton, New Jersey, 164

unanimity, 137–38, 340
unionist paradigm, 12–15
United Illinois and Wabash Company, 297
"Unite or Die" logo, 43–44, 46
U.S. Constitution of 1787, 58
uti possidetis, 268–69, 270, 274–76

Valcour Island, Battle of. *See* Champlain, Lake
Vandalia Company, 297, 299
Varnum, James Mitchell, 279, 286–87, 401n8
Vaughan, Benjamin, 331–32, 335
Vergennes, Comte de (Charles Gravier), *178*; and Austro-Russian mediation proposal, 301–2; and Franco-American alliance negotiations, 158, 177–79; Jay's appeal to, 314–15; Jay's break with, 327–31; on John Adams, 301; and peace negotiations, 269, 319–20, 322, 327–31,

Vergennes, Comte de (*continued*)
335, 337–38; and Spain, coordination with, 181, 268–69; and Spanish mediation offer, 205–7; and Treaty of Paris (1783) approval, 335, 337–38; and triple appliance hopes, 191–93, 194

Vermont: and abolition, 294; constitution of, 294; and domestic civil war fears, 4, 174, 231, 293–96; and Northern confederation fears, 356; and statehood tensions, 340, 341–42

Vimeur, Jean-Baptiste Donatien de. *See* Rochambeau, Comte de (Jean-Baptiste Donatien de Vimeur)

violence: British violence as unifying colonies, 22, 47–48; and fears of lawlessness with war, 27, 381n11

Virginia: and Articles of Confederation ratification, 188; and capital site selection, 362–65; debts of, 346; deference to, 30–33; emancipation in, 112, 113; and embargo proposal, 52–56; fears of, 341–42; and federal financial powers, 346–47; and independence, 42–43, 128; land cessions by, 275, 277–78, 293, 296–300, 358–61; and Mississippi river navigation rights, 248–49, 263–64, 272, 273–74, 275–80, 283–84; and partial confederation proposal, 231–32, 249; Pennsylvania boundary, 231; political convention (1776), 123–24; Remonstrance of the General Assembly of Virginia, 247–48; Resolution Instructing Delegates in Congress act, 248–49, 263–64, 272, 273–74, 278; resolution on confederation (1776), 123–24; Revolutionary War in, 113, 276–77, 282–86, 290–92, *291*, 293, 305–6; secession threats by, 36–39, 285–86; and Southern confederacy rumors, 357–58; state constitution, 124–25; and voting representation, 140–41; Williamsburg convention (1774), 52–54. *See also* territorial rights of Virginia

Virginia Capes, Battle of the, 290

voting representation: and Articles of Confederation, 140–41, 147, 173, 176, 186–87; in Franklin's Articles of Confederation proposal, 82; in Galloway's Plan of Union, 62; Jefferson on, 97; one state/one vote, 33–39, 97, 140–41, 147, 176; in Paine's Continental Charter, 104; and partial confederation, 249; proportional representation, 33–39, 82, 97, 140–41, 147; and slavery, 33–34; wealth-based, 38, 176. *See also* majority/supermajority voting

Walton, George, 269–70
war. *See* domestic civil war; French and Indian War; Revolutionary War
Ward, Samuel, 36, 37, 110–12, *111*, 120
Washington, George, *91, 369*; appointments of, 33, 90–93; and Black people in Continental Army, 109; on *Common Sense* (Paine), 106; as delegate, 22, 78; and dictator proposal, 255; fear of war with Britain, 22; and French and Indian War, 153; and French military aid, 259; and independence, 43; and Newburgh conspiracy, 353; New Jersey victories, 167; preparation for war, 76, 94; resignation and farewell address, 367–70; and South campaign, 6, 285–86, 289–92; and Yorktown siege, 290–92
Fort Washington, Battle of, 159
Watson-Wentworth, Charles. *See* Rockingham, Marquis de (Charles Watson-Wentworth)
western territories. *See* territorial rights
West Indies: and Franco-American alliance, 157, 196; and peace negotiations, 250, 324; and quadrangular trade, 224; and trade embargo, 66, 67, 75
West Virginia territory and Virginia's land cession, 277
Wharton, Thomas, 298
Whipple, William, 199, 251
White, Phillips, 350
Williams, William, 148, 164

Williamsburg convention (1774), 52–54
Williamson, Hugh, 354–55, 363–65
Willing, Thomas, 107, 137
Wilson, James, 127, 137, 147
Witherspoon, John, *145*; and domestic civil war fears, 4, 13, 145–46; and foreign alliances committee, 159; and Mississippi River navigation rights, 237, 246; on need for confederation, 4, 144–46; and peace negotiations, 302–3, 304; and Spanish mediation committee, 213

women, rights of, 100
Wyoming Valley, 4, 46, 110, 115, 382n24
Wythe, George, 127, 288

York, as Continental Congress site, 174
Yorktown, siege of, 290–92, *291,* 293

Zubly, John Joachim, 108